CULTURE ACROSS THE CURRICULUM

Culture Across the Curriculum provides a useful handbook for psychology teachers in the major subfields of the discipline. From introductory psychology to the foundations in such areas as social psychology, statistics, research methods, memory, cognition, personality, and development, to such specialized courses as language, sexuality, and peace psychology, there is something here for virtually every teacher of psychology. In addition to discussions of the rationale for inclusion of cultural context in their areas of specialization, these experienced teachers also offer advice and ideas for teaching exercises and activities to support the teaching of a psychology of all people.

KENNETH D. KEITH is Professor Emeritus of Psychological Sciences at the University of San Diego, and editor of the Cambridge University Press series *Elements of Psychology and Culture*. He is author or editor of a dozen books and more than 150 book chapters and articles, including *The Encyclopedia of Cross-Cultural Psychology, Cross-Cultural Psychology: Contemporary Themes & Perspectives*, and *Cross-Cultural Perspectives on Quality of Life*. Keith is a Fellow of the American Psychological Association, the Western Psychological Association, and the Association for Psychological Science, as well as a member of the International Association for Cross-Cultural Psychology and the recipient of numerous awards for teaching and for service to people with intellectual disabilities.

D1608559

CULTURE AND PSYCHOLOGY

Series Editor
David Matsumoto, *San Francisco State University*

As an increasing number of social scientists come to recognize the pervasive influence of culture on individual human behavior, it has become imperative for culture to be included as an important variable in all aspects of psychological research, theory, and practice. Culture and Psychology is an evolving series of works that brings the study of culture and psychology into a single, unified concept.

CULTURE ACROSS THE CURRICULUM

A Psychology Teacher's Handbook

EDITED BY

KENNETH D. KEITH

University of San Diego

CAMBRIDGE
UNIVERSITY PRESS

CAMBRIDGE
UNIVERSITY PRESS

University Printing House, Cambridge CB2 8BS, United Kingdom

One Liberty Plaza, 20th Floor, New York, NY 10006, USA

477 Williamstown Road, Port Melbourne, VIC 3207, Australia

314–321, 3rd Floor, Plot 3, Splendor Forum, Jasola District Centre, New Delhi – 110025, India

79 Anson Road, #06–04/06, Singapore 079906

Cambridge University Press is part of the University of Cambridge.

It furthers the University's mission by disseminating knowledge in the pursuit of education, learning, and research at the highest international levels of excellence.

www.cambridge.org
Information on this title: www.cambridge.org/9781107189973
DOI: 10.1017/9781316996706

© Cambridge University Press 2018

First published 2018

Printed in the United States of America by Sheridan Books, Inc.

A catalogue record for this publication is available from the British Library.

Library of Congress Cataloging-in-Publication Data
NAMES: Keith, Kenneth D. (Kenneth Dwight), 1946– editor. | Keith, Kenneth D.
TITLE: Culture across the curriculum : a psychology teacher's handbook / edited by Kenneth D. Keith.
DESCRIPTION: New York : Cambridge University Press, 2018. | Series: Culture and psychology
IDENTIFIERS: LCCN 2017054433 | ISBN 9781107189973 (hardback) |
ISBN 9781316639764 (paperback)
SUBJECTS: LCSH: Ethnopsychology–Study and teaching (Higher)–Textbooks. | Psychology–Study and teaching (Higher)–Textbooks. | Psychology teachers–Training of.
CLASSIFICATION: LCC GN270 .C87 2018 | DDC 155.8071/1–dc23
LC record available at https://lccn.loc.gov/2017054433

ISBN 978-1-107-18997-3 Hardback
ISBN 978-1-316-63976-4 Paperback

For Dave and Heather
with thanks, respect, and love

Contents

Figures

Tables

Contributors

CARL MARTIN ALLWOOD University of Gothenburg

JAMES ATHANASOU University of Sydney

ALYSSA BENEDICT The Chicago School of Professional Psychology

DIANA BOER University of Koblenz–Landau

CHANDRA DONNELL CAREY University of North Texas

KIM A. CASE University of Houston–Clear Lake

TYLER COLLETTE Texas A&M University–Kingsville

KRISTY K. DEAN Grand Valley State University

VIVIANE DE CASTRO PECANHA The Chicago School of Professional Psychology

PATRICK DEVLIEGER University of Leuven

TINASHE DUNE Western Sydney University

LEONIE ELPHINSTONE Queensland University of Technology

AFSHIN GHARIB Dominican University of California

JUDITH L. GIBBONS St. Louis University

PETER J. GIORDANO Belmont University

REGAN A. R. GURUNG University of Wisconsin–Green Bay

KATJA HANKE GESIS-Leibniz Institute for the Social Sciences

DEBRA HARLEY University of Kentucky

MICHAEL R. HULSIZER Webster University

NORIYUKI INOUE Waseda University

KENNETH D. KEITH University of San Diego

CHU KIM-PRIETO The College of New Jersey

MARY E. KITE Ball State University

ANNE M. KOENIG University of San Diego

DAVID S. KREINER University of Central Missouri

JACLYN KUKOFF The College of New Jersey

DAVID MATSUMOTO San Francisco State University

RICHARD L. MILLER Texas A&M University–Kingsville

ADRIANA MOLITOR University of San Diego

ELIAS MPOFU University of Sydney

SUSAN A. NOLAN Seton Hall University

WILLIAM L. PHILLIPS Dominican University of California

KATELYN E. POELKER Hope College

AARON S. RICHMOND Metropolitan State University of Denver

ANDREW F. SIMON Seton Hall University

MICHAEL STEVENS The Chicago School of Professional Psychology

JOSEPHINE C. H. TAN Lakehead University

JUNKO TANAKA-MATSUMI Kwansei Gakuin University

LACOUNT J. TOGANS Ball State University

CHRISTIN-MELANIE VAUCLAIR University Institute of Lisbon

QI WANG Cornell University

LINDA M. WOOLF Webster University

Foreword

Although psychologists have been studying psychological processes and behaviors across cultures for over a century, the study of the relation between culture and psychology has grown exponentially in the past several decades. Today this area of research has made valuable contributions to our knowledge in all areas of study, including cognition, emotion, personality, abnormal, social, developmental, and organizational psychology. Cross-cultural research has pushed the envelope in the development of new and exciting research methodologies and statistical techniques, and the knowledge generated from this area of research has fundamentally changed the way psychologists think about, study, and understand psychological processes and human behaviors.

Thus, it is not surprising that the topic of culture has been increasingly infused across the psychology curriculum. This movement has reflected not only developments in the field, but also the increasing cultural and ethnic diversity in our student populations. One of the many questions students ask when they take psychology classes is, "does this apply to me?" And for many years, that increasingly diversifying student body raised questions of the applicability of psychological knowledge and principles taught to them based on monocultural studies. This trend has also occurred in secondary schools, where psychology courses are increasingly found as part of the curriculum, too.

Despite this evolution in knowledge in psychology vis-à-vis culture, and despite the increasing need to teach about the fruits of this evolution in university and secondary school classrooms, to date there has been a dearth of resources for teachers out on the front lines teaching this material. Certainly there have been a few books, study guides, and readers developed over the years, but what the field sorely needed was a single, comprehensive handbook specifically designed for teachers of this important material.

It is within this backdrop that this handbook is a breath of fresh air, addressing a significant gap in the literature. Ken Keith has lined up a stellar cast of scholars, all of them outstanding teachers and/or researchers themselves, to provide their insights related to the teaching of this important material. The content covers all the major research areas on which culture has made an impact, and the areas most relevant to students across the country and around the world. Moreover, the book is structured into reasonable and easy-to-understand sections, namely Basic Concepts and Teaching across the Psychology Curriculum, with the latter broken down into sections titled In the Beginning, Research and Statistics, Biological Connections, Development, Cognition, Social Psychology, Health and Well-Being, and Personality, Disability, and Disorders. Professor Keith wraps up the book with an incisive, forward-looking synthesis and integration of the material.

This handbook promises to make a strong contribution to the literature. But more importantly, it will be a welcome resource for the many teachers of this area. Equally significant is the notion that this work is the all-important beginning of a living body of work, one that will need to be adjusted as new research on culture and psychology provides new insights into human behavior, and these can be combined with important developments in teaching methodologies and pedagogies.

I offer my congratulations to Professor Keith for this very welcome resource. And I offer my heartfelt gratitude and appreciation to the many teachers of culture and psychology for all of their hard work, efforts, and hours dedicated to a labor of love. You truly are the unsung heroes of academia and scholarship.

David Matsumoto
San Francisco, CA, USA

Preface

A few years ago, in the preface to an earlier book, I wished for a future in which cross-cultural psychology would not be taught just as a stand-alone course, but for one in which culture would be pervasive in the study of behavior. It would be, I hoped, an integral aspect of the mainstream psychology curriculum, embedded in all our courses. With each passing year, we move a step toward that goal. This book is an effort to take us a little further in the direction of a psychology of all people.

For millennia, people have formed groups and have interacted across groups, sometimes peaceably, and sometimes in conflict. They have faced challenges of communication, stereotyping, aggression, fear, and curiosity – all the stuff of culture. Yet, as my friend Walt Lonner has noted, researchers have sometimes considered culture simply "noise" – prompting him to wonder how such a profound part of people's lives could be so easily dismissed, and leading John Berry to observe that culture is not noise, but music. Lonner, too, has thought of culture as music, likening its rich composition and texture to that of an opera, and John Dewey, in his *Art as Experience*, noted that we exist not in a void, but in ongoing interaction with environment – with culture.

My hope is that this book brings together some of the key sections of the orchestra that comprise the teaching of psychology. Sometimes our efforts have been isolated, sometimes discordant, but as we strive to bring harmony to the process, blending the local with the international, the culture bound with the universal, the biological with the contextual, we make incremental progress toward a more complete understanding. In the light of the challenges faced by people living in this twenty-first-century world, to do otherwise would be irresponsible. We owe it to our students, to our children and grandchildren, and to our sisters and brothers around the globe to do our part to broaden our comprehension and to bring our science to bear on the problems they face, now and in the future.

There is something here for teachers of most of the courses found in typical psychology curricula and in most introductory psychology classes. To see further integration of contextual, cultural knowledge in these areas would indeed be music to the senses. And to paraphrase Shakespeare, if culture be the music of life, play on, play on.

Acknowledgments

I owe thanks to the authors who have contributed to this volume. They are committed to a psychology of all people, and I am grateful for their contributions to great teaching. Matt Bennett at Cambridge University Press supported and encouraged this project from the start; a team of anonymous reviewers provided comments and suggestions that helped to make the book better; and copy editor JaNoel Lowe worked patiently and capably to bring it to completion. They all have my thanks.

For many years Walt Lonner has been an example and an inspiration to scholars with interest in the relation between culture and psychological science. I am grateful for his advice, his wisdom, and his friendship. Finally, for more than a half century, Connie Keith has been my traveling companion, sage critic, and best friend – I do not have sufficient words to say what she has meant to me.

Prologue
A Psychology of All People
Kenneth D. Keith

For far too long, Western psychology, while assuming the universality of its findings, has taught a worldview based largely on data gathered from European Americans, many of them students. As teachers, we have too often failed to encourage our students to ask key questions, among them these:

Are there truly psychological principles or processes found universally across cultures? Do they transcend ethnic, racial, cultural, or national boundaries?

Are some principles or processes limited to the cultural or ethnic groups in which they are found? Might people of differing backgrounds experience basic psychological phenomena (e.g., emotion, cognition, development, sexuality) differently?

We have also too often failed to ask important questions of ourselves, for example:

Do I have cultural preconceptions or biases that I bring to my teaching?
What do I believe about the role of culture and context in my understanding of human behavior?
Am I prepared to adequately discuss the role and influence of cultural context in my specialty area?

North Americans make up roughly 6 percent of the world's population, and Europeans about 10 percent. Yet it is Euro-American psychology that has long dominated our understanding of human behavior. The time has come for us to look seriously to the role of psychology teachers in broadening the scope of the field and of the knowledge and imaginations of our students.

Backdrop

It has been two decades since Segall, Lonner, and Berry (1998) marveled that it was still necessary, after so many years, to advocate for the importance of taking culture into account when studying human behavior. And we are approaching three decades since Lonner (1990) found that culture was largely absent, or at best an afterthought, in most undergraduate psychology textbooks. Earlier, Cole (1984) lamented the fact that, in his own education, it was the methods and achievements of American experimental psychology that had seemed paramount, and that the curricula of such diverse cultures as Japan and the then Soviet Union were dominated by the American model. Well into the twenty-first century, the hegemony of this model, including its organization of the field around presumed universal mental processes at the expense of the applied domains of life – those aspects we might call culture – dominated Western psychology (e.g., Rozin, 2006).

The cultural limitations of much of our psychology are indeed long-standing, as Albee (1988) showed in discussing the prejudicial and ethnocentric views of a number of our forebears, including such luminaries as G. Stanley Hall, Francis Galton, and Robert Yerkes. These limitations have included not only the subject matter of the field but also the individuals whose behavior psychological scientists have studied, the people who have been research participants. Arnett (2008) found, for example, in an analysis of several mainstream journals of the American Psychological Association (APA), that authors sometimes did not report the ethnicity of their samples, and that when they did, the preponderance were European American. Perhaps this would be understandable if American psychologists were interested only in Americans, but as Sue (1999) noted, we often mistakenly assume American findings to be universal. We may thus find ourselves in the position of believing that 5 percent or less of the world's population can provide the basis for a universal understanding (Arnett, 2008).

We might assume that modern teachers of psychology would be alert to these limitations, and perhaps in their own research take pains to model a more inclusive approach to the design of studies intended to further broadly applicable pedagogical techniques. However, in a review of a quarter century of articles appearing in the journal *Teaching of Psychology*, Ocampo et al. (2003) found that only 7 percent (of more than 2,000) dealt with "diversity," and of those, the single largest number concerned gender. The categories of international and racial/ethnic together comprised only 1.3 percent (26 articles).

Furthermore, in an analysis of four leading teaching of psychology journals, Richmond, Broussard, Sterns, Sanders, and Shardy (2015) found that nearly a quarter of empirical studies reported no demographic data (other than college class level), and that fewer than one in six reported ethnicity of their samples. Among the 40 percent of teaching studies that reported sex of participants, women were significantly overrepresented, and in the studies reporting ethnicity, Caucasians were significantly overrepresented with other ethnicities significantly underrepresented. Finally, it is interesting to note that Richmond et al. found that over the five-year period from 2008 to 2013, the teaching journals they reviewed actually showed a decrease in reporting of demographic data on research samples.

Thus, it appears not only that the content of much of our research is culture limited but also that investigations of teaching are similarly restricted in their scope. Yet the American Psychological Association (APA, 2013), in its guidelines for the undergraduate psychology major, has endorsed the importance of incorporation of sociocultural factors, including such student skills as recognition of cultural and personal bias and identification of the limitations inherent in generalizing from Western research. The guidelines also address the need for infusion of cultural content across the curriculum. It is incumbent upon us as teachers to more adequately address the role of culture in the shaping of our knowledge, our teaching, and ultimately, our discipline.

Teaching and Culture

Teaching about culture in the context of psychology courses not only allows for achievement of curricular goals like those espoused by the APA but also enables students and teachers to more thoroughly address some of psychology's big questions, such as the role of culture in shaping the human psyche and in the evolution of human behavior (Morling, 2015). And despite the fact that cultures may differ in a variety of ways – economic, religious, social, or psychological – all cultures nevertheless face such common challenges as safety, health, reproduction, and survival (Matsumoto, 2009).

Cultural understanding is particularly crucial in an era in which we face a wide range of intercultural conflicts, not least among them fundamental governmental, political, and religious differences; the global challenges of climate change and inequitable distribution of resources; and the burgeoning revolution in electronic technology use. A broader understanding of culture and psychology can help as we deal with these daunting problems, and cultural understanding must come not just from specialized courses in cultural or cross-cultural psychology but also from the subfields that comprise the broader discipline of psychological science.

Textbooks

Early psychology textbooks (e.g., James 1892/1961; Ladd, 1894) often did not refer to cultural concepts, and even by the mid-twentieth century, popular introductory psychology books (e.g., Morgan & King, 1966) had very limited cultural content, sometimes with a brief focus on cultural or racial differences in intelligence, or cultural anthropology in so-called "backward" or "primitive" cultures. This limited coverage of culture and cultural concepts persisted at least until the 1980s in introductory psychology textbooks (Lonner, 2003; Quereshi, 1993), and perhaps even longer in textbooks on educational psychology (Snowman, 1997) and the history of psychology (Furumoto, 2003). In addition, as late as the 1990s, coverage of diverse cultural subgroups, though to some extent expanding, was nevertheless limited (Hogben & Waterman, 1997). More recently, introductory psychology textbooks have often presented a sociocultural perspective (Eaton & Rose, 2013), although analyses of introductory textbook content (e.g., Nairn, Ellard, Scialfa, & Miller, 2003) have sometimes not mentioned culture at all as a core concept.

Current introductory psychology textbooks may mention or actually define cultural or cross-cultural psychology (see, e.g., Gray & Bjorklund, 2014; Myers & DeWall, 2015), and their content often includes discussion of cultural aspects of a variety of psychological and behavioral phenomena, including such topics as attractiveness, development, emotion, intelligence, mental health, parenting, perception, and personality. As we might expect, contemporary social psychology textbooks may contain a significant amount of cultural material (e.g., Aronson, Wilson, Akert, & Sommers, 2016; Kassin, Fein, & Markus, 2014), and authors (e.g., Pickren & Rutherford, 2010) of history of psychology textbooks have begun to discuss the history of the field in relation to its cultural context. As David Matsumoto has noted, our textbooks have in fact become better in their coverage of cultural material; yet success in integrating culture in the teaching of psychology also depends critically upon the knowledge, viewpoint, and biases of the instructor (Hill, 2000).

What to Teach

The idea of integrating cultural content in the teaching of psychology is not new. Psychologists have for some years discussed the importance of teaching about gender and multicultural issues (often describing approaches to inclusion of cultural and subcultural groups within the

United States (see, e.g., Bronstein & Quina, 2003; Mio, Barker-Hackett, & Tumambing, 2007). Furthermore, integration of cultural and cross-cultural content in undergraduate psychology, including the introductory course, is an idea that has been with us for at least two or three decades (Hill, 2000; Triandis & Brislin, 1984).

Yet as teachers of psychology, we may wonder whether we are competent to teach cultural material, or what exactly it might mean to integrate cultural content in our courses. There are probably no clear and obvious answers to these questions, but there may be some wisdom in the oft-repeated Greek aphorism "Know thyself." Are we, for example, aware of the possibility that some research findings may be culture bound? That others may be universal? Or that there may be dynamic interplay between people and their cultural environments? (See, for example, Lonner, 2003). We can explore such questions as these, and in so doing, expand our personal horizons and self-knowledge.

The subsequent chapters of this volume offer a rich array of ideas for teaching the various subfields of the discipline of psychological science, and they provide resources and references reflecting a wide-ranging literature focused on the role of culture in these subfields. These sources reflect not only the evolving *content* of an inclusive psychology but also the need for shifts in *methodological* thinking and teaching that accompany cultural and cross-cultural research interests (e.g., Byrne et al., 2009; Trimble & Vaughn, 2013; Valsiner, 2013).

If we were to take a traditional approach to the question of what to teach, we might try to teach students *about* culture as a distinct entity, treating culture as a subject matter unto itself. This approach, the teaching of culture as a subject matter, is perhaps the inevitable first step, and many colleges and universities have developed courses devoted specifically to the teaching of cross-cultural psychology, some of them (e.g., Akimoto, 2016; Morling, 2015) including excellent teaching suggestions and resources. Yet, as we have seen, the American Psychological Association (2013) guidelines suggest integration of culture across the curriculum, and as we will see in Chapter 1 of this volume, current thinking may expand even beyond the concept of culture to a broader contextual perspective.

Conceptualizing Culture and Psychology

We might think of culture across the curriculum much as past authors have described writing across the curriculum (e.g., Fulwiler, 1984; Nodine, 1990) or ethics across the curriculum (e.g., Davis, 1993; Matchett, 2008). Just as those movements aspired to make writing and ethics integral to the teaching of all classes, so can we aim to make the role of cultural context a part of the natural flow of our teaching across the psychological science curriculum.

Thus, just as all teachers are in a sense teachers of writing or ethics, so too might we all become teachers of culture and context. I would suggest, along with other writers and researchers, that we should not aspire to study and to teach about only WEIRD (Western, educated, industrialized, rich, democratic) populations (Henrich, Heine, & Norenzayan, 2010). Sternberg (2014), in a cogent discussion of the relevance of culture to an understanding of cognitive development, argued that culture is not merely nice, but is in fact necessary to an understanding of intelligence. The history of our field arises from the indigenous work of psychological scientists, not only in Europe and North America, but in all places where individuals have attempted to articulate their understanding of the connection between their behavior and the world around them (Pickren & Rutherford, 2010).

In a sense then, we are all cultural psychologists, as Wang (2016) has argued we should be. An understanding of culture, she suggested,

> functions as a mirror that compels psychologists to reflect on their work and critically evaluate their theories and findings, to go beyond the surface and convenience to question what truly matters, and to embrace the complexity of human experiences with an open mind and open heart. (p. 592)

Nearly a century ago, John Dewey (1922) observed that the maintenance of a way of life depends upon the transmission of the meaning of the environment we inherit from our forerunners. Despite the fact that the nature and meaning of our environment is inherent in the culture in which we find ourselves, psychologists interested in culture have in the past noted reasons for the neglect of culture in our teaching. These reasons have included (Albert, 1988):

A relative lack of experience with other cultures
A tendency to try to simplify behavioral events and explanations
Overlooking cultural variability in an effort to avoid stereotyping
Concern that finding between-group differences leads to discrimination
Fear that a focus on group differences is inconsistent with egalitarian values
Ethnocentric tendencies that may engender resistance to study of cultural variables

However, in a world made smaller by electronic communication and international travel, we can no longer afford to overlook the importance of cultural context. In addition to the need for enhanced understanding of people across cultures, increasing access to higher education by subcultural groups within countries also makes cultural competence essential for the teachers delivering that education (Leiper, Van Horn, Hu, & Upadhyaya, 2008). Such cultural competence may in fact be an ethical necessity for psychology teachers (Tracey, 2005).

Our Task

One of the aims of this book is to provide resources and advice for psychology teachers who wish to more effectively highlight and integrate the role of culture in their various classes. The authors of the remaining chapters in this book take seriously the American Psychological Association (2013) *Guidelines* in their efforts to infuse sociocultural influences throughout the curriculum and the recognition in the *Guidelines* of "the urgency of producing culturally competent individuals" (p. 39).

So, in the words of Lewis Carroll's (1872) immortal walrus, the time has come to talk of many things. And as we speak of the multifaceted field we know as psychological science, let us truly hear all its voices, see all its faces, and savor all that cultural understanding can do to enrich our lives and those of our students. It is a conversation that may begin in the classroom, but which students may carry on for a lifetime.

References

Akimoto, S. (2016). Teaching cross-cultural psychology: Insights from an internationalized on-campus course. In D. Gross, K. Abrams, & C. Z. Enns (Eds.), *Internationalizing the undergraduate psychology curriculum: Practical lessons learned at home and abroad* (pp. 181–197). Washington, DC: American Psychological Association. doi:10.1037/14840-011

Albee, G. W. (1988). Foreword. In P. Bronstein & K. Quina (Eds.), *Teaching a psychology of people: Resources for gender and sociocultural awareness* (pp. vii–x). Washington, DC: American Psychological Association.

Albert, R. D. (1988). The place of culture in modern psychology. In P. Bronstein & K. Quina (Eds.), *Teaching a psychology of people* (pp. 12–18). Washington, DC: American Psychological Association.

American Psychological Association. (2013). *APA guidelines for the undergraduate psychology major*. Washington, DC: Author.

Arnett, J. J. (2008). The neglected 95%: Why American psychology needs to become less American. *American Psychologist, 63*, 602–614. doi:10.1037/0003-066X.63.7.602

Aronson, E., Wilson, T. D., Akert, R. M., & Sommers, S. R. (2016). *Social psychology* (9th ed.). Boston, MA: Pearson.

Bronstein, P., & Quina, K. (Eds.). (2003). *Teaching gender and multicultural awareness*. Washington, DC: American Psychological Association.

Byrne, B. M., Oakland, T., Leong, F. T. L., van de Vijver, F. J. R., Hambleton, R. K., Cheung, F. M., & Bartram, D. (2009). A critical analysis of cross-cultural research and testing practices: Implications for improved education and training in psychology. *Training and Education in Professional Psychology*, *3*, 94–105. doi:10.1037/a0014516

Carroll, L. (1872). *Through the looking glass, and what Alice found there*. London: Macmillan.

Cole, M. (1984). The world beyond our borders: What might our students need to know about it? *American Psychologist, 39,* 998–1005. doi:10.1037/0003-066X.39.9.998

Davis, M. (1993). Ethics across the curriculum: Teaching professional responsibility in teaching courses. *Teaching Philosophy, 16,* 205–235.

Dewey, J. (1922). *Human nature and conduct*. New York, NY: Henry Holt.

Eaton, A. A., & Rose, S. M. (2013). The application of biological, evolutionary, and sociocultural frameworks to issues of gender in introductory psychology textbooks. *Sex Roles, 69,* 536–542. doi:10.1007/s11199-013-0289-9

Fulwiler, T. (1984). How well does writing across the curriculum work? *College English, 46,* 113–125.

Furumoto, L. (2003). Beyond great men and great ideas: History of psychology in sociocultural context. In P. Bronstein & K. Quina (Eds.), *Teaching gender and multicultural awareness* (pp. 113–124). Washington, DC: American Psychological Association.

Gray, P., & Bjorklund, D. F. (2014). *Psychology* (7th ed.). New York, NY: Worth.

Henrich, J., Heine, S. J., & Norenzayan, A. (2010). The weirdest people in the world? *Behavioral & Brain Sciences, 33,* 61–83. doi:10.1017/S0140525X0999152X

Hill, G. W., IV. (2000). Incorporating a cross-cultural perspective in the undergraduate psychology curriculum: An interview with David Matsumoto. *Teaching of Psychology, 27,* 71–75. doi:10.1207/S15328023TOP2701_14

Hogben, M., & Waterman, C. K. (1997). Are all of your students represented in their textbooks? A content analysis of coverage of diversity issues in introductory psychology textbooks. *Teaching of Psychology, 24,* 95–100. doi:10.1207/s15328023top2402_3

James, W. (1961). *Psychology: The briefer course*. New York, NY: Harper & Row. (Original work published 1892)

Kassin, S., Fein, S., & Markus, H. R. (2014). *Social psychology* (9th ed.). Belmont, CA: Wadsworth.

Ladd, G. T. (1894). *Primer of psychology*. New York, NY: Charles Scribner's.

Leiper, J., Van Horn, E. R., Hu, J., & Upadhyaya, R. C. (2008). Promoting cultural awareness and knowledge among faculty and doctoral students. *Nursing Education Perspectives, 29,* 161–164.

Lonner, W. J. (1990). The introductory psychology text and cross-cultural psychology: Beyond Ekman, Whorf, and biased I.Q. tests. In D. Keats, D. Monro, & L. Mann (Eds.), *Heterogeneity in cross-cultural psychology:*

Selected papers from the ninth international conference of the International Association for Cross-Cultural Psychology (pp. 4–22). Lisse: Swets & Zeitlinger.

(2003). Teaching cross-cultural psychology. In P. Bronstein & K. Quina (Eds.), *Teaching gender and multicultural awareness* (pp. 169–177). Washington, DC: American Psychological Association.

Matchett, N. J. (2008). Ethics across the curriculum. *New Directions for Higher Education, 142,* 25–38. doi:10.1002/he.301

Matsumoto, D. (2009). Teaching about culture. In R. A. R. Gurung & L. R. Prieto (Eds.), *Getting culture: Incorporating diversity across the curriculum* (pp. 3–10). Sterling, VA: Stylus.

Mio, J. S., Barker-Hackett, L., Tumambing, J. S. (2006). *Multicultural psychology: Understanding our diverse communities.* Boston, MA: McGraw-Hill.

Morgan, C. T., & King, R. A. (1966). *Introduction to psychology* (3rd ed.). New York, NY: McGraw-Hill.

Morling, B. (2015). Teaching cultural psychology. In D. S. Dunn (Ed.), *The Oxford handbook of undergraduate psychology education* (pp. 599–611). Oxford: Oxford University Press.

Myers, D. G., & DeWall, C. N. (2015). *Psychology* (11th ed.). New York, NY: Worth.

Nairn, S. L., Ellard, J. H., Scialfa, C. T., & Miller, C. D. (2003). At the core of introductory psychology: A content analysis. *Canadian Psychology, 44,* 93–99. doi:10.1037/h0086930

Nodine, B. F. (Ed.). (1990). Psychologists teach writing. [Special issue]. *Teaching of Psychology, 17,* 1–61.

Ocampo, C., Prieto, L. R., Whittlesey, V., Connor, J., Janco-Gidley, J., Mannix, S., & Sare, K. (2003). Diversity research in teaching of psychology: Summary and recommendations. *Teaching of Psychology, 30,* 5–18. doi:10.1207/S15328023TOP3001_02

Quereshi, M. Y. (1993). The contents of introductory psychology textbooks: A follow-up. *Teaching of Psychology, 20,* 218–222.

Pickren, W. E., & Rutherford, A. (2010). *A history of modern psychology in context.* Hoboken, NJ: Wiley.

Richmond, A. S., Broussard, K. A., Sterns, J. L., Sanders, K. K., & Shardy, J. C. (2015). Who are we studying? Sample diversity in teaching of psychology research. *Teaching of Psychology, 42,* 218–226. doi:10.1177/0098628315587619

Rozin, P. (2006). Domain denigration and process preference in academic psychology. *Perspectives on Psychological Science, 1,* 365–376. doi:10.1111/j.1745-6916.2006.00021.x

Segall, M. H., Lonner, W. J., & Berry, J. W. (1998). Cross-cultural psychology as a scholarly discipline: On the flowering of culture in behavioral research. *American Psychologist, 53,* 1101–1110.

Snowman, J. (1997). Educational psychology: What do we teach, what should we teach? *Educational Psychology Review, 9,* 151–170. doi:10.1023/A:1024740512959

Sternberg, R. J. (2014). The development of adaptive competence: Why cultural psychology is necessary and not just nice. *Developmental Review, 34,* 208–224. doi:10.1016/j.dr.2014.05.004

Sue, S. (1999). Science, ethnicity, and bias: Where have we gone wrong? *American Psychologist, 54,* 1070–1077. doi:10.1037/0003-066X.54.12.1070

Tracey, M. D. (2005). Cultural competence: An ethical must in teaching and research. *Monitor on Psychology, 36*(11), 47.

Triandis, H. C., & Brislin, R. W. (1984). Cross-cultural psychology. *American Psychologist, 39,* 1006–1016. doi:10.1037/0003-066X.39.9.1006

Trimble, J. E., & Vaughn, L. (2013). Cultural measurement equivalence. In K. D. Keith (Ed.), *The encyclopedia of cross-cultural psychology* (Vol. 1, pp. 313–319). Chichester: Wiley-Blackwell.

Valsiner, J. (2013). Cultural psychology. In K. D. Keith (Ed.), *The encyclopedia of cross-cultural psychology* (Vol. 1, pp. 319–327). Chichester: Wiley-Blackwell.

Wang, Q. (2016). Why should we all be cultural psychologists? Lessons from the study of social cognition. *Perspectives on Psychological Science, 11,* 583–596. doi:10.1177/1745691616645552

PART I

Basic Concepts

The foundation of a meaningful psychological science depends, of necessity, on scientific literacy in psychology, including not only an understanding of the technical content and methods of the field, but also the context in which such knowledge is acquired and applied. As the world becomes figuratively smaller, culture and context become increasingly important to the science of psychology and to the teaching of the science. In Chapter 1, Stevens, Benedict, and de Castro Pecanha present the idea of a contextualized global psychology as an aspiration and a response to the imposition of Western theoretical frameworks on psychology in the rest of the world. Teaching, they suggest, is not limited to the basic skills of psychological literacy; it can, and should, nurture the skills students need to assume their roles as successful, responsible global citizens.

In the global community, it is inevitable that individuals will communicate and work with people of diverse cultural backgrounds – people with differing languages, customs, and worldviews. If it is true, as many authorities have predicted, that the internationalization of psychology is inevitable, the skills to navigate this increasingly interconnected world will be essential, and cannot depend upon assumptions of the universality of the familiar. In Chapter 2, Elphinestone discusses the need for teachers, clinicians, and other professionals to move beyond rigid conceptual viewpoints and cultural stereotypes to the kind of competence that recognizes both differences across cultures and variations within cultures. For teachers, this means recognizing the significance of experiential learning as well as the skills that can be gained in the classroom.

These two conceptual notions – a broad, contextualized global psychology, and the competence to negotiate complex and wide-ranging cultural variations – mark a fitting beginning point and a relevant framework for those setting out to teach a psychology of all people.

CHAPTER I

Foundation and Parameters of a Contextualized Global Psychology Education

Michael Stevens, Alyssa Benedict, and Viviane de Castro Pecanha

> *For when it comes to the investigation and examination of psychological functioning, there probably is no way to get rid of all the other stuff, even in the lab.*
>
> Richard Shweder (1989, p. 8)

As is often stated, all psychologies are indigenous. Given this perspective, the discipline of psychology must be understood as having a local ecology. That is, psychology in all its branches is situated in a complex array of intersecting contexts that shape the local form and focus of its science and practice, such as culture; geography; history; religion; and economic, political, and social systems. Psychology "addresses the individual as an active biopsychosocial being involved in dynamic interaction with a context, be it proximal or distal" (Silbereisen & Ritchie, 2014, p. 5). This definition can – and should – be expanded to include small and large groups (e.g., family, nation) as well as small and large contexts (e.g., socioeconomic status, culture). If context, broadly speaking, is inseparable from individual and group functioning, it follows (a) that psychology must welcome the contribution of allied disciplines to the understanding of individual and group functioning through their distinctive conceptual frameworks, research methods, and applied practices and (b) that psychology education must partner with allied disciplines by including those same informative frameworks, methods, and practices. The focus of this chapter is on the second implication of psychology as a contextually bound, global discipline, one that we believe constitutes an educational imperative. Psychology education must address similarities and differences in the underlying principles and overt expressions of individual and group functioning in diverse cultures and contexts around the world if it is to prepare students to become psychologically literate global citizens (Cranney & Dunn, 2011b; Leask, 2015; Leong, Pickren, Leach, & Marsella, 2012; Rich, Gielen, & Takooshian, 2017). Psychological literacy may be defined as the capacity to use psychological knowledge adaptively and responsibly (Butler & Halperin, 2012; Cranney & Dunn, 2011a; Cranney, Morris, & Botwood, 2015; Leask, 2015). Psychological literacy requires, at a minimum, knowledge of core and cutting-edge disciplinary content, critical and ethical thinking, research and communication skills, respect and empathy for all forms of diversity, and a sense of social responsibility (McGovern et al., 2010). Psychological literacy also demands critical self-reflection and integrative interdisciplinary as well as global perspectives. These student-learning outcomes translate into indispensable competencies for effecting socially responsible action directed toward the common good (Stevens & McGrath, 2017).

Progress has been made in integrating student-learning goals and outcomes related to psychological literacy within formal guidelines for undergraduate psychological education in the United States (American Psychological Association, 2013) and elsewhere (International Project on Competence in Psychology Work Group, 2016). However, a recent survey of national representatives from 49 member countries of the International Union of Psychological Science spanning six continents revealed that cultural and cross-cultural psychologies need to receive greater weight in psychology education (Pinquart & Bernardo, 2014). Advocates for a greater integration of culture in psychology education argue that such a focus is essential if students are (a) to question unfounded assumptions about human functioning based mainly upon Western psychological science[1] and (b) to understand and appreciate more fully the relation between culture and human functioning (Berry, 1999, 2013; Berry, Poortinga, Breugelmans, Chasiotis, & Sam, 2011). We extend the recommendation for a more culturally informed psychology education by including additional diversities found in contexts other than culture (Huguet, 2014). Not only does greater contextual inclusiveness help to avoid the intellectual fallacies and tautologies of cultural reductionism, but it also makes explicit the multiple and occasionally more relevant global contexts that bear on individual and group functioning. Global contextual inclusion is what contemporary psychology education needs.

This chapter is organized into four sections. The first provides a rationale for a more contextually inclusive global psychology education. It summarizes current deficiencies in psychology education in the United

---

[1] In this context, we use the word *Western* not to connote countries in the Western hemisphere, but rather in reference to countries that represent the culturally constructed and bounded intellectual heritage of what is generally considered to be mainstream psychology.

States along with the value in and worldwide efforts to globalize the psychology curriculum. The second section addresses matters of definition. It articulates the aims and scope of a contextualized global psychology; clarifies the relationship of a contextualized global psychology to cultural, cross-cultural, and intercultural psychologies; and demonstrates that a contextualized global psychology is more than a culturally enlightened psychology. The third section provides examples of how Western psychology can at times be parochial and even ethnocentric. Examples of this are drawn from literature in disciplinary fields not featured elsewhere in this book. The final section offers a broad orientation to teaching methods and resources aimed at enhancing the contextually inclusive and globally integrative foundation of psychology education. It includes a guiding framework, foundational literature, learning environments and pedagogy, and strategic planning. It is intended for psychology educators interested in designing and teaching contextualized global psychology courses at the undergraduate or graduate level.

Rationale for a Contextualized Global Psychology Education

Past as Prologue

During psychology's formative years as a discipline, psychologists in the United States actively partook in international communication and collaboration (Hogan & Vaccaro, 2007; Lutsky, Velayo, Whittlesey, Woolf, & McCarthy, 2005; Pickren & Rutherford, 2010). Although largely confined to Europe, this research and practice exchange, which frequently involved US students, facilitated the growth and maturity of the discipline. However, after World War II, US psychology turned inward, focusing ever more on a nativist version of psychology grounded in logical positivism and relying less on international input and partnership (Arnett, 2008; Hogan & Vaccaro, 2007; Pickren & Rutherford, 2010). In the decades that followed, this inward orientation coincided with the rapid development of US psychology (Pickren & Rutherford, 2010). Furthermore, the emergence of the United States as a global economic and military superpower lent authority, if not primacy, to the psychology that it developed. What constituted legitimate theoretical, methodological, and practical knowledge in psychology was dominated by a Western, mainly US-oriented perspective (Arnett, 2008; Danziger, 2006). This globally decontextualized psychology was exported to and initially welcomed by the majority world (Marsella, 1998).

At first, countries at the geographic and intellectual periphery lacked the resources to mount their own research and practice agendas, and hence were delayed in establishing their own indigenous formulations of psychology (Arnett, 2008; Baker, 2012; Danziger, 2006; Hogan & Vaccaro, 2007). However, this is changing. Both Western and non-Western psychologists have increasingly questioned the indiscriminate and decontextualized application of US psychology across borders and cultures. Indigenous psychologies showcase new concepts, methodologies, and practices, and non-Western literatures (e.g., Asian psychology) feature enriching perspectives on many aspects of human functioning (Arnett, 2008; Gergen, 2001). Psychology as a science and practice has a significant presence in 47 countries, and an increasing percentage of scholarship abstracted in PsycINFO is by non-US authors (Adair, Coelho, & Luna, 2002; Piocuda, Smyers, Knyshev, Harris, & Rai, 2015). Psychology's significant growth in many different countries and the extensive membership of various national and international psychology organizations attest to the robustness of psychology worldwide (Adair & Huynh, 2012; Baker, 2012; O'Gorman, Shum, Halford, & Ogilvie, 2012).

The pendulum is swinging back to the international exchanges that were the cornerstone of early US psychology (Arnett, 2008). Moreover, the field is amassing an impressive body of politically and ethically reflexive literature that examines extant psychological understandings and their impact on, as well as their expression of, the contexts in which they are situated (Downey & Chang, 2014; Fox, Prilleltensky, & Austin, 2009; Gergen, 2001). Postmodern dialogues, guided by the intellectual movements of social constructionism and critical psychology among others, permit fresh analyses of established theories, research methods, and applications in virtually every disciplinary specialty (Gergen, 2001). Social constructionism identifies all knowledge as created through social interaction and embedded in a matrix of cultural, political, and social dynamics (Pickren & Rutherford, 2010). As such, social constructionism repositions psychology itself as the object of study (Gergen, 2001) and challenges theoretical forestructures (Kuhn, 1970) that are central to psychology at any given time. Critical psychology confronts the discipline's claims of scientific objectivity and political neutrality, highlighting how US psychology has overemphasized autonomy and the individual at the expense of mutuality and community, and legitimized unjust institutions and societal practices. It insists that US psychology do justice to the complexity of its subject matter, draw on contextually sensitive methodologies, and defy the status quo, including racism, sexism, heterosexism, and ableism that perpetuate injustice (Arnett, 2008; Fox et al., 2009).

These and other perspectival frameworks offer important discursive resources across disciplinary specialties. They invite psychology educators to engage in the essential process of self-reflexivity and model this process for students. "Modelling reflexivity in our teaching, research and supervision is an important component not only of building this capacity in our students, but of shaping our own practice as educators, so that what we teach is reflected in the process by which we teach it" (Rodgers, 2012, p. 411). Students can be empowered to consider, perhaps for the first time, the economic, historical, political, religious, social, and other contexts out of which psychological explanations have arisen and to access psychological knowledge from diverse sources. Such an inclusive learning orientation will prepare students to become psychologically literate global citizens and participate in the work of psychology with curiosity, empathy, humility, respect, awareness, knowledge, and responsibility. Perspectival frameworks serve to curtail the tendency to homogenize, and encourage international involvement and intercultural dialogue that are the face of a contextualized global psychology.

Progress at Home and Abroad

Unsurprisingly, the growth of psychology worldwide and the availability of innovative pedagogical technologies are transforming psychology education. Psychology education is flourishing around the world (Bullock, 2012; Stevens & Zeinoun, 2013; Takooshian, Gielen, Rich, & Velayo, 2016), and psychology educators are integrating the perspectives and contributions of diverse cultures and contexts into the curriculum. For example, Mexico, Phillippines, and South Korea have infused indigenous psychological theories, research methods, and applied practices into coursework (Takooshian, Gielen, Plous, & Rich, 2016).

Calls for a globally contextualized curriculum in the United States extend to many different disciplines and degree programs, although approaches (e.g., add-on, infusion, transformation) and commitment to globalizing higher education vary from one institution to another (American Council on Education, 2012). The latest trend report mapping strategies for globalizing education reveals that the undergraduate curriculum is the least globalized (American Council on Education, 2012). In a knowledge-driven, competence-led world, a contextualized global education that offers a coherent learning experience for students should not be introduced in graduate school, but rather at the undergraduate level, if not earlier. Psychology education in the United States must further adjust its content and methods in order to better prepare students to understand, appreciate, and practice a contextualized global psychology.

The American Psychological Association has taken several steps to build upon psychology's early history as a global discipline. For example, the *Report and Recommended Learning Outcomes for Internationalizing the Undergraduate Curriculum* acknowledges that, "the mission of psychology is inherently international" (Lutsky et al., 2005, p. 2). One of the five learning goals in the American Psychological Association's (2013) *Guidelines for the Undergraduate Psychology Major, Version 2.0* is ethical and social responsibility in a diverse world, with learning outcomes that include the adoption of values that build community at local, national, and global levels. More recently, Takooshian, Gielen, Plous, et al. (2016) advanced 14 recommendations for globalizing psychology education. Instead of relying on a separate course to build students' competencies as psychologically literate global citizens, Takooshian, Gielen, Plous, et al. advise psychology educators to adapt existing courses (e.g., integrate psychological science and practice from around the world) and experiment with Internet-based communication platforms for delivering transnational courses and hosting international lectures.

Heeding the worldwide call for a more globally contextualized psychology education (Pinquart & Bernardo, 2014), international psychology organizations have collaborated to identify and advance a set of globally applicable core competencies in professional psychology that can be adapted to the national and cultural contexts in which psychology is locally practiced. The *International Declaration on Core Competences in Professional Psychology* (International Project on Competence in Psychology Work Group, 2016) provides a general framework to guide the education and training of psychologists in applied practice around the world, ensuring a coherent global professional identity and standards of quality. Core competencies are divided into three clusters: psychological knowledge and skills that undergird core competencies, professional behavior competencies, and professional activities competencies. Each competency cluster includes descriptions of aspired-to attitudes, knowledge, and skills. Competencies that are particularly relevant for contextualized global training in professional psychology include the ability (a) to recognize the impact of personal values, beliefs, and experiences, (b) to identify, acknowledge, and respect all forms of diversity, and (c) to work with knowledge and understanding of the multiple contexts of colleagues and clients.

It is instructive for psychology educators to examine how diverse countries are globally contextualizing psychology education. Appreciation of their successes and failures and the circumstances in which their approaches are situated can open new pathways to a contextualized global psychology education in the United States. One such country is Brazil. Like many other academic disciplines in Brazil, psychology was born globalized with theories, research methods, and applied practices introduced by philosophers, physicians, and social scientists from other countries, particularly from Western Europe and North America (Hutz, Gauer, & Gomes, 2012; Hutz, McCarthy, & Gomes, 2004; Lo Bianco, 2009). Until recently, efforts to develop a contextualized global psychology in Brazil mainly involved attending international conferences, growing international networks and exchange programs, and supporting cross-cultural research (Hutz et al., 2004). It is important to emphasize that a majority of these activities were marked by the unilateral movement of Brazilian psychologists seeking international knowledge and training (Lo Bianco, 2009). In the past decade, Brazil has become a more visible and equal partner on the global stage. A combination of events and forces have contributed to Brazil's current status as a psychology powerhouse, including the beneficial effects of globalization on existing normative practices (Cardoso, 2008), economic ascension (ranked among the 10 largest national economies; Cardoso, 2008), disentanglement from Western psychology coupled with acceleration of culturally and contextually Brazilian research and practice (e.g., test construction and validation, adaptation of psychotherapy; Hutz et al., 2004, 2012), and improvement in the quality of higher education (e.g., the formation of government agencies to monitor and evaluate graduate psychology programs; Gomes & Fradkin, 2015).

The Brazilian psychological literature of the past 10 years attests to various initiatives aimed at growing the discipline of psychology within its borders and supporting the development of a contextualized global psychology education (Araújo, 2012; Comissão de Aperfeiçoamento de Pessoal do Nível Superior, 2011; Costa, Coelho-Lima, Pereira da Costa, de Souzsa Seixas, & Yamamoto, 2014; Dutra & Azevedo, 2016; Feitosa, 2007; Macedo et al., 2014; Menandro, Linhares, Bastos, & Dell'Aglio, 2015; Tourinho & Bastos, 2010). These initiatives include (a) publication of psychology books in Portuguese that acknowledge the production of both local and global knowledge as valuable to psychology education, (b) development of government policies promoting cross-cultural initiatives to contextually globalize education in several disciplines, including psychology, (c) dual and joint degree programs that permit the interdisciplinary transfer of course credits, (d) facilitating the global mobility of psychology faculty, students, and administrative staff with the intent of enlarging their perspectives through cross-cultural immersion and ongoing dialogue, and (e) the formation of transnational academic partnerships to support mutually beneficial opportunities for collaborative research and training. These initiatives have given rise to a new era in Brazilian psychology, one that features worldwide horizontal disciplinary and interdisciplinary cooperation and blends Western and indigenous Brazilian perspectives on individual and group functioning. It is this hybrid that constitutes the contextualized global psychology education now offered to Brazilian psychology students.

Aims and Scope of a Contextualized Global Psychology

For better or worse, globalization continues to transform the world. The transnational movement of goods and capital; increased contact with people of vastly different backgrounds, experiences, and worldviews; and access to information through sophisticated communication technologies all underscore how compressed and interconnected the world has become. One outcome of globalization has been the call to contextualize the science and practice of psychology, given concerns about the relevance and utility of the prevailing Western paradigm. Reconfiguring the discipline within a global context requires an adjustment in perspective, which can be difficult and even contentious. In this section, we offer our definition of a contextualized global psychology. As previously stated, a contextualized global psychology is in part culturally situated; however, economic, geographic, historical, political, religious, social, and many other contexts also bear on the focus and scope of the discipline. It is not our intention to diminish the contribution of culture to psychology – culture matters. Rather, we seek to avoid the traps of cultural reductionism by acknowledging the multiple, diverse, and occasionally more germane contexts that contribute to scientific and applied psychology. Moreover, we do not find it helpful to stretch the term *culture* to incorporate other contexts or to use the terms *culture* and *context* interchangeably. Elastic construction of the term *culture* needlessly reduces clarity and meaning when reference is made to specific contexts in which psychological phenomena occur. Similarly, we dare not opine about the causal primacy of any one context in determining psychological phenomena, nor do we believe we can easily unpack culture from other intersecting contextual conditions and forces. Our task is simply to incorporate context, globally speaking, into the conversation about psychology education.

Definition of a Contextualized Global Psychology

Using terms such as *international psychology*, *global psychology*, and *global-community psychology*, many have attempted to define psychology from a more contextualized and global perspective (Berry, 1999, 2013; Bullock, 2012, 2015; Stevens & Zeinoun, 2013; Takooshian, Gielen, Rich, et al., 2016; van de Vijver, 2013), hence, our affinity for the term *contextualized global psychology*. Some emphasize pressing worldwide challenges, others highlight psychology as it is constituted in different countries, whereas still others underscore culture as the foundation for all human functioning (Pickren, Marsella, Leong, & Leach, 2012). Variations in the definitions of a contextualized global psychology suggest that the discipline is mired in a protracted developmental crisis, struggling to establish a more mature identity. Unfortunately, these conflicting definitions have also triggered confusion and ambivalence in psychology educators who are thinking about contextually globalizing their courses. The time is ripe to settle upon a definition that honors multiple perspectives and propels the field forward. Our definition of a contextualized global psychology synthesizes core elements of extant definitions into two complementary components: global psychology and globalizing psychology.

Global psychology can be thought of as a vision to which the discipline aspires, that is, the creation of a contextualized, internationally relevant, and responsive psychology. It involves:

> understanding challenging contemporary topics that are not geographically bound and which have a psychological dimension (cause, effect, mediation, moderation), and designing contextualized, ethical, and socially responsible actions that address these challenges and support individual and social well-being. (Stevens & McGrath, 2017)

Globalizing psychology can be viewed as a corrective process that safeguards the discipline against provincialism and obsolescence by monitoring and promoting contextualization. It is an essential response to the imposition of Western explanatory frameworks on psychological phenomena, and involves:

> mapping psychological phenomena in all branches of the discipline through the derivation of cross-cultural consistency (universals) or diversity (particulars) in the constructs and processes that underlie such phenomena. (Stevens & McGrath, 2017)

Our twofold definition has several implications. A contextualized global psychology seeks to understand the multiple intersecting contexts in which

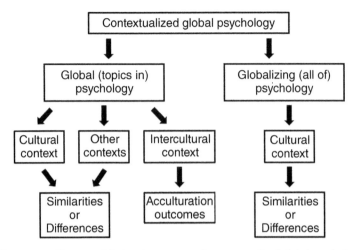

Figure 1.1   Contextual foci and outcomes of a contextualized global psychology

psychological phenomena – and psychology itself – are constructed and applied. A contextualized global psychology offers diverse interdisciplinary approaches to knowing, researching, and practicing that inform each other and that may or may not explicitly incorporate culture. A contextualized global psychology is ecologically more inclusive than cultural, cross-cultural, and intercultural psychologies (see Figure 1.1), making it contextually and globally applicable. As for psychology education, our twofold definition can guide the design of contextualized global psychology courses that expand students' intellectual and experiential horizons by exposing them to unfamiliar conditions and forces that they – and their instructors – may not have considered germane to human functioning. A contextualized global psychology curriculum can shape the attitudes, impart the knowledge, and even nurture the skills needed for psychological literacy and for working and living as responsible and successful global citizens (Cranney & Dunn, 2011b; Leask, 2015, Leong et al., 2012; Stevens & McGrath, 2017).

Interface between Contextualized Global Psychology and Other Psychologies

Figure 1.1 depicts the relation between our twofold definition of a contextualized global psychology – global and globalizing – and cultural, cross-cultural, and intercultural psychologies with which it intersects. Because cultural and indigenous psychologies are alike in conceptual content (Shweder, 2000), for efficiency, we will subsume indigenous psychology within cultural psychology. Whereas cultural and cross-cultural psychologies are familiar fields, intercultural psychology needs clarification. Intercultural psychology emphasizes the nature of contact between cultures at personal, community, and institutional levels; studies acculturation processes and outcomes of recent immigrants and refugees; and advocates policies and programs that support inclusive participation and intergroup harmony (Berry, 2015). In this sense, intercultural psychology resembles contemporary multicultural psychology in its global reach and application, particularly as it is understood outside the United States (Lowman, 2013).

If global psychology subsumes challenging topics that manifest across borders and have a psychological dimension (e.g., intergroup conflict, multinational organizational leadership, environmental sustainability), such topics should be conceptualized, studied, and addressed with relevant contexts in mind. Depending on the topic and focus of global interest, a relevant context may be cultural, intercultural, and/or something else entirely, with outcomes that reflect cross-contextual similarities or differences, or level of acculturative adjustment. For instance, DeSouza, Stevens, and Metivier (2011) focused on cultural context in exploring similarities and differences between Peruvian and US participants in their support for government retaliation after a terrorist attack. Berry and Hou (2016) focused on intercultural context in examining well-being as an acculturative outcome of the degree to which immigrants to Canada feel they belong to their host and heritage cultures. Stevens (2012) focused on economic and political contexts in showing that level of national development mediated the relationship of economic and political freedom to psychologists per population and their research productivity across 71 countries. Globalizing psychology, on the other hand, involves deriving cross-cultural similarities or differences in the observable indicators and underlying mechanisms of psychological phenomena in all specialty fields. Park, Haslam, Kashima, and Norasakkunkit (2016) focused on cultural context in discovering that, unlike Australians, Japanese who recalled instances of empathizing with others were less likely to self-humanize and more inclined to appreciate others' humanity. The effect of empathy on self-focus may be tied to culture.

Finally, given the likelihood that expressions of human functioning reflect the simultaneous operation of multiple intersecting contexts, it is essential to examine these contexts together. Overlooking their misguided presumption that all contextual factors are derivative of culture, Georgas, van de Vijver, and Berry (2004) unpacked the role of culture by showing that clusters of discrete contextual factors (affluence and religion) were systematically linked to psychological outcomes across countries (well-being). Specifically, "although economic development moves societies in a common direction, distinctive culture zones persist in which religious values are a constituent element" (p. 92). Although it remains unclear which contexts can legitimately be nested within culture, there are contexts that make seemingly independent contributions to psychological outcomes.

When Psychology Fails to Adopt a Contextualized Global Perspective

Thoughts, feelings, behavior, and even neurochemical action are influenced by the multiple intersecting contexts in which human beings are situated and, as autonomous agents, these same humans shape their ambient contexts through ongoing interaction. We are the creators and products of the worlds in which we live. The conceptual frameworks, research methods, and applied practices of Western psychology, like those of any indigenous psychology, are inherently limited in their capacity to predict and explain the global variation in human functioning. This is not to diminish the contributions of Western psychological research and practice, but rather to acknowledge that its rigid application, with little regard for global context, is parochial and, therefore, bound to constrain opportunities for accurate and meaningful understanding of psychological phenomena, particularly that which is unfamiliar and falls outside its contextual range of convenience (Kelly, 1955). A psychology based on 5–12% of the world's population (Arnett, 2008), situated in Western, educated, industrialized, rich, democratic (WEIRD) contexts (Henrich, Heine, & Norenzayan, 2010), and insistent that "people anywhere can be taken to represent people everywhere" (Arnett, 2008, p. 610), cannot always be right.

The following literature is drawn from psychological fields not covered elsewhere in this book: professional ethics, family psychology, organizational psychology, traffic and transportation psychology, and the psychology of women. This literature illustrates how assumptions grounded in Western psychology do not necessarily hold when extended to psychological phenomena situated in other global contexts. Other studies exemplify the use of Western psychology as an entry into global contexts that have been neglected or untouched by that same psychology.

These examples strengthen the case for a more contextually inclusive and globally integrative psychology education.

Professional Ethics

Ethics codes in psychology mirror the values and customs of the normative systems in which they are found (Stevens, 2008), yet psychologists have painstakingly crafted universal guidelines for the ethical practice of psychology. Contrasting the *Universal Declaration of Ethical Principles for Psychologists* (Ad Hoc Joint Committee, 2008) with the viewpoint that psychology is a contextualized discipline raises questions about the actual conduct of psychologists given the normative expectations prevailing in their local milieu: Will psychologists from contextually diverse corners of the world accept, reject, or respond ambivalently to universal ethical principles in their professional activities (Stevens, 2010)?

Whereas globalization has weakened national boundaries, local normative systems persist, growing stronger in response to perceived threats (Inglehart & Baker, 2000; Moghaddam & Harré, 1996). In spite of the inclusiveness with which the *Universal Declaration* was constructed and the availability of a contextually sensitive model for applying it to the development of national ethics codes (Gauthier, Pettifor, & Ferrero, 2010), its broad suitability and practicality have not been determined. As an example, although respect for the individual is made explicit in China's *Code of Ethics for Counseling and Clinical Practice* (Chinese Psychological Society, 2007), the code also reminds Chinese psychologists that they are responsible for ensuring social order and, under imprecisely worded conditions, required by law to violate confidentiality. How will Chinese psychologists resolve the ethical dilemma of balancing the rights and needs of the individual against those of society as stipulated by the *Universal Declaration* versus the Confucian virtues and political doctrine infused into the Chinese ethics code? Because ethics are foundational to the discipline, psychology educators may wish to globally contextualize all course modules on ethics by examining how the competing forces of globalization and localization affect trends in the ethical practice of psychology in the United States and elsewhere.

Family Psychology

Family psychology is embedded in larger ecological realities. How families form and function is influenced by cultural norms and various other contextual factors, such as economics, geography, and public policy. Expanding a Western frame and adopting a contextualized global psychology lens facilitates a comprehensive exploration of key aspects of family functioning, including appropriate roles and responsibilities of family members and the conditions that create or reduce family stress. Doing so also helps avoid premature and inaccurate conclusions about the components and optimizers of family well-being.

A particularly salient topic in family psychology concerns the optimal roles for and activities of children. Non-Western models of family and parenting/caregiving challenge Western assumptions and offer alternative views of family functioning and health, the role of the family as a socializing and educating agent for children, and appropriate roles and responsibilities of children in their families and communities. For example, in parts of the world where formal schooling has historically not been a primary activity of childhood, many children learn by being integrated into the community and engaging in contribution-oriented activities at an early age (Correa-Chávez, Mangione, & Black, 2015). Indigenous Peruvian Matsingenka toddlers practice heating their own food with fire under the supervision of family members; by the time they are three, many start practicing cutting wood and grass with machetes and knives (Ochs & Izquierdo, 2009). Measured against Western norms, these practices may be erroneously viewed as irresponsible and dangerous.

One of the most contentious issues regarding children's role in the family and community is their engagement in work. Individuals in more affluent Western settings may view any type of child labor, especially early on, as disruptive to healthy child development, assume that it is exploitative, and make uninformed judgments about why child labor is practiced by some families and communities around the world. Cross-cultural research highlights the multiple, interrelated contexts that lead to various types of child labor, and makes important distinctions between its exploitative and non-exploitative forms (Antony & Gayathri, 2002). Parental decisions regarding child labor are not a matter of cultural preference or restricted to the characteristics of parents and their households; rather, they are influenced by multiple contexts in a child's ecology (Webbink, Smits, & de Jong, 2013). For example, Krauss (2016) assessed the effects of individual, household, community, regional, and national contexts on child labor in Ghana, and found that child labor was linked to several intersecting contextual factors: the agrarian economy, demographics and social norms, geographic isolation of particular groups, perceptions in rural areas that basic education does not change economic circumstances, and the low priority of and capacity to enforce antichild-labor laws. Interviews helped to identify specific interdependencies between child labor and schooling, and highlighted the economic and societal demand for children to work (Krauss, 2016). Other researchers have identified additional contextually relevant factors, such as the availability of jobs for children to support their families and the absence and poor quality of schools (Webbink et al., 2013).

From a contextualized global psychology perspective, these conditions offer psychology students opportunities to appreciate the value of a comprehensive, contextually informed analysis of families. Students can become aware of and strive to remove cultural blinders, avoid reducing differences in family functioning to culture, and adopt investigatory methods that shed light on the larger network of intersecting contexts that impact family life.

Organizational Psychology

Organizational psychologists around the world are tasked with balancing global standardization against local customization (Ryan & Gelfand, 2012). They study and address manifestations of strikingly different and deeply rooted worldviews and how they impact work climate, productivity, and well-being. They often are members of multinational and multicultural teams of human resource professionals. Global companies headquartered in the United States and elsewhere have encountered attitudinal and behavioral challenges as the diverse values and traditions of their global workforce collide. For example, unionized US automobile workers have objected to mandatory morning exercises imposed by Japanese management. Whereas the company's rationale for adding exercise to the daily routine is rooted in data that it improves worker productivity in Japan and forms a culturally based obligation to the organization, US workers experienced exercising in front of Japanese managers as humiliating, in addition to violating their contractually negotiated rights (Gelfand et al., 2001). As with this case, context plays a critical role in the dynamics of organizations, including employee motivation and reward preferences, attitudes toward teams and teamwork, and leadership behavior (Ryan & Gelfand, 2012).

A major topic in organizational psychology is selecting and training leaders, one that assumes even greater importance when it involves global organizations with diverse workforces. Project GLOBE (House, Hanges, Javidan, Dorfman, & Gupta, 2004) seeks to identify common attributes of effective leaders and determine how leadership varies across contexts. Based on data from over 1,000 organizations in 62 countries, Project GLOBE has found that most organizations place little value on gender equality in terms of leadership opportunities. An exception to this is in East European (Albania, Georgia, Greece, Hungary, Poland, Russia, Slovenia) organizations. Gender equality scores for East European organizations are higher than those of organizations in ostensibly more socially progressive English-speaking countries (Australia, Canada, Ireland, New Zealand, United Kingdom, United States). Psychology educators can draw on this surprising finding, and invite their students to speculate about the contextual reasons for this difference (e.g., economic and political histories) and how they would empirically test their hypothesized explanations.

Traffic and Transportation Psychology

Traffic and transportation psychology is relatively unknown in the United States. However, it is well established internationally, having its own division in the International Association of Applied Psychology. Traffic and transportation psychology subsumes the attitudinal and behavioral dimensions of road safety, such as compliance with seat belt use, road signs, and speed limits. From a global health perspective, traffic accidents are the ninth leading cause of death worldwide and leading cause of death for people 15–29 years old (World Health Organization, 2015). Moreover, 90% of traffic fatalities occur disproportionately in low-to-middle income countries, and are estimated to result in economic losses of 5% of GDP (World Health Organization, 2015). The United Nations Agenda for Sustainable Development–Goal 3.6 aims to halve the worldwide number of fatalities and injuries from traffic accidents by 2020 (United Nations General Assembly, 2015). Yet data from Ethiopia show a steep incline in traffic fatalities (World Health Organization, 2015).

Recognizing the pitfalls of transferring Western psychology to non-Western contexts, Mamo and Haney (2004) nonetheless introduced the theory of planned behavior as a framework for examining the relation between attitudinal and behavioral compliance with traffic regulations in Ethiopia. They proposed that the intentions of minibus drivers to comply with traffic regulations would predict observed violations of those regulations. Mamo and Haney also measured years of driving experience and average distance driven each day. The results confirmed that intentions to comply with traffic regulations predicted violations of those regulations above and beyond driving experience and amount of daily driving. However, only a small proportion of traffic violations was predicted. Although the theory of planned behavior identified a narrow set of determinants of road safety in Ethiopia, it could not accommodate other contextual variables linked to compliance with traffic regulations. Regulatory compliance by drivers in low-to-middle income countries like Ethiopia also rests on economic pressures: circumventing traffic regulations is a financial imperative for many drivers, who not only must fulfill the terms of their employment, but also provide for their families. Vendors who peddle their wares in the midst of traffic also make it difficult to comply with traffic regulations. Psychology educators can present research like this to demonstrate the reasonableness of initially exporting a Western conceptual framework for understanding psychological phenomena in an unfamiliar global context, yet appreciating how such exports seldom prove entirely adequate.

Psychology of Women

Western feminist scholarship has made important contributions to the evolution of psychology as a discipline by critiquing conventional psychological theories and research for having omitted the female experience, measured women's psychological health against a male standard, and pathologized women, including their orientation toward connection (Belenky, Clinchy, Goldberger, & Tarule, 1986; Gilligan, 1982). Nevertheless, hegemonic forms of feminist psychology have been criticized for not addressing the experiences and psychological trajectories of women in diverse cultures and contexts, including those highlighted by different strains of feminist theory, such as critical race feminism, Black feminism, Latina feminism, Indigenous feminism, third-world feminism, and multiracial feminism (Bastian Duarte, 2012; Butler, 1995; Carby, 1997; Potter, 2015). Expansive discourses, as well as cultural and cross-cultural studies, highlight girls' and women's diverse conceptualizations (e.g., of self, body, relationship), as well as the different economic, political, and social contexts that shape their perceptions, beliefs, and behaviors.

Two conceptual frameworks – intersectionality theory and transnational feminist psychology – extend the contributions of early Western feminist psychology and can guide psychology educators as they explore gender, girls'/women's psychology, and the unique development and experiences of diverse and marginalized groups. Intersectionality theory demonstrates how hegemonic feminist psychology tends to overlook the ways in which women's race, class, and other identities become intertwined and create different contexts of experience as well as *axes of inequality* (Collins, 1993;

Crenshaw, 1991; Weber, 2007). Transnational feminist psychology seeks to decolonize hegemonic feminist psychology discourse, which prematurely universalizes the experiences of women, and to facilitate "new forms of feminist cross-border organizing" (Kurtis & Adams, 2015, p. 392). Dominant feminist discourses have often prioritized the concerns of White, heterosexual, Western, and middle-class women (Kurtis & Adams, 2015). They can "reflect and reproduce forms of racial and cultural hegemony that silence or pathologize experiences of people across various majority-world settings" (Kurtis & Adams, 2015, p. 389), and preclude discovery of how culture and other contextual factors impact women's psychological development and expression. For example, conventional feminist psychology may view self-restraint and silence in relationships as a global indicator of gender oppression. However, in some contexts, self-restraint or silence may be adaptive. For Turkish women, self-silencing was unrelated to depression and predicted greater relationship satisfaction, thus challenging North American theory and research that links self-silencing to depression and low relationship satisfaction (Kurtis & Adams, 2013). Transnational feminist psychology accesses context-sensitive research in diverse Western and majority-world settings, and extends the vision of pioneering feminist theorists to "reimagine forms of relationality that may better serve the interests of liberation" (Kurtis & Adams, 2015 p. 40).

Psychology educators can leverage intersectional and transnational feminist frameworks to shift the analytical focus from narrow and essentialist Western understandings of gender and women to intersecting identities and the systemic contexts that impact them. Exploring girls' and women's diverse realities and accessing insights from their experiences, including those related to struggle and resistance, can deepen psychology students' understanding of women's psychology and, perhaps, the human condition in general.

Teaching a Contextualized Global Psychology

The final section of this chapter addresses the pedagogy required for a contextualized global psychology education. It (a) includes an overarching framework to guide the design and delivery of contextualized global psychology courses, (b) identifies the general goals and student-learning outcomes for such courses, (c) delineates the foundational literature for a contextualized global psychology and explains its importance, (d) describes learning environments and instructional approaches to facilitate the attainment of student-learning goals and outcomes, and (e) discusses the need for strategic planning by psychology educators interested in developing and teaching contextually globalized courses.

Guiding Framework

Social constructionism offers a useful framework for psychology educators (Rodgers, 2012) designing and teaching contextualized global psychology courses and preparing students to take their place as citizens and workers in a complex, globalized world (Killick, 2015; Leask, 2015). It prompts psychology educators to remain aware of the relativistic, relational, and contextualized construction of knowledge (Rodgers, 2012) and to support students in accessing diverse perspectives that can enrich the knowledge they acquire about psychology and themselves (Killick, 2015). In a constructionist framework, psychology education becomes a process of bringing knowledge forth versus passing knowledge on, as in the traditional positivist approach to learning (Rodgers, 2012). Students are encouraged to step out of their zones of comfort and familiarity and engage in critical analyses of the contextual origins of psychological theories, research methods, and applied practices, as well as their own normative beliefs and actions (Rodgers, 2012; Stevens & McGrath, 2017). Such critical engagement is a key element of psychological literacy (Cranney & Dunn, 2011b), as it is to the general learning goal of enlarging perspectives (Krathwohl, 2002). A constructionist approach to a contextualized global psychology education also empowers educators to monitor the environment in which learning occurs, including the larger cultural and social context; classroom space, be it live or virtual; the learning processes of students; and, perhaps most importantly, the "crucible of interpersonal interaction in which the potentially transformative experience of professional education takes place" (Rodgers, 2012, p. 412). Leveraging the power of these interrelated spaces, psychology educators can guide their students to become more fully engaged critical thinkers, able to seek and apply diverse perspectives as individuals and as members of groups, integrating rather than dismissing information and experience that challenge their prevailing assumptions and biases (Butler & Halperin, 2012).

Learning Goals and Outcomes

Beyond oversimplified efforts to acknowledge diversity and cultural competence in the psychology curriculum, the overarching goals of a contextualized global psychology education are to empower students to reflexively consider their own beliefs and values, enhance their capacity for critical and flexible thinking, and cultivate awareness of how psychology in all its specialty fields is contextually situated (Rodgers, 2012; Stevens & McGrath, 2017). Psychology educators can design courses and use instructional methods that help students to (a) critically evaluate the suitability and consequences of applying Western psychological theories, research methods, and applied practices globally, (b) become familiar with non-Western models, methods, and applications and their relevance to understanding and addressing real-world phenomena, (c) cultivate awareness of how global events and forces impact the psychosocial and sociocultural realities of their lives and the lives of diverse peoples, (d) discover global topics of personal interest (e.g., globalization, migration, terrorism), and (e) use digital technologies to learn about the worldwide activities of psychologists and psychology organizations and to communicate and collaborate internationally (Stevens & McGrath, 2017).

Important learning outcomes connected to a contextualized global psychology education include, but are not limited to (a) awareness of different psychological and contextual perspectives (e.g., culture) with an appreciation of diversity in all its forms, (b) recognition that psychological constructs developed in one context may differ in substance and expression across contexts, (c) contextualized global psychology competencies (i.e., attitudes, knowledge and comprehension, skills, internal and external outcomes; Deardorff, 2009), (d) recognition of the role that psychology can have in addressing global concerns, and (e) an orientation toward global citizenship (Leask, 2015; Stevens & McGrath, 2017). With these learning goals and outcomes in mind, psychology educators can reconfigure their courses and teaching style to better prepare students to become psychologically literate and effective global citizens, wherever their lives take them (Cranney & Dunn, 2011b).

Foundational Literature

Foundational literature represents the essential body of knowledge upon which an entire discipline, disciplinary field, or topic within a disciplinary field rests. Analogous to a personal construct, there is a foundational literature that establishes the focus and range of convenience of a contextualized global psychology (Kelly, 1955; Stevens & McGrath, 2017). This foundational literature draws from conceptual, methodological, and applied material that together support a perspectival approach for best understanding, studying, and practicing psychology wherever it is constituted. The foundational literature also includes scholarship that demarcates the scope of a contextualized global psychology, that is, the contexts that set limits to the descriptive and explanatory power of scientific and applied psychology. In line with our twofold definition of a contextualized global psychology, the foundational literature serves to (a) inform our psychological understanding of and solutions to pressing topics that are not confined to any one geographic area, and (b) guide efforts to discover empirical similarities and differences in expressions of human functioning found in all branches of psychology.

For psychology educators seeking to introduce or deepen the contextualized global orientation and content of their courses, it is necessary to become acquainted with the foundational literature of this psychology. Psychology students benefit academically and personally from graduated exposure to this literature. The foundational literature of a contextualized global psychology will enable psychology educators and students to more fully appreciate the extent to which psychological science and practice around the world are inherently ecological and how researchers and practitioners approach psychological phenomena in highly diverse and intricately linked contexts (Stevens & McGrath, 2017). Most importantly, researchers and practitioners will begin to question their previously unchallenged, often Western, assumptions about individual and group functioning. Influential books in the extensive foundational literature of contextualized global psychology include the *International Handbook of Psychology* (Pawlik & Rosenzweig, 2000), *Handbook of International Psychology* (Stevens & Wedding, 2004), and *Toward a Global Psychology: Theory, Research, Intervention, and Pedagogy* (Stevens & Gielen, 2007). Other volumes feature the approaches of closely aligned disciplines to the contextually informed study and global application of psychology, such as *Cross-Cultural Psychology: Research and Applications* (Berry et al., 2011), *The Cambridge Handbook of Acculturation Psychology* (Sam & Berry, 2006), and *Critical Psychology: An Introduction* (Fox et al., 2009).

Learning Environments and Pedagogy

Based on the twofold definition of a contextualized global psychology, psychology education should prioritize the development of attitudes, knowledge, and skills that are aligned with efforts to understand and address long-standing and emerging global challenges (e.g., intergroup conflict, multinational organizational leadership, environmental sustainability). Psychology education must also offer learning environments that enable students to examine and critically reflect upon the similarities and differences in psychological processes and their expression in diverse cultures and contexts. These learning environments should encourage students to initiate dialogue with allied disciplines (e.g., anthropology, history, sociology) that broaden and deepen their understanding of individuals and peoples through multiple intersecting contextual lenses (e.g., cultural, economic, political, religious, social) without favoring any one context over another.

Psychology departments are urged to review their curricula in order to align their program and course learning outcomes with the expectations of a contextualized global psychology education, the most important of which is the expansion of students' intellectual and experiential understanding of conditions and forces that bear on individual and group functioning (Stevens & McGrath, 2017). In creating learning environments that nurture the development of psychologically literate global citizens, attention must also be given to instructional and learning strategies best suited to the preferences of millennial students for personally relevant material and technological engagement (Howe & Strauss, 2007).

Learning environments that have proven effective in engaging millennial students include opportunities for active and interactive experiential and service learning (Howe & Strauss, 2007; Price, 2009). Such learning is closely tied to innovative online instructional technologies, specifically synchronous and asynchronous multimedia teaching approaches (Anderson, 2008; Takooshian, Gielen, Plous et al., 2016). Asynchronous approaches include, but are not limited to, interactive quizzes, individual and group reflective writing assignments, voice-over recorded PowerPoint or Prezi presentations, YouTube videos and TED talks, and discussion forums with text and audio posts. Synchronous multimedia approaches are illustrated by on-ground encounters with diverse real-world conditions (e.g., poverty), live chat rooms, and video conferencing.

Active and interactive experiential learning should not rely solely on multimedia technologies. Williams and Falk (2010) confirmed that millennial students benefit from service-learning experiences that involve in vivo exposure to, assessment of, and solutions for real-world problems situated in multiple intersecting contexts. Service-learning experiences can expand and strengthen psychology students' intellectual, personal, social, and global citizenship competencies (Conway, Amel, & Gerwien, 2009). In teaching millennials, it is imperative that educators offer a combination of active and interactive experiential and service-learning activities, and actively participate in those activities, if their students are to achieve learning outcomes associated with a contextualized global psychology education (e.g., critical self-reflection, understanding how psychology-in-context can facilitate understanding of human functioning and global concerns). Whether delivered as lecture or seminar, on ground or online, or in synchronous or asynchronous formats, active and interactive experiential and service learning should touch upon accessible and meaningful global topics. Sample topics include (a) the psychosocial and sociocultural consequences to Europe of the humanitarian crisis in Syria, (b) the impact on low-and-middle income countries of international sanctions aimed at preserving the environment, (c) the importance of multidisciplinary, multisectoral, and multicultural outreach in curbing violence against women, and (d) the effectiveness of public policies in diverse countries for combating human trafficking.

The process of becoming a psychologically literate global citizen is completed when students mature into global change agents able to feel comfortable with, appreciate, empathize with, and seek opportunities to operate within diverse worldviews and to contribute to meaningful personal and work-related encounters with individuals, groups, and institutions around the world.

Strategic Planning

Despite recommendations from scholars and from domestic and international psychology organizations, globalizing the curriculum is a priority for approximately half of higher educational institutions in the United States (American Council on Education, 2012; for an example, see Pecanha & McGrath, 2015). Although recognition by university administrators of the urgency and value of a contextualized global curriculum is essential, grassroots efforts by faculty are needed to create the momentum and coursework for such a curriculum. There are personal and professional benefits to psychology educators in designing contextually inclusive, globally integrative courses. For instance, there are opportunities for mutually rewarding collaboration between academic departments, universities, and professional organizations, along with fresh outlooks on teaching. However, there also are daunting challenges. Many have called for a reinvigorated approach to psychology education that would prepare psychologically literate global citizens who possess the attitudes, knowledge, and skills needed to operate appropriately, effectively, and ethically in their work and private lives (Cranney & Dunn, 2011b; Leask, 2015; Leong et al., 2012; Rich et al., in press). Almost two decades ago, Anthony Marsella (1998) proposed a global-community psychology consisting of conceptual perspectives, research methods, and applied practices, having multidisciplinary, multisectoral, multicultural, and multinational origins, and being global in scope and utility. Regrettably, such innovative proposals for a contextualized global psychology curriculum in the United States have too often been scuttled (Pickren et al., 2012; Pinquart & Bernardo, 2014). Within higher education, resistance to a contextualized global psychology education can be found at student, instructor, and administrator levels, and reflects the presence of personal, structural, and systemic obstacles (Stevens & McGrath, 2017). For psychology instructors, resistance to a contextual global psychology education may be due to time constraints, coupled with personal and professional demands that interfere with attempts at curricular change. Structurally, psychology educators may encounter inertia, conflicting agendas, or a lack of incentives for globally contextualizing courses within their department or college. University-wide, psychology educators may be hampered by underdeveloped global expertise and inadequate or dysfunctional cross-departmental and administrative communication.

While our task is not to provide specific guidance on how to bring global contextual inclusiveness to the psychology curriculum, psychology educators who are wondering whether or not to reconfigure their courses may find it helpful to ask themselves (Halperin & Butler, 2015):

1. *Why should I rethink how I educate psychology students?*
2. *What is and what should be taught and learned in psychology courses?*
3. *What are the desired outcomes for a psychology education given current domestic and global realities?*

In entertaining these questions, we invite psychology educators to document the need to globally contextualize the content and instructional methods of their courses and the benefits of such reconfigured courses to themselves, their students and colleagues, and other people and communities with whom they may connect domestically and abroad. We further encourage psychology educators to lobby for institutional support for faculty development, funding, and release time to contextually globalize their courses. As with any plan meant to achieve a specific objective, it is imperative that psychology educators approach the global contextualization of their courses with awareness of the values and traditions of the academic system in which they work (contextual competencies are indispensable for psychology educators as change agents), anticipate unintended positive or negative outcomes of their actions to themselves and any collaterals who may be affected, and tailor their subsequent responses to emergent circumstances. If most or all conditions are favorable, psychology educators will surely find themselves and their teaching revitalized.

A Final Thought

The internationalization of higher education and specific efforts to context-ually globalize psychology are a call to action for educators in the United States and throughout the world. Psychology educators can acknowledge the strengths and limitations of psychological theory, research, and practice; endeavor to revitalize their instructional philosophy and methods; free themselves to collaborate across departments, institutions, specialties, dis-ciplines, and nations; and in so doing, become architects of the discipline's future. Education becomes a *practice of freedom*, whereby individuals "deal critically and creatively with reality and discover how to participate in the transformation of the world" (Shaull, 2000, p. 34).

References

Adair, J. G., Coelho, A. E. L., & Luna, J. R. (2002). How international is psychology? *International Journal of Psychology, 37,* 160–170. doi:10.1080/00207590143000351

Adair, J. G., & Huynh, C. L. (2012). Internationalization of psychological research: Publications and collaborations of the United States and other leading countries. *International Perspectives in Psychology: Research, Practice, Consultation, 1,* 252–267. doi:10.1037/a0030395

Ad Hoc Joint Committee. (2008). *Universal declaration of ethical principles for psychologists.* Retrieved from www.am.org/iupsys/ethics/univdecl2008.html

American Council on Education. (2012). *Mapping internationalization on U.S. campuses.* Retrieved from www.acenet.edu/news-room/Pages/Mapping-Internationalization-on-U-S-Campuses.aspx

American Psychological Association. (2013). *APA guidelines for the undergraduate psychology major: Version 2.0.* Retrieved from www.apa.org/ed/precollege/about/psymajor-guidelines.pdf

Anderson, T. (2008). *The theory and practice of online learning.* Athabasca: Athabasca University Press.

Antony, P., & Gayathri, V. (2002). Child labour: A perspective of locale and context. *Economic and Political Weekly, 37,* 5186–5189.

Araújo, S. F. (2012). *História e filosofia da psicologia: Perspectivas contemporâneas [History and philosophy of psychology: Contemporary perspectives].* Juiz de Fora: Editora Universidade Federal de Juiz de Fora.

Arnett, J. J. (2008). The neglected 95%: Why American psychology needs to become less American. *American Psychologist, 63,* 602–614. doi:10.1037/0003-066X.63.7.602

Baker, D. B. (Ed.). (2012). *The Oxford handbook of the history of psychology: Global perspectives.* New York, NY: Oxford University Press.

Bastian Duarte, A. I. (2012). From the margins of Latin American feminism: Indigenous and lesbian feminisms. *Signs, 38,* 153–178. doi:10.1086/665946

Belenky, M. F., Clinchy, B. M., Goldberger, N. R., & Tarule, J. M. (1986). *Women's ways of knowing: The development of self, voice, and mind.* New York, NY: Basic Books.

Berry, J. W. (1999). On the unity of the field of culture and psychology. In J. Adamopoulos & Y. Kashima (Eds.), *Social psychology and cultural context* (pp. 7–15). Thousand Oaks, CA: Sage. doi:10.4135/9781452220550.n2

(2013). Achieving a global psychology. *Canadian Psychology/Psychologie canadienne, 34,* 55–61. doi:10.1037/a0031246

(2015). Living successfully in two cultures. *International Journal of Intercultural Relations, 29,* 697–712. doi:10.1016/j.ijintrel.2005.07.013

Berry, J. W., & Hou, F. (2016). Immigrant acculturation and well-being in Canada. *Canadian Psychology/Psychologie canadienne, 57,* 254–264. doi:10.1037/cap0000064

Berry, J. W., Poortinga, Y. H., Breugelmans, S. M., Chasiotis, A., & Sam, D. L. (2011). *Cross-cultural psychology: Research and applications* (3rd ed.). New York, NY: Cambridge University Press. dx.doi.org/10.1017/CBO9780511974274

Bullock, M. (2012). International psychology. In D. K. Freedheim & I. B. Weiner (Eds.), *Handbook of psychology* (2nd ed., pp. 562–596). New York, NY: Wiley. doi:10.1002/9781118133880.hop201027

(2015). Internationalization in psychology: A process, not an outcome. *Psiencia. Latin American Journal of Psychological Science, 7,* 105–108.

Butler, H. A., & Halperin, D. F. (2012). Educating psychologically-literate students: The importance of critical thinking. In S. McCarthy, K. L. Dickson, J. Cranney, A. Trapp, & V. Karandashev (Eds.), *Teaching psychology around the world: Volume 3* (pp. 231–246). Newcastle: Cambridge Scholars Publishing.

Butler, J. (1995). Contingent foundations: Feminism and the question of "postmodernism." In S. Benhabib, J. Butler, D. Cornell, & N. Fraser (Eds.), *Feminist contentions: A philosophical exchange* (pp. 35–57). London: Routledge.

Carby, H. (1997). White woman listen! Black feminism and the boundaries of sisterhood. In R. Hennessy & C. Ingraham (Eds.), *Materialist feminism: A reader in class, difference, and women's lives* (pp. 110–128). New York, NY: Routledge.

Cardoso, F. H. (2008). Um mundo surpreendente [An amazing world]. In O. De Barros & F. Giambiagi (Eds.), *Brasil globalizado: o Brasil em um mundo surpreendente* (pp. 1–62). São Paulo: Elsevier.

Chinese Psychological Society. (2007). *Code of ethics for counseling and clinical practice.* Retrieved from www.am.org/iupsys/ethics/ethic-com-natl-list.html

Collins, P. H. (1993). Toward a new vision: Race, class, and gender as categories of analysis and connection. *Race, Sex, and Class, 1,* 25–45.

Comissão de Aperfeiçoamento de Pessoal do Nível Superior. (2011). *Ciência sem Fronteiras: Um programa especial de mobilidade internacional em ciência, tecnologia e inovação [Science without Borders: A special program of international mobility in science, technology and innovation]*. Retrieved from www.capes.gov.br/images/stories/download/Ciencia-sem-Fronteiras_ DocumentoCompleto_julho2011.pdf

Conway, J. N., Amel, E., & Gerwien, D. P. (2009). Teaching and learning in the social context: A meta-analysis of service learning's effects on academic, personal, social, and citizenship outcomes. *Teaching of Psychology, 36,* 233–245. doi:10.1080/00986280903172969

Correa-Chávez, M., Mangione, H., & Black, K. (2015). In and out of the classroom: The intersection of learning and schooling across cultural communities. In L. A. Jenson (Ed.), *The Oxford handbook of human development and culture: An interdisciplinary perspective* (pp. 292–306). New York, NY: Oxford University Press.

Costa, A. L. F., Coelho-Lima, F., Pereira da Costa, J., de Souzsa Seixas, P., & Yamamoto, O. H. (2014). Internacionalização da pós-graduação em psicologia: Estudo comparativo dos cursos de doutorado no Brasil e na Espanha [Internationalization of graduate programs in psychology: A comparative study of doctorates in Brazil and Spain]. *Revista Brasileira de Pós-Graduação, 11,* 789–818. doi:10.21713/2358-2332.2014.v11.548

Cranney, J., & Dunn D. S. (2011a). Psychological literacy and the psychologically literature citizen: New frontiers for a global citizen. In J. Cranney & D. S. Dunn (Eds.), *The psychologically literate citizen: Foundations and global perspectives* (pp. 3–12). New York, NY: Oxford University Press. doi:10.1093/acprof:oso/9780199794942.003.0014

(Eds.). (2011b). *The psychologically literate citizen: Foundations and global perspectives.* New York, NY: Oxford University Press. doi:10.1093/acprof: oso/9780199794942.001.0001

Cranney, J., Morris, S., & Botwood, L. (2015). Psychological literacy in undergraduate psychology education. In D. S. Dunn (Ed.), *The Oxford handbook of undergraduate psychology education* (pp. 863–872). New York, NY: Oxford University Press.

Crenshaw, K. (1991). Mapping the margins: Intersectionality, identity politics, and violence against women of color. *Stanford Law Review, 43,* 1241–1299. doi:10.2307/1229039

Danziger, K. (2006). Universalism and indigenization in the history of modern psychology. In A. C. Brock (Ed.), *Internationalizing the history of psychology* (pp. 208–225). New York, NY: New York University Press.

Deardorff, D. (2009). *The Sage handbook of intercultural competence.* Thousand Oaks, CA: Sage.

DeSouza, E. R., Stevens, M. J., & Metivier, R. M. (2011). Government retaliation against terrorism: A cross-national study. *Behavioral Sciences of Terrorism and Political Aggression, 3,* 1–19. doi:10.1080/19434472.2010.512216

Downey, C. A., & Chang, E. C. (2014). History of cultural context in positive psychology: We finally come to the start of the journey. In

J.T. Pedrotti & L. M. Edwards (Eds.), *Perspectives on the intersection of multiculturalism and positive psychology* (pp. 3–16). New York, NY: Springer. doi:10.1007/978–94-017–8654-6_1

Dutra, R. C. A., & Azevedo, L. F. (2016). Programa "Ciência sem Fronteiras": geopolítica do conhecimento e o projeto de desenvolvimento brasileiro [Science without Borders program: Geopolitics of knowledge and the Brazilian development project]. *Ciências Sociais Unisinos, 52,* 234–243. doi:10.4013/csu.2016.52.2.10

Feitosa, M. A. G. (2007). Implicações da internacionalização da educação para a formulação de currículos em psicologia [Implications of internationalizing education for the design of curricula in psychology]. *Temas em Psicologia, 15,* 91–103.

Fox, D., Prilleltensky, I., & Austin, S. (Eds.). (2009). *Critical psychology: An introduction* (2nd ed.). Thousand Oaks, CA: Sage.

Gauthier, J., Pettifor, J., & Ferrero, A. (2010). The universal declaration of ethical principles for psychologists: A culture-sensitive model for creating and reviewing a code of ethics. *Ethics and Behavior, 20*(3&4), 1–18. doi:10.1080/10508421003798885

Gelfand, M. J., Nishii, L. H., Holcombe, K. M., Dyer, N., Ohbuchi, K., & Fukumo. M. (2001). Cultural influences on cognitive representations of conflict: Interpretations of conflict episodes in the United States and Japan. *Journal of Applied Psychology, 86,* 1059–1074. doi:10.1037/0021–9010.86.6.1059

Georgas, J., van de Vijver, F. J. R., & Berry, J. W. (2004). The ecocultural framework, ecosocial indices, and psychological variables in cross-cultural research. *Journal of Cross-Cultural Psychology, 35,* 64–96. doi:10.1177/0022022103260459

Gergen, K. J. (2001). Psychological science in a postmodern context. *American Psychologist, 56,* 803–813. doi:10.1037/0003–066X.56.10.803

Gilligan, C. (1982). *In a different voice.* Cambridge, MA: Harvard University Press.

Gomes, W. B., & Fradkin, C. (2015). Historical notes on psychology in Brazil: The creation, growth and sustenance of postgraduate education. *Psicologia: Reflexão e Crítica, 28*(S), 2–13. doi.org/10.1590/1678–7153.2015284002

Halperin, D. F., & Butler, H. A. (2015). How to create a better future using the quality principles for undergraduate education. In D. S. Dunn (Ed.), *The Oxford handbook of undergraduate psychology education* (pp. 853–861). New York, NY: Oxford University Press.

Henrich, J., Heine, S. J., & Norenzayan, A. (2010). The weirdest people in the world? *Behavioral and Brain Science, 33,* 61–83. doi:10.1017/S0140525X0999152X

Hogan, J. D., & Vaccaro, T. P. (2007). International perspectives on the history of psychology. In M. J. Stevens & U. P. Gielen (Eds.), *Toward a global psychology: Theory, research, intervention, and pedagogy* (pp. 39–67). Mahwah, NJ: Erlbaum.

House, R. J., Hanges, P. J., Javidan, M., Dorfman, P. W., & Gupta, V. (Eds.). (2004). *Culture, leadership, and organizations: The GLOBE study of 62 societies*. Thousand Oaks, CA: Sage.

Howe, N., & Strauss, W. (2007). What to do? In N. Howe & W. Strauss (Eds.), *Millennials go to college: Strategies for a new generation on campus* (pp. 85–153). Great Falls, VA: Lifecourse Associates.

Huguet, P. (2014). Commentary on 'Bridging scientific universality and cultural specificity in PET'. In R. Silbereisen, P. J.-L. Ritchie, & J. Pandey (Eds.), *Psychology education and training* (pp. 164–166). Hove: Psychology Press.

Hutz, C. S., Gauer, G., & Gomes, W. B. (2012). Brazil. In D. B. Baker (Ed.), *Oxford library of psychology global perspectives* (pp. 34–50). New York, NY: Oxford University Press. doi:10.1093/oxfordhb/9780195366556.013.0003

Hutz, C. S., McCarthy, S., & Gomes, W. (2004). Psychology in Brazil: The road behind and the road ahead. In M. J. Stevens & D. Wedding (Eds.), *Handbook of international psychology* (pp. 127–144). New York, NY: Brunner-Routledge.

Inglehart, R., & Baker, W. E. (2000). Modernization, cultural change, and the persistence of traditional values. *American Sociological Review, 65*, 19–51. doi:10.2307/2657288

International Project on Competence in Psychology Work Group. (2016). *International declaration on core competences in professional psychology*. Retrieved from www.asppb.net/news/297538/International-Project-on-Competence-in-Psychology-IPCP-.htm

Kelly, G. A. (1955). *The psychology of personal constructs*. New York, NY: Norton.

Killick, D. (2015). *Developing the global student: Higher education in an era of globalization*. New York, NY: Routledge.

Krathwohl, D. R. (2002). A revision of Bloom's taxonomy: An overview. *Theory into Practice, 41*, 212–264. doi:10.1207/s15430421tip4104_2

Krauss, A. (2016). Understanding child labour beyond the standard economic assumption of monetary poverty. *Cambridge Journal of Economics, bew019*. dx.doi.org/10.1093/cje/bew019

Kuhn, T. S. (l970). *The structure of scientific revolutions*. Chicago, IL: University of Chicago Press.

Kurtis, T., & Adams, G. (2013). A cultural psychology of relationship: Toward a transnational feminist psychology. In M. K. Ryan & N. R. Branscombe (Eds.), *The Sage handbook of gender and psychology* (pp. 251–267). Thousand Oaks, CA: Sage. doi:10.4135/9781446269930.n16

(2015). Decolonizing liberation: Toward a transnational feminist psychology. *Journal of Social and Political Psychology, 3*, 388–413. doi:10.5964/jspp.v3i1.326

Leask, B. (2015). *Internationalizing the curriculum*. New York, NY: Routledge.

Leong, F. T. L., Pickren, W. E., Leach, M. M., & Marsella, A. J. (Eds.). (2012). *Internationalizing the psychology curriculum*. New York, NY: Springer. doi:10.1007/978-1-4614-0073-8

Lo Bianco, A. C. (2009). Da globalização inevitável à internacionalização desejável [From inevitable globalization to desirable internationalization]. *Revista Latinoamericana de Psicopatologia Fundamental, 12*, 445–453. doi:10.1590/S1415-47142009000300002

Lowman, R. L. (Ed.). (2013). *Internationalizing multiculturalism: Expanding professional competencies in a globalized world.* Washington, DC: American Psychological Association.

Lutsky, N., Velayo, R., Whittlesey, V., Woolf, L., & McCarthy, M. (2005). *APA Working Group on Internationalizing the Undergraduate Psychology Curriculum: Report and recommended learning outcomes for internationalizing the undergraduate curriculum.* Retrieved from www.apa.org/ed/precollege/about/international.pdf

Macedo, J. P., Dimenstein, M., Pereira de Sousa, A., Carvalho, D. M., Magalhães, M. A., & Silva de Sousa, F. M. (2014). Novos cenários de formação em psicologia no Brasil [New scenarios of training in psychology in Brazil]. *Avances en Psicología Latinoamericana, 32*, 321–332. dx.doi.org/10.12804/apl32.2.2014.10

Mamo, W. G., & Haney, D. (2014). Attitudes and behaviors regarding traffic regulations in Addis Ababa, Ethiopia. *International Perspectives in Psychology: Research, Practice, Consultation, 3*, 37–47. dx.doi.org/10.1037/a0035244

Marsella, A. J. (1998). Toward a global-community psychology: Meeting the needs of a changing world. *American Psychologist, 53*, 1282–1291. doi:10.1037/0003-066X.53.12.1282

McGovern, T. V., Corey, L. A., Cranney, J., Dixon, Jr., W. E., Holmes, J. D., Kuebli, J. E., . . . Walker, S. (2010). *Psychologically literate citizens.* In D. F. Halperin (Ed.), *Undergraduate education in psychology: A blueprint for the discipline's future* (pp. 9–28). Washington, DC: American Psychological Association.

Menandro, P. G. M., Linhares, M. B. M., Bastos, A. & Dell'Aglio, D. B. (2015). The Brazilian psychology postgraduate system and the internationalization process: Critical aspects, evaluation indicators and challenges for consolidation. *Psicologia: Reflexão e Crítica, 28*, 57–65. dx.doi.org/10.1590/1678-7153.2015284009

Moghaddam, F. M., & Harré, R. (1996). Psychological limits to political revolutions: An application of social reduction theory. In E. Hasselberg, L. Martienssen, & F. Radtke (Eds.), *Der dialogbegriff am ende des 20 jahrhunderts [The concept of dialogue at the end of the 20th century]* (pp. 230–240). Berlin: Hegel Institute.

Ochs, E., & Izquierdo, C. (2009). Responsibility in childhood: Three developmental trajectories. *Ethos, 37*, 391–413. doi:10.1111/j.1548-1352.2009.01066.x

O'Gorman, J., Shum, D. H. K., Halford, W. K., & Ogilvie, J. (2012). World trends in psychological research output and impact. *International Perspectives in Psychology: Research, Practice, Consultation, 1*, 268–283. doi:10.1037/a0030520

Park, J., Haslam, N., Kashima, Y., & Norasakkunkit, V. (2016). Empathy, culture and self-humanizing: Empathizing reduces the attribution of greater humanness to the self more in Japan than Australia. *International Journal of Psychology, 51*, 301–306. doi:10.1002/ijop.12164

Pawlik, K., & Rosenzweig, M. R. (Eds.). (2000). *The international handbook of psychology*. Thousand Oaks, CA: Sage.

Pecanha, V. de C., & McGrath, B. (2015, June). Master of arts in international psychology curriculum development. In F. Uslu (Ed.), *Proceedings of SOCIOINT15 – 2nd international conference on education, social sciences and humanities* (pp. 332–342). Istanbul: International Organization Center for Academic Research.

Pickren, W. E., Marsella, A. J., Leong, F. T. L., & Leach, M. M. (2012). Playing our part: Crafting a vision for a psychology curriculum marked by multiplicity. In F. T. L. Leong, W. E. Pickren, M. M. Leach, & A. J. Marsella (Eds.), *Internationalizing the psychology curriculum* (pp. 307–321). New York, NY: Springer.

Pickren, W. E., & Rutherford, A. (2010). *A history of modern psychology in context*. Hoboken, NJ: Wiley.

Pinquart, M., & Bernardo, A. B. I. (2014). Results of the IUPsyS survey of psychology education and training worldwide. In R. Silbereisen, P. J.-L. Ritchie, & J. Pandey (Eds.), *Psychology education and training* (pp. 21–44). Hove: Psychology Press.

Piocuda, J. E., Smyers, J. O., Knyshev, E., Harris, R. J., & Rai, M. (2015). Trends of internationalization and collaboration in U.S. psychology journals 1950–2010. *Archives of Scientific Psychology, 3*, 82–92. doi:10.1037/arc0000020

Potter, H. (2015). *Intersectionality and criminology*. London: Routledge.

Price, C. (2009). Why don't my students think I'm groovy? *The Teaching Professor, 23*, 7–8.

Rich, G., Gielen, U. P., & Takooshian, H. (Eds.). (2017). *Internationalizing the teaching of psychology*. Charlotte, NC: Information Age Publishing.

Rodgers, N. (2012). Social constructionism and graduate professional training: Challenges for teaching, supervision and research. In S. McCarthy, K. L. Dickson, J. Cranney, A. Trapp, & V. Karandashev (Eds.), *Teaching psychology around the world: Volume 3* (pp. 410–422). Newcastle: Cambridge Scholars Publishing.

Ryan, A. M., & Gelfand, M. (2012). Going global: Internationalizing the organizational psychology curriculum. In F. T. L. Leong, W. E. Pickren, M. M. Leach, & A. J. Marsella (Eds.), *Internationalizing the psychology curriculum* (pp. 245–262). New York, NY: Springer.

Sam, D. L., & Berry J. W. (Eds.). (2006). *The Cambridge handbook of acculturation psychology*. New York, NY: Cambridge University Press. doi:10.1017/CBO9780511489891

Shaull, R. (2000). Foreword. In P. Freire, *Pedagogy of the oppressed*. New York, NY: Continuum.

Shweder, R. (1989). Cultural psychology: What is it? In J. Stigler, R. Shweder, & G. Herdt (Eds.), *Cultural psychology: The Chicago symposia on culture and development* (pp. 1–46). New York, NY: Cambridge University Press.

(2000). The psychology of practice and the practice of the three psychologies. *Asian Journal of Social Psychology, 3*, 207–222. doi:10.1111/1467–839X.00065

Silbereisen, R., & Ritchie, P. L.-J. (2014). Introduction to psychology education and training: A global perspective. In R. Silbereisen, P. J.-L. Ritchie, & J. Pandey (Eds.), *Psychology education and training* (pp. 3–17). Hove: Psychology Press.

Stevens, M. J. (2008). Professional ethics in multicultural and international context. In U. P. Gielen, J. G. Draguns, & J. M. Fish (Eds.), *Principles of multicultural counseling and therapy* (pp. 135–166). Mahwah, NJ: Erlbaum.

(2010). Etic and emic in contemporary psychological ethics. *Europe's Journal of Psychology, 6*(4), 1–7. doi:10.5964/ejop.v6i4.219

(2012). Psychological ethics and macro-level change. In M. M. Leach, M. J. Stevens, G. Lindsay, A. Ferrero, & Y. Korkut (Eds.), *The Oxford handbook of international of psychological ethics* (pp. 375–393). New York, NY: Oxford University Press. doi:10.1093/oxfordhb/9780199739165.013.0027

Stevens, M. J., & Gielen, U. P. (Eds.). (2007). *Toward a global psychology: Theory, research, intervention, and pedagogy.* Mahwah, NJ: Erlbaum.

Stevens, M., & McGrath, B. (2017). A stand-alone course on international psychology. In G. Rich, U. P. Gielen, & H. Takooshian (Eds.), *Internationalizing the teaching of psychology* (pp. 23–38). Charlotte, NC: Information Age Publishing.

Stevens, M. J., & Wedding, D. (Eds.). (2004). *Handbook of international psychology.* New York, NY: Brunner-Routledge.

Stevens, M. J., & Zeinoun, P. (2013). International psychology. In K. Keith (Ed.), *The encyclopedia of cross-cultural psychology* (pp. 758–764). Hoboken, NJ: Wiley-Blackwell. doi:10.1002/9781118339893.wbeccp303

Takooshian, H., Gielen, U. P., Plous, S., & Rich, G. J. (2016). Internationalizing undergraduate psychology education: Trends, techniques, and technologies. *American Psychologist, 71*, 136–147. doi:10.1037/a0039977

Takooshian, H., Gielen, U. P., Rich, G. J., & Velayo, R. S. (2016). International psychology. In D. S. Dunn (Ed.), *Oxford bibliographies.* New York, NY: Oxford University Press. doi:10.1093/obo/9780199828340–0184

Tourinho, E. Z., & Bastos, A. V. B. (2010). Desafios da pós-graduação em psicologia no Brasil [Challenges to graduate courses in psychology in Brazil]. *Psicologia: Reflexão e Crítica, 23*, 35–46. doi:10.1590/S0102–79722010000400005

United Nations General Assembly. (2015). *Transforming our world: The 2030 agenda for sustainable development* [GA document A/RES/70/1]. Retrieved from www.un.org/ga/search/view_doc.asp?symbol=A/RES/70/1& Lang=E

van de Vijver, F. J. R. (2013). Contributions of internationalization to psychology: Toward a global and inclusive discipline. *American Psychologist, 68*, 761–770. dx.doi.org/10.1037/a0033762

Webbink, E., Smits, J., & de Jong, E. (2013). Household and context determinants of child labor in 221 districts of 18 developing countries. *Social Indicators Research, 110*, 819–836. dx.doi.org/10.1007/s11205-011-9960-0

Weber, L. (2007). Foreword. In B. Landry (Ed.), *Race, gender and class: Theory and methods of analysis* (pp. xi–xiv). Upper Saddle River, NJ: Pearson Education. doi:10.1016/j.advenzreg.2007.01.003

Williams, P. H., & Falk, A. (2010). Service learning and millennial students: Benefits and challenges to a team-based approach. *Professional Development: The International Journal of Continuing Social Work Education, 13*, 16–24.

World Health Organization. (2015). *Global status report on road safety 2015.* Retrieved from www.who.int/violence_injury_prevention/road_safety_status/2015/en/

Cultural Competence for Teachers and Students

Leonie Elphinstone

Globalization and increasing mobility of individuals and groups have resulted in increased diversification within nations as well as an increasing prevalence of intercultural relationships. These trends are in turn producing generations of individuals with multiple ethnic/cultural backgrounds and increasingly complex cultural identities. Such developments provide for an exciting future in terms of cultural interactions, while potentially further complicating communication between individuals from culturally diverse backgrounds. Working and teaching in psychology will bring increasing challenges associated with a diversity of clients and students, as well as those of other professionals with whom we work. As psychologists, we must be capable in a variety of areas, and increasingly one of these is cultural competence (DeAngelis, 2015; Hassim & Sedick, 2016; D. Sue, 2001; S. Sue, 2003, 2006; Sue, Arrendondo, & McDavis,1992).

Reflecting on the internationalization of psychology, van de Vijver (2013) noted that in the last 40 years, psychology has become more international as a consequence of both external and internal influences, including globalization, international migration, number of international conferences, cultural diversity of research participants, increased interest in comparisons across cultures, and a resulting increase in cross-cultural studies. van de Vijver concluded that the process of internationalization of psychology is irreversible and requires further development to make psychology, and particularly in psychological constructs, more inclusive and universally applicable. His call is for all psychologists to become conscious of the importance of culture in practice as well as in research

Similarly, D. Sue (2001) suggested that calls for incorporation of cultural competence in psychology have been hindered by belief in the universality of psychological findings that are largely Euro-American, by a lack of agreement on the definition of cultural competence, and by the lack of a framework for organizing its dimensions. van de Vijver (2013) reiterated Sue's concerns that psychological concepts and theories have developed from a predominately Euro-American context.

More recently, there has been increasing recognition that interactions between professionals in clinical and helping professions and their clients may be significantly hampered by rigid conceptual frameworks and lack of acknowledgement of the significance of cultural backgrounds. Kirmayer (2012) noted, for example, that encounters between professionals and clients are shaped by differences in cultural knowledge and identity, language, and religion. Furthermore, culture affects clinical services at a variety of levels, from access through service and relationships, including power relationships inherent in these contexts.

A number of authors (Danso, 2016; Garneau & Pepin, 2015; Kirmayer, 2012) have asserted that improving cultural competence of helping professionals can enhance cultural responsiveness, appropriateness, and effectiveness of clinical services. Cultural competence is increasingly recognized as essential for all mental health professionals (Sue, Zane, Nagayama Hall, & Berger, 2009), as well as for educators (Keith, 2012; Leiper, Van Horn, Hu, & Upadhyaya, 2008) and students (Cranney & Dalton, 2012; Velayo, 2012). Recognition of the need for cultural competence is demonstrated by the number of edited books and reviewed articles on cultural or intercultural competence published over the past decade (e.g., Deardorff, 2009; Hark & Delisser, 2009; Lonner, 2013; Truong, Paradies, & Priest, 2014), as well as the appearance of special issues of the *Journal of Cross-Cultural Psychology* (vol. 44, no. 6, 2013) and the *International Journal of Intercultural Relations* (vol. 48, 2015, pp. 1–136). The range of disciplines represented indicates recognition of the broad significance of cultural competence to a wide variety of helping professions and more broadly to business and other professions, in addition to education.

Until recently, the cultural competence focus has been predominantly on individuals moving from their own culture to another, and on issues related to adaptation, adjustment, and associated issues of culture shock (Chiu, Lonner, Matsumoto, & Ward, 2013). The role of psychologists working within their own context, and the development of cultural competence relevant to working with culturally diverse populations have received less emphasis, despite the well-established need for cultural competence in psychological practice (DeAngelis, 2015; Lonner, 2013).

As D. Sue (2001) noted, lack of clarity in the conception of the term *cultural competence* and a strong focus on evidence-based practice within the Anglo-Eurocentric model may perhaps account in part for the lack of established practice in this area. Relevant questions might include the following:

- What is the meaning of the concept of cultural competence? And more specifically, what does cultural competence mean for psychologists and for teachers of psychology?
- Can we develop cultural competence, and, if so, how?
- Can cultural competence be assessed, and, if so, how?

Answers to these questions lie in the history of the concept and in work in a range of related disciplines.

What Is Cultural Competence?

Background: Views of Culture

Early research on cultural competence was the product of globalization trends in business, resulting in the movement of expatriates around the world and the accompanying concerns of multinational companies with the success and the commercial outcomes of these placements (Mendenhall & Oddou, 1985). Much of this work related to what writers at the time termed *cross-cultural awareness and adjustment*. Concerns were predominantly associated with host and home cultures and with assumptions of internal consistency within cultures, and focused on adaptation to differences between cultures. Efforts to achieve such adaptation were largely knowledge based on and often assumed that an injection of cultural awareness training would do the trick. The seminal research of Edward Hall (1966) and Geert Hofstede (1980), focusing on cultural value dimensions, was a focal point for much of the work at that time. Hofstede's research in particular tended to position the perception of cultures in an essentialist frame (Garneau & Pepin, 2015) that was central to the way individuals were trained in cultural awareness to work in other cultures. This perspective saw cultural values as internally consistent within cultures or nations, suggesting that one could look at a culture and make generalized predictions about the values and behaviors of people from that culture/nation.

Although Hofstede's essentialist perspective has received criticism, it remains relevant in light of research reinforcing the broad notion of cultural values dimensions (e.g., House, Hanges, Javidan, Dorfman, & Gupta, 2004). Nevertheless, more recent research has demonstrated greater variation in individual differences within cultures than across cultures (Hofstede, Garibaldi de Hilal, Malvezzi, Tanure, & Vinken, 2010; Tay, Woo, Klafehn, & Chiu, 2010). The critical issue here is that although such value dimensions as individualism-collectivism and power distance continue to be relevant for understanding interactions and relationships, we should not assume that they necessarily define all individuals from a particular culture or nation. Similarly, an understanding of Hall's (1966) cultural notions, including high- and low-context, monochronic and polychronic approaches to time, and high and low territoriality, is useful background for individuals working with students or clients, but these are only part of a complex array of diversity factors and are not necessarily representative of cultural or national groups.

The essentialist cultural paradigm (Garneau & Pepin, 2015; Garran & Werkmeister Rozas, 2013; Gray & Thomas, 2006), in which culture is seen as objective, stable over time, and defining the differences between people risks ignoring other intracultural complexities now often identified as diversity, and may overlook the challenges associated with internal variation within cultures. Furthermore, teachers and others must acknowledge individuals with multiple cultural and/or ethnic identifications, as well as the processes of acculturation (Berry, 2005) – the individual (or group) culture change occurring when people encounter different cultures (Nguyen, 2013).

Recognition of individual variations within cultures has brought with it a move to a more flexible, dynamic view that sees culture as a social construction (Garneau & Pepin, 2015). Thus, according to Carpenter-Song, Nordquest Schwallie, and Longhofer (2007), culture is a dynamic relational process in which shared meanings originate in interactions between individuals – individuals who share information gained from social learning (Heine, 2012). Individuals are agents who influence and are influenced by conditions such as traditions, as well as by a broader sociopolitical backdrop (Lynam, Browne, Reinmer Kirkham, & Anderson, 2007). Thus, we must consider culture in historical, social, political, and economic contexts (Gregory, Harrowing, Lee, Doolittle, & O'Sullivan, 2010).

Apart from the challenges associated with defining culture in a more constructivist frame, there is another significant issue: As a result of biological relationships, migration, and acculturation processes, individuals increasingly identify with more than one culture (Berry, 2005). Hence, the complexity of identifying which culture(s) an individual's behavior or values may represent is heightened, making a prediction or diagnosis based on assumed cultural background fraught with difficulty and potentially stereotypical responses. Hassim and Sedick (2016) provided multiple examples of the complexity of interpretation of behaviors arising from different cultural identifications if seen from an Anglo-European frame of reference. For instance, behaviors interpreted as psychotic in one context are seen as "normal" in another, and in fact may be transitory in nature. Similarly, cultural assumptions about education and teaching may impede the teaching-learning process; as Hofstede and Hofstede (2005, p. 333) observed, "Information is more than words. It is words that fit into a cultural framework." For the purposes of this chapter, I favor a constructivist cultural perspective, recognizing that not all members of a cultural group will behave in similar ways or hold the same values, and that identity refers to what we *do*, not simply who we *are* (Hassim & Sedick, 2016).

Cultural competence. Having established a working definition of culture, it is also important to consider the meaning of the word competence. Kirmayer (2012, p. 156) defined competence in broad terms as "the ability to do things well, to achieve desired goals, and to act appropriately for the context." Within the framework of psychology and culture, the context may include individuals or settings that vary along both linguistic and cultural dimensions. Lonner (2013, p. 301), for example, defined cultural competence as "a psychological construct usually understood to consist of a set of attitudes, knowledge, and skills that together form a personal attribute that facilitates smooth and effective communication and interaction with people who are culturally and linguistically different."

Hammer, Gudykunst, and Wiseman (1978), in an early effort to understand cultural competence, identified 24 relevant abilities that contributed to a three-factor model involving the ability to manage psychological stress, communicate effectively, and establish interpersonal relationships. And although there is not strong consensus on a single definition of cultural competence (Chiu et al., 2013), a number of researchers (e.g., Chen & Starosta, 1997, 2000; Deardorff, 2006; Lum, 2011) have subsequently described such common features as effective, respectful interaction; communication; openness to cultural difference; sensitivity to others' worldviews (perspective taking); and emotional regulation. Definitions of cultural competence encompass both personal attributes (e.g., attitudes and knowledge; Lonner, 2013) and specific skills (e.g., shopping, communicating) necessary to functioning in a new context (Wilson, Ward, & Fischer, 2013).

Danso (2016), focusing on those working in helping professions within their own culture, suggested that the term *cultural competence* emerged in the 1980s in United States as a framework for addressing the ethno-cultural diversity produced by immigration. The need for health professionals to address the increasing diversity of their client groups has also been highlighted by other researchers (Blunt, 2007; Kirmayer, 2012). Writers and researchers in various fields of study, including transcultural medicine (Crampton, Dowell, Parkin, & Thompson, 2003; Kirmayer, 2012); nursing, social work, and occupational therapy (Danso, 2016; Harrison & Turner, 2011; Jani, Pierce, Ortiz, & Sowbel, 2011); as well as the teaching of psychology (Keith, 2012), have tried to define and address issues associated with cultural competency using a range of models.

Although it may be useful to teach cultural competence, in venues such as workshops for faculty and students (e.g., Velayo, 2012), development of cultural competence is likely to be an ongoing lifelong process (Rosenjack-Burcham, 2002; Garneau & Pepin, 2015). It encompasses effective, respectful response to people of all cultures, languages, classes, races, ethnic backgrounds, religions, spiritual traditions, immigration status, and other diversity factors in a manner that recognizes, affirms, values, and preserves their dignity (Lum, 2011).

Models of Cultural Competence

In an effort to understand why and how some people thrive in intercultural situations and to identify more clearly the potential models that might explain this, Leung, Ang, and Tan (2014) reviewed theoretical conceptions of what they referred to as *intercultural competence*. These investigators identified a variety of models drawn from researchers and practitioners in international leadership, management, personality, international education, and counseling. The review by these authors identified more than 30 intercultural competence models and more than 300 related constructs identifying features and behaviors of individuals considered culturally competent – in other words, individuals who are considered *successful* in intercultural interactions. Leung et al. distilled this research into three major content domains: intercultural traits, intercultural attitudes and worldviews, and intercultural capabilities. Each of these domains reflects a way of viewing an individual's propensity to develop and/or display cultural competence. Each also reflects potential models of assessment (Matsumoto & Hwang, 2013) of intercultural/cultural competence, which I will address later in the chapter.

Intercultural traits. There is a long history of traits (e.g., conscientiousness, extraversion, agreeableness) being positively correlated with sociocultural adaptation as well as with increased training ability, cultural awareness, and successful interpersonal behavior (Wilson et al., 2013). Leung et al. (2014) agreed that intercultural traits, like personality traits (Costa & McCrae, 1992), refer to enduring personal characteristics that might predict an individual's behaviors in situations involving interactions with others from different cultural backgrounds. According to Leung et al., examples of these traits, in addition to those noted earlier, include dissimilarity openness (Lloyd & Härtel, 2010), flexibility (Matsumoto et al., 2001; van der Zee & van Oudenhoven, 2000), tolerance of ambiguity (Bird, Mendenhall, Stevens, & Oddou, 2010; Deardorff, 2006), cognitive complexity (Lloyd & Härtel, 2010), inquisitiveness (Bird et al., 2010), quest for adventure (Javidan & Teagarden, 2011), emotional resilience (Kelley & Meyers, 1995), and open-mindedness (van der Zee & van Oudenhoven, 2000).

Some writers have suggested that these various traits may be antecedents rather than necessarily indicators of cultural competence (Chiu et al., 2013). Nevertheless, they may be significant contributors to training and to development of cultural competence, when combined with other factors that may be less rigid and more open to development (Wilson et al., 2013).

Worldviews. Individuals differ in perception of other cultures and information outside their own cultural experience (Leung et al., 2014). Bennett's (1986, 1993) focus on developmental dimensions of worldviews, from ethnocentric to ethnorelative, illustrates how variation between individuals may be observed both in attitudes and related behaviors. Individuals may have positive or negative attitudes toward other cultures or intercultural interactions, and we might predict that individuals who are highly culturally competent would have positive attitudes toward intercultural contact and other cultures.

According to Bennett's (1986, 1993) individual worldviews may be ethnocentric, and thus see the world from their own cultural perspective, or they may emphasize the complexity and contradictions of different cultures and countries as well as the similarities beneath surface-level differences. Individuals who are highly culturally competent are likely to have sophisticated, rather than simplistic construals of cultural differences and similarities. Constructs that capture such individual differences include cosmopolitan outlook (Bird et al., 2010; Javidan & Teagarden, 2011), category inclusiveness (Bird et al., 2010), and ethnocentric-ethnorelative cultural worldviews (Bennett, 1986, 1993; Hammer, 2011). Researchers are interested in the degree to which these conceptual views of the world can influence potential development and training in the area of cultural competence. Does a worldview, for instance, make an individual more or less open and receptive to training in the area of cultural competence?

Individual capabilities. Research on individual capabilities is a more recent area of interest and has a stronger focus on trainable skills and approaches. Leung et al. (2014) identified these as capabilities that a person can use when required in a particular situation. Earley and Ang (2003) identified intercultural capabilities as skills a person can use to be effective in intercultural interactions. These might include a basic knowledge level; an understanding of factors about a country/culture (Javidan & Teagarden, 2011); metacognitive, motivational, and behavioral cultural intelligence (Ang et al., 2007; Earley & Ang, 2003); linguistic skills (Imahori & Lanigan, 1989); social flexibility (Bird et al., 2010); and adaptability to communication (Gudykunst, 1993; Lloyd & Härtel, 2010).

Metacognition, identified as a key factor of the cultural intelligence (CQ) model (Ang et al., 2007; Earley & Ang, 2003), is a significant contributor to an individual propensity to adapt to and learn from situations presenting challenges to expectations and behavioral reactions (Klafehn, Chenchen, & Chui, 2013). Individual capabilities would seem highly relevant to psychologists working with individual clients in ambiguous contexts. However, this area also presents significant challenges in terms of assessment (Klafehn et al., 2013).

A combined model. Each of these models adds to our understanding of the antecedents for cultural competence and how individuals might demonstrate such competence. Furthermore, aspects of each of these three models may be required for an individual to demonstrate the skills, knowledge, behavior, and propensity for lifelong learning required for cultural competence. Following this reasoning, Leung et al. (2014) proposed a model combining the three, recognizing that intercultural traits predispose individuals to particular intercultural attitudes and worldviews and to intercultural capabilities. Together, Leung et al. suggested, these three models lead to intercultural effectiveness, or what might be termed *cultural competence* (Figure 2.1). Intercultural traits, they suggested, influence attitudes, worldviews, and capabilities, which in turn enable cultural competence.

Assessment of Cultural Competence

Matsumoto and Hwang (2013) reviewed ten cultural competence assessment tools, including measures related to the first three models described

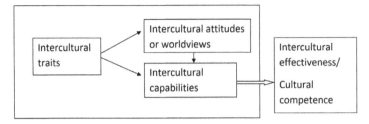

Figure 2.1   Model of intercultural effectiveness (cultural competence).
Adapted from Leung et al. (2014, p. 498).

previously (and by extension, the combined model), evaluating content, construct, and ecological validity of each assessment tool. Leung et al. (2014) also evaluated available assessment tools, reviewing predictive outcomes.

Individual traits model. In relation to the individual traits model, both research groups identified and reviewed outcomes associated with the Multicultural Personality Inventory (MPQ) (van der Zee & van Oudenhoven, 2000). The MPQ uses a five-factor scoring procedure, with scales labeled Emotional Stability, Social Initiative, Open Mindedness, Cultural Empathy, and Flexibility. Matsumoto and Hwang (2013) and Leung et al. (2014) reported a variety of studies suggesting that the MPQ may predict or be associated with sociocultural adjustment, psychological well-being, mental health, physical health, international aspirations, expatriate job satisfaction, performance of students working in culturally diverse teams, multicultural activities, international orientation, self-ratings and aptitude for an international career, number of foreign languages spoken (and self-rated proficiency), and experience living abroad. Other studies reported by Matsumoto and Hwang (2013) suggested that the MPQ may predict more traditional and direct measures of adaptation and adjustment, including satisfaction with life, social interactions, academic achievement, job satisfaction, team commitment, anxiety, positive and negative affect, reactions to hypothetical scenarios concerning acculturation strategies, team identification and affect in diverse teams, responses to critical incidents, and self-ratings of intercultural experiences.

The MPQ was one of three tests that Matsumoto and Hwang (2013) identified as having incremental ecological validity, demonstrating that it can predict cross-cultural outcomes beyond standard personality and intelligence; however, there are limitations in terms of breadth of predictive outcomes and other factors. Clearly, many of the outcomes predicted by the MPQ may be relevant to psychologists training and working in culturally diverse contexts.

Worldviews model. Matsumoto and Hwang (2013) reviewed the Intercultural Development Inventory (IDI), developed by Hammer, Bennett, and Wiseman (2003) based on Bennett's (1986) Developmental Model of Intercultural Sensitivity. This model proposes six stages of development reflecting how an individual moves from a stage of ethnocentrism to ethnorelativism. Reviewing ecological validity of the IDI, Matsumoto and Hwang reported that few studies have provided evidence of correlation with such demographic variables as intercultural experience, friends from other cultures, language study age, father's education, years spent in another culture, or length of time attending international school, suggesting that exposure to other cultures may be a relevant factor.

Leung et al. (2014) reported that, based on IDI scores, level of intercultural development significantly and positively predicts satisfaction with study abroad, percentage of intercultural friends, and effectiveness in meeting diversity and inclusion staffing goals. They also reported that people with higher levels of intercultural development are less anxious in intercultural situations. However, pre–post tests using the IDI to assess training efficacy have achieved mixed results (Matsumoto & Hwang, 2013).

Individual capabilities model. The individual capabilities model is perhaps the one most strongly represented by research in the area of CQ (Ang, Van Dyne, & Koh, 2005). Ang et al. (2005) defined CQ as an individual's capability to deal effectively in situations characterized by cultural diversity. The CQ is based on Earley and Ang's (2003) four-component theoretical model characterizing CQ as comprising metacognitive, cognitive, motivational, and behavioral CQ. Metacognitive CQ refers to the processes by which individuals acquire and understand cultural knowledge, whereas cognitive CQ is general knowledge about culture; motivational CQ is the magnitude and direction of energy applied toward learning and functioning in cross-cultural situations; and behavioral CQ is the capability to exhibit appropriate actions when interacting with people of different cultures (Ang & Van Dyne, 2008; Ang et al., 2007).

Based on a review of outcome studies related to use of the CQ scale, Leung et al. (2014) indicated that CQ consistently predicts "psychological outcomes such as intercultural adjustment, behavioral outcomes such as idea sharing and development of social networks with culturally different others, and performance outcomes such as task performance and cross-border leadership effectiveness" (p. 495). These investigators further noted that empirical evidence suggests that although all four factors are significantly and positively correlated with psychological and performance outcomes, motivational cultural intelligence is more strongly correlated with psychological outcomes, and metacognitive and behavioral cultural intelligence are more strongly correlated with performance outcomes.

Matsumoto and Hwang (2013) reported that scores on the CQ have predicted cross-cultural judgment and decision making, general and interactional adjustment and well-being, task performance on a problem-solving simulation, work performance, culture shock, and work performance; organizational innovation and transformational leadership behaviors; leader and team performance; cooperative relationship management behaviors; cultural adjustment; and psychological adjustment and sociocultural adaptation. Pre- and post-tests of the efficacy of intercultural training using the CQ as an outcome measure have provided mixed results, but with some useful evidence regarding potential training of students (Elphinstone, 2016). Additionally, Matsumoto and Hwang (2013) reported that several studies provided evidence that CQ predicts adjustment or adaptation above and beyond variables related to personality, demographics, and emotional intelligence.

A recent summary of relevant research (Van Dyne, Ang, & Tan, 2017) demonstrated the wide range and depth of research supporting the development and application of CQ, and this, combined with practical application of CQ (Livermore, 2016; Livermore & Van Dyne, 2015), seems to position it in the forefront of work in the area of cultural competence. Ang et al. (2005) reported that the Big Five personality trait of openness to experience predicts all four CQ capabilities, whereas extraversion predicts cognitive CQ, motivational CQ, and behavioral CQ. Conscientiousness predicts metacognitive CQ, and agreeableness and emotional stability predict behavioral CQ. Leung et al. (2014) concluded that the CQ model and the multicultural personality model have thus far provided the most promising evidence as intercultural competence models, suggesting that some combination of these may actually provide the most comprehensive model for explanation of factors significant for cultural competence.

Teaching for Cultural Competence

Reviews of the validity and reliability of tools for measuring cultural competence have suggested that the CQ, and the MPQ have significant potential for predicting behaviors critical for cultural competence

(Matsumoto & Hwang, 2013). The CQ, with its focus on capabilities rather than traits, appears to have the most potential for teaching students to build cultural competence.

The four components of the CQ model that can guide training are metacognitive CQ, cognitive CQ, motivational CQ, and behavioral CQ (Livermore, 2016; Livermore & Van Dyne, 2015).

Earley and Ang (2003) developed questions that individuals might ask of themselves as they prepare to deal with people from multicultural backgrounds, and Molina (2012/2013) adapted these questions for use by teachers. The questions align with the four CQ components, and are useful in guiding students as they develop cultural competence.

Metacognitive CQ. Metacognitive CQ focuses on the ability to reflect on one's own behavior and that of others, and, as a result, to adjust perceptions and actions. Sieck, Smith, and Rasmussen (2013) attempted to identify the processes involved in metacognition in cultural interactions and highlighted five potential processes. These are: notice anomalies (cultural surprises that seem unusual to an outsider); instantiate a general cultural schema (a potential general explanation of the surprising behavior); inquire as to causes (ask questions about why the behavior occurs); consider alternative explanations (exploring different possible causes can reduce overconfidence); and suspend judgment (don't rush to judgment in trying to explain surprising cross-cultural behavior). Sieck et al. (2013) compared experts to novices in dealing with cultural scenarios and found that all of these strategies except noticing anomalies differentiated among the groups. Interestingly, these researchers, including Leung et al. (2014), raised the possibility that personality or intercultural traits such as openness and flexibility may be important antecedents to the ability and willingness of individuals to consider alternative explanations and to suspend judgment.

Sieck et al. (2013) argued that these metacognitive strategies can be taught, and that they can be learned, even by individuals with little cross-cultural background. The metacognitive self-evaluation questions developed by Earley and Ang (2003) encompassed such dimensions as checking for accuracy of one's own cultural knowledge, adjusting cultural knowledge when interacting with individuals from an unfamiliar culture, and self-awareness of cultural knowledge used in interacting with people from different cultures.

Cognitive CQ. The cognitive area focuses on knowledge of cultures, cultural values, world religions, and much of the traditional material associated with cultural awareness; it is possible to address this area relatively easily in courses and training (Elphinstone, 2016). However, the uptake and acceptance of this knowledge base is influenced by the other three components of the model. Additionally, assumptions that this knowledge can be gained without real exposure to other cultures, either by immersion in a culturally diverse environment or extensive travel, seem questionable (Elphinstone, 2016).

Effective development of cognitive CQ requires a focus on a constructivist approach to culture, recognizing diversity within cultures and avoiding stereotypes suggesting that all people from a particular culture hold similar values or behave in the same way. Some useful avenues of self-reflection within the cognitive CQ area include knowledge of cultural values and religious beliefs, nonverbal behaviors of other cultures, the rules of other languages, and the marriage practices of other cultures (Earley & Ang, 2003).

Motivational CQ. Motivational CQ has been related to self-determination (Devitt, 2014) and encompasses both confidence and interest in effective intercultural functioning (Van Dyne et al., 2017). Research has suggested that motivated individuals learn more from cross-cultural experience (Yunlu & Clapp-Smith, 2014), and that motivational CQ is associated with cultural well-being of students who study abroad (Peng, Van Dyne, & Oh, 2015).

Useful self-reflection questions concern the ability to deal with stresses of a new culture, attitude toward interacting with people of other cultures, confidence in socializing with people of an unfamiliar culture, and likely enjoyment of living in another culture (Earley & Ang, 2003; Molina, 2012/2013). Changing student motivation may prove challenging for teachers of psychology, although there is some evidence to suggest that such activities as intercultural service learning activities may be helpful (e.g., Borden, 2007).

Behavioral CQ. Specific actions are an important aspect of cultural intelligence, and cross-cultural training can build cross-cultural competency skills (Kealey & Protheroe, 1996). Important behaviors can include appropriate use of accent and tone in verbal behavior, variation in the rate of speaking, effective use of silence and pauses when communicating, and the ability to change facial expressions appropriately (Earley & Ang, 2003). Cushner (1987) and Brislin, Cushner, Cherrie, and Yong (1986) reported that exposure to scenarios depicting cross-cultural incidents could aid not only in effecting specific responses, but also increased knowledge and empathy in students.

Role-playing can be an effective way to enhance skills in interpersonal interaction (Feinstein, Mann, & Corsun, 2002), and Bücker and Korzilius (2015) found that role-playing increased behavioral CQ of students in a cross-cultural study. Exposure to cross-cultural scenarios and critical incidents can improve both adjustment to foreign settings and interpersonal problem-solving skills (Cushner, 1987).

Teaching Activities

This section presents two approaches to providing students with classroom experiences designed to challenge cultural assumptions and knowledge in a relatively risk-free situation. In each case, students can test their cultural knowledge and skills, and receive feedback intended to improve their cultural awareness and intercultural facility.

BaFá BaFá. Simulations and gaming activities have long been recognized as aids to teaching and learning (e.g., Peterson, Glover, Romero, & Romero, 1978). The longest standing and most widely used simulation for exposing students to cultural concepts, increasing knowledge and skills for relating to unfamiliar cultures, and dealing with diversity issues, is BaFá BaFá (Shirts, 1969, 1977). This simulation involves dividing the class into two groups (cultures) with distinctly different values and ways of behaving, and then having individuals from each group observe and visit the other, with the aim of learning the rules of the other culture. Participants engage in debriefing, with emphasis on the apprehensions, misperceptions, and stereotypes they may have formed, and their conclusions about the necessity of such attitudes and behaviors as open-mindedness and cooperation (Dunn, Meine, & Dunn, 2011).

Studies of the BaFá BaFá simulation have suggested that participants may become less dogmatic and more tolerant of ambiguity (Peterson et al., 1978) and experience enhanced cultural insight (Koskinen, Abdelhamid, & Likitalo, 2008). Students learn how it feels to be "different," and can learn about the process of acculturation (Swift & Denton, 2003). In responding to similar classroom simulations, students have reported an increased understanding of cultural norms and enhanced sensitivity to the effects of their own behavior in cultural situations (Myers, Buoye, McDermott, Strickler, & Ryman, 2000). All of these outcomes are consistent with improved cultural competence. The BaFá BaFá stimulation can take 2–3 hours to complete, and materials are available from Simulation Training Systems (www.simulationtrainingsystems.com).

Culture-general assimilator. Brislin et al. (1986) developed the culture-general assimilator (CGA), comprising a set of 100 critical incidents introducing culture-general concepts. Each incident is a brief story leading to a conclusion embodying a misunderstanding or miscommunication between individuals from different cultural backgrounds (Brislin, 1986; Cushner, 1987). Following the story, students read a set of alternative explanations for the cultural conflict, and rate each explanation according to how well they believe each explains the situation. Each choice leads to feedback, helping the students to evaluate and understand their own ratings and the preferred explanation.

Research has shown that students trained using the CGA, compared to controls using a traditional cultural orientation, more competently recognized the dynamics of cross-cultural interactions and adjustment. They were also more efficient in interpersonal problem solving , and were better able to apply their knowledge in intercultural interactions (Cushner, 1989).

These simulation activities can provide students valuable cultural competence preparation before embarking upon international study or travel, and can enhance understanding and appreciation of cultural materials and information. Furthermore, they offer meaningful cultural exposure and practice in a safe setting with the opportunity for helpful feedback and support.

Conclusion

There is clearly a long way to go in terms of fully defining what cultural competence may mean for psychologists; however the CQ model offers potential as a framework for focusing on approaches and capabilities that will be relevant. It is an inescapable fact that in our professional lives we will all work with people of increasing diversity in settings requiring effective mindsets and skills. Reflecting on the challenges of training psychologists in cultural competence, Derald Sue observed:

> There are two issues here. First, formal training through workshops and academic work is required. However, that is not enough. Cultural competence is more than cognitive and intellectual understanding. If psychologists believe they need only specialized training, they will never become culturally competent. Cultural competence must be obtained through experiential reality .... . Psychologists must realize that cultural competence is not acquired just through book learning and skills training alone. (Tracey, 2006, p. 49)

Gaining cultural competence is likely to be a nonlinear dynamic process that is never ending and ever expanding – a process of lifelong learning (Deardorff, 2008).

Resources

BaFá BaFá: Educational Edition. www.simulationtrainingsystems.com
Cushner, K., & Brislin, R. W. (1996). *Intercultural interactions: A practical guide* (2nd ed.). Thousand Oaks, CA: Sage.
Deardorff, D. K. (Ed.). (2009). *The Sage handbook of intercultural competence.* Thousand Oaks, CA: Sage.
Landis, D., Bennett, J., & Bennett, M. (Eds.). (2004). *Handbook of intercultural training* (3rd ed.). Thousand Oaks, CA: Sage.

References

Ang, S., Van Dyne, L., & Koh, C. S. K. (2005). Personality correlates of the four-factor model of cultural intelligence. *Group and Organization Management, 31,* 100–123. doi:10.1177/1059601105275267
Ang, S., & Van Dyne, L. (Eds.). (2008). *Handbook of Cultural Intelligence.* New York, NY: Sharpe.
Ang, S., Van Dyne, L. V., Koh, C., Ng, K. Y., Templer, K. J., Tay, C., & Chandrasekar, N. A. (2007). Cultural intelligence: Its measurement and effects on cultural judgment and decision making, cultural adaptation and task performance. *Management and Organization Review, 3,* 335–371. doi:10.1111/j.1740-8784.2007.00082.x
Bennett, M. J. (1986). A developmental approach to training intercultural sensitivity. *International Journal of Intercultural Relations, 10,* 179–186. doi:10.1016/0147-1767(86)90005-2
  (1993). *Towards ethnorelativism: A developmental model of intercultural sensitivity* (2nd ed.). In R. M. Paige (Ed.), *Education for the intercultural experience* (pp. 21–71). Yarmouth, ME: Intercultural Press.
Berry, J. (2005). Acculturation: Living successfully in two cultures. *International Journal of Intercultural Relations, 29,* 697–712. doi:10.1016/j.ijintrel.2005.07.013
Bird, A., Mendenhall, M., Stevens, M. J., & Oddou, G. (2010). Defining the content domain of intercultural competence for global leaders. *Journal of Management Psychology, 25,* 810–828. doi:10.1108/02683941011089107
Blunt, A. (2007). Cultural geographies of migration: Mobility, transnationality and diaspora. *Progress in Human Geography, 31,* 684–694. doi:10.1177/0309132507078945
Borden, A. W. (2007). The impact of service-learning on ethnocentrism in an intercultural communication course. *Journal of Experiential Education, 30,* 171–183. doi:10.1177/105382590703000206
Brislin, R. (1986). A culture general assimilator: Preparation for various types of sojourns. *International Journal of Intercultural Relations, 10,* 215–234. doi:10.1016/0147-1767(86)90007-6
Brislin, R., Cushner, K., Cherrie, C., & Yong, M. (1986). *Intercultural interaction: A practical guide.* Beverly Hills, CA: Sage.

Bücker, J. J. L. E., & Korzilius, H. (2015). Developing cultural intelligence: Assessing the effect of the Ecotonos cultural simulation game for international business students. *International Journal of Human Resource Management, 26*, 1995–2014. doi:10.1080/09585192.2015.1041759

Carpenter-Song, E. A., Nordquest Schwallie, M., & Longhofer, J. (2007). Cultural competence reexamined: Critique and directions for the future. *Psychiatric Services, 58*, 1362–1365. doi:10.1176/appi.ps58.10.1362

Chen, G. M., & Starosta, W. J. (1997). A review of the concept of intercultural sensitivity. *Human Communication, 1*, 1–16.

(2000). The development and validation of the Intercultural Sensitivity Scale. *Human Communication, 3*, 1–15.

Chiu, C.-Y., Lonner, W. J., Matsumoto, D., & Ward, C. (2013). Cross-cultural competence: Theory, research, and application. *Journal of Cross-Cultural Psychology, 44*, 843–848. doi:10.1177/0022022113493716

Costa, P. T., & McCrae, R. R. (1992). *Revised NEO Personality Inventory (NEO PI-R) and New Five-Factor Inventory (NEO FFI) professional manual.* Odessa, FL: Psychological Assessment Resources

Crampton, P., Dowell, A., Parkin, C., & Thompson, C. (2003). Combating effects of racism through a cultural immersion medical education program. *Academic Medicine: Journal of the Association of American Colleges, 78*, 595–598. doi:10.1097/00001888-200306000-00008

Cranney, J., & Dalton, H. (2012). Optimizing adaptive student behaviors. In J. E. Groccia, M. A. T. Alsudairi, & W. Buskist (Eds.), *Handbook of college and university teaching: A global perspective* (pp. 60–76). Los Angeles, CA: Sage.

Cushner, K. H. (1987). Teaching cross-cultural psychology: Providing the missing link. *Teaching of Psychology, 14*, 220–224. doi:10.1207/s15328023top1404_7

(1989). Assessing the impact of a culture-general assimilator. *International Journal of Intercultural Relations, 13*, 125–146. doi:10.1016/0147-1767(89)90002-3

Danso, R. (2016, June 22). Cultural competence and cultural humility: A critical reflection on key cultural diversity concepts. *Journal of Social Work.* Published online. doi:10.1177/1468017316654341v

DeAngelis, T. (2015). In search of cultural competence. *Monitor on Psychology, 46*(3), 64.

Deardorff, D. K. (2006). The identification and assessment of intercultural competence as a student outcome of internationalization at institutions of higher education in the United States. *Journal of Studies in International Education, 10*, 241–266.

(2008). Intercultural competence: A definition, model, and implications for education abroad. In V. Savicki (Ed.), *Developing intercultural competence and transformation: Theory, research, and application in international education* (pp. 32–52). Sterling, VA: Stylus.

Deardorff, D. K., (Ed.). (2009). *The Sage handbook of intercultural competence.* Thousand Oaks, CA: Sage.

Devitt, P. J. (2014). *Cultural intelligence and the expatriate teacher: A study of expatriate teachers' constructs of themselves as culturally intelligent.* (Unpublished doctoral thesis). University of Exeter.

Dunn, T. P., Meine, M. F., & Dunn, S. L. (2011). The Bafá Bafá simulation revisited: A new way to address diversity issues in public administration initiatives that involve citizen engagement. *International Journal of Diversity in Organisations, Communities and Nations, 10,* 221–229. doi:10.18848/1447-9532/CGP/v10i06/38949

Earley, P. C., & Ang, S. (2003). *Cultural intelligence: Individual interactions across cultures.* Stanford, CA: Stanford University Press

Elphinstone, L. (2016, July). *Building cultural competence in undergraduate students.* Paper presented at the conference of the International Association for Cross-Cultural Psychology, Nagoya, Japan.

Feinstein, A. H., Mann, S., & Corsun, D. L. (2002). Charting the experiential territory: Clarifying definitions and uses of computer simulation, games, and role play. *Journal of Management Development, 21,* 732–744. doi:10.1108/02621710210448011

Garneau, A. B., & Pepin, J. (2015). Cultural competence: A constructivist definition. *Journal of Transcultural Nursing, 26,* 9–15. doi:10.1177/1043659614541294

Garran, A. M., & Werkmeister Rozas, L. (2013). Cultural competence revisited. *Journal of Ethnic and Cultural Diversity in Social Work, 22,* 97–111. doi:10.1080/15313204.2013.785337

Gray, D. P., & Thomas, D. J. (2006). Critical reflections on culture in nursing. *Journal of Cultural Diversity, 13,* 76–82.

Gregory, D., Harrowing, J., Lee, B., Doolittle, L., & O'Sullivan, P. S. (2010). Pedagogy as influencing nursing students' essentialised understanding of culture. *International Journal of Nursing Education and Scholarship, 7,* 30. doi:10.2202/1548-923X.2025

Gudykunst, W. B. (1993). Toward a theory of effective interpersonal and intergroup communication. In R. J. Wiseman & J. Koester (Eds.), *Intercultural communication competence, international and intercultural communication annual* (Vol. 16, pp. 3–17). Newbury Park, CA: Sage

Hall, E. T. (1966). *The hidden dimension.* New York, NY: Anchor Press.

Hammer, M. R. (2011). Additional intercultural validity testing of the Intercultural Development Inventory. *International Journal of Intercultural Relations, 35,* 474–87. doi:10.1016/j.ijintrel.2011.02.014

Hammer, M. R., Bennett, M. J., & Wiseman, R. (2003). Measuring intercultural sensitivity: The Intercultural Development Inventory. *International Journal of Intercultural Relations, 27,* 421–443. doi:10.1016/j.ijintrel.2011.02.014

Hammer, M. R., Gudykunst, W. B., & Wiseman, R. L. (1978). Dimensions of intercultural effectiveness: An exploratory study. *International Journal of Intercultural Relations, 2,* 382–393. doi:10.1016/0147-1767(78)90036-6

Hark, L., & Delisser, H. (Eds.). (2009). *Achieving cultural competency: A case-based approach to training health professionals.* Chichester: Wiley-Blackwell.

Harrison, G., & Turner, R. (2011). Being a "culturally competent" social worker: Making sense of a murky concept in practice. *British Journal of Social Work*, *61*, 333–350. doi:10.1093/bjsw/bcq101

Hassim, J., & Sedick, S. (2016). Developing cultural competencies in collectivist contexts. In K. Lowell (Ed.), *Cultural competence: Elements, developments and emerging trends* (pp. 21–48). New York, NY: Nova Science Publishers.

Heine, S. J. (2012). *Cultural psychology* (2nd ed.). New York, NY: Norton.

Hofstede, G. (1980). *Culture's consequences: International differences in work-related values*. Beverly Hills CA: Sage

Hofstede, G., Garibaldi de Hilal, A. V., Malvezzi, S., Tanure, B., & Vinken, H. (2010). Comparing regional cultures within a country: Lessons from Brazil. *Journal of Cross-Cultural Psychology*, *41*, 336–352. doi:10.1177/0022022109359696

Hofstede, G., & Hofstede, G. J. (2005). *Cultures and organizations: Software of the mind*. New York, NY: McGraw-Hill.

House, R. J., Hanges, P. J., Javidan, M., Dorfman, P. W., & Gupta, V. (Eds.). (2004). *Culture, leadership, and organizations: The GLOBE study of 62 societies*. Thousand Oaks, CA, Sage.

Imahori, T. T., & Lanigan, M. L. (1989). Relational model of intercultural communication competence. *International Journal of Intercultural Relations*, *13*, 269–286. doi:10.1016/0147-1767(89)90013-8

Jani, J. S., Pierce, D., Ortiz, L., & Sowbel, L. (2011). Access to intersectionality, content to competence: Deconstructing social work education diversity standards. *Journal of Social Work Education*, *47*, 283–301. doi:10.5175/JSWE.2011.200900118

Javidan, M., & Teagarden, M. B. (2011). Conceptualizing and measuring global mindset. *Advances in Global Leadership*, *6*, 13–39. doi:10.1108/S1535-1203(2011)0000006005

Kealey, D. J., & Protheroe, D. R. (1996). The effectiveness of cross-cultural training for expatriates: An assessment of the literature on the issue. *International Journal of Intercultural Relations*, *20*, 141–165. doi:10.1016/0147-1767(96)00001-6

Keith, K. D. (2012). Culture and teaching: Lessons from psychology. In J. E. Groccia, M. A. T. Alsudairi, & W. Buskist (Eds.), *Handbook of college and university teaching: A global perspective* (pp. 156–170). Los Angeles, CA: Sage.

Kelley, C., & Meyers, J. (1995). *Intercultural adaptability inventory (manual)*. Minneapolis, MN: National Computer Systems.

Kirmayer, L. J. (2012). Rethinking cultural competence. *Transcultural Psychiatry*, *49*, 149–164. doi:0.1177/1363461512444673

Klafehn, J., Chenchen, L., & Chiu, C.-Y. (2013). To know or not to know, is that the question? Exploring the role and assessment of metacognition in cross-cultural contexts. *Journal of Cross-Cultural Psychology*, *44*, 963–991. doi:10.1177/0022022113492893

Koskinen, L., Abdelhamid, P., & Likitalo, H. (2008). The simulation method for learning cultural awareness in nursing. *Diversity in Health and Social Care, 5,* 55–63.

Leiper, J., Van Horn, E. R., Hu, J., & Upadhyaya, R. C. (2008). Promoting cultural awareness and knowledge among faculty and doctoral students. *Nursing Education Perspectives, 29,* 161–164.

Leung, K., Ang, S., & Tan, M. L. (2014). Intercultural competence. *Annual Review of Organizational Psychology and Organizational Behavior, 1,* 489–519. doi:10.1146/annurev-orgpsych-031413-091229

Livermore, D. (2016). *Driven by difference: How great companies fuel innovation through diversity.* New York, NY: AMACOM.

Livermore, D., & Van Dyne, L. (2015). *Cultural intelligence: The essential intelligence for the 21st century.* Alexandria, VA: SHRM Foundation.

Lloyd, S., & Härtel, C. (2010). Intercultural competencies for culturally diverse work teams. *Journal of Management Psychology, 25,* 845–875. doi:10.1108/02683941011089125

Lonner, W. J. (2013). Cultural competence. In K. D. Keith (Ed.), *The encyclopedia of cross-cultural psychology* (Vol. I, pp. 301–303). Chichester: Wiley-Blackwell.

Lum, D. (Ed.). (2011). *Culturally competent practice: A framework for understanding diverse groups and justice issues* (4th ed.). Belmont, CA: Brooks/Cole.

Lynam, M. J., Browne, A. J., Reinmer Kirkham, S., & Anderson, J. M. (2007). Re-thinking the complexities of culture: What might we learn from Bourdieu? *Nursing Inquiry, 1,* 23–34. doi:10.1111/j.1440-1800.2007.00348.x

Matsumoto, D., & Hwang, H. C. (2013). Assessing cross-cultural competence: A review of available tests. *Journal of Cross-Cultural Psychology, 44,* 849–873. doi:10.1177/0022022113492891

Matsumoto, D., LeRoux, J., Ratzlaff, C., Tatani, H., Uchida, H., Kim, C., & Araki, S. (2001). Development and validation of a measure of intercultural adjustment potential in Japanese sojourners: The Intercultural Adjustment Potential Scale (ICAPS). *International Journal of Intercultural Relations, 25,* 483–510. doi:10.1016/S0147-1767(01)00019-0

Mendenhall, M., & Oddou, G. (1985). Dimensions of expatriate acculturation: A review. *Academic Management Review, 10*(1), 39–47. doi:10.5465/AMR.1985.4277340

Molina, S. C. (2012/2013). Romanticizing culture: The role of teachers' cultural intelligence in working with diversity. *CATESOL Journal, 24*(1), 220–244.

Myers, D. J., Buoye, A. J., McDermott, J., Strickler, D. E., & Ryman, R. G. (2000). Signals, symbols, and vibes: An exercise in cross-cultural interaction. *Teaching Sociology, 29,* 95–101.

Nguyen, A.-M. T. (2013). Acculturation. In K. D. Keith (Ed.), *The encyclopedia of cross-cultural psychology* (Vol. I, pp. 7–12). Chichester: Wiley-Blackwell.

Peng, A. C., Van Dyne, L., & Oh, K. (2015). The influence of motivational cultural intelligence on cultural effectiveness based on study abroad: The moderating role of participant's cultural identity. *Journal of Management Education, 39*, 572–596. doi:10.1177/1052562914555717

Peterson, C., Glover, J. A., Romero, D., & Romero, P. (1978). The effects of a cross-cultural simulation game on participants' personal characteristics. *Social Behavior and Personality, 6*, 21–26. doi:10.2224/sbp.1978.6.1.21

Rosenjack-Burcham, J. L. (2002). Cultural competence: An evolutionary perspective. *Nursing Forum, 37*(4), 5–16. doi:10.1111/j.1744-6198.2002.tb01287.x

Shirts, R. G. (1969). *BaFá BaFá – A cross-cultural simulation.* La Jolla, CA: Simile II. (1977). *BaFá BaFá – A cross-cultural simulation.* Del Mar, CA: Simile II.

Sieck, W. R., Smith, J. L., & Rasmussen, L. J. (2013). Metacognitive strategies for making sense of cross-cultural encounters. *Journal of Cross-Cultural Psychology, 44*, 1007–1023. doi:10.1177/0022022113492890

Sue, D. W. (2001). Multidimensional facets of cultural competence. *Counselling Psychologist, 29*, 790–821. doi:10.1177/0011000001296002

Sue, D. W., Arrendondo, P., & McDavis, R. J. (1992). Multicultural counseling competencies and standards: A call to the profession. *Journal of Counselling and Development, 70*, 477–486. doi:10.1002/j.1556-6676.1992.tb01642.x

Sue, S. (2003). In defense of cultural competency in psychotherapy and treatment. *American Psychologist, 58*, 964–970. doi:10.1037/0003-066X.58.11.964
    (2006). Cultural competency: From philosophy to research and practice. *Journal of Community Psychology, 34*, 237–245. doi:110.1002/jcop.20095

Sue, S., Zane, N., Nagayama Hall, G. C., & Berger, L. K. (2009). The case for cultural competency in psychotherapeutic interventions. *Annual Review of Psychology, 60*, 525–548. doi:10.1146/annurev.psych.60.110707.163651

Swift, C. O., & Denton, L. (2003). Cross-cultural experiential simulation in the global marketing classroom: Bafa Bafa and its variants. *Marketing Education Review, 13*(3), 41–51. doi:10.1080/10528008.2003.11488839

Tay, L., Woo, S. E., Klafehn, J., & Chiu, C.-Y. (2010). Conceptualizing and measuring culture: Problems and solutions. In E. Tucker, M. Viswanathan, & G. Walford (Eds.), *The handbook of measurement: How social scientists generate, modify and validate indicators and scales* (pp. 177–201). Thousand Oaks, CA: Sage.

Tracey, M. D. (2006, February). Q&A with Derald Sue: Gaining cultural competence. *Monitor on Psychology, 37*(2), 49.

Truong, M., Paradies, Y., & Priest, N. (2014). Interventions to improve cultural competency in healthcare: A systematic review of reviews. *BMC Health Services Research, 14*, 99. doi:10.1186/1472-6963-14-99

van de Vijver, F. J. R. (2013). Contributions of internationalization to psychology: Toward a global and inclusive discipline. *American Psychologist, 68*, 761–770. doi:10.1037/a0033762

van der Zee, K. I., & van Oudenhoven, J. P. (2000). The Multicultural Personality Questionnaire: A multidimensional instrument of multicultural effectiveness. *European Journal of Personality, 14*, 291–309. doi:10.1002/1099-0984(200007/08)14:4%3C291::AID-PER377%3E3.0.CO;2-6

Van Dyne, L., Ang, S., & Tan, M.-L. (2017). *Cultural Intelligence.* Oxford Bibliographies. Oxford, Oxford University Press. doi:10.1093/OBO/9780199846740-0115

Velayo, R. S. (2012). Internationalizing the curriculum. In J. E. Groccia, M. A. T. Alsudairi, & W. Buskist (Eds.), *Handbook of college and university teaching: A global perspective* (pp. 268–278). Los Angeles, CA: Sage.

Wilson, J., Ward, C., & Fischer, R. (2013). Beyond cultural learning theory: What can personality tell us about cultural competence? *Journal of Cross-Cultural Psychology, 44,* 900–927. doi:10.1177/0022022113492889

Yunlu, D. G., & Clapp-Smith, R. (2014). Metacognition, cultural psychological capital and motivational cultural intelligence. *Cross Cultural Management, 21,* 386–399. doi:10.1108/CCM-07-2012-0055

PART II

Teaching across the Psychology Curriculum

In 2013, the American Psychological Association published its *Guidelines for the Undergraduate Psychology Major*. A major section of those guidelines is titled "Sociocultural Learning Outcomes: The Infusion Approach." Unlike an earlier version of the *Guidelines*, which embodied a stand-alone approach to the teaching of sociocultural concepts, the 2013 edition calls for a diversity-rich approach to culture and context across the curriculum.

The authors of the following chapters have taken on the task of describing their efforts to infuse a broad range of cultural data, methods, and conceptual material in coursework in their specialties throughout the psychology curriculum. Their styles and approaches to teaching in their various areas differ, but all have the same aim: to convey the idea that psychological science is conducted and learned in a context and that that context is strongly cultural in nature. As Sam Sommers noted in the title of his aptly named book, *Situations Matter*, environment is a powerful force. Sommers went on, in his subtitle, to add: *Understanding How Context Transforms Your World*. As the authors in this volume make clear, culture is a major determinant of that context.

In the Beginning

We know that psychological science recognizes the importance of beginnings in many ways – for example, the first day of class, the attention-getting first line of a presentation, and the tendency (in some cultures) to remember the first item on a list. In this section, we consider two types of beginnings, both important to students of psychology: the beginnings and history of the discipline and the introductory course, which is the beginning point for students studying the field.

In its early days, psychology enjoyed a certain cultural and cross-cultural aspect. This is evident in Wilhelm Wundt's *Völkerpsychologie*, W. H. R. Rivers's Cambridge expedition, and W. G. Sumner's *Folkways*. Prominent early US psychologists studied in Germany, and William James was widely traveled and well versed in languages. Yet psychology in the United States evolved for some decades toward a focus on Western interests controlled largely by White men. During the same era, introductory psychology often offered little acknowledgment of the influence of culture whether on the definition of the field or the problems and data it chose to take up. Chapters 3 and 4 attempt to explore some of the ways we might help students to grasp the importance of cultural context and its contribution to beginnings: the beginnings of the discipline and their own as budding psychological scientists.

CHAPTER 3

Culture and Introductory Psychology

Kenneth D. Keith

In the United States alone, well over 1 million college students take psychology classes each year (Munsey, 2008), many of them introductory psychology, and about 300,000 high school students take the college-equivalent Advanced Placement introductory psychology course (APA, 2017). The introductory course is the entry point and the foundation for those who intend to continue in the discipline, and for other students, it may be a singular opportunity to gain a basic understanding of psychological science and its relevance to their lives. In this chapter, I briefly discuss some historical aspects of the course and the textbooks psychologists have developed for use in the introductory course with an eye to the evolution of the role of culture. I then provide some examples of the kinds of questions that might guide discussion of culture and its place in the beginning course and then conclude with some practical suggestions for teaching activities and resources for psychology teachers.

The First Century

Introductory (general) psychology and introductory psychology textbooks have a fairly long history, especially since near the end of the nineteenth century, when the teaching of psychological science emerged from its backdrop in philosophy (see Fuchs, 2000). The textbooks of the day (e.g., James, 1892; Ladd, 1898; Titchener, 1897) contained many topics that would look familiar today. However, these books contained no explicit reference to culture – a pattern that continued through the first half of the twentieth century, although such culture-related topics as social psychology began to emerge during that period (e.g., Webb, 1991). After the mid-twentieth century, culture began to appear in the indexes of introductory textbooks; for example, one popular book of the era (Morgan & King, 1966) included references to cultural changes, cultural determiners of personality, culture and intelligence, cultural patterns, and a definition of culture. However, Berthold (1977), analyzing the scientific sources cited by authors of 34 introductory texts, found no citations of journals that can be recognized as cultural or cross-cultural (e.g., *Journal of Cross-Cultural Psychology, International Journal of Psychology*).

Near the end of the twentieth century, Hogben and Waterman (1997) and Kowalski (2000) advocated improved inclusion of such culture-related topics as gender, race, and ethnicity, and Griggs, Jackson, and Christopher (1999) analyzed content of introductory textbooks. Their methodology was limited to the extent that topics they called "diversity and sex/gender" were coded only if they received coverage exceeding one-third of a chapter. Nevertheless, Griggs et al. reported that, of 37 textbooks examined, 12 (32 percent) included sufficient diversity or gender content to be included. By 1997, Cush and Buskist found that publishers of introductory psychology textbooks predicted cross-cultural content would be the area with the most increased emphasis in the ensuing decade.

The New Century

The trend toward greater inclusion of cultural content has continued into the twenty-first century as numerous introductory textbooks (e.g., Bernstein, Penner, Clarke-Stewart, & Roy, 2008; Weiten, 2008) have included a broadening array of cultural material. As introductory textbooks have continued to evolve, they sometimes include definitions of cultural or cross-cultural psychology as well as sections on the relation of culture to such psychological constructs as attractiveness, development, emotion, intelligence, mental health, parenting, perception, personality, and self (e.g., Gray & Bjorklund, 2014; Myers & DeWall, 2015). And, despite the fact that culture did not appear as a "core concept" in a study of textbooks conducted by Nairn, Ellard, Scialfa, and Miller (2003), an analysis encompassing 40 introductory textbooks (Lonner & Murdock, 2012) found dramatic increases in cultural coverage from 1988 to 2008.

It seems clear that our introductory texts continue to expand their coverage of culture and its relevance to the various subject matters of introductory psychology, although we still have plenty of room, not only in our books, but more importantly, in our classrooms, to infuse our work with culture. This means recognizing the limitations of many of our traditional teachings, understanding that too much of our knowledge has come from a limited range of experience (Arnett, 2008, 2009) and that we still have far to go in such subcultural areas as disability (Goldstein, Siegel, & Seaman, 2010) in our introductory psychology classes. As technology and travel make the world a smaller place, it is increasingly essential that all students appreciate the influence of culture and the global context on human behavior. In the words of Lonner and Murdock (2012, p.14), "World-wide we owe beginning students the challenge and pleasure of learning how the powerful forces of culture shape all of our lives."

Asking the Right Questions

A key perspective to bear in mind in attempting to bring culture to the introductory course is *integration*. We are likely to be more effective and to provide students not only with academic knowledge but also with life skills if we can integrate culture into the various subject matters of introductory psychology. Culture should be not an add-on unit but a natural, integral part of each aspect of the course. Here I will suggest the kinds of questions students should learn to ask as they make their way through the course; I will not try to cover every topic that you might present, but I will make suggestions for eight areas that are likely to be present in nearly every introductory psychology class. Additional ideas for the subfields typically taught in introductory psychology appear in other chapters throughout this book.

Research methods. Every introductory course includes at least some introduction to research methods, and every introductory psychology textbook cites large numbers of research studies and sources. Understanding the methods of science and learning to evaluate sources are important skills for students (Keith & Beins, 2017), and students should learn to question at least three aspects of research sources: the researchers, the research participants, and the instruments used to collect data. To this end, some important questions for students are these:

1. **Do researchers have a cultural bias?** Researchers are themselves the product of a cultural and contextual background, and sometimes they have an agenda (Keith & Beins, 2017). For example, more than a century ago, Goddard (1913) became zealous in his effort to identify mental deficiency in immigrants at Ellis Island, claiming that he could identify "deficient" people with 90 percent accuracy and that as many as 80 percent of some ethnic groups were mentally deficient. Goddard's claims were of course exaggerated and went far beyond the quality of his data. Researcher bias can also be subtle. If, for instance, an American researcher studies the mental health of another culture

and finds that people of that culture underreport symptoms, is it possible that the researcher's conclusion is colored by ethnocentrism (judging another culture by one's own standards)? Perhaps it would be equally valid to say that Americans overreport the same phenomenon.

2. **Who are the research participants?** As Arnett (2008) noted, most of the participants in research published in mainstream psychology journals are Americans, the majority of them White European Americans. It is not reasonable, Arnett argued, to generalize to all people from research based on 5 percent of the world's population. Earlier, Quinones-Vidal, Lopez-Garcia, Penaranda-Ortega, and Tortosa-Gil (2004) reported findings similar to those of Arnett, Heine, and Norenzayan (2006) suggested that a biased database undermines the ability of researchers to draw conclusions about psychological universals.

3. **Might people of different cultures respond differently to research instruments?** People of varied backgrounds may respond in differing ways to research instruments or questions. Thus, research participants of some countries are more likely than others to use the extreme score options on rating scales (Bachman & O'Malley, 1984; van Herk, Poortinga, & Verhallen, 2004); to compare themselves to members of their own group (which may be different from other groups) when completing ratings (Peng, Nisbett, & Wong, 1997); and to be self-enhancing or self-effacing in rating themselves (Miller & Madani, 2013). Matsumoto & Juang (2013) provided a review of these and other method biases.

4. **Are research instruments linguistically equivalent?** As researchers gather data across cultures, they of course encounter the need for instruments (e.g., questionnaires, tests, surveys) produced in different languages. It is important for students to realize that simply translating words is not adequate (consider, for example, a term like *hot dog*. In US English, it typically means a type of frankfurter sandwich, but could also mean someone behaving or performing in an ostentatious way. Yet to a non-native speaker, it might literally mean a warm canine mammal!). Researchers have typically dealt with the equivalence problem through back-translation or committee consensus (Matsumoto & Juang, 2013), but must also take into account both cultural and psychological equivalence as well as language equivalence (Tanzer, 2013).

Developmental psychology. Human development is another topic appearing in every introductory psychology textbook. The textbooks have long reported the significance of the work of such key figures as Jean Piaget and the importance of central themes (e.g., temperament, attachment, cognitive development). Although authors have with increasing frequency acknowledged sociocultural influences on development (e.g., the work of Lev Vygotsky), students may nevertheless erroneously conclude that some findings are universal. Their understanding will be better served if they learn to question their own assumptions:

1. **Do classic processes (e.g., temperament and attachment) play out in the same ways across cultures?** The work of Alexander Thomas and Stella Chess has long been central to an understanding of the fact that infants are born with individual differences in personality and temperament; despite the homogeneity of their sample, these researchers (e.g., Thomas, Chess, & Birch, 1970) believed their work to be generalizable across cultures – a conclusion that other researchers have questioned and that has been contradicted by more recent research showing cross-cultural differences (see Molitor & Hsu, 2011, for a review). Similarly, the groundbreaking work of John Bowlby (1969) and Mary Ainsworth (1977) led to the conclusion that secure infant attachment is universally desirable. However, although attachment between infants and parents is universal, researchers have questioned the cultural values inherent in the terms *secure* and *insecure*, and attachment behaviors may vary across cultures (e.g., van IJzendoorn & Sagi, 1999).

2. **Are the classic theories (e.g., Piaget, Erikson, Kohlberg) robust across cultures?** Although Piaget may well have believed his theory of cognitive development represented universal patterns of thought (Dasen, 1994), research evaluating his theory across cultures has produced mixed results. For example, whereas the Piagetian stages of cognitive development may follow a universal order, the sequence of skills developing within each stage may vary across cultures (Dasen, 1975). Furthermore, when measured in typical ways, Piaget's final stage of cognitive development (formal operations) may not occur in some cultures; however, in culture-appropriate tasks, formal reasoning may well be apparent (Saxe, 1981; Tuklin & Konner, 1973). It appears not only that culture influences cognitive development, but also that culture and the human brain may well have co-evolved (Cole & Packer, 2011). Researchers investigating other stage theories have reported more or less similar patterns of universal/culture-specific findings for the work of Erik Erikson (see Molitor & Hsu, 2011) and Lawrence Kohlberg

(Gibbs, Basinger, Grime, & Snarey, 2007; Keller, Edelstein, & Schmid, 1998). Each of these classic developmental theories has universal aspects, but numerous culture-specific aspects, as well.

Cognition, learning, memory, and perception. A number of the units in a typical introductory psychology course fall within the broad rubric of cognition. Some of the topics here are particularly intriguing to students, and there is fascinating cross-cultural research on many of them. Questions of particular interest within the culture realm include:

1. **Do we all perceive the world in similar ways?** More than a century ago, W. H. R. Rivers embarked upon the Cambridge expedition, a journey that would take him from England to the Torres Straits. There, and in rural India, Rivers recorded the responses of people to the Müller-Lyer illusion, with the aim of comparing data from these "less civilized" cultures to those of people in England. He expected that islanders in the Torres Straits and the rural people in India would be more susceptible to the angular Muller-Lyer illusion, and thus make more errors in judging the length of the lines presented in the illusion. To his surprise however, the English proved more susceptible to the illusion than the other groups – a finding that Rivers believed to be due to culture. Rivers's findings, as well as those of later replications, gave rise to the *carpentered world hypothesis* (Segall, Campbell, & Herskovits, 1966), the notion that people who experience life in rectangular structures develop different perceptions of size and distance than those of individuals living in different types of environments. Other authors have reported similar perceptual differences in reactions to photographs or drawings (Eddy, 2001; Livingstone, 1857) and in perceptions of distance in open spaces (Turnbull, 1961). Numerous other similar cross-cultural observations can provide interesting classroom material for the study of perception.

2. **Do we all categorize the world in the same way?** It might seem self-evident that people would see various ways of categorizing objects (e.g., by color, shape, or function) in similar ways. However, this is not always the case. Roberson, Davidoff, Davies, and Shapiro (2005) found that people who speak different languages may make different judgments about color categories, depending upon the language they speak; African adults tend to use color as a category for grouping objects (Greenfield, Reich, & Oliver, 1966); and adults in Western cultures are more likely to group by function (e.g., animals together,

tools together; Bruner, Oliver, & Greenfield, 1966). There is also evidence that Chinese individuals may categorize people according to relationships (e.g., parent–child), whereas Americans tend to group according to individual characteristics (e.g., children with children, adults with adults; Chiu, 1972; Ji, Zhang, & Nisbett, 2004). It thus seems clear that people of different cultures may see (and group) objects and people in different ways.

3. **Do all people remember in the same ways?** Although researchers seem to agree that the inability of adults to remember personal experiences before age three is probably universal, there are cultural differences in the age of onset of personal (autobiographical) memory, with Americans reporting earlier (and more specific) childhood memories than Asians (Wang, 2003; Wang & Ross, 2007). Investigators have also found cross-cultural differences in the occurrence of the serial position effect, with schooling, either within (e.g., Wagner, 1980) or across cultures (Cole & Scribner, 1974), predicting skill in remembering lists. These cultural differences in memory are illustrative of a wider range of interesting findings, some of which Matsumoto and Juang (2013) have summarized.

4. **Do cultures define intelligence in similar ways?** Western culture has often valued what Sternberg (1996) called inert intelligence – the abilities needed for performance on IQ tests, Scholastic Aptitude Tests, and other measures that correlate with academic achievement or with other tests, but that may not lead to successful lives (Wigdor & Garner, 1982). The Western approach to intelligence may value not only school-related skills and intellectual processing, but may also emphasize speed. On the other hand, intelligence in African cultures can be reflected in participation in family life (Super & Harkness, 1982); cooperativeness, obedience, and social responsibility (Serpell, 1974); or contribution to harmonious group relations (Ruzgis & Grigorenko, 1994). In Eastern cultures, the components of intelligence may include social skills (Azuma & Kashiwagi, 1987), as well as feelings, opinions, determination, and effort (Sternberg & Kaufman, 1998). Without doubt, the abilities that characterize intelligence vary widely across cultures, and it is difficult to conceive of intelligence without consideration of cultural context (Heine, 2012).

Sex and gender. The biological makeup of women and men determines, to a large extent, the sex roles that each may play. However, gender roles are largely culturally determined, and while they may be closely related to sex roles, this is not necessarily the case. Gender roles and their relation to culture may give rise to interesting questions for students to ponder and explore.

1. **Are there universal behavioral and psychological differences between women and men?** Investigation of gender roles across cultures has shown wide variation in perceptions of appropriate behavior for men and women (Williams & Best, 1990). Men tended generally to hold more traditional views of the role of women, and Muslims were more likely than Christians to hold traditional views about gender. However, although perceptions of appropriate gender roles varied from culture to culture, women and men within a particular culture tended to hold similar views (Williams & Best, 1990), suggesting a cultural influence on perceptions of gender roles. Research has suggested that men and women differ universally in some personality traits (Costa, Terracciano, & McCrae, 2001), and that men are more aggressive (Brislin, 1993). However, more recent work (Forbes, Zhang, Doroszewicz, & Haas, 2009), while finding cultural differences in direct and indirect aggression, concluded that gender was a weak contributor to aggression levels. Finally, in a study investigating factors underlying independence and interdependence across cultures (Eastern and Western) and genders, Kashima et al. (1995) found cultural differences for all the variables (agency, assertiveness, collectivism, and relatedness), but gender differences for only the relatedness measure (women scored higher). Men and women clearly differ in many ways – but understanding the differences requires that we also understand the cultural milieu.

2. **What aspects of gender roles are culture-limited?** Research has typically shown universal gender roles in such areas as division of household labor (e.g., Georgas, Berry, van de Vijver, Kagitcibasi, & Poortinga (2006). However, in studying gender division of labor among the Qhawqhat Lahu of China, Du (2000) found gender unity, with a high level of joint gender roles. There are also fairly dramatic differences in views of gender equity across cultures, ranging from the view that men and women should be treated equally to the notion that men should clearly have more rights than women (Williams & Best, 1990). The research on gender roles also offers a cautionary note about the tendency to assume that all Western (or Eastern) cultures are the same: Hunt, Piccoli, Gonsalkorale, & Carnaghi (2015), in a study of two "Western" cultures (Australia and Italy), reported some

interesting differences in the degree to which women endorsed feminine norms. Finally, Archer (2006), in a study of 52 cultures, found differences in domestic aggression between partners, with women victimized less (and men more) in individualistic countries. (This topic could also be discussed, of course, in relation to aggression.)

Health, disorders, and treatment. Students seem often to assume that physical and psychological well-being are essentially the same around the world. The idea that health and illness, adjustment and abnormality, might be linked to culture is an important concept, and one that has received a significant amount of attention in the research literature. Some sample questions:

1. **Does the American biomedical approach to health reflect cultural bias?** The Western evidence-based biomedical approach to health and health care has become dominant in the world (Gurung, 2011), often in its contemporary form, the biopsychosocial model (Engel, 1977). Historically, the Western approach has defined health as the absence of illness, with a comparatively recent emphasis on such factors as lifestyles, happiness, relationships, quality of life, and socioeconomic conditions. Despite the dominance of this Western perspective, other cultural approaches to health find favor with many of the world's people. A number of these have their basis in the notion of balance – balance between positive and negative forces (*yin* and *yang*), as in Chinese philosophy (Kaptchuk, 2000) or a balance between hot and cold, as in Latin American views (MacLachlan, 1997). Western medicine is one approach, but certainly not the only way that cultures conceptualize health and illness.

2. **Is abnormality the same across cultures?** A few psychological disorders are considered universal. Among these are depression (World Health Organization, 1983), and schizophrenia (World Health Organization, 1973) which, despite being universal, may show culture-related differences in symptoms. Many disorders are closely linked to cultural customs and practices, and culture serves to define what constitutes a disorder. Thus, notions of what might be "abnormal" vary across cultures. See López and Ho (2013) for discussion of a wide range of culture-bound syndromes.

Language and communication. Language is a fundamental characteristic of humans in social groupings, and present in all cultures. Introductory psychology students are sometimes surprised to learn that language plays an important role in human thought, and that languages vary in important ways. Some of these features of language are reflected in these questions:

1. **How does language differ across cultures?** Languages share a number of universal characteristics across cultures (Kreiner, 2011). However, languages also differ in important ways. The Japanese language, for example, is often indirect; uses honorifics and changing ingroup/outgroup contexts to indicate deference and relationships in conversations; and employs different self-referents, depending on age, gender, and context (Jordan & Noda, 1987). Other languages (e.g., German, Spanish, French) group nouns according to gender, although not in the same way across all languages (Nastase & Popescu, 2009). These language differences, and many others, reflect cultural values and practices, and some awareness of them can aid intercultural understanding.

2. **How does language influence thought?** Introductory textbooks vary in their coverage of the Sapir-Whorf (linguistic relativity) hypothesis, and many researchers have concluded that strong versions of the hypothesis (that language determines thought) may be too extreme. Nevertheless, research has shown that people are likely to classify objects consistently with the grammatical gender assigned by their language (e.g., Flaherty, 2001; Sera et al., 2002), or in ways consistent with terms used to discuss specific objects (Carroll & Casagrande, 1958). Furthermore, individuals seem better able to discriminate colors for which their languages have distinct words (Roberson, Davies, & Davidoff, 2000). The extent to which language affects thinking continues to be studied, but there can be little doubt that the two are connected in important ways.

Personality. Personality, as it appears in many introductory psychology textbooks, is primarily a Western construct. However, as Giordano (2011; Chapter 24 of this volume) has shown, other traditions have produced intriguing ways to consider the self and its relationship to the cultural context. Students might well wonder the extent to which views of personality are generalized; or are they unique to particular cultures?

1. **Do different cultures see personality differently?** Recent years have seen a strong emphasis on trait theory, and in particular the Five-Factor theory (e.g., McCrae & Costa, 1997, 1999). Research in many cultures has suggested the universality of the so-called Big Five traits (openness to experience, conscientiousness, extraversion, agreeableness, and

neuroticism), and investigators have even reported these traits in non-human animals (Gosling & John, 1999). However, data from several countries, including Spain, China, and the Philippines, have caused researchers to question whether the Big Five traits fully encompass characteristics of all people (Zhou, Saucier, Gao, & Liu, 2009; see Heine, 2012, for a review). Giordano (2011), noting the Western origins of the trait approach to personality, reviewed Eastern perspectives, suggesting the relevance of Buddhism and Taoism to an understanding of personality.

2. **Are there indigenous (culture-specific) aspects of personality?** The dominance of trait theory may prompt students to ask whether there is anything truly culturally unique about personality. Researchers, too, have asked the same question. The translation and use of Western personality assessment tools represents what some researchers (e.g., Cheung & Leung, 1998) have called the "imposed etic" approach. Some psychologists have developed tools for measurement of specific aspects of personality in their own cultures while recognizing the possibility that their findings might converge with the traits comprising the Big Five (Guanzon-Lapeña, Church, Carlota, & Katigbak, 1998). But others, noting that most Big Five studies have been conducted in literate urban settings, have produced findings suggesting the existence of indigenous personality characteristics among illiterate indigenous South American farmers (Gurven, von Rueden, Massenkoff, Kaplan, & Lero Vie, 2013), and have argued that use of a mainstream personality inventory (MMPI-2) may unfairly pathologize the indigenous worldview of American Indians (Hill, Pace, & Robbins, 2010). It seems important that students recognize the value of respect for unique indigenous cultures, and the risks of over-generalized use of Western assessments in understanding personality across cultures.

Social psychology. Perhaps nothing in the introductory course is more interesting to beginning students than social behavior and its relation to the environmental context. The power of situations is great (Sommers, 2011), and no situation is more complex or intriguing than the culture that surrounds and shapes us. As they begin to grasp the importance of culture, students wonder about its role in molding our views of others and their behavior, as well as ourselves and our own behavior.

1. **Do people around the world view themselves in the same ways?** Nothing is more central to the study of human behavior than the concept of self, and the ways people of different cultures view

themselves can make for fascinating study. In one of the most frequently cited articles in the cross-cultural literature, Markus and
Kitayama (1991) explored the idea of self-construal. They discussed
two very different views of self, one associated with Western individualistic cultures (*independent self*), and the other associated with non-
Western collectivistic cultures (*interdependent self*). The independent
self is autonomous, separate, and focused on the individual: personal
goals, characteristics, and achievements. The interdependent self, on
the other hand, is defined in relation to important others, fitting in
with the group, and meeting social responsibilities. In contrast to the
autonomy of the independent self, the interdependent self-construal
lacks clear boundaries and depends on context. In various studies
comparing Americans to Asians, Americans have tended to describe
themselves in terms of unique or internal characteristics, whereas
Asians are more likely to describe themselves in terms of relationships
with others.

2. **Do people obey and conform in the same ways around the world?**
    The classic studies of obedience are, of course, Stanley Milgram's
    (1974) investigations of response to authority. Investigators across
    cultures have made numerous attempts to replicate Milgram's studies,
    with widely varying results, probably dependent not only on cultural
    variations, but also on differences in demographics of participants and
    other methodological discrepancies. Some have argued that obedience
    is likely lower in individualistic cultures, but this too has come under
    scrutiny (Twenge, 2009). It is perhaps noteworthy that in a French
    television show "replication," participants obeyed at levels similar to
    those of Milgram's participants (Beauvois, Courbet, & Oberlé, 2012).
    The picture is also quite variable for conformity across cultures, where
    researchers have attempted to replicate the frequently cited work of
    Asch (1955), with wide variations in reported levels of conformity. In
    a large meta-analysis (Bond & Smith, 1996) of studies conducted in
    17 countries, higher rates of conformity were found in collectivistic
    countries than in those that were more individualistic.

3. **Do people across cultures make attributions in the same ways?**
    Individuals commonly attribute the behavior of others to internal
    (dispositional) characteristics of those others – a phenomenon known
    as the *correspondence bias* – that may occur even when the behavior of
    the other is influenced by external (situational) events (Koenig &
    Dean, 2011). Early research on such attributions suggested that the
    correspondence bias was stronger in people from Western cultures

than in those from Eastern cultures, as Miller (1984) found in a comparison of Americans and Hindus. Miller reported, for example, that Hindu people were likely to use relational or contextual behavioral explanations ("He lives far away from school") whereas Americans used internal, dispositional explanations ("He's a self-absorbed person"). More recent findings have indicated that the bias occurs in both Eastern and Western people, although those from Eastern cultures are more likely to reduce the bias when situational influences are made obvious (Koenig & Dean, 2011). Westerners, on the other hand, continue to make internal attributions even when situational causes are clear (Jones & Harris, 1967). When explaining our own behavior, as Westerners, we may engage in a different form of bias, attributing our own successes to personal characteristics (intelligence, athletic ability), while explaining our failures as the product of external causes (bad luck, other people); this is, of course, the self-serving bias (Miller & Ross, 1975). People of some (but not all) Eastern cultures, however, may engage not in the self-serving bias, but in self-effacement, with more modest self-oriented attributions, instead crediting success to relationships with others (Miller & Madani, 2013). We can thus see in this brief summary that explanations for behavior, whether our own or that of others, may be related to the cultural backdrop, and may be quite different, depending upon that backdrop.

This section has presented only an illustrative sampling of areas in which instructors can help students begin to ask questions that might illuminate and clarify the role of culture in the various conceptual and empirical topics they encounter in introductory psychology. Similar inquiry is possible (and desirable) in any of the subfields addressed in the course, and the other chapters of this book provide a rich source of ideas to guide the effort.

Teaching Activities

There are many aspects of the introductory psychology course that lend themselves to meaningful activities and demonstrations. Some of these are available in published form (e.g., Goldstein, 2008), and others can be easily generated by instructors and students. These are just a few examples:

1. **Analyze research.** Ask students to find a published research article dealing with a cultural or cross-cultural issue. The students can then evaluate basic aspects of the sampling and design of the study: Who are the participants? How were the participants selected? What cultural

groups or subgroups do the participants represent? Is culture treated as an independent variable, and if so, is this legitimate (e.g., can people be randomly assigned a culture)? Does the research employ research instruments, and if so, did participants complete them in a second language in a translated or back-translated version? These kinds of questions can form the basis of useful discussion about the realities and difficulties of conducting and interpreting cultural research.

2. **Personal space**. Drawing on such sources as Hall's (1990/1966) study of proxemics, students can develop activities to demonstrate various ways that culture may influence use of space. For example, if at lunch a student gradually and imperceptibly edges his or her eating utensils nearer the space of the person seated adjacent, at what point does that person begin to edge away? Is the result different for international students of different cultures? Or what can we learn from observing how people use space in public seating, at a train station or airport? How closely do individuals sit to others?

3. **Child behavior.** While a student in a border community, Downey (2004) conducted observations of children's playground behavior in two settings, one in Mexico and one in the United States. She coded the children's behavior and described it in such categories as sharing, social play, community play, and aggression. Adaptations of this type of observation, whether in playgrounds, community centers, preschools, or other settings, can provide interesting perspectives on the relation between culture and development.

4. **Self-serving bias**. Instructors can easily arrange a simple demonstration that allows students to compare their own views of self to those of people of other cultures. Devise, for example, a simple questionnaire, asking students to compare themselves on a continuum ranging from "Far below Average" to "Far above Average" on a range of attributes (friendliness, intelligence, generosity, honesty, understanding, compassion). Many students will rate themselves above average, and the exercise can lead to interesting discussion of the likely universality of self-serving bias and cultural variations that researchers have reported (e.g., Choi, Nisbett, & Norenzayan, 1999; Mezulis, Abramson, Hyde, & Hankin, 2004).

Resources

Many generic resources intended for the teaching of undergraduate psychology in general, and the introductory course in particular, may be easily adapted to include illustrations of the role of culture in our understanding of psychological phenomena. There are also numerous resources specifically intended to aid in the teaching of culture and psychology. These are just a few:

Goldstein, S. (2016). *Cross-cultural explorations: Activities in culture and psychology* (2nd ed.). New York, NY: Routledge.

This activities workbook provides numerous classroom activities designed to illustrate cultural and cross-cultural processes and effects. Many of these are engaging, interactive, and appropriate for introductory psychology.

Tobin, J. J., Hsueh, Y., & Karasawa, M. (2009). *Preschool in three cultures revisited: China, Japan, and the United States*. Chicago, IL: University of Chicago Press.

This book reports the work of Chinese, Japanese, and US researchers who studied preschools in the three cultures. The authors discuss how preschools reflect and pass on cultural values.

Tobin, J. J., Hsueh, Y., & Karasawa, M. (Directors). (2009). *Preschool in three cultures revisited: China, Japan, and the United States* [Video recording].

This video, intended to complement the book noted above, shows both daily activity in preschools in the three cultures, and commentary of teachers of each culture watching the video of the other groups. It provides a fascinating cross-cultural sample of child behavior and education. Faculty from many institutions can access the video at www.kanopystreaming.com/product/preschool-three-cultures-revisited. It is also available at joetobin.net

Lonner, W. J., Keith, K. D., & Matsumoto, D. (in press). Culture and the psychology curriculum: Foundations and resources. In D. Matsumoto & H. C. Hwang (Eds.), *Handbook of culture and psychology* (2nd ed.). Oxford: Oxford University Press.

This chapter presents background for the teaching of culture in psychology, discusses resources, and provides links to organizations that offer materials.

Online resources for the teaching of culture and psychology are available from the Society for the Teaching of Psychology, through its Office of Teaching Resources in Psychology (http://teachpsych.org/page-1603066) and from the International Association for Cross-Cultural Psychology, through the Online Readings in Psychology and Culture (https://scholarworks.gvsu.edu/orpc).

Conclusion

If we are to integrate culture in a meaningful way with the teaching of psychology, and if we intend to infuse culture throughout the curriculum, introductory psychology must be the beginning. The content of introductory psychology is a guide to the curriculum, mirroring in many ways, the content of the courses leading to the undergraduate psychology degree. It seems essential then, that if we are to teach a psychology of all people, it starts here, at the beginning.

References

Ainsworth, M. D. S. (1977). Attachment theory and its utility in cross-cultural research. In P. H. Leiderman, S. R. Tulkin, & A. Rosenfeld (Eds.), *Culture and infancy: Variations in the human experience* (pp. 49–67). San Diego, CA: Academic Press.

APA. (2017). Enrollment data. Retrieved from www.apa.org/ed/precollege/about/enrollment.aspx

Archer, J. (2006). Cross-cultural differences in physical aggression between partners: A social-role analysis. *Personality and Social Psychology Review, 10*, 133–153. doi:10.1207/s15327957pspr1002_3

Arnett, J. J. (2008). The neglected 95%: Why American psychology needs to become less American. *American Psychologist, 63*, 602–614. doi:10.1037/0003-066X.63.7.602

(2009). The neglected 95%: A challenge to psychology's philosophy of science. *American Psychologist, 64*, 571–574. doi:10.1037/a0016723

Asch, S. E. (1955). Opinions and social pressure. *Scientific American, 193*, 31–35. doi:10.1038/scientificamerican1155-31

Azuma, H., & Kashiwagi, K. (1987). Descriptions for an intelligent person: A Japanese study. *Japanese Psychological Research, 29*, 17–26.

Bachman, J. G., & O'Malley, P. M. (1984). Black-White differences in self-esteem: Are they affected by response styles? *American Journal of Sociology, 90*, 624–639. doi:10.1086/228120

Beauvois, J.-L., Courbet, D., & Oberlé, D. (2012). The prescriptive power of the television host: A transposition of Milgram's obedience paradigm to the context of a TV game show. *European Review of Applied Psychology, 62*, 111–119. doi:10.1016/j.erap.2012.02.001

Bernstein, D. A., Penner, L. A., Clarke-Stewart, A., & Roy, E. J. (2008). *Psychology* (8th ed.). Boston, MA: Houghton Mifflin.

Berthold, H. C. (1977). Psychology and the introductory text: The view from the reference section. *Teaching of Psychology, 4*, 36–39. doi:10.1207/s15328023top0401_8

Bond, R., & Smith, P. B. (1996). Culture and conformity: A meta-analysis of studies using Asch's (1952b, 1956) line judgment task. *Psychological Bulletin, 119*, 111–137. doi:10.1037/0096-3445.131.3.377

Bowlby, J. (1969). *Attachment and loss: Vol. 1. Attachment.* New York, NY: Basic Books.

Brislin, R. (1993). *Understanding culture's influence on behavior.* Fort Worth, TX: Harcourt Brace Jovanovich.

Bruner, J. S., Oliver, R., & Greenfield, P. (1966). *Studies in cognitive growth.* New York, NY: Wiley.

Carroll, J. B., & Casagrande, J. B. (1958). The function of language classifications in behavior. In E. E. Maccoby, T. M. Newcomb, & E. L. Hartley (Eds.), *Readings in social psychology* (pp. 18–31). New York, NY: Holt.

Cheung, F. M., & Leung, K. (1998). Indigenous personality measures: Chinese examples. *Journal of Cross-Cultural Psychology, 29,* 233–248. doi:10.1177/0022022198291012

Chiu, L. H. (1972). A cross-cultural comparison of cognitive styles in Chinese and American children. *International Journal of Psychology, 7,* 235–242. doi:10.1080/00207597208246604

Choi, L., Nisbett, R., & Norenzayan, A. (1999). Causal attribution across cultures: Variation and universality. *Psychological Bulletin, 125,* 47–63. doi:10.1037/0033-2909.125.1.47

Cole, M., & Packer, M. (2011). Culture and cognition. In K. D. Keith (Ed.), *Cross-cultural psychology: Contemporary themes and perspectives* (pp. 133–159). Malden, MA: Wiley-Blackwell.

Cole, M., & Scribner, S. (1974). *Culture and thought: A psychological introduction.* New York, NY: Wiley.

Costa, P. T., Terracciano, A., & McCrae, R. R. (2001). Gender differences in personality traits across cultures: Robust and surprising findings. *Journal of Personality and Social Psychology, 81,* 322–331. doi:10.1037/0022-3514.81.2.322

Cush, D. T., & Buskist, W. (1997). Future of the introductory psychology textbook: A survey of college publishers. *Teaching of Psychology, 24,* 119–122. doi:10.1207/s15328023top2402_7

Dasen, P. (1994). Culture and cognitive development from a Piagetian perspective. In. W. Lonner & R. Malpass (Eds.), *Psychology and culture* (pp. 145–149). Boston, MA: Allyn and Bacon.

Dasen, P. R. (1975). Concrete operational development in three cultures. *Journal of Cross-Cultural Psychology, 6,* 156–172. doi:10.1177/002202217562002

Downey, K. B. (2004). At the playground: Cultural differences in the play behavior of Mexican and Euro-American children. *Journal of Psychological Inquiry, 9,* 7–3.

Du, S. (2000). 'Husband and wife do it together': Sex/gender allocation of labor among Qhawqhat Lahu of Lancang, Southwest China. *American Anthropologist, 102,* 520–537. doi:10.1525/aa.2000.102.3.520

Eddy, W. H. (2001). *The other side of the world.* Enfield, NH: Enfield Publishing.

Engel, G. (1977). The need for a new medical model: A challenge for biomedicine. *Science, 196,* 129–136. doi:10.1126/science.847460

Flaherty, M. (2001). How a language gender system creeps into perception. *Journal of Cross-Cultural Psychology, 32,* 18–31. doi:10.1177/002202210103200105

Forbes, G., Zhang, X., Doroszewicz, K., & Haas, K. (2009). Relationships between individualism-collectivism, gender, and direct or indirect aggression: A study in China, Poland, and the US. *Aggressive Behavior, 35*, 24–30. doi:10.1002/ab.20292

Fuchs, A. H. (2000). Teaching the introductory course in psychology circa 1900. *American Psychologist, 55*, 492–495. doi:10.1037//0003-066X.55.5.492

Georgas, J., Berry, J. W., van de Vijver, F. J. R., Kagitcibasi, C., & Poortinga, Y. H. (2006). *Families across cultures: A 30 nation psychological study.* New York, NY: Cambridge University Press.

Gibbs, J., Basinger, K., Grime, R., & Snarey, J. (2007). Moral judgment development across cultures: Revisiting Kohlberg's universality claims. *Developmental Review, 27*, 443–500. doi:10.1016/j.dr.2007.04.001

Giordano, P. J. (2011). Culture and theories of personality: Western, Confucian, and buddhist perspectives. In K. D. Keith (Ed.), *Cross-cultural psychology: Contemporary themes and perspectives* (pp. 423–444). Chichester: Wiley-Blackwell.

Goddard, H. H. (1913). The Binet tests in relation to immigration. *Journal of Psycho-Asthenics, 18*(2), 105–110.

Goldstein, S. (2008). *Cross-cultural explorations: Activities in culture and psychology* (2nd ed.). New York, NY: Routledge.

Goldstein, S. B., Siegel, D., & Seaman, J. (2010). Limited access: The status of disability in introductory psychology textbooks. *Teaching of Psychology, 37*, 21–27. doi:10.1080/00986280903426290

Gosling, S. D., & John, O. P. (1999). Personality dimensions in nonhuman animals: A cross-species review. *Current Directions in Psychological Science, 8*, 69–75. doi:10.1111/1467-8721.00017

Gray, P., & Bjorklund, D. F. (2014). *Psychology* (7th ed.). New York, NY: Worth.

Greenfield, P. M., Reich, L. C., & Oliver, R. R. (1966). On culture and equivalence: II. In J. S. Bruner, R. R. Oliver, & P. M. Greenfield (Eds.), *Studies in cognitive growth* (pp. 270–318). New York, NY: Wiley.

Griggs, R. A., Jackson, S. L., & Christopher, A. N. (1999). Introductory psychology textbooks: An objective analysis and update. *Teaching of Psychology, 26*, 182–189. doi:10.1207/S15328023TOP260304

Guanzon-Lapeña, M. A., Church, A. T., Carlota, A. J., & Katigbak, M. S. (1998). Indigenous personality measures: Philippine examples. *Journal of Cross-Cultural Psychology, 29*, 249–270. doi:10.1177/0022022198291013

Gurung, R. A. R. (2011). Cultural influences on health. In K. D. Keith (Ed.), *Cross-cultural psychology: Contemporary themes and perspectives* (pp. 259–273). Malden, MA: Wiley-Blackwell.

Gurven, M., von Rueden, C., Massenkoff, M., Kaplan, H., & Lero Vie, M. (2013). How universal is the Big Five? Testing the five-factor model of personality variation among forager-farmers in the Bolivian Amazon. *Journal of Personality and Social Psychology, 104*, 354–370. doi:10.1037/a0030841

Hall, E. T. (1990/1966). *The hidden dimension.* New York, NY: Anchor Books.

Heine, S. J. (2012). *Cultural psychology* (2nd ed.). New York, NY: Norton.

Heine,S. J., & Norenzayan, A. (2006). Toward a psychological science for a cultural species. *Perspectives on Psychological Science, 1,* 251–269. doi:10.1111/j.1745-6916.2006.00015.x

Hill, J. S., Pace, T. M., & Robbins, R. R. (2010). Decolonizing personality assessment and honoring indigenous voices: A critical examination of the MMPI-2. *Cultural Diversity and Ethnic Minority Psychology, 16,* 16–25. doi:10.1037/a0016110

Hogben, M., & Waterman, C. K. (1997). Are all of your students represented in their textbooks? A content analysis of coverage of diversity issues in introductory psychology textbooks. *Teaching of Psychology, 24,* 95–100. doi:10.1207/s15328023top2402_3

Hunt, C. J., Piccoli, V., Gonsalkorale, K., & Carnaghi, A. (2015). Feminine role norms among Australian and Italian women: A cross-cultural comparison. *Sex Roles, 73,* 533–542. doi:10.1007/s11199-015-0547-0

James, W. (1892). *Psychology: The briefer course.* New York, NY: Holt.

Ji, L. J., Zhang, Z., & Nisbett, R. (2004). Is it culture or is it language? Examination of language effects in cross-cultural research on categorization. *Journal of Personality and Social Psychology, 87,* 57–65. doi:10.1037/0022-3514.87.1.57

Jones, E. E., & Harris, V. A. (1967). The attribution of attitudes. *Journal of Experimental Social Psychology, 3,* 1–24. doi:10.1016/0022-1031(67)90034-0

Jordan, E. H., & Noda, M. (1987). *Japanese: The spoken language. Part I.* New Haven, CT: Yale University Press.

Kaptchuk, T. (2000). *The web that has no weaver: Understanding Chinese medicine.* New York, NY: McGraw-Hill.

Kashima, Y., Yamaguchi, S., Kim, U., Choi, S., Gelfand, M., & Yuki, M. (1995). Culture, gender, and self: A perspective from individualism-collectivism research. *Journal of Personality and Social Psychology, 69,* 925–937. doi:10.1037/0022-3514.69.5.925

Keith, K. D., & Beins, B. C. (2017). *The Worth expert guide to scientific literacy: Thinking like a psychological scientist.* New York, NY: Worth.

Keller, M., Edelstein, W., & Schmid, C. (1998). Reasoning about responsibilities and obligations in close relationships: A comparison across two cultures. *Developmental Psychology, 34,* 731–741. doi:10.1037/0012-1649.34.4.731

Koenig, A. M., & Dean, K. K. (2011). Cross-cultural differences and similarities in attribution. In K. D. Keith (Ed.), *Cross-cultural psychology: Contemporary themes and perspectives* (pp. 475–493). Chichester: Wiley-Blackwell.

Kowalski, R. M. (2000). Including gender, race, and ethnicity in psychology content courses. *Teaching of Psychology, 27,* 18–24. doi:10.1207/S15328023TOP2701_3

Kreiner, D. S. (2011). Language and culture: Commonality, variation, and mistaken assumptions. In K. D. Keith (Ed.), *Cross-cultural psychology: Contemporary themes and perspectives* (pp. 383–399). Malden, MA: Wiley-Blackwell.

Ladd, G. T. (1898). *Primer of psychology.* New York, NY: Charles Scribner's Sons.

Livingstone, D. (1857). *Missionary travels and researches in South Africa.* London: Royal Geographic Society. Retrieved from www.gutenberg.org/files/1039/1039-h/1039-h.htm

Lonner, W. J., & Murdock, E. (2012). Introductory psychology texts and the inclusion of culture. *Online Readings in Psychology and Culture, 11*(1). dx.doi. org/10.9707/2307–0919.1115

López, I., & Ho, A. (2013). Culture-bound (or culturally salient?): The role of culture in disorder. In K. D. Keith (Ed.), *The encyclopedia of cross-cultural psychology* (Vol. 1, pp. 355–362). Chichester: Wiley-Blackwell.

MacLachlan, M. (1997). *Culture and health.* Chichester: Wiley.

Markus, H. R., & Kitayama, S. (1991). Culture and the self: Implications for cognition, emotion, and motivation. *Psychological Review, 98,* 224–253. doi:10.1037/0033-295X.98.2.224

Matsumoto, D., & Juang, L. (2013). *Culture and psychology* (5th ed.). Belmont, CA: Wadsworth.

McCrae, R. R., & Costa, P. T. (1997). Personality trait structure as a human universal. *American Psychologist, 52,* 509–516. doi:10.1037/0003-066X.52.5.509

(1999). A Five-Factor theory of personality. In L. A. Pervin & O. John (Eds.), *Handbook of personality: Theory and research* (2nd ed., pp. 139–153). New York, NY: Guilford.

Mezulis, A. H., Abramson, L. Y., Hyde, J. S., & Hankin, B. L. (2004). Is there a universal positivity bias in attributions? A meta-analytic review of individual, developmental, and cultural differences in the self-serving attributional bias. *Psychological Bulletin, 130,* 711–747. doi:10.1037/0033-2909.130.5.711

Milgram, S. (1974). *Obedience to authority.* New York, NY: Harper & Row.

Miller, D. T., & Ross, M. (1975). Self-serving biases in the attribution of causality: Fact or fiction? *Psychological Bulletin, 82,* 213–225. doi:10.1037/h0076486

Miller, J. G. (1984). Culture and the development of everyday social explanation. *Journal of Personality and Social Psychology, 46,* 961–978. doi:10.1037/0022-3514.46.5.961

Miller, R. L., & Madani, Y. (2013). Self-effacement. In K. D. Keith (Ed.), *The encyclopedia of cross-cultural psychology* (Vol. III, pp. 1141–1143). Chichester: Wiley-Blackwell.

Molitor, A., & Hsu, H.-C. (2011). Child development across cultures. In K. D. Keith (Ed.), *Cross-cultural psychology: Contemporary themes and perspectives* (pp. 75–109). Malden, MA: Wiley-Blackwell.

Morgan, C. T., & King, R. A. (1966). *Introduction to psychology* (3rd ed.). New York, NY: McGraw-Hill.

Munsey, C. (2008). Charting the future of undergraduate psychology. *Monitor on Psychology, 39*(8), 54.

Myers, D. G., & DeWall, C. N. (2015). *Psychology* (11th ed.). New York, NY: Worth.

Nairn, S. L., Ellard, J. H., Scialfa, C. T., & Miller, C. D. (2003). At the core of introductory psychology: A content analysis. *Canadian Psychology, 44,* 93–99. doi:10.1037/h0086930

Nastase, V., & Popescu, M. (2009, August). *What's in a name? In some languages, grammatical gender.* Proceedings of the 2009 Conference on Empirical

Methods in Natural Language Processing, 1368–1377. Retrieved from www.aclweb.org/anthology/D09-1142

Peng, K., Nisbett, R. E., & Wong, Y. C. (1997). Validity problems comparing values across cultures and possible solutions. *Psychological Methods, 2,* 329–344. doi:10.1037/1082-989X.2.4.329

Quinones-Vidal, E., Lopez-Garcia, J. J., Penaranda-Ortega, M., & Tortosa-Gil, F. (2004). The nature of social and personality psychology as reflected in JPSP, 1965–2000. *Journal of Personality and Social Psychology, 86,* 435–452. doi:10.1037%2F0022-3514.86.3.435

Roberson, D., Davidoff, J., Davies, I., & Shapiro, L. (2005). Colour categories in Himba: Evidence for the cultural relativity hypothesis. *Cognitive Psychology, 50,* 378–411. doi:10.1016/j.cogpsych.2004.10.001

Roberson, D., Davies, I. R. L., & Davidoff, J. (2000). Color categories are not universal: Replications and new evidence in favor of linguistic relativity. *Journal of Experimental Psychology: General, 129,* 369–398. doi:10.1037/0096-3445.129.3.369

Ruzgis, P., & Grigorenko, E. L. (1994). Cultural meaning systems, intelligence, and personality. In R. J. Sternberg & P. Ruzgis (Eds.), *Personality and intelligence* (pp. 248–270). New York, NY: Cambridge University Press.

Saxe, G. (1981). When fourth can precede second: A developmental analysis of an indigenous numeration system among Ponam Islanders in Papua New Guinea. *Journal of Cross-Cultural Psychology, 12,* 37–50. doi:10.1177/0022022181121003

Segall, M., Campbell, D., & Herskovits, M. J. (1966). *The influence of culture on visual perception.* New York, NY: Bobbs-Merrill.

Sera, M. D., Elieff, C., Forbes, J., Burch, M. C., Rodriguez, W., & Dubois, D. P. (2002). When language affects cognition and when it does not: An analysis of grammatical gender and classification. *Journal of Experimental Psychology: General, 131,* 377–397. doi:10.1037/0096-3445.131.3.377

Serpell, R. (1974). Aspects of intelligence in a developing country. *African Social Research, 17,* 578–596.

Sommers, S. (2011). *Situations matter: Understanding how context transforms your world.* New York, NY: Riverhead Books.

Sternberg, R. J. (1996). *Successful intelligence: How practical and creative intelligence determine success in life.* New York, NY: Simon & Schuster.

Sternberg, R. J., & Kaufman, J. C. (1998). Human abilities. *Annual Review of Psychology, 49,* 479–502. doi:10.1146/annurev.psych.49.1.479

Super, C. M., & Harkness, S. (1982). The infants' niche in rural Kenya and metropolitan America. In L. L. Adler (Ed.), *Cross-cultural research at issue* (pp. 47–55). New York, NY: Academic Press.

Tanzer, N. H. (2013). Linguistic equivalence. In K. D. Keith (Ed.), *The encyclopedia of cross-cultural psychology* (Vol. II, pp. 819–822). Chichester: Wiley-Blackwell.

Thomas, A., Chess, S., & Birch, H. G. (1970). The origin of personality. *Scientific American, 223,* 102–109. doi:10.1038/scientificamerican0870-102

Titchener, E. B. (1897). *An outline of psychology*. New York, NY: Macmillan.

Tuklin, S., & Konner, M. (1973). Alternative conceptions of intellectual functioning. *Human Development, 16*, 33–52. doi:10.1159/000271265

Turnbull, C. M. (1961). Some observations regarding the experiences and behavior of the BaMbuti Pygmies. *American Journal of Psychology, 74*, 304–308. doi:10.2307/1419421

Twenge, J. W. (2009). Change over time in obedience: The jury's still out, but it might be decreasing. *American Psychologist, 64*, 28–31. doi:10.1037/a0014475

van Herk, H., Poortinga, Y. H., & Verhallen, T. M. M. (2004). Response styles in rating scales: Evidence of methods bias in data from six EU countries. *Journal of Cross-Cultural Psychology, 35*, 346–360. doi:10.1177/0022022104264126

van IJzendoorn, M. H., & Sagi, A. (1999). Cross-cultural patterns of attachment: Universal and contextual dimensions. In J. Cassidy & P. R. Shaver (Eds.), *Handbook of attachment: Theory, research, and clinical applications* (pp. 713–724). New York, NY: Guilford Press.

Wagner, D. A. (1980). Culture and memory development. In H. C. Triandis & A. Heron (Eds.), *Handbook of cross-cultural psychology. Vol. 4: Developmental psychology* (pp. 187–232). Boston, MA: Allyn & Bacon.

Wang, Q. (2003). Infantile amnesia reconsidered: A cross-cultural analysis. *Memory, 11*, 65–80. doi:10.1080/741938173

Wang, Q., & Ross, M. (2007). Culture and memory. In S. Kitayama & D. Cohen (Eds.), *Handbook of cultural psychology* (pp. 645–667). New York, NY: Guilford.

Webb, W. B. (1991). History from our textbooks: Boring, Langfeld, and Weld's introductory texts (1935–1948+). *Teaching of Psychology, 18*, 33–35. doi:10.1207/s15328023top1801_9

Weiten, W. (2008). *Psychology: Themes and variations – Briefer version* (7th ed.). Belmont, CA: Thomson/ Wadsworth.

Wigdor, A. K., & Garner,W. R. (Eds.). (1982). *Ability testing: Uses, consequences, and controversies*. Washington, DC: National Academy Press.

Williams, J., & Best, D. (1990). *Sex and psyche: Gender and self viewed cross-culturally*. Beverly Hills, CA: Sage.

World Health Organization. (1973). *The international pilot study of schizophrenia*. Geneva: Author.

(1983). *Depressive disorders in different cultures: Report of the WHO collaborative study of standardized assessment of depressive disorders*. Geneva: Author.

Zhou, X., Saucier, G., Gao, D., & Liu, J. (2009). The factor structure of Chinese personality terms. *Journal of Personality, 77*, 363–400. doi:10.1111/j.1467-6494.2008.00551.x

CHAPTER 4

History of Psychology in Cultural Context

Kenneth D. Keith

If any date stands out in the minds and memories of undergraduate psychology students, it is likely 1879, a year that appears in virtually every introductory psychology textbook, and one that authors often cite as the starting point for scientific psychology. That year, of course, saw creation, by Wilhelm Wundt, of the first university-based laboratory of psychology (Goodwin, 2015). Both introductory and history of psychology textbooks also generally include discussion of earlier European philosophers and physiologists who were instrumental in setting the stage for scientific psychology – such figures as Descartes, Fechner, Helmholtz, Hume, Locke, Mill, and Weber (e.g., Benjamin, 2007; Goodwin, 2015; Gray & Bjorklund, 2014). And some authors acknowledge the role of the ancient Greeks as the scientific forebears of scientific psychology (e.g., Greenwood, 2009; Myers & DeWall, 2015).

The textbooks also generally detail the profound influence of Charles Darwin before making the metaphorical leap across the ocean to the work of James, Hall, Titchener, and others in North America. All these important contributors to our history have in common certain character-istics: They were men, and they were WEIRD (i.e., they were from **W**estern, **e**ducated, **i**ndustrialized, **r**ich, and **d**emocratic cultures) (Hen-rich, Heine, & Norenzayan, 2010). They were also White. Although these men and many others certainly played fundamentally significant roles in establishing and building the science we call psychology, it is also the case that for much of its history, those of us in the West have taught psychological science as a primarily Euro-American discipline, and we have often overlooked the contributions of psychologists who were not White Western men. In this chapter, I will suggest some avenues for integration of various cultural dimensions into the teaching of history of psychology.

What about Cultural Perspectives?

So-called "mainstream psychology," some observers (e.g., Misra & Gergen, 1993) have argued, while pursuing the goals of controlling and predicting behavior and identifying abstract universal principles, has also sacrificed sensitivity to intra- and intercultural variations. This criticism has arisen in large part because early interest in cross-cultural psychology frequently resulted in efforts by Western psychologists to collect data (often using Western instruments) in other cultures and then comparing and contrasting results across the different cultures. The imposition (or superposition) of mainstream methodology upon indigenous cultures often had the effect of overlooking the existence of local psychologies (Hwang, 2013). Yet, as Stevens, Benedict, and de Castro Pecanha point out in Chapter 1 of this volume, all psychologies are indigenous; psychology is always situated in a cultural context. Thus, North American and European psychologies are indigenous to their particular settings, just as surely as those of Filipinos (Yacat, 2013), Indians (Sinha, 1994), or Russians (Chebotareva & Novikova, 2013). And some of these indigenous perspectives existed long before the arrival of Western scientific psychology (e.g., Sinha, 1994).

People have been interested in human behavior and its connection to context literally for millennia. In a story told by Herodotus (Hunt, 1994), we hear of the Egyptian Pharaoh Psamtik I, ruler in the seventh century B.C.E. Convinced that Egyptians constituted the world's oldest culture, he designed an experiment intended to prove it. Psamtik believed that people had an inborn facility for language, and thus reasoned that a child isolated from birth would naturally learn, eventually, to speak its innate language. That language, he assumed, would be the first language of humans – Egyptian, obviously! Taking two infants from their mother, Psamtik sent them to live in a place where they would receive basic care, but would hear no spoken language. Eventually, the children did learn to speak, but to Psamtik's dismay they spoke not Egyptian, but the language of Phrygia – an ancient region of the country that is now Turkey. As crude (and cruel) as his experiment was, Psamtik had to conclude that the Phrygian culture was older than that of Egypt. As primitive as it might seem by today's standards, Psamtik's worldview was in essence an indigenous psychology that was then informed by cross-cultural experience.

In the twentieth century, historians of psychology took some notice of the significance of cultural perspectives, but sometimes treated them as footnotes to the central thrust of history. For example, in a classic book, Marx and Hillix's (1963) *Systems and Theories in Psychology*, discussions of

European psychology, Soviet psychology, and Oriental psychology were in appendices (not in the main text), and the word *culture* did not appear in the index. More recently, Pickren and Rutherford (2010) have undertaken a history of psychology that makes a deliberate effort to place the evolution of the discipline in cultural context, including discussion of internationalization, indigenization, and examples of indigenous psychologies; and Benjafield (2010) discussed the contributions of Confucian and Taoist ideas to early thought (also see Giordano, this volume).

These various approaches to culture and its relation to psychology have given rise to perspectives that easily lend themselves to inclusion in the history of psychology course. The most prominent of these perspectives are cross-cultural psychology, cultural psychology, and indigenous psychology, and each deserves a bit more discussion.

Cross-cultural psychology. When W. H. R. Rivers embarked upon his famous Cambridge expedition around the turn of the twentieth century, he took with him an apparatus designed to evoke responses allowing him to test the effect of the well-known illusion created by the German Franz Müller-Lyer. Rivers (1905) compared the visual perceptions of people living near the Torres Straits, along with those of the Todas of southern India, to the perception of English people. Rivers's work was an early example of *cross-cultural* research. Cross-cultural psychology involves investigation of "similarities and differences in individual psychological and social functioning in various cultures and ethnic groups" (Kağitçibaşi & Berry, 1989), and cross-cultural psychologists have traditionally been interested in seeking universal behavioral principles that hold true across cultures (Sinha, 2002). This work has thus resulted in efforts to identify whether psychological phenomena are culture specific or more broadly experienced across multiple cultures (Triandis, 2000). As Rivers and many others have done, cross-cultural psychologists have often designed research to test Western theories and Western methods with people of other cultures (Adamopoulos & Lonner, 2001; Laungani, 2002; Yang, 2000), sometimes confirming the universality of psychological principles.

Cross-cultural researchers have also attempted cross-cultural comparisons, often treating culture more or less as an independent variable (e.g., Heine, 2012) – and have encountered methodological difficulties. Investigators cannot, for example, randomly assign research participants to different cultures, thus making true experiments impossible, causal inferences difficult (Leung & van de Vijver, 2008; Lonner, 1974), and conclusions sometimes flawed (Ratner & Hui, 2003). Nevertheless, much of the work of cross-cultural researchers has employed the methods and designs of mainstream psychology, and some have suggested that perhaps cross-cultural psychology should be considered not a separate field, but rather a special method (e.g., Lonner, Keith, & Matsumoto, 2018). However cross-cultural work is conceptualized, many psychological universals have emerged (e.g., Brown, 1991; Heine, 2012). Thus, although they may play out differently in different cultures, such cross-cultural phenomena as aggression (Archer, 2006), gender roles (Williams & Best, 1990), orientation to time (Hofstede, 2001), and intelligence (Sternberg, 2004), among many others, are important in the lives of people around the world.

Cultural psychology. In contrast to cross-cultural psychologists, *cultural* psychologists are more likely to see culture as internal or integral to the individual, and to be less interested in traditional experimental or quasiexperimental methods (Triandis, 2000). The problems of interest to cultural psychology are those that arise from the activities of particular cultures, and are universal to the extent that culture is assumed to exist in every person (Valsiner, 2013). Cultural psychology has historical links to the *Völkerpsychologie* of Wundt (1900–1920; Benjafield, 2010) and to continental Europe, and emphasizes the relations between psychological characteristics of individuals and their cultures. Thus, cultural psychologists are likely to study the everyday activities and problems of a culture, often using such qualitative methods as ethnography, and with a lesser emphasis on comparisons across cultures (Greenfield, 2000).

Whereas cross-cultural psychologists may bring psychological principles (or methods, or instruments) *to* a cultural context, cultural psychologists are interested in phenomena occurring within, or arising *from*, the natural context (Triandis, 2000). Cultural psychology is closely related to anthropology (Yang, 2000), and may define psychology in terms of culture- or context-bound concepts. Perhaps most important, cultural psychologists have more interest in psychological principles originating from culture than in those imposed upon it (Segall, Lonner, & Berry, 1998).

Indigenous psychology. *Indigenous* psychologies are ways of thinking that arise from individual cultures, resulting in scientific viewpoints corresponding to the particular context (Berry, Poortinga, Segall, & Dasen, 2002). Thus, the focus is on an understanding of psychology deriving from the unique characteristics of a particular culture (Allwood & Berry, 2006), and indigenous psychologists are less interested in universal principles, and more concerned with the particular culture as a psychological system (Sinha, 2002). Although indigenous psychology is often associated with non-Western cultures, the indigenization movement has been a worldwide phenomenon during the past three or four decades (Allwood & Berry, 2006).

Indigenous psychologies have developed as a reaction to the perceived hegemony of mainstream psychology (Hwang, 2013). However, indigenization has not always meant a wholesale rejection of Western psychology. In India, for example, where the indigenous psychology movement is strong, there has been a process of modifying and combining British, European, and American psychology into Indian culture (indigenization from without), along with a homegrown psychology that takes into account long-standing traditions and historical texts (indigenization from within; Pickren & Rutherford, 2010). The reliance on the fabric of unique cultures and their traditions allows for both rich description (Matsumoto & Juang, 2013) and a bottom-up approach to theory building, based on local findings and experience (Hwang, 2013).

It is worth noting that there are other cultural and cross-cultural perspectives, including such fields as psychological anthropology, ethnic psychology, and (within broader national or cultural jurisdictions) multicultural psychology. Generally speaking, psychological scientists working within all these subfields seem increasingly to identify with more than one perspective (e.g., Morling, 2015), and there is room in the "big tent" for them all (Lonner et al., 2018). Lonner (2013) provided a useful history and chronology of the rise of interest in culture and psychology, and the organizations that have evolved to further that interest.

Whose Psychology Is It?

Western psychology was long the province of White men, often to the exclusion of women, people of color, and those arriving from other cultures. In this section, I provide a brief sampling of some key historical issues and examples, including some key individuals whom I believe deserve a place in the teaching of history of psychology. (There are, of course, many more whose lives and contributions could/should be recognized.) These people and issues are only representative of a range of subcultural groups and concerns that make up a culturally integrated picture of our past as a discipline.

The role of women. In 1905 Mary Whiton Calkins became the first woman to lead the American Psychological Association (APA) as its president. This honor did not, however, come easily. In 1890, the Harvard

Corporation had begrudgingly allowed Calkins to attend classes with William James, while making clear that she was not entitled to register as a regular student (Benjamin, 2006). Later, despite her successful completion of the requirements for the Ph.D. degree, Harvard authorities remained adamant in refusing to recognize her accomplishment. According to Scarborough and Furumoto (1987, p. 46), this occurred despite James's declaration that Calkins had completed "the most brilliant examination for the Ph.D. that we have had at Harvard." Several years later, in recognition of her work at Harvard, Radcliffe College offered Calkins a Ph.D. As a matter of personal conviction, citing her belief that Radcliffe's offer of a degree did not serve "the best ideals of education" (Benjamin, 2006, p. 121), Calkins declined the offer.

A second woman, Margaret Floy Washburn, became APA president in 1921. Washburn began graduate studies at Columbia University, where she attended classes taught by James McKeen Cattell. However, Columbia, like Harvard, refused to accept women as regular students. Realizing Washburn's high ability, Cattell advised her to transfer to Cornell University, where she would be allowed to study for a degree (Scarborough & Furumoto, 1987). In 1894 Washburn became the first student to receive the Ph.D. under the supervision of E. B. Titchener, and the first woman to earn a Ph.D. in psychology (Goodwin, 2008). Interestingly, although Titchener was willing to admit women as students, he denied them access to the elite organization, The Experimentalists, that he founded in 1904; he wanted the men to be able to speak freely and to smoke (Boring, 1967). The Experimentalists' ban on women persisted until after Titchener's death in 1927, and there would not be another female APA president until Anne Anastasi assumed the office in 1972.

In the early twentieth century, such psychological luminaries as G. Stanley Hall, E. H. Clark, and Hugo Münsterberg believed women to be constitutionally inferior to men. They thought the stress of menstruation would make the rigors of higher education dangerous (Birke, 1986), that education would impair childbearing (Shields, 1975), and that their irrational nature made women unfit to serve on juries (Hale, 1980). According to Galton (1907), women were intellectually inferior to men – an assumption that some attributed to superior variability in the behavior of men. It took the research of a woman, Leta Stetter Hollingworth, to dispel these myths about women and their capabilities (Benjamin, 1975; Hollingworth, 1914). Hollingworth was a pioneer in the psychology of women, and her work disputed the idea that women were dysfunctional during menstrual cycles or were inferior to men. Although she is most often remembered for her work on sex differences, Hollingworth went on to also make important contributions to clinical and educational psychology and to the field of special education.

Many other women have, of course, bucked the cultural tides to achieve distinction in the history of psychology. Scarborough and Furumoto (1987) documented the lives of important early contributors in the United States, and the website Psychology's Feminist Voices (www.feministvoices .com/history-of-women-in-psychology/) provides sources of information on others (mainly American and European).

Even the rat was white. In the early part of the twentieth century, the field of psychology was not particularly hospitable to minorities. The psychological testing movement brought numerous efforts to prove the intellectual inferiority of a variety of groups, including Blacks, Mexican Americans, and Native Americans (Guthrie, 1998), and it was the era of Henry Goddard (1912, 1913), who purported to show that large numbers of immigrants were mentally defective. Increasing numbers of immigrants experienced deportation due to ostensible "feeblemindedness," and nearly 80 percent of some groups (e.g., Hungarians, Italians, Jews, Russians) found themselves labeled defective (Hunt, 1994). The prominent psychologist Lewis Terman, writing in 1916, claimed that:

> High-grade or borderline deficiency ... is very, very common among Spanish-Indian and Mexican families of the Southwest and also among negroes. Their dullness seems to be racial, or at least inherent in the family stocks from which they come. (pp. 91–92)

Terman's words were an echo of those of Bruner (1912), who, in summarizing work on so-called "primitive races," said that while young Negro children were alert and eager, in adolescence they became "dull and stupid, and further development appears to be confined to the physical" (p. 388).

Another influential early psychologist, G. Stanley Hall, harbored his own ideas about racial differences, but nevertheless supported the education of minority students, including Francis Cecil Sumner, who, in 1920 at Clark University, became the first African American to receive a Ph.D.in psychology (Greenwood, 2009). In fact, according to Guthrie (1998), during this era, Clark educated more Black students than all other White colleges combined. Nevertheless, it would be more than a decade until the first African American woman to earn a psychology Ph.D., Inez Beverly Prosser, would receive her degree in 1933 at the University of Cincinnati. Tragically, her productive career was cut short when Prosser died in a car crash within a year of receiving her Ph.D. (Benjamin, Henry, & McMahon, 2005).

Most early Black psychologists were educators, and many were members of the American Teachers Association (ATA), an organization formed in reaction to the refusal of southern chapters of the National Education Association to accept Black members. Psychologists organized within the ATA, meeting at the 1938 ATA convention to establish ATA Division 6, the Department of Psychology (Guthrie, 1998). As World War II intervened and diverted attention away from the organizational effort, momentum lagged and the post-war APA failed to address the concerns of minority psychologists. By the 1960s, as the United States became more diverse, mainstream psychology continued its focus on the effort to establish universal principles based largely on the WEIRD society described in the introduction to this chapter (Pickren & Rutherford, 2010). As the title of Guthrie's (1976) book so aptly noted, *Even the Rat Was White.*

Yet it was an African American couple, Mamie and Kenneth Clark, who contributed to one of the most profound social changes of the twentieth century. For years, seventeen American states and the District of Columbia had maintained racially segregated schools, based on the so-called "separate but equal" doctrine. As graduate students, the Clarks studied the effects of segregation on the self-esteem and attitudes of children, and Kenneth Clark later contributed a paper on the effects of prejudice and discrimination on personality development to a major White House Conference on Children and Youth (Benjamin, 2006). Kenneth Clark testified in several court cases challenging the separate but equal doctrine; when the cases were combined into *Brown v. Board of Education*, the resulting landmark 1954 Supreme Court decision, in striking down the segregation laws, referred to the importance of social science testimony (Goodwin, 2008). This marked the first time the Supreme Court had cited psychological evidence in changing a law. And Kenneth Clark's White House paper was specifically noted in a footnote supporting the decision (Benjamin, 2006).

At the annual APA convention in 1968 in San Francisco, a group of concerned Black psychologists agreed to establish an organization. The group became the Association of Black Psychologists (ABPsi; www.abpsi .org/), and today asserts that "Black/African Centered psychology is ultimately concerned with understanding the systems of meaning of human beingness, the features of human functioning, and the restoration of normal/natural order to human development . . . to resolve personal and social problems and to promote optimal functioning" (Association of Black Psychologists, n.d.). In 1969, a year after the founding of the ABPsi, Black students challenged the APA to respond to their concerns – a development that led to recognition of the Black Students in Psychology organization and ultimately to changes in a variety of aspects of graduate training issues and opportunities for ethnic students (Guthrie, 1998). Kenneth Clark, in 1971, became the first African American elected president of the APA.

Groups soon following the lead of the ABPsi included the Network of Indian Psychologists and the American Indian Interest Group (which later merged and became the Society of Indian Psychologists (SIP; Trimble & Clearing-Sky, 2009). SIP (www.aiansip.org/) has worked to increase the number of American Indians in psychology, through such programs as Indians into Psychology Doctoral Education. Its mission is to be an organization for Native American people to advocate for the mental well-being of Native people. In 1986 Logan Wright, of the Osage Nation, became the first Native American elected president of the APA (Pickren & Rutherford, 2010).

Other key groups representing the interests of minority psychologists include the Asian American Psychological Association (AAPA; https:// aapaonline.org/), established in 1972 by San Francisco Bay area psychologists (Leong & Okazaki, 2009). Among its aims, the AAPA works to advance knowledge of, and concerns, including mental health and well-being, of Asian Americans. The AAPA maintains publications, including the *Asian American Journal of Psychology*. AAPA leaders have also been important influences in the work of the APA, including Richard Suinn, who in 1999 became the first Asian American psychologist to serve as APA president (Leong & Okazaki, 2009).

Hispanic psychology has a long history (e.g., Padilla, 1980), and there is long-standing concern about the mental health of Hispanic Americans and their underrepresentation in mental health professions (e.g., Rogler, 1997). In 1970, Hispanic psychologists at the APA convention in Miami established the Association of Psychologists por La Raza (APLR). Over several years, the APLR grew and evolved, first into the National Hispanic Psychological Association, and then the National Latina/o Psychological Association (NLPA; Pickren & Rutherford, 2010). The mission of NLPA is to advance psychological education and training, science, and practice for benefit of Hispanic/Latina/o groups (NLPA, 2012). Cuban American Antonio Puente served as APA president in 2017.

Many psychologists have written about the role of women, immigrants, and ethnic and racial groups in the development of Western psychology. And of course, cross-cultural texts and international sources have documented a variety of psychological perspectives and key players. Many of these individuals appear in history of psychology textbooks, but many do not, and those who do are not always presented in the context of their cultural heritage and its relation to their lives and contributions. Here I have touched only the tip of the figurative iceberg, in suggesting starting points for exploring some of these contributors.

There are plenty of rich possibilities, and I am reluctant to try to list names. But think of such people as Ruth Benedict, Urie Bronfenbrenner, Pierre Dasen, Lillian Gilbreth, Rogelio Díaz-Guerrero, Geert Hofstede, Matatoro Matsumoto, Shoma Morita, George Peter Murdock, Durganand Sinha, William Graham Sumner, Lev Vygotsky, and a hundred more. You will not find time or space to include them all. But if we branch out a bit, we can come to appreciate new perspectives and their cultural foundations. We can also think of old standards in the same way: Ainsworth, Descartes, Anna and Sigmund Freud, Horney, Koffka, Köhler, Lewin, Montessori, Pavlov, Piaget, Titchener, Turing, Wertheimer, Wundt, Zeigarnik, and all the rest – all have a cultural story just waiting to be told. Some of those stories will recount the influence of their personal context on development of the theories and viewpoints that we take to be important, insightful, or forward thinking. Other stories will tell the tale of cultural influences producing ideas that, by today's standards, seem horribly racist, sexist, or ethnocentric. Just as novels and movies can be funny, scary, horrific, or moving, so too are the stories of the people and events that define the ongoing saga of culture and history.

Teaching Activities

Make a new friend. It would be easy, in teaching history of psychology, to stick with a tried and true list of prominent psychologists – the ones who appear in all the textbooks, and whose names have become familiar to students. But it can be both interesting and enjoyable to make new historical and cultural acquaintances. Here's one way to do it:

1. Prepare a list of people who have made important contributions to psychological science, but who may not be household names for students. These could be important historical figures in psychology in other countries, immigrant psychologists whose cultural background might not be obvious in their scientific work, or perhaps more familiar native-born psychologists whose cultural influences might be particularly interesting (e.g., Stanley Milgram was profoundly influenced by his Jewish heritage).

2. Assign each student a name from the list (or allow each to choose a name). The activity is more interesting if there are no duplicates – that is, each student works with a different name.
3. Assign students the task of conducting historical/cultural research on the person whose name they have chosen. This will likely involve library and online investigation to learn about the individual's personal and cultural history. This step can also involve directly contacting the individual; most psychologists are remarkably generous in responding to emailed student requests for assistance with projects.
4. On an appointed day, each student introduces his or her new "friend" to the class. This should involve a brief description of the individual's work, as well as key personal/cultural experience that may have been influential in the person's life and work. The presentations can be enlivened by such aids as PowerPoint photographs or other visual materials.
5. If this is a graded activity, I suggest assessment not only of the class presentation, but also evaluation of a written paper based on the student's research.

Hire a new professor. Students sometimes wonder what it would be like to be a student in Wundt's laboratory, to study Morita therapy in Japan, or to conduct multinational surveys for major corporations. Wouldn't it be interesting, they might think, if Freud were on the faculty of my department. One way to capitalize on this line of thought is to make students members of a virtual faculty search committee. Here's how:

1. Prepare a faculty position description of the type that your department might typically use in hiring a new member. You will include the usual particulars, including rank, departmental characteristics, specialty area (or, for this assignment, maybe an "open" area of emphasis), contact information (perhaps listing yourself as chair of the search committee), and the position description (a combination of teaching, research, advising, or whatever seems appropriate for your department – but including the requirement that the person must bring an interesting cultural perspective or area of expertise, or significant international experience, as well).
2. Provide students with the position description.
3. Ask students to conduct research to find an individual from the history of psychology (living or dead) who would be a strong applicant.
4. Each student, after identifying an appropriate individual, should prepare a set of application documents, as if they were their chosen

psychologist. The packet should include a curriculum vitae, teaching statement, and research statement.

5. During the appointed class period, divide the class into small groups; try to be sure that no two people in any one group are representing the same historical figure.

6. Within each group, ask the students to discuss their "applications," and decide, for the group, which is the strongest applicant to become a finalist for the advertised position.

7. For each group, ask the person who prepared the "winning" application to present it to the entire class.

8. After hearing the presentations from the finalists, poll the entire class to determine whom they would hire to fill the faculty position.

I have used this assignment on numerous occasions, with varying (but always interesting) results. Sometimes the class chooses an obvious, prominent name (e.g., William James – after all, he wrote a book for teachers and he spoke multiple languages!). On other occasions, they may choose someone lesser known, but for powerful reasons (e.g., Harry Kirke Wolfe – Wundt's second American Ph.D. student, with a reputation as an extraordinary teacher).

Read all about it. This is a variant of an assignment devised and reported by Bryant and Benjamin (1999), and is a good way to simulate immersion in the cultural milieu of the time and place of an important event in the history of psychology.

1. Ask students to pick an important event in the history of psychology (e.g., Wundt establishes his lab; Binet develops a new test; Goddard begins testing immigrants), preferably one originating in another country, or that has obvious cultural dimensions.

2. Write a brief report of the important psychological event.

3. Conduct sufficient research to write brief reports of other things happening in the particular culture and the world on that date (e.g., when Yerkes's team developed the Army Alpha and Beta tests, Europe was at war, and the United States was on the verge of entering the war).

4. Each student then prepares a newspaper (using software, or the old-fashioned way: with paper and scissors!), including the psychological news, as well as other cultural and world events appropriate to the time.

5. During the appointed class period, students bring their newspapers and display them for the class to view. I have done this more or less like a poster session, with students having the opportunity to move around the room to see each other's work, ask questions, and engage in discussion.

If you grade this assignment, you may want to prepare a rubric including the aspects you consider most important (e.g., interest and accuracy of the psychological content, the cultural/national content, quality of the visual presentation). This is an activity that combines history, psychology, and culture in a way that students typically find engaging, and their creativity in identifying both psychological and cultural events of interest is sometimes fascinating.

Resources: Books and Articles

There are many helpful print resources for the teaching of both history and culture, and some good ones that provide information for both history and culture. This list includes a few that I have found particularly useful.

Benjamin, L. T., Jr. (2006). *A history of psychology in letters* (2nd ed.). Malden, MA: Blackwell.

It is one thing to know that Freud and Jung had a falling out, or that Kenneth and Mamie Clark contributed to desegregation of American schools. It is quite a different thing to read the letters in which they discussed the context, the related experiences, and their feelings about these events. Benjamin has compiled a fascinating collection of excerpts from the letters of historical figures, along with context-setting commentary.

Bronstein, P., & Quina, K. (Eds.). (2003). *Teaching gender and multicultural awareness: Resources for the psychology classroom.* Washington, DC: American Psychological Association.

This edited volume contains chapters discussing integration of multicultural perspectives in the teaching of various courses, and includes a chapter by Laurel Furumoto on teaching history of psychology in sociocultural context.

Gross, D., Abrams, K., & Ennis, C. Z. (2016). *Internationalizing the undergraduate psychology curriculum: Practical lessons learned at home and abroad.* Washington, DC: American Psychological Association.

The sixteen chapters of this book, all written by experienced teachers, comprise a wealth of practical information and ideas for those seeking support for integration of culture in their courses. Although not specifically addressing history of psychology, the perspectives of these authors are helpful.

Guthrie, R. V. (1998). *Even the rat was white: A historical view of psychology* (2nd ed.). Boston, MA: Pearson.

Robert Guthrie was the first African American psychologist whose papers were deposited at the Cummings Center for the History of Psychology at the University of Akron. In this book, originally published in 1976, starting with the views of European explorers and slavers, and Africans themselves, Guthrie explores the history of what it has meant to be Black and to be a Black psychologist. Every student should read this book, whether in history of psychology or elsewhere.

Keith, K. D. (Ed.). (2013). *The encyclopedia of cross-cultural psychology.* Chichester: Wiley-Blackwell.

With more than 600 entries by more than 300 international authors, this three-volume work provides information on many key international contributors to psychology and its history, descriptions of numerous indigenous psychologies, and reports on many important concepts and perspectives in the realm of culture and psychology.

Lee, R. (Ed.). (2009). History of racial and ethnic minority psychology [Special issue]. *Cultural Diversity and Ethnic Minority Psychology, 15*(4).

Lonner, W. J. (2013). Chronological benchmarks in cross-cultural psychology. Foreword. In K. D. Keith (Ed.), *The encyclopedia of cross-cultural psychology* (Vol. I, pp. xl–li). Chichester: Wiley-Blackwell. Also available at http://scholarworks.gvsu.edu/orpc/contents.html

Scarborough, E., & Furumoto, L. (1987). *Untold lives: The first generation of American women psychologists.* New York, NY: Columbia University Press.

This book tells the stories of twenty-five female psychologists, chosen by virtue of their membership in APA or James McKeen Cattell's 1906 *American Men of Science.* These are wonderful accounts of the cultural challenges posed by the demands of unwelcoming academe, discriminatory university practices, the demands of family, and the weight of history.

Resources: Electronic

Cummings Center for the History of Psychology: www.uakron.edu/ahap/

This Center, located at the University of Akron, houses a huge array of print material, memorabilia, and artifacts associated with the history of psychology. The website provides information concerning access to archives and other materials.

Office of Teaching Resources in Psychology (OTRP) of the Society for the Teaching of Psychology: http://teachpsych.org/page-1603066#

This is a free online resource that includes resources for a variety of courses and teaching concepts, including cross-cultural psychology, diversity, and history.

Online Readings in Psychology and Culture of the International Association for Cross-Cultural Psychology: http://scholarworks.gvsu.edu/orpc/

This free online compendium of materials dealing with the interface between culture and psychology includes units on historical issues and a unit on teaching. The site is sponsored by the International Association for Cross-Cultural Psychology.

Project Syllabus of the Society for the Teaching of Psychology: http://teachpsych.org/otrp/syllabi/index.php

This is a free online resource sharing syllabi for various psychology courses. Among these are syllabi for courses in history and in culture.

Psychology's Feminist Voices: www.feministvoices.com/history-of-women-in-psychology/

This website provides extensive resources about the contributions of women and the role of gender in the history of psychology.

References

Adamopoulos, J., & Lonner, W. J. (2001). Culture and psychology at a crossroad: Historical perspective and theoretical analysis. In D. Matsumoto (Ed.), *The handbook of culture and psychology* (pp. 11–34). New York, NY: Oxford University Press.

Allwood, C. M., & Berry, J. W. (2006). Origins and development of indigenous psychologies: An international analysis. *International Journal of Psychology*, *41*, 243–268. doi:10.1080/00207590544000013

Archer, J. (2006). Cross-cultural differences in physical aggression between partners: A social-role analysis. *Personality and Social Psychology Review*, *10*, 133–153. doi:10.1207/s15327957pspr1002_3

Association of Black Psychologists. (n.d.) What is Black psychology? Retrieved from www.abpsi.org/#

Benjafield, J. G. (2010). *A history of psychology* (3rd ed.). Don Mills: Oxford University Press.

Benjamin, L. T., Jr. (1975). The pioneering work of Leta Hollingworth in the psychology of women. *Nebraska History*, *56*, 493–505.

(2006). *A history of psychology in letters* (2nd ed.). Malden, MA: Blackwell.

(2007). *A brief history of modern psychology*. Malden, MA; Blackwell.

Benjamin, L. T., Jr., Henry, K. D., & McMahon, L. R. (2005). Inez Beverly Prosser and the education of African Americans. *Journal of the History of the Behavioral Sciences*, *41*, 43–62. doi:10.1002/jhbs.20058

Berry, J. W., Poortinga, Y. H., Segall, M. H., & Dasen, P. R. (2002). *Cross-cultural psychology: Research and applications* (2nd ed.). Cambridge: Cambridge University Press.

Birke, L. (1986). *Women, feminism, and biology.* New York, NY: Methuen.

Boring, E. G. (1967). Titchener's experimentalists. *Journal of the History of the Behavioral Sciences, 3,* 315–325. doi:10.1002/1520-6696(196710)3:4%3C315::AID-JHBS2300030402%3E3.0.CO;2-D

Brown, D. E. (1991). *Human universals.* Philadelphia, PA: Temple University Press.

Bruner, F. G. (1912). The primitive races in America. *Psychological Bulletin, 9,* 380–390. doi:10.1037/h0072417

Bryant, W. H. M., & Benjamin, L. T., Jr. (1999). Read all about it! Wundt opens psychology lab: A newspaper assignment for history of psychology. In L. T. Benjamin, Jr., B. F. Nodine, R. M. Ernst, & C. Blair-Broeker (Eds.), *Activities handbook for the teaching of psychology* (Vol. 4, pp. 47–49). Washington, DC: American Psychological Association.

Chebotareva, E. J., & Novikova, I. A. (2013). Russian psychology: Ethnic and cross-cultural. In K. D. Keith (Ed.), *The encyclopedia of cross-cultural psychology* (Vol. III, pp. 1111–1115). Chichester: Wiley-Blackwell.

Galton, F. (1907). *Inquiries into the human faculty and its development.* London: Dent.

Goddard, H. H. (1912). *The Kallikak family: A study in the heredity of feeblemindedness.* New York, NY: Macmillan.

(1913). The Binet tests in relation to immigration. *Journal of Psycho-Asthenics, 18*(2), 105–110.

Goodwin, C. J. (2008). *A history of modern psychology* (3rd ed.). Hoboken, NJ: Wiley.

(2015). *A history of modern psychology* (5th ed.). Hoboken, NJ: Wiley.

Gray, P., & Bjorklund, D. F. (2014). *Psychology* (7th ed.). New York, NY: Worth.

Greenfield, P. M. (2000). Three approaches to the psychology of culture: Where do they come from? Where can they go? *Asian Journal of Social Psychology, 3,* 223–240. doi:10.1111/1467-839X.00066

Greenwood, J. D. (2009). *A conceptual history of psychology.* Boston, MA: McGraw-Hill.

Guthrie, R. V. (1976). *Even the rat was white: A historical view of psychology.* New York, NY: Harper and Row.

(1998). *Even the rat was white: A historical view of psychology* (2nd ed.). Boston, MA: Pearson.

Hale, M. (1980). *Human science and order: Hugo Munsterberg and the origins of applied psychology.* Philadelphia, PA: Temple University Press.

Heine, S. J. (2012). *Cultural psychology* (2nd ed.). New York, NY: Norton.

Henrich, J., Heine, S. J., & Norenzayan, A. (2010). The weirdest people in the world? *Behavioral and Brain Sciences, 33,* 61–83. doi:10.1017/S0140525X0999152X

Hofstede, G. H. (2001). *Culture's consequences: Comparing values, behaviors, institutions, and organizations across nations* (2nd ed.). Thousand Oaks, CA: Sage.

Hollingworth, L. S. (1914). Variability as related to sex differences in achievement. *American Journal of Sociology, 19*, 510–530. doi:10.1086/212287

Hunt, M. (1994). *The story of psychology*. New York, NY: Anchor Books.

Hwang, K.-K. (2013). Indigenous psychology. In K. D. Keith (Ed.), *The encyclopedia of cross-cultural psychology* (Vol. II, pp. 716–718). Chichester: Wiley-Blackwell.

Kağitçibaşi, Ç., & Berry, J. W. (1989). Cross-cultural psychology: Current research and trends. *Annual Review of Psychology, 40*, 493–531. doi:10.1146/annurev.ps.40.020189.002425

Laungani, P. (2002). Cross-cultural psychology: A handmaiden to mainstream Western psychology. *Counselling Psychology Quarterly, 15*, 385–397 doi:10.1080/09515070310000069392

Leong, F. T. L., & Okazaki, S. (2009). History of Asian American psychology. *Cultural Diversity and Ethnic Minority Psychology, 15*, 352–362. doi:10.1037/a0016443

Leung, K., & van de Vijver, F. J. R. (2008). Strategies for strengthening causal inferences in cross-cultural research: The consilience approach. *International Journal of Cross Cultural Management, 8*, 145–169. doi:10.1177/1470595808091788

Lonner, W. J. (1974, April). *The past, present, and future of cross-cultural psychology*. Paper presented at the annual convention of the Western Psychological Association, San Francisco, CA.

(2013). Foreword. In K. D. Keith (Ed.), *The encyclopedia of cross-cultural psychology* (Vol. I, pp. xl–li). Chichester: Wiley-Blackwell.

Lonner, W. J., Keith, K. D., & Matsumoto, D. (2018). Culture and the psychology curriculum: Foundations and resources. In D. Matsumoto & H. C. Hwang (Eds.), *The Oxford handbook of culture and psychology*. New York, NY: Oxford University Press.

Marx, M. H., & Hillix, W. A. (1963). *Systems and theories in psychology*. New York, NY: McGraw-Hill.

Matsumoto, D., & Juang, L. (2013). *Culture and psychology* (5th ed.). Belmont, CA: Wadsworth.

Misra, G., & Gergen, K. J. (1993). On the place of culture in psychological science. *International Journal of Psychology, 28*, 225–243. doi:10.1080/00207599308247186

Morling, B. (2015). Teaching cultural psychology. In D. S. Dunn (Ed.), *The Oxford handbook of undergraduate psychology education* (pp. 599–611). New York, NY: Oxford University Press.

Myers, D. G., & DeWall, C. N. (2015). *Psychology* (11th ed.). New York, NY: Worth.

NLPA. (2012). Our mission. Retrieved from www.nlpa.ws/our-mission

Padilla, A. M. (1980). Notes on the history of Hispanic psychology. *Hispanic Journal of Behavioral Sciences, 2,* 109–128. doi:10.1177/07399863000200401

Pickren, W. E., & Rutherford, A. (2010). *A history of modern psychology in context.* Hoboken, NJ: Wiley.

Ratner, C., & Hui, L. (2003). Theoretical and methodological problems in cross-cultural psychology. *Journal for the Theory of Social Behavior, 33,* 67–94. doi:10.1111/1468-5914.00206

Rivers, W. H. R. (1905). Observations on the senses of the Todas. *British Journal of Psychology, 1,* 321–396.

Rogler, L. H. (1997). Fulfilling a promise. *Contemporary Psychology, 42,* 497–498. doi:10.1177/07399863000200401

Scarborough, E., & Furumoto, L. (1987). *Untold lives: The first generation of American women psychologists.* New York, NY: Columbia University Press.

Segall, M. H., Lonner, W. J., & Berry, J. W. (1998). Cross-cultural psychology as a scholarly discipline: On the flowering of culture in behavioral research. *American Psychologist, 53,* 1101–1110. doi:10.1037/0003-066X.53.10.1101

Shields, S. A. (1975). Functionalism, Darwinism, and the psychology of women: A study in social myth. *American Psychologist, 30,* 739–754. doi:10.1037/h0076948

Sinha, D. (1994). Origins and development of psychology in India: Outgrowing the alien framework. *International Journal of Psychology, 29,* 695–705. doi:10.1080/00207599408246559

    (2002). Culture and psychology: Perspective of cross-cultural psychology. *Psychology and Developing Societies, 14,* 11–25. doi:10.1177/097133360201400102

Sternberg, R. J. (2004). Culture and intelligence. *American Psychologist, 5,* 325–338. doi:10.1207/s15327957pspr1002_3

Terman, L. M. (1916). *The measurement of intelligence.* Boston, MA: Houghton Mifflin.

Triandis, H. C. (2000). Dialectics between cultural and cross-cultural psychology. *Asian Journal of Social Psychology, 3,* 185–195. doi:10.1111/1467-839X.00063

Trimble, J. E., & Clearing-Sky, M. (2009). An historical profile of American Indians and Alaska natives in psychology. *Cultural Diversity and Ethnic Minority Psychology, 15,* 338–351. doi:10.1037/a0015112

Valsiner, J. (2013). Cultural psychology. In K. D. Keith (Ed.), *The encyclopedia of cross-cultural psychology* (Vol. I, pp. 319–327). Chichester: Wiley-Blackwell.

Williams, J. E., & Best, D. L. (1990). *Measuring sex stereotypes: A multination study.* Beverly Hills, CA: Sage.

Wundt, W. (1900–1920). *Völkerpsychologie* (Vols. 1–10). Leipzig: W. Engelmann.

Yacat, J. (2013). Filipino psychology (sikolohiyang Pilipino). In K. D. Keith (Ed.), *The encyclopedia of cross-cultural psychology* (Vol. II, pp. 551–556). Chichester: Wiley-Blackwell.

Yang, K.-S. (2000). Monocultural and cross-cultural indigenous approaches: The royal road to the development of a balanced global psychology. *Asian Journal of Social Psychology, 3,* 241–263. doi:10.1111/1467-839X.00067

Research and Statistics

Thinking like a psychological scientist involves a complex of skills that are useful for anyone, not just psychologists or psychology students. Among these skills are the ability to evaluate claims using critical thought and analysis, to understand data and the context from which they arise, to judge the generalizability of findings, and to recognize different types of research and research methodologies. Many students will not have considered the possibility that culture matters when studying statistics (Chapter 5) or research design (Chapter 6), and yet, as we see in this section, the issues are both complex and fascinating. And no topic is more fundamental to the integrity of cross-cultural research than measurement (Chapter 7).

Often, the essence of useful research lies not in having the right answers, but in asking the right questions, and asking the right questions frequently depends upon mastery of a methodology relevant to the task. Conducting research across cultures often requires new ways of thinking – about variables, about measurement, about validity, about everything we may have thought we knew about culture. Research involving culture can tax ingenuity, and it presents challenging logistical obstacles. The authors of these chapters bring both enthusiasm and vast experience to the task, and they present a variety of perspectives that will be useful to teachers of psychology.

CHAPTER 5

Why Culture Matters in Teaching Statistics

Susan A. Nolan and Andrew F. Simon

Think, for a moment, of the average person.
Who comes to mind?

How would you describe the person you're imagining in terms of gender, race, ethnicity, age, religion, and disability? What does she do for a living? What are his hobbies? Is she married? Does he have children? What does she look like? How does he dress? What is her financial situation? How many years of education has he completed? How many friends does she have? Chances are that your "average person" is different from everyone else's on a number of variables. Your perspective on "average" depends on your experiences, including those related to culture. Indeed, even the concept of average seems to differ based on culture. For example, in the United States, there's a higher emphasis on superlatives than on average-ness, with every small town bragging that it has the highest waterfall or largest ball of string. Even Normal, Illinois, a town with a name that itself evokes typicality, touts its Steak 'n Shake restaurant as the first in the world (O'Keefe, 2005). Yet just across the border, government officials in Saanich, British Columbia, brag about their district's average-ness, stating that "being 'average' means we are a community where most young people are well balanced, pleasant people who contribute to the community in numerous ways" (O'Keefe, 2005, p.22).

Why Include Culture in Statistics Courses?

We argue that an emphasis on culture in statistics courses is valuable for at least the following three reasons. First, our cultural backgrounds inform our perceptions about the world – including what the average person is like or even whether it's better to be average or exceptional. Understanding that our perceptions are grounded in our experiences can help us to accept that we need the objectivity of statistics. In the case of the average person, statistics help identify actual means, medians, and modes in terms of both characteristics and behaviors. We are not objective thinkers, in part because of cultural experiences, and statistics help us move toward an objective understanding of the world. By debunking some of our misconceptions, we can start to accept the forces that shape our biased thinking in the first place, including those related to culture.

Second, cultural differences and similarities are inherently fascinating to many of us. Statistics instructors can harness students' interest in culture to introduce sophisticated statistical concepts in an engaging way. We'll come back later to our discussion of the average person, one in which our students readily engage. We introduce both central tendency and variability through an activity based on what each student imagines for the typical person, how that differs across students in the class, and how that is likely to vary across countries and cultures. The conversations about means, medians, modes, and standard deviations are, we can assure you, livelier than when we have used a more traditional topic to illustrate these calculations.

Moreover, cultural research is not just interesting to students – it's also research that they may have learned about previously. Research has demonstrated that students learn new information more readily when it is linked with information with which they are already familiar. For example, in one study, students retained more new information about a familiar historical figure than about an unfamiliar person (Ambrose & Lovett, 2014). A discussion about familiar aspects of culture might provide similar scaffolding for new statistical concepts.

Third, an important pursuit of research psychology is an understanding of culture and how it influences thinking and behavior. Statistics is a key ingredient in research that helps us understand ourselves and our environment in cultural and global context. A cultural approach to teaching statistics can help students understand cross-cultural research findings by helping them evaluate the pros and cons of various statistical approaches. It can help them develop an appropriate skepticism of statistical findings coupled with, we hope, a respect for the relative objectivity that statistics helps to bring to the cross-cultural research process.

We understand that there also are important considerations related to how culture shapes statistics and research methods more generally. These valuable discussions often center on western ways of doing research, including criticisms of the presentation of aggregate – rather than individual-level – data, as well as of the quantification of information about people divorced from cultural context (Tafreshi, Slaney, & Neufeld, 2016). Tafreshi and her colleagues argued, for example, that even rigorously applied statistical techniques "may not be enough when a particular culture does not share the basic assumptions of Western psychology such as those that underlie the quantitative imperative" (p. 244).

We agree that these considerations are important ones, and we encourage an ongoing dialog about both how culture shapes statistical approaches and how statistical approaches can hinder a full understanding of culture. However, the focus of this chapter will be the integration of culture into a traditional statistics course. Most statistics courses currently take a traditional approach, and we will offer suggestions on how to increase coverage of the convergence of culture and statistics without an instructor having to completely revamp her or his course.

The Central Role of Variability

We believe that several key concepts of statistics – and particularly the concept of variability – may be misunderstood if not presented against the background of culture. Statistics, ultimately, is based on variability – among individuals within a group and among groups. Means, for example, are dependent on the variability of the distribution they describe. Variability measures themselves are affected by certain characteristics of a distribution, including when there are outliers or when the distribution is not unimodal. The primary goal of most visual displays of data, an essential component of statistics courses, is to depict variability, whether within groups, among groups, or over time.

Moreover, null hypothesis significance testing (NHST) is based directly on variability. In analysis of variance (ANOVA), for example, the F statistic is calculated by dividing between-groups variability by within-groups variability. There is always variability within any group. Only when variability among groups is large enough compared to variability within groups do we reject the null hypothesis. For example, Matsumoto and Hwang (2015) examined reactions of people in the United States, India, Ecuador, Mexico, Bolivia, China, and South Korea to a set of videos showing crimes being committed. The researchers assessed whether the variability of emotional reactions to the videos across countries was large enough relative to the variability within each country that they could reject the null hypothesis. They found that the intensity of negative reactions differed, on average, based on country. Although observers across all countries experienced anger, contempt, and disgust, the intensity of these emotions varied to a greater extent across countries than within each country to a degree that the researchers could conclude that there were significant differences.

For those reasons, variability is arguably *the* key concept underlying statistical methods. But variability also is a key concept in cultural understandings of psychology. Tying statistics and culture together through variability creates, we believe, a discussion that allows students to better understand both constructs. In the next section, we will introduce a variability-based approach to teaching some of the most central statistical concepts through the infusion of topics rooted in cultural psychology.

Teaching Statistical Topics through Cultural Examples

In this section, we introduce a cultural/cross-cultural approach to the following topics: measures of central tendency; measures and visual displays of variability; standardization; Type I and Type II errors and the replication crisis; effect size; confidence intervals; correlation, regression, and covariates; and (briefly) reliability, validity, and factor analysis. For each of these concepts, we'll describe a teaching activity, demonstration, or discussion that highlights culture while teaching a statistical idea or technique.

Measures of central tendency. Findings from cultural psychology often fly in the face of the idea of central tendency. Calculating a mean, median, or mode is useful only if there is a center to be found. We can see the challenge of identifying a center when researchers utilize an instrument created in a culture different from the one under study. If the true average for people in a particular culture is different from the true average of the people on whom the instrument was normed, the validity of the instrument is called into question. That is, we cannot necessarily conclude whether we are measuring true differences in a particular construct or if the differences are a reflection of the bias toward the culture from which the instrument emerged. Such a discussion, about the often-illusory nature of a true mean, can help students better understand the concept of central tendency.

In class, we might use the example of the Issa, Falkenbach, Trupp, Campregher, and Lap (2017) assessment of the Psychopathic Personality Inventory – Revised (PPI-R) with a sample of Lebanese college students. In comparison to the US sample on which the PPI-R was normed, the Lebanese students' responses showed different statistical patterns. This led to uncertainty as to what it means to demonstrate psychopathy in one culture versus another. Issa and colleagues (2017) pointed out that their findings raise questions "as to whether the construct or the instrument is the issue in the measurement of psychopathy in the Arab world.

The underlying mechanisms of psychopathy may be analogous, but expressed differently cross-culturally" (p. 68), with different means and different variabilities around that mean. This example demonstrates the challenges researchers face when attempting to understand populations with different center points.

To highlight both the pitfalls in trying to pin down a central tendency and the importance of turning to statistics to thwart our tendencies toward bias, we also use the activity based on the average person that we mentioned earlier. As instructors in the United States, we ask students to imagine the typical American and write a paragraph describing that person. We then give them a list of some of 140 characteristics that author Kevin O'Keefe (2005) used in his real-life search for the average American, and ask them to indicate where their average American falls on each criterion.

Following this exercise, we break our class into pairs or small groups to share their ideas, and then come back to the larger class to talk about similarities and differences across students. We ask students what might account for some of their different ideas, guiding the discussion toward issues of cultural and other experiences. We then introduce O'Keefe's average American. O'Keefe (2005) undertook a painstaking and (usually) statistically driven search for the average American, a search he described in *The Average American: The Extraordinary Search for the Nation's Most Ordinary Citizen*. Using data from the 2000 US Census and other sources, O'Keefe ventured into the field to track down the single American person who was closest to average in 140 different characteristics. From a methodological perspective, O'Keefe cut a lot of corners in his search, but he produced concrete details that can drive a discussion. O'Keefe (2006) described average Americans as people who . . .

> weigh between 135 and 205 pounds and support both Roe v. Wade and a citizen's right to bear arms. They live in an unattached, owner-occupied house with a minimum of two people, one registered voter and one pet, in a suburb within three miles of a McDonald's, 20 minutes of a Wal-Mart and 100 miles of an ocean. They believe in gambling for money and support stricter enforcement of environmental regulations.

As O'Keefe added each new criterion, it became harder and harder to find the single individual who was perfectly average on every trait. In fact, just about all of the almost 100 finalists failed on at least one criterion. As a book reviewer noted: "One by one, his prospects flunk the test. One has too many cars. Another lacks a pet. And so it goes, down to the wire" (Grimes, 2005, para. 9).

O'Keefe (2006) eventually found Bob Burns in a statistically average Connecticut suburb. Burns, "who lives in a five-room house near the end of a cul-de-sac, was the only person in the community to nail all 140 qualifications – he matched everything from having a high school diploma to attending church regularly, from being better off financially than his parents to living within five miles of his workplace" (O'Keefe, 2006, para. 12). As for Bob, an American in a land of hyperbole, did he chafe at the "average" label? On the contrary. As O'Keefe (2005) reported: "'What an honor," [Bob] said softly," and then invited O'Keefe to go fishing with him (p. 222).

We turn again to our students with questions. How does Burns match up with their ideas? What are the benefits of O'Keefe's statistically driven process? What are the drawbacks in understanding the people of the United States? How and why would the average person differ across cultures within the United States and across countries? We end by pointing out that the exercise of questioning the usefulness of a given measure of central tendency is always a valuable one, regardless of the data. What does it mean if someone has a perfectly average reaction time, IQ score, or depression level? What information is missing with only a measure of central tendency and no information on variability? How might a report of a central tendency limit our full understanding of the many people behind that one number?

Measures and visual displays of variability. As we noted, variability is the linchpin of statistical analysis, as well as central to understanding people across cultures. Psychologist Qi Wang (2016) noted that "upon observing group variations in a psychological construct of interest within a multicultural sample, a researcher who dismisses the variations, partials them out in analysis as meaningless noise, or simply accepts them as is may lose potentially groundbreaking findings" (pp. 585–586). It is, then, attention to variability that can deepen our understanding of cultural similarities and differences, as well as uncover the mechanisms behind any differences.

One way to understand variability is to create data visualizations. In class, we have students explore different ways of graphing the same group difference using increasingly complex tools. Imagine a statistical comparison of a construct that elicits a mean difference between two cultural groups. First, we have students create a bar graph that depicts the group difference. Second, we have students add error bars to give a sense of the variability within each group. Third, they create side-by-side box plots that offer additional subtlety, allowing us to see the interquartile range for each of the groups. But the individual differences within each group might help us to understand the group difference better. As Wang (2016) observed, "cultural psychology by no means downplays the importance of individual differences" (p. 587). So, as a fourth step, we have students create a dot plot so that they can see the distribution of every individual data point. (We do a similar exercise with correlational data; students contrast the regression line with the scatterplot. The latter allows students to more easily understand why a given finding is just an aggregate finding, not true for every individual.)

To further emphasize the value of visualizing data at the individual level, we also use Dustin Cable's (2013) striking interactive online map of the United States, The Racial Dot Map: (http://demographics.coopercenter .org/racial-dot-map/). The map includes more than 300 million separate dots, color coded by race, one for every person included in the 2010 US Census. Students can easily see what parts of the country are integrated and what parts are segregated. Students enjoy playing with the map, zooming in on places they have lived, but also testing their own hypotheses about the racial makeup of different regions of the country, of rural versus urban areas, and so on. An activity based on Cable's map leads to rich discussions about both culture, such as how varying racial distributions might affect people's experiences, and statistics, including the importance of considering the individuals behind any set of data.

Any discussion of variability and difference is not complete without a discussion of similarity (Wang, 2016). Moghaddam (2012) discussed the many intergroup problems that have emerged because of increased globalization. Most notably, we may consider terrorism to be an effect of groups coming into contact with one another relatively quickly and without adequate preparation. Moghaddam (2012) offered an approach to educating people by starting with a focus on the many attributes groups around the world share with one another, noting the enormous number of similarities. Only after this is done should attention be given to group differences and to the value of diversity. Engagement with the individual data points – and the people behind them – can help students see the overlap among different groups and the fact that there are never hard and fast differences that apply across all group members.

Standardization. Once students understand central tendency and variability, they can use these concepts to standardize data. The most commonly used method to standardize scores is to calculate z scores by subtracting the mean from each score, and then dividing by the standard deviation. The resulting data tell us where each score falls in terms of standard deviation from the mean. Standardizing is particularly useful when we are trying to understand how a given construct plays out across cultures. Indeed, in their classic book on cross-cultural statistics and research methods, van de Vijver and Leung (1997) argued that "culture-level analyses can yield strikingly dissimilar results for standardized and nonstandardized data" (p. 88). By standardizing data, we are able to examine a given construct in the absence of any cross-cultural differences in means and standard deviations. Standardization might be especially useful when the ways in which people respond across cultures differ, but the underlying patterns remain.

A pair of classic studies highlights the potential utility of standardization in cultural research. David Buss and his colleagues (1990) found that, across samples from thirty-seven cultures, women gave higher mean ratings than men to the value of earning potential in a mate – that is, women placed a higher emphasis on a potential partner's economic resources. The researchers presented these data as part of an evolutionary explanation for mating behaviors. Using these same data, Alice Eagly and Wendy Wood (1999) documented variations in this mean difference across cultures. In cultures with more gender equality, women's ratings of the importance of their partners' earning potential tended to be lower. So, if a researcher were interested only in the general pattern of gender differences in mate preferences across cultures, he or she might want to standardize the rating scores for each culture. An analysis of standardized scores would give a sense of the gender difference within each culture in terms of standard deviations rather than raw scores, thus controlling for many aspects of culture. On the other hand, if a researcher were interested in cultural variations, it would make more sense to examine raw scores. As Eagly and Wood did with the variable of gender equality, that researcher could then begin to explore what variables might account for any variability in a particular gender difference across cultures.

Type I and Type II errors and the replication crisis. A statistically significant cross-cultural research finding could reflect a true difference. Or it could be a Type I error, a significant finding when there really is no difference. Similarly, a nonsignificant finding could indicate that there is no true difference (although we are always careful not to accept the null hypothesis). Or it could represent a Type II error, a failure to detect a real difference. In either case – a significant finding or lack thereof – we never know the underlying truth. These can be tricky concepts for students to grasp. The cross-cultural research literature supplies a wealth of contradictory findings that can spur discussion: Does the significant finding reflect a real difference or a Type I error? Does the failure to reject the null hypothesis reflect the lack of a real difference or a Type II error? More importantly, what are the ramifications of Type I and Type II errors when discussing cross-cultural differences and similarities?

These questions have taken on increased urgency as many well-known studies have failed to replicate (Diener & Diener-Biswas, n.d.). If we repeat a study with a new sample and get the same results, it is more likely that those results are accurate and can generalize. But if we do not get the same results, it may be either that the initial results were a Type I error or that there's something different about the second sample – and that "something different" could be tied to culture. That's the exciting opportunity presented by replication. As psychologist Lisa Feldman Barrett (2015) explained, the "failure to replicate is not a bug; it is a feature. It is what leads us along the path – the wonderfully twisty path – of scientific discovery" (para. 14).

Nonreplication may mean that the initial study's finding was a Type I error. For example, Ramsay, Tong, Pang, and Chowdhury (2016) conducted two experiments to examine whether priming people in Singapore to think of God and religion influenced the way they perceived ingroup and outgroup members. The researchers were curious to see whether there was a difference between men and women with respect to how the primes influenced them. An initial study provided support for a gender difference, identifying a tendency for women to rate members of outgroups more negatively when primed with the words "religion" and "God." To explore this trend more carefully, the researchers conducted a second study, focusing exclusively on perceptions of outgroup members. This time, no difference was found between women and men. As Ramsay and colleagues concluded: "Since the unanticipated gender effect observed in study 1 was not replicated in a second sample, it seems prudent to conclude that the gender effect observed in study 1 is likely to have been a false positive" (p. 13).

But nonreplication may also open the door for new culturally based hypotheses. Kemmelmeier and Malanchuk (2016) examined self-enhancement in an individualist culture and a collectivist culture. They sought to determine whether self-enhancement, viewing oneself as better than others, was different in Western Ukraine, historically oriented toward the individualism of Europe, than in Eastern Ukraine, historically oriented toward the collectivism of Russian culture. They looked at the "Muhammad Ali" effect, people's belief, often seen in individualist cultures, that they are more moral, but not necessarily smarter, than others.

Although the researchers found that those in Western Ukraine scored higher in independence and self-enhancement, on average, than those in the Eastern region, the Muhammad Ali effect was not found in either culture. The failure to replicate the effect, however, led not to the discounting of the previous finding, but rather to a number of new culturally driven hypotheses. Kemmelmeier and Malanchuk (2016) speculated that this nonfinding may have occurred because, on the whole, Ukraine, is more collectivist than the individualist cultures where the effect has been identified previously. They also hypothesized that Ukrainians may not view honesty as a more valued trait than they view intelligence, thus negating a self-enhancement of one over the other. Students can more readily generate alternative explanations for different findings in different cultures than for different findings where the new sample is less easily distinguished from the previous sample.

Effect size. Geoff Cumming's groundbreaking 2012 book, *Understanding the New Statistics,* was essentially a campaign to publicize an academic discussion of the pitfalls of null hypothesis significance testing and got everyone – well, every social scientist at least – talking about it. Cumming put forward an approach to analyzing and reporting data that emphasizes the "new statistics," including effect size and confidence intervals, which are decidedly not new, though their mainstream use may be. Since Cumming's push, there have been statements from a number of academic journals and professional associations, including the American Statistical Association, encouraging or even requiring the use of the new statistics in place of or in addition to null hypothesis significance testing (e.g., Association for Psychological Science, 2014; Trafimow & Marks, 2015; Wasserstein & Lazar, 2016).

We believe that the new statistics offer a particular benefit to an understanding of cross-cultural research, given the dangers of misinterpreting statistically significant differences between cultural groups. Indeed, cross-cultural researchers have described these dangers; specifically, errors in interpretation of null hypothesis significance testing . . .

> have several implications. Theoretically, they may lead to the construction of knowledge based on stereotypes. Research is then created to test this bias, which is perpetuated because of the continued use of limited data analytic techniques. Practically, programs for intercultural sensitivity, training, competence, adjustment, and the like are based on cultural stereotypes, providing consumers with incorrect guidelines that may be more harmful than helpful. (Matsumoto, Kim, Grissom, & Dinnel, 2011, p. 246)

For these reasons, we believe that cultural research is particularly suited to illustrate those hazards and help students better understand techniques that can help. Students, we find, can "get" the very real human effects that might derive from cross-cultural misunderstandings. With that in mind, we'll explore two of the new statistics in this chapter – effect sizes here and confidence intervals in the next section.

One of the most prominent of the new statistics, effect size, essentially quantifies the overlap between groups. Let's consider the effect size for a two-group comparison, Cohen's *d*, which is easily understood by students. It's simply the difference between two groups in terms of standard deviation, and it allows us to estimate the degree of overlap between two distributions. Jacob Cohen (1988), who developed Cohen's *d*, published guidelines – or conventions – to interpret the statistic. A Cohen's *d* of 0.2, indicating just 0.2 standard deviations difference between the two group means, is considered small. It coincides with an estimated overlap of 85 percent between the distributions. So, we can imagine two normal curves that are almost entirely overlapping. It's not all that helpful to draw conclusions about individuals in that case. A medium effect size of 0.5 indicates 67 percent overlap. Even a large effect size of 0.8 – close to 1 standard deviation of difference between means – indicates about 53 percent overlap.

One pitfall in statistical thinking involves the interpretation of a difference between groups – including cultural groups – as relevant for all or most people in these groups. Crocetti and colleagues (2015), for example, found variations in adolescent boys' and girls' experiences of generalized anxiety disorder across six countries, with girls showing more severe symptoms, on average, than boys across all but one country. These findings might lead some people to expect intuitively that all girls with the disorder in those five countries would express more severe symptoms than all boys with the disorder. But there are two problems with this intuition. First, there is always overlap between distributions. Second, that overlap can be quantified.

In this study, effect sizes for those differences fell in the small-to-moderate range, so the overlap between the distribution for boys and the distribution for girls would be extensive (Crocetti et al., 2015). This finding does not give us much information about individual girls or boys in these countries. Thus, without knowledge of effect size, an assumption could be made about differences between the girls and boys that would exaggerate differences. A deeper understanding of effect size (and confidence intervals, too, which are discussed in the next section) can save us from making such overgeneralized assumptions.

It's also important to note that effect size is highly dependent on sample size. Imagine that someone told you that he assessed two people in Japan and two people in the United States and found that the Japanese people were happier when experiencing positive feelings as related to engaging with others. This would show up as friendliness, for instance. Imagine that you also found that the two Americans are happier when experiencing positive emotions as related more to themselves than to their engagement with others. This could show up, for instance, as personal pride (Kitayama, Markus, & Kurokawa, 2000). (These are real findings, although with a lot more than just two people. And in the actual study, there was a medium effect size.) Let's say that these differences were about 0.1 standard deviation, equating to very small Cohen's d's. You'd probably roll your eyes and say that such a small sample is unlikely to be representative and can't tell us anything. Besides, those are tiny effects. And in this case, you would not find a statistically significant difference between means with just four people.

Now imagine that someone told you that she had assessed 1 million people in Japan and 1 million people in the United States (much more than in the actual study) and found the same findings. This time the Cohen's d's of 0.1 would be accompanied by findings of a statistically significant difference between means. You wouldn't roll your eyes anymore, because these are statistically significant. But don't forget the effect sizes. They're still tiny. Just because a difference seems to be a real one doesn't mean it's meaningful or important. In a cross-cultural study with a large sample size, it's particularly important to pay attention to the effect size before drawing grand conclusions, particularly at the individual level.

Cross-cultural researchers encourage the use of large samples for two reasons; they are often more representative of the overall population and they tend to produce results that replicate more easily in future studies (Matsumoto et al., 2011). However, these researchers also caution that, because of the heavy influence of sample size on statistical significance, we want to pay particular attention to effect size in cross-cultural work. A large sample size can lead to statistically significant findings even when there is just a small effect. Cross-cultural research is an area in which an exaggerated interpretation of a finding can lead to stereotypes and very real ramifications for people belonging to the groups in question. Let's look at a real-life example.

Lalonde and colleagues (2015) explored the link between gender and intergenerational conflict across cultural groups. They looked at emerging adults in South Asian Canadian (immigrant) cultures and European

Canadian (non-immigrant) cultures, and focused on issues of parent–child conflict, such as expectations regarding cultural traditions, education, and dating. The research team expected to find higher mean levels of conflict among women than men, and among immigrant than non-immigrant families. As expected, they found statistically significant gender differences, but the differences between cultural groups were either nonsignificant or had small effects. As Lalonde et al. concluded, "We can only comfortably state that there are *small* cultural differences between South Asian Canadians and European Canadians in their reported levels of intergenerational conflict and that the overall pattern suggests that they are *similarly* reporting moderate levels of conflict" (p. 532).

Examination of findings like this one can help students, and all of us, to temper our very natural tendency to essentialize a difference. Other researchers make the same argument, framed in terms of similarities rather than differences (Wang, 2016). Ball, Cribbie, and Steele (2013) attempted to quantify similarity by asking, "What is the largest difference between the population means that would *not* be meaningful in the context of the study?" (p. 150). They encourage researchers to note the point at which groups may differ on a measure but do so in a way that is so small it shows the groups to be, in fact, quite similar to one another.

Confidence intervals. Another way in which we can fight people's tendency to think of a mean difference as one that applies to most members of a group is to report interval estimates instead of point estimates (Matsumoto et al., 2011). Cumming (2012) pointed out that other sciences, like physics, routinely report interval estimates, such as "the melting point of the plastic was $85.5 \pm 0.2°C$" (p. ix). Interval estimates help in two ways; they provide a range of plausible variables and they remind us of the fact that statistics are just probability-based estimates.

Yet despite the utility of intervals, in the social sciences, we typically report point estimates, such as means (or differences between means), along with the standard deviations, for the comparison groups. In this case, the reader will often pay sole attention to the means (or differences between means), failing to register the variability around them. On the other hand, interval estimates, such as confidence intervals around a mean (or difference between means), force people to register the variability among groups. This premise is supported by research; in one study, researchers interpreted data based on either an interval estimate or an interval estimate alongside hypothesis testing; those who had only the interval estimate tended to be more accurate in their interpretations (Coulson, Healey, Fidler, & Cumming, 2010).

For this reason, it is important to instill in students a sense of the importance of reporting confidence intervals, and effect sizes, too, of course. As we noted with effect sizes, we believe an emphasis on statistical interpretation is particularly important with cross-cultural research where the ramifications of interpreting differences in an overly broad way can lead to potentially damaging stereotypes. Let's look at an example of a case that can be used in class, one in which confidence intervals help convey the finding in a more accurate way.

Researchers studied cultural display rules, norms that guide how people express emotion publicly, across cultures (Matsumoto et al., 2008). In a later discussion of how they used effect sizes and confidence intervals in reporting the data from this study, Matsumoto and his colleagues (2011) focused on findings from four of the countries studied: Australia, Japan, South Korea, and the United States. The researchers reported a small effect size for the difference between the United States and Australia; they also reported the 95 percent confidence interval around the difference between means: −0.025 to 0.043. This confidence interval includes zero, which indicates that it is plausible that there is no difference, but it also gives us a sense that the difference might be non-zero, although small. On the other hand, the confidence interval for the difference between the means for South Korea and the United States was 0.091 to 0.155. This interval does not include zero, so it is not plausible that there is no difference. It also reminds us that there is no single estimate for the difference between means, and that there is variability among the individuals in the samples within the two countries. Incidentally, there was a large effect size for this difference. We refer readers back to the discussion of effect size for an understanding of the reasons that both effect sizes and confidence intervals are important when making interpretations. We want to rein in exaggerations of the meaningfulness of differences, as they can lead to exaggerated beliefs about differences across cultures.

Correlation, regression, and covariates. Correlation and simple linear regression also can help us to understand differences across cultures. For example, one study that we sometimes discuss in class found statistically significant negative correlations between measures of loneliness and life satisfaction in people from three cultural groups – Italian, Chinese Canadian, and Anglo-Canadian, an indication that the presence and direction of the relation between these constructs was consistent across cultures (Goodwin, Cook, & Yung, 2001). The researchers, however, observed statistically significant differences in the strengths of these correlations. The relation was strongest among the Chinese Canadian sample

(r = -0.54), followed by the Italian sample (r = -0.48), and then by the Anglo-Canadian sample (r = -0.34). The researchers concluded that people in collectivist cultures, such as those in the Chinese Canadian culture, are more affected by loneliness and social exclusion than are those living in individualist cultures.

Thus, correlation – as well as its statistical partner, simple linear regression – can help us to understand how variables associate with each other in different cultural contexts. Cross-cultural correlational findings can lead students to ask thoughtful questions about why there might be differences in the strengths of various correlations. Conversely, cross-cultural research can help students to understand correlation coefficients and standardized (or beta) coefficients. Cultural findings also can provide a context in which to think about what is meant by a positive or negative correlation, how strength is independent of direction, and what it means for a coefficient to be closer to zero or closer to 1.

The thoughtful questions that students ask about why a particular association may vary across cultures often have statistical answers. We can explore the effects of third variables in correlation and regression, but we can also examine the association of a third variable, a covariate, with a dependent variable in a range of statistical tests, including t tests and ANOVAs. van de Vijver and Leung (1997) offered a hypothetical example. If researchers found that subjective well-being differed, on average, across countries, it may be based on variability in mean income rather than some cultural aspect of the countries of interest. In this case, the researchers could include mean income or other possible third variables – sometimes called *context variables* – as a covariate in the statistical analysis. Including income as a covariate would allow us to control for its influence, essentially comparing subjective well-being across countries for each level of income. This correction allows us to statistically eliminate potential confounding variables that cannot be manipulated experimentally. If a difference across countries disappears when controlling for income, then the effect can be explained by income rather than country. van de Vijver and Leung explained that the inclusion of a covariate like income is "highly useful in cross-cultural research because of the frequent presence of such experimentally controllable differences" (p. 119).

Teaching students about third variables in the context of culture encourages critical thinking both in generating possible third variables and in questioning which possibilities are more or less likely to have an impact. Such an approach enhances students' understanding of statistics at the same time that it fosters a critical mind-set toward cross-cultural psychology.

Reliability, validity, and factor analysis. Psychometric analyses provide another fruitful set of statistical topics for the introduction of culture. Culture helps us ask what reliability and validity actually mean. If an instrument – measuring, say, satisfaction in the workplace – has been found valid and reliable in one cultural context, it may lose its meaning in another because cultural contexts vary. Similarly, a discussion of culture when introducing factor analysis leads us to ask whether the categories of any given construct are the same across cultures. For an excellent and detailed discussion of the important role of culture in psychometric analysis, we refer you to Chapter 7 in this volume.

Resources

Instructors emphasizing the relevance of culture in statistics have a number of resources available to support these efforts. General discussions and lessons linking psychology and culture can be found on websites of the American Psychological Association (APA). For instance, The Society for the Psychological Study of Culture, Ethnicity and Race (Division 45 of APA) maintains a web page devoted to the teaching of cultural and cross-cultural issues. Specifically, the "Teaching Resources" section contains a range of exercises and suggestions from and for instructors focusing on such lessons (http://division45.org/resources/teaching-resources/). Also, a search through the web page of the APA's Society for the Teaching of Psychology (Division 2) yields syllabi from instructors teaching courses in cultural and cross-cultural psychology (http://teachpsych.org/page-1588384). Both sites provide valuable material for introducing and framing lessons around the link between psychology and culture.

We also encourage instructors to visit websites that specifically address the use of statistics as applied to issues of international import. In addition to discussing the applicability of statistical analyses, many of these sites also provide data sets. We have found that statistics instructors often create their own data sets or seek those that would be interesting to students so as to facilitate the learning of key concepts and formulas. To this end, we encourage instructors to visit sites that supply real-world, culturally relevant data for such lessons. The following information is provided to guide in these efforts.

- The World Health Organization (2017) provides statistical information and data sets for countries around the world. Students can see how statistics are used to understand health information globally by reading various summary reports (www.who.int/gho/countries/en/).

Instructors can open the "Data Repository" link to access a range of data sets covering issues such as substance abuse, communicable diseases, mortality, and reproductive health.

- The United Nations Children's Fund (UNICEF) (2017) provides data on literacy rates among children internationally (https://data.unicef .org/topic/education/literacy/). By opening the "Access to Data" link, instructors can find data on children's literacy categorized by gender within country, and clustered according to regions of the world (e.g., Middle East and North Africa, South Asia).

- The website UNdata (2017) provides country-by-country data on the legal age by which men and women can marry without consent (http:// data.un.org/Data.aspx?d=GenderStat&f=inID:19). These data may be especially interesting to college students as they allow them to compare themselves with peers around the world.

We conclude by reinforcing the value of tying culture to the instruction of statistics. From Kevin O'Keefe's (2005) solitary search for the single average American to worldwide big-data explorations of millions of social media data points, statistics are central to understanding people and cultures. More than ever before, our students, upon graduation, will be entering a world with an emphasis on globalization and cross-cultural connections. Central to the successful navigation of this world will be the ability to understand statistical reports as they address a broad array of countries and cultures. Those who have learned to apply and interpret statistical analyses will be better equipped to think critically about the information they are given. And they will be better equipped to lead others in gathering, interpreting, and visualizing data that accurately reflect the growing complexity of our interconnected world.

References

Ambrose, S. A., & Lovett, M. C. (2014). Prior knowledge is more than content: Skills and beliefs also impact learning. In V. A. Benassi, C. E. Overson, & C. M. Hakala (Eds.), *Applying science of learning in education: Infusing psychological science into the curriculum*. Retrieved from the Society for the Teaching of Psychology website, http://teachpsych.org/ebooks/asle2014/ index.php

Association for Psychological Science. (2014). Business not as usual. *Psychological Science, 25*, 3–6. doi:10.1177/0956797613512465

Ball, L. C., Cribbie, R. A., & Steele, J. R. (2016). Beyond gender differences: Using tests of equivalence to evaluate gender similarities. *Psychology of Women Quarterly, 37*, 2, 147–154. doi:10.1177/0361684313480483

Barrett, L. F. (2015, September 1). Psychology is not in crisis. *The New York Times*. Retrieved from www.nytimes.com

Buss, D. M., Abbott, M., Angleitner, A., Asherian, A., Biaggio, A., Blanco-Villasenor, A., . . . & Ekehammar, B. (1990). International preferences in selecting mates: A study of 37 cultures. *Journal of Cross-Cultural Psychology*, *21*, 5–47.

Cable, D. A. (2013). *The racial dot map*. University of Virginia. Retrieved from http://demographics.coopercenter.org/racial-dot-map/

Cohen, J. (1988). *Statistical power analysis for the behavioral sciences* (2nd ed.). Hillsdale, NJ: Erlbaum.

Coulson, M., Healey, M., Fidler, F., & Cumming, G. (2010). Confidence intervals permit, but do not guarantee, better inference than statistical significance testing. *Frontiers in Psychology: Quantitative Psychology and Measurement*, *1*, 1–9. doi:10.3389/fpsyg.2010.00026

Crocetti, E., Hale, W. W., Dimitrova, R., Abubakar, A., Gao, C-H., & Pesigan, I. J. A. (2015). Generalized anxiety symptoms and identity processes in cross-cultural samples of adolescents from the general population. *Child Youth Care Forum*, *44*, 159–174. doi:10.1007/s10566-014-9275-9

Cumming, G. (2012). *Understanding the new statistics: Effect sizes, confidence intervals, and meta-analysis*. New York, NY: Routledge.

Diener, E., & Diener-Biswas, R. (n.d.). The replication crisis in psychology. *Noba Project*. Retrieved from http://nobaproject.com/modules/the-replication-crisis-in-psychology

Eagly, A. H., & Wood, W. (1999). The origins of sex differences in human behavior: Evolved dispositions versus social roles. *American Psychologist*, *54*, 408–423.

Goodwin, R., Cook, O., & Yung, Y. (2001). Loneliness and life satisfaction among three cultural groups. *Personal Relationships*, *8*, 225–230. doi:10.1111/j.1475–6811.2001.tb00037.x

Grimes, W. (2005, November 18). Winnowing the field of America to one representative. *The New York Times*. Retrieved from www.nytimes.com

Issa, M.-A., Falkenbach, D. M., Trupp, G. F., Campregher, J. G., & Lap, J. (2017). Psychopathy in Lebanese college students: The PPI-R considered in the context of borderline features and aggressive attitudes across sex and culture. *Personality and Individual Differences*, *105*, 64–69. doi:10.1016/j.paid.2016.09.035

Kemmelmeier, M., & Malanchuk, O. (2016). Greater self-enhancement in Western than Eastern Ukraine, but failure to replicate the Muhammad Ali effect. *International Journal of Psychology*, *51*, 78–82. doi:10.1002/ijop.12151

Kitayama, S., Markus, H. R., & Kurokawa, M. (2000). Culture, emotion, and well-being: Good feelings in Japan and the United States. *Cognition and Emotion*, *14*, 1, 93–124. doi:10.1080/026999300379003

Lalonde, R. N., Cila, J., Lou, E., & Cribbie, R. A. (2015). Are we really that different from each other? The difficulties of focusing on similarities in cross-cultural research. *Peace and Conflict: Journal of Peace Psychology*, *21* (4), 525–534. doi:10.1037/pac0000134

Matsumoto, D., & Hwang, H.C. (2015). Emotional reactions to crime across cultures. *International Journal of Psychology, 50* (5), 327–335. doi:10.1002/ijop.12103

Matsumoto, D., Kim, J. J., Grissom, R. J., & Dinnel, D. L. (2011). Effect sizes in cross-cultural research. In D. Matsumoto & F. J. R. van de Vijver (Eds.), *Cross-Cultural research methods in psychology*. New York, NY: Cambridge University Press.

Matsumoto, D., Yoo, S. H., Fontaine, J., Anguas-Wong, A. M., Arriola, M., Ataca, B., . . . & Zengeya, A. (2008). Mapping expressive differences around the world: The relationship between emotional display rules and individualism versus collectivism. *Journal of Cross-Cultural Psychology, 39,* 55–74. doi:10.1177/0022022107311854

Moghaddam, F. M. (2012). The omnicultural imperative. *Culture and Psychology, 18* (3), 304–330. doi:10.1177/1354067X12446230

O'Keefe, K. (2005). *The average American: The extraordinary search for the nation's most ordinary citizen*. New York, NY: Public Affairs.

(2006). An average surprise. *The New York Times*. Retrieved from www.nytimes.com/2006/11/12/opinion/12CT-OKeefe.html

Ramsay, J. E., Tong, E. M. W., Pang, J. S., & Chowdhury, A. (2016). A puzzle unsolved: Failure to observe different effects of God and religion primes on intergroup attitudes. *Public Library of Science, 11* (1), 1–21. doi:10.1371/journal.pone.0147178

Tafreshi, D., Slaney, K. L., & Neufeld, S. D. (2016). Quantification in psychology: Critical analysis of an unreflective practice. *Journal of Theoretical and Philosophical Psychology, 36,* 233–249. doi:10.1037/teo0000048

Trafimow, D., & Marks, M. (2015). [Editorial]. *Basic and Applied Social Psychology, 37,* 1–2., doi:10.1080/01973533.2015.1012991

UNdata. (2017, March 29). Retrieved from http://data.un.org/Data.aspx?d=GenderStat&f=inID:19

United Nations Children's Fund. (2017, March 29). Retrieved from https://data.unicef.org/topic/education/literacy/

van de Vijver, F. J. R., & Leung, K. (1997). *Methods and data analysis for cross-cultural research*. Thousand Oaks, CA: Sage Publishers.

Wang, Q. (2016). Why should we all be cultural psychologists? Lessons from the study of social cognition. *Perspectives on Psychological Science, 11,* 583–596. doi:10.1177/1745691616645552

Wasserstein, R. L., & Lazar, N. A. (2016). The ASA's statement on p-values: Context, process, and purpose, *The American Statistician*. doi: 10.1080/00031305.2016.1154108

World Health Organization. (2017, March 29). Retrieved from www.who.int/gho/countries/en/

CHAPTER 6

Approaches to Culture-Oriented Research and Teaching

Carl Martin Allwood

We live in an increasingly globalized world, one in which interaction between people with different cultural backgrounds is increasingly common and expected. Still, communication between people from different parts of the world is often plagued by misunderstanding and feelings of estrangement. Possible contributing factor s are that people simply assume that people from the other culture make similar assumptions and think in the same way as themselves, and that they act on the basis of their prior stereotypic preconceptions about people from the other culture. Important questions in this context are how research can help improve communication between cultures and how people can be helped to understand the results of culture-oriented research in a realistic way.

Knowledge about culture in different societies and how culture influences people can help us broaden our understanding of the social reality we live in. Therefore, it is important that culture-oriented research is carried out in an appropriate way and that the public has a sufficient level of literacy in reading and understanding research. Readers may lack the motivation and time to understand what researchers want to communicate, and popular scientific renderings of research results are often written in an oversimplified way. An important way to help improve this situation is to give students a good opportunity to understand the fascination of culture-oriented research and to understand the strengths and weakness of such research.

This chapter will discuss different aspects and issues of culture-oriented research in psychology and provide suggestions for teaching students about such issues. First, as a background, I will briefly discuss some aspects of what is meant by culture and different approaches to culture-oriented psychological studies. Next follows a discussion of methodological issues, and the chapter ends with some suggestions for teaching.

Approaches to Culture and Culture-Oriented Research

Although researchers over time have developed specialized methodological approaches to their subject matter, background culture may influence research in more or less subtle ways. This is also the case for culture-oriented research in psychology, where research on culture and people has been conducted under various labels such as cross-cultural psychology (CCP), cultural psychology (CP) and indigenous psychology (IP). These approaches overlap, and each exists in different versions, but they still tend to differ in how they understand culture. It should also be noted that how to best define culture remains a controversial issue.

Definitions of culture range from narrow to broad. Narrow cultural concepts have usually focused only on the culture members' understanding of their world, under the assumption that people's understanding of their world is what forms their behavior and their creation of artifacts. Broader definitions of culture not only focus on how people understand the social and material world, but also commonly include human behavior and human-made objects, in general called *artifacts* (e.g., totem poles, watches, and computers). Although these components of culture are assumed to interact, often less attention has been given to the specifics of their concrete interaction and how the components create conditions for one another.

For example, two of the pioneers in cross-cultural psychology summarized their view on culture as follows: "[T]here are certain aspects that almost all researchers see as characteristics of culture. First, culture emerges in adaptive interactions between humans and environments. Second, culture consists of shared elements. Third, culture is transmitted across time periods and generations" (Berry & Triandis, 2006, p. 50). This definition hints at a foremost structural understanding of culture. It emphasizes cultural understanding as *shared* in a society and as fairly stable over time, thus stressing the importance of *tradition* as inherited over generations, while de-emphasizing cultural understanding derived from other societies during a person's lifetime.

The ongoing research program of Hofstede and colleagues illustrates how culture has been researched in terms of abstract, structural aspects. This research compares whole nations' cultures in terms of a small number of dimensions, originally four, but later expanded to six: power distance (small to large), uncertainty avoidance (weak to strong), individualism/collectivism, masculinity/femininity, long-/short-term orientation, and indulgence/restraint, assumed to be fairly stable over time (Hofstede, Hofstede, & Minkov, 2010). Moreover, culture in this type of research tends to be seen as something apart from the individual and as acting on the individual, whereas the reverse, that individuals change culture, has been de-emphasized (Atran, Medin, & Ross, 2005).

Research conducted on the basis of the preceding described understanding of culture, primarily in CCP, has been criticized for a tendency to be too abstract, context free and therefore overgeneralized, and for failing to provide information that allows predicting when and where its results apply. CCP often compares large units, such as parts of nations, whole nations, continents, or binary distinctions such as Western and non-Western cultures, on a small number of dimensions. A similar critique of this research has been that it compares entities that are difficult to compare. For example, social categories may not compare well between different types of societies (see, e.g., Boesch, 1996). However, researchers behind this research are in general well aware of the methodological difficulties of their enterprise. For example, one of the pioneers in CCP, Harry Triandis (1980), wrote "Cross-cultural psychology has all the methodological problems as research done by psychologists in a homogeneous culture, plus additional ones that arise because it is cross-cultural." (p. xv). Sometimes ways of handling these difficulties have been developed, but the reasons for the differences found between the compared groups are often still hard to understand. As an effect of this recognition, CCP researchers have attempted to develop methods that diagnose the presence of "irrelevant" features in the research that make the results difficult to compare. These methods are described elsewhere in this book and some are briefly discussed in this chapter.

In *cultural psychology* (CP), the value and importance of studying people *within* their cultural context tends to be recognized, and one is often skeptical with respect to the possibility of making quick comparisons between cultures (Cole, 1996). In order to get better knowledge of the local cultural situation, cultural psychologists have often used research approaches that bear similarity to those traditionally used in social anthropology, which have then been extended with research methods from psychology. In addition, they often use a Vygotskian perspective (see, e.g., Cole, 1996) or frameworks from situated cognition and similar approaches. Thus, cultural psychologists often present their results for one country at a time. This makes it more difficult to compare results from different parts of the world, but interesting conclusions about important concepts can still be drawn. Scribner and Cole's (1981) study of different forms of literacy among the Vai of Liberia and the skills that developed as a result of this literacy is a fine example of this type of research. In general, CP research has convincingly shown that mental abilities are primarily developed within the specific domains and contexts in which they are trained. This can be summarized as "intelligence as cultural practice" (Laboratory of Comparative Human Cognition [LCHC], 1982). However, the critics have not been silent. Atran et al. (2005) argued that culture in parts of CP is seen as too stable and too shared, and that CP has had a tendency to overgeneralize results *within* cultures. A relevant illustration could be the research by Nisbett, Peng, Choi, and Norenzayan (2001). These researchers subscribed to Cole's version of CP and compared thinking styles between Western (analytic, abstract style) and East Asian (holistic) cultures.

Shweder (1990) formulated another program for cultural psychology. He argued that research on culture in psychology should be based on an understanding of human beings as meaning seeking and intentional in an existentially uncertain situation. This conception seems to imply the importance of people's *life world*, as formulated in Husserl's phenomenological philosophy, that is, of people's *experienced* everyday world. In line with this, Shweder also wrote "Intentional things are causally active, but only by virtue of our mental representations of them" (p. 2). People act from their understanding of things as they appear to them. Shweder also emphasized the importance of diversity and that the CP he advocated "is an interdisciplinary human science" (p. 3).

A third type of culture-oriented psychology is the *indigenous psychology* (IP). IP exists in many versions (Allwood & Berry, 2006) and is a reaction, mostly in non-Western countries such as Taiwan, Hong Kong, the Philippines, India, and Mexico, against the dominance of mainstream psychology (MP). MP is seen as a Western indigenous psychology and as representing Western individualistic, materialistic, and liberal values. A study by Arnett (2008) illustrated the Western dominance in psychology. He found that 96 percent of participants in the articles in top-notch psychological journals from 2003 to 2007 were from Western nations where 12 percent of the world's population lives. In brief, the IPs argue that MP has *imposed* concepts and ideas from Western culture on non-Western societies and cultures (see, e.g., Berry, 1989) and that the IPs will contribute to a more complete *global psychology*.

In line with this, the IP approach stresses the importance of research based on each country's own culture and social conditions. Thus, research in the IPs should be based on phenomena, research problems, methods, concepts, and theories that derive from one's own culture and society (Allwood, 1998). In order to be in line with the experiences and training of the participants, these methods are often of an ethnographic kind (e.g., for the Philippines, see

Church & Katigbak, 2002). Indigenous methods are seen as key to producing research results that are tailor-fitted (useful and easily applicable) to the local society. In spite of the emphasis on local conditions, and on the work of researchers such as Bandura and Shweder, researchers in the IPs still often see culture as shared and quite stable over time (e.g., Kim & Park, 2006; Kim, Yang, & Hwang, 2006), although this may be changing.

In contrast to more structural, abstract, understandings of culture, more recent conceptualizations of culture stress the concrete causal links between meaning content and the social and material context of the culture. This type of cultural concept has inspired research that attends to the local causal connections between meaning content represented in memory, behavior, and artifacts. Thus, this research has emphasized the *process* aspect, rather than the structure aspect of culture (e.g., Allwood, 2011; Atran, 2001; Atran et al., 2005; Kashima, 2005). This type of more locally anchored approach bears similarity to the approach of Wittgenstein (1953), who argued that words' meaning develops on the basis of the concrete communication events and the contexts the words are used in.

More recent views on culture have also stressed that understanding in a society is diverse (heterogeneous) and distributed. The degree to which different types of cultural content are shared is seen as an interesting empirical question, and "the variable distribution of ideas is treated as signal, not noise" (Atran et al., 2005, p. 751). Accordingly, cultural content is seen as shared to various extents, both within and outside the borders of the society in question (compare, e.g., modern science, films and TV series, food traditions, fight sports, and religious content). Thus, in brief, these views of culture see it as dynamic, emphasizing its locally dependent, interactive, and changing aspects. The development of culture is seen as dependent on concrete conditions, such as other people and artifacts, and on how people activate goals and other forms of meaning content.

The stance taken with respect to culture has implications for research. If one tends to see culture in a society as homogeneous and shared, it may be seen as easier to compare societies. However, if one emphasizes that cultural meaning is causally linked to people in their concrete environment, it is reasonable to see it as distributed and possibly as making up a locally varied, socially collective (aggregated) memory. Given this, it will also be interesting to study *how* meaning spreads between people. It may also seem inviting to study how cues from the local environment (including Internet) selectively activate contents in people's memory and for this purpose to use research methodology developed in memory research and in research on judgment and decision making.

Taken together, this opens the door for the use of a range of research methods. Whether these methods are labeled qualitative or quantitative may be less important than whether the research methods bring forth new, relevant, and useful understanding about culture and how it is handled by humans (for a critique of the often fuzzily made distinction between qualitative and quantitative approaches to research, see Allwood, 2012).

In addition to the three described approaches, researchers in other subfields of psychology have also developed an interest in culture, for example in judgment and decision making (JDM) and in work psychology. In JDM some researchers have described their approach as *constructivistic* (Weber & Morris, 2010). This approach focuses on the effect of cues from the social environment, including people and artifacts, and on decision makers' context sensitivity. By focusing on conditions for decision makers' memory activation, the researchers are able to take context-specific factors into consideration and thereby understand the effects of culture in a dynamic and flexible way (see, e.g., Savani, Cho, Baik, &, Morris, 2015). This work has used an understanding of culture where the effects of culture are seen as determined by the local context, and thus, it has favored a more process-oriented, dynamic culture concept. Other work has also used priming in order to activate participants' culture-typical memory contents, but has assumed a more structural culture concept (see, e.g., Oyserman & Lee, 2008).

Research Methods in Culture-Oriented Psychology

Each of the approaches to cultural psychology is useful in relation to specific types of research questions. The methods used vary from methods that stress the data collection phase and the local context dependence of the phenomenon studied, to methods that compare what are taken to be "different" cultures and that use statistics and measurement theory. However, no method is exclusive to any of the approaches mentioned and in practice many kinds of methods are used in each of the approaches. It is also relevant, although not treated here, that culture-oriented psychological research, like all research, has an ethical dimension (see, e.g., Byrne et al., 2009).

Exploring Culture: Soft and Contextual Oriented Methods

Research methods for getting to know specific cultures are usually more cumbersome and take more time to use than the methods used for comparing cultures. The classical method used in social anthropology is a form of ethnography, *participant observation*. Here the researcher shares the lives of the people studied over a longer time period, from many months to a year or more, without actively interfering with their life process (Spradley & McCurdy, 1980). Researchers who do not know the local language have to rely on a translator, and if not well acquainted with the community, they need help from local community members. Often the researcher employs the same person as both translator and fixer.

Participant observation has occasionally proven to be difficult and to raise moral conundrums for the researcher. A first problem is, as in much research, to get access to the field site (or the community) where the data are to be collected. Thus, the researcher's presence and activities in the community have to be accepted by the people living there, and this often has to be negotiated with some person or group. The people in the community are then likely to see the researcher as associated with this person or group, so it is important that this choice is made strategically, especially in relation to the specific categories of people the researcher wants to get into contact with. Other aspects that might cause difficulties are the extent to which the researcher should share his or her property with the community, and how the researcher should relate to violence or conflicts between community members (see, e.g., Fowler & Hardesty, 1994).

For efficiency reasons, researchers often use methods that are more time effective than participant observation. Such approaches also fall under the label ethnography and can include visiting the field site more occasionally and making prebooked interviews with people. It can also mean doing sporadic but systematic observations in the community. However, both for ethical reasons and other reasons, it is usually prudent to inform people ahead of making observations; otherwise people may suspect that the researcher is, for example, a representative of the authorities sneaking around.

A specific method to carry out observations is so-called *shadowing*, also called *tag-along*. Shadowing can be carried out in different ways and basically means to follow a representative of a specific category of people (e.g., medical healers as they see their patients, or local money lenders who see their clients) and observe their interactions. A variant is *guided tours*, where the informant takes the researcher on a guided visit to selected parts of the informant's everyday world. With these methods, there is always a risk that people in the environment adjust and change their behavior when they notice the presence of the researcher. Often the researcher needs to have, or to develop, a good memory, because it can often be inappropriate or cumbersome to write down observations on the spot.

Interviews are also an important research method, but for space reasons, only some brief observations are given here. In general, the researcher can interview one or many persons at a time. I first discuss interviews of one person. If more well-considered and reflected answers are desired, the researcher can inform the interviewee about the questions in advance. Alternatively, the researcher can ask the questions on the spot and get more spontaneous and less reflected answers. Researchers also have to choose whether to ask specific questions and thereby get the information they want, or to let the informant talk more freely about some more general theme. In the latter case, unsuspected, new information may come forth. Thus, the researcher needs to plan in advance which type of answers is desired. In general, it is usually good if the person to be interviewed is calm and in a good mood.

In *focus groups,* many people are interviewed at the same time (see, e.g., Braun & Clarke, 2013). This can be done in many ways. For example, a fairly general theme or phenomenon may first be introduced by the researcher and then discussed more or less freely by the group. Apart from possible time efficiency, an advantage with focus groups is that the researcher gets an insight into what the informants consider appropriate to say in a social context with other people. The researcher will also get an insight into how expressions of social values are triggered in the group by what other people in the group say. Thus, focus groups often serve to inform researchers about what is considered socially appropriate to say in a community. A drawback is that people may not express personal opinions that they feel are not acceptable in the group. Thus, it can be good to add individual interviews after a focus group, and in these to ask follow-up questions about what was said in the focus group. However, it is important to see to it that this does not become embarrassing for the informants, for example, if they feel committed to what they said in the focus group but in fact really have another opinion. A practical challenge with focus groups is that it may be difficult, for example when the group is tape-recorded, to hear what is being said if many people talk at the same time. Accordingly, in order to structure the interchange, the researcher may choose to act as a chairperson in the group, allocating speech opportunity to one speaker at a time. However, this may hinder the informants' spontaneity.

Other ways to learn more about people's understanding include asking them to draw pictures of objects, events, or people in their surroundings. However, drawing skills are to a large extent a matter of training; thus, this may not be a good method in all types of societies without prior training (Cox & Bayraktar, 1989). Finally, equipping people with cameras and asking them to take photos, for example of important parts of their daily life, is also likely to produce interesting results.

Softer contextually oriented methods can be good to use in combination with more context-free statistically oriented methods. Atran et al. (2005) illustrated a creative method for investigating how people understand parts of their environment and how their understanding compares to that of other people. They asked members of three Amerindian groups in Guatemala about how they understood the relation between different types of plants and animals in the jungle. For a list of twenty-eight plants, they asked how each helped or hurt each of twenty-nine animals, and vice versa. They then compared how people in the three groups understood these relations, for example by comparing the factorial structures resulting from submitting the data to a principal component analysis (a cluster method that utilizes all variance in the data). The amount of explained variance for the first factor (that is, the factor with the largest explanatory value) is interpreted as showing the amount of shared understanding in the investigated content domain. An *individual's* factor loading on the first factor is seen to show the degree of overlap between the individual's understanding and the understanding most shared in the investigated group. The following factors are interpreted as showing the shared understanding of different subgroups of people. This approach is based on a method called *cultural consensus*, developed by Romney, Weller, and Batchelder (1986).

Atran et al. (2005) also illustrated the use of *social network analysis*, a method that can be used to explore how knowledge and understanding are spread in a society or community, in this case between men and women, within, and between, the three Guatemalan Amerindian groups. The researchers could draw conclusions about, for example, what different categories of people one talked to in order to learn about nature in the jungle and whom they saw as experts on these topics.

Comparing Results across Cultures

Generally speaking, when comparing entities, it is important that they are similar in the ways assumed. Otherwise, conclusions from the research results may be misleading. Greenfield (1997), and others have argued that culture-free tests are not possible (also called *culture-fair* or *culture-reduced* tests, i.e., tests that do not rely on knowledge specific to a particular experiential background). In line with this, Viswanathan (2005) argued "Whether a construct, its dimensionality, or its measurement applies to a new population should be viewed with a large dose of skepticism" (p. 284).

A fundamental reason for this is that all understanding, including the understanding researchers use when they create tasks and questionnaires, is grounded in local conditions and such conditions most likely differ across societies.

Thus, tests' similarity in different cultures should be seen as a matter of degree, and this should be weighed when interpreting results. Today it is still the case that most so-called culture-free tests are developed in Western countries, which means they are based on conditions specific to Western countries, or at least to more modern forms of life. Much has been written about what is important to consider when testing people from back-grounds that differ from those where the tests were developed (Cronbach, 1990; Greenfield, 1997; Smith, Bond, & Kağitcibasi, 2006; van de Vijver & Tanzer, 2004; Viswanathan, 2005). In addition, methods to assess potential differences with respect to features of items and their relation to other items in a test and to other properties in the research situation are available. Thus, it is at least to some degree possible to understand the extent to which tests measure the same thing in the compared groups. By use of such methods, researchers can identify many sources of irrelevant variance in their results. These methods are well described in other chapters in this book and by, for example, van de Vijver and Tanzer (2004) and Viswanathan (2005). Therefore, I will describe only some brief observations on what is commonly classified as main sources of error variance.

In general, measurements, for example of personality and cognitive features such as ability or cognitive style, are assumed to be affected both by the property or ability the researcher attempts to measure and by other factors (called *error* or *noise*) seen as irrelevant, extraneous, and as causing measurement bias (Viswanathan, 2005). The property that the researcher attempts to measure has different names. For example, it is called *theoretical construct* in the psychometric literature, *true value* in measurement theory, and in general statistics, the same, or similar, idea is also called *latent value* (underlying, hidden value, in contrast to the *manifest* value, that is, the *measured* value). However, because these names occur in somewhat different contexts, their associational value may differ somewhat. A general issue is how the theoretical construct is related to the measured value. Borsboom, Mellenbergh, and van Heerden (2003) argued that a framework in terms of causality and ontological realism is the best approach in this context.

Researchers in culture-oriented psychology commonly (at least initially) take a somewhat reified, essentialist approach with respect to theoretical constructs. This means that the construct is assumed to correspond to a kernel of properties that has some stability over time, and possibly over places, in external reality. However, the extent to which this is actually the case is an empirical question and this question is in focus in research that compares two or more cultures with respect to human properties. Thus, important questions for research that compares features between cultures are to what extent does the exact construct the researcher aims to measure exist in each of the compared cultures, and to what extent is it easily activated by the participants in all groups? I will briefly discuss some of the main sources of measurement error identified in cross-cultural research.

One source of measurement error involves differences between the samples that are seen as irrelevant to what the researcher wants to measure, *sample bias*. For example, the socialization environment of the participants may have given them different opportunities for training skills that are relevant to the studied task, or to answering questions presented by the researcher, or to handling the format of the task they are given. Here, the notion of intelligence as cultural practice developed in cultural psychology (e.g., Laboratory of Comparative Human Cognition, 1982), is relevant to remember. Accordingly, people and tasks as sources of measurement bias are difficult to separate. For example, participants in two cultures may differ in their experience of answering questions presented in a context-free format and of tasks that pose time constraints or demand a speedy response.

Other differences between participants that are commonly seen as irrelevant relate to the participants' response style. For example, researchers have found that participants from different cultures may differ in their use of extreme scale ends or scale midpoints, and in *desirability* tendency, for example in the form of *acquiescence*, the tendency to agree with proposed assertions (see, e.g., Viswanathan, 2005).

A problem not discussed so much in cross-cultural research is that research participants in non-Western countries are often students who tend to be more modern and Westernized than other people in their societies. On the same note, Chinese participants from Hong Kong often show more similar results to Westerners than participants from other parts of China (e.g., Nisbett, 2003).

Participants who understand various aspects of the research procedures differently from what the researcher intended can also cause measurement noise. This can, at least partly, be seen as an effect of how the research session is carried out, that is, as *administration bias*; norms for social interactions differ between societies and cultures, for example, depending on the age and gender of each of the parties to the research communication. In many communities, there are expectations about appropriate behavior in contacts between same or different categories of older and younger people and men and women, with respect to good manners concerning how to talk and what to talk about. In some communities, children should not respond to adults or look at them directly (Greenfield, 1997). To ask questions can be a show of weakness. The extent to which such expectations are fulfilled in the research session may have consequences for how the participants react and what information they will disclose. For participants with little contact with modern democracy and modern education systems, interview or test situations may be unfamiliar and can be perceived as threatening or perhaps even a police interrogation. If an interpreter is needed, it is important that the interpreter is thoroughly informed about what the research situation and the role of interpreter entail and how the session should be carried out.

Various aspects of the content of the items also have consequences for the level of noise in the measurement. This is called *instrument bias*. Differences in understood content between the compared groups can be at hand when the measurement instrument is translated from one language into another and if the translation does not capture the nuances in the translated-to language. Translation techniques, such as *back-translation*, have been developed to ameliorate these problems. Other aspects of the measurement scale, such as choice of a free-answer format or fixed-answer alternatives formulated by the researcher, can also influence the results, usually in ways seen as irrelevant.

An easy way to diagnose whether an instrument functions differently in two groups is to compare the correlations between the items in a scale (Cronbach's alpha) between the researched groups. Other methods of diagnosing sources of variance in the measurement values are described elsewhere in this book. In general, modern advanced statistical methods such as structural equation modeling (SEM) and multilevel modeling (MLM) are relevant to use in this context.

Use of Experimental Research Designs in Cultural Comparisons

In order to study whether an assumed causal factor has the same effect in two cultures, the results of two experiments, one carried out in each of the two cultures, can be compared. When true experiments (randomized allocation of participants to experimental conditions) are compared between two cultures, it is important that the participants in the two cultures do not differ in irrelevant ways. Shadish, Cook, and Campbell (2002) provided a thorough introduction to quasiexperimental design.

Use of the Web

Culture-oriented research is increasingly conducted on the worldwide web. Many companies can provide the researcher with access to participants who have declared themselves willing to fill in researchers' questionnaires or carry out experimental tasks for a low compensation. These companies can usually take care of emailing or linking the questionnaire or programmed task to the participants on the Internet. This opens up many exciting possibilities but it also adds new challenges to those described above. For example, the participants in net-based research are often likely to be unrepresentative of their society.

Teaching Research Methods in Culture-Oriented Psychology

As described, many types of methods are used in culture-oriented research. A further question is how students can best be helped to get a deeper understanding of how culture can be researched in psychology in ways that provide reliable and trustworthy conclusions. This includes helping students to understand the assets and limitations of various methodological approaches and how things tend to become still more complicated when research is carried out in practice. Different writers are likely to provide different answers to the learning issues covered here. However, a generally good approach to learning is *learning by doing*. In addition, in order to capture the students' attention, it is good to work with *concrete examples* either of asserted features of specific cultures or of interesting (asserted) cultural differences.

In addition, a golden rule for all researchers is to have good knowledge about the phenomenon one is researching. Therefore, given that students may not be able to visit a number of foreign Western and non-Western cultures, they should at least be encouraged to read anthropological monographs describing everyday life in places dissimilar to their own. A nice example is Shostak's (1983) depiction of the life of a woman from !Kung, a hunter-gatherer people in the Kalahari desert. Finally, it is also important that students are helped to achieve improved understanding of central theoretical concepts in cultural research methodology.

It is beyond the scope of this chapter to describe in detail all the various research issues and methods that are relevant for cultural research.

However, a number of teaching activities can be used to illustrate different aspects of the fascination and difficulties of culture-oriented research in psychology. In the following sections, I present such activities, as well as further relevant text sources and database material relevant to the issues I have discussed in this chapter.

Teaching Activities for Culture-Oriented Research Methods

I first discuss activities that aim to increase students' awareness of the conventions governing how phenomena in their everyday lives are named and described as an effect of the culture in which they live. These activities have relevance for students' understanding of the vagaries related to issues related to *construct validity* in research on culture in psychology (Shadish et al., 2002).

Improved Description Awareness

Necker cube activity. The first activity is intended to increase students' awareness that there are many ways to describe reality. This approach was described by the post-phenomenological philosopher Don Idhe (1977). First, I display a Necker cube (Figure 6.1) and instruct the students to say what it is. In my own teaching experience, the students are initially likely to say "a cube" or "a three-dimensional cube" and then that the cube can be seen from two angles, from the left or from the right; then some answers like "lines on the board" or "wooden box" are likely to come. Thereafter, silence tends to follow. I have seldom heard other more creative suggestions from students in this exercise. In the next step, I ask students to notice the feeling of being stuck in their own automated categorization system. After this, I suggest other interpretations of the Necker cube figure, such as "a diamond seen from the top," or "looking out from the bottom of an Indian tent" (both three-dimensional interpretations); "an

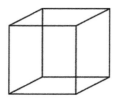

Figure 6.1   Necker cube

angular spider with legs in a box [the box is the outer lines]," "two divining rods, in opposite directions in a box" (both two-dimensional examples). Many other, more or less well-fitting, interpretations can be found, indicating the potential richness in how reality can be described. And, of course, similar exercises are possible with other suitable ambiguous stimulus items.

Taking photographs. A way to attempt to increase students' awareness of the "cultural-ness" of their everyday environment is to ask each of them to take two or three pictures and to explain what is culturally significant about them, either in class or as a written task to be handed in to the teacher.

Content Analysis

There are many more or less advanced computer programs (such as *NVivo* and *Atlas.ti*) for computer-aided content analysis of data in the form of texts of different kinds. Many forms of content analyses of interviews and written material exist. However, it is often illuminating to ask students to do a simple form of content analysis by hand.

Coding content. In this example, pairs of students are asked to separately code the contents of a few short interviews or written texts related to a specific research question, for example, what the participants mean by "a respected politician." In one version of the exercise, the teacher first prepares the material by identifying, for example, five to seven coding content categories to be used by the students when they code the material. In order to structure the task, the teacher can also specify exact sections, or parts, of the text where only one coding category of the different categories prepared should be used. In more ambitious versions of the exercise, the students are also asked to formulate (identify) the coding categories to be used and to delimit successive parts of the written material where the coding categories should be applied. The more advanced and realistic versions of this exercise will obviously take a longer time.

Interjudge reliability analysis. Issues of coding reliability are pertinent in the context of content analyses of different types of written or visual material from different cultures, and exercises for students can be formulated in this context. When both students in a pair have coded the material, they can compare their codings and calculate the percentage of identical codings. Above 70–80 percent common codings is often thought to be satisfactory, and what this means can be discussed with the students. There are also slightly more complicated ways to calculate interjudge reliabilities which, for example, do better justice to the effects of chance in the overlap of two coders' codings, such as the *kappa* coefficient (see, e.g., van Someren, Barnard, & Sandberg, 1994). Pros and cons of different ways of calculating the interjudge reliability of the two coders' codings can be discussed with the students.

Using Media

Sometimes it is difficult to find suitable participants in other countries for cross-cultural research. One possibility can then be to establish contact on the Internet with other schools or university departments with an interest in culture-oriented research in other countries and to start a collaborative cultural research practice exercise with them. The groups in the two countries can serve as participants in the other group's research exercise project, or in a joint research exercise. Thus, members of each group can be interviewed or asked to fill in questionnaires developed by the other group. They can also be interviewed, or provide written reports, about how they understand the questions or specific terms in the questions in the questionnaires.

Another use of the Web or paper media is to ask the students to analyze differences and similarities in different sorts of media in the students' home country and the corresponding media in other countries. Newspapers in countries using the same language as that spoken by the students may be best. For example, for students in English-speaking countries, English-speaking press in countries such as India, Sri Lanka, or Malaysia would work. Content analysis can be made of different types of contents in daily newspapers, for example similarities and differences in features of matrimonial contact ads, house-for-sale advertisements, rentals-wanted and room-to-let advertisements, ads for new cars, or family pages.

Furthermore, analyses can be made of how men and women are written about, and in what contexts they are written about in newspapers, weekly journals, or home pages for state authorities. Home pages for state authorities with text in a language that the students can understand can also be analyzed from other perspectives, as can the home page of the nation's government or leader. Finally, differences in various aspects of the content in open discussion fora on the Internet in the students' home country and the other country can be compared. Such fora may, for example, discuss problems experienced with taking care of babies, bringing up children, or other common personal problems.

Similar exercises can be made with respect to internet publications of, for example, newspapers or women's or men's journals, published in the context of different ethnicities in the same country, for example the United States or the United Kingdom. Here the class can discuss why immigrated ethnic minorities may differ less from the majority culture in a country than the corresponding ethnic group in their home country. When English written material is not available, the students can be asked to analyze visual material, for example, pictures of men and women in newspapers, in order to analyze different aspects of how men and women are rendered.

Exploring the Meaning of Theoretical Concepts

As noted, it is likely to be useful for students to more explicitly consider the meaning of theoretical concepts that are important for cultural research. The students can be asked to discuss the pros and cons of different definitions of concepts such as *culture, meaning, context, true value, error component, generalization, item-measurement non-equivalence*, and *structural non-equivalence*. This discussion can take place directly in written home assignments, or the students can first discuss the concepts in class and then be asked to prepare written reports describing the class discussions and these reports can later be discussed in class, for example, by students reviewing other students' reports. In order to make the discussions more concrete, examples of cultural research in psychology and from other disciplines such as anthropology can be used as contexts for the discussions.

An important topic to discuss with students concerns the meaning of *"true"* value (in contrast to *noise*, or *error variance*) in research comparing cultures or describing cultural properties. For example, Hofstede's (e.g., Hofstede et al., 2010) research on cultural dimensions (e.g., the individualism/collectivism, long-/short-term orientation feature in the United States) can be used as a concrete example on which to focus the discussion. This discussion can cover questions such as: How *stable* over time, context, and person categories are true values assumed to be in different forms of cultural research in psychology, and what is realistic to expect about stability in practice? Similarities and differences between stability issues in cross-cultural psychology and in the context of the trait-situation debate in personality psychology and the so-called replication crisis in social psychology can be discussed (e.g., Earp & Trafimow, 2015; Mischel, 1979). This theme can also be elaborated by asking students to identify how the true value of the measured cultural property is defined in a specific research paper. What aspects are identified as "noise" when measuring the true value and why?

In this context also, early "miscarriages" of research can be discussed. For example, early research in psychology concluded that Westerners were in general more intelligent than non-Westerners. The class can analyze how this research was conducted methodologically, and what the weaknesses of this research were. Examples of research that has improved earlier weaker research by taking further contextual factors into account are Cole and Scribner (1974) and Shebani, van de Vijver, and Poortinga (2008).

More or Less Complete Research Tasks

It is useful to give students smaller or larger research tasks. Such tasks can be used to increase student awareness of the difficulties of culture-oriented research. Smaller tasks can involve asking students to devise methods (for example, involving questionnaires, interviews, or observations) to study how people understand concepts that are likely to have a different meaning in different cultures (e.g., "youth," "family," "father"). Or students can be asked to plan questionnaires or interviews with people with different cultural backgrounds and to record and discuss the most important methodological considerations along the way as they consider choice and formulation of questions, recruitment of respondents, and collection of data. What limitations can they see with their suggestions?

For example, a useful initial approach may be to problematize conventional truths about people in some part of the world such as "the French are romantic" or "people from the United States are boisterous," and discuss what type of information such assertions provide and what the limits are to their trustworthiness. The teacher can also ask the students to consider how the truth of, for example, the assertion that "Brits are polite" can best be studied, and what the limitations are with respect to how results from the suggested research could be generalized.

Here, I offer a more complete version of a research task in eight steps. However, steps can be deleted, and steps can be carried out more or less ambitiously, depending on the needs of the class and how much time the class has at its disposal.

First step. Identify a suitable concept or task to examine. Formulate the research question. Examples of possible suitable concepts are a good home, good upbringing, good teacher, good boss, good human being. A possible task explores the participants' associations to, for example, a Buddha statue.

Second step. Identify the category of participants who will be asked to participate in the study. Some possible issues to discuss are: How large should the group be? What types of conclusions can be drawn from smaller or larger samples? How will participants be recruited? Can any aspect of how the participants are recruited affect how they understand what the research is about and thus influence their answers?

Third step. Identify suitable research methods/instruments for examining how people understand the concept or solve the task. Examples of different alternatives are questionnaires (open- or closed-answer alternatives), interviews (what type of interviews, for example, preset questions, preset questions with free follow-up questions, or totally free interview except that the topic is given to the informant), or request that participants make a drawing of a typical example of the concept and give their free associations to the object (e.g., statue). Discuss benefits and drawbacks with each alternative in relation to the intended participants.

Fourth step. Discuss how the data should be analyzed and what types of conclusions would be possible to draw from different ways of analyzing the results.

Fifth step. Prepare the research instrument.

Sixth step. Critique the prepared research instrument. This critique should also include assessments of how interpretable the results will be. Alternatively, students can first hand in written reports with their critique of the prepared instrument to be read by teacher and/or other students.

Seventh step. USE the instrument on small groups inside or outside the classroom.

Eighth step. Analyze results and write the report. Discuss pros and cons of different ways of presenting the results, for example, with respect to their generalization and trustworthiness.

Additional Teaching Resources and Materials

The Human Relations Area Files (HRAF; http://hraf.yale.edu/) is an extremely rich database with information about the world's cultures, be they small or large. It is somewhat advanced but comes complete with a special introduction for students (/resources/students/) to "topics that students may find useful before embarking on a research project involving *eHRAF World Cultures* or *eHRAF Archaeology.*" One needs to become a member if one's university is not.

The website of the International Association for Cross-Cultural psychology hosts a link to *Online Readings in Psychology and Culture (ORPC)* "designed to serve as a resource for researchers, teachers, students, and anyone who is interested in the interrelationships between Psychology and Culture." The link is http://scholarworks.gvsu.edu/orpc/. *Subunit 2.2 - Methodological Issues in Psychology and Culture* is especially relevant for the present chapter.

Gannon, M. J., & Pillai, R. (2016). Understanding global cultures. Metaphorical journeys through 34 nations, clusters of nations, continents and diversity (6th ed.). Los Angeles, CA: Sage.

Inspired by Hofstede's dimensional framework, this book takes a metaphorical approach to culture in different nations and clusters of nations. The book also comes with online teaching materials. It exemplifies a *quick tour approach* to different nations' cultures and is useful for discussing the assets and limitations of such an approach.

References

Allwood, C. M. (1998). The creation and nature(s) of indigenized psychologies from the perspective of the anthropology of knowledge. In S. Gorenstein (Ed.), *Knowledge and society* (Vol. 11, pp. 153–172). Greenwich, CT: Jai.
(2011). On the foundation of the indigenous psychologies. *Social Epistemology*, 25, 3–14. doi:10.1080/02691728.2010.534564
(2012). The distinction between qualitative and quantitative research methods is problematic. *Quality & Quantity, 46*, 1417–1429. doi:10.1007/s11135-011-9455-8
Allwood, C. M., & Berry, J. W. (2006). Origins and development of indigenous psychologies: An international analysis. *International Journal of Psychology, 41*, 243–268. doi:10.1080/00207590544000013
Arnett, J. J. (2008). The neglected 95%: Why American psychology needs to become less American. *American Psychologist, 63*, 602–614. doi:10.1037/0003-066X.63.7.602

Atran, S. (2001). The trouble with memes inference versus imitation in cultural creation. *Human Nature, 12*, 351–381. doi:10.1007/s12110-001-1003-0

Atran, S., Medin, D. L., & Ross, N. O. (2005). The cultural mind: Environmental decision making and cultural modeling within and across populations. *Psychological Review, 112*, 744–776. doi:10.1037/0033-295X.112.4.744

Berry, J. W. (1989). Imposed etics-emics-derived etics: The operationalization of a compelling idea. *International Journal of Psychology, 24*, 721–735. doi:10.1080/00207598908247841

Berry, J. W., & Triandis, H. C. (2006). Culture. In K. Pawlik & G. d'Ydewalle (Eds.), *Psychological concepts: An international historical perspective* (pp. 47–62). Hove: Psychology Press.

Boesch, E. E. (1996). The seven flaws of cross-cultural psychology: The story of a conversion. *Mind, Culture and Activity, 3*(1), 2–10. doi:10.1207/s15327884mca0301_2

Borsboom, D., Mellenbergh, G. J., & van Heerden, J. (2003). The theoretical status of latent variables. *Psychological Review, 110*, 203–219. doi:10.1037/0033-295X.110.2.203

Braun, V., & Clarke, V. (2013). *Successful qualitative research.* Los Angeles, CA: Sage.

Byrne, B. M., Oakland, T., Leong, F. T. L., van de Vijver, F. J. R., Hambleton, R. K., Cheung, F. M., & Bartram, D. (2009). A critical analysis of cross-cultural research and testing practices: Implications for improved education and training in psychology. *Training and Education in Professional Psychology, 3*, 94–105. doi:10.1037/a0014516

Church, A. T., & Katigbak, M. S. (2002). Indigenization of psychology in the Philippines. *International Journal of Psychology, 37*, 129–148. doi:10.1080/00207590143000315

Cole, M. (1996). *Cultural psychology: A once and future discipline.* Cambridge, MA: Harvard University Press.

Cole, M., & Scribner, S. (1974). *Culture and thought.* New York, NY: Wiley.

Cox, M. V., & Bayraktar, R. (1989). *A cross-cultural study of children's human figure drawings.* Presented at the Tenth Biennial Conference of the International Society for the Study of Behavioral Development, University of Jyväskylä, Finland.

Cronbach, L. J. (1990). *Essentials of psychological testing* (5th ed.). New York, NY: Harper & Row.

Earp, B. D., & Trafimow, D. (2015). Replication, falsification, and the crises of confidence in social psychology. *Frontiers in Psychology, 6*(621), 1–11. doi:10.3389/fpsyg.2015.00621

Fowler, D. D., & Hardesty, D. L. (Eds.). (1994). *Others knowing others: Perspective on ethnographic careers.* Washington, DC: Smithsonian Institution Press.

Greenfield, P. M. (1997). You can't take it with you: Why ability assessments don't cross cultures. *American Psychologist, 52*, 1115–1124. doi:10.1037/0003-066X.52.10.1115

Hofstede, G., Hofstede, G. J., & Minkov, M. (2010). *Culture and organizations: Software of the mind* (3rd ed.). New York, NY: McGraw Hill.

Idhe, D. (1977). *Experimental phenomenology: An introduction.* New York: Putnam.

Kashima, Y. (2005). Is culture a problem for social psychology? *Asian Journal of Social Psychology, 8,* 19–38. doi:10.1111/j.1467-839X.2005.00154.x

Kim, U., & Park, Y.-S. (2006). The scientific foundation of indigenous and cultural psychology. In U. Kim, K.-S. Yang, & K.-K. Hwang (Eds.), *Indigenous and cultural psychology: Understanding people in context* (pp. 27–48). New York, NY: Springer. doi:10.1007/0-387-28662-4_2

Kim, U., Yang, K.-S., & Hwang, K.-K. (2006). Contributions to indigenous and cultural psychology: Understanding people in context. In U. Kim, K.-S. Yang, & K.-K. Hwang (Eds.), *Indigenous and cultural psychology: Understanding people in context* (pp. 3–25). New York, NY: Springer. doi.org/10.1007/0-387-28662-4_1

Laboratory of Comparative Human Cognition (LCHC). (1982). Culture and intelligence. In R. Sternberg (Ed.), *Handbook of human intelligence* (pp. 642–719). Cambridge, MA: Cambridge University Press.

Mischel, W. (1979). On the interface of cognition and personality: Beyond the person-situation debate. *American Psychologist, 34,* 740–754. doi:10.1037/0003-066X.34.9.740

Nisbett, R. E. (2003). *The geography of thought: How Asians and Westerners think differently . . . and why.* New York, NY: The Free Press.

Nisbett, R. E., Peng, K., Choi, I., & Norenzayan, A. (2001). Culture and systems of thought: Holistic versus analytic cognition. *Psychological Review, 108,* 291–310. doi:10.1037//0033-295X.108.2.291

Romney, A. K., Weller, S. C., & Batchelder, W. H. (1986). Culture as consensus: A theory of culture and informant accuracy. *American Anthropologist, 88,* 313–338. doi:10.1525/aa.1986.88.2.02a00020

Oyserman, D., & Lee, S. W. S. (2008). A situated cognition perspective on culture: Effects of priming cultural syndromes on cognition and motivation. In R. M. Sorrentino & S. Yamaguchi (Eds.), *Handbook of motivation and cognition across cultures* (pp. 237–265). New York, NY: Elsevier. doi:10.1016/b978-0-12-373694-9.00011-8

Savani, K., Cho, J., Baik, S., & Morris, M. W. (2015). Culture and judgment and decision making. In G. Wu & G. Keren (Eds.), *Blackwell handbook of judgment and decision making* (pp. 456–477). Oxford: Blackwell. doi:10.1002/9781118468333.ch16

Scribner, S., & Cole, M. (1981). *The psychology of literacy.* Cambridge, MA: Harvard University Press. doi:10.4159/harvard.9780674433014

Shadish, W. R., Cook, T. D., & Campbell, D. T. (2002). *Experimental and quasi-experimental designs for generalized causal inference.* Boston, MA: Houghton Mifflin.

Shebani, M. F. A., van de Vijver, F. J. R., & Poortinga, Y. H. (2008). Memory development in Libyan and Dutch school children. *European Journal of Development Psychology, 5,* 419–438. doi:10.1080/17405620701343204

Shostak, M. (1983). *Nisa: The life and words of a !Kung woman.* New York, NY: Random House.

Shweder, R. (1990). Cultural psychology – What is it? In J. Stigler, R. Shweder, & G. Herdt (Eds.), *Cultural psychology: Essays on comparative human development* (pp. 1–43). New York, NY: Cambridge University Press. doi:10.1017/cbo9781139173728.002

Smith, P. B., Bond, M. H., & Kagitcibasi, C. (2006). *Understanding social psychology across cultures.* London: Sage. doi:10.4135/9781446212028

Spradley, J. P., & McCurdy, D. W. (1980). *Anthropology: The cultural perspective* (2nd ed.). New York, NY: Wiley.

Triandis, H. C. (1980). Preface. In H. C. Triandis & W. Lonner (Eds.), *Handbook of cross-cultural psychology: Vol. 3. Basic processes* (pp. viii–xix). Boston, MA: Allyn & Bacon. doi:10.1525/aa.1982.84.2.02a00060

van de Vijver, F. J. R., & Tanzer, N. K. (2004). Bias and equivalence in cross-cultural assessment: An overview. *Revue Européenne de Psychologie Appliquée, 54,* 119–135. doi:10.1016/j.erap.2003.12.004

van Someren, M. W., Barnard Y. F., & Sandberg, J. A. C. (1994). *The think aloud method: A practical guide to modelling cognitive processes.* London: Academic Press.

Viswanathan, M. (2005). *Measurement error and research design.* Thousand Oaks, CA: Sage. doi:10.4135/9781412984935

Weber, E. U., & Morris, M. W. (2010). Culture and judgment and decision making: The constructivist turn. *Perspectives on Psychological Science, 5,* 410–419. doi:10.1177/1745691610375556

Wittgenstein, L. (1953). *Philosophical Investigations.* Oxford: Blackwell.

CHAPTER 7

Teaching Psychological Measurement: Taking into Account Cross-Cultural Comparability and Cultural Sensitivity

Christin-Melanie Vauclair, Diana Boer, and Katja Hanke

Ask your students to imagine that they are taking an intelligence test and are asked the following questions[1]:

1. If BAD is written 214, how would you write DIG in the same secret writing? _____
2. What does it mean if someone says "she's buffed"?
   a. She's got a cute rear-end;
   b. She's overweight;
   c. She's wearing leather;
   d. She's got polished manners.
3. Which word is most out of place here?
   a. splib;
   b. blood;
   c. gray;
   d. spook;
   e. black.
4. What number comes next in the sequence: one, two, three, _____?
5. We eat food and we _____ water.

If your students come from a Western culture and have a middle-class background, they probably found it easy to answer question 1. However, they may have struggled to figure out the meaning of the words in questions 2 and 3, which are taken from intelligence tests designed for African Americans in the United States (Dove, 1971; Redden & Simon, 1986). These items assessed the knowledge of African American "street language," and students familiar with this subculture usually scored well on these tests. Yet average White middle-class college students have been

---

[1] Correct answers: 1. 497; 2. b; 3. c.; 4. many; 5. eat.

sometimes scored so poorly that they could be classified as intellectually disabled according to "street norms." Your students may also be surprised to learn that their answers to questions 4 and 5, which appear to be very simple, are wrong in this test. These two questions come from an intelligence test developed for the Edward River Australian Aboriginal community in North Queensland.[2] The correct answer to question 4 is "many," because in kuuk thaayorre language, counting only goes to three: *thana, kuthir, pinalam, mong*, etc. The word *mong* is best translated as "many," because it can mean any number between four and nine. The correct answer to question 5 is "eat," because there is no distinction between "eating" and "drinking" in the kuuk thaayorre language – the same verb is used to describe both functions. How many of these questions did your students get right?

This little exercise provides a good starting point for class discussions on psychological measurements and culture. You could ask students how they would feel if these kinds of tests were used as standardized intelligence tests or if such a test would be used to decide whether they should be admitted to a graduate school or hired for a new job. Such a discussion stimulates students' perspective taking and makes them aware of the cultural knowledge they usually take for granted. They may not be sensitive to the biases that are part of standardized intelligence tests, because their own middle-class background does not disadvantage them for these tests. By taking these culture-specific intelligence tests, which make nonmainstream cultural assumptions, students can come to experience some of the difficulties and issues involved with culturally biased methods of testing intelligence.

The issue of cultural bias is not restricted only to intelligence tests. In fact, psychological tests play an integral part in Western societies, helping decision makers arrive at informed decisions in many different domains (e.g., development of new policies or psychological diagnoses and treatments). Furthermore, measuring psychological characteristics (e.g., attitudes) is at the heart of most quantitative psychological studies. It is crucial that assessment of these characteristics is reliable (consistent across time, individuals, and researchers) and valid (i.e., measuring what it is intended to measure). The development of reliable and valid psychological measurements is the fruit of a rigorous research enterprise in which the measures are subjected to various tests. The objective is to ascertain that something is measured well enough to have scientific validity for the population in which the test is applied. This process becomes somewhat

---

[2] www.wilderdom.com/personality/intelligenceCulturalBias

more complex when the population is culturally diverse, and the aim is to develop or use a psychological measure that is not culturally biased.

In this chapter, we will emphasize the importance of culture when it comes to psychological measurements and identify some key measurement concepts in this context. Taking into account culture in psychological measurements brings with it a whole host of methodological issues that go beyond monocultural studies. Due to space constraints, we expect that students are already familiar with basic measurement theory (classical test theory) and its key concepts (reliability and validity). In the end, we also provide examples of teaching activities that can be used to explain cultural concepts in psychological measurement.

The Role of Culture in Psychological Measurement

The twenty-first century is an era of increased cultural diversity due to globalization and greater facility of traveling, living, and working elsewhere. Given the fact that societies have become more multicultural, it becomes crucial to develop psychological measurements that are culturally inclusive. Another important aspect is the fact that an increasing amount of *research* is today directed at understanding the role of culture in influencing different aspects of people's behavior, thought, and attitude. In fact, one of the main quests of cultural and cross-cultural psychology is to gather evidence from different cultures to better understand which aspects of the human mind and behavior are universal or culture specific. However, in order to draw scientifically valid conclusions about cultural differences, the measurement of people's minds and behaviors must be accurate, which is not as straightforward as it is for monocultural studies.

It may be helpful to remind students that measurement is actually pervasive in our everyday lives. We measure our weight by stepping on a bathroom scale, and judge whether we have a fever by using a thermometer. However, when psychologists undertake measurements, they are usually interested in assessing mental capacities and processes, which are called *latent psychological constructs* (e.g., intelligence, personality, attitudes) because they are somewhat hidden and elusive. This renders their measurement a tricky undertaking because one cannot use scales or thermometers to directly assess these constructs. Instead, psychologists use a systematic procedure for assigning scores to individuals so that these scores represent the characteristic of interest. This procedure, called *psychometrics*, has developed in Western cultures, and it bears some challenges when individuals come from another culture. In fact, it has become clear that research results and psychological measures are not always valid in non-Western cultures.

The validity of research results for populations other than those that have been studied is referred to as *external validity*. In other words, it is the degree to which research results can be generalized beyond one's sample. This is a crucial concept when dealing with different cultures. Psychologists often assume that certain aspects of the human mind and behavior are universal; however, the vast majority of psychological studies have relied on samples from so-called WEIRD societies (Western, Educated, Industrialized, Rich, and Democratic; Henrich, Heine, & Norenzayan, 2010), which challenges the assumption that the results are generalizable. In fact, Henrich and colleagues showed that some of the key findings in psychology, which were based on WEIRD samples and assumed to be universal, do not generalize to samples from other cultures. Today, an increasing number of studies compares multiple cultural groups with each other on psychological variables of interest in order to examine cultural similarities and differences (Matsumoto & van de Vijver, 2011).

Emic and Etic Approaches

In the psychological study of culture, two strategies can be distinguished. The first strategy looks at one culture specifically and investigates its specific characteristics, expressions, behaviors, or ways of thinking. In-depth bottom-up analysis reveals this culture's psychological constructs, which can be used for describing the culture, to develop interventions or to derive measures. This approach is called *emic* and it intends to reveal culture-specific constructs; it does not intend to uncover universals or culturally comparable constructs. The researchers discover the structure and meaning of concepts instead of predicting or imposing them. For example, culture-bound syndromes are culture-specific psychological disorders that can only be fully understood within a specific cultural context. This is the case for the culture-specific syndrome of *hikikomori* in Japan (Sakai, Ishikawa, Takizawa, Sato, & Sakano, 2004). It describes mainly male adolescents or adults who completely withdraw from social life, often seeking extreme degrees of isolation and confinement over a period of several months or even years. *Hikikomori* resembles different DSM-IV-R syndromes in Western cultures, such as social phobia, obsessive-compulsive disorder, depression, and schizophrenia, but does not fit into a single category and has several culture-specific manifestations. This example underscores the importance of conducting culture-specific analyses of psychological phenomena.

One specific emic approach investigates indigenous cultures and is called *indigenous psychology*. Yang (2000), a renowned Chinese indigenous psychologist, argued that current mainstream psychology is dominated by a Western perspective, so that Western psychological theories are culture specific and not applicable to other parts of the world. In fact, current mainstream psychology could be seen as a Western indigenous psychology. Yang further suggested building a cross-cultural indigenous research agenda in order to develop a more balanced global psychology.

The second strategy, called *etic*, aims to uncover psychological universals. This approach is mostly quantitative, views culture as an independent variable, and does not intend to include culture-specific features. The researchers determine the structure of psychological constructs, and the main aim is to compare cultures in order to test theories or hypotheses. Hence, etic studies attempt to establish the external validity of the phenomena studied. Both approaches come with advantages and disadvantages, and this is why Berry (1989) proposed to combine their strengths in order to derive psychological constructs that are applicable in a multitude of cultures. He called the approach *derived etics*, which first discovers emic constructs in various cultures and then combines their comparable features into a derived etic construct. This approach contrasts with another possible strategy in cross-cultural psychology, which is called *imposed etics*. It uses constructs derived in only one culture (generally Western), which are then assumed to be applicable in other cultures.

Cheung, van de Vijver, and Leong (2011) in their study of personality argued for a combined emic-etic approach, which (similar to Berry's derived etic) is an integrative strategy aiming to describe a psychological construct covering universal as well as culture-specific aspects. The combined emic-etic approach has been used, for example, to establish the South African Personality Inventory (SAPI). The SAPI project showed that the Big Five factor structure of personality, developed in the United States, was well represented in South Africa, but culture-specific social and relational aspects of personality were also revealed (Cheung et al., 2011).

One may ask now which approach to take when conducting (cross-) cultural psychological research. The decision on whether to use an emic, etic, or a combined emic-etic approach will largely depend on the topic of research whereas some psychological concepts are more universal, others may be truly culture specific. Furthermore, the specific research question may imply that one approach is more appropriate than another. Emic approaches advance our understanding of psychological mechanisms rooted in one particular culture whereas culture-comparative etic approaches assume similarities in psychological phenomena across cultures and can at the same time provide insight into cultural differences regarding the expression of these phenomena based on cultural values, environmental factors, or other culture-relevant components (e.g., crisis, history, political development).

Issues of Comparability: The Role of Bias and Equivalence

One of the most common ways of comparing cultures is to employ surveys in the form of anonymous questionnaires when participants are asked for their responses on rating scales to a series of questions (Heine, 2008). The great challenge for self-report measures lies in using psychological measures that are *equivalent* and unbiased across cultures, so that scores or associations between variables can be compared across cultures. Measurements may not be comparable across cultures, for example, because they have not been translated well, the items do not measure the same latent construct across cultures, culture-specific concepts do not exist in other cultures (e.g., the concept of counting beyond three), or individuals from some cultures show a specific response style (e.g., tending to use the midpoint of the response scale). We will come back to these issues in more detail.

Test bias is a form of systematic (i.e., nonrandom) error, which leads to the phenomenon that respondents from one culture have an unwarranted advantage over respondents from another culture. There are various sources of test bias in cross-cultural research (construct, instrument, and method bias), which can jeopardize the cross-cultural validity of a measure. If a measure is biased, it threatens the equivalence of measurement outcomes across cultures, meaning that the results may not be comparable across the sampled cultures and are, therefore, uninterpretable, or even misleading. In fact, bias and equivalence are two sides of the same coin: cross-cultural equivalence requires the absence of bias and the presence of cross-cultural bias results in some form of non-equivalence (van de Vijver & Leung, 1997). In order to make sure that we are not comparing apples and oranges when comparing measurement outcomes across cultures, we must ascertain that the measures are valid, not biased, and therefore equivalent across cultures.

The earlier intelligence test example illustrates how individuals from certain subcultures will probably score better on this test than the average White middle-class college student, because the test assesses cultural knowledge that is not accessible to the latter. As such, it is neither fair nor scientifically valid to conclude that White middle-class students' low scores on this test mean that they are unintelligent. In this case, the *external validity* of the test is compromised by its lack of cross-cultural equivalence as well as the presence of test bias.

A Taxonomy of Biases

Construct bias. *Construct bias* means that the construct measured is not identical across cultures. It refers to the cultural specificity of a psychological construct and means that there is an incomplete overlap of definitions of the construct across cultures, differential appropriateness of (sub)test contents (e.g., specific skills do not belong to the repertoire of one of the cultural groups), or inadequate sampling of relevant contents and incomplete coverage of the construct (van de Vijver, 2013a). The latter is also referred to as *domain underrepresentation*, which occurs when a measure misses important aspects of a construct in a specific cultural setting. For example, intelligence is defined as including social competence in some Asian cultures, such as Taiwan, Japan, and China, and therefore should be incorporated in tests assessing intelligence in these cultures (Smith, Fischer, Vignoles, & Bond, 2013). This is also an issue of *content validity*, which refers to the extent to which a measure presents all facets of a given construct. One way to overcome construct bias is *cultural decentering* – a procedure through which cultural specific contents are removed and items are formulated independently from the context, so that the instrument's appropriateness is maximized for all involved cultural groups (van de Vijver, 2013a).

Construct bias can compromise the *construct validity* of a measure in a specific cultural population. Construct validity refers to the degree to which a variable has been operationally defined so that it captures the essence of a latent psychological construct. For example, is the intelligence test a good measure of intelligence across different cultures? If the answer is yes, the measure has good construct validity. If the answer is no, any cross-cultural research conclusions drawn from the use of the measure are limited (Woolf & Hulsizer, 2011).

Method bias. Even if a construct is identical across cultures, method bias may be an issue. It includes the administration process, the instrument itself, and the sampling. These have been discussed as the main sources of method bias in cross-cultural research, while response sets are still disputed in the literature as a form of method bias or a true cultural phenomenon (i.e., a culture-specific communication style).

Administration bias. This includes influences due to the administration of the given instrument (e.g., the test environment, instructions, tester/interviewer effects, communication problems). Even if test situations are kept constant across participants, bias may occur because of uncontrollable events. For example, administration bias can arise when data collection takes place at the respondents' home and is disrupted by noise or other interfering events. Another source of administration bias can occur due to the test instructions. It is possible that differences in the instructions (e.g., one cultural sample may need more explanation in comparison to another) can lead to an overall method bias because the test conditions are not held constant across the cultural samples.

Administration bias is directly related to the issue of *internal validity* of the research results. Internal validity in cross-cultural research refers to the extent to which it is possible to draw the conclusion that culture has a causal effect on the observed phenomenon. In fact, a primary concern in psychological studies is to control all extraneous or confounding variables that may be part of an administration bias. However, achieving internal validity is difficult in cross-cultural research because these studies are quasiexperimental by nature and, therefore, limited in regard to cause and effect conclusions in the first place. Culture cannot be manipulated by the researcher because participants are already enculturated when they participate in the study. Moreover, using standardized administration procedures in some cultures can even introduce a cultural bias, if the test situation is not compatible with local customs and cultural standards. For example, indigenous psychologists in the Philippines have pointed out that standardized test administrations limit the interaction between participants and researchers, which is an undesirable test situation for Filipino respondents (Pe-Pua, 2006). They prefer a casual and nondirected conversation that is driven by the respondent rather than the researcher. The methodology that corresponds to this cultural preference has been called *pagtatanong-tanong*, which means "casually asking around." Hence, using a standardized procedure may jeopardize the validity of the research results in this culture.

Sampling bias. This term means that samples are not comparable and variations in samples from one cultural context to the other can confound the observed scores. For example, if educational levels in minority and majority members of a sample are not controlled or corrected for, a comparison of psychological constructs will confound cultural and educational differences (van de Vijver, 2013a). Because realistically speaking, random sampling rarely occurs, researchers have to be careful when interpreting their findings and making attempts to generalize.

Instrument bias. This kind of bias relates to instrument characteristics (van de Vijver, 2013b). An instrument developed in a Western setting and then exported to a non-Western context may cause issues with item familiarity, response modes (e.g., familiarity with computers), or response formats (e.g., multiple-choice formats; He & van de Vijver, 2013).

Response styles. Also referred to as *response sets*, response styles are systematic tendencies to respond to questions in a particular way, mostly to give a good impression of oneself. This is especially the case when participants are giving answers to self-report measures, such as attitudes. Four different kinds of response styles have been studied. A very common impression management strategy to portray oneself in a favorable light is referred to as social desirability, which has been widely studied (Paulhus, 1991). Additionally, there are other styles of impression management, such as the tendency to agree regardless of the content of the questions (acquiescence response style), the tendency to use the extreme end points of a scale (extreme response style), and the tendency to overuse the middle point of a scale (midpoint response style).

The challenge of how to manage different response sets has been a subject for debate for decades. Usually response sets are considered a part of measurement error (Johnson, Kulesa, Cho, & Shavitt, 2005). Thus, some have suggested correcting for response sets in survey research (He & van de Vijver, 2013, 2015), because they can have an impact on the measurement structure, means of scales, and associations between variables (Welkenhuysen-Gybels, Billiet, & Cambré, 2003). Whereas the more conventional perspective views response styles as a nuisance factor that should be corrected (see Hui & Triandis, 1989), others hold the view that response styles are a reflection of culture-moderated communication filters (Smith, 2004) and response sets thus have meaning and do not need to be corrected for (He & van de Vijver, 2013). For example, research has shown that East Asian cultures favor midpoint response options (van de Gaer, Grisay, Schulz, & Gebhardt, 2012) and that cultural values can explain some of the cultural response tendencies (Johnson et al., 2005). Consequently, the cultural context adds another layer of complexity to response sets.

Recent research questioned the debate about whether cultural response styles are nuisances that need to be corrected. In large-scale studies, He and van de Vijver (2013, 2015) provided empirical evidence that correcting for response sets does not necessarily increase the validity of cross-cultural comparisons and concluded that response sets are often used as communication styles in order to moderate or amplify responses.

Item bias. This bias type refers to poor item translation, inadequate item formulation (e.g., complex wording), nuisance factors (e.g., item[s] may invoke additional traits or abilities), incidental differences in appropriateness of the item content (e.g., topic of item of educational test not in the curriculum in one cultural group), and cultural specifics (e.g., connotative meaning and/or appropriateness of item content). For example, van de Vijver (2013c) argued that if two people from different cultures have the same levels on the latent construct (e.g., they have the same level of intelligence), but their responses result in differences in mean scores on the measures, then it is very likely that the items are biased.

In sum, a number of different biases can hamper the meaning and validity of cross-cultural research results. In order to overcome some of these biases, an adequate cultural adaptation and translation of the measure is crucial.

Translation and Adaptation

Adequate translation is key to ensuring the validity of the measurements used in different cultural settings. The most commonly used method to translate a source survey into a target survey is the translation-back-translation procedure and translations are carried out as part of an "Ask-the-Same-Question" (ASQ) model (Harkness, 2003). However, this procedure is no longer recommended, because it has some serious limitations (see Mohler, Dorer, de Jong, & Hu, 2016). Harkness (2003) used an example of how translation-back-translation procedures can fail: The German item "Das Leben in vollen Zügen genießen" can be translated by a naïve translator into "Enjoy life in full trains!" This translation is literal and has face value. However, because this is a German expression of enjoying life to the fullest, the literal translation would simply be wrong.

The procedure for a translation-back-translation approach consists of various steps. First, the initial translation is carried out for a specific target population. This translation is then back-translated into the source language (e.g., source language: English; target language: Chinese). The next step is to compare the two translations of the source language in order to find any translation issues. The cross-cultural survey guidelines recommend producing the best possible translation and then making a direct evaluation in the target language.[3] According to the guidelines, translation-back-translation approach is considered an indirect comparison that is

---

[3] http://ccsg.isr.umich.edu/index.php/chapters/translation-chapter

vulnerable to misleading insights and eventually to lower quality translations (see Harkness et al., 2010).

A recommended alternative to the translation-back-translation procedure is the team approach, also referred to as the *committee approach*. It
requires a team of knowledgeable bilingual experts who produce the best
possible translation in a team effort and directly evaluate the solution
within the committee. The translation of the measure is completed when
the committee achieves a consensus about the appropriateness of the
translation.

The cultural adaptation of measures goes beyond mere translation (Behr
& Shishido, 2016). The issue of appropriateness of research material needs
to be considered here specifically, because it will affect the quality of cross-
cultural research. For example, imagine you are asking your students to
respond to the following question: "To which religious group do you
belong?" and you provide them with a categorical response option regarding
the religious groups *Muslim Sunni, Muslim Shia, Hinduism, Bahá'i Faith,
Sikhism, Shintoism, Daoism, Traditional, none,* and *other (specify)*. Assuming
that your students have a Western background, you can discuss with them
the appropriateness of this question in their cultural setting.

A key question in the cultural adaptation of psychological measures is
whether it captures the psychological construct adequately, representa-
tively, and comprehensively. Hence, an important consideration in this
process is to reflect carefully from which cultural context the measure is
coming (source) and to which culture it should be applied (target). For
example, a survey that originated from the United States and includes
questions about schooling and politics that make sense only in this setting
becomes meaningless when used with another cultural sample. Hence, it is
important to adapt the items in such a way that they make sense in the
target population. According to van de Vijver and Leung (1997, 2011),
there are two ways that this can be achieved: (a) by adapting the material in
a way that it is adequate for the culture of interest or (b) by assembling and
designing a new instrument (i.e., referred to as *indigenization*). The
problem with the latter option is that it is difficult to make cross-cultural
comparisons if the instrument is different.

Equivalence. Why can't we simply compare measurement scores between
cultures and interpret the difference as culturally meaningful? The reason
is that we first need to be very sure that the same underlying latent
construct was measured and hence is indeed comparable. If the construct
is meaningless, differently defined, or not comparable (i.e., inequivalent),

comparisons are baseless. Equivalence is defined as the level of comparability of scores across cultures. When testing the equivalence of psychological measures across cultures, there is a hierarchy of different levels of equivalence that can be statistically examined: functional, structural, metric, and scalar equivalence.

Functional equivalence requires an in-depth understanding of each cultural context and extensive qualitative and conceptual work. It is the most abstract level of equivalence and, therefore, difficult to prove whether the exact same constructs are captured exhaustively. This type of equivalence also taps into issues of *linguistic equivalence*, which refers to the extent to which the construct of interest has been adequately translated. Functional equivalence is often assumed and not tested, whereas the remaining levels heavily rely on being statistically tested and should not be assumed (van de Vijver & Poortinga, 1997).

Structural equivalence – sometimes also referred to as *construct equivalence* – refers to indicators that tap adequately the construct of interest in a culturally meaningful way. Those indicators need to be relevant and representative of the construct in each cultural setting. This level of equivalence is the basis for all cross-cultural comparisons and needs to be established before higher levels of equivalence can be tested (see Table 7.1).

Metric equivalence is needed in order to compare relative patterns in the data (e.g. correlation-based analyses) between two or more cultural groups. Psychometric tests are employed to identify and remove problematic items from the scale. Metric equivalence is defined as having the same measurement unit across cultures, but not the same origin (He & van de Vijver, 2013). This means that it is possible to compare correlations and investigate associations with regressions, but it is not possible to make mean-level comparisons.

Scalar (or *full score*) *equivalence* is the highest level of equivalence and the most difficult one to establish statistically. It occurs when measures have the same measurement unit and origin. Only if scalar equivalence is established, is it possible to directly compare mean scores between two or more cultural groups using *t* tests or analysis of variance.

Multigroup confirmatory factor analysis is the most common procedure to test for structural, metric, and scalar equivalence. More recently, other procedures have been suggested that seem to be more appropriate for testing equivalence across cultures (e.g., Bayesian structural equation modeling; for an overview, see Boer, Hanke, & He, in press).

In this chapter, we have discussed the role of culture in psychological research and what we need to consider if we want to make meaningful

Table 7.1 *Overview of the Different Types of Equivalence, Their Sources of Bias, and Analytical Procedures*

Type of Equivalence	Definition	Source of Bias	How to Establish This Type of Equivalence
Functional Equivalence	The same construct exists in the cultural groups	Construct has different functions or is interpreted differently across cultures	Appropriate translation and domain representation
Structural Equivalence	Same indicators can be used to measure a construct in different cultural groups	Rough factor loading structure is not similar across cultures – some factor loadings are not significant in some cultural groups but in others it is	Analytical tools For example: exploratory factor analysis, multigroup confirmatory factor analysis
Metric Equivalence	Indirect comparisons possible between groups, such as correlation-based analysis (e.g., regression models), but no multilevel models	Factor loadings are not identical across cultures	Some analytical tools: Strict (exact) test: Multigroup confirmatory factor analysis (same factor loadings) Approximation test (tolerant toward trivial measurement unit differences): Bayesian structural equation modeling
Scalar (or Full Score) Equivalence	Direct comparisons of (latent) mean scores across cultures are possible (e.g., *t* tests, ANOVA, etc.)	Factor loadings and indicator intercepts differ across cultures	Some analytical tools: Strict (exact) test: Multigroup confirmatory factor analysis (same intercepts) Approximation test (tolerant toward trivial measurement unit differences): Bayesian structural equation modeling

Adapted from Boer, Hanke, & He (in press).

comparisons across cultures. We introduced the different approaches to studying culture in psychology: emic and etic approaches and the fact that derived etic and combined emic-etic approaches seem most fruitful, because they embrace universality and culture specificity at the same time. We have summarized the different kinds of biases that can occur and what can be done to reduce bias. We have also summarized the controversial role of response sets in cross-cultural research. Because adequate translation is one important way to ensure item quality and reduce item bias, we explained why the committee approach is the most recommended procedure. Furthermore, we introduced the different levels of equivalence (functional, structural, metric, and scalar equivalence), which should be tested before any cross-cultural comparisons are made. In the following section, we suggest some useful teaching exercises to apply the contents of this chapter.

Exercises and Examples

EXERCISE 1.   TRANSLATION AND LINGUISTIC EQUIVALENCE

Let the students get together in teams of two or three and ask them to translate some items using the translation-back-translation and the committee approaches. Discuss and compare the translations using the two different approaches. This assignment requires bilinguals.

EXERCISE 2.   DISTINGUISHING CULTURE-SPECIFIC (EMIC) AND
UNIVERSAL CONCEPTS (ETIC)

This exercise aims to sensitize students for culture-specific and universal concepts with cross-cultural differences.

Task 1. Ask the students to identify a music style specific to their local area or region. The students then describe the origin and characteristics of the music as well as the specific context in which people listen to it. Although most music styles are hybrids with many different cultural influences, they are usually not directly comparable to other music styles due to their historical and regional specificity. Note that there are regions in the world where music is not described in terms of *genres* as is the case in China. Here, bands (particularly Chinese-Pop or, for short, C-Pop bands) are phenomena that are similar to genres. In these contexts, bands rather than particular music genres could be described.

Task 2. The next exercise is suitable for multicultural classrooms. Students are asked to identify a characteristic of people in their country, which seems distinctive to their cultural identity. The group then discusses whether this characteristic is indeed a culture-specific construct. There is a chance that most mentioned characteristics overlap across cultures. A discussion may then reveal that the actual culture-specific aspect lies in the importance that is attributed to cultural characteristics in specific contexts. This means that the construct can be universal, whereas its significance and manifestation in specific contexts can vary across cultures. One example would be that the Brazilian national identity seems particularly linked to Samba and to music in general. Brazilians are not the only culture in which music is associated with national identity and in which Samba is liked. However, the *strong meaning* of Samba is culture specific in Brazil.

EXERCISE 3. DEVELOPING A CULTURALLY SENSITIVE AND WIDELY APPLICABLE MEASURE

This exercise puts the contents of this chapter into practice. The task is to develop a research plan for development of a psychological measure that captures the functions of music listening. The measure should be culturally sensitive as well as applicable in a wide range of different cultures. Groups of three to six students should work on this task. The task given to students may read as follows: *Your task is to develop a culturally sensitive measure that captures "the functions of music listening." The measurement is supposed to be applicable to young people around the globe. How would you come up with the items? Who would you ask to provide input? Which functions and which contexts of music listening would you consider? The research agenda may entail different stages and research methodologies.*

One possible research agenda solving this task is presented in the following example. It can be used for discussing and evaluating the proposals provided by student groups. A critical reflection of the provided example could also be part of the in-class discussion.

EXAMPLE. PROCESS OF DEVELOPING A NEW CULTURALLY SENSITIVE AND WIDELY APPLICABLE MEASURE

Aiming to derive a holistic framework of functions of music listening, the second author used a mixed-methods design (Boer, 2009; see also Boer & Fischer, 2012; Boer et al., 2011, 2012). The research agenda followed a two-stage procedure. First, a qualitative culturally decentered study set out to identify the reasons why people like to listen to music, the meaning of music in their personal and social lives as well as in their families and cultures. The data were used for development of a psychological measure that was then validated in a second stage.

The first research stage utilized a qualitative online survey aiming to capture various personal, social, and cultural functions of music from people hailing from different cultures and nations. This strategy intended to maximize the cultural diversity in regard to music usage and rituals, while trying to avoid domain underrepresentation of certain music functions. Multiple questions were used to capture each of three contexts of music listening functions:

Exercises and Examples (cont.)

1. **Personal.** What does music mean to you? Please write your thoughts about the role music plays in your life. How does music influence your life? Think about one specific situation when you were listening to music in the last 3 days. Please describe what you thought, felt, and did in that situation.
2. **Social.** What role does music play when you are hanging out with your friends? What is the meaning of music for your family members?
3. **Cultural.** What is the meaning of music in your home country? What is the meaning of music in your cultural community?

Each participant answered three of those questions (one on each context), which were presented as open-ended questions without space limitations. The questionnaire was available in English and German.

The qualitative study was conducted online with samples of young people from four cultural clusters: South America, (South) East Asia, Anglo-Saxon regions, and Europe. The link to the survey was disseminated via discussion boards of music-related websites, because people highly committed to music were sought to provide most valuable insights about their involvement with music and the reflected reasons for music listening in various contexts. In total, 222 participants from thirty-one countries contributed their qualitative answers to this study. The data were analyzed using thematic analysis. The analysis revealed seven main functions of music listening: music in the background, memories through music, music as diversion, emotions and self-regulation through music, music as reflection of self, and social bonding through music (for more detail see Boer, 2009; Boer et al., 2011). For each main function, multiple subfunctions were identified.

In the second research stage, the aim was to develop a measure that captures these several main functions of music. The qualitative input of study 1 was used to generate items. Item generation was mostly based on phrases provided by the participants of the qualitative study. An initial set of 229 items was derived. Their usefulness and applicability were assessed in a multicultural committee, who checked all items for clarity and translatability as well as congruence and consistency in content. The remaining 74 items were translated from English to German and Spanish using the translation-back-translation approach.

The set of seventy-four items was administered in quantitative surveys in Spanish, English, and German to student participants in Mexico, New Zealand, and Germany (see Boer, 2009; Boer et al., 2011). The parallel assessment of the measure in three languages and cultural groups aimed to enhance the cultural sensitivity and cross-cultural applicability of the resulting item selection. The data were analyzed using principal component analysis. Items with clear factor loadings were identified and items were removed that had double loadings, formed single factors, or loaded inconsistently across the three samples. This resulted in thirty-six final items measuring ten functions of music listening: emotions, social bond with friends, family bond, venting, dancing, background, focus, values, political attitudes, and cultural identity. In order to assess the cross-cultural comparability of the measure's factor structure, its equivalence was tested across the sampled cultures. The results showed that the scale meets structural equivalence across the three cultural samples (see Boer, 2009; Boer et al., 2012). The scale was named RESPECT-Music[4] (Ratings of Experienced Social, PErsonal, Cultural Themes of Music Functions).

The learning goals of this exercise are threefold. First, students will discuss in-depth which issues need to be considered when developing and testing a new culturally sensitive measure. The familiarity with the topic (music listening) will provide a fairly easy entry point for in-depth discussions based on personal experiences. Second, this task engages students in considering different cultural perspectives in the development of one measure that aims to be applicable across cultures. Third, the complexity of developing culturally sensitive scales will become apparent. The class can discuss and evaluate the different approaches and solutions developed by the groups as well as the exemplary solution presented here. This will emphasize the fact that a research question may be answered in different ways.

References

Behr, D., & Shishido, K. (2016). The translation of measurement instruments for cross-cultural surveys. In C. Wolf, D. Joye, T. W. Smith, & Y. Fu (Eds.), *The SAGE Handbook of Survey Methodology* (pp. 269–287). London: Sage.

Berry, J. W. (1989). Imposed etics-emics-derived etics: The operationalization of a compelling idea. *International Journal of Psychology*, 24, 721–735. doi:10.1080/00207598908246808

Boer, D. (2009). *Music makes the people come together: Social functions of music listening for young people across cultures.* (Unpublished doctoral dissertation). Victoria University of Wellington, New Zealand). Retrieved from http://researcharchive.vuw.ac.nz/bitstream/handle/10063/1155/

Boer, D., & Fischer, R. (2012). Towards a holistic picture of functions of music: A culturally decentred qualitative approach. *Psychology of Music*, 40, 179–200. doi:10.1177/0305735610381885

Boer, D., Fischer, R., de Garay Hernández, J., González Atilo, M. L., Moreno, L., Roth, M., & Zenger, M. (2011). The functions of music-listening across cultures: The development of a scale measuring personal, social and cultural functions of music. In F. Deutsch, M. Boehnke, U. Kühnen, & K. Boehnke

---

[4] The RESPECT-Music scale in its current form is available in nine languages so far and has been assessed in fifteen countries. It is download available at www.uni-koblenz-landau.de/de/koblenz/fb1/institut-psychologie/abteilungen/sozial%20und%20organisationspsychologie/research/

(Eds.), *Rendering borders obsolete: Cross-cultural and cultural psychology as an interdisciplinary, multi-method endeavor*. Bremen: International Association for Cross-Cultural Psychology.

Boer, D., Fischer, R., Tekman, H. G., Abubakar, A. A., Njenga, J., & Zenger, M. (2012). Young people's topography of musical functions: Personal, social and cultural experiences with music across genders and six cultures. *International Journal of Psychology, 47,* 355–369. doi:10.1080/00207594.2012.656128

Boer, D., Hanke, K., & He, J. (in press). On handling systematic measurement error in cross-cultural research: A review and critical reflection on equivalence and invariance tests. *Journal of Cross-Cultural Psychology*.

Cheung, F. M., van de Vijver, F. J., & Leong, F. T. (2011). Toward a new approach to the study of personality in culture. *American Psychologist, 66*(7), 593. doi:10.1037/a0022389

Dove, A. (1971). The "Chitling" test. In L. R. Aiken, Jr., *Psychological and educational testings*. Boston: Allyn and Bacon.

Harkness, J. A. (2003). Questionnaire translation. In J. A. Harkness, F. van de Vijver, & P. Ph. Mohler (Eds.), *Cross-cultural survey methods* (pp. 35–56). Hoboken, NJ: John Wiley.

Harkness, J. A., Edwards, B., Hansen, S. E., Miller, D. R., & Villar, A. (2010). Designing questionnaires for multipopulation research. In J. A. Harkness, M. Braun, B. Edwards, T. P. Johnson, L. E. Lyberg, P. Ph. Mohler, B-E. Pennell, & T. W. Smith (Eds.), *Survey methods in multinational, multicultural, and multiregional contexts* (pp. 33–58). Hoboken, NJ: John Wiley.

He, J., & van de Vijver, F. J. R. (2013). Methodological issues in cross-cultural studies in educational psychology. In G. A. D. Liem & A. B. I. Bernardo (Eds.), *Advancing cross-cultural perspectives on educational psychology: A festschrift for Dennis McInerney* (pp. 39–56). Charlotte, NC: Information Age.

Heine, S. J. (2008). *Cultural psychology*. New York, NY: W.W. Norton.

Henrich, J., Heine, S. J., & Norenzayan, A. (2010). The weirdest people in the world? *Behavioral and Brain Sciences, 33,* 111–135. doi:10.1017/S0140525X0999152X

Hui, C., & Triandis, H. C. (1989). Effects of culture and response format on extreme response style. *Journal of Cross-Cultural Psychology, 20,* 296–309. doi:10.1177/0022022189203004

Johnson, T., Kulesa, P., Cho, Y. I., & Shavitt, S. (2005). The relation between culture and response styles: Evidence from 19 countries. *Journal of Cross-Cultural Psychology, 36,* 264–277. doi:10.1177/0022022104272905

Matsumoto, D., & van de Vijver, F. (Eds.). (2011). *Cross-cultural research methods in psychology*. Cambridge: Cambridge University Press.

Mohler, P., Dorer, B., de Jong, J., & Hu, M. (2016). *Translation: Overview. guidelines for best practice in cross-cultural surveys*. Ann Arbor, MI: Survey Research Center, Institute for Social Research, University of Michigan.

Paulhus, D. L. (1991). Measurement and control of response bias. In J. P. Robinson, P. R. Shaver, & L. S. Wrightsman (Eds.), *Measures of personality and social psychological attitudes* (pp. 17–59). San Diego, CA: Academic Press.

Pe-Pua, R. (2006). From decolonising psychology to the development of a cross-indigenous perspective. In U. Kim, K. S. Yang, & K. K. Hwang (Eds.), *Indigenous and cultural psychology: Understanding people in context* (pp. 109–137). New York: Springer.

Redden, P. M., & Simons, J. A. (1986). *Manual for the Redden Simons "Rap" Test.* Ankeny, IA: Des Moines Area Community College.

Sakai, M., Ishikawa, S., Takizawa, M., Sato, H., & Sakano, Y. (2004). The state of hikikomori from a family's point of view: Statistical survey and the role of psychological intervention. *Japanese Journal of Counseling Science, 37,* 168–179.

Smith, P. B. (2004). Acquiescent response bias as an aspect of cultural communication style. *Journal of Cross-Cultural Psychology, 35,* 50–61. doi:10.1177/0022022103260380

Smith, P. B., Fischer, R., Vignoles, V. L., & Bond, M. H. (Eds.). (2013). *Understanding social psychology across cultures: Engaging with others in a changing world* (2nd ed.). Thousand Oaks, CA: Sage.

van de Gaer, E., Grisay, A., Schulz, W., & Gebhardt, E. (2012). The reference group effect: An explanation of the paradoxical relationship between academic achievement and self-confidence across countries. *Journal of Cross-Cultural Psychology, 43,* 1205–1228. doi:10.1177/0022022111428083

van de Vijver, F. J. R. (2013a). Construct bias. In K. Keith (Ed.), *The encyclopedia of cross-cultural psychology* (pp. 233–235). Hoboken, NJ: Wiley. doi:10.1002/9781118339893

(2013b). Method bias. In K. Keith (Ed.), *The encyclopedia of cross-cultural psychology* (pp. 878–880). Hoboken, NJ: Wiley.

(2013c). Item bias. In K. Keith (Ed.), *The encyclopedia of cross-cultural psychology* (pp. 772–774). Hoboken, NJ: Wiley.

van de Vijver, F. J. R., & Leung, K. (1997). *Methods and data analysis of comparative research.* Thousand Oaks, CA: Sage.

van de Vijver, F. & Leung, K. (2011). Equivalence and bias: A review of concepts, models, and data analytic procedures. In D. Matsumoto & F. van de Vijver (Eds.), *Cross-cultural research methods in psychology* (pp. 17–45). Cambridge: Cambridge University Press.

van de Vijver, F. J. R., & Poortinga, Y. H. (1997). Towards an integrated analysis of bias in cross-cultural assessment. *European Journal of Psychological Assessment, 13,* 29–37. doi:10.1027/1015-5759.13.1.29

Welkenhuysen-Gybels, J., Billiet, J., & Cambré, B. (2003). Adjustment for acquiescence in the assessment of the construct equivalence of Likert-type score items. *Journal of Cross-Cultural Psychology, 34,* 702–722. doi:10.1177/0022022103257070

Woolf, L. M. & Hulsizer, M. R. (2011). Why diversity matters: The power of inclusion in research methods. In K. D. Keith (Ed.), *Cross-cultural psychology: Contemporary themes and perspectives* (pp. 56–72). Oxford, UK: Wiley-Blackwell.

Yang, K. S. (2000). Monocultural and cross-cultural indigenous approaches: The royal road to the development of a balanced global psychology. *Asian Journal of Social Psychology, 3*, 241–264. doi:10.1111/1467-839X.00067

Biological Connections

What does it mean that gene variants are found across cultures? Can culture influence the brain? Is it true that there is more variation within cultures than between cultures? How do cultural practices influence the occurrence of diseases within groups? Does the language we speak affect the structure of the brain? Is brain function the same for the same tasks across cultures? These are simply representative examples of the kinds of questions that make the gene-culture and culture-brain intersections fascinating study material for psychology students and their teachers, and that make Chapter 8 a fine resource for teachers of biological psychology – whether in a stand-alone course or in the introductory course.

Most students can grasp the fact that perception may vary across cultures – after all, it involves interpretation and related cognitive processes. But what about sensation? Are sensory processes susceptible to change with cultural experience? The relations among environment, sensation, and perception are both fascinating and complex – and the subject of Chapter 9 in which Phillips provides numerous examples of teaching activities and ideas designed to enliven the classroom or laboratory, and to provoke curiosity in student learners.

CHAPTER 8

Incorporating Culture into Biological Psychology Courses

Afshin Gharib

We can all agree that it is desirable to increase the cross-cultural content in psychology courses, both because cultural variation was historically neglected in the development of our field, and because fostering cultural sensitivity and cross-cultural knowledge is increasingly important in an interdependent world. That said, some courses in the psychology curriculum, such as social psychology, lend themselves more easily and directly to cross-cultural theory and research. It may seem like a challenge or an unnecessary diversion to include cross-cultural research into a biological psychology course. For the instructor of a biological psychology course, there are two challenges – first, the question of whether cross-cultural material is relevant for a physiologically oriented course, and second, how cross-cultural material can be incorporated in an interesting and engaging way, given limited resources for undergraduate biological psychology courses. After all, few of us have access to a functional magnetic resonance imaging (fMRI) machine for in-class demonstrations.

The first question is whether cross-cultural material has a place in a physiologically oriented psychology course. As teachers of biological psychology, we often begin our classes with a discussion of evolutionary similarities between species. Physiologically, there are more similarities than differences, not only across human cultural groups but across species, and a typical starting point for biological psychology is a discussion of how "neurons are neurons and brains are brains," which after all is the justification for using animal models in physiological research. It is the similarities in physiology that allow us to study neurons in invertebrates and draw conclusions about synaptic processes in humans. If traditional approaches to teaching biological psychology stress commonalities so strongly, why would we want to spend the time to discuss cultural differences?

While on the one hand we stress the commonalities among people, brains, and physiology, we also readily acknowledge that brains and behavior are sensitive to experience. The nature versus nurture question is a recurring theme in psychology courses, including biological psychology. One of the most important developments in our modern conception of brain function is an appreciation of the plasticity of the nervous system. For example, few discussions of the role of the hippocampus in memory fail to include a mention of the classic finding that London taxi drivers, as a result of having to memorize the complex street map of London in order to be licensed, show increases in the size of their hippocampi (Maguire, Woollett, & Spiers, 2006), a clear demonstration that lifestyle influences biology. In fact, as the following review of some of the relevant cross-cultural research highlights, culture influences physiology and physiology influences culture. Far from being irrelevant, the argument made here is that cross-cultural research can be a central component of a biological psychology class.

There are at least six good reasons for biological psychology instructors to include cross cultural material:

1. Because different versions of some genes occur in different frequencies in some cultural groups, discussing cross-cultural research can highlight individual differences in genetic and physiological processes – something that is often overlooked in our courses.
2. The fact is that cross-cultural research in psychology as a whole is increasing dramatically and influencing every aspect of the discipline (Keith, 2013). The more physiological areas of psychology are no exception, with research on gene-culture interactions leading to new insights on human evolution (Durham, 1991), and the new area of cultural neuroscience leading to cross-cultural research on brain function (Chiao, Li, Seligman, & Turner, 2016).
3. Recent research in cross-cultural psychology supports the conclusion that to some extent, there is a relation between cultural background and variations in physiological functioning. The brain is plastic, and culture, like other aspects of the environment, can alter brain activity. After all, culture is information that is stored in the brain, and it is not surprising that differences in cultures are related to differences in brain activity.
4. These findings lead to conclusions that are important for the field of biological psychology, for example, highlighting the plasticity of the nervous system, and illustrating the interaction between genetics and the environment.
5. As instructors, we need to acknowledge the diversity of students in our classes, and including cross-cultural research makes the course content more relevant to students of diverse cultural backgrounds.

6. While the research may be cross-cultural, there is more diversity within cultures than between them, so, for example, findings described here on differences between individualist and collectivist cultures apply just as much to more or less individualist members of any cultural group. Similarly, gene variants are found across cultures, so a discussion of the consequences of a particular allele that happens to be prevalent in one population for brain function or behavior generalizes to people with the same allele in other groups.

This last point is one that needs to be emphasized both in reviewing the research in this area and in discussing the implications of these findings with students. One exercise that I have found helpful is to have everyone in class take a measure of collectivism/individualism early in the term. For example, the original Triandis and Gefland (1998) individualism and collectivism scale is a short sixteen-item measure that students can score for themselves. We then have a discussion in class of how variable individual scores are, even for students from the same cultural background. What I have found every time I have done this exercise is that several of my students from traditional Western cultural backgrounds are surprised at their high collectivism scores. This discussion can also be used to highlight how, when we talk about cultural differences, we are always talking about averages, not about individuals. Students find it interesting later in the course, when we discuss some of the research in cross-cultural neuroscience comparing individualist and collectivist cultures, to consider how they would perform in the experiments based on their scores. Of course, the same caution needs to be stressed in discussing genetic differences between ethnic populations – there is more genetic variability within any ethnic group than there is between groups, and when findings of genetic differences between human populations are introduced, it is important to remind students that the differences are only average differences and no conclusions can be reached about any one individual of that ethnicity.

This question of genetic differences between populations is a particularly important and sensitive issue in discussions of cultural differences in a biologically oriented course because of the historic misuse of biological theories in supporting eugenic policies. I find it a valuable use of class time to dedicate one class meeting early in the semester to discussing some of these abuses in the context of discussing research methods and ethics. I assign students Stephen Jay Gould's (1977) very brief essay, "The Nonscience of Human Nature," as supplementary reading, and talk about the dangers of drawing broad conclusions about a particular population based on average differences, and how this applies just as much to research on the genetics of alcohol metabolism, or brain areas involved in perceptual judgments as it does to scores on IQ tests.

In the following sections, I will review cross-cultural findings that can be incorporated into a standard biological psychology course. The review is organized in terms of the topics that are usually covered in an upper-division undergraduate course, and some recent as well as classic research in these areas is outlined. Note that this review is not at all comprehensive; the focus is on research articles that could be assigned as readings to undergraduate students, and findings that highlight some of the advantages of incorporating cultural information into a biological psychology course. One way to use this information is to assign individual students or groups the topics to investigate in the context of cross-cultural research. Students can be given the original research articles to read and then present the research to the class. For many of the articles reviewed here, while students would not be able to replicate the physiological research in my classes, I encourage them to create their own versions of the stimuli used in the studies to present to the class as part of their class project. At the end, I review some suggestions for how to incorporate this information into courses.

Evolution and Genetics

The first few meetings of my biological psychology class, and parts of the first chapter of many textbooks, focus on evolutionary processes and genetics. This is an opportunity to introduce research on the role of human culture in shaping human evolution, and the physiological and behavioral consequences of variations in allele frequencies across different populations.

In terms of the influence of culture on evolutionary history, Durham (1991) provided an excellent book-length discussion of some interesting examples of how cultural practices have led to unique selection pressures on particular genes, which in turn contributed to cultural change in human evolutionary history. O'Brien and Laland (2012) provided a shorter and more recent review of the field that can be assigned as supplementary reading for an undergraduate course.

The best-known example of the coevolution of genes and culture is that of lactose tolerance. While in most mammals the production of lactase, the enzyme that metabolizes the carbohydrate lactose in milk declines after weaning, a significant proportion of the human population (about 35 percent) continues to produce lactase into adulthood. There is wide variation across populations in the proportion of people with the lactose persistence

(LP) trait, with rates of 90 percent and higher in Scandinavian countries and the United Kingdom. The prevalence of LP in a population is related to the cultural practice of dairy farming. LP is caused by a single gene mutation in Northern Europeans, and that mutation originated in humans after the domestication of cattle and spread with the prevalence of dairy farming and the practice of consuming milk (Gerbault et al., 2011). Cultures that do not have a tradition of dairy farming have low levels of the LP trait.

A second well-studied example of cultural practices influencing the spread of genetic traits is the case of the sickle cell trait in West Africa. The cultural practice of clearing forests for yam farming created environments (standing pools of water) that led to increases in the population of mosquitoes that carry malaria. The spread of yam farming and the increase in malaria in turn led to selection for the sickle cell allele for hemoglobin, which causes sickle cell anemia in homozygous individuals but provides protection against malaria in heterozygous carriers (Durham, 1991).

These are just two examples of how cultural practices influence evolutionary selection for particular alleles of genes that confer an advantage to individuals living in those cultures. A particularly interesting further example of possible interaction between evolutionary processes and cultural forces, especially in the context of research on differences between individualist and collectivist cultures to be discussed later, is the theory put forward by Fincher, Thornhill, Murray, and Schaller (2008) that collectivism as a cultural value system, with its relatively greater emphasis on ingroup versus outgroup distinctions and conformity within the group, may itself be an evolved adaptation to higher risk of disease due to higher prevalence of pathogens.

It is important to always stress for students that there is more genetic variation within any culture or population than there is among populations. It is not the case that everyone from a dairy farming culture has the LP trait. There are lactose-intolerant people from cultures with a long tradition of dairy farming, and many people from nondairying cultures have the LP trait. For example, 36 percent of people among the Beni Amir pastoralists in Africa are lactose intolerant, even though they are from a culture with a long history of milk consumption, and 20 percent of the neighboring tribe of Dounglawi have the LP trait even though the Dounglawi are a nondairying culture (Gerbault et al., 2011). Within any group of students, it is likely that there will be several lactose-intolerant individuals, and a discussion of the ethnic background of the class in the context of lactose tolerance would be illustrative because it is likely that many of the lactose-intolerant and lactose-tolerant individuals are from the same ethnic background.

Neurons, Neurotransmitters, and Psychopharmacology

Another early topic in a physiological psychology course would be nerve cells, neurotransmitters, and psychopharmacology. This area offers a number of opportunities to continue to discuss genetic variability between populations and the interaction between genes and culture. For example, neurotransmitters and receptors for neurotransmitters are the products of genes, and genetic polymorphisms influence how neurotransmitters function.

One genetic polymorphism that has been well studied is the variation in the serotonin transporter gene (5-HTT), particularly the so-called short (S) and long (L) alleles. The S allele results in a less efficient protein and higher levels of serotonin left in the synapse due to less serotonin reuptake. One finding that is frequently mentioned in biological psychology courses is the relation between the serotonin transporter gene and increased risk of anxiety and mood disorders. In individuals who are carriers of the S allele (either heterozygous or homozygous), childhood stressful events predict adult depression, while those homozygous for the L allele do not show the same relation between stressful events and mood disorders (Caspi et al., 2003). One interesting feature of this genetic polymorphism is that the S allele has been found to be more prevalent in collectivistic cultures than in individualistic ones (Chiao & Blizinsky, 2010). Given that the S allele increases the risk of a variety of mental health problems, including mood and anxiety disorders, one interpretation of this geographic co-distribution of the S allele and collectivist cultures is that collectivism, with its emphasis on group cohesion, cooperation, and harmony, may be an adaptive response to a heightened sensitivity to stress in S allele carriers by creating a social environment that decreases and mitigates the effects of stress (Chiao & Blizinsky, 2010). Reviews by Chiao and Blizinsky (2010) and Nomura (2016) of the cross-cultural research in this area would be valuable course readings.

The serotonin transporter gene is not the only example of a genetic polymorphism that seems to vary with culture. A discussion of polymorphism in the oxytocin receptor gene can be found later in this chapter. Other well-known examples are the genes for alcohol dehydrogenase and acetaldehyde dehydrogenase, the key enzymes in the metabolism of alcohol (Peng et al., 1999). Variants of genes for these two enzymes that are particularly prevalent in East Asians result in a buildup of acetaldehyde after drinking alcohol, which is unpleasant for the drinker and as a result reduces alcohol consumption. This genetic makeup may be a protective factor against alcoholism and may explain the relatively low rates of alcohol use disorders in many parts of Asia compared to the rest of the world (Chen & Yin, 2008). Within East Asian populations, those who metabolize alcohol less efficiently have lower rates of alcohol use disorders compared to more efficient metabolizers. In fact, being homozygous for some of these alleles seems to provide full protection against developing alcoholism (Peng et al., 1999). Although more prevalent among East Asians, these alleles are found in other ethnic groups as well, and not all East Asians carry the same alleles. A discussion of alcohol metabolism is also an opportunity to discuss the difference between ethnicity and culture. High rates of intolerance to alcohol lead to low rates of alcohol use disorders in certain groups, not only in Asia, where, for example, the rate of alcoholism in Taiwan is eight times lower among ethnic Han Chinese (among whom the less efficient forms of the enzyme are prevalent) compared to other ethnic groups on the island (Chen et al., 1999), but also among Asian Americans compared to other ethnic groups in the United States (46).

Genetic variation in alcohol metabolism is just one example of how physiological differences among populations can result in differences in reactions to drugs. The case of individual variation in metabolism and response to psychotherapeutic drugs is discussed later in the chapter; however, as one further example, researchers have found that rates of lung cancer are lower among Asian smokers compared to other ethnic groups. This discrepancy is due in part to genetic differences in rate of nicotine metabolism resulting from variation in efficiency of the CYP2A6 enzyme. Asians are more likely to have alleles of the CYP2A6 enzyme that leads to slower metabolism of nicotine, which in turn leads to less nicotine intake per cigarette and lower risk of lung cancer (Benowitz, Perez-Stable, Herrera, & Jacob, 2002).

Neuroanatomy

Another foundational topic covered early in a biological psychology course is discussion of neuroanatomy and brain structure. Given clear evidence that experience can alter brain structure (Maguire et al., 2006), it would be surprising if culture did not influence brain anatomy. Discussing cross-cultural research in this area is particularly valuable in an undergraduate course because it is natural for us to discuss functional neuroanatomy as if different brain regions are as clearly delineated in real life as they are in the figures in textbooks and anatomical models. Cross-cultural evidence teaches the important lesson that there is always a great deal of individual variation, not only in behavior and genetics, but also in brain structure and function. While research on the effect of culture on functional differences in brain activity is only just starting (see Park & Huang, 2010, for a review), there are some interesting findings that can be incorporated into a class discussion, particularly in the context of the effects of speaking different languages.

Crinion et al. (2009) looked for neuroanatomical differences between speakers of tonal languages compared to those nontonal language speakers. In tonal languages such as Chinese, pitch conveys meaning, while in nontonal languages, pitch when speaking a word does not alter the word's meaning. Speakers of Chinese showed increases in gray and white matter in right temporal lobe regions associated with pitch perception and in sections of the left insula, which play a role in discriminating tones in Chinese words. Importantly, these differences in brain anatomy were found not only in native speakers of Chinese but also in native English speakers who were learning Chinese as adults. These findings suggest that the differences in the brains of speakers of tonal languages were due to learning and experience, highlighting the plasticity of the brain. Further research on the effects of language on brain function are discussed subsequently.

Sensation and Perception

The finding that the language we speak can affect the size of specific brain regions is powerful evidence of the plasticity of the brain and the importance of experience. In fact, cultural factors influence many aspects of brain function, even the relatively simple processing of perceptual information (see Goh & Park, 2009).

Kitayama, Duffy, Kawamura, and Larsen (2003) developed a task known as the framed-line test, in which participants viewed a line within a square frame. They were then given a square frame of a different size and asked to draw either a line of the same absolute length or one of the same relative length (relative to the size of the new frame). When comparing the performance of American and Japanese participants, the researchers found that although American participants were better at drawing lines of the same absolute length as the target, suggesting that they were ignoring the contextual information of the frame, Japanese participants were more accurate in drawing lines of the same relative length, revealing greater attention to contextual information. Using a similar task in a fMRI study, Hedden, Ketay, Aron, Markus, and Garbrieli (2008) found that while similar areas of the brain showed increased activation when East Asian and

European American participants had to make judgments about whether a line was either the same absolute length as a target or the same relative length given the size of the frame, for each group, activity in parts of the frontal and parietal lobes believed to be involved in attentional control was greater when they were performing the more culturally difficult task – that is, East Asians had a greater increase in activity in the frontal and parietal lobes when making absolute length judgments, while Americans showed greater activation in these areas when they needed to take contextual information into account. One important lesson from this research is that even if the same brain areas are used in the performance of a task across cultures, culture can still influence the relative effort required to complete a task and the amount of activation in those brain areas.

An influential theory in cross-cultural psychology is that people from Western cultures tend to focus on central components of a scene, while people from Asian cultures engage in more holistic processing, incorporating more contextual information (Kitayama et al., 2003). This theory can explain the cultural differences in performance on the framed-line test, and the distinction between holistic and object-centered processing has also been shown to influence the processing of more complex visual scenes. Gutchess, Welsh, Boduroğlu, and Park (2006), in an fMRI study of East Asian and American participants viewing photographs of natural scenes, found that Americans showed greater activity in parts of the brain's visual processing network associated with identifying objects (the so-called ventral "what" pathway that includes parts of the occipital and temporal lobes) when encoding central objects in photographs compared to East Asians. In a later fMRI study, Goh et al. (2007) found that compared to both young and old American and younger East Asian participants, elderly East Asian participants showed less adaptation within the same brain pathways when shown a series of pictures where the central object stayed the same while its background changed, suggesting less efficient processing of central objects in visual scenes.

Jenkins, Yang, Goh, Hong, and Park (2010) further demonstrated that culture can influence not only the attention paid to stimuli, but also the processing of visual information in an interesting study that makes a good demonstration for a class discussion. Chinese and American participants viewed pictures that were either congruent in terms of the central object and its background (a stove pictured in a kitchen) or incongruent (a stove pictured in the middle of a field). Chinese participants showed greater adaptation in the ventral "what" visual pathway to the repeated incongruent images compared to Americans, suggesting greater processing of the background and more attention to the incongruity. As a class project, students can create congruent and incongruent images themselves to illustrate the study's procedures and finding.

Not only do Easterners attend to and process the context of a visual scene more than Westerners, but also there is evidence that cultures can influence the amount of processing of specific types of visual information. Goh et al. (2010) found greater activation of the fusiform face area in Westerners when looking at same-race faces (as opposed to houses) compared to that of East Asians, and more lateralized (right hemisphere) processing of face information in East Asians. The researchers interpreted these differences in terms of a more analytic style of processing face information in Westerners, and more holistic processing in East Asians.

Sleep and Rhythms

The study of sleep and biological rhythms is an area that has emphasized cross-cultural comparisons. Cultures differ in norms related to sleep; for example, in some cultures, an afternoon nap is the norm, but in others, it is not (Flaskerud, 2015). Given persistent problems with sleep, including the prevalence of insomnia and chronic sleeplessness that are features of the modern urban, industrialized lifestyle, researchers have been interested in understanding sleep patterns in other cultures and societies.

For example, in a particularly interesting recent study, Yetish et al. (2015) provided activity trackers to members of three hunter-gatherer groups (the Hadza and San in Africa, and the Tsimane of Bolivia) in order to collect extensive data on sleep patterns and to address the question of whether sleep patterns may have been substantially different in the pre-industrial past. The surprising conclusion of the study was that across the different populations, sleep patterns were not very different from those in Western industrialized cultures, with people typically sleeping 7 to 8 hours per night. In light of various theories suggesting that modern sleep patterns are very different from those in the distant past, the results of this study provide a good example of the value of cross-cultural research as a way of testing our assumptions.

Hormones

A classic area of biopsychological investigation done in another culture and one of the few to be frequently cited in physiological psychology textbooks is the study of males with 5α-reductase deficiency in villages in the

Dominican Republic. Individuals with this condition are born with ambiguous genitalia and would sometimes be raised as girls in childhood. Testosterone at puberty would masculinize their genitals. In an important set of studies, Imperato-McGinley, Guerrero, Gautier, and Peterson (1974) and Imperato-McGinley, Peterson, Gautier, and Sturla (1979) found that most of these genetically male individuals chose to live as males after puberty, with a male gender identity and assuming male gender roles. These studies were important evidence against the theory of gender neutrality which argued that gender identity is determined by early social-ization and how children are raised. The research by Imperato-McGinley et al. is an example of how cross-cultural research can contribute important knowledge about universal physiological processes, as 5α-reductase defi-ciency occurs with higher frequencies in certain families in some cultures. The finding that in these populations individuals raised as females assume the gender identity of males after puberty supports the theory that early hormone exposure is a key factor in the development of gender in all cultures.

A hormone that has been the focus of interest more recently is oxytocin. The role of oxytocin in promoting attachment, empathy, and trust is a topic of frequent discussion in biological psychology classes. An interesting series of studies has investigated the role of a particular allele of the oxytocin receptor gene OXTR rs53576. There are two important alleles of this gene, the G and A alleles. Research has shown that carriers of the G allele may be more sensitive parents and more empathetic (LeClair, Sasaki, Ishii, Shinada, & Kim, 2016). Kim et al. (2010) found that American carriers of the G allele (either homozygous or heterozygous) who had experienced recent psychological distress were more likely to seek emotional support compared to Americans homozygous for the A allele. Interestingly, this effect of the G allele on emotional support seeking was not found in native Korean participants, although Korean Americans showed the American typical pattern. This finding is interpreted in terms of the impact of cultural norms – seeking emotional support is a cultural norm in American culture – while collectivist cultures tend to be more concerned about the possible negative interpersonal consequences of seek-ing support and are less likely to seek social support (Kim et al., 2010). This finding suggests that culture can influence how a gene is expressed as a behavioral phenotype. In individualist cultures, the G allele leads to more support seeking, but in collectivist cultures it does not.

In a follow-up study, Kim et al. (2011) studied the interaction between the OXTR G allele and culture in emotional suppression. Individualist and collectivist cultures differ not only in terms of norms for seeking emotional support, but also in social norms for expressing emotions. Unlike individualists, collectivists encourage emotion suppression as an emotion regulation strategy. Americans homozygous for the G allele of the oxytocin receptor gene were less likely to report suppressing emotions than Americans homozygous for the A allele, while the opposite was found in native Koreans: Those with the G allele were more likely to suppress emotions than those with the A allele. These findings suggest that having the G allele made carriers more sensitive to the social norms of their particular culture, whichever culture they were in. Individualistic G carriers acted more like individualists and collectivistic G carriers acted more collectivist in suppressing emotions.

LeClair et al. (2016) recently found that Americans homozygous for the G allele of the OXTR gene reported less loneliness and a more secure attachment style than Americans homozygous for the A allele. Among Japanese participants, those homozygous for the G allele of the OXTR gene reported more loneliness and a more insecure attachment style than Japanese homozygous for the A allele. Again, this reversal between cultures can be explained in terms of cultural norms. American culture encourages less interpersonal caution, leading to larger social networks and less loneliness, while the opposite is true in Japan where greater caution in establishing interpersonal connections is the social norm. Similarly, the authors suggested that insecure attachment is more of a cultural norm in collectivist cultures that encourage dependency and emotional closeness between parent and child. Again, these results suggest that carrying the G allele of OXTR makes individuals more sensitive to their particular culture's norms.

The research on the polymorphisms of the oxytocin receptor are important to discuss in a biological psychology course, as this research clearly demonstrates in a concrete example how genetics and culture – nature and nurture – interact. We frequently discuss the importance of both nature and nurture, and in this case we can clearly demonstrate to our students how the same allele, in different cultures, leads to very different behaviors.

Emotion

A fair amount of cross-cultural research has focused on differences in emotional expression between cultures, and recent research has started to explore cross-cultural differences in the emotional brain. The amygdala in particular is an important brain structure in the processing of emotional information (LeDoux, 1996). In an fMRI study, Chiao et al. (2008) found that native Japanese participants had greater amygdala activation in response to fearful Japanese faces compared to European faces, while European Americans showed the opposite pattern of greater amygdala activity when viewing fearful European faces compared to Japanese faces. This finding matches behavioral data showing that people are better at recognizing emotional expressions of people from their own culture.

This same-culture advantage in sensitivity to emotional expressions applies even to very subtle cues. Adams et al. (2010) used the Reading the Mind in the Eyes task in an fMRI study, in which participants view photographs of only the target's eyes and attempt to judge the emotion the target is expressing. The researchers found that there was a same-culture advantage in judgments of emotions based only on information from the eyes – native Japanese were more accurate in judging the emotions from Japanese eyes, European Americans were better at judging the emotions of European eyes. When performing the task, both groups of participants showed increased activity in the posterior superior temporal sulci, but the increase in activity was greater when viewing same-culture eyes. This finding again shows that even when the same brain areas are involved in a task, culture can influence the amount of brain activity.

A particularly enjoyable article to assign for a class presentation is one that used an emotional face/voice Stroop task. Liu, Rigoulot, and Pell (2015) presented native Chinese and North American participants in an event-related potential (ERP) study a Stroop-like task requiring them to view photographs of same-ethnicity faces expressing either sadness or fear while listening to a voice making word-like utterances in their own languages that were either in a fearful or sad tone. The participants had to ignore either the facial expression or the tone of voice when judging whether the other stimulus was fearful or sad. For both groups of participants, there was a Stroop effect, in that they were faster making emotion judgments when the face and voice were congruent, but there was also an effect of culture, in that for Chinese participants it did not matter if they were instructed to ignore the face or voice, while North Americans had a harder time ignoring faces than ignoring voices. In addition, the North American participants also showed a greater N 400 ERP response when trying to ignore faces than when ignoring voices, an ERP that is sensitive to mismatches between stimuli. The Chinese participants did not show a difference in ERP between having to ignore faces and having to ignore voices. These findings may reflect a cultural difference in how much emotion is typically expressed in faces – Chinese participants may have found it easier to ignore facial cues of emotions because suppressing facial expressions is a cultural norm in Asian cultures. For a class presentation, students can try creating their own face/voice Stroop task, using either photographs or short films of a target face expressing one emotion and an overlaid voice expressing either the same or different emotion.

Lidaka and Harada (2016) conducted another interesting study of the influence of culture on the processing of emotional information in the brain. Testing only native Japanese participants, they first gave individuals a measure of self-concept to identify relative levels of individualism and collectivism for each participant. Participants then viewed emotionally arousing photographs of insects. The researchers hypothesized that more collectivist individuals would be more sensitive to negative, emotionally arousing stimuli, and indeed they found that the more collectivist the participant, the greater the activation in the right amygdala when viewing the emotionally arousing stimulus compared to a neutral one. In a second experiment, participants were primed to either a more collectivist or individualist outlook by first reading a story that either highlighted social connections or individual initiative. They found that the priming influenced amygdala reactivity, so that those primed to a collectivist orientation showed increased activity in the right amygdala when viewing the emotionally arousing pictures while those primed to an individualist orientation did not. This study is an interesting one to discuss; it shows both how within any cultural group there are individuals who are more or less individualist or collectivist, and how easily these orientations can be altered and how that change in turn is reflected in neural activity. Both culture and the brain show plasticity.

Learning and Memory

Much less cross-cultural research has explored the brain areas involved in learning and memory compared to emotion, but interest in the question of whether there are cultural differences in these areas is increasing. When covering learning in a biological psychology course, it is common to discuss the role of the so-called reward circuit of the brain (unless this topic is covered under the discussion of emotions). There is evidence that different sorts of social cues are reinforcing in different cultures. In an fMRI study, American and Japanese participants passively viewed male body outlines in either dominant or submissive poses. For Americans, viewing the dominant poses increased activity in parts of the brain reward circuit (the caudate and the medial prefrontal cortex), while for the

Japanese participants, viewing the subordinate poses increased brain activity in these areas. In addition, participants self-reported tendencies toward dominance or subordination correlated with brain activity, so that participants with higher subordinate scores had greater brain activation when viewing the subordinate poses and higher dominance scores were correlated with more activation when viewing the dominance pose (Freeman, Rule, Adams, & Ambady, 2009). As part of a class presentation, students can not only prepare their own versions of dominant and subordinate stimuli, but can also take the dominance/subordination measure provided in the article to predict how their reward circuits would react to the stimuli.

There is evidence for cross-cultural differences in memory. For example, people from individualist societies typically remember more autobiographical memories and from an earlier age than people from collectivist cultures (for a review, see Gutchess & Huff, 2016; Ross & Wang, 2010). However, little work has appeared on cultural differences in brain areas related to memory (e.g., the hippocampus). Gutchess et al. (2006) found differences in brain areas activated when Americans, compared to East Asians, encoded central objects in an image, even though the groups did not differ in recognition of the images after a 10-minute delay. This finding suggests that there can be differences in brain activity even if behavioral performance is the same between cultures. As a group project, the Gutchess et al. (2006) article can be used as an assignment for a class presentation for memory (rather than sensation and perception). In preparing their own versions of the stimuli used in that study, students can take photographs and using editing software either remove the central object from the background or remove the background, leaving only the central object, as Gutchess et al. (2006) described.

In view of the fact that the hippocampus was one of the first areas shown to be plastic based on environmental experience (e.g., Maguire, Intraub, & Mullally, 2016), the lack of published cross-cultural research in the neuroscience of memory is interesting in itself, and another class activity could include reviewing cross-cultural memory differences and discussing predictions that could be made about potential differences in brain activity.

Cognition, Judgment, and Decision Making

A number of cross-cultural neuroscience studies have investigated differences in higher level cognitive processing and have found that culture may influence neural functioning across a variety of tasks and levels of cognitive processing. At a simple level, for example, when native Japanese and Americans are asked to perform a simple go/no-go judgment task (respond to all letters except one), both groups show increased activity in brain areas associated with inhibitory control when withholding responses, but activity in one of those areas – the left inferior frontal gyrus – was greater in native Japanese than in either Caucasian Americans or Japanese Americans, consistent with the hypothesis that people in collectivist cultures develop stronger inhibitory processes and self-control (Pornpattananangkul et al., 2016).

A particularly important set of studies has examined how individualist and collectivist cultures differ in how people view themselves. A defining feature of the collectivist-individualist dimension is that in collectivist cultures, people tend to view themselves in terms of interdependent relationships, while individualists have a more independent and autonomous view of the self. These differences in cultural values relate to differences in both behavior and neural activity. In an fMRI study, Chinese and Western participants made judgments about either their own personality attributes or the attributes of their mother, and after scanning, completed a recognition memory test of the adjectives. Although Westerners recognized more of the traits used in the self-judgment task than the traits used in the mother judgment task, Chinese participants recognized both sets of traits equally (a finding that could also be included in a discussion of memory). In addition, during the judgment tasks, Westerners had greater activity in the medial prefrontal cortex when making judgments about themselves compared to making judgments of their mothers, but for Chinese participants, medial prefrontal activity was similar when making self-judgments and judgments about their mothers (Zhu, Zhang, Fan, & Han, 2007). For the Chinese participants, representations both of the self and of a close other involve the medial prefrontal cortex, while for Westerners, this region of the brain is exclusively activated by self-representations. These findings suggest that difference between cultures in interdependence is reflected in brain activity.

In a follow-up fMRI study, Chiao et al. (2010) used cultural priming with bicultural Asian American participants to prime either a more collectivist or more individualist self-representation. Participants underwent scans as they made judgments concerning statements about themselves in general or statements about themselves in a social context. When given an individualist prime, participants showed more activity in the medial prefrontal and posterior cingulate cortex when making general judgments about themselves compared to making contextual judgments. They showed the opposite pattern of greater activity in these regions when making judgments about themselves in a social context compared to general judgments about the self, when given a collectivist prime. These two studies showed that culture can shape how we construe ourselves (either as autonomous or interdependent), that this self-construal is associated with activity in specific brain areas, and that this construal and brain activation are both plastic.

Finally, there has been a great deal of interest in recent years in the neural basis of theory of mind. Native Japanese bilingual adults tested on a false belief story task, either in Japanese or in English, showed similar increases in brain activity in several brain areas, including the medial prefrontal cortex and anterior cingulate cortex, regardless of the language the story was presented in, and these increases were similar to the changes in brain activity in English-language monolinguals tested in English. However, there were also changes in activity in some brain areas that were specific to either the monolinguals, the bilinguals tested in English, or the bilinguals when tested in Japanese, suggesting that there are some brain regions that are involved in Theory of Mind across cultures, but there are also linguistically and culturally unique patterns of brain activity when performing Theory of Mind tasks (Kobayashi, Glover, & Temple, 2006). A subsequent study found similar general and culture-specific effects in 9-year-old bilingual Japanese children (Kobayashi, Glover, & Temple, 2007).

One difference between individualist and collectivist cultures is that collectivists put greater emphasis on group cohesion. This in turn may lead to differences in the ability to take the perspective of members of one's ingroup compared to an outgroup. In a study comparing native Korean and Caucasian American participants' reactions to images of people expressing distress, Korean participants reported greater empathy toward pictures of Asians expressing pain than pictures of Europeans expressing pain, and greater activity in the left temporo-parietal junction, one of the brain areas implicated in theory of mind (Cheon et al., 2011). An interesting feature of this study was that the pattern of brain activity and difference in empathy were related not only to culture, but also to scores on the social dominance scale (Pratto, Sidanius, Stallworth, & Malle, 1994). Social dominance orientation – a preference for hierarchy over egalitarianism – was higher in Koreans than in Americans, and was positively correlated with greater empathy for ingroup distress compared to outgroup. For a class project, students can present the study, prepare their own versions of the stimuli, and have the class take the Pratto et al. (1994) social dominance scale so that students can consider what their own level of empathy for outgroup individuals may be.

Language

A classic contribution of research done in other cultures to our understanding of brain function has been work studying acquired dyslexia in Japanese readers. Written Japanese is unique in having two very different scripts – Kana is a phonetic alphabet, while Kanji is composed of logographic symbols. Damage to the left frontal lobe (Broca's area) results in difficulties in reading and writing Kana, while leaving reading and writing ability in Kanji largely intact. On the other hand, damage to the temporoparietal area causes deficits in Kanji, leaving Kana ability intact (Sasanuma, 1974, 1975). The unique nature of Japanese writing allows for dissociation of the functions of these two brain areas. A recent fMRI study of Chinese developmental dyslexics supports the idea that different writing styles depend on activity in different brain areas. In a comparison of normal and dyslexic Chinese readers, the brain area showing the most consistent difference in activity during reading was the left frontal lobe, rather than the temporoparietal region implicated in developmental dyslexia in English readers (Siok, Perfetti, Jin, & Tan, 2004).

More recent research has supported the idea that different writing styles depend on activity in different brain areas. A study of Chinese children comparing the meanings of pairs of Chinese characters found that while many of the brain areas active during the task, such as the left inferior parietal lobe, were similar to areas previously found to be important in semantic judgments in English readers, there were also areas of increased activation more posterior in the parietal lobe that were unique to Chinese readers. This may be due to more complex mapping from orthography to word meaning in Chinese (Chou, Chen, Fan, Chen, & Booth, 2009). A related finding is that as children become more proficient readers of English, they show increasing activity in the left inferior parietal lobe, an area believed to be important in processing phonological information. As children become more proficient readers of Chinese, on the other hand, they show greater brain activity in more posterior areas of the cortex, areas involved in visual processing, perhaps because there is less of a connection between Chinese characters and specific speech sounds; proficiency in reading Chinese depends more on visual processing of the characters (Cao, Brennan, & Booth, 2015).

When analyzing more similar spoken and written languages, we can expect greater overlap of brain activity. However, given that all languages are different from each other, some differences may be expected even between related languages. This idea gained support from a positron emission tomography (PET) study comparing reading ability in Italian- and English-speaking dyslexics. One difference between written Italian and English is that Italian is a more transparent written language, with letters more likely to be uniquely mapped to speech sounds, while in written English, the mapping between a letter and a sound is more varied and ambiguous. Although brain activation was largely similar between the Italian and English readers, the Italian dyslexics showed less of a reading deficit due to the greater ease of reading Italian (Paulesu et al., 2001). One interesting feature of this study is the dissociation between brain activity and behavior – even though brain activity was similar across cultures, the Italian readers outperformed the English readers due to the specific features of the two written languages.

Psychopathology

Cultures can differ greatly in how they view mental illness and how they attribute the causes of mental illness (Watters, 2010), but research has yet to show whether these cultural differences in attitudes lead to differences in brain function, either in those who hold those attitudes or those who experience mental illness. On the other hand, there has been a great deal of research on ethnic differences in response to psychiatric medication because these differences have important implications for patient treatment.

For example, a wide variety of psychotherapeutic drugs (including antidepressant, antianxiety, and antipsychotic medications) are metabolized in the liver by the cytochrome – P450 family of enzymes, and there are population-based variations in prevalence of certain alleles for these enzymes (Lin, Smith, & Ortiz, 2001). For example, one allele – CYP2D6*4 – is prevalent in Caucasians who have problems with metabolism of drugs, but rare in other populations. A different allele – CYPD6*10 – is the leading cause of poor drug metabolism in East Asians, but very rare in other populations. In addition, a variety of nutrients in foods and chemicals in herbal medications can increase or decrease the production of these enzymes, and as a result, cultural variations in diet and reliance on traditional medicines can change the response to medications (Lin et al., 2001). One example is St John's wort, a popular herbal remedy, which can cause negative side effects in patients taking a variety of medications, including antidepressants. These ethnic and cultural variables highlight the necessity of taking culture into account when considering treatments for mental disorders.

Health and Stress

There is evidence that different cultures cope differently with stress (Tweed, White, & Lehman, 2004; Watters, 2010). For example, collectivist and individualist cultures differ in how much they externalize their coping. Collectivists rely more on internally targeted coping strategies such as reappraisal of the situation, while individualists rely more on externally targeted coping strategies such as attempting to change the stressful situation (Tweed et al., 2004). Collectivists are also less likely to seek social support in response to stress compared to individualists (Chiang, Saphire-Bernstein, Kim, Sherman, & Taylor, 2012). These cultural differences impact physiological responses to stress. European American college students show an inverse relation between their sense of social support and immune inflammation (a biological marker of stress), reflecting the relative importance of social support for coping with stress in individualists. Asian Americans do not show the same relation between social support and a decreased stress response, which suggests that social support is less important as a coping mechanism when dealing with stress (Chiang et al., 2012).

It is possible that some of these differences in response to stress have a biological, genetic basis. As a final topic in my class, I try to close the circle on the discussion of the role of culture on physiological processes by returning to the topic of cultural impacts on human evolution, in the context of health (see Sasaki, LeClair, West, & Kim, 2016, for a review). A long-standing theory about how culture may have shaped human biology, known as the thrifty gene hypothesis, was first proposed by Neel (1962). According to this theory, there is evolutionary selection for genes that promote more efficient food metabolism and weight gain in populations that face frequent risks of famine (Diamond, 2003, provides an engaging review). Such conditions would have been common in groups that migrated frequently and over long distances, for example, the ancestors of modern Pacific Islanders, and this selection for "thrifty genes" leads, in modern environments of easily available calories, to a variety of health problems known as metabolic syndrome, including obesity, diabetes, high blood pressure, and high cholesterol. An interesting example of this phenomenon to discuss in class is the case of the Pima Indians of the Southwest United States. There are two distinct populations of the Pima, one group that lives in the United States and a second group living a more traditional lifestyle in Mexico. Compared to their Mexican counterparts, the Pima in the United States, with readily available high-calorie food and a sedentary lifestyle, show much higher rates of metabolic syndrome (Valencia et al., 2005).

Bringing Culture into the Biological Psychology Classroom

This review has highlighted how a biological psychology class would be less complete without consideration of culture and cross-cultural research. Far from being irrelevant to the discussion of biological approaches in psychology, culture can be a central component of such a course. Including cross-cultural research allows for a deeper understanding of everything from evolutionary processes to functional localization in the brain. Discussions of cross-cultural research also raise important ethical issues around how biological information can be misused. In addition, incorporating cross-cultural research is an effective way of resolving some common misconceptions for students in biological psychology courses. One misconception, reinforced by the way we commonly discuss localization of function, is the idea that there are clearly marked, easy-to-identify brain regions "for" specific functions. One thing cross-cultural research clearly demonstrates is differences in localization of function between different individuals. These findings also highlight the plasticity of the nervous system and the effect of experience on neural functioning. This area of research stresses the important influence of experience and the environment on physiological functioning, something that should always be stressed in our courses. It should be noted that this review is organized in terms of the way that I would present the material in different sections of the course. Many of the studies discussed could easily be presented at other points in the course; for example, research I include on oxytocin under hormones could instead be presented while discussing emotions, so individual instructors can choose to organize the presentation of the research to fit their courses.

The next question is how to best incorporate some of this research into a typical biological psychology course. One of the things I do during the first week or so of class is give everyone in class a measure of collectivism/ individualism. Students can score these measures for themselves, or the instructor can score them and provide students their scores. There are a number of convenient and quick measures available; I use either Triandis and Gelfand (1998), a sixteen-item scale, or Sivadas, Bruvold, and Nelson's (2008) fourteen-item scale because both are short and can be completed quickly. Then, when we discuss some of the cross-cultural research during the rest of the course, I remind the class that there is variability in every population, and even in a group of students from a typically individualist culture there is a range of scores on measures of collectivism/individualism. Students can then consider how they (and their brains) would respond if they were participants in the research we study.

In a large lecture class, probably the easiest approach to covering the research findings would be to assign some of the articles reviewed here as readings each week and discuss the research as part of the lecture on that topic. If this is not feasible, for example, if there are already other readings assigned in addition to a textbook, an alternative would be to give one review article for the class to read early in the course and then discuss the individual research findings during lectures. There are a number of excellent, readable reviews of this field, including those by Ambady and Bharucha (2009); Park and Huang (2010); Rule (2014); Rule, Freeman, and Ambady (2013); Chiao (2009); Han & Northoff (2008); Sasaki et al. (2016); and Goh and Park (2009).

Smaller classes are conducive to group or individual projects. I have found it best to use group projects so that students can cooperate in reviewing the more challenging research. Each group can be assigned a topic or an individual research article to review and present to the class. I have found it best to go over the early, more foundational material in lecture – covering the cross-cultural research on evolution, neural transmission, and neuroanatomy myself, and assigning later subjects to groups of students to present in class. The advantage of having students present the cultural neuroscience research as class presentations is that the groups can be encouraged to develop their own versions of some of the stimuli used in the studies to present in class. Students enjoy the task of preparing and presenting their stimuli, for example, using photo editing software to remove background or foreground objects as in the study by Gutchess et al. (2016), creating their own Reading the Mind's Eye stimuli as in Chiao et al. (2008), creating congruent or incongruent pictures as in Jenkins et al. (2010), or creating their own face/voice Stroop task as in Liu, Rigoulot, & Pell (2015).

It may seem at first that discussing cultural differences in a biological psychology class is unnecessary. However, almost every area covered in a typical biological psychology class could benefit from including a cultural perspective. In fact, the role of culture in shaping our biology and physiology could be an organizing theme for a biological psychology class, enriching the content of the course and broadening students' understanding of the interaction of "nature" and "nurture."

References

Adams, R. B., Rule, N. O., Franklin, R. J., Wang, E., Stevenson, M. T., Yoshikawa, S., ... Ambady, N. (2010). Cross-cultural reading the mind in the eyes: An fMRI investigation. *Journal of Cognitive Neuroscience, 22,* 97–108. doi:10.1162/jocn.2009.21187

Ambady, N., & Bharucha, J. (2009). Culture and the brain. *Current Directions in Psychological Science, 18,* 342–345. doi:10.1111/j.1467-8721.2009.01664.x

Benowitz, N., Perez-Stable, E., Herrera, B., & Jacob, P. (2002). Slower metabolism and reduced intake of nicotine from cigarette smoking in Chinese-Americans. *Journal of the National Cancer Institute, 94,* 108–115. doi:10.1093/jnci/94.2.108

Cao, F., Brennan, C., & Booth, J. R. (2015). The brain adapts to orthography with experience: Evidence from English and Chinese. *Developmental Science, 18,* 785–798. doi:10.1111/desc.12245

Caspi, A., Sugden, K., Moffitt, T. E., Taylor, A., Craig, I. W., Harrington, H., ... Poulton, R. (2003). Influence of life stress on depression: Moderation by a polymorphism in the 5-HTT gene. *Science, 301*(5631), 386–389. doi:10.1126/science.1083968

Chen, C. C., Lu, R. B., Chen, Y. C., Wang, M. F., Chang, Y. C., Li, T. K., & Yin, S. J. (1999). Interaction between the functional polymorphisms of the alcohol metabolism genes in protection against alcoholism. *American Journal of Human Genetics, 65,* 795–807. doi:10.1086/302540

Chen, C. C., & Yin, S. (2008). Alcohol abuse and related factors in Asia. *International Review of Psychiatry, 20,* 425–433. doi:10.1080/09540260802344075

Cheon, B. K., Im, D., Harada, T., Kim, J., Mathur, V. A., Scimeca, J. M., ... Chiao, J. Y. (2011). Cultural influences on neural basis of intergroup empathy. *Neuroimage, 57,* 642–650. doi:10.1016/j.neuroimage.2011.04.031

Chiang, J. J., Saphire-Bernstein, S., Kim, H. S., Sherman, D. K., & Taylor, S. E. (2012). Cultural differences in the link between supportive relationships and proinflammatory cytokines. *Social Psychological and Personality Science, 4,* 511–520. doi:10.1177/1948550612467831

Chiao, J. Y. (2009). Cultural neuroscience: A once and future discipline. *Progress in Brain Research, 178,* 287–304. doi:10.1016/S0079-6123(09)17821-4

Chiao, J. Y., & Blizinsky, K. (2010). Culture-Gene coevolution of individualism collectivism and the serotonin transporter gene. *Proceedings: Biological Sciences, 277*(1681), 529–537. doi:10.1098/rspb.2009.1650

Chiao, J. Y., Harada, T., Komeda, H., Li, Z., Mano, Y., Saito, D., ... Iidaka, T. (2010). Dynamic cultural influences on neural representations of the self. *Journal of Cognitive Neuroscience, 22,* 1–11. doi:10.1162/jocn.2009.21192

Chiao, J. Y., Iidaka, T., Gordon, H. L., Nogawa, J., Bar, M., Aminoff, E., ... Ambady, N. (2008). Cultural specificity in amygdala response to fear faces. *Journal of Cognitive Neuroscience, 20,* 2167–2174. doi:10.1162/jocn.2008.20151

Chiao, J. Y., Li, S., Seligman, R., & Turner, R. (2016). *The Oxford handbook of cultural neuroscience.* New York, NY: Oxford University Press.

Chou, T., Chen, C., Fan, L., Chen, S., & Booth, J. R. (2009). Testing for a cultural influence on reading for meaning in the developing brain: The neural basis of semantic processing in Chinese children. *Frontiers in Human Neuroscience, 3,* 1–9. doi:10.3389/neuro.09.027.2009

Crinion, J. T., Green, D. W., Chung, R., Ali, N., Grogan, A., Price, G. R., ... Price, C. J. (2009). Neuroanatomical markers of speaking Chinese. *Human Brain Mapping, 30,* 4108–4115. doi:10.1002/hbm.20832

Diamond, J. (2003). The double puzzle of diabetes. *Nature, 423,* 599–602. doi:10.1038/423599a

Durham, W. H. (1991). *Coevolution: Genes, culture, and human diversity.* Stanford, CA: Stanford University Press.

Fincher, C., Thornhill, R., Murray, D., & Schaller, M. (2008). Pathogen prevalence predicts human cross-cultural variability in individualism/collectivism. *Proceedings: Biological Sciences, 275*(1640), 1279–1285. doi:10.1098/rspb.2008.0094

Flaskerud, J. H. (2015). The cultures of sleep. *Issues in Mental Health Nursing, 36,* 1013–1016. doi:10.3109/01612840.2014.978960

Freeman, J. B., Rule, N. O., Adams, R. J., & Ambady, N. (2009). Culture shapes a mesolimbic response to signals of dominance and subordination that associates with behavior. *Neuroimage, 47,* 353–359. doi:10.1016/j.neuroimage.2009.04.038

Gerbault, P., Liebert, A., Itan, Y., Powell, A., Currat, M., Burger, J., ... Thomas, M. (2011). Evolution of lactase persistence: An example of human niche construction. *Philosophical Transactions: Biological Sciences, 366*(1566), 863–877. doi:10.1098/rstb.2010.0268

Goh, J. O., Chee, M. W., Tan, J. C., Venkatraman, V., Hebrank, A., Leshikar, E. D., ... Park, D. C. (2007). Age and culture modulate object processing and object-science binding in the ventral visual area. *Cognitive, Affective & Behavioral Neuroscience, 7,* 44–52. doi:10.3758/CABN.7.1.44

Goh, J. O., & Park, D. (2009). Culture sculpts the perceptual brain. *Progress in Brain Research, 178,* 95–111. doi:10.1016/S0079-6123

Goh, J. S., Leshikar, E. D., Sutton, B. P., Tan, J. C., Sim, S. Y., Hebrank, A. C., & Park, D. C. (2010). Culture differences in neural processing of faces and houses in the ventral visual cortex. *Social Cognitive and Affective Neuroscience, 5,* 227–235. doi:10.1093/scan/nsq060

Gould, S. J. (1977). *Ever since Darwin: Reflections in natural history.* New York, NY: Norton.

Gutchess, A. H., & Huff, S. (2016). Cross-cultural differences in memory. In J. Y. Chiao, S. Li, R. Seligman, R. Turner, J. Y. Chiao, S. Li, ... R. Turner (Eds.), *The Oxford handbook of cultural neuroscience* (pp. 155–169). New York, NY: Oxford University Press.

Gutchess, A. H., Welsh, R. C., Boduroğlu, A., & Park, D. C. (2006). Cultural differences in neural function associated with object processing. *Cognitive, Affective & Behavioral Neuroscience, 6,* 102–109. doi:10.3758/CABN.6.2.102

Han, S., & Northoff, G. (2008). Culture-sensitive neural substrates of human cognition: A transcultural neuroimaging approach. *Nature Reviews Neuroscience, 9*, 646–654. doi:10.1038/nrn2456

Hedden, T., Ketay, S., Aron, A., Markus, H. R., & Gabrieli, J. E. (2008). Cultural influences on neural substrates of attentional control. *Psychological Science, 19*, 12–17. doi:10.1111/j.1467-9280.2008.02038.x

Imperato-McGinley, J., Guerrero, L., Gautier, T., & Peterson, R. (1974). Steroid 5α-reductase deficiency in man: An inherited form of male pseudohermaphroditism. *Science, 186*, 1213–1215. doi:10.1126/science.186.4170.1213

Imperato-McGinley, J., Peterson, R., Gautier, T., & Sturla, E. (1979). Androgens and the evolution of male-gender identity among male pseudohermaphrodites with 5α-reductase deficiency. *New England Journal of Medicine, 300*, 1233–1237. doi:10.1056/NEJM197905313002201

Jenkins, L. J., Yang, Y., Goh, J., Hong, Y., & Park, D. C. (2010). Cultural differences in the lateral occipital complex while viewing incongruent scenes. *Social Cognitive and Affective Neuroscience, 5*, 236–241. doi:10.1093/scan/nsp056

Keith, K. D. (2013). *The encyclopedia of cross-cultural psychology, Vols. 1–3.* Chichester: Wiley-Blackwell. doi:10.1002/9781118339893

Kim, H. S., Sherman, D. K., Mojaverian, T., Sasaki, J. Y., Park, J., Suh, E. M., & Taylor, S. E. (2011). Gene–culture interaction: Oxytocin receptor polymorphism (OXTR) and emotion regulation. *Social Psychological and Personality Science, 2*, 665–672. doi:10.1177/1948550611405854

Kim, H. S., Sherman, D. K., Sasaki, J. Y., Xu, J., Chu, T. Q., Ryu, C., . . . Taylor, S. E. (2010). Culture, distress, and oxytocin receptor polymorphism (OXTR) interact to influence emotional support seeking. *PNAS Proceedings of the National Academy of Sciences of the United States Of America, 107*, 15717–15721. doi:10.1073/pnas.1010830107

Kitayama, S., Duffy, S., Kawamura, T., & Larsen, J. T. (2003). Perceiving an object and its context in different cultures: A cultural look at new look. *Psychological Science, 14*, 201–206. doi:10.1111/1467-9280.02432

Kobayashi, C., Glover, G. H., & Temple, E. (2006). Cultural and linguistic influence on neural bases of "theory of mind": An fMRI study with Japanese bilinguals. *Brain and Language, 98*, 210–220. doi:10.1016/j.bandl.2006.04.013

(2007). Cultural and linguistic effects on neural bases of "theory of mind" in American and Japanese children. *Brain Research, 1164*, 95–107. doi:10.1016/j.brainres.2007.06.022

LeClair, J., Sasaki, J., Ishii, K., Shinada, M., & Kim, H. (2016). Gene–culture interaction: Influence of culture and oxytocin receptor gene (OXTR) polymorphism on loneliness. *Culture and Brain, 4*, 21–37. doi:10.1007/s40167-016-0034-7

LeDoux, J. E. (1996). *The emotional brain: The mysterious underpinnings of emotional life.* New York, NY: Simon & Schuster.

Lidaka, T., & Harada, T. (2016). Cultural values modulate emotional processing in human amygdala. In J. Y. Chiao, S. Li, R. Seligman, R. Turner, J. Y.

Chiao, S. Li, ... R. Turner (Eds.), *The Oxford handbook of cultural neuroscience* (pp. 107–120). New York, NY: Oxford University Press.

Liu, P., Rigoulot, S., & Pell, M. D. (2015). Culture modulates the brain response to human expressions of emotion: Electrophysiological evidence. *Neuropsychologia, 67,* 1–13. doi:10.1016/j.neuropsychologia.2014.11.034

Lin, K., Smith, M. W., & Ortiz, V. (2001). Culture and psychopharmacology. *Psychiatric Clinics of North America, 24,* 523–538. doi:10.1016/S0193-953X(05)70245-8

Maguire, E. A., Intraub, H., & Mullally, S. L. (2016). Scenes, spaces, and memory traces: What does the hippocampus do? *Neuroscientist, 22,* 432–439. doi:10.1177/1073858415600389

Maguire, E. A., Woollett, K., & Spiers, H. J. (2006). London taxi drivers and bus drivers: A structural MRI and neuropsychological analysis. *Hippocampus, 16,* 1091–1101. doi:10.1002/hipo.20233

Matsushita, S., & Higuchi, S. (2017). Use of Asian samples in genetic research of alcohol use disorders: Genetic variation of alcohol metabolizing enzymes and the effects of acetaldehyde. *American Journal on Addictions, 26,* 469–476. doi:10.1111/ajad.12477

Neel, J. V. (1962). Diabetes mellitus: A "thrifty" genotype rendered detrimental by "progress"? *American Journal of Human Genetics, 14,* 353–362.

Nomura, M. (2016). Genes, brain, and culture through a 5-HTT lens. In J. Y. Chiao, S. Li, R. Seligman, R. Turner, J. Y. Chiao, S. Li, ... R. Turner (Eds.), *The Oxford handbook of cultural neuroscience* (pp. 121–128). New York, NY: Oxford University Press.

O'Brien, M., & Laland, K. (2012). Genes, culture, and agriculture: An example of human niche construction. *Current Anthropology, 53,* 434–470. doi:10.1086/666585

Park, D. C., & Huang, C. (2010). Culture wires the brain: A cognitive neuroscience perspective. *Perspectives on Psychological Science, 5,* 391–400. doi:10.1177/1745691610374591

Paulesu, E., Démonet, J., Fazio, F., McCrory, E., Chanoine, V., Brunswick, N., ... Frith, U. (2001). Dyslexia: Cultural diversity and biological unity. *Science, 291*(5511), 2165–2167. doi:10.1126/science.1057179

Peng, G., Wang, M., Chen, C., Luu, S., Chou, H., Li, T., & Yin, S. (1999). Involvement of acetaldehyde for full protection against alcoholism by homozygosity of the variant allele f mitochondrial aldehyde dehydrogenase gene in Asians. *Pharmacogenetics, 9,* 463–476.

Pornpattananangkul, N., Hariri, A. R., Harada, T., Mano, Y., Komeda, H., Parrish, T. B., ... Chiao, J. Y. (2016). Cultural influences on neural basis of inhibitory control. *Neuroimage, 139,* 114–126. doi:10.1016/j.neuroimage.2016.05.061

Pratto, F., Sidanius, J., Stallworth, L. M., & Malle, B. F. (1994). Social dominance orientation: A personality variable predicting social and political attitudes. *Journal of Personality and Social Psychology, 67,* 741–763. doi:10.1037/0022-3514.67.4.741

Ross, M., & Wang, Q. (2010). Why we remember and what we remember: Culture and autobiographical memory. *Perspectives on Psychological Science*, *5*, 401–409. doi:10.1177/1745691610375555

Rule, N. O. (2014). Cultural Neuroscience: A historical introduction and overview. *Online Readings in Psychology and Culture*, *9*. dx.doi.org/ 10.9707/2307-0919.1128

Rule, N. O., Freeman, J. B., & Ambady, N. (2013). Culture in social neuroscience: A review. *Social Neuroscience*, *8*, 3–10. doi:10.1080/17470919.2012.695293

Sasaki, J. Y., LeClair, J., West, A. L., & Kim, H. S. (2016). The gene-culture interaction framework and implications for health. In J. Y. Chiao, S. Li, R. Seligman, R. Turner, J. Y. Chiao, S. Li, . . . R. Turner (Eds.), *The Oxford handbook of cultural neuroscience* (pp. 279–297). New York, NY: Oxford University Press.

Sasanuma, S. (1974). Impairment of written language in Japanese aphasics: Kana versus Kanji Processing. *Journal of Chinese Linguistics*, *2*(2), 141–158. Retrieved from www.jstor.org/stable/23752907

(1975). Kana and kanji processing in Japanese aphasics. *Brain and Language*, *2*(3), 369–383. doi:10.1016/S0093-934X(75)80077-0

Siok, W. T., Perfetti, C. A., Jin, Z., & Tan, L. H. (2004). Biological abnormality of impaired reading is constrained by culture. *Nature*, *431*(7004), 71–76. doi:10.1038/nature02865

Sivadas, E., Bruvold, N. T., & Nelson, M. R. (2008). A reduced version of the horizontal and vertical individualism and collectivism scale: A four-country assessment. *Journal of Business Research*, *61*, 201–210. doi:10.1016/j. jbusres.2007.06.016

Triandis, H. C., & Gelfand, M. J. (1998). Converging measurement of horizontal and vertical individualism and collectivism. *Journal of Personality and Social Psychology*, *74*, 118–128. doi:10.1037/0022-3514.74.1.118

Tweed, R. G., White, K., & Lehman, D. R. (2004). Culture, stress, and coping: Internally- and externally-targeted control strategies of European Canadians, East Asian Canadians, and Japanese. *Journal of Cross-Cultural Psychology*, *35*, 652–668. doi:10.1177/0022022104270109

Valencia, M., Weh, J., Nelson, R., Esparza, J., Schulz, L., Ravussin, E. & Bennett, P. (2005). Impact of lifestyle on prevalence of kidney disease in Pima Indians in Mexico and the United States. *Kidney International*, *68*, S141–S144. doi:10.1111/j.1523-1755.2005.09724.x

Watters, E. (2010). *Crazy like us: The globalization of the American psyche*. New York, NY: Free Press.

Yetish, G., Kaplan, H., Gurven, M., Pontzer, H., Manger, P. R., Wilson, C., . . . Seigel, J. M. (2015). Natural sleep and its seasonal variations in three pre-industrial societies. *Current Biology*, *25*, 2862–2868. doi:10.1016/j. cub.2015.09.046

Zhu, Y., Zhang, L., Fan, J., & Han, S. (2007). Neural basis of cultural influence on self-representation. *Neuroimage*, *34*, 1310–1316. doi:10.1016/j. neuroimage.2006.08.047

CHAPTER 9

Sensation and Perception: Why Culture Matters

William L. Phillips

There is a simple answer to the question, "Why is culture important to the teaching of sensation and perception?" Examining the influence of culture (in any domain) makes us realize that there exist several perspectives when interpreting our world – which is the first step in creating a global community, as well as understanding the person sitting next to us. The intent of this chapter is to provide you with lecture ideas, research examples, and student projects that lead to a better understanding of how culture influences the processes of sensation and perception.

Culture, Perception, and Sensation

I am constantly quizzing my students on the definition of psychology (the scientific study of behavior and mental processes), and I keep reminding them that the definition means that anything affecting our behavior or how we think is fair game to be studied by psychologists. This in turn makes all of us psychologists at some point: We have all wondered what someone *meant* by saying or doing *that*. Often, someone in class retorts, "but almost *everything* affects our behavior and thinking at some point!" I gleefully respond, "Yes, it does ... welcome to psychology – the study of *everything!*" Now, it is quite easy to get students to make the connection between culture and psychology; culture obviously affects our behavior and the way we think. And in turn, how do we come to know our culture? Can you learn all you need to know about a culture by reading about it? Must it be experienced? Are we born with it? (This can morph into a discussion of Plato's *rationalism* versus Aristotle's *empiricism*, and of Descartes' *dualism* versus Locke's *monism*.)

If culture is learned through experience, it must come first by way of some sensory input (sensation), and the interpretation of those inputs (perception). But alas, our culture affects our interpretation (thinking), and thereby our perception, and in one mighty fell swoop of logic, culture affects our perception!

> **Suggested in-class exercise.** Draw the components (sensation, perception, behavior, thinking, and culture) on the board and have the class connect them – keeping in mind that many of the arrows will go both ways. Foster a discussion about the connections, the directions the arrows should point, and whether anything is missing.

However, what of culture and the study of sensation? At first glance, it may seem that exploring cultural differences as they relate to sensation is not necessary. Regardless of culture, all members of the human species are similar with respect to physiology. We are all born with the senses of sight, hearing, touch, taste, and smell (note that not all of these are necessary for learning about one's culture). The development of these sensory systems is in fact dependent upon interaction with the environment, as Hubel and Wiesel (1959) showed in their research on the visual development of cats. As you recall, their research showed that feature detectors in the occipital cortex could be influenced by the environment. Moreover, single-cell neural recordings of particular areas of monkeys' occipital lobes revealed that neurons may be sensitive to features as complex as another monkey's face (Bruce, Desimone, & Gross, 1981).

Because the environment has been shown to influence neural processing, and culture is part of one's environment, logic dictates that it, too, may influence sensory processes. Gislén et al. (2003) examined an example of culture influencing sensory processes. Gislén had heard from a friend about a tribe of sea nomads in Southeast Asia (the Moken people) who live in boats and stilted huts along the waters off the coast of Myanmar and Thailand. As sea nomads, the Moken people are excellent fishermen, and the sea furnishes much of their food needs. Gislén et al. were most interested in what they had heard about the vision of the Moken children. The children are tasked with diving for shellfish and other food sources that live on the ocean floor (to depths of 10–15 feet) without the use of scuba gear or masks. Gislén's friend noticed that the Moken children's underwater vision was superior to hers, even though she was wearing a diving mask (Handwerk, 2004)!

Gislén, Warrant, Dacke, and Kröger (2006) designed a study to test the Moken children's vision, comparing it with a group of similar aged European children. They found that on land, the vision of the two groups of children was similar, as was the basic structure of the eyes. When tested underwater, however, the Moken children had *twice* the acuity of the European children; their underwater vision was much more clear (they could see twice as far underwater) than that of the European children. Upon taking eye measurements of both groups of children underwater, Gislén et al. (2003) discovered that the lenses of the eyes of the Moken children are able to accommodate (change shape) to a larger degree, allowing more refraction (and focusing) of light onto the retina. Furthermore, the Moken children's pupils could constrict to a pinhole size 22 percent smaller than that of their European counterparts. These two adaptations, lens accommodation and pupil constriction, allow the Moken children to see better underwater.

A question still remains: Are these adaptations due to genetics (nature) or to the environment (nurture/culture)? To determine the answer, Gislén et al. (2006) once again tested European children. Four children ages 9–13 received 11 eleven training sessions over 33 days, each session lasting for 2 hours. The children would dive underwater, and were asked to report the orientation of several gratings at differing distances. Measurement of acuity improved from Day 1 to Day 33, and when tested 4 months and 8 months later (without training), the underwater acuity performance of these four participants improved to that of the Moken children. Though this does not completely rule out genetic factors, the experiment showed that experience (training) is sufficient to account for differences in underwater acuity.

Suggested in-class exercise. Before describing the Gislén et al. (2006) study, divide the class into groups and ask students to design the study to show that it is the Moken children's culture that is responsible for their increased underwater acuity. (Note that the students should have already learned the basic physiology of the eye, which was covered in an earlier lecture.)

This example illustrates how the demands of culture can influence sensation by changing physiology (*bottom-up processing*). Examples such as this make it more plausible that culture can have even more prominent effects on perception (*top-down processing*). Difficulty understanding the difference between top-down and bottom-up processing arises when you tell students that "previous experience" can affect our perception. When they hear the story of the Moken children, they will likely (incorrectly) label the change in accommodation and pupil constriction as top-down, rather than bottom-up, processing due to the requirement of experience. Explain that there is no *cognition* necessary for the vision to improve, making this example bottom-up (a *physiological* change), and that "experience," as it relates to top-down processing, has its influence through *memory* and *expectations*.

Demonstrations and Projects Emphasizing the Role of Culture in Perception

Vision and a brief history lesson in cross-cultural research. Probably the most frequently cited example of cross-cultural perception research (appearing in almost every perception and introductory psychology textbook) concerns the *carpentered world hypothesis* proposed by Segall, Campbell, and Herskovits (1966). These researchers systematically studied seventeen groups of adults and children from ten countries in Africa, the Philippines, and the United States, comparing performance differences on several types of illusion-provoking stimuli (most notably, the Müller-Lyer illusion). Segall et al. found that the European and American samples were the most susceptible to the illusion. Moreover, the data supported the hypothesis that varying degrees of exposure to an environment composed of squared buildings and city-block metrics results in more susceptibility to the Müller-Lyer illusion.

Another highly cited study, focusing on color perception, seldom appears in perception texts, but almost always occurs in cognitive psychology texts. Rosch (1973) studied color discrimination of the Dani tribe of New Guinea, which has only two words for color in their language – one for dark colors and one for light colors. Despite having only two labels for color, the Dani were able to discriminate several colors from one another, evidence that directly refuted the *Whorf hypothesis* concerning *linguistic determinism* – that language determines our thought (and therefore, our perception).

Interestingly enough, both the Segall et al. (1963) and Rosch (1973) studies were extensions of research performed by W. H. R Rivers (Slobodin, 1978), who is rarely cited in textbooks. (Have you heard of him?) Rivers (considered by some to be the first cross-cultural experimental psychologist) studied the peoples of the Torres Straits region (near New Guinea) in the early 1900s. Operating with the hypothesis that the native peoples would be more susceptible to the Müller-Lyer illusion (after all, they were "less-civilized"), his research revealed that they were actually *less* susceptible to the illusion. Rivers also studied the color language of the Torres Strait island communities, many of which had only two or three words in their language for color (e.g., black, white, and red). When sorting color tiles, the islanders would group blue and green tiles together. These research findings were later used to develop the Whorf hypothesis (for a manageable summary of the research performed by Rivers, Rosch, and Segall, Campbell, and Herskovits (1966), see Phillips, 2011).

Suggested homework. Assign students (in groups) to read one of the sections (Color Perception, The Müller-Lyer Illusion, The Ponzo Illusion, Picture Perception: Perceiving Depth in Pictures, or Picture Perception: Context and Wholeness) from Chapter 8 of *Cross Cultural Psychology: Contemporary Themes and Perspectives* (Keith, 2011) and have them present and lead a discussion of the research to the rest of the class.

More recent research: Analytic versus holistic perception. Masuda, Gonzalez, Kwan, and Nisbett (2008) conducted several studies revealing aesthetic differences in pictures and photographs between persons of Eastern and Western cultures. These projects are easy to replicate, and provide students the experience of presenting research that they do on their own. Each of the following tasks shows differences between East Asians and Westerners with respect to attention paid to the context and background (*holistic*) compared with attention paid to the individual or salient object (*analytic*).

Drawing a Simple Picture

Forty-three Americans and forty-six East Asian international students attending the University of Michigan were given 5 minutes to draw a picture of a landscape that included a house, a person, a river, a tree, and a horizon, as well as any other objects they wanted to include (Masuda et al., 2008). Comparison of the drawings showed that East Asians drew the horizon much higher on the page, allowing for inclusion of more background objects in the scene. Of particular note was the difference in size of the person; in the Western drawings, the person tended to be very large in comparison to other objects (e.g., the house or tree), whereas the Eastern drawings included much more contextual detail, and the person in the picture was drawn more to scale in comparison of the other objects (see Figure 9.1).

Taking and Choosing the Best Photograph

In a second study, Masuda et al. (2008) asked the same participants from the drawing study to take four portrait photographs of a model in four different settings, each at a constant distance of 9 feet. All

Figure 9.1   Examples of drawings like those of participants in the
Masuda et al. (2008) study
(courtesy of William L. Phillips)

participants used the same digital camera, and were shown how the zoom function worked before taking their photos. The main dependent variable was the size of the model in the photos. Results revealed that overall (in all four settings), East Asians took photos in which the model was 33 percent smaller than in the photos taken by their American counterparts. This indicated that the East Asian participants were including more background in their photos than the American participants.

Suggested research project. The two studies just described are easy to replicate. Divide students into groups of two to four persons (depending on the size of the class) and ask them to replicate one of those summarized. The students can add independent variables or conditions. For example, the drawing study could add different cultures, different scenes (urban versus rural), sites on campus, or classrooms. For the photograph study, one might add different cultures, settings/objects, indoors/outdoors, gender (male taking photo of a female versus a male, a female taking photo of a male versus a female), or photos of groups. A group of my students asked participants on campus to take four photos at an outside campus location, and then had each participant choose the photo he or she preferred. The students replicated the results of Masuda et al. (2008), even though the participants were Asian American rather than East Asian international students. Examples of the photos from this study appear in Figure 9.2.

Figure 9.2   Photograph by an American participant (a) and photograph by Asian
American participant (b)
(courtesy of William L. Phillips)

Touch. One of the most common textbook examples of cultural differences regarding touch is one describing pain perception. Based on a
cultural ritual in Paravur, Kerala, India (called *Garuda thookam*), hooks
are placed in the backs of dancers, who are then hung from a cart and
wheeled around the town. It is an honor to be selected, practitioners report
feeling little pain, and the wounds are reported to heal quickly (Melzak,
1973; for great pictures, see Google for *Garuda thookam*).

Although the following example is often considered cross-cultural com-
munication, I use it to discuss cultural differences in touch. McDaniel and
Andersen (1998) cited the works of Hall, Dodd, Jandt, and Patterson, who
all concluded that peoples of Northern Europe, the United States, and
Northeast Asia tend to be "low contact" (avoiding touch), and peoples of
Southern Europe, Latin America, the Middle East, India, and Southeast
Asia to be "high contact," especially when interacting with close friends or
family.

To better understand cultural differences surrounding touching, McDaniel
and Andersen (1998) studied public displays of affection (PDA) among
opposite-sex couples at a large airport located on the west coast of the
United States. The researchers observed same-race couples and recorded
the types of touching they exhibited before one member of the couple
departed to the boarding gate. After scoring the touch (see McDaniel
and Andersen (1998), the researchers interviewed the remaining member
of the couple to determine the country of origin and relationship status.

Contrary to the reports of earlier authors, American and Northern European couples engaged in the most touching (had the highest scores), while Northeast and Southeast Asians had the lowest scores, with Latin Americans falling in the middle (there were too few couples from other regions to do an analysis with these groups). Clearly, these findings indicated that opposite-sex touching was more socially acceptable to individuals from the United States and Northern Europe than to those from Northeast or Southeast Asia.

In business situations, there are also cultural differences in practices that should be adhered to. Munter (1993) reported that in Latin American, Mediterranean, and Middle Eastern societies, an embrace or shoulder pat following a handshake is expected, whereas in the United States and Australia, a firm handshake is appropriate. In Thailand and Laos, "prayer hands" and a bow are sufficient, but bowing in Japan may be insulting if the intricacies are not followed correctly. Finally, in Muslim and Hindi cultures, shaking or touching with the left hand could be considered an insult, as is touching the head in many African and Asian cultures.

Suggested in-class exercise. Ask half of the class to place their heads down on their desks. On the board (or as a PowerPoint slide), inform the other half that you will pair them with a "heads-down" student. They are to approach their heads-down partner and shake his or her hand, using *both* hands. Ask each group to describe what they felt and thought about the handshakes that occurred between female–female pairs, male–female pairs, and male–male pairs.

Audition. One of the more difficult concepts in the typical audition chapter is the equal loudness curve (the fact that tones of different frequencies must be played at different decibel levels to be perceived as having the same loudness). An interesting lab project (or simply as part of lecture) is to present several different frequencies and ask the class whether they can hear them. There are many such tests available online (e.g., www .noiseaddicts.com/2010/10/hearing-loss-test/) that make this easy to do. To begin, play a 1,000 Hz tone and use the computer's volume control (the 🔊 button on the keyboard) to set a "standard" sound pressure level (spl). Click on this icon and set it at 33. (Note that these are not actual "decibels," but they will serve as an abstract quantitative measure of sound pressure scores). Next, set the speaker volume control to a level that makes the standard 1,000 Hz tone loud but not piercing (this volume control will henceforth not be adjusted; it will remain constant). Only the volume control on the computer should be used to adjust volume from this point forward. Tell the students that the loudness rating they should assign the 1,000 Hz tone is 50 units. Then play a few of the low- and high-frequency tones and ask students to rate their loudness, comparing them to the loudness of the 1,000 Hz tone standard.

Suggested in-class exercise. Students can complete the entire list of tones as either a lab assignment (if you have access to a lab) or as a take-home assignment. Instruct the students to rate each tone in the list, comparing its loudness to the 1,000 Hz standard tone (make sure they play each tone alongside the standard). Have students record their loudness ratings in a table such as the following one.

Stimulus Frequency	Loudness Rating	Volume	Stimulus Frequency	Loudness Rating	Volume	Stimulus Frequency	Loudness Rating	Volume
20 Hz			500 Hz			15 KHz		
30 Hz			1 KHz			16 KHz		
40 Hz			2 KHz			17 KHz		
50 Hz			5 KHz			18 KHz		
60 Hz			8 KHz			19 KHz		
100 Hz			10 KHz			20 KHz		
200 Hz			12 KHz					

Next (for each tone), the Volume column should be used to record the value on the computer's volume control necessary to hear the test frequency at the same loudness as the 1,000 Hz tone. Ask students to bring their results to the next class meeting to compare their responses. This laboratory task will help the students understand the equal loudness curve, as well as introduce individual differences (and perhaps age differences, as you compare your own hearing to that of the students).

Once you have discussed individual differences, you can then introduce the work of Deutsch, Henthorn, Marvin, and Xu (2006), who studied the ability to perceive absolute pitch in children. Absolute pitch (or perfect pitch) is the ability to produce or name a musical note without the aid of a reference tone. Its occurrence is rather rare, with roughly 1 in 10,000 people in the United States possessing this ability (Deutsch et al., 2006). It had been widely known that many famous composers had the ability, and that it was related to musical talent. Deutsch and her colleagues studied several children attending a music conservatory in the United States, and discovered that 14 percent of the American children had absolute pitch, while 60 percent of the speakers of a tonal language (such as Mandarin and Vietnamese) had this ability. Deutsch et al. concluded that learning musical tones at a young age (during the language critical period) is similar to that of learning a second tonal language. It seems clear in this case that cultural experience is vital to perception.

Taste and smell. In most sensation and perception texts, taste and smell are presented together as the "chemical" senses, and I tend to lecture about them together, rather than separately. After discussing the physiology associated with each (which is rather daunting), it is a good idea to present the students with examples of how these processes work. The demonstrations I describe next are both interesting and entertaining.

When discussing the five basic taste receptors, I show students the map of the different tastes as they were once believed to appear on the tongue, along with how the taste of Umami was left out of the taste literature for over one hundred years, having been identified as glutamate in 1908 by Kikunae Ikeda (Lindemann, Ogiwara, & Ninomiya, 2002). Glutamate adds a "savory" flavor to foods by means of the acids influencing the salts of a dish (Lindemann et al., 2002). Although glutamate had been used in cooking for centuries (and not just in Eastern cultures), it was not "scientifically" accepted as a basic taste until 1985, probably due to its Eastern origins (making it a topic for cross-cultural discussion).

The discussion of specialized taste receptors for the basic tastes allows you to demonstrate evidence for specific taste receptors using Gymnema sylvestre. In India, Gymnema leaves have been used for medicinal purposes, including treatment of intestinal and liver problems, for more than 2000 years (Healthline, 2016). Chewing the leaves has also served historically to treat inflammation, asthma, eye problems, and snakebite (Kanetkar, Singhai, & Kamat, 2007). A unique property of Gymnema is that it specifically blocks sweet receptors, accounting for its use to regulate sugar consumption (thereby controlling weight). In addition to its relevance to sensation and perception, discussion of Gymnema can contribute to understanding of medicinal practices across cultures.

Suggested demonstration. *Gymnema* tablets are available at any store where herbal supplements are sold (I recommend getting the 400 mg capsules, which can be easily broken and added to water to create a "tea"). You will also need to bring some candy to class (M&Ms are a good choice), and small 1–3 oz paper cups. Before class, break two capsules into a 750 ml bottle of water and shake vigorously to create the tea. Only about 1/2 oz of the tea is necessary to obtain the effect of blocking sweet receptors. Ask students to eat a few M&Ms, and then have them drink the tea, swirling it around in their mouths before swallowing (the tea is very bitter, but not horrible). Then ask the students to eat another handful of M&Ms; they will taste very bitter! (SweetTARTS or Jolly Ranchers also work well.) The effect will last for only about 45 minutes. This demonstration illustrates the importance of all the basic tastes in accounting for the flavor of a food or drink.

A question students often ask when discussing taste is "Why do some cultures have a high tolerance for spicy food?" It appears that this is due mainly to early exposure to those foods. Early exposure to spicy foods, which often contain capsaicin (the chemical that makes jalapeno peppers hot) slowly "kills off" nerve endings of pain fibers in the mouth (Thacker, 2013). Because food preference is highly dictated by culture, there are many cultural differences in tolerance for spicy food.

Perhaps my favorite demonstration involves a lecture involving taste, smell, flavor, and multimodal perception. Indeed, our experience with food is fully multimodal – food can look good (bright colors), sound good (sizzling bacon), feel bad (slimy texture), and, finally, smell and taste good. Students will often bring up several examples of foods they misjudged based on one of these qualities, making for a good discussion. Popular food choices (associated with different cultures) include sushi, seafood, and insects. I personally enjoyed a multimodal experience in a Japanese restaurant, where the people at the next table had ordered a pizza-looking dish that moved as the waiter brought it out! My friend and I were immediately curious, and so ordered our first "Dancing Katsuobushi" dish. Dried bonito fish flakes are sprinkled onto a baked dish, and the heat causes the flakes to move back and forth (much like maggots!). Thus, in the context of our cultural experience, this dish did not look good at all. It did not smell particularly good (very "fishy"), it sounded okay (a crisp sizzle), and it had a strange texture – yet the taste was delicious! This story always prompts others to share their experiences, making for a good lecture.

Next, to give students a full cultural taste experience, I introduce the "king of fruit" – the durian. During an episode of *Anthony Bourdain: Parts Unknown*, the well-traveled TV host was in Southeast Asia, commenting on the "worst-smelling fruit in the world." This was obviously something I had to look into for sensation and perception (S&P)! The durian is considered a dessert in Southeast Asia, even though it smells a bit like VERY dirty, smelly feet! The "king of fruit" is an apt moniker – the fruit is just under the size of a bowling ball, weighing 5–7 pounds, and has a shell of spikes, making it painful to simply hold onto very tightly. Rumor has it that during medieval conflicts, the durian was tied to a stick or rope and used as a mace-like weapon. (Okay, there is no citation for this because I made it up, but when you see and hold the durian, you cannot argue that it would not make a very effective weapon). In truth, only the spiked skin of the durian is smelly; the fruit inside is similar to a thick, somewhat stringy, mango-tapioca pudding. Some students no doubt would have eaten a durian before, but for others, it will be the first they have heard of it. After giving everyone the opportunity to taste the durian, you can continue the discussion of cultural influences on taste (really flavor) perception.

Suggested demonstration. Durian can typically be found at a Chinese grocery store. It is rather expensive (about $20), and will likely be partially frozen (to reduce the smell). Let it thaw for at least 24 hours before cutting into it. As long as you keep it wrapped in plastic and in a cool place, the smell will not be overwhelming. Rather than prepping the durian before class, I like to make a bit of a performance of it. You will need a pair of rubber cleaning gloves (to protect your hands from the smell and the spikes), a butcher knife (or small hatchet), 2–3 oz paper cups, newspaper, and plastic spoons. Before cutting into the durian, carry it around the classroom and allow students to smell and touch it. Some "super-smellers" may be completely disgusted; be sure to respect their aversion. Spread the newspapers generously onto a desk at the front of the room. Try to make a performance out of cutting open the durian. It will take a hearty stab to breech the thick skin. After making a 6–7 in incision down the center, you should be able to put both hands inside the durian and rip the shell the rest of the way (warning: the spikes are sharp!). You now will have two halves containing three to four compartments of the fruit. Dish the fruit into the cups as students line up for a taste. (I typically get only about a third of students willing to try it.)

Conclusion

The goal of this chapter was to give you some ideas that do not always appear in textbooks for research projects, lab assignments, and in-class demonstrations that illuminate the role culture plays in the process of perception. Remember that not all of the demonstrations are cross-cultural per se, but they can be used to introduce discussion of cross-cultural topics. Two important things that I have learned in more than 20 years of teaching are that (a) a story makes it better and (b) if you are not excited about teaching it, the students are not going to be excited about learning it. Take advantage of the story – and make it personal if you can. Everyone is a bit more engaged when information comes in the form of a story, and if you can incorporate yourself (through personal experience), students will get to know you better and become more comfortable. It's okay to embellish a story or two (take the durian weapon as an example).

In conclusion, the main point we want to get across to students is not just that there exist cultural differences in sensation and perception, but also that culture shapes how we sense and interpret the world around us. We should try to reframe the entire issue from "'look how different we are," to "look how similar we are," even as culture contributes to our uniqueness.

References

Bruce, C. J., Desimone, R., & Gross, C. G. (1981). Visual properties of neurons in a polysensory area in superior temporal sulcus of the macaque. *Journal of Neurophysiology*, *46*(2), 369–384. doi: 10.1152/jn.1981.46.2.369.

Deutsch, D., Henthorn, T., Marvin, E., & Xu, H. (2006). Absolute pitch among American and Chinese conservatory students: Prevalence differences, and evidence for a speech-related critical period. *Journal of the Acoustical Society of America*, *119*, 719–722. doi:10.1121/1.2151799

Gislén, A., Dacke, M., Kröger, R. H., Abrahamsson, M., Nilsson, D., & Warrant, E. J. (2003). Superior underwater vision in a human population of sea gypsies. *Current Biology*, *13*, 833–836. doi:10.1016/S0960-9822(03) 00290-2

Gislén, A., Warrant, E. J., Dacke, M., & Kröger, R. H. (2006). Visual training improves underwater vision in children. *Vision Research*, *46*, 3443–3450. doi:10.1016/j.visres.2006.05.004

Handwerk, B. (2004, May). Sea gypsies of Asia boast "incredible" underwater vision. Retrieved from http://news.nationalgeographic.com/news/2004/05/0514_040514_seagypsies.html

Healthline. (2016, September 30). *Is Gymnema the future of diabetes treatment?* Retrieved from www.healthline.com/health/diabetes/gymnema-future-treatment

Hubel, D. H., & Wiesel, T. N. (1959). Receptive fields of single neurons in the cat's striate cortex. *Journal of Physiology*, *148*, 574–591. doi:10.1113/jphysiol.1959.sp006308

Kanetkar, P., Singhai, R., & Kamat, M. (2007). Gymnema sylvestre: A memoir. *Journal of Clinical Biochemistry and Nutrition*, *41*(2), 77–81. doi:10.3164/jcbn.2007010

Keith, K. D. (Ed.). (2011). *Cross-cultural psychology: Contemporary themes and perspectives*. Chichester: Wiley-Blackwell.

Lindemann, B., Ogiwara, Y., & Ninomiya, Y. (2002, November). The discovery of umami. *Chemical Senses, 27*(9), 843–844. doi:10.1093/chemse/27.9.843

Masuda, T., Gonzalez, R., Kwan, L., & Nisbett, R. E. (2008). Culture and aesthetic preference: Comparing the attention to context of East Asians and Americans. *Personality and Social Psychology Bulletin, 34,* 1260–1275. doi:10.1177/0146167208320555

McDaniel, E. R., & Andersen, P. A. (1998). Intercultural variations in tactile communication. *Journal of Nonverbal Communication, 22,* 59–75. doi:10.1023/A:1022952509743

Melzak, R. (1973). *The puzzle of pain.* New York, NY: Basic Books.

Munter, M. (1993). Cross-cultural communication for managers. *Business Horizons, 36*(3), 69–78. doi:10.1016/S0007-6813(05)80152-1

Phillips, W. L. (2011). Cross-cultural differences in visual perception of color, illusions, depth, and pictures. In K. D. Keith (Ed.), *Cross-cultural psychology: Contemporary themes and perspectives* (pp. 160–180). Chichester: Wiley-Blackwell.

Rosch, E. H. (1973). Natural categories. *Cognitive Psychology, 4,* 328–350. doi:10.1016/0010-0285(73)90017-0

Segall, M. H., Campbell, D. T., & Herskovits, M. J. (1966). *The effects of culture on perception.* Indianapolis, IN: Bobbs-Merrill.

Slobodin, R. (1978). *W. H. R. Rivers.* New York, NY: Columbia University Press.

Thacker, A. (2013, June 10). FYI: Are people born with a tolerance for spicy food? Retrieved from www.popsci.com/science/article/2013-06/fyi-are-people-born-tolerance-spicy-food

Development

Classic developmental theories have achieved the status of universals in many classrooms over the years. Yet contemporary research has shown us the extent to which some aspects of these theories are context dependent, and scholars have reached out, beyond the traditional Western perspectives, to the work of researchers from other cultural perspectives. In addition to questioning the universality of the traditional theories, we might also ask whether our developmental language is culture dependent; for example, what does the term *preschooler* mean in a culture that does not have the kind of structured approach to schooling that exists in the United States? In Chapter 10, Molitor presents a contemporary perspective on the teaching of child development.

Although students may often think of adolescence as a phenomenon defined by biological markers, Gibbons and Poelker (Chapter 12) discuss the social/cultural construction of adolescence. It may also surprise students to learn that the vast majority of the world's adolescents live in so-called developing countries – often countries with cultural contexts very different from those of industrialized Western countries. Students may arrive to the class believing common misconceptions or myths about adolescence, and this chapter can help teachers develop approaches that will clarify their understanding. And, as in Chapter 8, here too we see the interplay between biology and culture, as adolescents may differ cross-culturally in their development.

CHAPTER 10

Teaching Child Development from a Cross-Cultural Perspective

Adriana Molitor

Developmental psychology instructors within the United States can readily forget that children around the world often grow up in very different circumstances than those we regularly witness during our modern, everyday lives. We may colloquially refer to young children as preschoolers or think of achievement motivation as encompassing college degree goals. Accordingly, it is no surprise that many of our students will not envision the cultural diversity that exists worldwide among developing children unless they are prompted to reflect on it. Many contemporary North American notions such as preschool, day care, supervised extracurricular activities, or electronic media are not a part of a child's life in some cultures around the world.

Jensen Arnett and Maynard (2013) pointed out that economically developed countries house fewer than 20 percent of the world's population; thus, many children around the globe do not even complete primary education and only half go on to receive any secondary schooling (United Nations Development Programme, 2006). Unfortunately, the majority of psychological studies, including those that address child development, typically sample from a limited slice of the world's population – those living in societies that some argue are WEIRD (Western, educated, industrialized, rich, and democratic; Henrich, Heine, & Norenzayan, 2010).

This limited cultural focus and population sampling prevents our field from fully knowing about the generalizability of many findings and theories concerning children or the variability in development that may exist but is not observed within our WEIRD slice of the world (Berry, Poortinga, Segall, & Dasen, 2002; Gardiner & Kosmitzki, 2011). The result usually is that our textbooks and lectures teach about child development from a narrow cultural perspective and insufficiently prompt important reflection about the extent to which we are encountering universal processes or phenomena. Nevertheless, scholars during the last half-century have conducted a sufficient number of cross-cultural studies of children to broaden our typically narrow view of child development and help us gain and share greater knowledge of a universal developmental psychology applicable to children across cultures (Berry et al., 2002; Gardiner & Kosmitzki, 2011). A review and discussion of cross-cultural child development research additionally can help students become more informed global citizens, obtain improved understanding of their own culture, and counteract often ethnocentric judgments about what is natural and good that are commonplace when we are culture bound in our views (Bornstein, 2010; Gardiner & Kosmitzki, 2011; Heine, 2012). Importantly, integration of a cultural perspective can aid students in comprehending some of the fundamental concepts that we explore in a standard child development course.

Examples of Concepts Benefitting from Cultural Context

Temperament. Temperament is a topic commonly addressed in most developmental courses. Infant temperament refers to genetically and biologically based individual differences in reactivity and self-regulation that are influenced over time by experience and maturation (Rothbart & Bates, 1998, 2006). In many discussions of temperament, the concept of goodness of fit is presented, yet it is often inadequately appreciated unless a review includes cultures beyond those in North America. Originally conceived by Thomas and Chess (Thomas, Chess, & Birch, 1968, 1970), *goodness of fit* refers to the match or dissonance between a child's temperament and the demands of his or her environment. These psychiatrists and researchers proposed that specific aspects or types of temperament do not necessarily place a young child at risk for later behavioral problems (e.g., irritable, highly negative infants do not necessarily become angry or aggressive children). Rather, Thomas and Chess argued that it is the extent and duration of mismatch between an infant's temperament and environmental demand characteristics that contribute to a risk for problems in later childhood and beyond. To illustrate, we can ask students to imagine two divergent primary caregivers in the United States – one who is comfortable and patient with an irritable infant and one who is distressed and/or insensitive to the same infant irritability. Students then can begin to foresee that the latter dyad will have difficult interactions that potentially lead to problems related to increasing child anger and even externalizing issues.

Yet the concept of goodness of fit can be more fully understood when an instructor points out that temperament preferences typically have differed among cultures and problems might readily ensue when an infant possesses temperamental qualities that contrast with cultural ideals. For example, students often are surprised to consider exuberant, social, smiling temperaments as undesirable at any developmental age or persistent negative emotions as suitable demeanors after infancy, yet Russian culture de-emphasizes positive emotional expressions and instead has a long-standing acceptance of negative affectivity (Gartstein, Slobodskaya, & Kinsht, 2003). One of my former students confirmed that she was rebuked by a tour guide during a recent visit to Russia for waving and smiling at preschool children in an endearing manner. The rebuke specifically disparaged American sentiments about raising children to be charming. Thus, within Russian culture, offspring with less sociable, affectively positive tendencies may actually be less out of step with their caregivers and peers, and their subsequent interactions may be more synchronous with social partners than otherwise anticipated from an American perspective.

In another example of poor goodness of fit, researchers have established that behaviorally inhibited (shy, anxious, reactive) infants and toddlers are frequently at pronounced risk in the United States and similar Western cultures for a host of later developmental problems such as peer rejection and internalizing disorders because shy-inhibited behaviors give the impression of social incompetence in cultures that value competiveness, confidence, and assertiveness (Chen, 2011; Rubin, Coplan, & Bowker, 2009). Yet students further comprehend the notion of dissonance versus matching of environmental demands when an instructor explains that behavioral inhibition has not customarily led to developmental problems among children in East Asian cultures such as China or Korea because these cultures traditionally have valued reserved behavior and therefore interpret young children with shy tendencies to be well behaved and mature (Chen, 2011; Chen, DeSouza, Chen, & Wang, 2006).

Interestingly, as China's urban centers during the twenty-first century increasingly reflect a competitive market economy, peers and adults in major cities are placing greater value on assertiveness. Thus, unlike their traditional rural counterparts, urban Chinese children with shy-inhibited temperaments now are facing increased problems in social and psychological adjustment (Chen, 2011; Chen, Cen, Li, & He, 2005; Chen, Wang, & Cao, 2011; Yang, Chen, & Wang, 2015).

Parenting styles. Students also may misunderstand elements of effective parenting styles if only American middle-class culture is reviewed. Diana Baumrind (1968, 1971) long ago popularized the distinction between authoritative and authoritarian parenting based on two important dimensions: warmth/acceptance and demandingness/control. Researchers continue to use this framework extensively for understanding parenting, and although scholars have modestly adapted it (Baumrind, 2013; Grolnick & Pomerantz, 2009; Maccoby & Martin, 1983; Skinner, Johnson, & Snyder 2005), most generally agree that warmth/acceptance is an important foundation for caregiving worldwide (Rohner, 1986, 1994; Rohner & Khaleque, 2013; Skinner et al., 2005). This dimension captures the ways parents express love and concern for their children. Unfortunately, some students can view this dimension through a narrow perspective that mostly reflects modern middle-class American culture, often thinking of it as expressed via robust physical displays of affection (e.g., hugs), verbal declarations (e.g., "I love you"), or effusive praise (e.g., "That was great" or "You're so smart").

Students need help placing these examples of warmth/acceptance in their proper context and might otherwise view parents from other cultures as cold or unloving. When students recall that we live in an individualistic versus collectivist culture where interpersonal communication rules take place in a low- versus high-context forum (Hall, 1976; Triandis, 1994), they begin to recognize that overt displays may be elicited from parents because our society does not share a unified implicit code for extracting meaning from subtle cues. Rohner (1994) vividly recounted when he first learned that parents in West Bengal peeled and seeded an orange for their child as a strong symbolic message of parental affection and approval. This example reminds students and instructors alike that there are diverse ways to express the parenting dimension of warmth. Within a homogeneous, high-context culture such as the traditional West Bengal setting encountered by Rohner, parental means of communication can be inconspicuous to cultural outsiders, yet perfectly understood by local children. By comparison, our low-context culture might require more explicit expressions of warmth because we have fewer agreed upon rules of communicating it; as such, it otherwise may go unnoticed by our children.

Integrating cultural research also can increase students' understanding of beneficial versus problematic elements of parenting style. For example, middle-class American parents frequently rely on praise to communicate warmth and approval; it is a well-established aspect of the authoritative parenting profile. Yet many cultures do not use praise as a means to express warmth (Jensen Arnett & Maynard, 2013). Moreover, American parental praise tends to be what Carol Dweck and her colleagues have referred to as generic, person-praise (e.g., "You're such a good dancer") that implies a stable personal quality instead of specific, process-praise that implies malleable behavior (e.g., "You really knew those dance steps"; Cimpian, Arce, Markman, & Dweck, 2007; Kamins & Dweck, 1999). As a result, Dweck and colleagues have found that American children are quite susceptible to forming a fixed mind-set that reduces future efforts to achieve improvement (Blackwell, Trzesniewski, & Dweck, 2007; Dweck, 2006, 2015; Rattan, Good, & Dweck, 2012). In contrast, within East Asian and South Asian cultures that do customarily use praise to communicate warmth/acceptance, adults and children both tend to share a growth mind-set that believes effort can incrementally improve many abilities, even intelligence (Rattan, Savani, Naidu, & Dweck, 2012).

Teaching Approach

Several instructional steps prepare students with a necessary orientation prior to incorporating cultural work into a child development course. These steps involve providing students with background concepts, helping students understand research limitations and approaches, and providing students with a framework for how culture infuses itself into the lives of children, affecting developmental processes and phenomena that psychologists typically try to understand. Instructors will vary in the amount of detail they choose to expound upon, but even minimal coverage of each orientation topic will provide students with a foundation for understanding studies presented by the instructor and for exploring cross-cultural child development research on their own.

The first step in orienting students to cross-cultural perspectives in child development is for instructors to briefly explain what is meant by culture and, although scholars do not completely agree upon definitions, how to distinguish this concept from related terms such as race or ethnicity. Similarly, students benefit from clarification of basic concepts from cultural studies such as *emic, etic, macroculture, worldview, bicultural,* and *multicultural* if they have not had prior exposure to this lexicon. Many textbooks in cross-cultural psychology or multicultural education address useful vocabulary in their introductory chapters, and students should obtain some understanding of how scholars differentiate among basic terms in order to aid in the precision of everyone's thinking. Most importantly, students appreciate a reminder that there is inherent diversity within many cultures, especially those with complex variation in ecologies or economic structure. Thus, using a single label to describe a wide-ranging group of individuals (e.g., "Italian," "Chinese") can feel much like stereotyping and is inherently overgeneralizing.

Preemptively acknowledging this pervasive problem of overgeneralization helps students view findings with appropriate caution. Related to the issue of using broad cultural groupings, instructors also should point out the dynamic nature of cultures. As cultures are constantly evolving, any trends or comparisons identified by researchers capture a single point in time and may not wholly reflect that same culture in the past or future. Heine (2012) elaborated extensively on cultural evolution and can provide a useful elucidation on the topic as instructors plan an orientation for their students.

As a second step in properly preparing students to review cross-cultural work in child development, instructors should address methodological issues and approaches unique to cross-cultural research. Although the body of cross-cultural studies in psychology is large and growing robustly, students need to be aware that these cross-cultural comparisons are often between industrialized cultures, particularly North Americans versus East Asians, primarily because psychologists pursuing such contrasts have fewer concerns about methodological appropriateness and equivalence, comparable meaning, implicit assumptions and knowledge, or differences in experimental control when their studies are confined to industrialized cultures (Heine, 2012). An instructor's review of these concerns makes students aware that psychologists often encounter immediate and import-ant limitations to their standardized tools and procedures when attempting to conduct primary research in some cultures. Thus, many of the world's cultures and children are not represented in the body of modern developmental psychology.

For a broader look into the development of children in non-industrialized or remote cultures, instructors and students should be open to reviewing anthropological studies. Students need to be aware of differ-ences in methodological approaches of modern developmental psychology (e.g., experimental paradigms, standardized measures) and its goals (e.g., objectivity, quantifiability; Gardiner & Kosmitzki, 2011) versus method-ology customarily used in cultural anthropology (e.g., ethnographies, qualitative analyses of narratives). Coverage of methodology should include strengths and problematic issues associated with the research approaches of each discipline. Preparing students for methodological dif-ferences will help them gain appropriate perspective when critiquing findings. For example, students should not expect to see large sample sizes in an in-depth qualitative linguistic analysis, but still can gain valuable insight into the development of children from this type of cultural work. Students also may notice increasing methodological overlap as well as increasing employment of multimethod techniques from each discipline (Gardiner & Kosmitzki, 2011; see also Ember & Ember, 2009).

Finally, students need an overarching framework for thinking about cultural influences. One common approach is to review Bronfenbrenner's ecological systems theory. Covered in most standard developmental textbooks, this framework places a child's development in a series of nested systems (e.g., microsystem, mesosystem, exosystem, macrosystem, and chronosystem) (Bronfenbrenner, 1977, 2005; Bronfenbrenner & Morris, 1998). The two latter systems help identify cultural ideologies and sociohistorical conditions that affect a child in important ways. Specifically, the macrosystem encompasses the beliefs, values, and customs of a child's culture that influence a child's and family's environments and relationships. The chronosystem captures the importance of timing of environmental events as well as how historical changes and contexts impact an individual's development (Bronfenbrenner, 1977, 2005; Bronfenbrenner & Morris, 1998). Bronfenbrenner's framework allows a flexible view into the multiple layers of influence on child development including, yet well beyond, the immediate parent–child relationship, and thus provides a natural entry point for discussing cultural differences and their effects on children.

Super and Harkness' (1986, 1994, 1997) concept of developmental niche provides a simple framework for understanding the role of culture in children's lives. The psychologist and anthropologist team proposed three interconnected components of culture as a working system to influence children's development. *Settings* encompass features of the daily physical and social environment in which a child resides. These include living spaces, objects, family composition, caretakers, and number and ages of peers. *Customs and practices* refer to normative and individual child-rearing practices within a culture that range from pragmatic parenting strategies (e.g., sleeping, feeding, work, and child care routines) to time-honored rituals (e.g., religious ceremonies, ways to acknowledge symbolic milestones). Practices also include interpersonal socialization experiences such as communication styles, play attitudes, teaching approaches, and disciplinary techniques.

Finally, caretaker psychology encompasses not merely the psychological attributes of a parent but also wider cultural belief systems, particularly shared understandings about children's needs and their development. These include implicit "ethnotheories" about how, when, and why abilities unfold, desired competencies, effective socialization techniques, and ultimate goals for development (Dasen, 2003; Harkness, Mavridis, Liu, & Super, 2015; Harkness & Super, 2006). Most developmental textbooks, even those incorporating cultural perspectives, do not discuss the concept of developmental niche, yet modern psychological researchers use it to address cultural or ethnic differences (e.g., Tamis-LeMonda, Nga-Lam Sze, Fei-Yin Ng, Kahana-Kalman, & Yoshikawa, 2013). Moreover, the framework and elements delineated by Super and Harkness (1986, 1994, 1997) provide students with a relatively accessible representation of how culture tangibly shapes socialization and environmental factors. For advanced courses, instructors may choose to present additional frameworks (e.g., Berry's ecocultural framework; see Berry, 2003) as well as theoretical attempts at their integration (see Dasen, 2003).

Example Teaching Activity

Super and Harkness (1997) argued that a child's development niche is organized as a congruent system; thus, the three components are not merely intended to exhaustively collect different aspects of culture. Rather, the three components work in a nonarbitrary, cohesive way to affirm consistent cultural messages to a developing child (although the system's open nature periodically translates into temporary inconsistencies between components; Harkness, 2002; Harkness, Super, Barry, Zeitlin, & Long, 2009; Super & Harkness, 1997). Students tend to grasp the meanings of each subsystem but not necessarily the overarching principle of coherence or cohesiveness. That is, students often can generate examples of each type of component yet not necessarily recognize systematic connections between them. An activity that helps students move from disconnected to connected subsystems is to have them reflect on the developmental niche of their own childhood and think of aspects from each of the three components (i.e., settings, practices, beliefs/values).

Using three side-by-side columns, students should list as many sample details that they can recall of each component, yet do so in an otherwise unstructured and spontaneous way so no connections are required. Instructors should then follow up with an illustration of the developmental niche as a coordinated system. One illustration by Super and Harkness comes from a comparative study of infants and young children from the United States and the Netherlands (Harkness, 2002; Super, Harkness, van

Tijen, van der Vlugt, Fintelman, & Dijkstra, 1996). These researchers found that Dutch parents shared a belief (i.e., caretaker psychology) that proper rest and schedule regularity ultimately controlled infants' and young children's arousal states, including daytime behavior and sleep quality (e.g., children's difficult behavior was typically attributed to a disrupted schedule, too much excitement, and lack of sleep). Thus, Dutch parents created a quiet, calm environment before and during sleep in order to support children's rest and regularity (e.g., physical and social settings). They also enforced early and strict bedtime schedules that included requiring children to stay in bed until a regulated wake-up time and kept to these schedules diligently (e.g., practices) (Harkness, 2002; Super & Harkness, 1994; Super et al., 1996).

Dutch parents' ethnotheories about the nature of infant sleep not only led to strict sleep management routines but also comparatively less parental stimulation during infants' wakeful moments. Ultimately, compared to their American counterparts, Dutch infants slept an average of 2 hours more per day with less night waking. In this example, there is clear organization among the beliefs, settings, and practices that structure the daily life of these Dutch infants. After offering this illustration and/or others, instructors should ask students to look at the lists they generated and draw lines connecting any examples from each subcomponent that supports a common theme.

Students may then contemplate how their own developmental niche reflected a harmonized system by elaborating on a coordinated aspect of their niche that is reflected within each of the three components. For example, one student with few siblings recognized that her parents enrolled her in preschool not because of a need for child care but because her parents placed a high value on socializing and learning social skills. Her parents also bought a home on a street with many children and scheduled many play dates. The student also recalled that her parents regularly talked to her about her play experiences and even coached her about her own and friends' feelings and perspectives, as well as possible solutions to social conflicts. Thus, what started as three separate lists with seemingly random elements came to be recognized as a coherent pattern imparting consistent cultural messages about the importance of social skills.

Resources

Video: Babies. To stimulate broad or initial interest in cross-cultural perspectives of child development, instructors should turn to visual resources available to the public rather than relying solely on an academic publisher; however, purchases may be required. For example, for a small price, instructors can have students view the documentary *Babies* (79 minutes; Chabat & Balmès, 2009). The film captures ordinary day-to-day as well as milestone moments from the first year of life of four babies: Ponijao in Namibia, Bayarjargal in Mongolia, Mari in Japan, and Hattie in California, United States. The riveting video and audio footage are presented without narration, so that it often feels as if the viewer is a nearby observer. Without commentary, the viewer's attention and mind are free to wander and make connections and contrasts between the lives of these four infants from their birth to their first steps. As a result, the documentary effectively communicates commonalities and dissimilarities in these infants' early development as well as cultures. If viewing occurs outside of a class meeting, instructors can motivate careful watching by asking for a written reflection on one of several possible themes (e.g., features of the babies' lives that a student found surprising, common behaviors that the babies displayed, or striking differences in parental behaviors).

Free materials. In terms of free content, the Internet offers instructors ready access to video segments and pictures of children's lives from throughout the globe. For example, YouTube provides a pictorial series featuring *The Bedrooms of Children around the World* (BuzzFeed Yellow, 2014) based on the book *Where Children Sleep* by photographer James Mollison (2014). This short footage (2:04) offers a striking contrast between children who grow up in cultural communities marked by great wealth versus those encumbered by extreme poverty. A similar pictorial essay by photographer Gabriele Galimberti (2014) titled *Toy Stories* features children around the world with their favorite toys (see www.gabrie legalimberti.com/toy-stories/). The latter series of photos can launch an open-ended discussion about the cultural milieu that the toys reveal. These and other media resources aptly set the tone for addressing cultural perspectives on child development without necessarily exemplifying specific course concepts.

Textbooks. Although many contemporary developmental textbooks incorporate some degree of cross-cultural research, few take an explicitly cultural focus. Several notable exceptions published by Pearson Higher Education are *Lives across Cultures: Cross-Cultural Human Development* by Harry Gardiner and Corinne Kosmitzki (6th ed., 2018), *Human Development: A Cultural Approach* (2nd ed., 2016) by Jeffrey Jensen Arnett, and

Child Development: A Cultural Approach (2nd ed., 2017) by Jeffrey Jensen Arnett and Ashley Maynard.

The text by Gardiner and Kosmitzki (2018) does not attempt to be comprehensive in coverage of developmental content; however, it offers an engaging and fully cultural perspective of child, adolescent, and adult development using a chronological within-topics approach to representative domains (e.g., language and cognition, the family, self and personality development). Instructors can use it as a core text although they likely will wish to supplement chapters with readings of primary research articles or in-depth reviews of particular topics. Alternatively, the textbooks authored by Jensen Arnett offer comprehensive chronological coverage of child development that is comparable to that within many standard texts, yet these texts incorporate cultural research findings liberally throughout each chapter. Supplemental articles can extend the cultural coverage but may not be necessary for lower-division courses. To accompany the Jensen Arnett textbooks, the publisher provides video clips illustrating specific developmental concepts (e.g., stranger anxiety, object permanence, theory of mind) as experienced by children from varying cultures.

Reference materials. An increasing number of publications and reference books can help instructors enhance their own understanding of child development across cultures before preparing their course curriculum and material. Those new to the field of cultural studies should refer to Barbara Rogoff's (2003) *The Cultural Nature of Human Development* for a compelling argument that child development is not universal and simply cannot be studied independently from culture. This seminal book presents research from psychology and anthropology that demonstrates that human development is a cultural process.

Likewise, instructors should consult Marc Bornstein's (2010) *Handbook of Cultural Developmental Science* to acquaint themselves with decades of cross-cultural research in child development. This comprehensive compendium first provides a summary of findings from cross-cultural psychological studies of children sorted into a full range of developmental domains (e.g., cognition, language, emotions, and temperament). The handbook then summarizes cross-cultural child development findings according to different world regions including Central and South America, Africa, Southeast Asia, and India.

Finally, instructors should consult *The Oxford Handbook of Human Development and Culture: An Interdisciplinary Perspective* by Lene Arnett Jensen (2015) for further updates on cross-cultural studies through adolescence, early adulthood, and the complete life span. This handbook blends both universal and cultural perspectives in understanding child and human development by offering an extensive collection of writings representing theoretical and empirical work from various disciplines. Although an instructor may additionally benefit from reviewing cultural chapters within other handbooks (e.g., *Handbook of Attachment, Wiley-Blackwell Handbook of Childhood Social Development, Handbook of Child Psychology and Developmental Science*), the earlier mentioned readings provide a strong foundation for any instructor wanting to obtain essential cultural knowledge on child development prior to preparing course material.

Summary

Studies of children from diverse cultures help students and experts alike to see the full scope of child development. Moreover, cultural research on children enables psychological scientists to further test and delineate the nature of developmental processes and phenomena that have been mostly understood within limited cultural settings. Bornstein (2010, p. xi) rightly claimed, "cultural developmental inquiry ... is critical to exploring and distinguishing cultural uniformity and cultural diversity of biopsychological constructs, structure, functions, and processes."

Mainstream psychologists now increasingly recognize the importance of cultural context to the field of child development, and experts share a common goal to create a more universal developmental psychology applicable to children across cultures (Berry et al., 2002; Gardiner & Kosmitzki, 2011). As a result, a substantial body of cultural developmental research not only exists but also has been commendably summarized for any interested consumer. A number of resources also are available to aid the instructor wishing to offer a more inclusive portrayal of child development. Thus, we might consider the present time an ideal opportunity to incorporate a truly cultural perspective into a child development course.

References

Arnett Jensen, L. (Ed.) (2015). *The Oxford handbook of human development and culture: An interdisciplinary perspective.* New York, NY: Oxford University Press.

Baumrind, D. (1968). Authoritarian vs. authoritative parental control. *Adolescence, 3*(11), 255–272.

   (1971). Current patterns of parental authority. *Developmental Psychology, 4*(1, Pt. 2), 1–103. doi:10.1037/h0030372

(2013). Authoritative parenting revisited: History and current status. In R. E. Larzelere, A. S. Morris, A. W. Harrist, R. E. Larzelere, A. S. Morris, A. W. Harrist (Eds.), *Authoritative parenting: Synthesizing nurturance and discipline for optimal child development* (pp. 11–34). Washington, DC: American Psychological Association. doi:10.1037/13948-002

Berry, J. W. (2003). Ecocultural perspective on human psychological development. In T. S. Saraswathi (Ed.), *Cross-cultural perspectives in human development: Theory, research, and applications* (pp. 51–69). Thousand Oaks, CA: Sage.

Berry, J. W., Poortinga, Y. H., Segall, M. H., & Dasen, P. R. (2002). *Cross-cultural psychology: Research and applications* (2nd ed.). New York, NY: Cambridge University Press.

Blackwell, L. S., Trzesniewski, K. H., & Dweck, C. S. (2007). Implicit theories of intelligence predict achievement across an adolescent transition: A longitudinal study and an intervention. *Child Development, 78,* 246–263. doi: 10.1111/j.1467-8624.2007.00995.x

Bornstein, M. H. (Ed.) (2010). *Handbook of cultural developmental science.* New York, NY: Psychology Press.

Bronfenbrenner, U. (1977). Toward an experimental ecology of human development. *American Psychologist, 32,* 513–531. doi:10.1037/0003-066X.32.7.513

(2005). The bioecological theory of human development. In U. Bronfenbrenner (Ed.), *Making human beings human: Bioecological perspectives on human development* (pp. 3–15). Thousand Oaks, CA: Sage.

Bronfenbrenner, U., & Morris, P. A. (1998). The ecology of developmental processes. In W. Damon (Series Ed.) & R. M. Lerner (Vol. Ed.), *Handbook of child psychology: Vol. 1. Theoretical models of human development* (5th ed., pp. 993–1028). New York, NY: Wiley.

BuzzFeed Yellow (Producer). (2014). *The bedrooms of children around the world* [YouTube video]. Available from www.youtube.com/watch?v=lJx4SkDhh7I

Chabat, A. (Producer), & Balmès, T. (Director). (2009). *Babies* (Motion picture). United States: Focus Features/NBC Universal.

Chen, X. (2011). Culture and children's socioemotional functioning: A contextual-developmental perspective. In K. H. Rubin (Series Ed.) & X. Chen & K. H. Rubin (Vol. Ed.), *Social, emotional, and personality development in context, Vol. 3: Socioemotional development in cultural context* (pp. 29–52). New York, NY: Guilford.

Chen, X., Cen, G., Li, D., & He, Y. (2005). Social functioning and adjustment in Chinese children: The imprint of historical time. *Child Development, 76*(1), 182–195. doi:10.1111/j.1467-8624.2005.00838.x

Chen, X., DeSouza, A., Chen, H., & Wang, L. (2006). Reticent behavior and experiences in peer interactions in Canadian and Chinese children. *Developmental Psychology, 42,* 656–665. doi:10.1037/0012-1649.42.4.656

Chen, X., Wang, L., & Cao, R. (2011). Shyness-sensitivity and unsociability in rural Chinese children: Relations with social, school, and psychological adjustment. *Child Development*, *82* (5), 1531–1543. doi:10.1111/j.1467-8624.2011.01616.x

Cimpian, A., Arce, H.-M. C., Markman, E. M., & Dweck, C. S. (2007). Subtle linguistic cues affect children's motivation. *Psychological Science*, *18*, 314–316. doi:10.1111/j.1467-9280.2007.01896.x

Dasen, P. (2003). Theoretical frameworks in cross-cultural developmental psychology: An attempt at integration. In T. S. Saraswathi (Ed.), *Cross-cultural perspectives in human development: Theory, research, and applications* (pp. 128–165). Thousand Oaks, CA: Sage.

Dweck, C. S. (2006). *Mindset: The new psychology of success.* New York, NY: Random House.

Dweck, C. S. (2015). Growth. *British Journal of Educational Psychology*, *85*(2), 242–245. doi:10.1111/bjep.12072

Ember, C., & Ember, M. (2009). *Cross-cultural research methods* (2nd ed.). New York, NY: Alta Mira.

Galimberti, G. (2014). *Toy stories: Photos of children from around the world and their favorite things.* New York, NY: Abrams.

Gardiner, H. W., & Kosmitzki, C. (2011). *Lives across cultures: Cross-cultural human development* (5th ed.). Boston, MA: Allyn & Bacon/Pearson.

 (2018). *Lives across cultures: Cross-cultural human development* (6th ed.). New York, NY: Pearson.

Gartstein, M., Slobodskaya, H., Kinsht, I. (2003). Cross-cultural differences in temperament in the first year of life: United States of America (US) and Russia. *International Journal of Behavioral Development*, *27*(4), 316–328. doi:10.1080/01650250244000344

Grolnick, W., & Pomerantz, E. (2009). Issues and challenges in studying parental control: Toward a new conceptualization. *Child Development Perspectives*, *3*(3), 173–175. doi:10.1111/j.1750-8606.2009.00101.x

Hall, E. T. (1976). *Beyond culture.* New York, NY: Doubleday.

Harkness, S. (2002). Culture and social development: Explanations and evidence. In P. Smith & C. Hart (Eds.), *Blackwell handbook of childhood social development* (pp. 60–77). Malden, MA: Blackwell.

Harkness, S., Mavridis, C. J., Liu, J. J., & Super, C. (2015). Parental ethnotheories and the development of family relationships in early and middle childhood. In L. Arnett Jensen (Ed.), *The Oxford handbook of human development and culture: An interdisciplinary perspective* (pp. 271–291). New York, NY: Oxford University Press.

Harkness, S., & Super, C. M. (2006). Themes and variations: Parental ethnotheories in Western cultures. In K. H. Rubin & O. B. Chung (Eds.), *Parenting beliefs, behaviors, and parent-child relations: A cross-cultural perspective* (pp. 61–79). New York, NY: Psychology Press.

Harkness, S., Super, C. M., Barry, D., Zeitlin, M., & Long, J. (2009). Assessing the environment of children's learning: The developmental niche in Africa.

In E. Grigorenko (Ed.), *Multicultural psychoeducational assessment* (pp. 133–155). New York, NY: Springer.

Heine, S. J. (2012). *Cultural psychology* (2nd ed.). New York, NY: W.W. Norton.

Henrich, J., Heine, S. J., & Norenzayan, A. (2010). The weirdest people in the world. *Behavioral and Brain Sciences, 33,* 61–83. doi:10.1017/S0140525X0999152X

Jensen Arnett, J. (2016). *Human development: A cultural approach* (2nd ed.). New York, NY: Pearson.

Jensen Arnett, J., & Maynard, A. (2013). *Child development: A cultural approach.* Upper Saddle River, NJ: Pearson.

(2017). *Child development: A cultural approach* (2nd ed.). New York, NY: Pearson.

Kamins, M., & Dweck, C. (1999). Person versus process praise and criticism: Implications for contingent self-worth and coping. *Developmental Psychology, 35,* 835–847. doi:10.1037/0012-1649.35.3.835

Maccoby, E., & Martin, J. (1983). Socialization in the context of the family: Parent-child interaction. In P. H. Mussen (Series Ed.) & E. M. Hetherington (Vol. Ed.), *Handbook of child psychology: Vol. 4. Socialization, personality, and social Development* (4th ed., pp. 1–101). New York, NY: Wiley.

Mollison, J. (2010). *Where children sleep.* London: Chris Boot.

Rattan, A., Good, C., & Dweck, C. S. (2012). "It's ok – not everyone can be good at math": Instructors with an entity theory comfort (and demotivate) students. *Journal of Experimental Social Psychology, 48,* 731–737. doi:10.1016/j.jesp.2011.12.012

Rattan, A., Savani, K., Naidu, N. R., & Dweck, C. S. (2012). Can everyone become highly intelligent? Cultural differences in and societal consequences of beliefs about the universal potential for intelligence. *Journal of Personality and Social Psychology, 103*(5), 787–803. doi:10.1037/a0029263

Rogoff, B. (2003). *The cultural nature of human development* (Reprint ed.). New York, NY: Oxford University Press.

Rohner, R. P. (1986). *The warmth dimension: Foundations of parental acceptance-rejection theory.* Thousand Oaks, CA: Sage.

(1994). Patterns of parenting: The warmth dimension in worldwide perspective. In W. Lonner & R. Malpass (Eds.), *Psychology and culture* (pp. 113–120). Boston, MA: Allyn & Bacon.

Rohner, R. P., & Khaleque, A. (2013). Parenting essentials: Parental warmth, behavioral control, and discipline. In K. D. Keith (Ed.), *The encyclopedia of cross-cultural psychology* (Vol. III, pp. 971–976). Chichester: Wiley-Blackwell.

Rothbart, M. K., & Bates, J. E. (1998). Temperament. In W. Damon (Series Ed.) & N. Eisenberg (Vol. Ed.), *Handbook of child psychology: Vol. 3. Social, emotional, and personality development* (5th ed., pp. 105–176). New York, NY: Wiley.

(2006). Temperament. In W. Damon & R. M. Lerner (Series Eds.) & N. Eisenberg (Vol. Ed.), *Handbook of child psychology: Vol. 3. Social, emotional, and personality development* (6th ed., pp. 99–166). New York, NY: Wiley.

Rubin, K. H., Coplan, R., & Bowker, J. (2009). Social withdrawal in childhood. *Annual Review of Psychology*, 60, 141–171. doi:10.1146/annurev.psych.60110707.163642

Skinner, E., Johnson, S., & Snyder, T. (2005). Six dimensions of parenting: A motivational model. *Parenting: Science and Practice*, 5(2), 175–235. doi:10.1207/s15327922par0502_3

Super, C. M., & Harkness, S. (1986). The developmental niche: A conceptualization at the interface of child and culture. *International Journal of Behavioral Development*, 9, 545–570. doi:10.1177/016502548600900409

(1994). The developmental niche and culture. In W. Lonner & R. Malpass (Eds.), *Psychology and culture* (pp. 95–99). Boston, MA: Allyn & Bacon.

(1997). The cultural structuring of child development. In J. Berry, P. Dasen, & T. S. Saraswathi (Eds.), *Handbook of cross-cultural psychology: Vol. 2. Basic processes and human development* (2nd ed., pp. 1–39). Boston, MA: Allyn & Bacon.

Super, C. M., Harkness, S., van Tijen, N., van der Vlugt, E., Fintelman, M., & Dijkstra, J. (1996). The three R's of Dutch childrearing and the socialization of infant arousal. In S. Harkness & C. M. Super (Eds.), *Parents' cultural belief systems: Their origins, expressions, and consequences* (pp. 447–466). New York, NY: Guilford.

Tamis-LeMonda, C., Nga-Lam Sze, I., Fei-Yin Ng, F., Kahana-Kalman, R., & Yoshikawa, H. (2013). Maternal teaching during play with four-year-olds: Variation by ethnicity and family resources. *Merrill-Palmer Quarterly*, 59(3), 361–398. doi:10.1353/mpq.2013.0016

Thomas, A., Chess, S., & Birch, H. (1968). *Temperament and behavior disorders in children*. New York, NY: New York University Press.

(1970). The origin of personality. *Scientific American*, 223(2), 102–109. doi:10.1038/scientificamerican0870-102

Triandis, H. (1994). Culture and social behavior. In W. Lonner & R. Malpass (Eds.), *Psychology and culture* (pp. 169–173). Boston, MA: Allyn & Bacon.

United Nations Development Programme (UNDP). (2006). *Human development report*. New York, NY: Author.

Yang, F., Chen, X., & Wang, L. (2015). Shyness-sensitivity and social, school, and psychological adjustment in urban Chinese children: A four-wave longitudinal study. *Child Development*, 86(6), 86, 1848–1864. doi:10.1111/cdev.12414

Teaching Adolescent Development from an International and Cultural Perspective

Judith L. Gibbons and Katelyn E. Poelker

Although Schlegel and Barry (1991) found nearly universal support for a developmental stage of adolescence among 173 societies, the experiences of adolescents vary widely internationally and cross-culturally. The physical and social environments of teenagers differ both within and between cultures. For many, between-culture differences are the first to come to mind. The goals and daily activities of a middle-class adolescent from the United States living in a big city differ from those of her rural Kenyan peer, a girl such as 15-year-old Lucy who is the caregiver for her three young nieces (UNICEF, 2009). With respect to within-culture diversity, an adolescent boy in Guatemala who comes from a family of wealthy business owners and attends private schools will likely have a much different future than his counterpart, Pizarro, who sells combs, playing cards, and toothbrushes on the streets of Guatemala City (Offit, 2008). The family of the latter child may value education just as much as the former, but its economic circumstances require that 14-year-old Pizarro contribute to the family's subsistence instead of going to school.

In other words, despite common biological markers that trigger the onset of adolescence by inducing puberty, what it means to be an adolescent is largely socially and culturally constructed. The length and content of the stage of adolescence change depending on culture. For the purpose of this chapter, we define *adolescence* as beginning with the biological onset of puberty and concluding with the assumption of adult roles, which are culturally dictated. Therefore, we argue that one cannot fully understand an adolescent's life without first examining the cultural context in which she or he lives.

There are approximately 1.8 billion 10–24-year-olds in the world today (United Nations, 2015), and about 90 percent of them live in majority world (sometimes known as *developing*) countries (UNICEF, 2011). In the world's forty-eight least developed countries, children and teenagers comprise the majority of the population (United Nations, 2015). At no time in our history have there been more young people, suggesting that youth-centered issues are critical, demanding our attention both now and in the future. The issues that need addressing, however, are dependent upon the adolescent's circumstances, varying both between and within cultural contexts.

In our experience, university students have found the study of adolescent development to be rewarding, and their quest for knowledge of this developmental period seems to be enhanced by better understanding culture's important role in shaping adolescents' daily lives. Anecdotally, students have shared that they understand themselves and close others better after spending a semester learning about the transitions adolescents face and the myths that prevail about this developmental stage. Some examples of myths include the storm and stress hypothesis and the inevitable and intense conflict with parents. Many students are eager to apply this knowledge to their respective careers as teachers, counselors, social workers, physical therapists, nurses, and physicians. By recognizing the ways in which culture contributes to adolescent development, students can take this knowledge and appreciation for cultural values and traditions and use it to be more culturally competent and empathic educators, therapists, and healthcare providers.

Key Concepts in Adolescent Development Situated in Cultural Context

A host of concepts would be misunderstood if not situated and explained in a cultural context. We highlight only two of those constructs here. Hall's (1904) storm and stress hypothesis, the notion that adolescence is a period characterized by inevitable conflict with parents, mood swings, and risky behavior, is one example. This view has been perpetuated, in part, by mainstream US media portrayals of adolescence as a time of crisis (Steinberg, 2001). There have been theoretical and empirical challenges to this hypothesis (e.g., Mead, 2001; Steinberg, 2001). Yet the stereotype of adolescents as unruly, disturbed, rebellious, and prone to risk taking persists among parents and mental health professionals in the United States and has consequences for adolescent well-being (Buchanan & Hughes, 2009; Offer, Ostrov, & Howard, 1981). There are within- and between-culture differences, however; adolescent storm and stress tends to be less common in majority countries than in minority countries, and in minority groups in the United States (Arnett, 1999). In China, where the stereotype of adolescence includes filial piety (responsibility and respect toward parents) as well as positive emotions, adolescents stayed in school, unlike in the United States where engagement in school declines through-out adolescence (Qu, Pomerantz, Wang, Cheung, & Cimpian, 2016).

Notably, even physical development, including the age at menarche (a woman's first menstrual period), varies cross-culturally and internationally. This phenomenon reflects both within- and between-country diversity. For example, in the United States, there are ethnic differences in the timing of menarche with African American girls beginning menstruation sooner than European American girls; girls living in South Europe achieve menarche earlier than do their counterparts in North Europe (Karapanou & Papadimitriou, 2010). Although genetics plays a role in this process, other factors like socioeconomic status, nutrition, and environmental stress must also be considered (Chisholm, Quinlivan, Petersen, & Coall, 2005; Karapanou & Papadimitriou, 2010). Beginning in the 1970s in the United States and other minority world countries, the age of menarche across ethnic groups began to decline due to increased access to better healthcare and nutrition – a phenomenon known as the *secular trend* (Eveleth & Tanner, 1990).

In general, despite ethnic differences, girls from families with a higher socioeconomic status reach menarche earlier than those with lower socio-economic backgrounds (Eveleth & Tanner, 1990). Girls with access to better nutrition reach the necessary fat threshold for menstruation sooner than girls who do not receive sufficient nutrients. Consequently, adolescent girls living in situations in which they are chronically undernourished are older when that threshold is reached. In Kenya, a lower middle-income country, age at menarche ranged from 13 to 18 in one study, compared to a range of 11–15 years in Australia, a high income country (Morabia, Costanza, & the World Health Organization, 1998). We argue that menarche is a powerful example for students because of its clarity. Furthermore, it helps unpack the notion that menarche is a universal process. At the basic biological level, the events of menarche and menstruation are similar across cultures, but the precursors and consequences are culturally constructed.

Approaches to Teaching Adolescent Development in Cultural Context

With respect to techniques that can be used throughout the course to promote the inclusion of cultural content in discussions of adolescence, it is critical to put students in a cultural mind-set at the start of the semester. Students should become accustomed to questioning research findings and theories with respect to their applicability to adolescents in other cultures. When the second author taught a course on adolescent psychology recently, she was pleased that, toward the end of the semester, students would ask her to explain whether a particular research finding was applicable to youth outside the United States

One way to set this tone is to use a textbook that regularly incorporates cultural implications into the examples used in the text. We have found Jeffrey Arnett's (2012a) text, *Adolescence and Emerging Adulthood: A Cultural Approach*, to be excellent in helping to achieve this goal. Instead of offsetting cultural content in colorful boxes that are not integrated with the rest of the text, Arnett consistently notes the role that culture plays in development. For example, he explains and includes photographs of the "coming of age" rituals for adolescents that commonly accompany the onset of puberty in many cultures, although they are not often celebrated in the United States.

Another excellent resource is Arnett's (2012b) edited book, *Adolescent Psychology around the World*. Even if instructors elect not to use it as a primary text, the book provides a series of profiles of adolescents spanning four world regions: Africa and the Middle East, Asia, the Americas, and Europe. In most cases, the chapters are authored by scholars from those countries and include topics such as how the period of adolescence is defined, education, work, religion, gender, the media, and unique issues for adolescents in that cultural context. A list of further readings is provided at the end of each chapter.

A more recent chapter by Poelker and Gibbons (2016) would also be helpful in putting both the instructor and the students in a cultural mindset. It highlights how culture influences all aspects of adolescents' lives from whether they are able to continue to attend school to how they spend their leisure time.

Use of Poignant Examples

We find the use of clear, vivid examples to be a powerful tool to illustrate the magnitude of culture's impact. They are especially powerful for students who have little exposure to other cultural groups or who are not well traveled.

One such example is the use of mobile or cell phones. Mobile phone use is widespread around the world among adolescents and young adults. In the United States, 85 percent of young adults (including late adolescents) have smart phones (Pew Research Center, 2015). Along with using the phones to seek information such as regarding health, perform online banking, text with friends, and look for a job, late adolescents report using their phones to avoid boredom or to ignore others around them. For young cattle herders in Kenya, a cell phone is most useful for finding good grazing sites and avoiding park authorities (Butt, 2015). Late adolescents and emerging adults in Ghana, on the other hand, use cell phones primarily for entertainment, such as listening to music (Akanferi, A. A., Aziale, L. K., & Asampana, I. 2014). In India, many worry that cell phone use has become an addiction (Nehra, Kate, Grover, Khehra, & Basu, 2012). Thus, cell phone use does not serve the same purposes or have the same developmental implications for adolescents and youth in different cultural settings.

Compelling examples of how adolescents' lives differ can also be gleaned from the ethnographic literature. The Harvard Adolescence Series includes studies of teenagers from urban Morocco, Nigerian Ijo societies, Aboriginal communities in Australia, and Inuit communities in Canada (Burbank, 1988; Condon, 1987; Davis & Davis, 1989; Hollos & Leis, 1989). For example, in Morocco, adolescents must learn *aql*, the ability to navigate social situations smoothly and responsibly. On the other hand, Inuit adolescents have a great deal of autonomy and authority in their daily lives; they often determine their family's sleeping arrangements, reserving individual rooms for themselves, and allocating other rooms to be shared by their parents and younger siblings. Additional ethnographic reports can be found about adolescents in Pacific Island societies (Herdt & Leavitt, 1998), Maori communities in New Zealand (Ausubel, 1959), urban Japan (White, 1994), and among Mescalero Apaches (Farrer, 1987).

Cultural Self-Study

One activity to orient students to the powerful implications of culture in adolescents' lives is to encourage them to examine their own cultural identities. We have used a cultural self-study exercise based on Weigl (2009) in which students reflect on how their own cultural backgrounds, values, and worldviews shape their attitudes and behaviors. This exercise has been particularly powerful for students who belong to majority groups in the United States and do not believe they carry a culture. In other words, they are like fish who do not recognize that they are in water. After reflecting upon how their own beliefs and worldviews have been influenced by their parents and values perpetuated in their homes and communities, students are better able to grasp the undeniable ways that culture shapes who we are.

BaFá BaFá Simulation

The BaFá BaFá simulation is an efficacious exercise that promotes active learning and intercultural understanding (Sullivan & Duplaga, 1997). Students are randomly divided into two groups – the Alphas and the Betas (Simulation Training Systems, 2016). They come to learn through experience that the Alpha culture promotes patriarchy, collectivistic values, and ingroup/outgroup thinking. The Beta culture, in contrast, is highly competitive and promotes an individualistic approach to interactions. The Betas also speak a foreign language. As students work through the exercise, they are tasked with learning the culture's rules and practices through scouts and visits, but without asking directly. Stereotypes and misunderstandings abound as the two cultures interact with one another. After the simulation ends, both the Alphas and the Betas reconvene to have a powerful discussion, facilitated by the course instructor, about the influence of our cultural groups in our daily lives and on our everyday decisions and interactions with others.

Resource Distribution Activity

Another impactful exercise is one concerning unequal resource distribution (Gibbons, 2010). Students are randomly divided into four groups. Each group's task is to construct a series of objects (e.g., a 3-in by 3-in square of white paper, a paper chain with four links each made from a different color paper) using only the materials inside the envelopes they are given. They are, however, allowed to talk with other groups and negotiate for supplies as needed. When the first group finishes, the instructor verifies that the group has indeed produced each of the objects to the correct specifications and then interviews the winning team as though they have just won a major athletic competition. Winners often explain their success by saying that they had good teamwork or that they were creative. After the winners have had a chance to "explain" their victory, the other groups are asked to explain why that group won. The nonwinning groups quickly (and accurately) explain that the winners had access to a key tool that was necessary to complete almost all of the tasks – a ruler. The groups are then asked to create a team name that describes the efforts of the other groups and their own team in the game. The discussion that ensues focuses on stereotypes (based on the team names they assigned to the groups), behavioral differences (i.e., negotiating behavior), and emotions.

Although originally implemented in a psychology of women course, this exercise is an engaging activity for students that reveals the implications of access to resources, particularly for members of marginalized groups. In a course on adolescent development, the conversation could focus on what this distribution might mean for adolescents living in difficult circumstances and for their access to education, quality healthcare, and nutrition. It could also be applied to discussions of gender, particularly regarding opportunities that may be more readily available to adolescent boys compared to adolescent girls in some cultures. More specifically, this exercise could be a powerful illustration of the concept that social worlds often broaden for boys during adolescence whereas they contract for many adolescent girls (Mensch, Bruce, & Greene, 1998).

Rewriting the Textbook

Although Arnett (2012a) does a superior job of incorporating cultural content into his text on adolescent development, not all textbook authors readily discuss cultural influences on development. To help students both recognize and correct this shortcoming, instructors can provide students with textbook passages that have been written without mention of cultural or international data (Goldstein, 2007). Students are then tasked with rewriting that section of the text so that it includes a cultural perspective. One advantage of this exercise is its flexibility. For instance, instructors could assign it more than once throughout the semester and the assignment could be completed individually or in small groups. Instructors also dictate the length of passage chosen from the text, with longer passages presumably more challenging than shorter ones. Furthermore, students could rewrite the passage in class with information from the lecture or their own experiences, or they could be required to conduct a literature search outside of class and incorporate empirical references into their revised passage. If this activity is assigned more than once, students could also compile their textbook rewrites into a writing portfolio at the end of the semester.

Three Developmental Domains

In teaching adolescent development, we have typically structured the course around three developmental domains: (a) biological/physical development, (b) cognitive development, and (c) socioemotional development. The domains are presented to students in that order with the biological/physical and cognitive domains taking up approximately the first half of the semester and the socioemotional domain spanning the remaining half. Of course, there are many ways to present this material that foster student engagement, and this approach represents only one of many strategies. Throughout this chapter, we will refer to those three domains of development and will present topics according to that framework.

The Physical Domain

The factors that pose risks to adolescents' physical well-being are intertwined; they include poverty, natural disasters, conflict, female gender, and threats to sexual and reproductive health. On the other hand, adolescents living in difficult conditions often show remarkable individual and collective resilience.

Menarche. As described, menarche is useful to illustrate the cultural variation in biological development during adolescence due to the role that access to nutritious food and quality healthcare play in preparing an adolescent girl's body for menstruation (Chisholm et al., 2005). For many girls, menarche is the formal start of puberty and depending on the girl's circumstances, can bring a series of challenges with respect to school attendance. For adolescent girls in Bangladesh, their schools did not have sufficient lavatory facilities to allow them to continue attending school while they were menstruating (UNICEF, 2013). When school administrators noticed a decline in the attendance in their adolescent female students (at the rate of 48 percent over 7 years), they took action to make the lavatory facilities better able to suit the needs of the 1,400 students. Administrators and volunteers have also received training on how to discuss and manage girls' menstruation, providing both emotional and material support.

Introducing university students to coming of age ceremonies, like the Latin American *quinceañera* tradition for 15-year-old girls, is a way in which instructors can reveal overlap in the three developmental domains by illustrating the social consequences of puberty in many adolescent cultures. As noted, Arnett (2012a) provides some vivid examples, and Price and Crapo (2002) have a short reading on those ceremonies for adolescent girls. Students can then be challenged to compare and contrast those traditions with more informal coming of age milestones in their own cultures and experiences.

Poverty. Poverty is a major stress for many adolescents around the world. In 2008, about 42 percent of the world's youth lived in poverty (on less than $2 per day), including 22 percent who lived in severe poverty (on less than $1 per day; Advocates for Youth, 2008). In Latin America in 2013, rates of poverty among young people were similar (40 percent; Pan American Health Organization, 2013). Poverty has severe consequences for adolescents. Teenagers who live in conditions of scarcity are more likely to drop out of school, either because parents cannot afford books, school uniforms, and supplies, or because the adolescent's labor is needed. One in five of the world's adolescents is out of school, sometimes pursuing a job (UNICEF, 2011). Even youth who work at jobs are likely to lack resources; more than one-third of working youth live on less than $2 per day (International Labour Organization, 2015). Although we tend to think of adolescents as being digitally connected, poverty impairs those opportunities as well. Poor youth have much less access to technology and the knowledge it affords than do wealthier young people (UNFPA, 2014).

"Poverty also exacerbates the exposure of young people to a range of human rights violations such as early and forced marriage, and sexual violence and coercion" (UNFPA, 2014, p. 43). Girls may be forced into prostitution. Access to and knowledge about healthcare can be impacted by poverty. For example, adolescents living in poverty are less likely to be informed about HIV than are wealthier teens (UNICEF, 2014). Worldwide, fewer than 20 percent of adolescent girls have knowledge about HIV and its transmission, yet young women face the highest risk of infection of any demographic group (UNICEF, 2014).

There are a number of resources that faculty can tap to highlight the pervasive effects of poverty. The exercise described about unequal resources (Gibbons, 2010) can be used to explore some of the psychological experiences of living without adequate resources. There is also a compelling online game, SPENT (Urban Ministries of Durham, 2011) that highlights the difficulty of surviving with a low income. Although aimed at adults in the United States, it is effective in showing the painful choices that low-income people have to make. For example, would you rather ignore your toothache or send your child to a birthday party without a present? In addition, UNICEF (2014) has provided a teaching unit based on the life of Shasha, a 14-year-old girl living in a tent for earthquake survivors in Haiti. The teaching unit, designed for high school teachers, includes provocative discussion questions and could be adapted for a university course.

Sexual and reproductive health. Komal, a 16-old-girl in India, loved school and dreamed of attending university but was forced by her parents to marry. Instead of continuing in school, she found herself quickly pregnant and confined to the home. She hopes things will be better for her daughter (UNFPA, 2013). Guadelupe, 16 years old and living in Mexico, had dropped out of school to address family problems, and found herself pregnant with her boyfriend's child. They now live together with their 1-year-old son in the house of the boyfriend's father (Stern, 2002).

Issues related to sexuality and reproductive health often come to the fore during adolescence. Sexual health risks are closely linked to other factors such as poverty, lack of access to education, child marriage, marginalization, and gender. Adolescent girls in majority world countries are more likely than those from the minority world to become mothers; in fact, 95 percent of births to adolescents occur in developing countries (UNFPA, 2013).

Adolescent motherhood (within or outside of marriage) has serious consequences (UNFPA, 2013). Complications of childbirth are a leading cause of death for adolescent girls. Physically immature adolescent girls may suffer long-term and debilitating complications of giving birth, such as obstetric fistula. Pregnant girls may also be at risk for unsafe abortions, which are more likely to lead to physical complications for adolescents than for adult women. Both adolescent boys and girls may contract sexually transmitted diseases, including HIV. In addition, babies born to young girls are likely to suffer a variety of health problems. Importantly, adolescent mothers are less likely to continue in school and more likely to live lives of poverty compared to women who delay childbearing. Coercive sex is not uncommon and can lead not only to pregnancy and sexually transmitted diseases, but also to psychological disorders such as depression and anxiety (Hindin & Fatusi, 2009; United Nations, 2012). Although girls suffer more consequences than do boys from early pregnancy, boys, like Guadelupe's boyfriend, who become fathers at a young age, also suffer social repercussions (Kato-Wallace, Barker, Sharafi, Mora, & Lauro, 2016). The economic cost to nations of girls leaving school early is also significant.

Disasters. Natural disasters, such as hurricanes, earthquakes, floods, tsunamis, and volcanic eruptions, are common in much of the world. People living in poor economic conditions and who are likely to have inadequate or poorly constructed shelter are more susceptible to the negative consequences of disasters. Children are more likely than adults to be injured or die from disasters. In addition, adolescent girls are vulnerable to trafficking and child marriage following disasters (United Nations Children's Fund, 2016). Thus, disasters unequally affect those already living in poverty and groups, such as adolescent girls, who are already vulnerable.

Adolescents also demonstrate awe-inspiring resourcefulness and resilience. They use those skills both for their own survival after disasters and to help others. Victor Israelsson was a Swedish adolescent who lost his entire family in the 2004 tsunami in the Indian Ocean. Yet today, he shows the post-traumatic growth and maturity that sometimes come from facing a serious trauma (Rafowitz, 2016). Youth resourcefulness has also been harnessed for assisting others in recovery following natural disasters. For example, after the 2004 tsunami, young people from around the world mobilized, using their creativity to offer help and provide solutions to those affected. After expressing their own shock and despair, they offered first support and then practical suggestions. Lucy, age 17 from Romania wrote, "Start some online courses with teachers all around the world (online volunteers) and learn because many schools from South Asia were destroyed and children and young people have no place where to go, they are isolated and lonely and can't continue their classes for the moment" (UNICEF, 2005, p. 10).

Conflict. Adolescents living in regions of armed conflict are vulnerable to injury, death, and exploitation. They may become separated from their parents and other family members. Armed conflict often disrupts schooling. Enrollment in secondary education is 20 percent lower in conflict-ridden countries and even lower for girls than for boys (Alam, Warren, & Applebaum, 2016; United Nations, 2015). As for most risks, the burden falls unequally on the poor and the marginalized. Adolescent boys are often recruited as child soldiers; girls may be trafficked or sold as "wives" of soldiers. Concy, a 14-year-old girl, was abducted into the Lord's Resistance Army (LRA) in Uganda and taken to Sudan. There she was given to a man who had killed his previous female partner. A.A., at 14 years of age, became separated from his parents during armed conflict. He voluntarily offered his help to the army, where he first served as a checkpoint attendant and then as a fighter. He became known as "Nasty Killer" for his violence and mutilation of victims (Action for the Rights of Children, 2002).

An article about child soldiers provides some insight into why adolescents who are poor or marginalized are vulnerable to becoming soldiers as well as developmental issues that might make participation in war and conflict attractive to them (Action for the Rights of Children, 2002). An exercise in Goldstein (2007) can also be used to help students understand the psychological needs that an army or rebel group might meet for teenagers caught up in conflict.

The Cognitive Domain

There is great variability internationally regarding adolescents' school attendance, and secondary school enrollment rates are considerably lower than those for primary school (UNICEF, 2011). A UNICEF (2012) report on progress for children revealed that there are 531 million adolescents (about 60 percent of adolescents in 2012) attending secondary school, which represents a significant increase from the 196 million in 1976. Furthermore, those adolescents not enrolled in school around the world come from the most disadvantaged and oppressed groups (Global Partnership for Education, 2014). Girls are overrepresented among out-of-school adolescents, at least in part because many girls do not have access to adequate restrooms during menstruation (Global Partnership for Education, 2014; UNICEF, 2013). Other barriers to school attendance are varied (e.g., inability to pay school fees, reliance on adolescent's work wages); unfortunately, until such challenges are better addressed, students' matriculation from primary to secondary school will likely remain problematic (Poelker & Gibbons, 2016).

Secondary school enrollment statistics have implications for Piaget's (1972) theory of cognitive development, as formal operational thinking, the highest level in his theory, is associated with educational level (Cole, 1996). Formal operational thinking, according to Piaget (1972), is the ability to think abstractly and to solve problems with multiple variables. Although the sequence of Piaget's stages may be universal, many adolescents are at a disadvantage with respect to reaching the formal operational stage, in large part because they have not received sufficient schooling (Cole, 1996; Dasen, 1972). This may not reflect their cognitive ability, but instead an inherent bias in Piaget's theory in that it reflects the developmental patterns of youth who consistently attended school.

Many students may erroneously think that a theory like Piaget's (1972) could be universally applied, at least in part because it is so well known and widespread. Using Piaget's cognitive development theory as an example of the limitations of psychology's grand theories will hopefully plant a seed of skepticism in students that transfers to central theories in other areas of psychology. In other words, it may help them to understand the confines of such theories and how they should be applied to other cultures with caution.

Giving students the opportunity to complete different types of intelligence tests is also a powerful way to explain how culture is related to intelligence and cognitive ability. Warren (2006) detailed a series of activities that reveal how both language and culture influence intelligence test scores. In one exercise, without any explanation or extra assistance, monolingual university students are asked to complete an intelligence test in Spanish. In another, the test is composed of items that rely on extensive cultural knowledge for correct answers (e.g., "One meter equals how many centimeters?" and "How many disciples did Jesus have?"). The first reflects the country in which one lives and the second is related to religion. After students try to answer the questions, instructors facilitate a discussion about which cultural factor is highlighted in the item and how that factor may put others at a disadvantage. For example, a student in France is likely to have an easier time answering the metric question than one in the United States, and a Christian will be more readily able to respond that Jesus had twelve disciples as opposed to a non-Christian.

Serpell (1993, 2011) has highlighted other cultural elements of schooling and education using examples from his work in rural Zambia. After interviewing parents and school teachers, Serpell concluded that they recognized two types of intelligence (*nzelu*): cleverness (*chenjela*) and social responsibility (*tumikila*). Parents responded that schools promoted the former, because that is the type of intelligence measured by academic tests, without teaching the latter. Parents' concerns stemmed from their worries that children with too much cleverness without a grounding in social responsibility would negatively impact their communities. Thus, Serpell argued, teachers are forced to act as bicultural mediators, advancing the agenda of Western education while maintaining local values and customs. We contend that for many university students, the notion that cultural values could be in conflict with the basic right to getting an education will come as a surprise and could serve as a catalyst for rich conversation. This discussion could be followed by adapting an activity by Goldstein (2007) on home and school fit. Although the activity is written about challenges that younger Hawaiian children face when their familial and cultural backgrounds clash with the demands of their school environment, it could be adapted to reflect adolescents' struggles (as opposed to younger children's).

To help students grasp the diversity of school missions around the world, instructors can ask students to look on the Internet for two school mission statements. Once they have identified them, students can compare and contrast mission statements, noting their similarities and differences. Students can share their results with the class to amplify the underlying message of the assignment – that schools around the world educate young people differently and with different objectives in mind.

One final tool to illustrate the cultural complexities in adolescents' academic experiences is the 54-minute documentary *2 Million Minutes*

(Compton & Heeter, 2008), which chronicles the high school careers of one boy and one girl from each of three countries: the United States, China, and India. Watching this documentary as a class has promoted excellent discussions on the strengths and weaknesses of the US education system, especially in comparison to how other countries approach secondary education and students' matriculation to university. For example, students learn that many of their peers in other countries do not hold part-time jobs during high school because they are so focused on their studies and preparation for national university entrance exams. International students in the class can enrich the conversation by sharing their secondary school experiences in their respective countries, which helps to provide a more balanced view of each approach.

The Socioemotional Domain

Identity and the self. The evolution of the self during adolescence has been a topic of interest to psychologists for decades (Harter, 2012; Rosenberg, 1986). Although adolescent fluctuations in and implications for self-esteem are often the focus of those efforts, here we emphasize adolescents' developments in self-concept. According to Rosenberg (1986), there are five central ways in which the self-concept transforms during adolescence. Those changes include an increased emphasis on psychological and abstract characteristics and a decreased focus on the physical exterior as well as a tendency to see oneself in relation to others (Rosenberg, 1986). While a 7-year-old boy would describe himself as "having a dog named Jake, being a very good soccer player, and liking the color red," his 16-year-old sister would explain that she is a "good daughter, shy in new situations, and a trustworthy friend" (Harter, 2012).

Cross-cultural research on the self indicates that one's cultural background influences the self-concept; such influences are evident during adolescence (Markus & Kitayama, 1991). In individualistic cultures, broadly speaking, the ways we differ from others are celebrated and "the squeaky wheel gets the grease" (Markus & Kitayama, 1991, p. 224). When adolescents from Sri Lanka and the United States were asked to complete a version of the Twenty Statements Test (TST; Kuhn & McPartland, 1954) by completing the prompt "I am . . ." twenty times, there were gender and cultural differences (Stiles, Gibbons, & de Silva, 1996). Girls, regardless of culture, were more likely than boys to describe themselves in relational terms. This type of description was particularly prevalent in younger (ages 11–13) Sri Lankan adolescent girls.

In one specific example highlighted for illustrative purposes, the responses to the "I am" prompt were compared for two 12-year-old girls, one from the United States and the other from Sri Lanka (Gibbons & Stiles, 2004; Stiles et al., 1996). They revealed considerable overlap as well as important differences. The Sri Lankan girl emphasized group membership to a greater degree than her US peer. Although both girls mentioned their families, the Sri Lankan adolescent specifically mentioned her role as a sister to her brother in addition to her school and religious affiliation. Many of the Sri Lankan girls also noted their nationality, which was a far less common occurrence among US youth.

To make this topic more interactive in the classroom, instructors could ask students to complete the TST themselves. After sharing their responses with the class or in small groups, students could hypothesize about how their responses might differ from or parallel those of peers from other cultures. They could also reflect on how their responses to the TST today might have changed since their own adolescence. Using popular sayings from different cultures (e.g., "The nail that stands up gets hammered down") may be a way to engage students in discussion on the topic of how the values of the culture shape the inner self. Markus and Kitayama (1991) provide additional examples of those types of sayings in their article.

Given that globalization continues to affect multiple aspects of adolescents' lives around the world, many young people adopt multiple identities to reflect their multicultural worlds (Jensen, 2003). Thus, adolescents must cope with the battle between tradition and the values perpetuated by globalization. Youth in India and Armenia have reported a rejection of traditional norms related to all facets of their identities, ranging from the foods they eat to arranged marriage (Huntsinger, 2013; Rao et al., 2013). Those choices reveal friction with the values of their parents and grandparents; one's sense of self is impacted by such decisions. Jensen (2003) argued that adolescents act intentionally with respect to their cultural identities, even though it is likely that friction between and among identities may occur. As technological advances continue to facilitate international connections for youth around the world, adolescents and those who care about them must confront the challenges that globalization brings for identity development, the central task of this developmental period (Erikson, 1968).

Adolescents' social worlds. One critical way in which adolescents' lives differ across cultures is how they spend their time. With that said, adolescents appear to spend their days engaged in one of three ways (or a combination thereof): in school, at work, or engaged in leisure activities (Lloyd, Grant, & Ritchie, 2008; Ritchie, Lloyd, & Grant, 2004). In our experience in the classroom, our students, US university students, reported that their own adolescent years were spent doing some of each: learning, working, and relaxing. Unlike Pizarro, the Guatemalan street vendor (Offit, 2008) or Lucy, the Kenyan girl who cared for her nieces (UNICEF, 2009), our students rarely worked to support their families. Instead, their part-time jobs were sources of spending money and instilled the values of responsibility and work ethic.

For many adolescents around the world, however, work is a major part of their daily lives. And although there is a multitude of reasons for low enrollment among secondary school students worldwide, having to leave school to contribute to the family's economic resources is often one of them. Thus, nonstudents are much more likely than students to work for money (Ritchie et al., 2004). In a study of adolescents from Pakistan, Nicaragua, Kenya, India, and South Africa, boys (regardless of enrollment status in school) enjoyed more leisure time and less work time than girls (Lloyd et al., 2008). However, those gender differences were lessened when the girls were enrolled in school, suggesting that education may be an equalizer for girls with respect to how they spend their time.

Adolescents' time use has social implications, too. In the United States, for example, adolescents spend less time on school work and more time engaged in leisure activities like time with friends when compared to their peers from other minority world countries (Larson, 2001). This point is clearly emphasized in the documentary 2 Million Minutes when the teens from the United States are compared to those from China and India (Compton & Heeter, 2008). The US teens are portrayed with vivacious social lives. In one scene, for example, they are studying for an exam while watching the popular television show Grey's Anatomy, making studying a social event. Meanwhile, their Chinese peers spent every waking moment sharpening their academic skills in preparation for the national university entrance example. The sharp contrast provides an excellent launching point for discussion of the advantages and disadvantages of both approaches and the implications of adolescents' time use. A study by Larson and Verma (1999) provides evidence for this pattern; youth in North America spent between 3.0 hours and 4.5 hours each day on schoolwork compared to their peers in Europe and East Asia who spent 4.0–5.5 hours and 5.5–7.5 hours on schoolwork each day, respectively. When it came to talking with peers, however, US students emerged in first place. Their 2–3 hours a day far surpassed the 45 minutes to 1 hour that

East Asian youth spent talking with peers (Larson & Verma, 1991). To help students connect with the possible ways that adolescents can spend their time, students could assume the role of a (hypothetical) parent and argue for how they would like their adolescent to spend her or his day, choosing from work, school, and leisure activities.

Future orientation, imagination, and creativity among adolescents. During adolescence, young people often use their advanced cognitive skills to imagine possible futures, including possible future selves (Markus & Nurius, 1986; Piaget, 1972). The content of those imagined futures differs across nations, cultures, and specific conditions of their lives (Macek, Jezek, & Vazsonyi, 2013; Nurmi, 1991). Teenagers' imagined futures are most often optimistic and idealistic, rather than realistic. Street children in Honduras imagined themselves as teachers and doctors (DiCarlo, Gibbons, Kaminsky, Wright, & Stiles, 2000). Inuit adolescents from a remote community expected to complete university education, although it was unlikely they would do so (Condon, 1987). At other times, adolescents use their imaginations and abilities to subvert the existing order, as Japanese teen girls who invented their own language without the markers of hierarchy that characterize the Japanese language (Wright, 2002), or, as in the case of Nigerian girls who endorsed polygamous marriages more than their male counterparts, recognize some advantages of traditional practices and reinforce cultural customs in their future plans (Hollos & Leis, 1989).

Adolescents often use their imaginations and creativity to advance societal well-being. Nicola Jacobs, 17 years old of South Africa, invented reflective material to post house numbers in a former township so that emergency personnel could respond more quickly (UNICEF, 2015). Manushi Nilesh Shah and Misha Patel, 17 of Kenya, invented a water purification system based on a cactus extract, a readily available and nontoxic substance (UNICEF, 2015). There is a long history of youth social activism, from anti-Nazi youth movements to animal rights activism (Sherrod, Flanagan, Kassimir, & Syvertsen, 2006). For example, members of opposing gangs in El Salvador formed Homies Unidos in an effort to stop gang violence and promote reintegration of repatriated youth into their Salvadorian communities (Ballvé, 2006). A brief exercise for students would involve their scanning the Internet for other examples of adolescents' positive contributions to society.

A study of over 8,000 adolescents from twenty different countries explored adolescents' views of the ideal man and ideal woman (Gibbons & Stiles, 2004). Adolescents' images often reflect their imagined future selves or their imagined future spouse. Overall, teenagers held prosocial attitudes; most important was that the ideal person be kind and honest, and like children. However, there were international and gender differences as well. It was more important that the ideal person be fun and sexy in individualistic countries whereas intelligence and popularity were more valued by teens in collectivist countries. Girls, more often than boys, drew the ideal person with others and smiling. An exercise that students might complete is to write a short list of the traits of the ideal man or women according to their own values and then compare those with research findings from adolescents in other countries. The essential lesson here is that there are cultural similarities as well as cultural differences. After all, international psychology is not only about a search for difference (Wang, 2017).

Conclusion

In sum, it is possible to heed the calls for better representation of the world's population in our courses (e.g., Arnett, 2008). Here we suggest exercises, films, and readings that can be used by instructors of adolescent psychology courses to broaden students' knowledge about the range of adolescent experiences around the world. As globalization proceeds, we and our students will be called upon to understand other cultures and others' experiences to foster better communication and understanding among global citizens. Young people, both the adolescents depicted here and our youthful students, represent talented agents of change for the future.

References

Action for the Rights of Children. (2002). Critical issues: Child soldiers. Retrieved from www.unicef.org/violencestudy/pdf/ARC_working_with_children.pdf

Advocates for Youth. (2008). *Youth and the state of the world.* Retrieved from www.advocatesforyouth.org/storage/advfy/documents/fsstateworld.pdf

Akanferi, A. A., Aziale, L. K., & Asampana, I. (2014). An empirical study on mobile phone usage among young adults in Ghana: From the viewpoint of university students. *International Journal of Computer Applications, 98,* 15–21. doi:10.5120/17178-7273

Alam, M., Warren, R., & Applebaum, A. (2016). Closing the gap: Adolescent girls' access to education in conflict-affected settings. Washington, DC: Georgetown Institute for Women, Peace and Security. Retrieved from https://giwps.georgetown.edu/sites/giwps/files/closing_the_gap_adolescent_girls_access_to_education_in_conflict-affected_settings.pdf

Arnett. J. J. (1999). Adolescent storm and stress reconsidered. *American Psychologist, 54,* 317–326. doi:10.1037/003-066X.54.5.317

(2008). The neglected 95%: Why American psychology needs to become less American. *American Psychologist, 63,* 602–614. doi:10.1037/0003-066X.63.7.602

(2012a). *Adolescence and emerging adulthood: A cultural approach.* (5th ed.) Upper Saddle River, NJ: Prentice-Hall.

(2012b). *Adolescent psychology around the world.* New York, NY: Psychology Press.

Ausubel, D. P. (1959). *Maori youth: A psychoethnological study of cultural deprivation.* New York, NY: Holt, Rinehart, and Winston.

Ballvé, T. (2006). Homies Unidos. In L. R. Sherrod, C. A. Flanagan, R. Kassimir, & A. K. Syvertsen (Eds.). *Youth activism: An international encyclopedia* (pp. 316–318). Westport, CT: Greenwood.

Buchanan, C. M., & Hughes, J. L. (2009). Construction of social reality during early adolescence: Can expecting storm and stress increase real or perceived storm and stress? *Journal of Research on Adolescence, 19,* 261–285. doi:10.1111/j.1532-7795.2009.00596.x

Burbank, V. K. (1988). *Aboriginal adolescence: Maidenhood in an Australian community.* New Brunswick, NJ: Rutgers University Press.

Butt, B. (2015). Herding by mobile phone: Technology, social networks and the "transformation" of pastoral herding in East Africa. *Human Ecology, 43,* 1–14. doi:10.1007/s10745-014-9710-4

Chisholm, J. S., Quinlivan, J. A., Petersen, R. W., & Coall, D. A. (2005). Early stress predicts age at menarche and first birth, adult attachment, and expected life span. *Human Nature, 16,* 233–265. doi:10.1007/s12110-005-1009-0

Cole, M. (1996). *Cultural psychology: A once and future discipline.* Cambridge, MA: Harvard University Press.

Compton, R. A., & Heeter, C. (2008). *2 million minutes* [Motion picture]. United States: Broken Pencil Productions.

Condon, R. G. (1987). *Inuit youth: Growth and change in the Canadian arctic.* New Brunswick, NJ: Rutgers University Press.

Dasen, P. R. (1972). Cross-cultural Piagetian research: A summary. *Journal of Cross-Cultural Psychology, 3,* 23–39. doi:10.1177/002202217200300102

Davis, S. S., & Davis, D. A. (1989). *Adolescence in a Moroccan town.* New Brunswick, NJ: Rutgers University Press.

DiCarlo, M. A., Gibbons, J. L., Kaminsky, D. C., Wright, J. D., & Stiles, D. A. (2000). The use of street children's drawings as windows into their life circumstances and aspirations. *International Social Work, 43,* 107–120. doi:10.1177/a010524

Erikson, E. (1968). *Identity, youth, and crisis.* New York, NY: Norton.

Eveleth, P., & Tanner, J. M. (1990). *Worldwide variation in human growth.* New York, NY: Cambridge University Press.

Farrer, C. R. (1987). Singing for life: The Mescalero Apache girls' puberty ceremony. In L. C. Mahdi, S. Foster, & M. Little (Eds.), *Betwixt & between: Patterns of masculine and feminine initiation.* (pp. 239–263). La Salle, IL: Open Court.

Gibbons, J. L. (2010). The power of resources: An exercise in inequality for teaching psychology of women. *Psychology of Women Quarterly, 34*, 127–130. doi:10.1111/j.1471-6402.2009.01549.x

Gibbons, J. L., & Stiles, D. A. (2004). *The thoughts of youth: An international perspective on adolescents' ideal persons*. Greenwich, CT: Information Age.

Global Partnership for Education. (2014). Out-of-school children. Retrieved from www.globalpartnership.org/focus-areas/out-of-school-children

Goldstein, S. (2007). *Cross-cultural explorations: Activities in culture and psychology*. London: Routledge.

Hall, G. S. (1904). *Adolescence: Its psychology and its relation to physiology, anthropology, sociology, sex, crime, religion, and education* (Vols. I & II). Englewood Cliffs, NJ: Prentice Hall.

Harter, S. (2012). *The construction of the self: Developmental and sociocultural foundations*. New York, NY: Guilford.

Herdt, G., & Leavitt, S. C. (Eds.) (1998). *Adolescence in Pacific Island societies*. Pittsburgh, PA: University of Pittsburgh Press.

Hindin, M. J., & Fatusi, A. O. (2009). Adolescent sexual and reproductive health in developing countries: An overview of trends and interventions. *International Perspectives on Sexual and Reproductive Health, 35*(2), 58–62. doi:10.1362/3505809

Hollos, M., & Leis, P. E. (1989). *Becoming Nigerian in Ijo Society*. New Brunswick, NJ: Rutgers University Press.

Huntsinger, C. (2013, October 23). Armenian adolescents and globalization. Society for Research on Adolescence. Retrieved from www.s-r-a.org/announcements/online-newsletter/2013-10-25-armenian-adolescents-and-globalization-0

International Labour Organization. (2015). Global employment trends for youth 2015. Retrieved from www.ilo.org/wcmsp5/groups/public/—dgreports/—dcomm/—publ/documents/publication/wcms_412015.pdf

Jensen, L. A. (2003). Coming of age in a multicultural world: Globalization and adolescent cultural identity formation. *Applied Developmental Science, 7*, 189–196. doi:10.1207/S1532480XADS0703_10

Karapanou, O., & Papadimitriou, A. (2010). Determinants of menarche. *Reproductive Biology and Endocrinology, 8*, 1–8. doi:10.1186/1477-7827-8-115

Kato-Wallace, J., Barker, G., Sharafi, L., Mora, L., Lauro, G. (2016). *Adolescent boys and young men: Engaging them as supporters of gender equality and health and understanding their vulnerabilities*. Washington, DC: Promundo-US. New York City: UNFPA.

Kuhn, M. H., & McPartland, D. S. (1954). An empirical investigation of self-attitudes. *American Sociological Review, 19*, 68–76. doi:qo.2307/2088175

Larson, R. W. (2001). How U.S. children and adolescents spend their time: What it does (and doesn't) tell us about their development. *Current Directions in Psychological Science, 10*, 160–164. doi:10.1111/1467-8721.00139

Larson, R. W., & Verma, S. (1999). How children and adolescents spend their time across the world: Work, play, and developmental opportunities. *Psychological Bulletin, 125*, 701–736. doi:10.1037/0033-2909.125.6.701

Lloyd, C. B., Grant, M., Ritchie, A. (2008). Gender differences in time use among adolescents in developing countries: Implications of rising school enrollment rates. *Journal of Research on Adolescence, 18*, 99–120. doi:10.1111/j.1532-7795.2008.00552.x

Macek, P., Jezek, S., & Vazsonyi, A. T. (2013). Adolescents during and after times of social change: The case of the Czech Republic. *Journal of Early Adolescence, 33*, 1029–1047. doi:10.1177/0272431613507758

Markus, H. R., & Nurius, P. (1986). Possible selves. *American Psychologist, 41*, 954–969. doi:10.1037/003-066X.41.9.954

Markus, H. R., & Kitayama, S. (1991). Culture and the self: Implications for cognition, emotion, and motivation. *Psychological Review, 98*, 224–253. doi:10.1037/0033-259X.98.2.224

Mead, M. (2001). *Coming of age in Samoa: A psychological study.* New York, NY: HarperCollins.

Mensch, B. S., Bruce, J., & Greene, M. E. (1998). *The unchartered passage: Girls' adolescence in the developing world.* New York, NY: The Population Council.

Morabia, A., Costanza, M. C., & the World Health Organization. (1998). International variability in ages at menarche, first livebirth, and menopause. *American Journal of Epidemiology, 148*, 1195–1205. doi:10.1093/oxfordjournals.aje.a009609

Nehra, R., Kate, N., Grover, S., Khehra, N., & Basu, S. (2012). Does the excessive use of mobile phones in young adults reflect an emerging behavioral addiction? *Journal of Postgraduate Medicine, Education and Research, 46*, 177–182. doi:10.5005/jp-journals-10028-1040

Nurmi, J.-E. (1991). How do adolescents see their future? A review of the development of future orientation and planning. *Developmental Review, 11*, 1–59. doi:10.1016/0273-2297(91)90002-6

Offer, D., Ostrov, E., & Howard, K. I. (1981). The mental health professional's concept of the normal adolescent. *Archives of General Psychiatry, 38*, 149–152. doi:10.1001/archpsyc.1981.01780270035003

Offit, T. A. (2008). *Conquistadores de la calle: Child street labor in Guatemala City.* Austin, TX: University of Texas Press.

Pan American Health Organization. (2013). *Reaching poor adolescents in situations of vulnerability with sexual and reproductive health.* Washington, DC: Author.

Pew Research Center. (2015). U.S. smartphone use in 2015. Retrieved from www.pewinternet.org/2015/04/01/us-smartphone-use-in-2015/

Piaget, J. (1972). Intellectual evolution from adolescence to adulthood. *Human Development, 15*(1), 1–12. doi:10.1159/000271225

Poelker, K. E., & Gibbons, J. L. (2016). Adolescents in the majority world. In U. P. Gielen & J. L. Roopnarine (Eds.). *Childhood and adolescence: Cross-cultural perspectives and applications* (2nd ed., pp. 263–296). Santa Barbara, CA: Praeger.

Price, W. F., & Crapo, R. H. (2002). *Cross-cultural perspectives in introductory psychology* (4th ed.). Pacific Grove, CA: Wadsworth.

Qu, Y., Pomerantz, E. M., Wang, M., Cheung, C., & Cimpian, A. (2016). Conceptions of adolescence: Implications for differences in engagement in school over early adolescence in the United States and China. *Journal of Youth and Adolescence, 45*, 1512–1526. doi:10.1007/s10964-016-0492-4

Rafowitz, M. (2016). Crashing down: A tsunami survivor tells his story. Retrieved from http://aplus.com/a/tsunami-survivor-university-of-miami?no_monetization=true

Rao, M. A., Berry, R., Gonsalves, A., Hostak, Y., Shah, M., Roeser, R. W. (2013). Globalization and the *identity remix* among adolescents. *Journal of Research on Adolescence, 23*(1), 9–24. doi:10.1111/jora.12002

Ritchie, A., Lloyd, C. B., & Grant, M. (2004). Gender differences in time use among adolescents in developing countries: Implications of rising school enrollment rates. *Policy Research Working Papers, 193*, 1–34.

Rosenberg, M. (1986). Self-concept from middle childhood through adolescence. In J. Suls & A. G. Greenwald (Eds.), *Psychological perspectives on the self* (Vol. 3, pp. 107–131). Hillsdale, NJ: Lawrence Erlbaum.

Schlegel, A., & Barry, H. (1991). *Adolescence: An anthropological inquiry.* New York, NY: Free Press.

Serpell, R. (1993). *The significance of schooling: Life-journeys in an African society.* Cambridge: Cambridge University Press.

(2011). Social responsibility as a dimension of intelligence, and as an educational goal: Insights from programmatic research in an African society. *Child Development Perspectives, 5*(2), 126–133. doi:10.1111/j.1750-8606.2011.00167.x

Sherrod, L. R., Flanagan, C. A., Kassimir, R., & Syvertsen, A. K. (Eds.) (2006). *Youth activism: An international Encyclopedia.* Westport, CT: Greenwood.

Simulation Training Systems. (2016). BaFa' BaFa'. Retrieved from www.simulationtrainingsystems.com/schools-and-charities/products/bafa-bafa/

Steinberg, L. (2001). We know some things: Parent-adolescent relationships in retrospect and prospect. *Journal of Research on Adolescence, 11*, 1–19. doi:10.1111/1532-7795.00001

Stern, C. (2002). Poverty, social vulnerability and adolescent pregnancy in Mexico: A qualitative analysis. Retrieved from www.cicred.org/Eng/Seminars/Details/Seminars/Bangkok2002/30BangkokStern.pdf

Stiles, D. A., Gibbons, J. L., & de Silva, S. S. (1996). Girls' relational self in Sri Lanka and the United States. *Journal of Genetic Psychology, 157*, 191–203. doi:10.1080/00221325.1996.9914857

Sullivan, S. E., & Duplaga, E. A. (1997). The Bafa Bafa Simulation: Faculty experiences and student reactions. *Journal of Management Education, 21*, 265–272. doi:10.1177/105256299702100212

UNICEF. (2005). Voices of hope: Adolescents and the tsunami. Retrieved from www.unicef.org/publications/files/Tsunami_newbackcover.pdf

(2009). Adolescents and youth. Retrieved from www.unicef.org/kenya/children_3793.htm

(2011). The state of the world's children 2011. Adolescence: An age of opportunity. Retrieved from www.unicef.org/sowc2011/pdfs/SOWC-2011-Main-Report_EN_02092011.pdf

(2012). Progress for children: A report card on adolescents. Retrieved from www.unicef.org/media/files/PFC2012_A_report_card_on_adolescents.pdf

(2013). Simple solutions to keep girls in school in Bangladesh. Retrieved from www.unicef.org/infobycountry/bangladesh_70622.html

(2014). How poverty affects children: Shasha's story. Retrieved from https://teachunicef.org/sites/default/files/documents/units-lesson-plans/shashas_story_full_unit_grades_9_to_12.pdf

(2015). The state of the world's children 2015: Executive summary. Retrieved from www.unicef.org/publications/files/SOWC_2015_Summary_and_Tables.pdf

United Nations. (2012). World population monitoring: Adolescents and youth, a concise report. Retrieved from www.un.org/en/development/desa/population/publications/pdf/fertility/12_66976_adolescents_and_youth.pdf

(2015). #YouthStats: Armed conflict. Retrieved from www.un.org/youthenvoy/armed-conflict/

United Nations Children's Fund. (2016). Country programme document Bangladesh. Retrieved from www.unicef.org/about/execboard/files/2016-PL10-Bangladesh_CPD-ODS-EN.pdf

UNFPA. (2013). Motherhood in childhood: Facing the challenge of adolescent pregnancy. Retrieved from www.unfpa.org/sites/default/files/pub-pdf/EN-SWOP2013-final.pdf

(2014). The power of 1.8 billion: Adolescents, youth, and the transformation of the future. Retrieved from www.unfpa.org/sites/default/files/pub-pdf/EN-SWOP14-Report_FINAL-web.pdf

Urban Ministries of Durham. (2011). SPENT. Retrieved from playspent.org

Wang, Q. (2017). Five myths about the role of culture in psychological research. *Observer, 30*(1), 20–24.

Warren, C. S. (2006). Incorporating multiculturalism into undergraduate psychology courses: Three simple active learning activities. *Teaching of Psychology, 33*, 105–109. doi:10.1207/s15328023top3302_5

Weigl, R. C. (2009). Intercultural competence through cultural self-study: A strategy for adult learners. *International Journal of Intercultural Relations, 33*, 346–360. doi:10.1016/j.ijintrel.2009.04.004

White, M. (1994). *The material child: Coming of age in Japan and America.* Berkeley, CA: University of California Press.

Wright, D. (2002). Japanese youth: Rewriting futures in the "no taboos" postbubble millennium. In J. Gidley & S. Inayatullab (Eds.). *Youth futures: Comparative research and transformative visions* (pp. 85–98). Westport, CT: Praeger.

Cognition

Evidence-based teaching practices for integration of culture in courses on cognition are a feature of Chapter 12, along with numerous teaching activities. In this chapter, Richmond also presents the case for the culture-cognition connection on the continuum from the broad (internationalizing the course) to the very specific (e.g., relation between culture and facial recognition). In Chapter 13, Wang uses a classic story to weave her own fascinating account of the relation between culture and memory, including important memory differences between members of Eastern and Western cultures and teaching activities to illustrate key concepts.

Inoue (Chapter 14) describes an international experiential approach to enliven an educational psychology course for teachers in training. The chapter is a first-hand report of the activities of students in a cross-cultural program and includes practical information as well as reflections on the nature and value of the experience.

Kreiner (Chapter 15) explores the importance of cultural context in the study of language, particularly in relation to pragmatics, and he discusses some surprising similarities in languages. An interesting feature for the teaching of language and culture is the relation between cultural expectations and violations of conversational rules.

CHAPTER 12

Where Tides Collide: Integrating Culture in Teaching Cognitive Psychology

Aaron S. Richmond

> Culture and the brain historically have often been the subjects of different forms of discourse. But a growing recognition of the extent of the brain's plasticity, of the evolutionary basis of cognition, and of the coevolution of culture and the brain makes clear that cultural and neural processes are interwoven.
>
> Ambady & Bharucha (2009, p. 342)

As illustrated in this quote, at times the terms *cognition* and *culture* were either completely at odds with one another or at best tidal currents fiercely mixing together. However, it seems that times are changing – or we (teachers of cognitive psychology) can start to change them. But first, what is the definition of *culture*? I am particularly fond of David Matsumoto who is not only an expert in cultural psychology but also strives to understand, investigate, and share best practices in teaching the psychology of culture. Matsumoto (2008) defined *culture* as "a unique meaning and information system, shared by a group and transmitted across generations, that allows the group to meet basic needs of survival, coordinate socially to achieve a viable existence, transmit social behavior, pursue happiness and well-being, and derive meaning from life" (p. 14). Given Matsumoto's definition, it is my belief that cognition plays an integral role in this process. For example, cognition is an information system of concepts, types of memories, and neural processing. Additionally, language transmits information across generations through such processes as working memory and executive functioning. I think the transposition of culture to cognition can go on and on. These are certainly not mutually exclusive concepts.

Considering the probability that culture and cognition are intertwined, the goal of this chapter is to further justify the need to infuse culture into the teaching of cognition and to discuss how to accomplish this task. Second, I will identify key cognitive concepts that have preexisting research and/or teaching resources that demonstrate the unique relation between culture and cognition. Within this section, I highlight four evidence-based practices that have demonstrated how to incorporate culture into cognition. Third, common cognitive concepts that have been misconstrued or misconceived from a cultural context will be identified and discussed. Fourth, I will describe use of a short, simple activity to demonstrate how culture influences face and name recognition. Fifth, I will discuss general strategies and principles on how to incorporate culture into a cognitive psychology course. I will conclude an "A" list of readings on how to incorporate culture into cognition.

On the Importance of Culture in Cognition

Why is it important to integrate culture into cognition? One way to investigate the issue is to understand how frequently cognitive psychology concepts are represented in textbooks. In 2013, Homa and colleagues were interested in understanding what content was covered in introductory psychology courses across the United States. Homa et al. solicited more than 150 syllabi from various types of institutions (community colleges and baccalaureate institutions). They evaluated the course content and student learning objectives within each syllabus. Of particular interest was the amount of time spent on each chapter/topic. Homa et al. reported that cognition is one of the most broadly covered topics in introductory psychology courses. Instructors spent 19.51 percent of their instructional time on the topic of cognition while topics such as cultural psychology were only briefly covered in the syllabi. Homa et al.'s findings are consistent with those of other studies reporting that cognitive psychology is widely represented in introductory psychology (Griggs & Bates, 2014; Griggs & Jackson, 2013). Considering how much time instructors spend on teaching cognition and potentially how little time is spent on cultural psychology, instructors have an incredible opportunity to embed cultural psychology (by providing cultural examples of cognition) into the curriculum – thereby increasing students' understanding of cultural similarities and differences.

A second reason why teachers of cognitive psychology should incorporate culture into their courses is student interest in and perception of the importance of cognition. Recent research has suggested that a large part of introductory psychology courses is dedicated to cognition. McCann, Immel, Kadah-Ammeter, and Adelson (2016) conducted a study of more than 320 students from across the United States to determine the importance of and interest in specific chapters of introductory psychology textbooks. Students were surveyed from all types of institutions (e.g., technical colleges, community colleges, and baccalaureate colleges and universities). McCann and colleagues found that of sixteen separate chapters, students considered memory to be the most important. Another cognitive chapter, thinking/language/intelligence was ranked as the seventh most important. Additionally, students were significantly more interested in memory than many other chapters (e.g., statistics, history of psychology). Given that students are both interested in cognitive concepts and believe them to be important, introducing culture (by personally connecting to students in the class) into the teaching of these concepts will likely increase student interest, learning, and belief of importance of cognitive psychology.

Another reason why culture should be infused into teaching cognitive psychology is the lack of culture and diversity throughout the psychology curriculum. In a study of articles published in the journal *Teaching of Psychology* over a 28-year period, Ocampo et al. (2003) investigated the degree of diversity (e.g., culture, gender, race, sexual orientation) that was studied. Ocampo et al. discovered that in 2,029 articles, only 9 percent (f = 194) mentioned or studied diversity. Based on their results, Ocampo and colleagues suggested that there needs to be an increased programmatic focus on diversity-related research, theory-driven empirical research, and most importantly, assessment of the ability of psychology teachers to address (and in so doing infuse) diversity in their instructional methods.

Recently, Richmond et al. (2015) studied the sample diversity of empirical articles published in the top journals of teaching of psychology (e.g., *Teaching of Psychology, Psychology Learning and Teaching, Teaching of Educational Psychology*, and *Training and Education in Professional Psychology*). In the 302 articles reviewed, published from 2008–2013, 79 percent of participants were Caucasian students, 72 percent were female, and most of the articles did not report basic cultural and diversity data (ethnicity).

Not only do diversity and culture have low representation in teaching of psychology research (Ocampo et al., 2003; Richmond et al., 2015), there is also evidence to suggest that culture is not covered in the major as well. In a study of more than 200 psychology programs across the United States, Fuentes and Shanon (2016) found that most programs offer cultural or multicultural psychology courses. However, very few of these courses are required. Additionally, only 28 percent of courses offered in psychology majors even briefly mention culture, and they give "very little attention to the intersectionality that exists among cultural factors" (Fuentes & Shanon, 2016, p. 197). Given this lack of diversity and culture as a focus in research on teaching of psychology and as a curricular focus, it is incumbent upon teachers to inculcate culture into the cognitive psychology classroom.

There is evidence to suggest that when diversity and culture are used in the classroom, students' epistemological beliefs toward psychology knowledge increase. In a large-scale study, Elicker, Snell, and O'Malley (2009) researched how beliefs about the use of diversity in the classroom are related to perceived level of learning. Elicker and colleagues found that when students perceived an increase in diversity in classroom practices, their perception of their understanding of psychology content also increased. Moreover, underrepresented groups self-reported less understanding when diversity was absent.

In the end, given the interest and emphasis in cognitive psychology, the lack of coverage and research on diversity and culture, and the effects of exposure to diversity and culture, it is evident that infusion of culture into cognitive instructional practices is a must. Furthermore, Matsumoto (2008) suggested that we should teach culture in cognitive psychology to avoid the cultural attribution fallacy (i.e., attributing cultural differences without empirical evidence) and that teachers of cognitive psychology should bolster their repertoire of teaching strategies by incorporating culture by teaching cultural differences in cognitive concepts, and, more importantly, by using innovative teaching strategies (e.g., experiential learning) that improve learning. Matsumoto said it best: "It [human culture] helps us to create and maintain social systems, create beliefs about the world, and communicate the meaning system to other humans and subsequent generations." (p. 15). What better way to accomplish this task than to infuse, integrate, and embrace culture in the teaching of cognitive psychology?

Infusing Culture into Concepts of Cognitive Psychology

When I first approached writing this chapter, I had the preconceived notion that finding an array of good examples, demonstrations, and studies might be difficult. Interestingly, as I conducted further research, I was pleasantly surprised to find that (even though well hidden at times) there are some amazing resources that will assist teachers in incorporating culture into cognition – so much so that I cannot cover them all (see below, "Four Evidence-Based Practices for Infusing Culture in Cognition," for a few examples) but can only curate some of the best examples and summarize how they apply to specific cognitive concepts. See Table 12.1 for a list of ways teachers can infuse culture into the teaching of cognition.

Table 12.1 *A List of Typical Cognitive Concepts Covered and Associated
Published Cultural Differences, Examples, and Activities*

Cognitive Concept	Published Cultural Differences, Examples, and Activities
Neural Basis for Cognition Diet on Cognition	Socioeconomic status effects on brain development (Hackman & Farrah, 2009) Cultural neuroscience (Ambady & Bharucha, 2009) Effects of breastfeeding, ethnic and cultural differences on brain development (Isaacs et al., 2010)
Visual Perception	Cultural differences in the Muller-Lyer illusion (Davis & Carlson, 1970)
Object Recognition Word Recognition	Object processing (Goto et al., 2010; Gutchess, A. H., Welsh, R. C., Boduroğlu, A., & Park, D. C. 2006) Socioeconomic status differences in word recognition (Fernald, A., Marchman, V. A., & Weisleder, A. 2013)
Attention Selective Attention Divided Attention	The cocktail party phenomenon (Clump, 2006) Attention allocation (Boduroglu et al., 2009) Attentional control (Hedden et al., 2008)
Learning Strategies Encoding Long-Term memory Metacognition Autobiographical Memory Implicit Memory Working Memory Episodic Memory	Greek mnemonics (Foer, 2011) Japanese mnemonics (Mori & Shimizu, 2007) Gender stereotype and memory (Ganske & Hebl, 2001) Long-term memory and stereotype threat (Hess et al., 2003) Bilingual differences in metacognition and working memory (Ransdell, Barbier, & Niit, 2006) Autobiographical memory (Conway et al., 2005) Implicit Association Test (IAT; Greenwald et al., 1998) Working memory deficits: Aging and cultural differences (Gutches et al., 2006) Cultural similarities and differences in episodic memories (Levy & Langer, 1994)
Language Biological Roots of Language	Cultural norms in language development (Axtell, 1993) Cross-cultural differences in verbal processing (Hill, 1998, 2004) Whorfian (or linguistic relativity) hypothesis (Hunt & Agnoli, 1991) Articulatory suppression differences (Flaherty & Moran, 2005) Biological and cognitive differences in mono-vs. bi-lingual (de Groot, 2011)
Visual Imagery and Knowledge	Visual processing and math (Cantlon & Brannon 2007)
Judgment and Reasoning	Gender and cultural differences in heuristic search (Swinks, 2003) Cultural differences in rule-based and associative reasoning (Norenzayan et al., 2002)

Table 12.1 (cont.)

Cognitive Concept	Published Cultural Differences, Examples, and Activities
Intelligence Problem Solving	Black Intelligence Test of Cultural Homogeneity (Williams, 1975) Cultural differences in verbal IQ (Kim, 2002) Culture in artificial intelligence (Pinker, 2016) Testing, assessments, and problem solving (Warren, 2006)
Conscious and Unconscious Thought	Cognition of time and culture (Goldstein, 2016) Cultural cognition quiz (Ropeik, 2011)
General Cognitive Resource Diversity Engagement General Explanation	Diversity bibliography (Rominger & Kolesar, 2008) How to engage students in cross-cultural psychology (Anderson & Miller, 2011; Cathey & Ross, 2011) Culture-cognition connection (Winerman, 2006) Culture-cognition: Social orientation hypothesis (Varnum et al., 2010) The contact hypothesis (Bradway & Atchley, 2008)

For example, one of my favorite cultural infusion activities is to demonstrate the effects that culture can play in intelligence testing. I use the Black Intelligence Test of Cultural Homogeneity (BITCH; Williams, 1975). After the test, students self-score and I map their scores onto a normal curve. Students, on average, score below the cut point for intellectual disability. We discuss why, and how many IQ tests can be culturally biased. There are several other examples listed in Table 12.1 that can be used in your classroom.

Four Evidence-Based Practices for Infusing Culture in Cognition

Although culture and cognition have been at a bit of odds for decades, there are several evidence-based practices on how to incorporate culture into the teaching of cognitive psychology. First, in 2000, Hoyert and O'Dell investigated the effects of contextualizing flashbulb memories with various student experiences (cultures). These researchers had students in an introductory psychology course record a memory of an event on the first day of class and subsequently recall the same memory 2 months later during the memory section of the course and diagnose their episodic memory based on Brown and Kulli's (1997) work. Specifically, Hoyert and O'Dell asked students what they were doing when they learned of Princess Diana's death. The activity demonstrated that memories are reconstructions of events rather than exact replicas. Hoyert and O'Dell then tested participants' knowledge of the elements of episodic memory and compared their scores to students in courses where they did not receive this activity. Hoyert and O'Dell found that students improved their knowledge of episodic and flashbulb memories and viewed the activity as valuable in their understanding of course material to those who did not receive the activity. Many of these memories were culturally, gender-stereotypical, and ethnically relative (Hoyert & O'Dell, 2000). It is a great opportunity to demonstrate the culture differences in episodic/flashbulb memories.

A second example of infusing culture into cognition comes from Warren's (2006) investigation of three simple activities to incorporate multiculturalism in study of the cognitive concept of intelligence. In the first activity, students completed a ten-item verbal intelligence test. Many of the words were culturally specific to Hispanic culture or were presented in Spanish. Students then calculated their "verbal IQ." They then discussed whether the test was a good measure of their intelligence or whether their language ability influenced their results. In the second activity, Warren presented a similar ten-item verbal IQ test, but biased toward English speakers and U.S. culture. Students briefly wrote on how race, gender, culture, socioeconomic status (SES), and age may influence performance on the IQ test. The last activity was a "performance IQ test" requiring students to recreate an origami paper crane. After completing the activity, students again considered whether the activity was a good IQ test and discussed it with classmates. Warren found that students increased their knowledge of cultural influence on IQ tests. This is a simple activity that teachers can incorporate into their classroom instruction to highlight the role that culture plays in IQ assessment.

A third example by Ganske and Hebl (2001) addresses the issue of gender stereotyping and memory performance. They asked students to read two stories (one masculine/male and one feminine/female). Like the classic telephone activity, students retold the story to another student in the class who, in turn, retold the story to another student in the class. After five retells, the entire class listened to the original story aloud. They discussed how they tended to recall gender-congruent aspects of the story. For example, male students retold the story (measure of recall) with more male stereotypical traits such as *aggressive* and *strong*. Ganske and Hebl found that students' understanding of gender stereotyping memories increased and that students enjoyed the activity. This is a simple 5–10 minute activity that can demonstrate gender stereotyping in memory.

Finally, Stiegler-Balfour (2013) described how instructors of cognitive psychology can infuse diversity into a lesson on autobiographical memory. First, prior to class, students read an article by Levy and Langer (1994). They studied the role of negative stereotypes and cultural differences on the effects of aging on memory. They had older and younger Chinese hearing, American deaf, and American hearing individuals complete a series of memory tasks. Younger American and Chinese participants performed similarly on the memory task. However, the older deaf and Chinese participants outperformed the older American hearing group. Levy and Langer concluded that negative stereotypes about aging contribute to memory loss in older individuals. After reading the article and during class, students had 20–30 minutes to discuss, in groups, the difference between Western and Asian cultures in how they view aging and memory, the perceived gender stereotypes on memory in the study, and cross-cultural research in autobiographical memory.

These are but a few ways to infuse culture in teaching cognition. As listed in Table 12.1, there are several other evidence-based methods to infuse culture, gender, SES, and other diversity variables into the teaching of cognition.

Common Cognitive Concepts That Are Misunderstood from a Cultural Context

Although the study of culture and the study of cognitive psychology have sometimes been different and unrelated (Ambady & Bharucha, 2009), there are key cognitive concepts that are often misunderstood if not presented in cultural context. First, it is a common misconception that *second language acquisition reduces executive functioning* (Bialystok, 2011). Not only does popular culture believe that learning a second language hinders facility in the first language and ergo executive functioning (EF), but many cognitive psychologists also believed this myth as well (Bialystok, 2011). Several studies have demonstrated not only that bilinguals do not suffer EF deficits but also in some cases have higher EF (Kroll, Dussias, Bogulski, & Kroff, 2012). Furthermore, there is evidence to suggest that in older people, fluent bilingualism is linked to prevention of declining EF in old age (Bialystok, Craik, Klein, & Viswanathan, 2004).

Another common misperceived cognitive concept is gender differences in verbal (language arts) and spatial and logical intelligence (math). That is, there is a misconception that boys/men are better in math because of their spatial and logical mathematical intelligence than girls/women, and conversely that girls/women are better in language arts because of their verbal intelligence. Several meta-analytic studies (Hyde, 2005; Hyde, Fennema, & Lamon, 1990; Hyde, Lindberg, Linn, Ellis, & Williams, 2008; Hyde & Linn, 1988; Hyde & Mertz, 2009; Spelke, 2005) concluded that slightly different abilities between genders are likely not due to biological factors but rather cultural factors. However, when differences do occur (most often during middle school years), they tend to disappear by the time students graduate high school. What does not seem to be a myth is the vocations/careers that men and women pursue (e.g., men tend to pursue more mathematical and science-oriented careers whereas women tend to pursue more social science careers).

There are several other cognition myths with cultural origins that should be discussed or debunked in the classroom. These include left-brain (males)/right-brain (females), SES and enriching environments during the sensitive period, vaccines cause autism, SES and classical music increase IQ, and gender differences in learning styles, among others (Dekker, Lee, Howard-Joes, & Jolles, 2012). Yet sometimes this list is greater than the content in the syllabus, so focusing on EF and bilingualism and gender differences in IQ is a good place to start.

Is It Fahim or Pierre? An Activity in Cultural Differences in Face Recognition

In searching for an activity to create, I wanted to pose an engaging and current example of culture in cognition. Therefore, a recent study by Zwebner, Sellier, Rosenfeld, Goldenberg, and Mayo (2017) on cultural similarities and differences in facial recognition caught my eye. In eight separate experiments in two different countries (France and Israel) and with both human subjects and computerized decision tasks, Zwebner et al. studied whether culture influenced how we match names to faces. They found that participants were significantly better at matching a name that was consistent with their own nationality (i.e., a person from France matched French names with pictures more consistently). Conversely, Hebrew participants were significantly worse at matching non-Hebrew names to stereotypical non-Hebrew faces.

For this activity, it is my goal that students understand the cognitive processes behind face and name recognition and how they may be influenced by cultural differences. This activity can be used in the visual perception chapter or the word recognition chapter. However, if you are daring, you may use it in your lesson about how culture effects cognition.

(a)   (b)

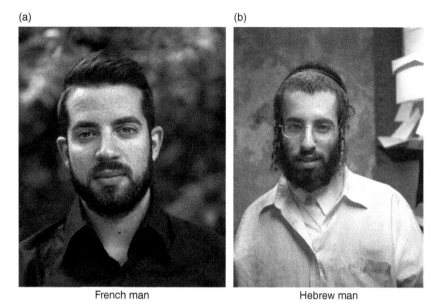

French man   Hebrew man

Figure 12.1   Sample photos for the stereotypical (a) French man (b) Hebrew man
What is the name of the male on the left _____ and what is the name
of the male on the right _____ ?

Choose from the list below:
1. Magnus
2. Pierre
3. Dan
4. Jon
5. Aaron
6. Hugo
7. Louis
8. Abel
9. Samuel
10. Fahim

To prepare for the activity, download ten black-and-white photos of either
male or female adults who could be considered culturally stereotypical
(e.g., French or Hebrew). See Figure 12.1 for an example of a stereotypical
French and Hebrew male. Additionally, create a list of ten to twenty
French and Hebrew male names. See Figure 12.1 for examples. Create
five to ten PowerPoint slides that ask students to either name individual
pictures or to choose two names for two corresponding pictures. You will
also need to create a scoring sheet. Start by explaining to students that you

would like them to match the picture with the name that they believe best matches the picture. Show the five to ten pictures or set of pictures. Have students self-score by giving a 1 for correctly matching a stereotypical Hebrew or French name to a stereotypical Hebrew or French picture. Scores should range from 0 to 10, with a higher score representing a more typical confirmation of cultural bias in face-name recognition. Have students turn in their score sheets and score. Typically, students will match a culturally specific name, for example, Fahim with (b) of Figure 12.1. To debrief the students, go through each slide and ask students how they answered and ask them to explain their choices. Finally, ask students to discuss why they think their answers may be stereotypical along cultural lines. You can discuss the research and cognitive processes behind both facial and name recognition.

General Strategies to Infuse Culture in Teaching Cognition

Beyond teaching culture in relation to specific cognitive concepts, there are two general strategies (internationalizing courses and multiculturalism) that a teacher may employ to infuse culture into the teaching of cognitive psychology. First, Bartolini, Gharib, and Phillips (2009) suggested that to infuse cognitive psychology with culture, teachers should *internationalize* their course. Bartolini and colleagues noted that teachers can do this in one (or both) of two ways by (a) introducing research on basic concepts that has been conducted in other countries and continents or (b)discussing how culture can affect cognitive processes. Bartolini et al. went so far as to develop a student learning objective (SLO) for cognitive psychology courses that emphasize culture in cognition: "Students will gain increased understanding for how culture affects cognitive processing, as well as the kind of cognitive research that is taking place in other countries" (p. 23). They suggested that to assess this SLO, students should find articles demonstrating cultural differences in cognitive processes (e.g., Flaherty & Moran, 2005).

Velayo (2011) also suggested internationalizing psychology courses, but with more general teaching strategies. For instance, have visiting scholars, international students, or study-abroad students come to your classroom and discuss various cognitive concepts and how they research or experience them differently. Or show films that exemplify the *international perspective* of various cognitive concepts. For example, the film *The Act of Killing* by Oppenheimer, Herzog, and Morris (2012) chronicles the perpetrators of the Indonesian killings of 1965–1966 and exemplifies the power of episodic memories and forgetting theories. Velayo also suggested that teachers should attend any international events that may be related to cognition.

Second, Kluck (2005) suggested that we should create cognitive psychology courses with multiculturalism in mind. When integrating multiculturalism into cognitive psychology courses, Kluck wrote that we should consider not only culture but also gender, ethnicity, nationality, religious or spiritual perspectives, SES, and mental abilities or disabilities. In cognitive psychology courses, there are numerous examples of gender, SES, ethnicity, and mental ability differences and similarities (see Table 12.1 for examples). Kluck pointed out that one of the best ways to make a cognitive course multicultural is to use the Implicit Attitudes Test (IAT). Teachers can use the IAT as an experiential assignment for students to understand reasoning, judgment, and decision making and how these cognitive concepts are influenced by implicit memories (e.g., biases). Kluck also suggested that cognitive psychology teachers should create an assignment requiring students to research whether classical cognitive psychology concepts were ever studied or researched with bias. For example, some researchers used the study of phrenology (the shape and size of the skull) as a predictor of IQ in the attempt to demonstrate racial dominance.

As suggested by Bartolini et al. (2009) and Velayo (2011), using the general strategy of internationalizing as well as Kluck's (2005) approach to infusing multiculturalism into your cognitive psychology course will undoubtedly increase understanding of the role that culture has in teaching cognition.

In Conclusion: Never Stop Reading!

It seems evident that there is a growing trend in both research and teaching that connects culture to cognition. Therefore, it is my hope that some of the information in this chapter may work toward teaching students this evolving intertwined relation. Whether you are using general strategies such as attempting to *internationalize* your psychology course or demonstrating how culture influences such specific phenomena as facial and name recognition, invariably your students will begin to understand the important role that culture plays in cognition. When tides collide, the water temperature changes, the currents mix and churn, waves break and crash, and ultimately something new is formed. Similarly, when we combine culture and cognition, something new is born, and it is incumbent upon us to usher in this change for the next generation of students and scholars.

I know that we all have a mighty tall stack of books on our nightstand, desk, or floor; however, I conclude with a reading list that would be helpful to teachers trying to develop a cultural focus in their cognition courses:

Resources

Berry, J. W. (1993). An ecological approach to understanding cognition across cultures. In J. Altarriba (Ed.), *Cognition and culture: A cross-cultural approach to cognitive psychology* (Vol. 103, pp. 361–375). Amsterdam, The Netherlands: North Holland/Elsevier Science.

Bradway, P. A., & Atchley, S. (2008). The contact hypothesis: Interviewing across cultures. In L.T. Benjamin, Jr. (Ed.), *Favorite activities for the teaching of psychology*. Washington, DC: American Psychological Association.

Cole, M., & Packer, M. (2011). Culture and cognition. In K. D. Keith (Ed.), *Cross-cultural psychology: Contemporary themes and perspectives* (pp. 133–159). Chichester: Wiley-Blackwell.

Goldstein, S. (2016). *Cross-cultural explorations: Activities in culture and psychology*. New York, NY: Routledge.

Heine, S. (2011). *Cultural psychology* (2nd ed.). New York, NY: W. W. Norton.

References

Ambady, N., & Bharucha, J. (2009). Culture and the brain. *Current Directions in Psychological Science, 18*, 342–345. doi:10.1111/j.1467-8721.2009.01664.x

Anderson, S. L., & Miller, R. L. (2011). Engaging students in cross-cultural psychology. In R. L. Miller, E. Balcetis, S. R. Burns, D. B. Daniel, B. K. Saville, & W. D. Woody (Eds.), *Promoting student engagement* (Vol. 2, pp. 9–14). Retrieved from the Society for the Teaching of Psychology, http://teachpsych.org/ebooks/pse2011/index.php

Axtell, R. E. (Ed.). (1993). *Do's and taboos around the world* (3rd ed.). New York, NY: Wiley.

Bartolini, L., Gharib, A., & Phillips, W. (2009). Internationalizing psychology courses. In S. A. Meyers & J. R. Stowell (Eds.), *Essays from e-xcellence in teaching* (Vol. 9, pp. 11–16). Retrieved from http://teachpsych.org/ebooks/eit2009/index.php

Bialystok, E. (2011). Coordination of executive functions in monolingual and bilingual children. *Journal of Experimental Child Psychology, 110*, 461–468. doi:10.1016/j.jecp.2011.05.005

Bialystok, E., Craik, F. I. M., Klein, R., & Viswanathan, M. (2004). Bilingualism, aging, and cognitive control: Evidence from the Simon Task. *Psychology and Aging, 19*, 290–303. doi:10.1037/0882–7974.19.2.290

Boduroglu, A., Shah, P., & Nisbett, R. E. (2009). Cultural differences in allocation of attention in visual information processing. *Journal of Cross-Cultural Psychology, 40*, 349–360. doi:10.1177/0022022108331005

Bradway, P. A., & Atchley, S. (2008). The contact hypothesis: Interviewing across cultures. In L. T. Benjamin, Jr. (Ed.), *Favorite activities for the teaching of psychology*. Washington, DC: American Psychological Association.

Brown, R., & Kulik, J. (1977). Flashbulb memories. *Cognition*, *5*, 73–99. doi: 10.1016/0010-0277(77)90018-X

Cantlon, J. F., & Brannon, E. M. (2007). Adding up the effects of cultural experience on the brain. *Trends in Cognitive Sciences*, *11*, 1–4. doi:10.1016/j.tics.2006.10.008

Cathey, C., & Ross, A. S. (2011). Teaching about diversity: Activities that promote student engagement. In R. L. Miller, E. Balcetis, S. R. Burns, D. B. Daniel, B. K. Saville, & W. D. Woody (Eds.), *Promoting student engagement* (Vol. 2, pp. 9–14). Retrieved from the Society for the Teaching of Psychology, http://teachpsych.org/ebooks/pse2011/index.php

Clump, M. A. (2006). An active learning classroom activity for the "cocktail party phenomenon." *Teaching of Psychology*, *33*, 51–53. doi:10.1207/s15328023top3301_9

Conway, M. A., Wang, Q., Hanyu, K., & Haque, S. (2005). A cross-cultural investigation of autobiographical memory on the universality and cultural variation of the reminiscence bump. *Journal of Cross-Cultural Psychology*, *36* (6), 739–749. doi:10.1177/0022022105280512

Davis, C. M., & Carlson, J. A. (1970). A cross-cultural study of the strength of the Muller-Lyer illusion as a function of attentional factors. *Journal of Personality and Social Psychology*, *16*, 403–410. doi:10.1037/h0030052

de Groot, A. M. B. (2011). *Language and cognition in bilinguals and multilinguals: An introduction*. New York, NY: Psychology Press.

Dekker, S., Lee, N. C., Howard-Jones, P., & Jolles, J. (2012) Neuromyths in education: Prevalence and predictors of misconceptions among teachers. *Frontiers in Psychology*, *3*, 429. doi:10.3389/fpsyg.2012.00429

Elicker, J. D., Snell, A. F., & O'Malley, A. L. (2009). Do student perceptions of diversity emphasis relate to perceived learning of psychology? *Teaching of Psychology*, *37*, 36–40. doi:10.1080/00986280903425706

Fernald, A., Marchman, V. A., & Weisleder, A. (2013). SES differences in language processing skill and vocabulary are evident at 18 months. *Developmental Science*, *16*, 234–248. doi:10.1111/desc.12019

Flaherty, M., & Moran, A. (2005). Articulatory suppression in bilingual and second language speakers. *International Journal of Cognitive Technology*, *10*, 38–46.

Foer, J. (2011, February 11). Secrets of a mind-gamer: How I trained my brain and became a world-class memory athlete. Retrieved from www.nytimes.com/interactive/2011/02/20/magazine/mind-secrets.html?_r=0

Fuentes, M. A., & Shannon, C. R. (2016). The state of multiculturalism and diversity in undergraduate psychology training. *Teaching of Psychology*, *43*, 197–203. doi:10.1177/0098628316649315

Ganske, K. H., & Hebl, M. R. (2001). Once upon a time there was a math contest: Gender stereotyping and memory. *Teaching of Psychology*, *28*, 266–268. doi:10.1207/S15328023TOP2804_07

Goldstein, S. (2016). *Cross-cultural explorations: Activities in culture and psychology.* New York, NY: Routledge.

Goto, S. G., Anduo, Y., Huan, C., Yee, A., & Lewis, R. S. (2010). Cultural differences in the visual processing of meaning: Detecting incongruities between background and foreground objects using the N400. *SCAN, 5,* 242–253. doi:10.1093/scan/nsp038

Greenwald, A. G., McGhee, D. E., & Schwartz, J. L. K. (1998). Measuring individual differences in implicit cognition: The Implicit Association Test. *Journal of Personality and Social Psychology, 74,* 1464–1480. doi: 10.1037/0022-3514.746.1464

Griggs, R. A., & Bates, S. C. (2014). Topical coverage in introductory psychology textbooks versus lectures. *Teaching of Psychology, 41,* 144–147. doi:10.1177/0098628314530347

Griggs, R. A., & Jackson, S. L. (2013). Introductory psychology textbooks: An objective analysis update. *Teaching of Psychology, 40,* 163–168. doi:10.1177/0098628313487455

Gutchess, A. H., Welsh, R. C., Boduroğlu, A., & Park, D. C. (2006). Cultural differences in neural function associated with object processing. *Cognitive, Affective, & Behavioral Neuroscience, 6*(2), 102–109. doi:10.3758/CABN.6.2.102

Hackman, D. A., & Farah, M. J. (2009). Socioeconomic status and the developing brain. *Trends in Cognitive Sciences, 13*(2), 65–73. doi:10.1016/j.tics.2008.11.003

Hedden, T., Ketay, S., Aron, A., Markus, H. R., & Gabrieli, J. D. (2008). Cultural influences on neural substrates of attentional control. *Psychological Science, 19,* 12–17. doi:10.1111/j.1467-9280.2008.02038.x

Hess, T. M., Auman, C., Colcombe, S. J., & Rahhal, T. A. (2003). The impact of stereotype threat on age differences in memory performance. *The Journals of Gerontology Series B: Psychological Sciences and Social Sciences, 58*(1), P3–P11. doi:10.1093/geronb/58.1.P3

Hill, G. W. (1998). Nonverbal communication through gestures. Activities and videos for teaching cross-cultural issues in psychology. Society for the Teaching of Psychology (APA Division 2), Office of Teaching Resources in Psychology (OTRP). Retrieved from http://teachpsych.org/resources/Documents/otrp/resources/hill98activities.pdf

(2004). *Cross-cultural verbal misunderstandings: Instructor's manual with test bank for Matsumoto and Juang's culture and psychology* (3rd ed.). Belmont, CA: Wadsworth.

Homa, N., Hackathorn, J., Brown, C. M., Garczynski, A., Solomon, E. D., Tennial, R. … & Gurung, R. A. (2013). An analysis of learning objectives and content coverage in introductory psychology syllabi. *Teaching of Psychology, 40,* 169–174. doi:10.1177/0098628313487456

Hoyert, M. S., & O'Dell, C. D. (2000). Examining memory phenomena through flashbulb memories. *Teaching of Psychology, 27,* 272–273. doi:10.1207/S15328023TOP2704_06

Hunt, E., & Agnoli, F. (1991). The Whorfian hypothesis: A cognitive psychology perspective. *Psychological Review, 98*, 377. doi.10.1037/0033–295X.98.3.377

Hyde, J. S. (2005). The gender similarities hypothesis. *American Psychologist, 60*, 581–592. doi:10.1037/0003-066X.60.6.581

Hyde, J. S., Fennema, E., & Lamon, S. (1990). Gender differences in mathematics performance: A meta-analysis. *Psychological Bulletin, 107*, 139–155. doi:10.1037/0033-2909.107.2.139

Hyde, J. S., & Linn, M. C. (1988). Gender differences in verbal ability: A meta-analysis. *Psychological Bulletin, 104*, 53–69.

Hyde, J. S., Lindberg, S. M., Linn, M. C., Ellis, A. B., & Williams, C. C. (2008). Gender similarities characterize math performance. *Science, 321*, 494–495. doi: 10.1126/science.1160364.

Hyde, J. S., & Mertz, J. E. (2009). Gender, culture and mathematics performance. *Proceedings of the National Academy of Sciences, 106*(22), 8801–8807. doi:10.1126/science.1160364

Isaacs, E. B., Fischl, B. R., Quinn, B. T., Chong, W. K., Gadian, D. G., & Lucas, A. (2010). Impact of breast milk on intelligence quotient, brain size, and white matter development. *Pediatric Research, 67*, 357–362. doi:10.1203/PDR.0b013e3181d026da

Kim, H. S. (2002). We talk, therefore we think? A cultural analysis of the effect of talking on thinking. *Journal of Personality and Social Psychology, 83*, 828–842. doi:10.1037//0022-3514.83.4.828

Kluck, A. S. (2005). Integrating multiculturalism into the teaching of psychology: Why and how? In T. Zinn, B. K. Saville, & J. E. Williams (Eds.), *Essays from e-xcellence in teaching* (Vol. 5). Retrieved from http://teachpsych.org/Resources/Documents/ebooks/eit2005.pdf

Kroll, J. F., Dussias, P. E., Bogulski, C. A., & Kroff, J. R. V. (2012). Juggling two languages in one mind: What bilinguals tell us about language processing and its consequences for cognition. In B. H. Ross (Ed.), *The psychology of learning and motivation* (pp. 229–262). San Diego, CA: Elsevier. doi:10.1016/B978-0-12-394393-4.00007-8

Levy, B., & Langer, E. (1994). Aging free from negative stereotypes: Successful memory in China and among the American deaf. *Journal of Personality and Social Psychology, 66*, 989–997. doi:10.1037/0022-3514.66.6.989

Matsumoto, D. (2008). Some thoughts about teaching issues of culture in psychology. In S. A. Meyers & J. R. Stowell (Eds.), *Essays from e-xcellence in teaching* (Vol. 7, pp. 14–17). Retrieved from http://teachpsych.org/ebooks/eit2007/index.php

McCann, L. I., Immel, K. R., Kadah-Ammeter, T. L., & Adelson, S. K. (2016). The importance and interest of introductory psychology textbook topics student opinions at technical college, 2-, and 4-year institutions. *Teaching of Psychology, 43*, 215–220. doi:10.1177/0098628316649477

Mori, Y., & Shimizu, H. (2007). Japanese language students' attitudes toward kanji and their perceptions on kanji learning strategies. *Foreign Language Annals, 40*, 472–490. doi:10.1111/j.1944-9720.2007.tb02871.x

Norenzayan, A., Smith, E. E., Kim, B. J., & Nisbett, R. E. (2002). Cultural preferences for formal versus intuitive reasoning. *Cognitive Science, 26,* 653–684. doi:10.1207/s15516709cog2605_4

Ocampo, C., Prieto, L. R., Whittlesey, V., Connor, J., Janco-Gidley, J., Mannix, S., & Sare, K. (2003). Diversity research in teaching of psychology: Summary and recommendations. *Teaching of Psychology, 30,* 5–18. doi:10.1207/S15328023TOP3001_02

Oppenheimer, J. (Director), Herzog, W. (Producer), & Morris, E. (Producer) (2012). *The act of killing.* Denmark: Final Cut for Real.

Pinker, S. (2016, August 12). AI won't takeover the world, and what our fears of the robopocalypse reveal. *Big Think.* Retrieved from http://bigthink.com/videos/steven-pinker-on-artificial-intelligence-apocalypse?utm_campaign=Echobox&utm_medium=Social&utm_source=Facebook#link_time=1488405438

Ransdell, S., Barbier, M., & Niit, T. (2006). Metacognitions about language skill and working memory among monolingual and bilingual college students: When does multilingualism matter? *International Journal of Bilingual Education and Bilingualism, 9*(6), 728–741. doi:10.2167/beb390.0

Richmond, A. S., Broussard, K., Shardy, J. C., Sanders, K. K., Sterns, J. L., & Lieberenz, S. K. (2015). Who are we studying? Sample diversity in teaching of psychology research. *Teaching of Psychology, 42,* 218–226. doi:10.1177/0098628315587619

Rominger, R., & Kolesar, A. (2008). Diversity related bibliography and resources. Retrieved from http://teachpsych.org/resources/Documents/otrp/resources/rominger08.pdf

Ropeik, D. (2011, March 9). Take the cultural cognition quiz. *Psychology Today.* Retrieved from www.psychologytoday.com/blog/how-risky-is-it-really/201103/take-the-cultural-cognition-quiz

Spelke, E. S. (2005). Sex differences in intrinsic aptitude for mathematics and science? A critical review. *American Psychologist, 60,* 950–958. doi:10.1037/0003-066X.60.9.950

Stiegler-Balfour, J. J. (2013). Memory. In S. E. Afful, J. J. Good, J. Keeley, S. Leder, & J. J. Stiegler-Balfour (Eds.). *Introductory psychology teaching primer: A guide for new teachers of Psych 101.* Retrieved from the Society for the Teaching of Psychology, http://teachpsych.org/ebooks/intro2013/index.php

Swinkels, A. (2003). An effective exercise for teaching cognitive heuristics. *Teaching of Psychology, 30,* 120–122. doi:10.1207/S15328023TOP3002_08

Varnum, M. E., Grossmann, I., Kitayama, S., & Nisbett, R. E. (2010). The origin of cultural differences in cognition the social orientation hypothesis. *Current Directions in Psychological Science, 19,* 9–13. doi:10.1177/0963721409359301

Velayo, R. S. (2011). Internationalizing your psychology course. In J. Holmes, S. C. Baker, & J. R. Stowell (Eds.), *Essays from e-xcellence in teaching* (Vol. 10, pp. 6–9). Retrieved from http://teachpsych.org/ebooks/eit2010/index.php

Warren, C. S. (2006). Incorporating multiculturalism into undergraduate psychology courses: Three simple active learning activities. *Teaching of Psychology, 33*, 105–109. doi:10.1207/s15328023top3302_5

Williams, R. L. (1975). *Black Intelligence Test of Cultural Homogeneity: Manual of directions.* St. Louis, MO: Williams.

Winerman, L. (2006). The culture-cognition connection. *Monitor on Psychology, 37*(2), 64. Retrieved from www.apa.org/monitor/feb06/connection.aspx

Zwebner, Y., Sellier, A. L., Rosenfeld, N., Goldenberg, J., & Mayo, R. (2017). We look like our names: The manifestation of name stereotypes in facial appearance. *Journal of Personality and Social Psychology, 112*, 527–554. doi:10.1037/pspa0000076

CHAPTER 13

Integration of Culture in the Teaching of Memory

Qi Wang

Approximately 85 years ago, in a social psychology laboratory at Cambridge University, psychologist Frederic Bartlett was testing the memories of his "educated and rather sophisticated" participants of an English background – Cambridge students. He was interested in social influences on the transformations or reconstructions of material in memory. He asked his participants to read the following story of a rather strange Native American folktale (Bartlett, 1932, p. 65):

The War of the Ghosts
One night two young men from Egulac went down to the river to hunt seals, and while they were there it became foggy and calm. Then they heard war-cries, and they thought: "Maybe this is a war party." They escaped to the shore, and hid behind a log. Now canoes came up, and they heard the noise of paddles, and saw one canoe coming up to them. There were five men in the canoe and they said:

"What do you think? We wish to take you along. We are going up the river to make war on the people."

One of the young men said: "I have no arrows."

"Arrows are in the canoe," they said.

"I will not go along. I might be killed. My relatives do not know where I have gone. But you," he said, turning to the other, "may go with them."

So one of the young men went, but the other returned home.

And the warriors went on up the river to a town on the other side of Kalama.

The people came down to the water, and they began to fight, and many were killed. But presently the young man heard one of the warriors say: "Quick, let us go home: that Indian has been hit." Now he thought: "Oh, they are ghosts," He did not feel sick, but they said he had been shot.

So the canoes went back to Egulac, and the young man went ashore to his house, and made a fire. And he told everybody and said: "Behold

I accompanied the ghosts, and we went to fight. Many of our fellows were killed, and many of those who attacked us were killed. They said I was hit, and I did not feel sick."

He told it all, and then he became quiet. When the sun rose he fell down. Something black came out of his mouth. His face became contorted. The people jumped up and cried.

He was dead.

After the participants read the story, Bartlett repeatedly tested their memories for it at different time intervals, ranging from 15 minutes to as long as 10 years. Bartlett expected that through repeated remembering, supernatural elements and unusual terms and events in the folktale would eventually be transformed into a "stereotyped form" familiar to the Cambridge students. That was indeed what he found: Many of the foreign elements of the story dropped out of memory or appeared in forms common to the participants' social group. For example, one participant later recalled the phrase "something black came out of his mouth" as "he foamed at the mouth." Another participant replaced "canoe" with "boat" and hunting seals with "fishing" in his recall. Most interestingly, the part about the ghosts, which was highly significant to the original story, was completely missed by all participants. As time went by, the strangeness of the folktale was entirely gone, and the content and style of the recalled stories became more and more familiar and stereotyped in line with the participants' cultural norms and expectations.

Bartlett's findings were groundbreaking at the time. They reveal the constructive nature of remembering: Memory is an active act of rationalization, interpretation, and transformation, rather than a faithful photocopy of the outside world or a mere recovery of information stored in the brain. People's general knowledge about the world influences how they perceive, understand, process, and remember new information. More important from the current perspective, memory reconstruction is deeply conditioned by the wealth of customs, institutions, and traditions of a group, such that "social organization gives a persistent framework into which all detailed recall must fit, and it very powerfully influences both the manner and the matter of recall" (Bartlett, 1932, p. 296). Bartlett's conviction in the sociocultural formulation of memory has been confirmed and extended in the past two decades of cross-cultural research (for a review, see Wang, 2013), which has provided both the convincing rationale and rich resources for integrating culture in the teaching of memory.

Culture in Remembering

The influence of culture on the constructive process of remembering is pervasive and overarching. To conceptualize the critical role of culture in remembering, Wang (2016b) proposed a cultural dynamic theory as the framework to understand and predict the effects of cultural variables on memory. In the theory, memory is construed as an open system that emerges, develops, and transforms under the multitude of influences of culture (for a detailed discussion, see Wang, 2016b). Specifically, the theory posits that memory takes place in the dynamic transaction between an active individual and his or her changing environment; it is situated in culturally conditioned time and space over a multitude of timescales; and it develops in the process of children acquiring cultural knowledge about the self and the purpose of the past through early socialization. These integrative premises lead to the predictions that there are cultural variations in memory components as a result of pertaining cultural variables; the cultural influences can be observed at different stages of remembering, from encoding to recall; and the cultural differences emerge early and originate from interactions between parents and children.

The cultural dynamic theory has been used as an explanatory framework to understand cultural influences on various aspects or components of memory, including memory content, structure, valence, subjectivity, accessibility, and functional usage (Wang, 2016b). For the purpose of illustrating the integration of culture in the teaching of memory, I focus here on *memory content* – the extent to which memory information concerns rememberers themselves versus others and social interactions (i.e., self-focus versus other focus) and *memory valence* – the extent to which memory information concerns positive versus negative past experiences. I present data from Western, particularly European American, and East Asian samples that have been frequently studied in cross-cultural research.

One cultural variable that has been found to be particularly responsible for shaping memory is culturally prioritized self-goals (for a review, see Wang 2013). Cognitive theories have emphasized the executive role of working self-goals in modulating the process of remembering (Conway & Pleydell-Pearce, 2000). These currently activated self-goals channel cognitive resources to encode and consolidate goal-consistent information into memory and later prioritize the selective retrieval of such information at recall, thus profoundly influencing what events and what aspects of the events are remembered. Critically, fundamental self-goals, such as autonomy, relatedness, self-enhancement, and self-improvement, although universally existing, are variably prioritized across cultures (Heine, Lehman, Markus, & Kitayama, 1999; Wang, 2013). The self-goals that are prioritized in a particular cultural context often remain chronically active to guide the remembering process. Thus, in cultures that prioritize autonomous self-goals, as European American culture often does, people may be motivated to focus on information concerning their own roles and perspectives that accentuates the uniqueness of the individual. Such information is likely to be well represented in memory and highly accessible during recall. In contrast, in cultures that prioritize relational self-goals, as East Asian cultures often do, people may focus on and remember information about collective activities and important others.

Consistent with this theoretical prediction, cross-cultural research has shown that when asked to recall recent or distant personal experiences, European American adults often recall memories of unique personal experiences with idiosyncratic details and cast themselves as the central character of the story (e.g., successes, fears, nightmares) whereas Asians and Asian Americans often recall memories focusing on the roles of others and social interactions (e.g., school activities, family outings, disputes with neighbors; Wang, 2001a, 2006, 2008; Wang & Conway, 2004). These cultural differences have been observed in children as young as preschoolers (e.g., Han, Leichtman, & Wang, 1998; Peterson, Wang, & Hou, 2009; Wang, 2004). The culturally prioritized self-goals are further related to memory content at the individual level such that, regardless of culture, people who exhibit more salient autonomous self-goals also tend to recall more self-focused and less socially orientated memories compared with those who exhibit more salient relational self-goals (Wang, 2001a, 2004).

Additional evidence for the influence of culturally prioritized self-goals on memory content came from studies that experimentally primed self-goals to increase the retrieval of memory content consistent with the self-goals (Wang, 2008; Wang & Ross, 2005; Wang, Shao, & Li, 2010). For instance, Wang and Ross (2005, Study 1) asked European American and Asian college students to describe themselves as either unique individuals (i.e., autonomous-self prime) or as members of social groups (i.e., relational-self prime). The students then recalled their earliest childhood memories. In both cultural groups, those whose autonomous self-goals were activated prior to the recall reported more self-focused memories whereas those whose relational self-goals were made salient recalled more socially oriented memories. In a follow-up study (Wang & Ross, 2005,

Study 2), participants received the same primes as in Study 1 and were asked to read a storybook that had only illustrations but no words. Participants then received a surprise memory test about the story shortly after the reading. Compared with those in the relational-self prime condition, those in the autonomous-self prime condition recalled more information about the protagonist and introduced fewer peripheral characters and fewer social interactions in their story memories. Thus, when remembering both personal experiences and story material, memory content reflected the particular self-goals being primed. These findings provide experimental evidence for the influence of cultural self-goals on memory content focus.

Importantly, the priming effects did not eliminate or even reduce the magnitude of cultural differences in either personal memory or story memory: European Americans recalled more self-focused and protagonist-focused memories than did Asians, regardless of priming manipulations (Wang & Ross, 2005). Thus, priming and culture exerted independent effects on memory. These findings suggest that the cognitive frame (i.e., activated self-goals) at the time of retrieval is not the sole determinant of recall and that cultural discrepancies in recall may reflect differences in how information is originally represented in memory. In other words, cultural self-goals may not only filter the information people retrieve from memory, but also directly act upon memory encoding by affecting people's attention, perception, emotion, and meaning analysis during an ongoing event, thus determining how, what, and whether at all event information is encoded in memory (Wang, 2013, 2016b).

Along the same line, self-goals for enhancement versus improvement are variously emphasized across cultures, which, in turn, influence the valence of memories. Western, particularly European American, cultures endorse to a greater extent self-enhancement goals that motivate individuals to pursue and maintain a positive sense of self whereas East Asian cultures prioritize self-improvement goals that motivate individuals to seek actual change and improvement in the self (Heine & Hamamura, 2007; Heine et al., 1999). As a result, Western individuals may tend to dwell on past events that boost their positive self-views whereas East Asians may attend to events that provide opportunities for self-reflection and improvement. Indeed, research has shown that whereas European Americans tend to exhibit a positive bias in memory, East Asians are often evenhanded in remembering positive and negative events and sometimes even focus more on negative experiences (Endo & Meijer, 2004; Oishi, 2002; Ross, Heine, Wilson, & Sugimori, 2005).

In Endo and Meijer (2004), for example, US and Japanese college students were asked to recall as many instances as they could of success and failure that they had experienced in their lives. Whereas Americans recalled considerably more success stories than failure stories, Japanese recalled slightly more failure stories than success stories. Similarly, Ross and colleagues (2005) asked Canadian and Japanese college students to recall events that either made them feel proud or embarrassed. Although Canadians found proud events easier to recall than embarrassing events, Japanese found no difference in recalling proud and embarrassing events. Oishi (2002) further found that whereas there was no cultural difference in people's actual emotional experiences on a daily basis, European Americans retrospectively recalled their experiences in a more positive light than did Asian Americans. Interestingly, people who exhibit greater self-enhancement goals, namely, people who perceive themselves more positively, also tend to recall more self-focused and less socially orientated memories, regardless of culture (Wang, 2001a, 2004). It appears that autonomy and self-enhancement motivations go hand in hand in affecting memory across individuals and cultures.

Cultural differences in memory valence may further reflect different cultural experiences people encounter in their daily lives and thus different types of information they encode in memory. In a study by Kitayama, Markus, Matsumoto, & Norasakkunkit (1997) using a situation sampling method, Japanese and American participants were asked to recall situations they had experienced in which their self-esteem either increased or decreased. A second group of Japanese and American participants were then asked to judge how much their self-esteem would have increased or decreased if they had been in those situations themselves. Both Japanese and Americans judged the Japanese self-esteem – decreasing situations as more condemning to their self-esteem than American ones, and judged the American self-esteem–increasing situations as more enhancing to their self-esteem than Japanese ones. Thus, life experiences that people regularly encounter in the United States are particularly effective in boosting positive self-views whereas life experiences that people regularly encounter in Japan afford opportunities for self-criticism. The different kinds of experiences can be subsequently encoded and retained in memory, contributing to cultural differences in memory valence.

Cultural differences in memory content and valence can be traced back to early narrative interactions between parents and their young children. Cross-cultural studies have consistently revealed differences in the structure, organization, and content focus of parent–child memory sharing in line with the prevailing self-goals in respective cultural contexts (Miller, Wiley, Fung, & Liang, 1997; Mullen & Yi, 1995; Sahin-Acar & Leichtman, 2015; Wang, 2001b; Wang, Leichtman, & Davies, 2000). Memory sharing between European American mothers and children often takes a child-centered approach, where the child remains the focal point of the conversation and the mother frequently refers to the child's roles and perspectives in the past event. In contrast, memory sharing in East Asian families often takes a mother-centered, hierarchically organized approach in which the mother sets the direction of the conversation and frequently refers to social interactions and group activities in the past event. Furthermore, European American mothers tend to observe a "looking good" principle, in which they frequently position their children in a positive light (Miller et al., 1997; Ochs, Smith, & Taylor, 1989). In contrast, East Asian mothers often adopt a "didactic mode" in which they bring about children's past transgressions as the focal point of the story and explicitly instruct children to follow rules (Miller et al., 1997; Muller & Yi, 1995; Wang, 2001b; Wang et al., 2000).

Consider the following conversation between a European American mother (M) and her 3-year-old daughter (C) about a recent visit to Grandma's house (Wang, 2013, p. 8):

M: Do you remember when we're at Nana's on vacation, and we went down to the dock at Grandmommy's? You went swimming?

C: Um-hum.

M: What did you do that was really neat?

C: Jump off the dock.

M: Yeah. That was the first time you've ever done that.

C: That was like a diving board.

M: You're right, it was. And where did Mommy have to stand?

A: In the sandy spot.

M: In the sandy spot, right. Mommy said, "Wait, wait, wait! Don't jump 'til I get into my sandy spot!"

A: Why?

M: 'Cause you remember how I told all the leaves pile up on the bottom of the lake? And it makes it a little mushy. And so, you jumped off the dock and then what did you do?

C: Swim.

M: To...

C: Nana.

M: Yeah. All by yourself with what on your back?

C: Bubbles.

M: Yeah.

This conversation focuses on what the little girl accomplished in the past event. The mother repeatedly talks about the child's roles, actions, and opinions and encourages the child to do so as well. During the conversational exchange, the mother and child assume an equal partnership, commenting and expanding on each other's responses and together keeping the conversation going. The end result is a coherent story with the child being a courageous little heroine. Such parent–child narrative interactions cultivate a sense of autonomy and uniqueness in the child on the one hand and boost the positivity of the child's self-views on the other. They further facilitate a culture-specific mode of remembering that highlights the individual as the central character of the story basks in glory and success.

The following conversation that occurred at dinnertime of a Chinese American family illustrates typical narrative interactions between East Asian parents and their children. Here, the mother (M) initiated a conversation in the presence of the father (F) about the misbehavior of the 4-year-old boy, Baobao (C), that took place earlier during the day (Wang, 2013, p. 19):

M: Baobao, did you tell papa what you did wrong today?
F: He made mistake again?
M: Did you tell Papa? Huh?
C: (makes noise, sounds like yes)
M: Huh?
C: Already told Papa.
M: You already told Mama, right?
C: Right.
M: Did you tell Papa? Papa doesn't know.
C: No.
M: What happened to you at Aunty Lee's house?
C: Baobao didn't want to go in.
M: Hmm ... you were at the door and didn't want to go in. And then what?
C: Didn't play with Edward.
M: Hmm ... you didn't want to play with Edward. Hmm ... anything else?
C: At the staircase, didn't say "bye-bye"
M: Hmm ...
C: Didn't close the door properly.
M: Hmm.... Did you hear, Papa?
F: I heard. Baobao told Papa already.
M: Already told Papa?
F: Papa already know. Next time (Baobao) will behave better, right?
M: Next time don't make mistakes, okay?

Apparently, Baobao is not eager at the beginning to talk about what he did wrong that day. In spite of his reluctance, his mother insists that Baobao report to his father each of his wrongdoings during a visit to a friend's house. With his mother's repeated questioning, Baobao finally gives in and does an excellent job in making his "confession." The conversation ends with a moral coda of future behavioral expectations. During this exchange, the mother plays a leading role in directing the conversation, situates the child in social contexts, and explicitly evaluates his behavior in relation to others. Such parent–child narrative interactions instill a sense of relatedness and belonging in the child on the one hand, and encourage self-examination and self-improvement on the other. They further facilitate a culture-specific mode of remembering that is centered on important others and relationships and on learning lessons from the past to ensure smooth social interactions.

Taken together, as the cultural dynamic theory predicts (Wang, 2016b), memory content and valence exhibit systematic variations in line with culturally prioritized self-goals that emphasize autonomy versus relatedness and those that emphasize self-enhancement versus self-improvement. Such variations reflect cultural influences on memory not only at recall but also at encoding. The variations further originate from early narrative inter-actions between parents and children that model to children what to remember, how to remember, and why to remember it in line with cultural norms and expectations. Thus, memory serves culture-specific goals and functions and reflects individuals' conscious or unconscious responses to varied cultural experiences (Alea & Wang, 2015).

Integrating Culture in the Teaching of Memory

I have reviewed research on cultural influences on memory content, memory valence, and the early narrative interactions between parents and children. I will provide an example of each case for the integration of culture in the teaching of memory. The topic of memory, especially personal memory, is directly relevant to people's daily experiences and can resonate with students personally. As a result, I have found that the most effective way of demonstrating cultural influences on memory is to directly involve students in the remembering process. Students often find the activities interesting and engaging, and are often surprised by the memory differences produced right in the class.

Example 1: Culture and memory content

This example activity involves cultural priming and subsequent assessment of personal memory. Divide the class into two groups (e.g., students sitting on the right side of the classroom as Group A and those sitting on the left side as Group B). Present the following story beginning (adapted from Trafimow, Triandis, & Goto, 1991, p. 652) on a slide to both groups (30 seconds):

> Sostoras, a warrior in ancient Sumer, was largely responsible for the success of Sargon I in conquering all of Mesopotamia. As a result, he was rewarded with a small kingdom of his own to rule. About 10 years later, Sargon I was conscripting warriors for a new war. Sostoras was obligated to send a detachment of soldiers to aid Sargon I. He had to decide whom to put in command of the detachment.

Then ask Group A to close their eyes and Group B to continue to read on the next slide the first (individual) version of the story-ending (30 seconds):

> After thinking about it for a long time, Sostoras eventually decided on Tiglath who was a talented general. This appointment had several advantages. Sostoras was able to make an excellent general indebted to him. This would solidify Sostoras's hold on his own dominion. In addition, the very fact of having a general such as Tiglath as his personal representative would greatly increase Sostoras's prestige. Finally, sending his best general would be likely to make Sargon I grateful.

Ask Group B to close their eyes and Group A to read on the next slide the second (social) version of the story ending (30 seconds):

> After thinking about it for a long time, Sostoras eventually decided on Tiglath who was a member of his family. This appointment had several advantages. Sostoras was able to show his loyalty to his family. He was also able to cement their loyalty to him. In addition, having Tiglath as the commander increased the power and prestige of the family. Finally, if Tiglath performed well, Sargon I would be indebted to the family.

Present both groups with the memory task (3–5 minutes):

- Think about ... [e.g., the moment when you received the admission letter from your university; the first day of this semester; the last Valentine's day]
- Use five sentences to describe what happened. Write them down.

After students finish their memories, post the following task on the next slide (1 minute):

- How many sentences focus on only yourself, and how many sentences include references to others?

Ask the students to raise their hands if they have three or more sentences concerning only themselves. Compare the numbers of hands between Groups A and B. Are there more students in Group B who read the individual version of the story ending, raising their hands, compared with those in Group A who read the social version of the story ending?

For further illustration, the following two memory examples can be presented to students. They were recalled by participants in a study that examined the influence of self-goals on memory content by priming the bicultural self in Asian Americans (Wang, 2008). Asian Americans, and immigrants in general, often develop a "double-identity" corresponding to the cultural belief systems of the host culture and their culture of origin (Devos, 2006; Ryder, Alden, & Paulhus, 2000). Whereas the "American identity" is associated with mainstream American values of independence and autonomy, the "Asian identity" is associated with Asian cultural values of mutual dependence and collective interest. Priming each identity presumably activates autonomous or relational self-goals, which then modulate access to memory information consistent with the activated self-goals. In the study (Wang, 2008), Asian American students were asked to describe themselves as being either American or Asian. They then each recalled two autobiographical events of personal importance. Students whose American identity was made salient were more likely to recall memories of exclusive personal experiences and focused more on their own roles and perspectives and less on social interactions and significant others when compared with those whose Asian identity was made salient.

The two memory examples both concern the time when the participants received the news of being accepted to Cornell, yet their content focus showed striking differences: The first memory, provided by a participant in the American identity condition, focuses on his own experience and personal emotions and predilections whereas the second memory, provided by a participant in the Asian identity condition, focuses on the shared experience and social interactions between him and significant others. Thus, the two memories, although about a similar event, differed in content as a function of the cultural identity and the associated self-goals activated at recall (Wang, 2008, pp. 748–749):

> I got the acceptance letter for Cornell. I did not like my high school at the time & most of the people in it, so this was very good news to me. I remember flipping up and down on my bed upon reading it, and then taking the car keys & going for a drive. I recall the Van Halen song, "Standing on Top of the World" being played on the Radio, and me singing along to it, with the window down. Then I remember getting out of my car in a big parking lot, and screaming at the top of my lungs. I was ecstatic. The hard work paid off, and I was getting out of this town.
>
> The day I got my letter of acceptance to Cornell gave me a sense of relief. I had made it. I thought this would make my parents pretty happy. Well, they were happy. But, they knew better than to abandon their caution. You'll have to work hard, they say. I know I do. So it's not the fact of accomplishing something that makes my parents happy or puts them at ease. It's the ability to plan and the existence of some sort of personal ambition. That's it.

Example 2: Culture and memory valence

A simple, in-class activity can be organized based on the methods used in cross-cultural research on memory valence (e.g., Endo & Meijer, 2004; Oishi, 2002; Kitayama et al., 1997; Ross et al., 2005). Divide the class into two groups (e.g., students sitting on the right side of the classroom as Group A and those sitting on the left side as Group B). Ask Group A to recall positive experiences and Group B to recall negative experiences. Then switch the task so that Group A now recalls negative experiences and Group B recalls positive experiences (3 minutes for each valence). In other words, this activity involves a within-subject design with the order of event valence counterbalanced.

The memory questions can be general or specific, taking into consideration the characteristics and interests of the students in the class. The timeline of the memories can be distant or across the entire lifespan, or from a recent life period. Here are some examples:

• Recall as many incidences as you can of success that you have experienced in your life.
• Recall as many incidences as you can of failure that you have experienced in your life.

Or

• List all the events that you have experienced in the past 2 weeks that made you feel good about yourself.
• List all the events that you have experienced in the past 2 weeks that made you feel bad about yourself.

Or

• List all the positive events that have happened to you since the beginning of the semester.
• List all the negative events that have happened to you since the beginning of the semester.

Or

• Recall as many past incidences as you can that made you feel particularly proud.
• Recall as many past incidences as you can that made you feel especially embarrassed.

After the students complete the recall, ask them to count the number of positive and negative events, respectively. Ask the students who have recalled more positive than negative events to raise hands, and then ask those who have recalled more negative than positive events to raise hands. Alternatively, ask the students to compute a positive-to-negative ratio score (i.e., the number of positive events divided by the number of negative events) and if the technology (e.g., clickers) is available, show the distribution of the ratio scores to the class. Then discuss past cross-cultural findings about memory valence (e.g., Endo & Meijer, 2004; Oishi, 2002; Kitayama et al., 1997; Ross et al., 2005), and explain the influences of self-goals for enhancement versus improvement that are variably emphasized in different cultures. Ask the students to discuss in small groups how their memories may be related to their appreciation for self-enhancement or self-improvement goals.

Example 3: Culture and parent–child memory sharing

To demonstrate cultural influences on how parents share memories with their children, ask students to recall their early interactions with their parents. The activity can focus on a memorable conversation that students had with their parents as a young child (3–5 minutes):

> Think back about a time when you were before age 8. Remember a conversation that you and your parents had about a past event that you experienced. What was it about? Recall as much detail as you can about how the conversation went.

After students complete the recall, ask individual students from different cultural backgrounds to share their memories with the class. Comment on the content focus and valence of the past event in the recalled conversation. Present cross-cultural findings on the different ways that parents in East Asian and Western cultures share memories with their children (Miller et al., 1997; Muller & Yi, 1995; Wang, 2001b; Wang et al., 2000). Show the students the conversational examples that I included in the last section.

Alternatively, the activity can focus on memory sharing more generally between students and their parents during their early childhood. The following instruction is adapted from a study in which parents were asked to report on the frequency, occasions, and reasons for sharing memories with their young children (Kulkofsky, Wang, & Koh, 2009).

> Think back about the time when you were at the preschool age. Did your parents talk with you about past events that you experienced? Estimate how many times per week you and your parents talked about the past (e.g., 0 times, 1–2 times, 3–4 times, 5–7 times, more than 7 times). Think about when and why your parents usually shared memories with you. Briefly describe each occasion.

Students can do this activity on their own, or discuss it with their neighbors (5 minutes). After they complete the task, ask individual students from different cultural backgrounds to share their answers with the class. Comment on the occasions and reasons for sharing memories (e.g., to make the child feel good or to help the child learn a lesson). The frequency of memory sharing is also an interesting topic for discussion. Kulkofsky and colleagues (2009) found in their study that all European American mothers reported talking about the past at least once a week, and approximately 40 percent of them reported talking about the past more than seven times a week. In contrast, Chinese mothers were more likely than European American mothers to report talking about the past one to two times per week. Some of the Chinese mothers reported never sharing memories, and none of them reported talking about the past more than seven times a week. In general, compared with Asian parents, Western parents have been found to share memories with their children more frequently and more elaborately, in line with their cultural emphasis on the importance of remembering personal experiences for establishing and affirming an autonomous sense of self (Muller & Yi, 1995; Wang, 2001b, 2007; Wang et al., 2000).

In sum, these hands-on, personally involved activities can effectively engage students and illustrate the central role of culture in shaping individual memory as well as shared memory between parents and children.

Suggested Teaching Resources

In addition to the articles cited in the last section that are directly related to the activities of integrating culture in the teaching of memory, the following readings may be useful for teachers in preparation for the class or to recommend to advanced undergraduate or graduate students.

Wang, Q. (2013). *The autobiographical self in time and culture*. New York, NY: Oxford University Press. doi:10.1093/acprof:oso/9780199737833.001.0001

> The author traces the developmental, social, cultural, and historical origins of the autobiographical self – the self that is made of memories of our past. By analyzing everyday family storytelling, autobiographical writings in Western and Chinese literature, memory data from controlled experiments in the laboratory, and personal narratives on blogs and Facebook, the author illustrates that our memories and our selves are conditioned by time and culture. She examines some of the most controversial issues in current psychological research of memory and analyzes the influences of the larger social, political, and economic forces on the autobiographical self.

Wang, Q. (2016a). Why should we all be cultural psychologists? Lessons from the study of social cognition. *Perspectives on Psychological Science*, *11*(5), 583–596. doi:10.1177/1745691616645552

The author calls the attention of psychologists to the pivotal role of cultural psychology in extending and enriching research programs. She argues that it is not enough to simply acknowledge the importance of culture, and urges psychologists to practice cultural psychology in their research. She deconstructs five assumptions about cultural psychology that seriously undermine its contribution to the building of a true psychological science. She discusses how cultural psychology can provide unique insights into psychological processes and further equip researchers with additional tools to understand human behavior.

Wang, Q. (2016b). Remembering the self in cultural contexts: A cultural dynamic theory of autobiographical memory. [Special issue: Memory and connection: Remembering the past and imagining the future in individuals, groups, and cultures]. *Memory Studies, 9*(3), 295–304. doi:10.1177/1750698016645238

People from different cultures often tell diverse stories about their past experiences. Research in the past two decades has revealed systematic differences in the content (self-focus versus other focus), structure (specific versus general), valence (positive versus negative), accessibility (memory density, detailedness), developmental origin (age and density of earliest childhood memories), and functional usage (self-definition, relationship maintenance, behavioral guidance, emotion regulation) of autobiographical memory across cultures. The author outlines a cultural dynamic theory of autobiographical memory that aims to synthesize the findings and provide a coherent guide to future investigation.

Ross, M., & Wang, Q. (2010). Why we remember and what we remember: Culture and autobiographical memory. *Perspectives on Psychological Science, 5*(4), 401–409. doi:10.1177/1745691610375555

The authors examine cultural (mainly East–West) differences in the functions and contents of autobiographical memory. They discuss how cultural differences in physical environments, self-views, the motivation to self-enhance, concerns for behavioral control, socialization, emotional regulation, and language affect the development and use of memory. Cultural influences take place at the individual level of cognitive schemata and memory strategies, as well as the interpersonal sphere of daily mnemonic practices and exchanges. The authors conclude that autobiographical memory is categorically cultural.

References

Alea, N., & Wang, Q. (2015). Going global: The functions of autobiographical memory in cultural context. *Memory*, *23*(1), 1–10. doi:10.1080/0965 8211.2014.972416

Bartlett, F. C. (1932). *Remembering: A study in experimental and social psychology.* Cambridge: Cambridge University Press.

Conway, M., & Pleydell-Pearce, C. W. (2000). The construction of autobiographical memories in the self-memory system. *Psychological Review*, *107*(2), 261–288. doi:10.1037/0033-295X.107.2.261

Devos, T. (2006). Implicit bicultural identity among Mexican American and Asian American college students. *Cultural Diversity and Ethnic Minority Psychology*, *12*, 381–402. doi:10.1037/1099-9809.12.3.381

Endo, Y., & Meijer, Z. (2004) Autobiographical memory of success and failure experiences. In Y. Kashima, Y. Endo, E. S. Kashima, C. Leung, & J. McClure (Eds.), *Progress in Asian Social Psychology* (Vol. 4, pp. 67–84). Seoul, Korea: Kyoyook-Kwahak-Sa.

Han, J. J., Leichtman, M. D., & Wang, Q. (1998). Autobiographical memory in Korean, Chinese, and American children. *Developmental Psychology*, *34*(4), 701–713. doi:10.1037/0012-1649.34.4.701

Heine, S. J., & Hamamura, T. (2007). In search of East Asian self-enhancement. *Personality & Social Psychology Review*, *11*, 4–27. doi:10.1177/1088868 306294587

Heine, S. J., Lehman, D. R., Markus, H. R., & Kitayama, S. (1999). Is there a universal need for positive self-regard? *Psychological Review*, *106*, 766–794. doi:10.1037/0033-295X.106.4.766

Kitayama, S., Markus, H. R., Matsumoto, H., & Norasakkunkit, V. (1997). Individual and collective processes in the construction of the self: Self-enhancement in the United States and self-criticism in Japan. *Journal of Personality and Social Psychology*, *72*, 1245–1267. doi:10.1037/0022-3514.72.6.1245

Kulkofsky, S., Wang, Q., & Koh, J. B. K. (2009). Functions of memory sharing and mother-child reminiscing behaviors: Individual and cultural variations. *Journal of Cognition and Development*, *10*, 92–114. doi:10.1080/15248370903041231

Miller, P. J., Wiley, A. R., Fung, H., & Liang, C. H. (1997). Personal storytelling as a medium of socialization in Chinese and American families. *Child Development*, *68*, 557–568. doi:10.2307/1131678

Mullen, M. K., & Yi, S. (1995). The cultural context of talk about the past: Implications for the development of autobiographical memory. *Cognitive Development*, *10*, 407–419. doi:10.1016/0885-2014(95)90004-7

Ochs, E., Smith, R., & Taylor, C. (1989). Detective stories at dinnertime: Problem solving through co-narration. *Cultural Dynamics*, *2*, 238–257. doi:10.1177/092137408900200206

Oishi, S. (2002). The experiencing and remembering of well-being: A cross-cultural analysis. *Personality and Social Psychology Bulletin*, *28*, 1398–1406. doi:10.1177/014616702236871

Peterson, C., Wang, Q., & Hou, Y. (2009). "When I was little": Childhood recollections in Chinese and European Canadian grade school children. *Child Development, 80*(2), 506–518. doi:10.1111/j.1467-8624.2009.01275.x

Ross, M., Heine, S. J., Wilson, A. E., & Sugimori, S. (2005). Cross-cultural discrepancies in self-appraisals. *Personality and Social Psychology Bulletin, 31*, 1175–1188. doi:10.1177/0146167204274080

Ross, M., & Wang, Q. (2010). Why we remember and what we remember: Culture and autobiographical memory. *Perspectives on Psychological Science, 5*(4), 401–409. doi:10.1177/1745691610375555

Ryder, A. G., Alden, L. E., & Paulhus, D. L. (2000). Is acculturation unidimensional or bidimensional? A head-to-head comparison in the prediction of personality, self-identity, and adjustment. *Journal of Personality and Social Psychology, 79*, 49–65. doi:10.1037/0022-3514.79.1.49

Sahin-Acar, B., & Leichtman, M. D. (2015). Mother-child memory conversations and self-construal in Eastern Turkey, Western Turkey and the USA. *Memory, 23*(1), 69–82. doi:10.1080/09658211.2014.935437

Trafimow, D., Triandis, H. C., & Goto, S. G. (1991). Some tests of the distinction between the private self and the collective self. *Journal of Personality and Social Psychology, 60*(5), 649–655. doi:10.1037/0022-3514.60.5.649

Wang, Q. (2001a). Culture effects on adults' earliest childhood recollection and self-description: Implications for the relation between memory and the self. *Journal of Personality and Social Psychology, 81*(2), 220–233. doi:10.1037/0022-3514.81.2.220

(2001b). 'Did you have fun?' American and Chinese mother-child conversations about shared emotional experiences. *Cognitive Development, 16*, 693–715. doi:10.1016/S0885-2014(01)00055-7

(2004). The emergence of cultural self-constructs: Autobiographical memory and self-description in European American and Chinese children. *Developmental Psychology, 40*(1), 3–15. doi:10.1037/0012-1649.40.1.3

(2006). Earliest recollections of self and others in European American and Taiwanese young adults. *Psychological Science, 17*, 708–714. doi:10.1111/j.1467-8721.2006.00432.x

(2007). 'Remember when you got the big, big bulldozer?' Mother-child reminiscing over time and across cultures. *Social Cognition, 25*, 455–471. doi:10.1521/soco.2007.25.4.455

(2008). Being American, being Asian: The bicultural self and autobiographical memory in Asian Americans. *Cognition, 107*, 743–751. doi:10.1016/j.cognition.2007.08.005

(2013). *The autobiographical self in time and culture.* New York, NY: Oxford University Press. doi:10.1093/acprof:oso/9780199737833.001.0001

(2016a). Why should we all be cultural psychologists? Lessons from the study of social cognition. *Perspectives on Psychological Science, 11*(5), 583–596. doi:10.1177/1745691616645552

(2016b). Remembering the self in cultural contexts: A cultural dynamic theory of autobiographical memory. [Special issue: Memory and connection: Remembering the past and imagining the future in individuals, groups, and cultures]. *Memory Studies*, *9*, 295–304. doi:10.1177/1750698016645238

Wang, Q., & Conway, M. A. (2004). The stories we keep: Autobiographical memory in American and Chinese middle-aged adults. *Journal of Personality*, *72*, *5*, 911–938. doi:10.1111/j.0022-3506.2004.00285.x

Wang, Q., Leichtman, M. D., & Davies, K. I. (2000). Sharing memories and telling stories: American and Chinese mothers and their 3-year-olds. *Memory*, *8*, 159–178. doi:10.1080/096582100387588

Wang, Q., & Ross, M. (2005). What we remember and what we tell: The effects of culture and self-priming on memory representations and narratives. *Memory*, *13*, 594–606. doi:10.1080/09658210444000223

Wang, Q., Shao, Y., & Li, Y. J. (2010). "My way or Mom's way?" The bilingual and bicultural self in Hong Kong Chinese children and adolescents. *Child Development*, *81*, 555–567. doi:10.1111/j.1467-8624.2009.01415.x

CHAPTER 14

Bringing Life to Educational Psychology through Cross-Cultural Experiences

Noriyuki Inoue

Introduction

Numerous authors have agreed that a wide variety of human psychological functioning has a social and cultural basis (Bruner, 1998; Cole, 1996). Because psychological processes take place in a context, the cultural context will heavily influence the ways we interact with the world, make meanings, set goals, and take actions (Markus & Kitayama, 1991; Reagan, 2004; Uttal, 1995). These processes include learning and teaching that take place in schools and other educational settings.

Educational psychology has traditionally focused on theories and research on human cognition and learning relevant to school learning. In this field, many new paradigms have emerged and been replaced by others, but in recent years, the field has truly embraced the cultural basis of learning and teaching as one of its domains. Teaching is a cultural activity, and without critically examining the cultural foundation, it would be difficult to comprehend the psychological processes that take place in real-life practices (Göncü & Gauvain, 2012).

However, one essential agenda in the field is an effort to overcome the division between theories and practice. Too much emphasis on the positivistic approach to conceptualize learning can make educational psychology a field that is overly abstract and disconnected from actual school contexts (Inoue, 2015). Without making connections to real-life school contexts, students could go into teaching without a full understanding of real-life dynamics of classroom contexts. This decontextualized facet of educational psychology can cause major problems in teacher education programs where educational psychology is often a required course.

Researchers in the field have compellingly argued that human cognition and learning are heavily situated in their social and cultural contexts (Brown, Collins, & Duguid, 1989; Lave, 1991). Given this nature of human learning, it can also be argued that educational psychology needs to expand its scope beyond Western contexts and mono-cultural learning situations to reflect diverse and globalized societies (Inoue, 2012; Portes, 1996). As is well known, comparative studies of teacher education and teaching practices suggest that embracing different cultural assumptions and practices can lead to improving teacher education and classroom learning (see Darling-Hammond & Lieberman, 2012). A few well-known examples include improving the quality of teaching practices through Japanese lesson study (Stevenson & Stigler, 1992), the Finish approach to teaching practices (Sahlberg, 2011), and the Singaporean curriculum to strengthen students' academic achievement (Ng, 2007). These popular cases point to the need to embrace cross-cultural perspectives to reconceptualize teacher education beyond local perspectives so that teachers can critically examine their own cultural assumptions by considering diverse epistemological and ontological stances.

The question is how it is possible to teach educational psychology in a way that truly requires students to examine their own assumptions and embrace multicultural perspectives for their future teaching. It would be easy to simply add new reading assignments and class discussions to the course contents, but that may not ensure that students encounter cognitive dissonance in real-life settings and reflect on their assumptions in relation to cultural contexts. Promoting students' critical reflections for the improvement of teaching would require a much more effective approach that is grounded in real-life educational practices.

The following section discusses a case in which a graduate-level educational psychology course included a global study travel experience in Japan so that students could critically reflect on their own assumptions on teaching and learning through cross-cultural experiences. I first introduce the program logistics and contents, and then discuss what the students learned in the program. Finally, I discuss educational implications of this approach.

Tokyo Program: A Global Study Course on Cognition and Learning

The Tokyo Program started as a part of a master's level teacher education program in 2010 at a private higher education institution in Southern California. The university implemented global study initiatives to support new endeavors to internationalize the curriculum. The Tokyo Program was developed as a part of such endeavors implemented in the teacher education program at the university.

In the teacher education program, students are required to fulfill the international requirement for graduation. The program offers multiple opportunities for students to fulfill that requirement, but most of the students meet it by taking a global study course that involves a short-term study abroad. Global study opportunities are typically offered as academic courses in the teacher education program. Each year, a few of the faculty members who teach in the program offer one of their academic courses as a global study course. By taking a global study course in this way, students fulfill the international requirement and accumulate credits toward graduation. Most of the global study courses are taught in the summer, and the duration of the trip is typically 1 or 2 weeks with required local presessions and postsessions at the university before and after the trip. Almost all the students who participate in the program are preservice teachers.

In implementing the global study requirement, the university made the decision to reduce the fees for global study courses to half the regular course tuition. In addition to the tuition, students pay hotel, air, and other travel expenses, but the total amount they pay for the global study courses is typically equal to or less than the cost of a regular course. The university created this financial structure as an incentive for students to participate in global study programs. The teacher education program offers various global study courses that involve various countries, including Lithuania, Mexico, and England as well as the Tokyo Program.

In the teacher education program, the Tokyo Program was offered as an educational psychology course titled Cognition and Learning. To offer the program, I proposed to teach the course as a summer global study course and gained departmental approval each year. The course covered a variety of cognitive and learning theories in relation to various aspects of teaching practices and decision making that teachers make in classroom contexts. Before I proposed the global study program, the cognition and learning course was usually taught in the spring and summer on the campus at the university. The global study was a summer course designed to help students engage in substantial reflection on their cultural assumptions about learning in relation to psychological theories and their cross-cultural experiences. In a sense, the course was a natural choice for a summer course in Tokyo because students could benefit from incorporating discussions of East Asian epistemology with human development and learning (see Inoue, 2012). For example, learning about mind-set theory is enriched by incorporating the Confucian view of human growth, learning about social affective cognition is enriched by incorporation of the Taoist concepts of *yin* and *yang*, and learning about constructivism is enhanced by inclusion of the Japanese concept of *kizuki* (conceptual change that cannot be reversed).

To register in the summer global study program, students submitted an application to the global study office at the university in early spring. The application materials included the application form, a copy of the student's passport, a deposit, and other documentation. The number of the students applying for the program has varied from six to twelve, averaging about eight per year. Students first applied for the program before the deadline in early spring, and then were accepted on a first-come, first-served basis. Nearly all the applicants were accepted to the program with the exception of a few cases involving visa restrictions and missing documentations.

Program Content

Since its inception nearly a decade ago, the Tokyo Program has operated annually except for one summer (2011) when it was suspended due to the great East Japan earthquake. Each year the program has improved incrementally based on previous years' experiences. Although there have been minor variations in its content and learning activities, the core content and learning activities remained unchanged. The following section describes the typical content and schedule across the years.

Presessions. Before traveling to Japan, students participated in six presessions resembling the form of the regular *cognition and learning* course. The presessions included reading, lecture presentations, and discussions. Because the course was normally offered on the campus twice each year – in spring and in summer – it was necessary to make the content of the summer offering for the global study program equivalent to the spring offering. The predeparture sessions thus took the form of an intensive summer course over 2 weeks during which students completed the same reading assignments, lectures and class discussions, group presentations, classroom video analyses, and a short take-home exam as students who took the regular course. The key assignment for each student was the completion of a small action research project with a K–12 student. Students completed these projects in their practicum sites, guided by cognitive theories and research covered in the course. The assignment served as the final project, and involved work both before and after the Japan trip.

The following is a schedule of key topics covered in the presessions. All presessions involved open lectures and discussions to help students examine their cultural assumptions while planning and conducting the final project.

Session 1   Introduction: Overview of the course
              Philosophical foundations of cognitive studies

Theory and you: Construction of meaning
Action research methodology and epistemology
Session 2 Behaviorism
Contingency and self-regulated learning
Limitations of behaviorism
Session 3 Problem solving in classrooms
Variability in thinking for cognitive development
Cognitive strategies and meta-cognition
Brain, cognition, and uncertainty
Contingency, qualia, and mirror neurons
Society of mind
Japan travel orientation
Session 4 Piaget's theory of cognitive development
Cognitive constructivism
Theorizing in reality
Radical constructivism
Comparative studies on cognition and learning
Neriage: Japanese inquiry lessons
Japanese lesson study
Session 5 Vygotskian/neo-Vygotskian theories
Social constructivism
Human cognition and the society
Motivation to learn
Learning identity, belief, and cognition
Japanese cultural epistemology
Session 6 Cognition and personal development
Language and cognition
Self-concept and culture
Social and personal development and learning
Community of learners and culture
Action research as reflective inquiry
Predeparture orientation

By the end of the presessions, students were expected to have developed an understanding that (a) human cognition and learning are not independent of cultural values, beliefs, and assumptions, (b) Japanese teachers regularly collaborate with each other for the sake of professional growth and development in the form of lesson study, (c) and the way Japanese teachers educate their students is quite different from the US way with more emphasis on holistic development of students and less emphasis on performance. The students developed their understanding of these issues based on readings, videos on Japanese schooling, and class discussions to get ready for the trip.

For almost all the students who participated in the program, it was their first visit to Japan, and for many, it was their first journey abroad. At the end of these six presessions, I offered a short orientation to explain the logistics of the Japanese travel. After the presessions, the students traveled to Japan with much excitement and anticipation.

Japan session. After the students arrived in Japan and checked into the hotel, they and the faculty leader (the author) met for the first evening dinner at a Japanese restaurant. This arrangement helped students get to know each other and to share their perspectives easily. The remainder of the Japan schedule follows:

> **Day 1.** On the morning of the first day, the students visited the Japanese partner university. After a brief campus tour, they met their Japanese university partners – Japanese students and their professor – in a classroom on the central Tokyo campus. The Japanese group included five to ten undergraduate and graduate students studying education as a part of their human science degree programs. After self-introductions, a few of the US students who volunteered to present their ongoing action research projects gave PowerPoint presentations followed by questions and answers, and open-ended discussions on educational implications. Then some of the Japanese students presented their ongoing research projects, again followed by questions and discussions. Both the US and Japanese faculty members facilitated the discussions, with simultaneous translations provided by the US faculty member.
>
> These cross-cultural research exchanges resulted in many interesting discussions on the ways both groups view and study education. One of the key differences was that the US students started the project to assist teachers at their partnership school from their *individual* perspectives based on their teaching experiences whereas the Japanese students started the project from a perspective based on their *collective* experience. This individualistic versus collectivistic origin of preparation was an interesting contrast, and was evident in the cross-cultural discussions. The US students offered their ideas individually whereas the Japanese students first looked at each other, whispered their idea for affirmation from their peers, and then spoke up. Although there were cross-cultural differences in the style of discussion, there were active exchanges on the nature of professionalism of teachers, different types

of reflections that teachers can engage in, and ways teachers make sense of different points in their lessons. During the session, there were also many laughs and vibrant exchanges between the two groups of students.

When the afternoon session was complete, the US group returned to the hotel together via train, observing the behavior of people in everyday commuting. Many of the students indicated that they were impressed with how clean and tidy train stations were and how people behaved quietly and politely in the crowded train – interesting cultural observations to end a full day.

Day 2. On the second day, the group experienced a half-day tour of Tokyo, visiting key historic landmarks such as the Imperial Palace, Meiji Shrine, and Asakusa Sensoji Temple in central Tokyo. During the tour, the professional guide taught them about historic figures, a few Japanese expressions, cultural manners, and recent cultural trends. As on the previous day, the students observed how people behaved and interacted on streets and public places while touring the city. The tour ended around lunch time at a station about a 20-minute train ride from the hotel. Students continued exploring Tokyo and returned to the hotel on their own.

In the evening, the students participated in a cafe meeting intended to debrief what they saw and experienced during the day. Group members shared what they saw and experienced in various parts of the city, and discussed with ttheir professor how their experiences related to Japanese schooling and what they had been learning in the course. There were many responses, but all suspected that people's politeness and public manners could result from how students are educated in Japanese schools. Many group members were exhausted from jet lag, but all of them were curious to know what they would learn in Japanese classrooms on the next day.

Day 3. The third day started early in the morning to visit a secondary public school in a suburban city of Tokyo. The arrangement was made by the Japanese university partner, who works with the school district on a regular basis. The school was in a middle-class district with a wide variety of children from diverse economic backgrounds.

Orientation. The visit started with a meeting with the principal and the vice principal in one of the school's meeting rooms. The principal gave a brief introduction to the Japanese education system, the school curriculum, and the teacher education system in Japan. The group learned that in Japanese schools are committed not only to academic achievement of the students but also to their social and personal development. The group learned that the goal of education was defined by the Japanese Basic Educational Law Article 1 as holistic development of students – or "the completion of human character." The students also learned about the Japanese national curriculum, and how teachers collaborate with each other and make efforts to improve their teaching formally and informally.

Observation. After a question-and-answer session, the group observed classrooms where mathematics, science, English, Japanese, and society study lessons were in progress. The classroom activities were diverse, consisting of whole-class instructions, group activities, and presentations. Students also observed art, music, and physical education classes. They learned that students are students everywhere, and they were impressed with the emphasis on nonacademic development in the public school curriculum through required art and physical education classes.

Teacher education. Following lunch together at a local restaurant, the students visited the teacher development center operated by the city's public school district. During the visit, teacher education specialists from the district explained aspects of the teacher education system, such as local- and school-based lesson study initiatives and national-, prefectural-, and district-based teacher development initiatives. The specialists related how the center promotes teacher development while helping teachers to overcome a variety of contemporary issues in schools, such as bullying and poverty. The session continued for the entire afternoon with questions and answers. One of the key comments made by a teacher educator at the center was that Japanese education aims at creating a chain reaction of happiness so that students can become happy and contribute to the society. She explained this by creating origami chains one by one as a metaphor. Many US students later indicated how impressed they were with the idea, given that their student-teaching experiences in the United States were very different.

At the end of day, the Japanese university partner hosted a welcome party in a local restaurant. The event involved students of both countries informally interacting with each other, and the Japanese teachers, principals, and teacher development center staff also joined the party and mingled with the US group. This activity, of course, served to help the Japanese and US participants to better know one another.

Day 4. The day started early with a visit to an elementary school in the school district where students from the Japanese university partner had been working as classroom aides.

Orientation. When the group arrived at the public elementary school, the principal welcomed the students and gave a short introduction to the school and to the concept of Japanese lesson study. In lesson study, teachers go through cycles to plan their lessons together, observe each others' lessons, and regularly reflect on them. After a brief question-and-answer session about the elementary school curriculum and the school, the group observed several classes.

Observation. One of the observed classes received instruction using the lesson study approach. The US and Japanese university students observed the same lesson in the morning while taking notes for later lesson analyses and reflections. The students wrote on stick-on notes about their observations (e.g., how the teacher asked questions and interacted with students, how the teacher used curriculum materials) with the understanding that their notes would be used in an afternoon lesson study session.

When the initial class period ended, the students went on to observe other classes, including arts, music, and crafts, where elementary students collaborated while receiving guidance from the teachers. These observations strengthened the students' understanding of the Japanese public education emphasis on holistic human development.

Teaching. One of the highlights of this day was the opportunity for the US students to teach a class to the elementary school children on English or the US culture. The students were free to teach anything in any form as long as it related to learning English. They were thus free to use music, videos, or computers in their lessons. The elementary school had requested this in advance, and the US group had made plans for the session. The US students formed groups of two or three and prepared for team teaching a 45-minute lesson for the class they were assigned. In preparing for the lesson, each group discussed the lesson plan and activities with the US faculty member serving as their mentor. Based on feedback from previous offerings of the program, students used games and kinesthetic activities that involved the use of English in meaningful and enjoyable ways.

In the final class hour before the lunch break, each group started teaching its lesson in the assigned classroom. The Japanese university students and Japanese teachers stayed in the classrooms to support the US students as they taught the Japanese children. The teaching session continued for 45 minutes with the US students teaching children – about thirty to forty in each classroom – using music, dance, and games. Although some of the US students were not very confident in their teaching in the beginning, the Japanese children clearly enjoyed the lessons. Though some of the groups needed support from the Japanese university students and teachers, the 45-minute class passed quickly with children engaging in learning activities and enjoying the lesson.

Through the classroom experience, the US students learned how language barriers can be overcome if lessons are made easier to understand with gestures, clear instructions, and most importantly, establishing rapport with children. The US students also learned to overcome the fear of teaching children whom they do not know very well. At the end of the teaching session, there was a sense of satisfaction and celebration with a new bond created between the US students and the Japanese children in each classroom.

Lunch. In Japanese schools, students eat together in their classrooms, carrying lunch from the school kitchen and serving each other. Each US group stayed in the classroom during the lunch period, which started as the Japanese children in charge of lunch time for the week brought lunch for everyone to the classroom. The children in the classroom then worked together to set up the lunch. The US students helped to prepare the lunch as they interacted informally with the Japanese children. The children recited together their appreciation (*Itadakimasu*) for the food and began their lunch. The classroom teacher was there but gave minimal assistance.

Recess. After the lunch, which continued for about 40 minutes, the Japanese children cleaned the dishes and utensils and returned them to the school kitchen. Again, the US students stayed in the classroom, helping the Japanese children. Following lunch, some of the US group joined the children in a 40-minute recess period, going to the school playground and playing soccer and other activities, while other groups mingled with the Japanese children inside the building. The Japanese students were not fluent in English, but communications were smooth with gestures and simple English and Japanese expressions.

Analysis. After the recess period, the US group gathered with the Japanese university students to analyze and discuss their observations from the morning. In groups of four to six US and Japanese university students, group members placed their stick-on notes from the morning observations on a large sheet on the group table. They then categorized the notes into meaningful themes. Each international group read everyone else's notes and considered what themes would emerge in the grouping process. This lesson analysis followed the KJ method (Scupin, 1997), an intuitive data analysis approach popular in Japan and consistent with Japanese culture. This session continued for about 60–90 minutes.

When the lesson analysis was complete, each group gave a short presentation of the themes that it had extracted. The teacher who taught the lesson, the principal, and the vice principal also joined the presentation session. Each group presented diverse ideas by illustrating them on the board and reflecting on the observed lessons. There were many good analyses from the cross-cultural groups, ranging from the way the teacher fostered student motivation and curiosity about the lesson contents in the first 5 minutes, how the teacher responded to students with respect without dismissing wrong answers, and how he encouraged the students to help others who had difficulty. There were good discussions on how the Japanese teacher interacted with the students to bring all class members together, and helped students learn the contents for the next lesson while addressing the needs of individual students as a part of the lesson. The presentations and discussions continued for about 90 minutes with the Japanese teacher who taught the lesson giving his reflection and the principal and vice principal giving supportive feedback.

Reflection. According to a later survey, the US group was most impressed with the humility and professionalism of the Japanese teacher who taught the lesson. The teacher carefully listened to each group's presentation, reflected on his need for improvement, and sincerely thanked them for their ideas. The group also learned that teachers regularly engaged in such reflections through lesson study, and considered many aspects of teaching, such as the overall curriculum map, each student's developmental history, and group dynamics as well as helping students grow academically, personally, and socially. Many US students gained insights about the ways they should approach the teaching profession after graduation.

The cross-cultural lesson study meeting ended with an opportunity for overall reflection for the day with only the US students and Japanese university students. Although the students were exhausted after the long day, there were many positive comments about the fruitfulness of such cross-cultural dialogues on learning and teaching. Comments from the US students included thoughts about the respectful behaviors of the children, how professional and humble the teachers were, and the emphasis that Japanese schools place on social and personal development of students. They reasoned that people's respectful behaviors in public places came from Japanese schooling in which teachers and principals make efforts to promote holistic human development of students at public schools. Many US students commented that they found a renewed motivation to pursue the teaching profession and they would like to make similar efforts in their classrooms after returning to the United States. The Japanese students also commented how much they learned from the US participants, such as freely volunteering their ideas and giving presentations in an engaging manner.

Days 5 and 6. The remaining two days were free days for the students to explore the city and other parts of the country on their own. They wholeheartedly immersed themselves in the Japanese culture as they toured various parts of the country and interacted with the people. They kept in touch with the Japanese university students whom they worked with in the program, and some of them got together.

On the final day, the students participated in an evening cafe meeting for debriefing. The US students shared many travel stories, such as how kind people had been when they got lost, how tidy and clean Japanese communities were, and how enjoyable it had been to communicate with the Japanese youth they had encountered. Students discussed their appreciation for the program and their perception that teaching can be such a rich profession that can contribute to the happiness of the people and the society. The day ended with a farewell party. The following day, some of the students returned to the United States while some chose to stay and tour the country a little longer.

Postsession. Following the Japan session, a postsession was held at the US university. Using their learning and experiences in Japan, the students completed their action research project by continuing to work with the student with whom they had been working before leaving for Japan. The post session was a 3-hour meeting in which the students presented their action research projects and reflected on their learning in Japan. The presentation was followed by class discussions on their takeaways from the global study course.

Most of the students shifted the focus of their action research projects from academic achievement toward linking their student proteges' personal and social development with academic learning, paying more attention to creating a respectful relationship and bond with the student. The students learned that cognitive processes and development have strong social, affective, and cultural foundations, and that making learning come alive requires commitment and professionalism. Submission of final papers marked the conclusion of the global study program.

Student Reflections

The final papers that the students submitted involved many themes. Because the purpose of this chapter is to discuss a case that exemplifies the benefit of incorporating culture into the teaching of educational psychology, I will not discuss comprehensive analyses and evaluations of the papers. Rather, I would like to introduce some of the students' comments that seem to represent their learning:

> Visiting Japan changed me as a person, and how I view the world. I was truly blown away seeing how much emphasis is placed on social emotional development of students in school and how this emphasis changes the climate of the classroom and the relationships in the classroom. I noticed that the students seemed very comfortable with their teachers, I even saw the students hanging on their teachers legs, holding their hands, and sitting on their laps while Sarah and I were giving our lesson. It was uplifting to see such relationships inside the classroom, and the community that is built during lunchtime. The children were given so many responsibilities, and were also given a lot of trust, which is something that is lacking in American schools. I wonder if we spent more time focusing on social emotional development, instead of making students perfect their reading and writing by age 7, if this would change how a student learns material?
>
> I loved visiting the schools, the classroom climate was warm and inviting. Students looked like they were having fun and learning at the same time. Teachers seemed more like a facilitator than an authority figure. I especially appreciate the community the schools fostered – cleaning classroom together, serving lunch, teachers eating with students. I would love to see this type of community and care in my future school (or at least classroom).
>
> My trip to Japan revealed the power in a collective approach to education. An approach that looks on improving the class as a whole and not just uplifting and celebrating the individual. That the good of the class or society as a whole is more important than the success of any one student.
>
> I absolutely loved visiting the schools and seeing what a community they have established throughout the school and in each individual classroom. You could see what a great relationship the students had with the teachers and their peers, which is something that I really want to strive for in my individual classroom. I think that establishing a good relationship and teaching empathy is so important to develop adults who really care about one another and can express their feelings safely. I also really like how in the

Japanese school systems they teach the students so many aspects of life and responsibility. For example, when we got to eat lunch with the students at the elementary school they set up everything for lunch, served each other and themselves, practiced dental hygiene, etc. These are important life-long skills that students should be learning at a young age, it is truly amazing how much more their school system does to prepare them for life after and outside of school. The overall culture in Japan was like nothing I have ever seen before.

I realized how important it is to establish a community first to give students a feeling of acceptance and empathy before they can explore individuality and autonomy with each other's support. This chain reaction of happiness, I feel, begins with the educator, it begins with me.

These comments testify to how infusing culture into teaching educational psychology can lead to a fruitful outcome. The students learned about the key principles that underlie teaching practices in Japanese schools as they observed classes and interacted with Japanese educators, Japanese university students, and others. Furthermore, students deepened their understanding of Japanese schooling by grounding it in their actual experiences in the culture. These holistic experiences in connection to academic learning in presessions served as the basis of the transformations that the students went through.

Lessons Learned

The process of planning the program, leading the group on the trip, and other logistical and financial considerations required much time and energy, but it turned out to be a highly rewarding endeavor. During the 7 years of operation of the program, the relationship with the Japanese university partner was sustained and strengthened, and the program has become richer and more fruitful as the years have passed.

One interesting by-product of the program was a strengthened bond among the participating US students. Many students indicated that they have never spent so much time, or engaged in deep conversations with, those who share similar professional aspirations. They not only collaborated with one another to go through the program activities but also engaged in adventures to explore the city and immerse themselves in an unfamiliar culture. This experience made them closer and helped them share different perspectives, feelings, and values in a way they had never done at home. In a way, they experienced the same close bonds with their fellows that Japanese teachers do in Japanese lesson study – an outcome they had never anticipated in the beginning.

Many of the students who participated in the program have kept in touch with each other after graduation, and have often returned to the university to share their experiences as new teachers, referring to what they learned and experienced in Japan. Each year, the students who have participated in the program in the previous year have shared their experiences with new students in the global study orientation in the spring. It is such human links that seem to have given a special spirit to sustain and enrich the Tokyo Program.

Implications

The global study project demonstrates how cross-cultural collaborations to infuse culture into teaching educational psychology can transform the nature of a course. It can ground learning educational psychology in a real-life cultural context (Göncü & Gauvain, 2012) as it creates opportunities for students to engage in critical reflections on their cultural assumptions on teaching (Darling-Hammond & Lieberman, 2012). It can also expand students' scopes beyond Western contexts and monocultural assumptions on education for their self-transformation (Inoue, 2015, 2012; Portes, 1996).

I have to note that these endeavors would not have been possible without the university's commitment to internationalize its curriculum and the collaboration of the Japanese partner. The global study program developed on a strong foundation through infusion of a pedagogically meaningful theme throughout, while considering the nature of the overall academic content, students' career aspirations and interests, and cultural differences and similarities.

The process required many creative decisions about the logistics and rationale of the program as well as frequent consultation with the Japanese partner about the details of the program. This multidimensional effort made this global study program possible. Such international collaboration is the key to success in cross-cultural endeavors. And perhaps this is true even when we teach educational psychology courses in local contexts; those with whom we partner and how we work with partners define the nature of the endeavor.

In sum, infusing culture can make educational psychology come alive for students. Taught in cultural context, educational psychology, like other psychology courses, is no longer an abstract and disconnected field for students hoping to teach. Use of available cultural contexts and cross-cultural collaborations can do much to elicit authentic learning and critical reflection in students. With so many cultures around the world, the potential may be limitless.

Acknowledgement

I thank Professor Tadashi Asada and his students at Waseda University, the teachers and principals at Tokorozawa City, and the teacher education staff at Tokorozawa Teacher Development Center, who have assisted the global study program over the years, for their kindness and generosity.

References

Brown, J. S., Collins, A., & Duguid, P. (1989). Situated cognition and the culture of learning. *Educational Researcher, 18*, 32–42. doi:10.17730/humo.56.2. x3359235511444655

Bruner, J. (1998). *The culture of education.* Cambridge, MA: Harvard University Press.

Cole, M. (1996). *Cultural psychology: A once and future discipline.* Cambridge, MA: Harvard University Press.

Darling-Hammond, D., & Lieberman, A. (2012). *Teacher education around the world: Changing policies and practices.* New York, NY: Routledge.

Göncü, A., & Gauvain, M. (2012). Sociocultural approaches to educational psychology: Theory, research, and application. In K. R. Harris, J. Brophy, G. Sinatra, & J. Sweller (Eds.), *APA educational psychology handbook, Vol. 1. Theories, constructs, and critical issues* (pp. 123–152). Washington, DC: American Psychological Association.

Inoue, N. (2012). *Mirrors of the mind: Introduction to mindful ways of thinking education.* New York, NY: Peter Lang.

(2015). *Beyond actions: Psychology of action research for mindful educational improvement.* New York, NY: Peter Lang.

Lave, J. (1991). *Situated learning: Legitimate peripheral participation.* New York, NY: Cambridge University Press.

Markus, H. R., & Kitayama, S. (1991). Culture and the self: Implications for cognition, emotion, and motivation. *Psychological Review, 98*, 224–253. doi:10.1037/0033-295X.98.2.224

Ng, P. T. (2007). Quality assurance in the Singapore education system in an era of diversity and innovation. *Educational Research for Policy and Practice, 6*, 235–247. doi:10.1007/s10671-007-9018-x

Portes, P. R. (1996). Ethnicity and culture in educational psychology. In D. Berliner & R. Calfee (Eds.), *Handbook of educational psychology* (pp. 331–357). New York, NY: Routledge.

Reagan, T. (2004). *Non-Western educational traditions: Indigenous approaches to educational thought and practice (sociocultural, political, and historical studies in education)* (3rd ed.). New York, NY: Routledge.

Sahlberg, P. (2011). Lessons from Finland. *Education Digest, 77*(3), 18–24.

Scupin, R. (1997). The KJ method: A technique for analyzing data derived from Japanese ethnology. *Human Organization, 56,* 233–237. doi:10.17730/humo.56.2.x33592351444655

Stevenson, H. W., & Stigler, J. W. (1992). *The learning gap: Why our schools are failing and what we can learn from Japanese and Chinese education.* New York, NY: Summit Books.

Uttal, D. H. (1995). Beliefs, motivation, and achievement in mathematics: A cross-national perspective. In M. Carr (Ed.), *Motivation in mathematics.* Cresskill, NJ: Hampton.

CHAPTER 15

Teaching about Language by Integrating Culture

David S. Kreiner

Language is a central topic in modern psychological science. George Miller (1990) summarized the importance of language, noting that "no general theory of psychology will be adequate if it does take account of language" (p. 7). In addition to long-standing interest in the psychology of language in its own right, language is an important topic within many subfields of psychology, such as developmental psychology, cognition, perception, neuroscience, comparative psychology, and multicultural psychology.

The study of language is also important because of its role in the historical development of psychology. Karl Lashley's (1951) classic paper on serial order in behavior was not confined to linguistic issues but included many examples of language, such as the need for hierarchical order in speech. Although it is an overstatement to say that Lashley's paper sparked the cognitive revolution, it did provide support for critiques of behaviorism (Bruce, 1994). In fact, Noam Chomsky (1959) referred to Lashley's work in his rejection of the behaviorist account of language. Chomsky's analysis of language indicated a need to infer cognitive structure and processes because principles of behavior alone could not explain how people produce and understand language. The argument that language could not be explained without reference to the mind was a key development in the history of modern psychology as a whole, not just the psychology of language. Thus, even faculty who do not teach courses that directly cover language as a topic have reason to be knowledgeable about the importance of the topic to psychology as a discipline.

The goal of this chapter is to provide background and advice on how the inclusion of cultural content can improve teaching about language. I will not be concerned with the teaching of particular languages (e.g., how to effectively teach French), but instead I will focus on teaching about the topic of human language in general. I intend for the chapter to be useful not only for those teaching a course in the psychology of language or psycholinguistics, but also in other courses in which language is a relevant topic. Language is certainly an appropriate topic for a history of psychology course for the reasons mentioned in the preceding paragraph.

Introductory psychology is another relevant course, as instructors may include a unit on language or on language and thinking. Other courses in which issues of language are often addressed include (but are not limited to) cognitive psychology, developmental psychology, and multicultural or cross-cultural psychology. In such courses, language may be covered as a separate topic in one or more chapters, or it may be a recurrent topic that arises at multiple points throughout the course. I hope that this chapter will be useful to instructors of any of these courses.

Why Culture Should Be Included in the Teaching of Language

Given that language is an important topic, we may question whether it is necessary or useful to include cultural concepts when teaching about it. I submit that the answer to both questions is a definite *yes*. First, language and culture are intertwined. Language is often considered a key element of culture. In fact, it can be difficult to tease the two apart (Everett, 2005).

Language appears to be both uniquely human and universal across humans. The need to use language is so strong that it may be viewed as a human instinct (Pinker, 1994) as evidenced by the spontaneous development of a language when a group of people lack a common way to communicate (Sandler, Meir, Padden, & Aronoff, 2005). Not only is the use of language common across cultures, but many features of language are also remarkably similar across different human languages, as revealed in the following discussion of linguistic universals.

Yet languages clearly differ from each other. People of different cultures may speak different languages or even different sets of languages. Furthermore, even when the same language is used, differences in dialect can occur across both cultures and subcultures. These differences can be substantial enough to make languages partially or completely incomprehensible to individuals of other cultures despite the fact that languages all follow the same basic blueprint. It is therefore not possible to fully describe similarities and differences across cultures without reference to language. Similarly, it is not possible to fully explore linguistic differences without reference to culture.

An interesting way to think about how culture and language are intertwined is to examine the Sapir-Whorf hypothesis. Learning about this hypothesis and the relevant evidence can help students understand why it is necessary to consider culture and language together. Briefly, the

Sapir-Whorf hypothesis is the claim that language affects how people think. The hypothesis has an interesting history that relates to anthropology and linguistics in addition to psychology. Although the scientific status of the hypothesis has varied over the last eight decades, there is now compelling evidence that supports it in some respects. For example, differences between languages predict cognition in areas such as memory and perception of time (Cook & Bassetti, 2011). Thus, cultural differences in the way people think about the world can arise from differences in their languages.

Two Examples of the Importance of Culture in Learning about Language

Next, I will review two important issues about language that highlight the necessity of considering culture. First, I consider how inaccurate attributions about languages have cultural implications. Second, I review why the pragmatic aspect of language use can be understood only by considering cultural similarities and differences.

The Myth of Primitives: Critical Thinking about Language Differences

Are some languages more primitive while others are more advanced? This question parallels the anthropological question of whether some cultures are primitive ones. It is commonly believed that "linguistic complexity is a reflection of differential cultural complexity" (Joseph & Newmeyer, 2012, p. 347), meaning that more complex cultures tend to have more complex languages, even though linguistics textbooks consistently refute this idea.

Let us consider what it would mean for languages to differ in their level of complexity or primitivity. An implication of this belief is that some languages are less functional than others in their capacity for allowing people to communicate. This idea of primitivity has a history among scholars who have studied language in addition to being an assumption that the lay public may make about different languages. For that reason, it will be of benefit to students for an instructor teaching about language to explicitly address the issue.

Languages are much more similar to each other than a superficial analysis would suggest. Students may be interested to learn about linguistic universals, features shared across languages, such as those proposed by Hockett (1966). One example of a linguistic universal is the use of hierarchy, meaning that smaller units are combined to make larger units.

For example, we combine speech sounds (*phonemes*) to make words, and we combine words into sentences. Another example of a linguistic universal is that all languages have grammatical categories, such as nouns and verbs, although the specific grammatical categories may vary across languages. Linguists have explored numerous other possible universals, although Hockett (1966) noted that it is impossible to prove that a characteristic occurs in all human languages without studying every language that exists and has ever existed.

Although it is often assumed that the associations in a language between sounds and meaning are arbitrary, recent research (Blasi, Wichmann, Hammarstrom, Stadler, & Christiansen, 2016) has suggested that there is some commonality in these associations within basic vocabulary terms and that the commonalities likely developed independently in different language groups. For example, the word for *nose* often includes an "n" sound. Thus, even for an aspect of language that logically could be arbitrary and thus highly variable across cultures, there is surprising similarity.

The relation of language diversity to culture is particularly apparent when considering how languages are learned. Although the ability to learn language has a genetic basis, we clearly have to learn the specific language(s) used in our environment. We learn language from individuals in the culture in which we live. Furthermore, language is an important tool in how we transmit the culture to the next generation. Unlike genetic evolution, cultural changes can be transmitted not only to offspring but horizontally among people in different groups (Krumov & Larsen, 2013). These cultural changes can include differences in the language and in how the language is learned by members of the culture. Thus, culture is an important factor in understanding both language acquisition and language change.

Students often find language development to be a particularly interesting topic. Instructors can capitalize on this interest by connecting to cultural concepts when teaching about how children learn a language. Studying the developmental sequence of language acquisition in children provides a prime opportunity to examine how cultural variation may or may not affect development. To the extent that the development sequence is similar across languages and cultures, we can assume the existence of linguistic universals that drive development. Yet cultures can differ dramatically in beliefs and practices related to how children learn language. Do such cultural differences correspond to variation in how children actually acquire language?

When teaching about language acquisition, instructors typically describe developmental milestones that are similar across normally developing children. Tables or charts illustrating such milestones are often included in textbooks (cf., Hoff, 2009). For example, at 6–9 months of age, infants begin to babble, meaning that they produce repeated syllables (e.g., *ba ba ba*). Children typically begin producing speech, one word at a time, at about 1 year of age. Combinations of words, usually two at a time (e.g., *want milk*), emerge at about 2 years of age.

An interesting critical thinking exercise is to consider how to determine whether similarity in language development is a result of similar environments across cultures or instead arises from universal, genetically programmed language learning mechanisms. Research indicates that adult caregivers may talk differently to children compared to how they talk to other adults, for example, speaking more slowly and melodically (Gathercole & Hoff, 2007). If this "motherese" affects language development, then differences in its use should predict children's development. But the evidence shows that children develop language even in the absence of motherese (Gathercole & Hoff, 2007).

Crago, Allen, and Hough-Eyamie (1997) examined language development in the Inuit culture of northern Canada in which the Inuktitut language is spoken. The language environment is quite different in Inuit culture than in British and North American cultures. Because the developmental milestones that are commonly presented in textbooks are based largely on studies of people in English-speaking cultures, it is important to determine whether Anglo-centric models of language acquisition hold up across different cultures. Crago et al. (1997) reported that Inuit children receive more language input from their peers and engage in relatively less parent–child language interaction than do children in British and American cultures. Linguistic interactions with adults tend to focus more on children understanding instructions given to them than on encouraging the children to speak. Do differences such as these require that we have different models of language acquisition for different cultures, or is language development similar despite the differences in environment?

The answer seems to be that it is some of both. Zhang, Jin, Shen, Zhang, and Hoff (2008) noted that, "From a distance, language development looks different in different cultures.... A closer look at the predictors and processes of language development, however, suggests it is much the same wherever it occurs" (p. 150). Inuit children produce single words at around 1 year and produce simple combinations at about 2 years of age. The application of grammatical rules increases rapidly after the age of 2.

These milestones are similar for both English and Inuktitut speakers despite the fact that the languages are quite different in structure. However, children acquiring Inuktitut start using passive constructions (e.g., *the drink was spilled*) earlier and more often than do speakers of English, German, or Hebrew (Crago et al., 1997). This difference may be related to the differing grammatical structure of the languages as well as differences in what language children hear as Crago et al. (1997) reported that adult speakers of Inuktitut frequently use passive constructions.

Although the sequence of language development is similar across cultures, the pace of development varies with environmental factors such as the amount of language input that children receive (Gathercole & Hoff, 2007). One might be tempted to infer that some cultures are more advanced at creating environments that support language development. The evidence points once again to similarity across cultures. Environmental factors that predict both vocabulary and grammatical development appear to be similar in different cultures (Zhang et al., 2008). For example, children in higher socioeconomic status (SES) homes tend to show faster language development, and SES predicts vocabulary development more than it predicts grammatical development. Both aspects of this finding appear to hold across North American, Western European, and Chinese cultures (Zhang et al., 2008).

Another way to think about commonality across human languages is to consider what distinguishes human language from other communication systems. Miller (1990) provided a succinct description of the two key properties that distinguish human language: communication and representation. There are other, nonlinguistic systems that people and other animals use for the purpose of communicating information. It is possible to have mental representations of the world that are not linguistic in nature, such as spatial representations. Only language combines the function of communicating with the function of providing mental representations of the world. Krumov and Larsen (2013) suggested another unique property of human language: that it provides a capacity to communicate our intentions to others and to allow us to infer the intentions of others. As I will show in the section on pragmatics later in this chapter, communicating intention is an important aspect of culture. Thus, at a broad level, human languages are much more similar to each other than they are to other communication systems.

We have seen that languages have much in common with each other despite their obvious differences in areas such as vocabulary and grammatical structure. What, then, would be the argument that some languages are more or less primitive than others? Scholars have sometimes argued that some languages are less sophisticated than others based on the number of words a language uses to express a particular concept. Such views were common in the nineteenth and early twentieth centuries (Hill, 1952). However, these views were based on inadequate linguistic analysis. Furthermore, those who made such claims overlooked important cultural characteristics.

Interestingly, the argument that some languages are primitive has been based both on claiming that a language lacks words for particular concepts and that a language has an excessive number of words for the same concept. A well-known example of the former is the claim that the Native American language Hopi lacks words for time, the purported consequence being that speakers of Hopi are unable to think about time. The claim is often attributed to the linguist Benjamin Whorf, but that attribution is inaccurate. Whorf (1950) instead claimed that the Hopi language did not have verb tenses for past, present, and future. His conclusion was that Hopi speakers thought about time *differently* than did speakers of languages that contain those verb tenses, not that they were *incapable* of thinking about time.

Language primitivity has also been attributed to a language having too many words for one concept. An example is the belief that the Cherokee language (also Native American) lacks a single, general word for *washing*, instead having over a dozen verbs for the action. Hill (1952) analyzed this claim, noting that the presumption was that the large number of words represented inefficiency in the language. Hill's analysis suggested that the conclusion was factually incorrect; he concluded that Cherokee has only two morphemes for *washing*. However, the more salient point is that the number of words for a concept is not a meaningful measure of linguistic efficiency. Morphemes, linguistic units of meaning such as root words, can be combined in systematic ways to produce different meanings. Such combination of units is characteristic of all human languages. Scancarelli (1994) later revisited the claim about the Cherokee language and concluded that it may contain three to four morphemes for *washing*. Scancarelli explained that the different conclusions about the number of morphemes were likely due to the fact that Hill did not have access to individuals who spoke Cherokee, which necessarily limited the quality of his data. Scancarelli agreed with Hill that the number of morphemes for a concept is not indicative of the primitiveness of a language but instead reflects the general property that languages are hierarchical. These examples highlight the need to think critically both about the data upon which claims are based and about assumptions concerning what constitutes primitivity.

There are cultural consequences to the misconceptions that some languages are better or worse than others and that the differences reflect cognitive abilities of the speakers. An instructive example is the way that African American Vernacular English (AAVE) has been parodied as "Mock Ebonics." In response to a school district's decision to incorporate knowledge of AAVE to help students improve their skills in English, many individuals posted offensive parodies of this dialect on the Internet (Ronkin & Karn, 1999). Ronkin and Karn (1999) analyzed the posted examples mocking Ebonics and noted that they framed the dialect as an inferior, less systematic version of English. For example, Mock Ebonics examples tended to insert the word *be* frequently and nonsystematically, whereas in AAVE, the word *be* is actually used systematically to make a distinction that is not made in Standard American English (SAE). Specifically, AAVE distinguishes between a continual state (*She be working*, meaning that she works in general) and a temporary state (*She working*, meaning that she is working at this moment), whereas in SAE, *She is working* is ambiguous about whether the action is temporary or ongoing. Similar patterns have occurred in denigrating other languages, such as in Mock Spanish.

Bias about languages has also extended to bilingualism. Individuals who speak more than one language often exhibit code-switching, which refers to switching between two (or more) languages within a conversation. For example, a Spanish-English bilingual may include some Spanish words in a sentence that is mostly in English. Parama, Kreiner, Stark, and Schuetz (2017) found that, although code-switching has historically been viewed negatively, monolingual speakers did not tend to perceive bilingual speakers as less competent than did bilingual speakers. However, Parama et al.'s findings suggested that monolingual speakers may be less aware than bilingual speakers of the sophisticated cognitive abilities required to accomplish code-switching.

We have seen that ideas about language primitivity are highly flawed. But the idea of "equal complexity" of languages is also problematic. A major difficulty in evaluating these claims is that there is no clear definition of language complexity (Joseph & Newmeyer, 2012).

It is difficult to measure language complexity because levels of complexity or simplicity vary within languages, not just between them. Joseph and Newmeyer (2012) discussed the idea of trade-offs in complexity. For example, a language that does not have many restrictions on word order may have a more complex system of inflecting words (e.g., adding prefixes or suffixes) to indicate syntactic roles. Similarly, languages that have less complex syllable structure may have more tonal differentiation between words. The concept of complexity trade-offs has sometimes been taken to support the idea of equal complexity of all languages, as if there is a rule that higher complexity in one feature must be matched by lower complexity elsewhere in the language. However, there appears to be little support for a law of equal complexity. Some languages do appear to be learned more easily by adults than others, implying differences in language complexity. For example, there is a consensus in linguistics that Creole languages can be viewed as simpler than non-Creole languages. Creole languages are those that are formed as combinations of existing languages when speakers of the different languages live in the same environment and must communicate without a common language. Although languages may indeed differ in complexity, depending on how complexity is defined, differences in linguistic complexity should not be assumed to reflect differences in the primitivity of cultures (Joseph & Newmeyer, 2012).

The complexity of a language is related to "factors such as its degree of contact or lack of contact with other languages, its relative prestige vis-à-vis its neighbours, its overall number of speakers, its role as a *lingua franca*, and other sociopolitical considerations" (Joseph & Newmeyer, 2012, p. 357). These factors are themselves reflective of cultural differences. Thus, failure to take culture into account can lead to unwarranted conclusions about language differences or similarities.

In addition to difficulties associated with evaluating the concept of language complexity, some assumptions about linguistic universals have been challenged. Everett (2005) has suggested that some languages could be notably different in complexity or even lack key features to qualify as "true" languages. Presumably, these communication systems would not be categorized as languages without revising the list of linguistic universals. After studying the Pirahã people of Brazil, Everett concluded that a culture places limits on how its people communicate. In particular, the Pirahã people confine their communication to immediate experience. It is this cultural constraint, Everett suggested, that explains why the language lacks a number of features present in other languages, such as number words. Everett notes that the Pirahã are monolingual despite living in proximity to speakers of other languages and argues that the monolingualism is itself a result of cultural differences. In Everett's view, it is necessary to study languages in the context of the culture because neither culture nor language can be understood in the absence of the other.

As one examines the interesting variations across languages and cultures, it becomes increasingly difficult to classify some languages, or even specific language features, as more or less primitive. The important lesson to be learned is that the concept of primitivity has no more meaning when comparing languages than it does when comparing cultures.

We have seen that human languages have much in common, although some purported universals may be disputed. The salient point from the preceding discussion is that a deep consideration of culture is necessary in order to fully understand the similarities and differences across different languages.

Language Is Not Just Words: Cultural Context and Pragmatics

At a phenomenological level, language generally feels easy to produce and to understand. Yet the cognitive machinery underneath that performance is complex. A basic understanding of the psychology of language requires learning about the various processes necessary in order to be a competent language user. Briefly, languages users must be competent in the phonology, syntax, semantics, and pragmatics of their language. *Phonology* refers to the level of speech sounds. The words *cat* and *hat* differ in the initial phoneme, "kuh" versus "huh," which results in a difference in meaning. It should be pointed out to students that phonology is a separate issue from spelling as children who do not yet know how to write can still distinguish words based on phonology. We should also note that not all languages rely on sound; sign languages do not have phonology but do contain parallel linguistic units related to gestural components.

Syntax refers to the rules for combining linguistic units, such as how morphemes are combined to produce intelligible sentences. For example, *the dog bit the cat* has a different meaning than *the cat bit the dog* even though the speech sounds and words are identical; the difference lies in which word is the grammatical subject or object.

The *semantic level* of language refers to the meanings that we extract. For example, *the dog ran down the street* has a different meaning than *the dog walked down the street* even though the syntax is identical. The difference is in the semantic value of the particular words used, in this case the two verbs.

Language also has a *pragmatic level*, which is the focus of this section. The pragmatic level refers to how speakers and listeners understand the purpose of the communication. Consider the question, *Can you open that window?* The person asking that question may intend for the listener to open the window or may intend for the listener to reply by indicating an ability to perform the task (*Why, yes I can!*). It is possible for a listener to misunderstand a speaker's purpose even when correctly processing the phonology, syntax, and semantics. In the remainder of this section, I will consider how cultural context is necessary for understanding the pragmatic level of language.

A key point for students is that meaning (semantics) depends heavily on context as demonstrated by the classic experiments of Bransford and Johnson (1972). They presented contextual information, such as a line drawing or a verbal topic, either before or after their participants listened to a descriptive passage. Participants displayed greater comprehension of the passage when the contextual information was presented first. For example, it was easier to understand sentences like *A seashore is a better place than the street* when participants knew in advance that the topic was kite flying. Bransford and Johnson's research often appears in textbook treatments of the psychology of language. I propose that the importance of context can be extended by the instructor to examples of cultural context in the form of differing pragmatic rules.

Grice (1978) proposed that in addition to the actual utterance (the particular words used), speakers may have particular implications in mind. Implications are present when a meaning is not explicitly stated but can be inferred. For example, *I went to the grocery store* may be taken to imply that I purchased groceries while I was there. Grice's cooperative principle and conversational maxims illustrate the pragmatic level of language. The cooperative principle is the idea that speakers and listeners cooperate in attempting to successfully communicate the speaker's purpose. Conversational maxims include quantity, meaning that the speaker should supply enough information to fulfill the purpose of the communication but not more; quality, meaning that the information being communicated should be correct or substantiated; relevance, meaning that the information provided should be related to the purpose of the conversation; and manner, meaning that the speaker should communicate in a clear and organized way in order to avoid ambiguity (Lee, 2005). A speaker may violate a maxim to create an implication, based on the assumption that the listener will try to infer the speaker's true purpose. For example, a person may ask, *Is it warm in here?* The statement itself may violate the maxim of manner because it appears to be a question for which the speaker's intended meaning might be, *It's too warm; let's open the window.* But these inferences depend on the listener and speaker sharing assumptions and following the same conversational habits. Lee (2005) noted that Grice's maxims may not be applied in the same way across cultures. For example, with respect to the maxim of quantity, the amount of information that is considered appropriate to share can vary depending on the cultural context.

Expectations about conversational rules are not constant across cultures. For example, saying "thank you" for a routine action may be expected in one culture but considered odd in another culture (Lee, 2005). Furthermore, a conversational maxim may be violated in order to follow cultural rules of politeness (e.g., not fully sharing information about another person's performance in order to spare the person's feelings). Wong (2010) provided an example concerning the maxim of quality: Singapore English speakers do not make the same distinction as do Anglo English speakers between statements of fact and statements of opinion. Anglo English speakers tend to use qualifiers or hedges (e.g., *In my opinion ...*) to indicate when their statements are opinions, whereas Singapore English speakers find it acceptable to make statements that *could* be true without qualifying them. Thus, by a strict reading of the maxim of quality, one might conclude that Singapore English speakers violate that maxim. Wong concluded instead that speakers of Singapore English follow a different rule or schema about quality of information: A statement can be assumed to be true unless there is evidence that contradicts it.

Another example of a cultural difference in conversational rules is the level of indirectness with which people speak. Holtgraves (1997) presented various conversational scenarios to undergraduate students and asked them to select direct or indirect conversational responses. One scenario was that a student had just completed a poorly done class presentation and asked for feedback. A direct response was, "I didn't think it was very good," whereas an indirect response was, "It's hard to give a good presentation for 30 minutes" (Holtgraves, 1997, p. 636). Indirectness in conversation is more common in collectivist cultures than in individualistic cultures; for example, Koreans tend to produce and understand indirect statements more than do Americans (Holtgraves, 1997). Lee (2005) encouraged teachers to learn what cultural assumptions relate to language use so that they can help students become aware of how these differences affect communication.

Students may find it interesting to consider how the pragmatic level of language can shed light on misunderstandings and how an understanding of cultural differences can prevent miscommunication. Roberts, Moss, Wass, Sarangi, and Jones (2005) studied miscommunication between doctors and patients in London medical offices. Almost one-third of the conversations included misunderstandings. Two-thirds of those misunder-standings occurred in conversations with patients who were non-native English speakers. The misunderstandings rarely had to do with differing cultural beliefs about health. Instead, misunderstandings occurred at the phonological, syntactic, semantic, and pragmatic levels of language. Examples included differences in pronunciations of words; use or lack of use of syntactic structure, stress, and intonation; and customs for how topics are introduced and changed.

Gass and Maronis (1991) analyzed types of miscommunication between native and non-native speakers. In some cases, the parties are aware that there was a misunderstanding, in which case, they may make attempts to correct the problem. In other cases, the parties may not even realize that the intended message was not the one that was perceived by the listener. When such a misunderstanding occurs, it may result in negative judg-ments (e.g., assuming that the other person in the conversation is rude or incompetent). It is particularly important to recognize cases of miscom-munication so that the correct intended meaning can be identified by all parties involved (Gass & Maronis, 1991).

Gass and Maronis (1991) noted that native language speakers may assume that a non-native speaker who demonstrates fluency also under-stands the pragmatic, cultural rules of the language. Thus, when a non-native speaker fails to follow one of those conventions, it may be perceived as an intentional violation rather than as a result of lack of familiarity with the culture. In contrast, violations of pragmatic rules by less fluent speakers are likely to be attributed to a lack of competence with the language rather than to intentional flouting of the rules. Gass and Maronis emphasized that the pragmatic level of language must be considered if we are to understand the causes of miscommunication.

The pragmatic level of language provides a natural opportunity for instructors to integrate cultural concepts into teaching about lan-guage. In fact, it is difficult to see how students could fully grasp the importance of pragmatics without considering cultural assumptions and expectations.

Infusing Cultural Examples into Teaching about Language

There is no shortage of cultural content that is relevant for teaching about language. However, instructors may be concerned about how to include additional material in a course without exceeding time constraints. I propose that instructors can integrate cultural concepts into a course without substantially reducing other content about language. An efficient way to integrate culture into the teaching of language is to use cultural examples as a tool for helping students understand language concepts. This approach supports effective teaching of language concepts via the integration of cultural content.

Instructors and textbook authors often use examples to illustrate concepts. Because psychology of language content is often abstract, it is helpful to provide activities and demonstrations to illustrate the concepts (Carroll, 2004). In one activity, students evaluate signs from American Sign Language on their iconicity, which refers to whether the sign resembles the concept to which it refers (Carroll, 2004). (Most signs, like spoken words, are not iconic.) Notice that this activity helps students learn about an abstract language concept, iconicity, by using cultural examples.

Diekhoff (2008) suggested an activity for helping students understand the role of expectations in language comprehension. The instructor reads aloud sentences that are grammatical and meaningful, grammatical but not meaningful, and ungrammatical and not meaningful, asking students to transcribe them. Students find it more difficult to perceive and transcribe the less meaningful sentences because they violate expectations about the language (Diekhoff, 2008). This activity could be adapted to include an emphasis on how expectations may differ across languages and cultures, possibly including examples that violate rules in one language but adhere to rules in a different language.

Instructors can use language concepts to illustrate multicultural issues and vice versa. For example, Dunn and Hammer (2014) discussed the challenges of teaching about group privilege, unearned advantages from which an individual may benefit as a result of membership in a group. One such example is the advantage of being a native speaker of the dominant language in a particular environment. Discussing examples like these can give students practice applying their knowledge of various language concepts such as syntactic and pragmatic rules while also broadening their understanding of cultural differences.

Another example is teaching about the power of labels for groups of people, *person with a disability* versus *disabled person* (Dunn & Hammer, 2014). Examples of these labels could be used to help students understand the Sapir-Whorf hypothesis by illustrating how such labels can limit or influence our thinking about other people. These examples may be more vivid and memorable than more commonly used examples to illustrate the Sapir-Whorf hypothesis, such as differences between languages in color words or time-related vocabulary.

Similarly, Kite and Whitley (2012) described an activity to raise awareness of stereotype-supporting language such as *Indian giver* or *Dutch treat*. Students read a list of stereotypical phrases, indicating whether they had used them and whether they were positive or negative. The students then discussed the phrases in groups. Kite and Whitley found that the activity helped students think about how language can communicate stereotypes even when the speaker is unaware of doing so.

One potential concern with asking students to generate relevant cultural examples is that members of majority groups may have difficulty thinking about their own culture. Language examples may be particularly useful in helping such students appreciate the relevance of cultural diversity. The instructor may ask the students to think about how they use language and whether they may be seen as different, inferior, or having minority status based on their dialect. For example, is a dialect of American English from one region of United States likely to lead to different attributions about the speaker than a dialect from a different region?

Until recently, little research existed supporting the effectiveness of examples for helping students learn concepts, but Rawson, Thomas, and Jacoby (2015) found that presenting examples could enhance conceptual understanding. Interestingly, whether the examples were presented before or after the relevant concepts did not seem to matter. They also found that interleaving examples of different concepts was more effective than blocked practice in which multiple examples of the same concept were presented before moving on to the next concept. However, this interleaving advantage did not occur when the definition of the concept was presented along with each example. A natural way to apply these findings would be to define a particular language concept and present with it examples of how that concept applies in different cultures, each time reminding students of the definition of the language concept. Alternatively, an interleaved presentation of different language concepts in the framework of a particular culture may be more efficient than presenting multiple examples of the same language concept.

A Sample Teaching Activity: Violating Conversational Rules

In this section, I will describe a class activity based on the strategy of using cultural concepts to illustrate concepts about language. I noted earlier in this chapter that the concept of pragmatics in language is important and cannot be properly understood without reference to culture. The class activity described in this section is based on that connection between language pragmatics and culture. The goals of the activity are to help students understand the importance of pragmatics and to help them identify how this language concept can illuminate cultural differences. Students may gain insight about potential causes of communication failures as well as develop strategies for more effective cross-cultural communication.

The instructor should first define the concept of pragmatics and then present the cooperative principle and Grice's four maxims as a framework (see the section "Language Is Not Just Words: Cultural Context and Pragmatics"). Students should then form small groups to begin the activity.

The initial task for each group is to construct an example of a conversation in which a speaker violates one or more of Grice's maxims. Each group should write out the dialogue and then identify one or more maxims that the speaker violated. I recommend that the instructor consult with each group to ensure that they are generating an applicable example.

Once all groups have completed their example conversations, they should trade scripts with a different group. Each group should read the conversation they receive and attempt to identify what maxim the conversants violated.

Finally, each group should discuss one or more cultural differences that could explain why apparent violations might be culturally appropriate and in fact signify adherence to the cooperative principle at a higher level. The instructor may wish to close the activity by inviting groups to share their analyses, providing additional examples for the class.

It may be helpful for the instructor to first present an example in order to clarify the process. In the following example, the conversation illustrates Wong's (2010) description of apparent violations of the maxim of quality in Singapore English:

SPEAKER A: How many exams do we have in the Intro Psych class?
SPEAKER B: We have six exams.
SPEAKER A: Wow, that seems like a lot!
SPEAKER B: Yes, but it could be four exams.
SPEAKER A: What do you mean? I thought you said it was six!

In this conversation, Speaker B appears to violate the maxim by providing questionable or inaccurate information about the number of exams. Speaker A interprets that answer to be a statement of fact and is surprised when Speaker B then indicates that it might be a different number of exams.

Without considering cultural differences, the example illustrates how violating a conversational maxim can lead to a misunderstanding. However, students should consider different cultural perspectives as they evaluate a conversation. When presenting the preceding example, the instructor can summarize Wong's (2010) analysis by indicating that, in Singapore English, a speaker is not expected to qualify a statement (with a phrase such as *I think it might be . . .*) when the statement *could* be true. Thus, the misunderstanding is more accurately described as a difference in cultural expectations rather than as a failure of one speaker to follow a conversational rule.

Each group should be able to create a conversation illustrating a miscommunication, identify one or more relevant maxims, and, most importantly, generate an explanation based on differences across cultures. Note that the activity requires students to take at least one cultural perspective other than their own. Practicing such perspective taking is important because "seeing the world from another's point of view is vital to eliciting critical thought and just actions" (Dunn & Hammer, 2014, p. 50).

Resources and Materials for Including Culture in Teaching about Language

- The Society for the Teaching of Psychology (STP) maintains an International Resources website. The site includes a Teaching Repository in addition to a variety of diversity information and articles. http://teachpsych.org/Diversity/International-Resources
- The Breaking Prejudice website ("Breaking the Prejudice Habit") is maintained by Awareness Harmony Acceptance Advocates (AHAA). The collection of songs may be useful for illustrating how diversity content is communicated through lyrics. The Teaching area includes assignments; see in particular the Language Activity and the Non-Verbal Communication Activity, both listed under Group Activities. http://breakingprejudice.org/teaching/
- The Understanding Prejudice Website, funded by the National Science Foundation and McGraw-Hill Higher Education, includes a wealth of resources for instructors. In particular, see Springboards for Discussing Prejudice in the Teacher's Corner. Several of the prompts could help start a discussion of prejudiced language. www.understandingprejudice.org/
- Online Readings in Psychology and Culture is a website published by the International Association for Cross-Cultural Psychology. Especially relevant resources include Subunit 4.2 – Language, Communication

and Culture. This subunit includes an article by Altarriba (2002) summarizing research on bilingualism and highlighting issues related to code-switching. An article by Chiu (2011) provides an overview of language and culture, focusing on their co-evolution and on how language may influence cognition. http://scholarworks.gvsu.edu/orpc/contents.html

• Carroll and Pinnow (2011) described the design, administration, and assessment of a creative project for a psychology of language class. The assignment could easily be adapted to include a cross-cultural focus. The chapter also contains an annotated bibliography of activities and demonstrations. http://teachpsych.org/ebooks/pse2011/vol2/index.php

• Fernald and Fernald (2008) described a class activity on the sequence of development. The instructor provides a list of developmental milestones to students, who then indicate the order in which they think they occur. Students also attempt to differentiate between abilities that develop as a result of biological maturation and abilities that require training.

References

Altarriba, J. (2002). Bilingualism: Language, memory and applied issues. *Online Readings in Psychology and Culture, 4*(2). doi:10.9707/2307-0919.1034

Blasi, D., Wichmann, S., Hammarstrom, H., Stadler, P., & Christiansen, M. (2016). Sound-meaning association biases evidenced across thousands of languages. *Proceedings of the National Academy of Sciences, 113*, 10818–10823. doi:10.1073/pnas.1605782113

Bransford, J. D., & Johnson, M. K. (1972). Contextual prerequisites for understanding: Some investigations of comprehension and recall. *Journal of Verbal Learning and Verbal Behavior, 11*, 717–726. doi:10.1016/S0022-5371(72)80006-9

Bruce, D. (1994). Lashley and the problem of serial order. *American Psychologist, 49*, 93–103. doi:10.1037/0003-066X.49.2.93

Carroll, D. (2004). Web-based assignments in the psychology of language class. *Teaching of Psychology, 31*, 204–206. www.teachpsych.org/top/index.php

Carroll, D., & Pinnow, E. (2011). Engaging students in the psychology of language. In R. L. Miller, E. Balcetis, S. R. Burns, D. B. Daniel, B. K. Saville, & W. D. Woody (Eds.), *Promoting student engagement* (Vol. 2, pp. 92–95). Retrieved from the Society for the Teaching of Psychology web site, http://teachpsych.org/ebooks/pse2011/vol2/index.php

Chiu, C. (2011). Language and culture. *Online Readings in Psychology and Culture, 4*(2). doi:10.9707/2307-0919.1098

Chomsky, N. (1959). Verbal behavior [Review]. *Language*, 35, 26–58. doi:10.2307/411334

Cook, V., & Bassetti, B. (2011). *Language and bilingual cognition*. New York, NY: Psychology Press.

Crago, M. B., Allen, S. E. M., & Hough-Eyamie, W. P. (1997). Exploring innateness through cultural and linguistic variation. In M. Gopnik (Ed.), *The biological basis of language* (pp. 70–90). Oxford: Oxford University Press.

Diekhoff, G. M. (2008). The role of expectancies in the perception of language. In L. T. Benjamin (Ed.), *Favorite activities for the teaching of psychology* (pp. 145–147). Washington, DC: American Psychological Association.

Dunn, D. S., & Hammer, E. D. (2014). On teaching multicultural psychology. In F. T. L. Leong (Ed.), *APA handbook of multicultural psychology: Vol. 1. Theory and research* (pp. 43–58). Washington, DC: American Psychological Association.

Everett, D. L. (2005). Cultural constraints on grammar and cognition in Pirahã. *Current Anthropology*, 46, 621–646. doi:10.1086/431525

Fernald, P. S., & Fernald, L. D. (2008). Early motor and verbal development. In L. T. Benjamin (Ed.), *Favorite activities for the teaching of psychology* (pp. 180–181). Washington, DC: American Psychological Association.

Gass, S. M., & Maronis, E. M. (1991). Miscommunication in nonnative speaker discourse. In H. G. N. Coupland, H. Giles, & J. M. Wiemann (Eds.), *"Miscommunication" and problem talk* (pp. 121–145). Newbury Park, CA: Sage Publications.

Gathercole, V. M., & Hoff, E. (2007). Input and the acquisition of language: Three questions. In E. Hoff, M. Shatz, E. Hoff, & M. Shatz (Eds.), *Blackwell handbook of language development* (pp. 107–127). Oxford: Blackwell. doi:10.1002/9780470757833.ch6

Grice, H. P. (1978). Further notes on logic and conversation. In J. A. Adler & L. J. Rips (Eds.), *Reasoning: Studies of human inference and its foundations* (pp. 765–773). Cambridge, MA: Cambridge University Press.

Hill, A. A. (1952). A note on primitive languages. *International Journal of American Linguistics*, 18, 172–177. doi:10.1086/464167

Hockett, C. (1966). The problem of universals in language. In J. H. Greenberg (Ed.), *Universals of language* (2nd ed., pp. 1–29). Cambridge, MA: Massachusetts Institute of Technology Press.

Hoff, E. (2009). *Language development* (4th ed.). Belmont, CA: Wadsworth.

Holtgraves, T. (1997). Styles of language use: Individual and cultural variability in conversational indirectness. *Journal of Personality and Social Psychology*, 73, 624–637. doi:10.1037/0022-3514.73.3.624

Joseph, J. E., & Newmeyer, F. J. (2012). "All languages are equally complex": The rise and fall of a consensus. *Historiographia Linguistica*, 2, 341–368. doi:10.1075/hl.39.2-3.08jos

Kite, M. E., & Whitley, B. E. (2012). Ethnic and nationality stereotypes in everyday language. *Teaching of Psychology*, 39, 54–56. doi:10.1177/0098628311430314

Krumov, K., & Larsen, K. S. (2013). The evolution of language and socio-culture. In K. Krumov & K. S. Larsen, *Cross-cultural psychology: Why culture matters* (pp. 109–142). Charlotte, NC: Information Age.

Lashley, K. S. (1951). The problem of serial order in behavior. In L. A Jeffress (Ed.), *Cerebral mechanisms in behavior: The Hixon Symposium* (pp. 112–146). New York, NY: Wiley.

Lee, J. S. (2005). Embracing diversity through the understanding of pragmatics. In K. Denham & A. Lobeck (Eds.), *Language in the schools: Integrating linguistic knowledge into K-12 teaching* (pp. 17–27). Mahwah, NJ: Lawrence Erlbaum.

Miller, G. A. (1990). The place of language in a scientific psychology. *Psychological Science, 1,* 7–14. doi:10.1111/j.1467-9280.1990.tb00059.x

Parama, K., Kreiner, D. S., Stark, K., & Schuetz, S. (2017). Monolingual and bilingual perceptions of code-switching: A difference in cognition but not competence. *North American Journal of Psychology, 19,* 87–102. http://najp.us/north-american-journal-of-psychology-index

Pinker, S. (1994). *The language instinct: How the mind creates language.* New York, NY: William Morrow.

Rawson, K., Thomas, R., & Jacoby, L. L. (2015). The power of examples: Illustrative examples enhance conceptual learning of declarative concepts. *Educational Psychology Review, 27,* 483–504. doi:10.1007/s10648-014-9273-3

Roberts, C., Moss, B., Wass, V., Sarangi, S., & Jones, R. (2005). Misunderstandings: A qualitative study of primary care consultations in multilingual settings, and educational implications. *Medical Education, 39,* 465–475. doi:10.1111/j.1365-2929.2005.02121.x

Ronkin, M., & Karn, H. E. (1999). Mock Ebonics: Linguistic racism in parodies of Ebonics on the internet. *Journal of Sociolinguistics, 3,* 360–380. doi:10.1111/1467-9481.00083

Sandler, W., Meir, I., Padden, C., & Aronoff, M. (2005). The emergence of grammar: Systematic structure in a new language. *Proceedings of the National Academy of Sciences, 102,* 2661–2665. doi:10.1073/pnas.0405448102

Scancarelli, J. (1994). Another look at a "primitive language." *International Journal of American Linguistics, 60,* 149–160. doi:10.1086/466227

Whorf, B. (1950). An American Indian model of the universe. *International Journal of American Linguistics, 16,* 67–72. doi:10.1086/464066

Wong, J. (2010). The "triple articulation" of language. *Journal of Pragmatics, 42,* 2932–2944. doi:10.1016/j.pragma.2010.06.013

Zhang, Y., Jin, X., Shen, X., Zhang, J., & Hoff, E. (2008). Correlates of early language development in Chinese children. *International Journal of Behavioral Development, 32,* 145–151. doi:10.1177/0165025407087213

Social Psychology

Among the various subfields of psychology, social psychology with its interest in the effects of groups on individual behavior has had a long-standing connection to culture. In this section of the book, the initial chapters (16 and 17) explore traditional social psychological phenomena (e.g., attribution, person perception, persuasion, self, and identity) with accompanying suggestions for teaching activities.

In Chapter 18, we explore a reality that may be unsettling for some students: the likelihood that we are all, in our own ways, ethnocentric, judging other cultures or groups by the standards of our own, and often finding the other to be inferior. The chapter also reviews some of the correlates of ethnocentrism, and influences that have been associated with its reduction.

The final two chapters (19 and 20) of this section address particularly timely topics: how cultures treat sexual minorities and the importance of the integration of culture and peace psychology. In each case, the authors provide interesting, contemporary ideas for teaching activities and for relating the subject matter to cultural context.

CHAPTER 16

Culture and Social Behavior

Richard L. Miller and Tyler Collette

According to Henrich, Heine, and Norenzayan (2010), social psychology is WEIRD in that much of our understanding of social behavior has largely been based on research conducted with college sophomores in Western, educated, industrialized, rich, and democratic countries. Arnett (2008) found that in recent issues of six top psychology journals, 68 percent of the participants were from the United States and an additional 28 percent were from other Western, industrialized countries.

In general, social psychologists examine how others influence our thoughts, feelings, and behaviors. A sociocultural perspective allows us to expand that analysis to include how membership in a particular cultural group can also influence social behavior. Although there are many universals of social behavior, the purpose of this chapter will be to identify ways in which culture modifies our understanding of social psychological phenomena. The need for this approach is evident in research by Amir and Sharon (1987) that failed to replicate six major social psychological studies when conducted with college students in Israel. In addition to examining how culture may change what we know, it is also true that adding culture to our list of variables can enrich our understanding of social behavior. For example, early studies of achievement motivation focused on the internal state of a person, which led to an ethnocentric construction of achievement motivation. Subsequently, culturally based conceptions of achievement motivation have enlarged our understanding of the role of locus of control, individualism/collectivism, and cultural context in how and why individuals are motivated to achieve (Maehr, 1974). Finally, culture has been shown to strengthen or weaken an effect first studied in a Western society. For example, Schacter et al. (1954) found that the *degree* to which deviates were rejected varied from country to country. Thus, a cross-cultural perspective can enrich our understanding of both classic and current research in the most important topics in the science of social behavior, including those discussed in this chapter: social cognition, person perception, self and identity, conformity, persuasion, interpersonal relations, group dynamics, aggression, helping, and prosocial behavior.

In addition to clarifying the knowledge base, a cross-cultural perspective allows us to better understand social change. In today's world, social behaviors are triggered by unprecedented levels of cross-national contact through travel, migration, social media, globalization, international educational opportunities, and worldwide media coverage of contemporary events. For example, with regard to migration, the move from rural to urban areas in many countries has changed what were once primarily collectivist countries into countries with urban pockets of individualism (see Du, Li, & Lin, 2015). In directing a study abroad trip to Peru, the senior author expected to find a largely collectivist population as indicated in Hofstede (2001). While that is certainly the case on Lake Titicaca where families take turns running the local tourist shops and the profits are shared among all of the residents, 85 percent of the participants in my students' research projects conducted in Lima were self-proclaimed individualists as defined by the Singelis (1994) scale.

Social Cognition

Social cognition is the study of how people process, store, and apply information about themselves, other people, and social situations. It examines the role that the cognitive processes involved in the perception, judgment, and memory of social stimuli play in social interactions. To this end, social psychologists studying social cognition focus on how social and affective factors influence information processing, attitudes, and behavior.

A key concept in the study of social cognition is Festinger's (1957) theory of cognitive dissonance, which suggests that when individuals experience inconsistency between two cognitions or between cognition and behavior, the discrepancy elicits aversive feelings of dissonance, which motivate individuals to try to reduce the inconsistency. Whereas Festinger was convinced that the need for cognitive consistency is a basic human need similar to hunger and thirst, the universality of cognitive dissonance has been challenged by cross-cultural researchers. Heine and Lehman (1997) found that after making a difficult decision, North Americans reduced dissonance by enhancing a chosen alternative and devaluing a rejected alternative. In contrast, East Asians did not show this pattern. Markus and Kitayama (1991) interpreted this cultural difference by arguing that dissonance stemming from counterattitudinal behavior may not be experienced by individuals with interdependent self-construals, who place less importance on internal attributes (e.g., attitudes) as self-defining characteristics compared to external attributes (e.g., social roles). As such, inconsistency between attitudes and behavior may be regarded as less significant in Eastern compared to Western cultures. Furthermore, Sakai (1981) found dissonance-related attitude change following public- but not private-induced compliance in an Asian sample.

Hoshino-Browne, Zanna, Spencer, & Zanna (2005) conducted four studies and found that both Easterners and Westerners experience cognitive dissonance, but that cultural differences shape the particular situations in which dissonance is aroused. In their research, European Canadians showed significant postdecisional justification when they made choices for themselves whereas Asian-Canadians only engaged in postdecisional justification when they made choices for their friends.

Research by Kitayama, Snibbe, Markus, and Suzuki (2004) illustrated the importance of cultural values in dissonance reduction. In four experiments, they found that after making a choice, individuals justified their decision in order to eliminate doubts about culturally sanctioned aspects of the self. For their North American participants, this aspect included competence and efficacy whereas among Japanese participants, it was positive appraisal by other people.

Other cultural factors can affect cognitive dissonance. Newburry and Yakinova (2006) found that individuals from high uncertainty avoidance, high power distance, and high context cultures prefer greater cognitive consistency. Another factor that can affect dissonance arousal is trust. In China, trust is bestowed on the extended family while those outside the family are often distrusted (Child & Möllering, 2003). This bias against members of the outgroup can affect elicitation of cognitive dissonance in collectivist cultures. In collectivist cultures, cognitive dissonance also may arise when decisions are made that are in conflict with the values or norms of the culture. Trompenaars (1994) identified several cultural dimensions that could affect cognitive dissonance, including universalism versus particularism (rules are to be applied universally versus rules are secondary to relationships), individualism versus communitarianism (whether individual interests should take precedence over group wishes and benefits), specific versus diffuse (getting to the point versus first establishing a relationship), and affective versus neutral display of emotions and achievement versus ascription (whether status is derived from a person's achievements versus her or his background).

Another important concept in the study of social cognition is regret. Regret is a negative reaction to something that one has either done or failed to do. This negative reaction can be expressed in the form of sadness, shame, depression, annoyance, embarrassment, or guilt. In a study by Shimanoff (1984), regret was the second most expressed emotion in everyday conversation after love.

Much of the literature on regret distinguishes between decisions to act (i.e., actions) and decisions not to act (i.e., inactions). Regret for actions occurs when a person does something (commission) that he or she wishes he or she had not done whereas regret for inaction occurs when a person did not do something (omission) that he or she wishes he or she had done. Regret for inaction can also include regret for missed opportunities.

Gilovich, Wang, Regan, and Nishina (2003) conducted five studies with participants from three collectivist cultures (China, Japan, and Russia) in which they asked participants to report their greatest regrets. They were then asked to identify whether their greatest regrets were due to something they did that they wished they had not done (action) or something they did not do that they wished they had (inaction). They found that in each of the collectivist cultures, inaction was regretted more than action.

Komiya, Miyamoto, Watabe, and Kusumi (2011) focused on the distinction between interpersonal and self-situations as well as between action and inaction regrets with Japanese and US students. Inaction regrets were recalled to a greater extent than action regrets in self-situations compared to interpersonal situations, and Americans recalled inaction regrets at a higher rate than did the Japanese. With regard to intensity, Japanese students displayed more regret in interpersonal situations compared to Americans. However, in self-situations, Americans and Japanese students reported equal levels of regret.

In a study by Zeelenberg, van der Pilgt, and Manstead (1998), a Dutch television show provided an opportunity for people to undo regrets that had occurred in social situations. They found that regret for action was more likely to result in an apology as a means to undo interpersonal transgressions than were regrets of inaction. Results also showed that the time between the regretted event and the apology is shorter for regrets of action than for regrets of inaction. The findings of this study support the temporal pattern of regret described by Gilovich and Medvec (1995). In general, people tend to experience more regret when they do something out of the ordinary than when they engage in normal behavior. Normality can be either intrapersonal (consistency within a person) or interpersonal (consistency between people). Kur, Roese, and Namkoong (2009) examined whether the impact of violating these two forms of normality on regret varies across cultures. These researchers also examined the effects of mutability, the extent to which an alternative to the norm violation was available. Among Korean participants (but not Americans), the impact of mutability on regret was greater when an intrapersonal norm was violated rather than the interpersonal norm. Kur et al. interpreted this finding as an indication of the greater collectivist emphasis in Korea as compared to the United States.

Teaching Activity to Illustrate Social Cognition

Clock time and event time. In this activity, students determine whether their culture is characterized by "clock time" or "event time" (i.e., time needed to complete an activity) and then spend a day living according to the opposite time orientation. They then write about their experiences, speculating about corresponding cultural values. According to Levine (1997), cultural differences in the pace of life constitute one of the most profound adjustments sojourners must make and can be observed when individuals move between urban and rural settings, corporate cultures, and ethnic groups. The goal of this activity is to increase students' awareness of cultural differences in how we think about time. For more information, see Goldstein (2008, pp. 329–331).

Person Perception

The study of person perception focuses on how we form impressions of other people based on their appearance, personality, or initial contact. A key concept in the study of person perception is the fundamental attribution error, which is the tendency to overestimate how much a person's behavior is due to dispositional factors and to underestimate how much it is due to situational factors. Dispositional factors refer to a person's internal characteristics, such as personality traits, abilities, and motives. Situational factors refer to external causes. In general, collectivists are less likely to make the fundamental attribution error than individualists. For example, Miller (1984) found that Indians were more likely to make situational attributions, such as role obligations, more often than dispositional attributions. Similarly, Morris and Peng (1994) found that a US newspaper was more likely to describe mass murders in terms of dispositional factors (such as a very bad temper) whereas Chinese newspapers were more likely to focus on situational factors (such as having been recently fired). A cultural factor that plays a role in differences in the fundamental attribution error is the prevalence of self-effacement in Asian cultures. Japanese respondents frequently attribute failure to internal factors, for example, lack of ability, and success to external factors, such as luck or circumstances (Kashima & Triandis, 1986). Lee and Seligman (1997) found a similar self-effacing bias among the Chinese.

Another aspect of person perception is the ability to recognize and remember other people's faces. Across many cultures, there exists a same-race bias in facial recognition. According to Meissner & Brigham (2001), this differential recognition ability may be due to attitudes toward those of a different race, task difficulty, social orientation, and experience, but not so much from lack of contact with others.

Teaching Activity to Illustrate Person Perception

Cultural display rules. Students keep a record of form and intensity of their emotions and how they expressed these feelings, including key information about each emotional situation, over a period of time (e.g., a week). They then individually answer a series of questions regarding their observations (specifically aimed toward assisting students in realizing display conventions). The goal of this activity is to consider the cultural beliefs and values that regulate the practice of emotion display and to help students identify the display rules that they use. For more information see Goldstein (2008, p. 179).

Self and Identity

Harry Stack Sullivan (1953) suggested that interaction with significant others, especially parents, is the primary source of a person's identity, and Eric Erikson (1964) conceptualized the process of achieving a stable identity as the most critical task of adolescence. Erikson suggested that individuals experience an identity crisis during adolescence, and resolution of this crisis requires individuals to balance the various self-images they experience with the social roles available to them as they mature. Erikson (1964, 1966) noted that their culture provides people with an appropriate range of social roles from which to select who they will become and also a process by which they can validate their identity. Similarly, Gardiner and Kosmitzki (2008) pointed out that successful resolution of a crisis at any stage of development will depend on how the culture views the crisis and the resolution.

Erikson (1966) also suggested that situational changes such as immigration to a new country could cause an imbalance between people and the cultural contexts in which they formed their identity. Those with strong identities are not likely to experience a renewed identity crisis, but Erikson noted that even those with a strong sense of who they are still respond to changes in cultural context. Expanding on Erikson's ideas, Marcia (1966) suggested that the process of identity development is not limited to adolescence, but continues throughout the life span as one's cultural context may change and develop. According to Marcia, a person's identity is influenced by personality, maturity, and cultural context. Marcia's identity status model (1966) proposed that identity is a result of two processes: exploration and commitment.

Erikson was not the only theorist to discuss the importance of cultural context in identity formation. Several researchers have noted the influence of contextual factors that are both immediate (one's present situation) and broad (the historical milieu) on the formation and experience of one's identity (Sellers, 1998). For example, if you are the only Hispanic person in a room of African Americans, you may become extremely aware of race, and that awareness will in turn affect your behavior and how you think of yourself. How situations can cause aspects of our identity to become more accessible has been demonstrated in several studies in which individuals were reminded of their cultural identity (e.g., Benet-Martinez, Leu, Lee, & Morris, 2002; Hong, Morris, Chiu, & Benet-Martinez, 2000).

Other theories that suggest that membership in a cultural group or groups will influence how individuals define themselves include social identity theory (Tajfel & Turner, 1986) and self-categorization theory (Turner, Hogg, Oakes, Reicher, & Wetherell, 1987). These theories suggest that as membership in a cultural group becomes salient, individuals model their social beliefs and behavior on those they perceive to be prototypical of the group.

In cross-cultural research, the term *self-construal* is often used instead of *identity*. A self-construal is the awareness of our thoughts and feelings that provides an understanding of our private inner selves: The theory of divergent self-construals (Markus & Kitayama, 1991) attempted to expand upon the limited "Western" view of the self held by many contemporary researchers. Drawing upon research delineating cross-cultural differences in the views of personhood, Markus & Kitayama (1991) proposed that self-construals could be divided into two distinct conceptual representations of the self: independent and interdependent. Although some aspects of the self may be universal, they asserted that the fundamental nature of the self-construal is inextricably bound to the culture in which the individual was reared. Independent self-construals are, according to Markus and Kitayama (1991), generally representative of individuals in Western cultures whereas individuals in non-Western cultures are more likely to possess interdependent self-construals.

Markus and Kitayama (1991) and Singelis (1994) provided definitions of independent and interdependent self-construals. Persons of the Western world (e.g., the United States, northern Europe) generally subscribe to strongly individualistic beliefs, emphasizing the uniqueness of every individual and encouraging development of an independent self-construal. The independent self-construal views the self as an autonomous entity whose own thoughts, feelings, and actions are of utmost importance. Other people are important largely as a basis for social comparison, and the realization of internal attributes and accomplishment of personal goals are viewed as highly desirable states. In contrast, many cultures categorized as non-Western (e.g., China) are characterized as collectivist, focusing on the inherent connectedness of the individual to others. The interdependent construal of self is derived from this belief, viewing the self as an integral part of the social relationships in which one is engaged, and recognizing that thoughts, feelings, and actions are directly related to those of others with whom the person interacts. Relationships with others are integral to self-definition as is the ability to maintain harmony in such social relationships. In one representative study, Parkes, Schneider, and Bochner (1999) administered the Twenty Statements Test (Kuhn & McPartland, 1954) to participants from nationalities classified as either individualist or collectivist (based upon Hofstede's Individualism Index, 2001). Their results indicated that individualists are more likely to employ autonomous self-descriptions (referring to their own internal attributes) whereas collectivists are more likely to describe themselves with social references (referring to group membership or to other people). Markus and Kitayama (1991) posited that these divergent views of the self maintain a crucial role in the organization of one's self-regulatory schemata and the interpretation of one's experiences, leading to a variety of consequences. One's self-construal can affect cognitive, emotional, and motivational processes. Likewise, the self is also a product of the social experiences to which it is exposed, especially those of culture, providing a continually evolving and dynamic presence (Cross & Madson, 1997).

Triandis (1995) pointed out that Markus and Kitayama's (1991) use of the terms *independent* and *interdependent* construal of self is more or less equivalent to the social patterns of individualism and collectivism. Within a culture, variation exists in the extent that either individualism or collectivism is emphasized above the other, but most members of a specific culture will tend toward the same view. In an individualistic culture, the definition of self is independent of the group; in a collectivistic culture, the definition of self is tied to the ingroup. Individualists promote personal goals whereas collectivists give priority to ingroup goals. Individualists rely more heavily upon attitudes as determinants of social behavior rather than norms, which are a key influence upon collectivists' social behaviors. Individualists maintain relationships that are personally advantageous and eliminate those that are costly to the individual, but collectivists will often maintain individually taxing relationships if they are beneficial to the ingroup. Triandis (1996) also identified factors that promote either individualism or collectivism within a particular culture. Heterogeneous societies that have a large number of role definitions but relatively fewer norms (complex and loose) promote individualism; homogeneous societies with fewer role definitions and a large number of norms foster the development of collectivism. High social class; migration, especially to urban areas; social mobility; and exposure to mass media also contribute to individualism.

Teaching Activities to Illustrate Self and Identity

Nicknaming across cultures. In this exercise, students interview three individuals each (preferably demographically diverse), and ask questions about nicknames. Students then individually determine the functions of these nicknames (e.g., individuating) and discuss cultural influences on nicknames and their functions. A classroom discussion can address how nicknames can reflect social class membership, regional identity, and other cultural differences. The students can then compare their answers to those provided by Skipper, Leslie, & Wilson (1990). The goal of this activity is to illustrate how nicknaming can reinforce cultural values.

Experience over materialism: Trying a consumer moratorium. A second exercise that can illustrate how we define ourselves relates to how our identity is related to material goods. While positive and pleasurable activities we engage in are ultimately more satisfying than the material goods we so often seek to own (e.g., Gilbert, 2006), individuals living in a postindustrial society spend a fair amount of time obtaining things. Giving up our tendency to be consumers can be a challenge, but some students may be willing to try to do so for a week or two and then report on the experience. All students need to do is to seek out positive experiences that are largely cost free (e.g., going to a park, playing a game, exercising, socializing with friends) and to refrain from making any consumer purchases beyond those that are necessary (e.g., food, transportation, health related). When the moratorium on shopping is over, the students can discuss their experiences and reactions in class or write a brief paper on their experiences.

Conformity

At some point in their lives, every American's parents have voiced the dilemma, "If all your friends jumped off a bridge, then would you jump off too?" It's a relatively common phrase indicating the dangers that can come from being a blind follower, a sheep, a conformist. However, had your parents been Japanese you might have heard the phrase "deru kugi wa utareru," which roughly translates as "the nail that sticks out is the one to get hammered." Conformity research has traditionally focused on why and when people conform (Fiske, 2014; Myers & Dewall, 2016). This anecdote allows for a glimpse into the importance of adding culture as not only another mechanism for psychologists to utilize in our search to understand conformity, but also as a mediator for the mechanisms we have traditionally studied.

One of the most salient early experiments was one conducted by Asch (1951), in which participants conformed to majority pressures when choosing corresponding line lengths. Early cross-cultural research on conformity focused on this particular aspect of individualism and collectivism, and largely found distinct differences between these two value systems on conformity (Bond & Smith, 1996; Huang & Harris, 1973; Triandis, Bontempo, Villareal, Asai, & Lucca, 1988), although much of the research done on this topic has examined how individuals conform when being pressured by strangers (e.g., Asch, 1951).

More recent research has found clear cultural distinctions in conformity. For example, Takono and Sogan (2008) found that Japanese participants were less likely to conform during a traditional Asch line experiment than their American counterparts. Williams and Sogan's (1985) research on Japanese conformity found that Japanese participants, traditionally collectivists, were less likely to conform when influenced by strangers than by ingroup members. Hitokoto and Uchida's (2015) research on subjective well-being found significant correlations between interdependent happiness, or happiness directly connected to one's relationships, and students' subjective well-being among Japanese students. This was not true for American students.

Conformity pressures change throughout time. Americans have become less likely to conform over the years (Bond & Smith, 1996). This is most evident in American consumer patterns. Over time, a drive to be unique has changed the nature of product development (Tian, Bearden, & Hunter, 2001). This shift can also be seen in countries like Japan but is explained on the basis of conforming to be unique, a phrase that is likely an oxymoron (Knight & Young Kim, 2007). In this case, the connection between culture change and traditional past is an important aspect of understanding conformity pressures. Reconceptualizing conformity for students then goes along with reconceptualizing culture for students (Oyserman, Coon, & Kemmelmeier, 2002).

Culture is ever changing, but there is an overlying persistence of traditional values that also influences how we interact with the world (Inglehart & Baker, 2000). For example, whereas conformity is often portrayed negatively in Western societies, Horike (1992) found that the Japanese identified conformity as the most important factor underlying their humanity. This interrelation between change and tradition is at the core of the necessity for teaching from a cultural lens.

Teaching Activity to Illustrate Conformity

Social graces in different cultures. In this activity, students examine conformity to normative expectations regarding social manners. Because socially acceptable behavior differs from culture to culture, instructors can create an exercise using items provided by Axtell (1993) and Dresser (1996) to illustrate gestures and behaviors that are acceptable in one culture and unacceptable in another. Students try to match each behavior with the culture in which it is appropriate. The goal of this activity is to make students aware of cross-cultural variation in social graces and the gestures that are rude in one culture and perfectly acceptable in another.

Persuasion

Aristotle once wrote "Persuasion is clearly a sort of demonstration, since we are most fully persuaded when we consider a thing to have been demonstrated" (Roberts, 2009, p. 1). While this may seem quite reasonable on the surface, is this how persuasion really works? Furthermore, are all people persuaded by the same things and under similar conditions? Are individuals in some cultures more persuadable than others? For the purpose of this chapter, we will focus on two major concepts that have been historically taught in social psychology courses, the Yale Attitude Change Approach and the elaboration likelihood model.

Persuasion is the deliberate use of a message to incite changes in beliefs, attitudes, or behaviors (Myers & Twenge, 2017). A popular technique still taught in most social psychology classrooms is the Yale Attitude Change Approach. According to this approach, there are three core components to attitude change. First is the nature of the source. This includes the attractiveness and the credibility of the communicator. Second is the nature of the message. This includes the genuineness and the quality of the message. Last is the nature of the audience. This includes age, political positions, intelligence, and many other characteristics that can affect how a message will be received by an audience (Hovland, Janis, & Kelley, 1953).

This model has produced many influential works over the past six decades (Hovland et al., 1953; Janis, 1967; Nabi, 1999; Petty & Brinol, 2010; Tesser, 1978). However, other researchers have found distinct cultural differences in how this model can be applied. One distinction, the source of the communication, can be conceptualized using power distance, one of Hofstede's cultural dimensions. Power distance is the degree to which individuals with less power accept or expect unequal distributions of power (Hofstede & Bond, 1984). This has a telling effect on the persuasiveness of a particular source. For example, Fikret Pasa (2000) found that Turkish individuals were more likely to be affected by the source if the communicator held higher status. Pornpitakpan and Francis (2000) found that people in Thailand, a high power distance country, were more likely to be affected by the communicator than those in America, a low power distance country. In another study, a source generated from a subculture was considered credible only if the audience was also an individual from that subculture (Brumbaugh, 2002). This is an important aspect of persuasion, because a credible source in one culture may very well be noncredible in another. For example, a person in a hierarchical society will be less influenced by an individual who has lower status, even if the individual possesses other characteristics of a good source, such as attractiveness (Fikret Pasa, 2000).

Sincerity and overall quality of a message are well researched and foundational areas of persuasion (Janis & Hovland, 1959; Nabi, 1999). However, is a persuasive message equally persuasive in any culture? The term *uncertainty avoidance*, coined by Hofstede (2011), is defined as the extent to which individuals within a culture feel uncomfortable with ambiguity and uncertainty. Countries who score high in uncertainty avoidance are less likely to be influenced by Internet advertising (Vishwanath, 2003). Furthermore, Lim, Leung, Sia, and Lee (2004) found that after controlling for factors such as GDP, crime, and income inequality, individuals from countries that scored high in uncertainty avoidance were less likely to shop online in comparison to their low uncertainty avoidance counterparts. Other research has found that those in high uncertainty avoidance cultures are likely to perceive messages from experts to be more influential than are people in low uncertainty avoidance cultures (Pornpitakpan & Francis, 2000).

Another important approach to attitude change is the elaboration likelihood model. This dual-process theory posits that there are two routes of persuasion – a central route focusing on the true merits of the information being presented, and a peripheral route focusing on positive or negative cues in the message (Petty & Cacioppo, 1984). Hong, Muderrisoglu, and Zinkhan (1987) found that in terms of central/informational routes to persuasion, there were no differences between individualist and collectivist cultures. However, Pornpitakpan and Francis (2000) found that collectivists were more likely to value persuasive arguments from a central route when coming from a credible source whereas individualists were more persuaded by peripheral routes regardless of credibility. There are clear cultural differences in the effectiveness of peripheral messages. For example, Korean consumers were more likely to be persuaded by products marketed with a peripheral stress on the family or ingroup benefits. In contrast, American consumers were more likely to be persuaded by a peripheral stress on individual benefits (Han & Shavitt, 1994).

Persuasion is not always successful. Individuals value their freedom and autonomy and will sometimes resist social influence. When social pressure becomes so blatant that individuals think that their freedom to think or do what they want is threatened or eliminated, they may experience psychological reactance (Brehm, 1966). This can cause a boomerang effect that may lead individuals to do the opposite of what is desired in order to restore their freedom of choice.

Cross-cultural research has found differences in individuals' likelihood of experiencing reactance. Worchel (2004) suggested that while psychological reactance can lead to attempts to restore freedom, it could also lead to attempts to reestablish one's sense of self. For example, Jonas et al. (2009) found that collectivists were less sensitive to a threat to their individual freedom than individualists but more sensitive if their collective freedom was threatened. Similarly, collectivists value the collective freedom of an ingroup more in the face of an outgroup threat than individualists whereas individualists are protective of their individual freedom, especially within an ingroup (Graupmann, Jonas, Meier, Hawelka, & Aichhorn, 2012).

Another interesting cultural variation in reactance sensitivity can be seen in individuals who are bicultural. Biculturals can be self-conscious about their identity and as a result may experience reactance against cultural cues that imply how they should behave. Thus, self-consciousness can result in overcorrection, leading to behaviors that provide contrast effects. Similarly, individuals who perceive their cultural identities to be in opposition can experience inner conflict that can result in reactance against cultural expectations (Benet-Martinez & Haritatos, 2005). In conclusion, there does not seem to be a universal desire for freedom of choice, nor are there consistent ways of responding to the loss of freedom.

Teaching Activity to Illustrate Persuasion

Redesigning public service announcements. Koch and Lomore (2009) describe how students in an introductory social psychology class redesigned a public service announcement so it would be more effective. The procedure described in their article can be readily adapted for use with a variety of community organizations (e.g., local food banks, animal protectors/shelters). Students reported that the exercises helped them understand the concepts involved in attitude change and persuasion, and that they found the activity to be enjoyable. To apply cultural concepts to the exercise, students could design announcements that would primarily appeal to individualists versus collectivists.

Group Dynamics

Think about the groups that you belong to, such as family, coworkers, or sports teams. Do you interact with each group in the same way? Your cultural background may play a large role in how you interact and experience these groups. In this section, we will expand on a few aspects of group dynamics to highlight how culture mediates group dynamics: group polarization, groupthink, and intercultural interactions.

Psychologists study group dynamics to help explain why groups make the decisions they do, and to understand particular behaviors like riots, inaction, and helping behaviors (Backstrom, Huttenlocher, Kleinberg, & Lan, 2006). Group polarization occurs when group members enhance an individual's preexisting attitudes or behaviors. There are some clear cultural differences that arise in the literature (Myers & Twenge, 2017). For example, South Koreans (collectivists) were more likely to make polarized and risky decisions when in a group than were Australians (individualists)

(Kim & Park, 2010). This can be explained by the nature of the risky shift, or making riskier decisions when in a group than when alone (Myers & Twenge, 2017). Collectivists tend to be more influenced by interactions within a group, particularly when the group comprises ingroup members (Kim & Park, 2010). Group polarization affects individuals who value group relations more than those who value individual preferences.

Another important group dynamic concept is groupthink. *Groupthink* is the psychological drive for consensus, whereby any dissent against group decisions is suppressed and the consideration of alternate decisions is undervalued (Fiske, 2014). Under this condition, groups might make decisions that are ultimately detrimental to the group because members are driven to make sure that a decision is supported fully by all members. Due to their value of maintaining group harmony, collectivist cultures are more likely to be affected by groupthink (Kameda & Sugimori, 1993). To combat this phenomenon, many Japanese businesses have developed a practice of designating a "devil's advocate," or someone designated to find faults with group decisions, to ensure that good decisions are made (Flynn, 1992).

Intercultural interactions can be a good way to highlight the importance of a cultural lens. In particular, research on sojourners has produced some telling variations in how people from different cultures deal with living among those of another culture (Church, 1982). Ward and Kennedy (1993) found that external locus of control was beneficial to adjusting to a new cultural environment. Social support systems within both cultures were an important aspect of adjusting to a new environment. Individuals also found transitioning to cultures with similar values much easier than transitioning to a culture with vastly different cultural values (Ward & Kennedy, 1993). Furthermore, collectivists are more likely to find a transition to another country more difficult if there are not other collectivists in the new culture (Rosenthal, Bell, Demetriou, & Efkledes, 1989).

Teaching Activity to Illustrate Group Dynamics

Acculturation. For this demonstration, divide students into two groups and through a series of activities, form distinct groups that simulate cultures. After the enculturation process, the groups experience acculturation by "sojourning" to the other "culture" and interacting with its members. Finally, students discuss their experiences. Formal evaluation of this activity indicated that students' knowledge of the acculturation process improved and their opinion of the exercise was very positive. The goal of this activity is to allow students to actively experience the acculturation process. For more information, see Tomcho and Foels (2002).

Helping/Prosocial Behavior

Two competing explanations have been put forward to account for altruistic behavior: sociobiology and education. In other words, are we genetically programmed to help one another or is it a learned behavior? Cross-cultural research has helped clarify the relative contributions of each. Much of the anthropological literature suggests substantial differences in the amount of generosity or helping behavior across cultures. For example, Margaret Mead (as cited by Mussen, 1977) described the differences between two New Guinea tribes, the Arapesh who were gentle, cooperative, generous, and responsive to the feeling and needs of others and the Mundugamor who were aggressive, uncaring, ruthless, and lacking in generosity and cooperation. Social psychological research in this area includes the work of the Whitings and their colleagues (Whiting & Edwards, 1988; Whiting & Whiting, 1975), who examined helping behavior in six countries. Their explanation for the differences in helping behavior centered on the extent to which children were given family responsibilities that promoted helpfulness, and provides support for the social learning hypothesis. Other studies have shown that in collectivist cultures, individuals are comparatively more likely to help members of the ingroup while those from individualist cultures are comparatively more likely to help members of the outgroup (Leung & Bond, 1984).

Another aspect of helping behavior is the extent to which we believe we are helpful. In a study of the *holier than thou* phenomenon, Balcetis, Dunning, and Miller (2009) found that respondents from individualist cultures overestimated the likelihood that they would act generously as compared to how they actually acted when redistributing a reward, donating money, or avoiding rude behavior whereas collectivists were accurate in their self-predictions. In contrast, both groups were roughly accurate in predicting their peers' behavior. Balcetis et al. also reported that collectivists were more accurate than individualists in their self-predictions even when both groups were sampled from the same cultural group. Why might this be? Perhaps members of collectivist cultures were more accurate when predicting both their own and others' behaviors because they are more motivated to fit in with normative group behavior and the expectations of others.

Financial education for refugees. Norvilitis (2010) described an activity in which students assisted refugee families in creating bank accounts and managing finances. Students kept a journal that documented their thoughts about ethnocentrism, stereotyping, and prejudice during the course of the project. Students gave positive reviews of the project and noted how meaningful the experience was. In addition, students reported that they gained a heightened awareness of the large number of refugees living within their community, and their needs.

Interpersonal Relationships

Why do we choose to form relationships with certain people, and do people around the world form bonds for the same reasons? Interpersonal relationships are a compelling concept to view through a cultural lens, because there does seem to be some universal similarities between cultures, even across species. However, the expression of these universal mechanisms can vary greatly.

Interpersonal relationships are the social connections or affiliations between individuals, either through a shared bond between two individuals or with a larger group. In this section, we will focus on three key concepts: basic attraction, the mere exposure effect, and high and low relational mobility.

Are the celebrities Ryan Gosling and Emma Watson considered attractive in any culture? The answer is yes, to a certain extent. People tend to be attracted to symmetrical faces no matter where you go in the world (Cárdenas & Harris, 2006; Thornhill, 1992). For evolutionary biologists, this is because of a perceived stability in genetic development, and an indicator that an individual is free of harmful genetic mutations (Thornhill & Gangestad, 1999). Furthermore, there tends to be a universal value for skin that is free of sores, blotches, rashes, or blemishes (Montagu, 1984). Again, evolutionarily, this is an indicator of perceived health, and potential for healthy offspring (Ford & Beach, 1951). In addition, we tend to like people who have average features. This is not to say we like average-looking people, but we like faces with average-sized eyes, noses, ears, and other features (Heine, 2016). Rhodes et al. (2005) found that participants rated average-featured faces higher regardless of ethnic or cultural background of the face. In fact, average faces with both Western and Eastern features were rated higher than any other combination (Rhodes et al., 2005).

Although there tends to be a universal value for certain features, there are distinct differences in what is considered attractive from a cultural perspective. For example, the Paduang in Thailand use a number of rings to slowly elongate their necks, the Mentawai of Indonesia file their teeth into sharp points, and American women in the United States paint their lips, darken their eyelids, and shave their eyebrows (Heine, 2016). Furthermore, ideal body size can vary widely from country to country. South American participants valued a fuller figure more than their North American counterparts (Furnham & Baguma, 1994). These ideals can change over time as well. Trends in North America have seen the ideal body go from fuller-figured to thinner and thinner from the 1940s to the 1980s (Garner, Garfinkel, Schwartz, & Thompson, 1980).

So if we have a universal standard for attractiveness and we have cultural differences in what we find attractive, how do we develop our cultural preferences? This might best be explained by the mere exposure effect. The more exposed we are to a particular characteristic or feature, the more positively it is rated (Heine, 2016). This effect can be used to further explain the effects of classical conditioning, whereby we find that over time, certain features are not threatening and therefore favorable (Zajonc, 1968).

Cultures can differ in terms of the cultural characteristics that are valued in relationships, and can help us understand why we form particular relationships. Cultures differ in terms of relational mobility. This is the freedom that individuals have for moving between relationships, or the extent to which individuals can form and end interpersonal relationships (Heine, 2016). A culture that has high relational mobility might see very flexible ties between individuals. Additionally, these cultures will have many opportunities to form new relationships, and individuals do not feel particularly tied to old relationships (Yuki, Maddux, Brewer, & Takemura, 2005). High relational mobility is more likely in individualistic cultures, and can predict the level of intimacy a person prefers when forming new relationships (Schug, Yuki, & Maddux, 2010). In contrast, low relational mobility, where individuals have fewer opportunities to form new relationships, leads to a value of maintaining harmony in current relationships (Heine, 2016). Collectivist cultures tend to have lower relational mobility. Furthermore, collectivists may be less likely to expose aspects about themselves when meeting new people, but more likely to expose aspects of themselves with old relationships (Schug, Yuki, & Maddux, 2010).

Teaching Activity to Illustrate Interpersonal Relations

Behavior in hierarchical versus egalitarian societies. Provide students a list of situations that individuals are likely to encounter in an organizational setting and have them write about how someone from an egalitarian society versus a hierarchical society (i.e., Hofstede's power distance dimension) would react to each situation, either as an individual writing exercise or in a class discussion. Students identify the type of society in which they were born based on their reactions to the situations. The goal of this activity is to encourage students to consider cultural differences in behavior in an organizational setting. For more information, see Okun, Fried, and Okun (1999, p. 149).

Aggression

Fiske (2014) defined *aggression* as any behavior intended to harm another individual. The first type of aggression we will discuss is physical aggression. Cohen, Nisbett, Bowdle, and Schwarz (1996) conducted three studies in the United States on the "southern culture of honor." Researchers intentionally bumped into participants as they walked through a hallway and called them an "asshole." Southern participants acted out aggressively, whereas northerners were less likely to react at all (Cohen et al., 1996). Cohen & Nisbett (1994) found that the southern view on aggression was only increased in specific situations including when one's honor has been shaken, when defending oneself (or more importantly another), and when socializing children. Furthermore, when others would call for less aggression in these types of situations, southerners are more likely to say aggression is warranted (Hayes & Lee, 2005).

Another type of aggression is indirect aggression. It includes spreading gossip, rumors, or lies about an individual with the intent to harm his or her reputation (Fiske, 2014). Most research on this type of aggression has found few cultural differences (Björkqvist, 1994; Österman et al., 1998; Richardson & Green, 2006). However, a distinct pattern does emerge related to gender. Österman et al. (1998) found that across both individualist and collectivist cultures, men were more likely to exhibit direct aggression, including verbal and physical aggression, than women. In contrast, women were more likely to exhibit indirect aggression. Toldos (2005) found similar results when sampling Spanish children. However, in this case, physical aggression by boys transformed into verbal aggression as children got older. There do not seem to be documented cultural differences in indirect aggression.

Although we do not see cultural difference in some types of aggression, there are particular types of aggressions that are less acceptable in some cultures than others. For example, Li, Wang, Wang, and Shi (2010) found that Chinese students who identified as collectivists were less likely to use relational aggression, or aggression with the intent to harm a person they knew. Chinese students who identified as individualists were more likely to exhibit aggression (Li et al., 2010). This finding was supported by Forbes, Zhang, Doroszewicz, and Haas (2009), who found that both indirect aggression and direct aggression were less likely to be seen in Chinese participants than their US counterparts when aggression was relational. A large-scale analysis of sixty-two countries' reports of student aggression found that, among students, there were no differences between individualist and collectivist cultures. However, there was a reported difference by school principals. Individualist principals reported more aggression than collectivist principals (Bergmüller, 2013). This may be due to a difference in the principals' records of punishing transgressions rather than a difference in actual aggressive behavior.

Teaching Activity to Illustrate Aggression

Analyzing insults. In this activity, each student interviews three individuals from different cultures and asks each one to produce several insulting statements. Students then individually code the insults they collected on the basis of individualism/collectivism, noting differences that emerge as a function of the interviewees' cultural contexts, considering cultural differences in the use of insults (i.e., individual versus relational aim). Students can compare their answers to those found by Semin and Rubin (1990) in their research on verbal abuse. The goal of this activity is to identify individualism/collectivism via derogatory verbal statements.

Exploring Cultural Variations Using Social Networking: A Teaching Technique

There are more than 200 social networking sites, and their success is largely a result of two human needs: the need to connect with others and the need to create a sense of identity. Social networking websites provide instructors with opportunities for increasing student interest and involvement with course materials. When students first join a social networking site such as MySpace or Facebook, they create a profile in which they can post pictures and provide information about themselves and their interests.

The design of this assignment facilitates students' awareness of cultural similarities and differences. In the assignment, students create a profile page for an imaginary person (i.e., an avatar) from a culture different from their own. Students craft the profile page to reflect the avatar's personality, preferences, and environment in which he or she lives. The students first provide a profile of the avatar and over the course of the semester write a blog (i.e., an online journal) about the avatar in terms of several psychological processes, including different aspects of social behavior that can include child development, identity formation, and gender differences. In each blog entry, students must cite sources from the scientific literature as well as Internet resources to support their descriptions. For example, in the child development blog, students typically address the parenting practices, temperament, attachment, cognitive development, and social development in their avatar's culture.

Social networking sites offer a great deal of flexibility in terms of the content students choose to include as well as how they present the information in the structure of their profile. In this multimedia environment, students can integrate popular music, videos, and multimedia representations into their avatar's profile to help articulate a cultural identity. Students often go beyond the assignment to include emblems, music videos, images, and pictures that reflect the life of their avatar. All of the students who have participated in this exercise have uploaded photos of their avatar and their avatar's society. The photos function as another tool of self-presentation as students think about what photos to use to articulate their avatar visually.

Student survey responses indicated that students perceived the social networking project to be a positive learning experience. Also, in the initial implementation of this project, students who participated scored higher on a comprehensive final exam than did those who prepared a literature review paper with similar learning goals covering the same topics.

By creating profile pages for characters from another culture, students can think about how identities are constructed (online or otherwise) and what kinds of interests their character might have that are not explicitly mentioned in the text. This assignment encourages students to step outside their cultural boundaries to construct a coherent identity within the online environment. In addition, it promotes engagement with all of the various facets of culture that a typical cross-cultural psychology course would cover in a manner that excites and interests students.

Teaching Resources

Pines, A. M., & Maslach, C. (2002). *Experiencing social psychology: Readings and Projects* (4th ed.). New York, NY: McGraw-Hill.

Short readings accompanied by several research projects covering each of the topics in this chapter.

Goldstein, S. (2008). *Cross-Cultural Explorations: Activities in Culture and Psychology* (2nd ed.) Boston, MA: Allyn & Bacon.

Activities, miniexperiments, case studies, and self-administered scales in three areas relevant to this chapter: culture and social behavior, intergroup relations, and intercultural interaction

Kremer, J., Sheehy, N., Reilly, J., Trew, K., & Muldoon, O. (2003). *Applying social psychology*. New York, NY: Palgrave Macmillan.

Provides applications of social psychological knowledge to several areas of everyday life. Each chapter provides two to five in-class activities that ask students to apply what they have learned in the chapter to a social issue.

Okun, B. F., Fried, J., & Okun, M. L. (1999). *Understanding diversity: A learning-as-practice primer*. Pacific Grove, CA: Brooks-Cole.

Information and exercises that help readers learn to assess cross-cultural situations and interact personally and professionally with others who are likely, because of their cultural backgrounds, to have different values, perceptions, behaviors, and expectations of how people should act toward them.

References

Amir, Y., & Sharon, I. (1987). Are social psychological laws cross-culturally valid? *Journal of Cross-Cultural Psychology, 18,* 383–470. doi:10.1177/0022002187018004002

Arnett, J. J. (2008). The neglected 95%: Why American psychology needs to become less American. *American Psychologist, 63,* 602–614. doi:10.1037/0003-066X.63.7.602

Asch, S. E. (1951). Effects of group pressure upon the modification and distortion of judgment. In H. Guetzkow (Ed.), *Groups, leadership and men* (pp. 222–236). Pittsburgh, PA: Carnegie Press.

Axtell, R. E. (Ed.). (1993). *Do's and taboos around the world* (3rd ed.). New York, NY: Wiley.

Backstrom, L., Huttenlocher, D., Kleinberg, J., & Lan, X. (2006, August). Group formation in large social networks: Membership, growth, and evolution. In *Proceedings of the 12th ACM SIGKDD International Conference on Knowledge Discovery and Data Mining* (pp. 44–54). New York, NY: ACM. doi:10.1145/1150402.1150412

Balcetis, E., Dunning, D., & Miller, R. L. (2009). Do collectivists "know themselves" better than individualists? Cross-cultural studies of the "holier than thou" phenomenon. *Journal of Personality and Social Psychology, 95,* 1252–1267. doi:10.1037/a0013195

Benet-Martinez, V., & Haritatos, J. (2005). Bicultural identity integration (BII): Components and psychosocial antecedents. *Journal of Personality, 73,* 1015–1050. doi:10.1111/j.1467-6494.2005.00337.x

Benet-Martinez, V., Leu, J., Lee, F., & Morris, M. (2002). Negotiating biculturalism: Cultural frame switching in biculturals with "oppositional" vs. "compatible" cultural identities. *Journal of Cross-Cultural Psychology, 33,* 492–516. doi:10.1177/0022022102033005005

Bergmüller, S. (2013). The relationship between cultural individualism–collectivism and student aggression across 62 countries. *Aggressive behavior, 39,* 182–200. doi:10.1002/ab.21472

Björkqvist, K. (1994). Sex differences in physical, verbal, and indirect aggression: A review of recent research. *Sex Roles, 30,* 177–188. doi:10.1007/BF01420988

Bond, R., & Smith, P. B. (1996). Culture and conformity: A meta-analysis of studies using Asch's (1952b, 1956) line judgment task. *Psychological Bulletin, 119,* 111. doi:10.1037/0033-2909.119.1.111

Brehm, J. W. (1966). *A theory of psychological reactance.* New York, NY: Academic Press.

Brumbaugh, A. M. (2002). Source and nonsource cues in advertising and their effects on the activation of cultural and subcultural knowledge on the route to persuasion. *Journal of Consumer Research, 29,* 258–269. doi:10.1086/341575

Cárdenas, R. A., & Harris, L. J. (2006). Symmetrical decorations enhance the attractiveness of faces and abstract designs. *Evolution and Human Behavior, 27,* 1–18. doi.org/10.1016/j.evolhumbehav.2005.05.002

Child, J., & Möllering, G. (2003). Contextual confidence and active rust development in the Chinese business community. *Organization Science, 14,* 69–80. doi.org/10.1111/j.1740-8784.2007.00081.x

Church, A. T. (1982). Sojourner adjustment. *Psychological Bulletin, 91,* 540–572. doi:10.1037/0033-2909.91.3.540

Cohen, D., & Nisbett, R. E. (1994). Self-protection and the culture of honor: Explaining southern violence. *Personality and Social Psychology Bulletin, 20,* 551–567. doi:10.1177/0146167294205012

Cohen, D., Nisbett, R. E., Bowdle, B. F., & Schwarz, N. (1996). Insult, aggression, and the southern culture of honor: An "experimental ethnography." *Journal of Personality and Social Psychology, 70,* 945–960. doi:10.1037/0022-3514.70.5.945

Cross, S. E., & Madson, L. (1997). Models of the self: Self-construals and gender. *Psychological Bulletin, 122,* 5–37. doi:10.1037/0033-2909.122.1.5

Dresser, N. (1996). *Multicultural manners: New rules of etiquette for a changing society.* New York, NY: Wiley.

Du, H., Li, X., & Lin, D. (2015). Individualism and sociocultural adaptation: Discrimination and social capital as moderators among rural-to-urban migrants in China. *Asian Journal of Social Psychology, 18,* 176–181. doi:10.1111/ajsp.12085

Erikson, E. H. (1964). *Childhood and society.* New York, NY: Norton.

  (1966). Identity and uprootedness in our time. In *Insight and responsibility: Lectures on the ethical implications of psychoanalytic insight* (pp. 83–107). London: Faber and Faber.

Festinger, L. (1957). *A theory of cognitive dissonance.* Stanford, CA: Stanford University Press.

Fikret Pasa, S. (2000). Leadership influence in a high power distance and collectivist culture. *Leadership & Organization Development Journal, 21,* 414–426. doi:10.1108/01437730010379258

Fiske, S. T. (2014). *Social beings: Core motives in social psychology (3rd ed.).* Hoboken, NJ: Wiley.

Flynn, B. B. (1992). Managing for quality in the US and in Japan. *Interfaces, 22,* 69–80. doi:10.1287/inte.22.5.69

Forbes, G., Zhang, X., Doroszewicz, K., & Haas, K. (2009). Relationships between individualism-collectivism, gender, and direct or indirect aggression: A study in China, Poland, and the US. *Aggressive Behavior, 35,* 24–30. doi:10.1002/ab.20292

Ford, C. S., & Beach, F. A. (1951). *Patterns of sexual behavior.* New York, NY: Harper and Row.

Furnham, A., & Baguma, P. (1994). Cross-cultural differences in the evaluation of male and female body shapes. *International Journal of Eating Disorders, 15,* 81–89. doi:10.1002/1098-108X(199401)15:1<81::AID-EAT2260150110>3.0.CO;2-D

Gardiner, H. K., & Kosmitzki, C. (2008), *Lives across cultures: Cross-cultural human development.* Boston, MA: Pearson.

Garner, D. M., Garfinkel, P. E., Schwartz, D., & Thompson, M. (1980). Cultural expectations of thinness in women. *Psychological Reports, 47,* 483–491. doi:10.2466/pro.1980.47.2.483

Gilbert, D. (2006). *Stumbling on happiness.* New York, NY: Alfred A. Knopf.

Gilovich, T., & Medvec, V. H. (1995). The experience of regret: What, when, and why. *Psychological Review, 102,* 379–395. doi:10.1037/0033-295X.102.2.379

Gilovich, T., Wang, R. F., Regan, D., & Nishina, S. (2003). Regrets of action and inaction across cultures. *Journal of Cross-Cultural Psychology, 34*, 61–71. doi:10.1177/0022022102239155

Goldstein, S. (2008). *Cross-Cultural Explorations: Activities in Culture and Psychology* (2nd ed.) Boston, MA: Allyn & Bacon.

Graupmann, V., Jonas, E., Meier, E., Hawelka, S., & Aichhorn, M. (2012). Reactance, the self, and its group: When threats to freedom come from the ingroup versus the outgroup. *European Journal of Social Psychology, 42*, 255–266. doi:10.1002/ejsp.857

Han, S. P., & Shavitt, S. (1994). Persuasion and culture: Advertising appeals in individualistic and collectivistic societies. *Journal of Experimental Social Psychology, 30*, 326–350. doi:10.1006/jesp.1994.1016

Hayes, T. C., & Lee, M. R. (2005). The southern culture of honor and violent attitudes. *Sociological Spectrum, 25*, 593–617. doi:10.1080/02732170500174877

Heine, S. J. (2016). *Cultural psychology* (3rd ed.). New York, NY: Norton.

Heine, S. J., & Lehman, D. R. (1997). Culture, dissonance, and self-affirmation. *Personality and Social Psychology Bulletin, 23*, 389–400. doi:10.1177/0146167297234005

Henrich, J., Heine, S. J., & Norenzayan, A. (2010). The weirdest people in the world. *Behavior and Brain Sciences, 33*, 61–83. doi:10.1017/S0140525X0999152X

Hitokoto, H., & Uchida, Y. (2015). Interdependent happiness: Theoretical importance and measurement validity. *Journal of Happiness Studies, 16*, 211–239. doi:10.1007/s10902-014-9505-8

Hofstede, G. (2001). *Culture's consequences: Comparing values, behaviors, institutions and organizations across nations.* Thousand Oaks, CA: Sage.

(2011). Dimensionalizing cultures: The Hofstede model in context. *Online readings in psychology and culture, 2*, 1–26. doi:10.9707/2307-0919.1014

Hofstede, G., & Bond, M. H. (1984). Hofstede's culture dimensions an independent validation using Rokeach's value survey. *Journal of Cross-Cultural Psychology, 15*, 417–433. doi:10.1177/0022002184015004003

Hong, J. W., Muderrisoglu, A., & Zinkhan, G. M. (1987). Cultural differences and advertising expression: A comparative content analysis of Japanese and US magazine advertising. *Journal of Advertising, 16*, 55–68. doi:10.1080/00913367.1987.10673061

Hong, Y. Y., Morris, M., Chiu, C. Y., & Benet-Martínez, V. (2000). Multicultural minds: A dynamic constructivist approach to culture and cognition. *American Psychologist, 55*, 709–720. doi:10.1037/0003-066X.55.7.709

Horike, K. (1992, July). *An investigation of the Japanese social skills: What is called "hito-atari-no-yosa" (affability).* Paper presented at the 25th International Congress of Psychology, Brussels, Belgium.

Hoshino-Browne, E., Zanna, A. S., Spencer, S. J., & Zanna, M. P. (2005). Investigating attitudes cross-culturally: A case of cognitive dissonance among East Asians and North Americans. In G. R. Maio & G. Haddock (Eds.), *Theoretical perspectives on attitudes for the 21st century: The Gregynog Symposium*. East Sussex: Psychology Press.

Hovland, C. I., Janis, I. L., & Kelley, H. H. (1953). *Communication and persuasion: Psychological studies of opinion change*. New Haven, CT: Yale University Press.

Huang, L. C., & Harris, M. B. (1973). Conformity in Chinese and Americans: A field experiment. *Journal of Cross-Cultural Psychology*, *4*, 427–434. doi:10.1177/002202217300400404

Inglehart, R., & Baker, W. E. (2000). Modernization, cultural change, and the persistence of traditional values. *American Sociological Review*, *65*, 19–51. doi:10.2307/2657288

Janis, I. L. (1967). Effects of fear arousal on attitude change: Recent developments in theory and experimental research. *Advances in Experimental social Psychology* (Vol. 3, pp. 166–224). doi:10.1016/S0065-2601(08)60344-5

Janis, I. L., & Hovland, C.I. (1959). *Personality and persuasibility*. New Haven, CT: Yale University Press.

Jonas, E., Graupmann, V., Niesta-Kayser, D., Zanna, M. P., Traut-Mattausch, E., & Frey, D. (2009). Culture, self, and the emergence of reactance: Is there a "universal" freedom? *Journal of Experimental Social Psychology*, *45*, 1068–1080. doi:10.1016/j.jesp.2009.06.005

Kameda, T., & Sugimori, S. (1993). Psychological entrapment in group decision making: An assigned decision rule and a groupthink phenomenon. *Journal of Personality and Social Psychology*, *65*, 282–292. doi:10.1037/0022-3514.65.2.282

Kashima, Y., & Triandis, H. C. (1986). The self-serving bias in attributions as a coping strategy: A cross-cultural study. *Journal of Cross-Cultural Psychology*, *17*, 83–97. doi:10.1177/0022002186017001006

Kim, D. Y., & Park, J. (2010). Cultural differences in risk: The group facilitation effect. *Judgment and Decision Making*, *5*, 380–390. doi:10.1.1.420.1090

Kitayama, S., Snibbe, A. C., Markus, H. R., & Suzuki, T. (2004). Is there any "free" choice? Self and dissonance in two cultures. *Psychological Science*, *15*, 527–533. doi:10.1111/j.0956-7976.2004.00714.x

Knight, D. K., & Young Kim, E. (2007). Japanese consumers' need for uniqueness: Effects on brand perceptions and purchase intention. *Journal of Fashion Marketing and Management: An International Journal*, *11*, 270–280. doi:10.1108/13612020710751428

Koch, E. J., & Lomore, C. D. (2009). "This is a public service announcement": Evaluating and redesigning campaigns to teach attitudes and persuasion. *Teaching of Psychology*, *36*, 270–272. doi:10.1080/00986280903175731

Komiya, A., Miyamoto, Y., Watabe, M., & Kusumi, T. (2011). Cultural grounding of regret: Regret in self and interpersonal contexts. *Cognition and Emotion*, *25*, 1121–1130. doi:10.1080/02699931.2010.516962

Kuhn, M. H., & McPartland, T. (1954). An empirical investigation of self-attitudes. *American Sociological Review*, *19*, 69–76. www.jstor.org/stable/2088175

Kur, T., Roese, N. J., & Namkoong, J-E. (2009). Regrets in the East and West: Role of intrapersonal versus interpersonal norms. *Asian Journal of Social Psychology, 12*, 151–156. doi:10.1111/j.1467-839X.2009.01275.x

Lee, Y. T., & Seligman, M. E. P. (1997). Are Americans more optimistic than the Chinese? *Personality and Social Psychology Bulletin, 23*, 32–40. doi:10.1177/0146167297231004

Leung, K., & Bond, M. H. (1984). The impact of cultural collectivism on reward allocation. *Journal of Personality and Social Psychology, 47*, 793–804. doi:10.1037/0022-3514.47.4.793

Levine, R. (1997). *A geography of time: The temporal misadventures of a social psychologist.* New York, NY: Basic Books.

Li, Y., Wang, M., Wang, C., & Shi, J. (2010). Individualism, collectivism, and Chinese adolescents' aggression: Intracultural variations. *Aggressive Behavior, 36*, 187–194. doi:10.1002/ab.20341

Lim, K. H., Leung, K., Sia, C. L., & Lee, M. K. (2004). Is eCommerce boundary-less? Effects of individualism–collectivism and uncertainty avoidance on Internet shopping. *Journal of International Business Studies, 35*, 545–559. doi:10.1057/palgrave.jibs.8400104

Maehr, M. L. (1974). Culture and achievement motivation. *American Psychologist, 29*, 887–896. doi:10.1037/h0037521

Marcia, J. E. (1966). Development and validation of ego identity status. *Journal of Personality and Social Psychology, 3*, 551–559. doi:10.1037/h0023281

Markus, H. R., & Kitayama, S. (1991). Culture and the self: Implications for cognition, emotion, and motivation. *Psychological Review, 98*, 224–253. doi:10.1037/0033-295X.98.2.224

Meissner, C. A., & Brigham, J. C. (2001). Thirty years of investigating the own-race bias in memory for faces: A meta-analytic review. *Psychology, Public Policy and Law, 7*, 3–35. doi:10.1037/1076-8971.7.1.3

Miller, J. G. (1984). Culture and the development of everyday social explanation. *Journal of Personality and Social Psychology, 46*, 961–978. doi:10.1037/0022-3514.46.5.961

Montagu, A. (1984). The skin, touch, and human development. *Clinics in Dermatology, 2*, 17–26. doi:10.1016/0738-081X(84)90043-9

Morris, M. W., & Peng, K. (1994). Culture and cause: American and Chinese attributions for social and physical events. *Journal of Personality and Social Psychology, 67*, 949–971. doi:10.1037//0022-3514.67.6.949

Mussen, P. H. (1977). *Roots of caring, sharing and helping. The development of prosocial behavior in children.* San Francisco, CA: W. H. Freeman.

Myers, D. G., & DeWall, C. N. (2016). *Exploring psychology.* New York, NY: Worth.

Myers, D. G., & Twenge, J. M. (2017). *Social psychology.* New York, NY: McGraw-Hill.

Nabi, R. L. (1999). A cognitive functional model for the effects of discrete negative emotions on information processing, attitude change, and recall.

Communication theory, *9*, 292–320. doi:10.1111/j.1468-2885.1999. tb00172.x

Newburry, W., & Yakinova, N. (2006). Standardization preferences: A function of national culture, work interdependence and local embeddedness. *Journal of International Business Studies*, *37*, 44–60. doi:10.1057/palgrave. jibs.8400179

Norvilitis, J. M. (2010). Financial education for refugees. *Social Psychology Network*. Retrieved from www.socialpsychology.org/action/2010hon or3.htm

Okun, B. F., Fried, J., & Okun, M. L. (1999). *Understanding diversity: A learning-as-practice primer*. Pacific Grove, CA: Brooks-Cole.

Österman, K., Björkqvist, K., Lagerspetz, K. M., Kaukiainen, A., Landau, S. F., Frączek, A., & Caprara, G. V. (1998). Cross-cultural evidence of female indirect aggression. *Aggressive Behavior*, *24*, 1–8. doi:10.1002/(SICI)1098-2337(1998)24:1<1::AID-AB1>3.0.CO;2-R

Oyserman, D., Coon, H. M., & Kemmelmeier, M. (2002). Rethinking individualism and collectivism: Evaluation of theoretical assumptions and meta-analyses. *Psychological Bulletin*, *128*, 3–72. doi:10.1037/0033-2909.128.1.3

Parkes, L. P., Schneider, S. K., & Bochner, S. (1999). Individualism-collectivism and self-concept: Social or contextual. *Asian Journal of Social Psychology*, 367–383. doi:10.1111/1467-839X.00046

Petty, R. E., & Brinol, P. (2010). Attitude change. In R. F. Baumeister & E. J. Finkel (Eds.), *Advanced social psychology: The state of the science* (pp. 217–259). New York, NY: Oxford University Press.

Petty, R. E., & Cacioppo, J. T. (1984). Source factors and the elaboration likelihood model of persuasion. *Advances in Consumer Research*, *11*, 668–672.

Pornpitakpan, C., & Francis, J. N. (2000). The effect of cultural differences, source expertise, and argument strength on persuasion: An experiment with Canadians and Thais. *Journal of International Consumer Marketing*, *13*, 77–101. doi:10.1300/J046v13n01_06

Rhodes, G., Halberstadt, J., Jeffery, L., & Palermo, R. (2005). The attractiveness of average faces is not a generalized mere exposure effect. *Social Cognition*, *23*, 205–217. doi:10.1521/soco.2005.23.3.205

Richardson, D. S., & Green, L. R. (2006). Direct and indirect aggression: Relationships as social context. *Journal of Applied Social Psychology*, *36*, 2492–2508. doi:10.1111/j.0021-9029.2006.00114.x

Roberts, W. R. (2009). The Internet Classics Archive | Rhetoric by Aristotle. Retrieved from http://classics.mit.edu/Aristotle/rhetoric.1.i.html

Rosenthal, D. A., Bell, R., Demetriou, A., Efklides, A. (1989). From collectivism to individualism? The acculturation of Greek immigrants in Australia. *International Journal of Psychology*, *24*, 57–71. doi:10.1080/00207594.1989.10600032

Sakai, H. (1981). Induced compliance and opinion change. *Japanese Psychological Research*, *23*, 1–8. doi:10.1111/1467-839X.00046

Schacter, S., Nuttin, J., de Monchaux, C., Maucorps, P. H., Osmer, D., Duijker, H., Rommetveit, R., & Israel, J. (1954). Cross-cultural experiments on threat and rejection: A study of the organization for comparative social research. *Human Relations, 7*, 403–439. doi:10.1177/001872675400700401

Schug, J., Yuki, M., & Maddux, W. (2010). Relational mobility explains between-and within-culture differences in self-disclosure to close friends. *Psychological Science, 21*, 1471–1478. doi:10.1177/0956797610382786

Sellers, R. M. (1998). Multidimensional model of racial identity: A reconceptualization of African American racial identity. *Personality and Social Psychology Review, 2*, 18–39. doi:10.1207/s15327957pspr0201_2

Semin, G. R., & Rubin, M. (1990). Unfolding the concept of person by verbal abuse. *European Journal of Social Psychology, 20*, 463–474. doi:10.1002/ejsp.2420200602

Shimanoff, S. B. (1984). Commonly named emotions in everyday conversations. *Perceptual and Motor Skills, 58*, 514. doi:10.2466/pms.1984.58.2.514

Singelis, T. M. (1994). The measurement of independent and interdependent self-construals, *Personality and Social Psychology Bulletin, 20*, 580–591. doi:10.1177/0146167294205014

Skipper, J. K., Leslie, P., & Wilson, B. S. (1990). A teaching technique revisited: Family names, nicknames, and social class. *Teaching Sociology, 19*, 209–213. www.jstor.org/stable/1318492

Sullivan, H. S. (1953). *The interpersonal theory of psychiatry*. New York, NY: Norton.

Takano, Y., & Sogon, S. (2008). Are Japanese more collectivistic than Americans? Examining conformity in in-groups and the reference-group effect. *Journal of Cross-Cultural Psychology, 39*, 237–250. doi:10.1177/0022022107313902

Tajfel, H., & Turner, J. C. (1986). The social identity theory of intergroup behavior. In S. Worchel & W. G. Austin (Eds.), *Psychology of intergroup relations* (pp. 7–24). Chicago, IL: Nelson-Hall.

Tesser, A. (1978). Self-generated attitude change. *Advances in experimental social psychology* (Vol. 11, pp. 289–338). doi:10.1016/S0065-2601(08)60010-6

Thornhill, R. (1992). Fluctuating asymmetry and the mating system of the Japanese scorpionfly, Panorpa japonica. *Animal Behaviour, 44*, 867–879. doi:10.1016/S0003-3472(05)80583-4

Thornhill, R., & Gangestad, S. W. (1999). Facial attractiveness. *Trends in Cognitive Sciences, 3*, 452–460. doi:10.1016/S1364-6613(99)01403-5

Tian, K. T., Bearden, W. O., & Hunter, G. L. (2001). Consumers' need for uniqueness: Scale development and validation. *Journal of Consumer Research, 28*, 50–66. doi:10.1086/321947

Toldos, M. P. (2005). Sex and age differences in self-estimated physical, verbal and indirect aggression in Spanish adolescents. *Aggressive Behavior, 31*, 13–23. doi:10.1002/ab.20034

Tomcho, T. J., & Foels, R. (2002). Teaching acculturation: Developing multiple "cultures" in the classroom and role-playing the acculturation process. *Teaching of Psychology, 29*, 226–229. doi:10.1207/S15328023TOP2903_11

Triandis, H. C. (1995). *Individualism & collectivism.* Boulder, CO: Westview.
  (1996). The psychological measurement of cultural syndromes. *American Psychologist, 51,* 407–415. doi:10.1037/0003-066X.51.4.407
Triandis, H. C., Bontempo, R., Villareal, M. J., Asai, M., & Lucca, N. (1988). Individualism and collectivism: Cross-cultural perspectives on self-ingroup relationships. *Journal of Personality and Social Psychology, 54,* 323. doi:10.1037/0022-3514.54.2.323
Trompenaars, F. (1994), *Riding the waves of culture: Understanding cultural diversity in business.* London: Irwin.
Turner, J. C., Hogg, M. A., Oakes, P. J., Reicher, S. D., & Wetherell, M. S. (1987). *Rediscovering the social group: A self-categorization theory.* Oxford: Blackwell.
Vishwanath, A. (2003). Comparing online information effects: A cross-cultural comparison of online information and uncertainty avoidance. *Communication Research, 30,* 579–598. doi:10.1177/0093650203257838
Ward, C., & Kennedy, A. (1993). Where's the "culture" in cross-cultural transition? Comparative studies of sojourner adjustment. *Journal of Cross-Cultural Psychology, 24,* 221–249. doi:10.1177/0022022193242006
Whiting, B. M., & Edwards, C. P. (1988). *Children of different worlds: The foundation of social behavior.* Cambridge, MA: Harvard University Press.
Whiting, B. M., & Whiting, J. W. (1975). *Children in six countries: A psychological analysis.* Cambridge, MA: Harvard University Press.
Williams, T. P., & Sogon, S. (1985). Group composition and conforming behavior in Japanese students. *Japanese Psychological Research, 26,* 231–234. doi:10.4992/psycholres1954.26.231
Worchel, S. (2004). The diamond in the stone: Exploring the place of free behavior in studies of human rights and culture. In R. A. Wright, J. Greenberg, & S. S. Brehm (Eds.), *Motivational analyses of social behavior: Building on Jack Brehm's contribution to psychology* (pp. 107–128). Mahwah, NJ: Erlbaum.
Yuki, M., Maddux, W. W., Brewer, M. B., & Takemura, K. (2005). Cross-cultural differences in relationship- and group-based trust. *Personality and Social Psychology Bulletin, 31,* 48–62. doi:10.1177/0146167204271305
Zajonc, R. B. (1968). Attitudinal effects of mere exposure. *Journal of Personality and Social Psychology, 9,* 1–27. doi:10.1037/h0025848
Zeelenberg, M., van der Pilgt, J., & Manstead, A. S. R. (1998). Undoing regret on Dutch television: Apologizing for interpersonal regrets involving actions or inactions. *Personality and Social Psychology Bulletin, 24,* 1113–1119. doi:10.1177/0146167298241008

CHAPTER 17

Teaching about Cultural Differences in the Correspondence Bias

Anne M. Koenig and Kristy K. Dean

Imagine a computer screen, all white, with a series of animated geometric figures. The circle and square drift toward each other, but are then diverted in opposite directions. The triangle and the rectangle track each other, both moving up, then down, and then to the left. The shapes stay in motion, sometimes coming into contact, sometimes drifting apart. How would you explain this scene? More than likely, you would attribute agentic, humanlike qualities to the shapes and perceive their actions as social in nature – the shapes are drawn together, they want to avoid each other, the circle is shy, the triangle is needy. Your social explanations for the movements of these geometric figures reflect an innate motivation to explain the world around you, and an inclination to draw on interpersonal processes to do so. This is the basis for Heider's (1958) concept of "naïve psychology" and the beginnings of the social psychological study of attribution – the inferences we make about the dispositional (i.e., internal – such as abilities, feelings, or personal characteristics) and situational (i.e., external – such as others' behaviors, context, or luck) causes of events.

Attribution theory is an important topic in social psychology. Ironically, at the same time students of introductory and social psychology are learning about the power of the situation to shape human behavior – the central premise of the field of social psychology – they are also learning that people tend to weigh internal qualities more heavily in the attributional process than external factors – the correspondence bias (e.g., Gilbert & Malone, 1995). The correspondence bias has become so ubiquitous within the research literature that Jones (1990) commented that it is "a candidate for the most robust and repeatable finding in social psychology" (p. 138). Indeed, many textbooks refer to the correspondence bias as the fundamental attribution error (although see Gawronski, 2004, for a discussion of distinctions between the two concepts). But the fundamental nature of the correspondence bias is questionable, especially when researchers return to the central premise of social psychology and consider the power of the situation, and the power of culture more specifically, in shaping our psychological processes. Like many contributors to this volume, we are excited to see researchers and instructors take a culturally informed approach in their work, but are mindful of the work that remains.

We designed this chapter with several goals in mind. First, as we summarize findings from the cross-cultural literature on attributions, we both describe how culture shapes the attributional process and explain why cultural similarities and differences occur. One goal of this section is to provide additional information, including sources, beyond what is conveyed in the typical introductory or social psychology textbooks. Within these descriptions, we also highlight potential approaches to teaching this content in line with the goal to support the integration of culture into teaching about attribution. In an attempt to provide maximum flexibility, we propose two different approaches – a "what" and a "why" that vary in terms of depth of coverage. Finally, we provide specific examples of activities and demonstrations that highlight the cultural nature of attribution. Overall, our approach is inspired by cross-cultural psychology's attempts to unpack cultural differences (see Oyserman & Lee, 2007, for a review) and is easily customizable to fit instructors' specific learning objectives. We want to provide flexibility for instructors to choose the best teaching strategy for them, as instructional choices depend on the specific level of coursework (introductory or social psychology), amount of time devoted to attributional theory and the correspondence bias, whether they plan to adopt a cultural approach to studying other course topics, and the extent to which the textbook and other reading materials communicate a cultural approach to the topic.

But first, two important notes. This chapter is specifically focused on cross-cultural differences and similarities in the correspondence bias. The actor–observer bias and the ultimate attribution error have received much less attention within the cultural literature, and the self-serving bias, despite implicating the attributional process, is arguably more relevant to discussions on self-enhancement and self-improvement motivations. We encourage readers interested in cultural variation in these biases to consult a previous chapter we wrote for an undergraduate audience (Koenig & Dean, 2011). Additionally, our summary of the accumulated cross-cultural literature on the correspondence bias uses the same cultural distinctions as the original research. That is, we reference comparisons between people from Western cultures (e.g., Western Europeans and people of European descent in the United States and Canada) and Eastern cultures (e.g., Japanese, Korean, and Chinese) throughout the chapter. These are arguably broad categorizations, and as the field of cultural psychology has evolved over time, it has attempted to transcend generalizations and identify the specific ways that culture "gets inside our heads" to shape psychology (Kitayama, Markus, Matsumoto, & Norasakkunkit, 1997). Most attempts to unpackage East–West differences in the correspondence bias center on cultural orientations of collectivism and individualism and the psychological orientations they encourage (Hofstede, 1980; Triandis, 1995). Specifically, Western cultures support an individualistic orientation that prioritizes the individual and personal concerns (e.g., distinctiveness, autonomy, individual rights and well-being) whereas Eastern cultures support a collectivistic orientation that prioritizes social relationships and groups and social concerns (e.g., connectedness, social obligations, maintaining social harmony). By extension, individualism orients people to think analytically, construe the self as independent, and perceive personality as fixed, whereas collectivism orients us toward holistic thinking, interdependent self-construal, and the perception of personality as flexible (Markus & Kitayama, 1991; Nisbett, Peng, Choi, & Norenzayan, 2001). In this chapter, we summarize both types of research studies – those that describe cross-cultural differences (the "what") and those that seek more proximal, causal explanations for these differences (the "why") – to provide instructors with flexibility in terms of how deeply they choose to employ a cultural approach in their coverage of this topic.

Teaching Cultural Differences and Similarities in the Correspondence Bias: The "What"

Research studies examining the correspondence bias in the United States and other Western cultures coalesce to show a tendency for people to emphasize internal, dispositional causes for a behavior relative to external, situational causes (Gilbert & Malone, 1995; Jones, 1979; Ross, 1977). This effect has emerged across different paradigms, including the classic attitude attribution paradigm in which people make attributions about another's attitude based on a chosen or forced essay (Jones & Harris, 1967), and the quiz role paradigm in which people are randomly assigned to write trivia questions, answer those questions, or observe the game and make attributions about the questioner's and contestant's intelligence (Ross, Amabile, & Steinmetz, 1977). Both of these paradigms are typically discussed in standard introductory and social psychology textbooks.

Research into the attributional process across cultures has yielded convincing evidence for cultural variation. For example, Miller (1984) investigated social explanations for prosocial and antisocial behaviors provided by US and Hindu Indians of varying ages. Young children (8- and 11-year-olds) employed internal and external attributions similarly across the two cultures; indeed, children from both cultural groups attributed prosocial behavior to external causes more than internal causes – a reversal of the correspondence bias. It was only as they increased in age – and became increasingly more socialized within their individualistic culture – that American participants shifted their attributional patterns to display a correspondence bias, weighing internal factors more heavily than external factors. For Hindu Indians, however, as age increased, they weighed external factors more heavily than internal factors. In general, the accumulated evidence confirms cultural variation in the degree to which people attribute the behavior of others to internal versus external sources (e.g., Choi, Nisbett, & Norenzayan, 1999). This statement, however, glosses over some interesting nuances within this literature.

Research examining internal and external attributions for "real-world," naturally occurring behavior consistently finds that Westerners make more internal attributions and fewer external attributions compared to Easterners. For example, research examining newspaper reports of high-profile murder cases, the outcomes of soccer matches, and various issues of international interest (e.g., the environment, refugees, resettlement) showed that reports emphasized different attributions in different cultures (Lee, Hallahan, & Herzog, 1996; Morris & Peng, 1994, Study 2). This pattern of findings also emerges in studies where participants from Eastern versus Western cultures generated their own scenarios (Miller, 1984), responded to scenarios crafted by experimenters (Choi, Dalal, Kim-Prieto, & Park, 2003; Morris & Peng, 1994, Study 3), and made attributions for nonhuman behavior (Morris & Peng, 1994, Study 1).

However, research laboratory studies that utilize the classic attitude attribution and quiz show paradigms often find cultural similarities rather than differences in the correspondence bias. Specifically, studies that replicate the original procedures for the attitude attribution paradigm show that Korean, Japanese, and Chinese participants continue to emphasize dispositions more than situational constraints when inferring the attitude of the essay writer in the forced choice condition (Choi & Nisbett, 1998; Kashima, Siegal, Tanaka, & Kashima, 1992, Study 2; Krull et al., 1999, Study 1; Masuda & Kitayama, 2004, Study 2). In the quiz show paradigm Krull et al. (1999, Study 2) also found that Chinese participants estimated the questioner's general knowledge as higher than that of the respondent. In another variation by Van Boven, Kamada, and Gilovich (1999), not only were participants randomly assigned to questioner and responder roles but the responder was also instructed by the experimenter to provide either altruistic or selfish responses to the questions. Despite knowing the situational constraints imposed by the experimenter, Japanese participants in the questioner role formed a more positive impression of the responder when he or she responded altruistically versus selfishly, maintaining a strong correspondence between personality and behavior. In sum, cross-cultural studies directly examining the correspondence bias confirm its presence in Eastern cultures.

However, in line with the idea of cultural variation, there is also ample evidence that the correspondence bias is more readily attenuated and thus a relatively weaker phenomenon in Eastern compared to Western cultures. One approach for reducing this bias involves highlighting the relevance of situational constraints. For example, when social constraints were highlighted by assigning participants to write a supportive or opposing essay before reading the target essay, mirroring the no choice condition in the attitude attribution paradigm, the correspondence bias was reduced among Korean, but not American, participants (Choi & Nisbett, 1998). A second approach for attenuating the correspondence bias involves reducing the relevance of dispositional information. Within the attitude attribution paradigm, this involves prompting participants to question whether the essay is truly diagnostic of the writer's attitude. Research shows that Japanese, but not American, participants questioned diagnosticity and subsequently displayed an attenuated correspondence bias after reading brief essays containing unpersuasive arguments (Miyamoto & Kitayama, 2002) and witnessing the actor read an essay written by someone else (Masuda & Kitayama, 2004).

Given all this information, how should an instructor approach incorporating cultural differences in attribution into their course? The answer is – as usual within social psychology – "it depends." At the most basic level, the "what" approach involves describing East versus West differences in attribution. Specifically, this approach identifies and describes cultural variation in the degree to which people emphasize internal versus external factors when making attributions. The most simplistic way to implement this approach is to focus on findings from studies examining attributions for naturally occurring behavior as these studies straightforwardly demonstrate Western dispositionalism and Eastern situationalism. Studies like those by Miller (1984), who studied differences in attribution across age groups, and Morris and Peng (1994), who studied differences across cultures with a variety of designs, are perhaps the most accessible and the most likely to be mentioned in introductory and social psychology textbooks. A more nuanced way of implementing this approach is to also discuss findings from studies employing the classic paradigms that directly examine the correspondence bias. Recall that these studies consistently find cultural similarities in the correspondence bias, but that cultural differences emerge when situational constraints are especially obvious (Choi & Nisbett, 1998) or the validity of dispositional forces is especially questionable (Masuda & Kitayama, 2004). This nuanced approach addresses attribution in more depth through discussion of contradictory findings and how variations in methodology and experimental conditions provide insight into when cultural differences versus similarities in attribution emerge. Our impression is that the "what" approach is most appropriate in introductory psychology where the inherent breadth of the course is more likely to limit depth of coverage, and where the introductory nature of the course encourages a heavier focus on psychological findings compared to psychological mechanisms.

It is also important to emphasize to students that these cultural variations are not value laden. Attributions are about one's perceptions of the cause of a behavior, not about the true cause of a person's behavior. The correspondence bias is considered a "bias" because it is a preference or overreliance on certain types of attributions, but the accuracy of those attributions is often unknown in real-life settings (although they could be manipulated in an experimental context). Thus, it is not that Eastern, collectivistic cultures are more accurate or less biased – they simply prefer other types of attributions in some contexts, the accuracy of which is also unknown for many behaviors.

Teaching Explanations for Cultural Differences and Similarities in the Correspondence Bias: The "Why"

Merely documenting *what* differs across cross-national groups does not necessarily get to the heart of *why* those psychological differences exist. The "why" approach to teaching cultural differences in the correspondence bias involves both description and explanation of cross-cultural differences in attribution. Specifically, this approach involves unpacking culture to discuss why cultural variation in attribution occurs. The simplest way to implement this approach is to explain cultural differences in attribution in terms of culture-level differences in individualistic and collectivistic orientations (Kitayama et al., 1997). As mentioned previously, cultural differences in the correspondence bias are often explained as reflecting the relative individualistic or collectivistic orientations of one's culture (Kitayama et al., 1997). Within Western cultures, the emphasis on the individual is thought to foster a general tendency to look inward to traits, dispositions, preferences, and feeling states that distinguish individuals from each other; this inward focus, then, fosters a tendency to make internal attributions. In contrast, within Eastern cultures, the collectivistic emphasis on the fundamental ties that bind individuals to each other within relationships and groups focuses attention outward to these social groups and the situational contexts in which they function; this external focus on the social context is argued to foster a stronger emphasis on the situational factors that influence behavior. The earlier that instructors introduce this cultural dimension the better if they are planning to draw on individualism and collectivism in coverage of other course topics. This cultural dimension provides a parsimonious framework for predicting and explaining cultural differences in various psychological phenomenon, not just attribution (see Fiske, Kitayama, Markus, & Nisbett, 1998, for a review). This basic "why" approach is entirely appropriate and achievable within introductory psychology; indeed, several popular introductory psychology textbooks describe cultural differences in attribution and explain them in terms of individualism/collectivism (e.g., Ciccarelli & White, 2017; Weiten, 2017).

However, quite obviously, culture is multifaceted. The concept of culture includes beliefs, values, mind-sets, languages, traditions, rituals, religious and political systems; the list is long, to be sure. Which specific aspects of culture are actively shaping our attributions? Individualistic and collectivistic orientations surely fuel this process however the cross-cultural literature has attempted to further unpack cultural differences by focusing on the more proximal, person-level psychological orientations that result from these broad, culture-level orientations (Choi et al., 1999; Oyserman & Lee, 2007). We encourage instructors to implement a more nuanced approach to explaining cultural variation in attribution by going beyond culture-level orientations to discuss the relevant research on person-level, causal psychological orientations like self-construals, thinking styles, and lay theories of personality (Oyserman & Lee, 2007).

Before discussing these person-level mechanisms, we want to highlight that cross-national comparisons are quasiexperimental studies that cannot assert causality because we cannot technically manipulate one's cultural experiences. However, we can manipulate the cognitive salience or accessibility of individualistic and collectivistic orientations as well as the accessibility of the psychological orientations they encourage. This experimental approach to culture is consistent with the situated cognition model of culture (Oyserman & Lee, 2007, 2008). Specifically, this model argues that individualistic and collectivistic orientations come to differently shape psychological processes of people within cultures because time and time again, across the many situations a person experiences in daily life, these situations emphasize individual versus collective concerns. However, every person, regardless of culture, experiences situations that emphasize both individual and collective concerns: Everyone has attempted to highlight her or his own unique attributes and distinguish the self from others at some point, and everyone has experienced moments of deep connection to loved ones or valued groups. In sum, culture can be conceptualized as both chronic and habitual as well as temporarily cued within specific situations. By conceptualizing culture as situationally fluid, the causal role of culture – in terms of general cultural orientations or more proximal psychological orientations – can be examined through experimental methodology.

One commonly covered person-level difference between individualistic and collectivistic cultures is that these cultures encourage distinct self-construals. Ample research has demonstrated that Western individualists tend to adopt independent self-construals and define the self in terms of distinctive personal attributes whereas Eastern collectivists adopt interdependent self-construals and define the self in terms of important relationships and group memberships (Markus & Kitayama, 1991). Consequently, because independent self-construals emphasize separateness based on internal traits and qualities, they should encourage attributions that are similarly focused on internal attributes; because interdependent self-construals emphasize one's embeddedness within relationships and groups, they should engender attributions that similarly highlight situational connections. To test this rationale, Kühnen, Hannover, Pohlmann, and Roeder (2013) manipulated the temporary accessibility of independent and interdependent self-construals and examined attributions for an essay writer's attitude when the essay was high versus low in diagnosticity. That is, Kühnen and colleagues examined whether priming distinct self-construals yielded the same pattern of attributions that emerged in Miyamoto and Kitayama's (2002) study of cross-national differences. The answer is yes; participants primed with interdependent, but not independent, self-construals displayed an attenuated correspondence bias after reading brief essays containing unpersuasive arguments, similar to the pattern of results for Japanese versus American participants in prior research.

A second mechanism identified within the literature is that individual-istic cultures tend to encourage an analytic thinking style in which focal objects are understood as separate from their contexts and defined by their properties or attributes whereas collectivistic cultures tend to adopt a holistic thinking style in which focal objects are closely bound to and understood in terms of their contexts (Nisbett et al., 2001). Consequently, an analytic style shapes attributions by emphasizing the importance of an actor's defining traits and dispositions whereas a holistic style shapes attributions by invoking external, situational factors that influence an actor's behavior. Although several studies identify thinking styles as playing a causal role in eliciting cross-cultural differences in the correspondence bias (see Choi et al., 1999, for a review; Masuda & Kitayama, 2004), this has never been directly tested. For example, Choi and colleagues (2003) measured tendencies to think holistically in Study 3, and found that Koreans reported higher holism scores than Americans. However, these researchers never examined whether this mediated the effect of culture on internal versus external attributions, nor has a research study experimen-tally manipulated the salience of analytic versus holistic thinking and assessed its effects on the types of attributions people make. That is, the literature is lacking direct evidence that cultural differences in attribution are directly caused by more proximal differences in thinking styles. It is worth noting, however, that thinking styles are also argued to underlie cultural differences in attention (Masuda & Nisbett, 2001), categorization (Chiu, 1972), and reasoning (Peng & Nisbett, 1999).

A third mechanism for cross-cultural differences in the correspondence bias is lay theories of personality. An entity theory conceptualizes personality as stable and unchangeable whereas an incremental theory conceptualizes personality as flexible and changeable by attempts at self-improvement (Dweck, Hong, & Chiu, 1993). Given Western versus Eastern differences in the emphasis on individuals and dispositions versus collectives and situations, it is unsurprising that American participants report stronger agreement with entity-based characterizations of personal-ity than do Korean participants, who instead report a strong incremental lay theory (Norenzayan, Choi, & Nisbett, 2002). The assumption, then, is that the correspondence bias is more readily attenuated in Eastern versus Western cultures because Easterners perceive situations as more diagnostic of behavior than dispositions, which they believe will change (Knowles, Morris, Chiu, & Hong, 2001). Unfortunately, the causal role of lay theories has not been examined within the cross-cultural literature. How-ever, research manipulating the salience of these distinct lay theories confirms that priming entity compared to incremental theories fosters a more dispositional focus when making attributions (Chiu, Hong, & Dweck, 1997; Poon & Koehler, 2006). That is, distinct cultural orientations appear to elicit distinct lay theories, and manipulating distinct lay theories elicits variation in the attribution process. Taken together, these findings provide indirect yet suggestive evidence that future research will reveal cultural differences in the correspondence bias driven by distinct lay theories.

In sum, research examining the psychological orientations that derive from individualistic versus collectivistic cultural orientations clarifies the process by which culture "gets inside our heads" to influence attributional processes. Regardless of whether the existing research evidence directly or indirectly supports the causal role of these person-level mechanisms, unpacking studies like these represent a new generation of cross-cultural research that is becoming more mainstream within the psychological literature. As such, a more in-depth "why" approach that discusses one or more of these person-level mechanisms is appropriate for upper-level courses like social psychology as is reflected in several popular textbooks (e.g., Aronson, Wilson, & Akert, 2017; Kassin, Fein, & Markus, 2017). It is important to keep in mind that this more in-depth "why" approach will require devoting more time to this topic because scaffolding is required. That is, instructors will first need to address cross-cultural differences (the "what") and then reflect on the cultural dimensions of individualism and collectivism (the basic "why") before transitioning to a discussion on one or more of the psychological orientations just described.

Activities for Teaching Cultural Influences on the Correspondence Bias

Regardless of whether instructors focus on the "what" or emphasize the "why," any classroom activity that demonstrates cultural influences on attribution requires two components: (a) a behavior to make attributions about and (b) a way to emphasize cultural differences in attribution processes. Table 17.1 outlines a variety of both of these ideas, separating them into the two parts of emphasizing cultural differences and demonstrating attributions. Instructors can mix and match these sets in ways that will work for them, or use their own correspondence bias demonstrations along with a cultural difference manipulation.

It may seem difficult to demonstrate cultural differences within the context of a traditional classroom where most students are from the same

Table 17.1 *Ways to Emphasize Culture*

Task	Specific Examples
Class Discussion	When having students generate internal and external attributions for an event/behavior, note any difference in the number or immediacy of different types of attributions. Discuss how the students' cultural background may play a role in what attributions first come to mind. Based on what students know about cultural differences, ask students to consider how they would respond if taking an individualistic or collectivistic orientation. Have the students create a hypothesis about how attributions might differ across cultures before revealing the results of a cross-cultural study and see if they can guess the outcome of the results.
Differential Instructions	Before making attributions about a person's behavior, give students different instructions (a) to focus on the individuals and their qualities or to evaluate their personality or (b) to focus on the situation and how the outcome is influenced by the situation or to evaluate the novelty and comfort (or other factors) of the situation. A control condition with no instructions could also be used, which would highlight which set of instructions is the "default" for students. Do not let students know there are different instructions. Then tally up the internal and external attributions created by each group. When discussing the outcome of the ratings, the different instructions should be revealed, emphasizing that the individual instructions are similar to individualistic default thinking whereas the situational instructions are prompting students to take a collectivistic orientation.
Similarities and Differences with Friends and Family Prime	Trafimow, Triandis, and Goto (1991) developed a task to prime individualism versus collectivism mind-sets, and following their example, individualism could be primed by asking students to think or write for a few minutes about what makes them different from their family and friends and what they expect of themselves whereas collectivism could be primed by asking students to think or write about what they have in common with their family and friends and what they expect of them.
Pronoun Circling Task Prime	Gardner and colleagues (Brewer & Gardner, 1996; Gardner, Gabriel, & Lee, 1999) developed a task in which people circle singular pronouns (I/me/my) to prime individualism and plural pronouns (we/us/ours) to prime collectivism. Various paragraphs have been used, including (for the collectivistic prime): *We* go to the city often. *Our* anticipation fills *us* as *we* see the skyscrapers come into view. *We* allow *ourselves* to explore every corner, never letting an attraction escape *us*. *Our* voice fills the air and street. *We* see all the sights, *we* window-shop, and everywhere *we* go *we* see *our* reflection looking back at *us* in the glass of a hundred windows. At nightfall *we* linger, *our* time in the city almost over. When finally *we* must leave, *we* do so knowing that *we* will soon return. The city belongs to *us*. (Note: plural pronouns are in italics for emphasis here but would be in plain text when used as a prime.)

Table 17.1 (cont.)

Task	Specific Examples
Sentence Unscrambling Task Prime	Sentence unscrambling tasks often involve lists of five words presented in a random order that people have to form into a four-word sentence (dropping one word). To prime individualism, singular pronouns or words such as *distinct, different, competitive, unique, alone, independence, individual,* and *separate* are used in the sentences, and to prime collectivism, plural pronouns or words such as *similar, cooperative, group, together, cohesive, connection, interdependence,* and *friendships* are used (see Dean & Gardner, 2014; Kühnen & Hannover, 2000). For example:

Please read each of the scrambled sentences below and identify the four words that can be rearranged to form a sentence. Write the new four-word sentence in the space provided.

Example: fiercely he a bike rides   He rides a bike_____

1. wrapped candy is individually deeply   _____
2. coffee dog alone the played   _____
3. lost book she her north   _____
4. the apart drifted birds finger   _____
5. were separated rivals yesterday the   _____
6. her boxes style unique is   _____
versus
1. joke we have together fun   _____
2. united were they boxes finally   _____
3. lost book she her north   _____
4. by won they cooperating taste   _____
5. friends deeply ate dinner the   _____
6. popular the group efficiently works   _____

Attribution Tasks

Task	Specific Examples
Current Event	Take a current world event and have students list possible internal and external attributions for the event, which makes them think about the difference between internal and external attributions and can emphasize the myriad of situational factors that Westerners tend to overlook. One example is attributions for gun violence. In the West, there are examples of politicians and journalists blaming individuals for their violent acts – that they are mentally ill or have violent personalities (see Editorial Board, 2015). Have students think about how differing attributions for violence might lead to different solutions – to taking away guns from individuals (with mental illness, with felony convictions, with domestic abuse convictions) versus changing societal norms (reducing media violence, making guns more difficult for anyone to purchase, finding support for those in financial trouble).
Video	Show a video in class that demonstrates a behavior (helping the homeless, aggression in a sports match, being anxious before an exam) and have

Table 17.1 (*cont.*)

Task	Specific Examples
	students list possible internal and external attributions for the behavior. One specific example (Bungay, 2009) appears in this chapter. As another example, a conformity video may be useful, especially in introductory psychology classes where conformity is also a likely topic in the same chapter. There are several videos displaying conformity, such as the Candid Camera elevator task (Prudential, 2013) or the Brain Games episode on conformity (in which people stand up when hearing a beep in an office waiting room; Davis et al., 2015). Because the situational factors may be more obvious once it becomes clear that many people conform (and thus the behavior cannot as easily be attributed to the person), we recommend showing only the first person in the video and having students make attributions about that person. After these attributions are discussed, the rest of the video could be played to demonstrate the power of conformity as a situational pressure.
Imagine Scenario	Have students imagine a scenario and make attributions for the imagined behavior. A specific example is described in this chapter in the scenario adapted from Johannesen-Schmidt (2008).
Quiz Show Activity	As in the Ross et al. (1977) quiz show paradigm, randomly assign students to write or answer questions or observe the game, and then have each student estimate each person's intelligence. Based on the correspondence bias, people in Western cultures would usually make higher internal attributions of intelligence for the questioner than the contestant, ignoring the situational factor that he or she was randomly assigned to write the questions.

or similar cultures, but there are ways to encourage students to grapple with cultural modes of thinking. Activities to demonstrate cultural differences can involve prompting students to think about different orientations before making attributions or priming different orientations in a more covert way, consistent with the situated cognition approach to culture. Oyserman and Lee's (2008) meta-analysis summarizes a range of strategies for priming collectivist versus individualist mind-sets that can be adapted for the classroom, several of which are included in Table 17.1. For example, students could write about how they are similar versus different from their friends and family or circle either singular or plural pronouns in a passage.

Within the context of attribution theory, these activities require pairing these cultural elements with demonstrations that elicit the correspondence bias. The main element of an attribution demonstration is having a behavior about which students make attributions. Many instructors may already use demonstrations that can be adapted for this purpose. Behaviors that have possible internal and external causes may work best in order to allow for variation across cultural primes. Common behaviors may include acts of helping behavior, aggression, conformity, or emotional states such as anxiety or anger. Introductory psychology instructors may especially wish to use behaviors that relate to other social psychology concepts covered in this chapter, such as conformity or the bystander effect of helping behavior. Current events might also provide fodder for attributions (e.g., gun violence, political protests, human-made disasters). Table 17.1 lists possibilities for how to create situations for students to make attributions about, including videos of behavior or imagined scenarios.

For example, one author of this chapter, teaching a social psychology course, paired the differential instructions with a video of aggressive behavior. The You Tube video was a short reel of a female soccer player who punched an opposing player in the back and yanked on another opposing player's hair, pulling her to the ground (Bungay, 2009). The reel was silent, cutting out any commentary, but more information about the player and her consequences can be found in other related videos (RcJ2, 2009). The written instructions given to students told them either to (a) evaluate the woman's behavior and "think about her personality, such as how intelligent, confident, and friendly" she is [individualistic instructions], (b) evaluate the situation and "think about the situation, such as how comfortable, stimulating, and unusual it is" [collectivistic instructions], or (c) watch the video [control condition]. The short video was played without any other commentary from the instructor, and then all students answered an open-ended question about why they thought the woman behaved this way and rated whether they thought the woman acted more because of her personal qualities or because of situational influences on a 7-point scale from 1 (*completely due to personal qualities*) to 7 (*completely due to situational influences*). Students often said that the soccer player was provoked or elbowed (a situational attribution), but many also mentioned that she must be an aggressive person or have a bad temperament. The numerical scores showed an average slightly below 4 (toward the person qualities end of the scale) for the instructions asking students to think about the woman's personality and slightly above 4 (toward the situational side) for the instructions asking students to think about situational forces. The control condition was similar to the situational instructions, even though the class was composed predominantly of American students. In this case, the activity occurred at the end of the class, and students' answers were collected by the professor, who discussed the results of the activity the next day when discussing cultural differences in attribution. At that point, attribution differences were tied to independent versus interdependent self-construal and analytic versus holistic thinking as part of a why-level analysis of culture. Other instructors may prefer that students code their own or another student's answers and the class can tally the proportion of internal and external attributions in each condition. Ideally, students will generate more internal than external attributions in the individualistic and control conditions but an equal number of internal and external attributions (or more external than internal) in the collectivistic condition.

Another demonstration used in a social psychology course was the sentence unscramble task paired with an imagined scenario. The instructor gave students a half sheet of paper; on the first side was the sentence unscramble task, with half of the students getting the individualistic prime and half the collectivistic prime (see Table 17.1). On the back was the imagine scenario, where students were asked to nominate an acquaintance they might run into near their residence and "Imagine you are carrying several bags of groceries or other products into your residence. One of the bags breaks and items spill onto the ground and some roll several feet away. You are gathering up the items and obviously have your hands full, when your acquaintance passes by. Your acquaintance waves at you, but doesn't stop to help" (adapted from Johannesen-Schmidt, 2008). Students were asked to write an explanation for why their acquaintance did not help and to rate on a 7-point scale whether their acquaintance acted more because of his or her personal qualities or because of situational factors (as described earlier). Unfortunately, perhaps because the individual was an acquaintance or because the class had just discussed the definitions and examples of internal and external attributions, there was no difference in attributions provided by students given the different primes. The average ratings for the two primes were on the situational end of the scale and nearly all students indicated the person was likely in a hurry or busy, although a couple of students did mention that it was possible the person was a jerk. Perhaps a scenario with positive behavior would work better, as students might be wary of labeling someone with negative traits. The activity was still useful, however, to get students thinking about different types of attributions, to explain a difference between individualistic and collectivistic cultures, and as an example of a prime (which was another topic being discussed in class).

Other instructors may have different preferences for the types of activities, the amount of time they would take, and how they relate to other course material. We hope instructors find the list in Table 17.1 useful and encourage them to combine the ways to emphasize culture with behavioral attributions in any way that makes sense to them. It is always possible that the demonstration does not "work" the way it was intended, but instructors can nevertheless use it to point out how different cultural and psychological orientations encourage different attributional patterns. Instructors could also discuss how students' knowledge of attribution may have attenuated the bias or changed their thinking about attributions.

Conclusion

Taking a cultural approach to understanding attributional processes provides new insights into how people make attributions within different cultural environments. First, it provides new insights by demonstrating cultural differences (i.e., the "what"). Second, it provides new insights by thoroughly examining when and why these cultural differences occur – which provides insight into the attributional process as it occurs in the East and West (i.e., the "why"). If instructors wish to emphasize culture even more strongly, they can include a discussion of the value of cross-cultural research not only to understanding others but also for understanding one's own culture. Indeed, a cross-cultural approach helps students appreciate the subjectivity of attributions by emphasizing that attributions convey just as much about our own cultural orientation and ways of thinking about the world as they do other people's behavior. We believe that attribution theory is a great place to emphasize how cultures think differently, explain multiple distinctions between individualistic and collectivistic cultures, and provide students with a strong connection to cultural psychology.

References

Aronson, E., Wilson, T., & Akert, R. M. (2017). *Social psychology* (8th ed.). Upper Saddle River, NJ: Pearson.

Brewer, M. B., & Gardner, W. L. (1996). Who is this "we"? Levels of collective identity and self-representations. *Journal of Personality and Social Psychology*, *71*, 83–93. doi:10.1037/0022-3514.71.1.83

Bungay, D. (2009, November 8). *Raw video – Soccer player throws fist and pulls hair*. Retrieved from www.youtube.com/watch?v=bjV2D4s2kDU

Chiu, C. Y., Hong, Y. Y., & Dweck, C. S. (1997). Lay dispositionism and implicit theories of personality. *Journal of Personality and Social Psychology*, *73*, 19–30. doi:10.1037/0022-3514.73.1.19

Chiu, L.-H. (1972). A cross-cultural comparison of cognitive styles in Chinese and American children. *International Journal of Psychology*, *7*, 235–242. doi:10.1080/00207597208246604

Choi, I., Dalal, R., Kim-Prieto, C., & Park, H. (2003). Culture and judgment of causal relevance. *Journal of Personality and Social Psychology*, *84*, 46–59. doi:10.1037/0022-3514.84.1.46

Choi, I., & Nisbett, R. E. (1998). Situational salience and cultural differences in the correspondence bias and in the actor-observer bias. *Personality and Social Psychology Bulletin*, *24*, 949–960. doi:10.1177/0146167298249003

Choi, I., Nisbett, R. E., & Norenzayan, A. (1999). Causal attribution across cultures: Variation and universality. *Psychological Bulletin*, *125*, 47–63. doi:10.1037/0033-2909.125.1.47

Ciccarelli, S. K., & White, J. N. (2017). *Psychology* (5th ed.). Boston, MA: Pearson.

Davis, A., Jacobs, D., Kolber, J. (Writers), & Nigro, M. (Director). (2015). Peer pressure. In P. C. Wells (Producer), *Brain Games*. National Geographic.

Dean, K. K., & Gardner, W. L. (2014). How will "I" vs. "we" perform? An investigation of future outlooks and self-construals. *Personality and Social Psychology Bulletin*, *40*, 947–958. doi:10.1177/0146167214532137

Dweck, C. S., Hong, Y. Y., & Chiu, C. Y. (1993). Implicit theories and individual differences in the likelihood and meaning of dispositional inference. *Personality and Social Psychology Bulletin*, *19*, 644–656. doi:10.1177/0146167293195015

Editorial Board. (2015, December). Don't blame mental illness for gun violence. *The New York Times*. Retrieved from www.nytimes.com/2015/12/16/opinion/dont-blame-mental-illness-for-gun-violence.html?_r=0

Fiske, A. P., Kitayama, S., Markus, H. R., & Nisbett, R. E. (1998). The cultural matrix of social psychology. In D. Gilbert & S. Fiske (Eds.), *The handbook of social psychology*, (Vol. 2, 4th ed., pp. 915–981). Boston, MA: McGraw-Hill.

Gardner, W. L., Gabriel, S., & Lee, A. Y. (1999). "I" value freedom, but "we" value relationships: Self-construal priming mirrors cultural differences in judgment. *Psychological Science*, *10*, 321–326. doi:10.1111/1467-9280.00162

Gawronski, B. (2004). Theory-based bias correction in dispositional inference: The fundamental attribution error is dead, long live the correspondence bias. *European Review of Social Psychology*, *15*, 183–217. doi:10.1080/10463280440000026

Gilbert, D. T., & Jones, E. E. (1986). Perceiver-induced constraint: Interpretations of self-generated reality. *Journal of Personality and Social Psychology*, *50*, 269–280. doi:10.1037/0022-3514.50.2.269

Gilbert, D. T., & Malone, P. S. (1995). The correspondence bias. *Psychological Bulletin*, *117*, 21–38. doi:10.1037/0033-2909.117.1.21

Heider, F. (1958). *The psychology of interpersonal relations*. New York, NY: Wiley. doi:10.1037/10628-000

Hofstede, G. (1980). *Culture's consequences: International differences in work-related values*. Beverly Hills, CA: Sage.

Johannesen-Schmidt, M. (2008). *Instructor's resource manual to social psychology* (6th ed.). Upper Saddle River, NJ: Pearson Education.

Jones, E. E. (1979). The rocky road from acts to disposition. *American Psychologist*, *34*, 107–117. doi:10.1037/0003-066X.34.2.107

(1990). *Interpersonal perception*. New York, NY: Freeman.

Jones, E. E., & Harris, V. A. (1967). The attribution of attitudes. *Journal of Experimental Social Psychology*, *3*, 1–24. doi:10.1016/0022-1031(67)90034-0

Kashima, Y., Siegel, M., Tanaka, K., & Kashima, E. S. (1992). Do people believe behaviors are consistent with attitudes? Towards a cultural psychology of attribution processes. *British Journal of Social Psychology*, *31*, 111–124. doi:10.1111/j.2044-8309.1992.tb00959.x

Kassin, S., Fein, S., & Markus, H. R. (2017). *Social psychology* (10th ed.). Boston, MA: Cengage.

Kitayama, S., Markus, H. R., Matsumoto, H., & Norasakkunkit, V. (1997). Individual and collective processes in the construction of the self: Self-enhancement in the United States and self-criticism in Japan. *Journal of Personality and Social Psychology*, *72*, 1245–1267. doi:10.1037/0022-3514.72.6.1245

Knowles, E. D., Morris, M. W., Chiu, C.-Y., & Hong, Y.-Y. (2001). Culture and the process of person perception: Evidence for automaticity among East Asians in correcting for situational influences on behavior. *Personality and Social Psychology Bulletin*, *27*, 1344–1356. doi:10.1177/0146167201271010

Koenig, A. M., & Dean, K. K. (2011). Cross-cultural differences and similarities in attribution. In K. D. Keith (Ed.), *Cross-cultural psychology: Contemporary themes and perspectives* (pp. 475–493). Malden, MA: Wiley-Blackwell.

Krull, D. S., Loy, M. H., Lin, J., Wang, C. F., Chen, S., & Zhao, X. (1999). The fundamental fundamental attribution error: Correspondence bias in individualist and collectivist cultures. *Personality and Social Psychology Bulletin*, *25*, 1208–1219. doi:10.1177/0146167299258003

Kühnen, U., & Hannover, B. (2000). Assimilation and contrast in social comparisons as a consequence of self-construal activation. *European Journal of Social Psychology*, *30*, 799–811. doi:10.1002/1099-0992(200011/12)30:6<799::AID-EJSP16>3.0.CO;2-2

Kühnen, U., Hannover, B., Pohlmann, C., & Roeder, U. (2013). How self-construal affects dispositionalism in attributions. *Social Cognition*, *31*, 237–259. doi:10.1521/soco.2013.31.2.237

Lee, F., Hallahan, M., & Herzog, T. (1996). Explaining real-life events: How culture and domain shape attributions. *Personality and Social Psychology Bulletin*, *22*, 732–741. doi:10.1177/0146167296227007

Markus, H. R., & Kitayama, S. (1991). Culture and the self: Implications for cognition, emotion, and motivation. *Psychological Review, 98*, 224–253. doi:10.1037/0033-295X.98.2.224

Masuda, T., & Kitayama, S. (2004). Perceiver-induced constraint and attitude attribution in Japan and the US: A case for the cultural dependence of the correspondence bias. *Journal of Experimental Social Psychology, 40*, 409–416. doi:10.1016/j.jesp.2003.08.004

Masuda, T., & Nisbett, R. E. (2001). Attending holistically versus analytically: Comparing the context sensitivity of Japanese and Americans. *Journal of Personality and Social Psychology, 81*, 922–934. doi:10.1037/0022-3514,81.5.922

Miller, J. G. (1984). Culture and the development of everyday social explanation. *Journal of Personality and Social Psychology, 46*, 961–978. doi:10.1037/0022-3514.46.5.961

Miyamoto, Y., & Kitayama, S. (2002). Culture and correspondence bias: Is the road from act to disposition rockier in Japan? *Journal of Personality and Social Psychology, 83*, 1239–1248. doi:10.1037/0022-3514.83.5.1239

Morris, M. W., & Peng, K. (1994). Culture and cause: American and Chinese attributions for social and physical events. *Journal of Personality and Social Psychology, 67*, 949–971. doi:10.1037/0022-3514.67.6.949

Nisbett, R. E., Peng, K., Choi, I., & Norenzayan, A. (2001). Culture and systems of thought: Analytic versus holistic cognition. *Psychological Review, 108*, 291–310. doi:10.1037/0033-295X.108.2.291

Norenzayan, A., Choi, I., & Nisbett, R. E. (2002). Cultural similarities and differences in social inference: Evidence from behavioral predictions and lay theories of behavior. *Personality and Social Psychology Bulletin, 28*, 109–120. doi:10.1177/0146167202281010

Oyserman, D., & Lee, S. W. S. (2007). Priming "culture": Culture as situated cognition. In S. Kitayama & D. Cohen (Eds.), *Handbook of cultural psychology* (pp. 255–279). New York, NY: Guilford Press.

(2008). Does culture influence what and how we think? Effects of priming individualism and collectivism. *Psychological Bulletin, 134*, 311–142. doi:10.1037/0033-2909.134.2.311

Peng, K., & Nisbett, R. E. (1999). Culture, dialectics, and reasoning about contradiction. *American Psychologist, 54*, 741–754. doi:10.1037/0003-066X.54.9.741

Poon, C. S. K., & Koehler, D. J. (2006). Lay personality knowledge and dispositionist thinking: A knowledge-activation framework. *Journal of Experimental Social Psychology, 42*, 177–191. doi:10.1016/j.jesp.2005.04.001

Prudential. (2013, May 13). *Prudential: Everybody's doing it*. Retrieved from www.youtube.com/watch?v=BgRoiTWkBHU

RcJ2. (2009, November 6). *Elizabeth Lambert of New Mexico Lobos suspended*. Retrieved from www.youtube.com/watch?v=PJiRQsyrBoI

Ross, L. (1977). The intuitive psychologist and his shortcomings: Distortions in the attribution process. In L. Berkowitz (Ed.), *Advances in experimental social psychology* (pp. 173–220). New York, NY: Academic Press. doi:10.1016/s0065-2601(08)60357-3

Ross, L., Amabile, T. M., & Steinmetz, J. L. (1977). Social roles, social control, and biases on social-perception processes. *Journal of Personality and Social Psychology, 35,* 485–494. doi:10.1037/0022-3514.35.7.485

Trafimow, D., Triandis, H., & Goto, S. (1991). Some tests of the distinction between the private self and the collective self. *Journal of Personality and Social Psychology, 60,* 649–655. doi:10.1037/0022-3514.60.5.649

Triandis, H. C. (1995). *Individualism and collectivism.* Boulder, CO: Westview.

van Boven, L., Kamada, A., & Gilovich, T. (1999). The perceiver as perceived: Everyday intuition about the correspondence bias. *Journal of Personality and Social Psychology, 77,* 1188–1199. doi:10.1037/0022-3514.77.6.1188

Weiten, W. (2017). *Psychology: Themes and variations* (10th ed.). Boston, MA: Cengage.

CHAPTER 18

Ethnocentrism: Our Window on the World

Kenneth D. Keith

A frog in a well, according to the old Asian proverb, is quite happy. He can see a bit of the sky, and it is a perfectly fine bit of sky; he has a bit of water, and it is a perfectly fine bit of water. His is a perfectly fine well, giving him no reason to wish to see any other place. What could be better than the place he calls home?

It is a common, and probably universal, tendency to hold up our own place or culture as the standard by which we judge others (LeVine & Campbell, 1972). We know this tendency as *ethnocentrism* (e.g., Berry, Poortinga, Segall, & Dasen, 2002), and it has long been a topic of discussion in cross-cultural research. The contemporary literature on ethnocentrism is extensive, and it appears in such diverse realms as willingness to buy domestic products (Guo & Zhou, 2017), the causes of riots (Fasel, Sarrasin, Green, & Mayor, 2016), attitudes toward immigration (Banks, 2016), and religion (Banyasz, Tokar, & Kaut, 2014).

Nevertheless, the idea of ethnocentrism is not new, and dates at least from the work of W. G. Sumner (1906), who used the term to describe divisions between ingroups and outgroups in such groups as the Papuans of New Guinea and the Greeks and Romans, among others. Indeed, Darwin (1874) discussed the tendency of tribes to favor their own groups, and more than two millennia ago, Hecataeus of Miletus wanted to divide the world into Europe and Asia – "us" and "them" (Durant, 1939). In this chapter, I will discuss some characteristics and causes (or at least correlates) of ethnocentrism, and some ideas teachers have found useful in reducing it. In the effort to integrate culture in the teaching of psychology, ethnocentrism has its obvious place in social psychology and in introductory psychology. However, an understanding of ethnocentrism is a crucial foundation in other areas as well, including clinical and counseling psychology, educational psychology, school psychology, and organizational psychology.

Understanding Ethnocentrism

What is ethnocentrism? Ethnocentrism derives its meaning from language connoting judgments or feelings that are centered (hence *centrism*) in one's own cultural or ethnic (*ethno*) setting (Brislin, 2000). Ethnocentrism is often characterized by negative perceptions of outsiders (Price & Crapo, 2002), and a tendency to favor members of one's own group (Taylor & Jaggi, 1974). We naturally want to be with people who are like us, and we feel different from, and perhaps even afraid of, those who are not like us (Strickland, 2000). We are enculturated in the society into which we are born, learning its rules, its way of doing things, and its expectations. As we learn to behave in culturally appropriate ways, we also learn to observe and interpret the behaviors of others, and thus notice and judge others' behavior; the rules of our culture become second nature (Matsumoto & Juang, 2013).

It is perhaps natural, as we learn what is "right" in our own culture, that the differences we notice between our group (ingroup) and other groups (outgroups) are seen as deficiencies (Berry et al., 2002). Although various authorities have long debated whether research investigating cultural differences must include ethnocentrism (e.g., Herskovits, 1948), it seems inevitable that virtually everyone, researcher and tourist alike, may find it difficult to avoid imposing familiar standards and norms on the behavior of members of other groups. We see the world through familiar lenses (Matsumoto & Juang, 2013), and if those around us, other members of our own culture, are viewing through the same lenses, we may be shaped toward a limited worldview with little awareness of the shaping process. We, like the Asian frog, will come to believe that ours is a perfectly good well.

When positive feelings for the ingroup are accompanied by negative views of the outgroup, the result is the classic ethnocentrism that Sumner (1906) described, an ethnocentrism characterized by feelings of superiority to the outgroup (Hooghe, 2008) and feelings of superior virtue on the part of the ingroup (Hammond & Axelrod, 2006). The greater the difference between the groups, the greater becomes the likelihood of negative judgment of the other (Berry et al., 2002). The view that positive judgment of the ingroup is accompanied by negative attitudes toward the outgroup may have arisen from the fact that Sumner (1906) described clearly defined cultural groups that literally fought one another for survival. He wrote, for example, about villages that maintained their separation not only by virtue of differing languages and religions, but also by such practices as cannibalism and head hunting. Consistent with this early perspective, Pratto and Glasford (2008) discussed the fact that when groups are in competition, they value the lives of ingroup members over those of people from the outgroup.

Researchers have not always found the type of classic ethnocentrism that Sumner described. For example, Khan and Lieu (2008), studying Pakistanis and Indians, found more ingroup support than outgroup disfavor. And Brewer (1999, 2007), while noting that research has generally supported the notion of a reciprocal ingroup favor/outgroup disfavor relation, groups may sometimes hold positive ingroup feelings without offsetting hostility or disdain toward the outgroup. Raden (2003), in a large sample of US citizens, found that ingroup bias without negative views of the outgroup was more prevalent than classic ethnocentrism (with hostility toward the outgroup).

Who is ethnocentric? The short answer to this question might be simply "everyone." This is an important point for students to understand; although we may take steps to try to ameliorate our ethnocentrism, we all see the world from where we stand. At least some degree of ethnocentrism is virtually inevitable.

Sumner (1906) listed many cultural and national groups whose people believed themselves to be uniquely human or "chosen." Among these groups were Caribs, Greenlanders, Jews, Kiowa, Lapps, and Seri. However, although ethnocentrism may be universal (e.g., LeVine & Campbell, 1972), levels of ethnocentrism vary across cultures (e.g., Pan, 2007).

Researchers have investigated ethnocentrism in a wide range of settings, including people across nationalities (Beswick, 1972; Cashdan, 2001; Neuliep, Chaudoir, & McCroskey, 2001); American ethnic minorities (Gittler, 1972; Hraba, 1972; Mutisya & Ross, 2005; Prothro,1952; Raden, 2003); consumers across cultures (Fischer & Zeugner-Roth, 2017; Guo & Zhou, 2017; He & Wang, 2015); and people with disabilities (Chesler, 1965; Gorman & Cross, 2014). Researchers have also found ethnocentrism in judgments of attractiveness and competence of people across cultures (Neuliep, Hintz, & McCroskey, 2005) and across ethnic groups (Stephan & Langlois, 1980), Finally, it is interesting to note that investigators have studied musical ethnocentrism – examining the association of music with national identity (Boer et al., 2013) – and ethnocentrism directed toward nonhuman species (Bizumic & Duckitt, 2007).

What are the origins of ethnocentrism? One important line of reasoning concerning the etiology of ethnocentrism is rooted in *evolutionary* theory.

The practice of dividing the world into "us" and "them" and avoiding or fighting the "other" may have contributed to the survival of groups that might otherwise have been victim of aggression or other forms of tribal behavior (Wilson, 1978). It is also likely, some writers (e.g., Thayer, 2004) have proposed, that humans have an adaptive affinity for those individuals to whom they are biologically related. A logical outcome of this would be that individuals would first support or protect immediate family members, then other biological relatives, then their ethnic group, and eventually others – a kind of hierarchical model of evolutionary ethnocentrism. Such family ties may, according to Freedman (1984), serve human evolution as groups reach a maximum population density and family units split off to form new groups – with the advantage that family-based groups can reasonably precisely track kinship. The kinship notion does not, of course, mean that environmental/cultural forces are not important; however, some evidence exists to support the notion that cultures with more ethnic homogeneity (and therefore more presumed biological similarity) are also more ethnocentric (Thayer, 2004).

Another potential biological/evolutionary explanation for ethnocentrism has its basis in the biological costs and benefits of interacting with ingroup members versus outgroup members. An important rationale here is that ingroup members are likely to have been exposed to and developed immunity to pathogens present within the group. Following this line of reasoning, Navarrete and Fessler (2006) designed research showing that ethnocentrism increased as a function of perceived disease vulnerability. This finding was consistent with the work of Faulkner, Schaller, Park, and Duncan (2004), who also concluded that perceived disease vulnerability may lead to negative attitudes toward outgroups. In another test of the disease-threat model, Navarrete, Fessler, and Eng (2007) concluded that pregnant women were most ethnocentric during the first trimester of pregnancy, when the fetus is most vulnerable (Health Encyclopedia, 2017). Park, Faulkner, and Schaller (2003) also proposed a model linking the disease-threat model to prejudice against people with physical disabilities.

The role of biological evolution in the development of ethnocentrism is not clear, and some research has failed to support an evolutionary conclusion. For example, Roberts (1997), studying the relation between reproductive success and ethnocentrism across ethnic groups in India, failed to find a significant correlation between these two measures. It is also possible, of course, that cultures may evolve in their social structure, even if not biologically (e.g., Ross, 1991). This is of course a topic that could be discussed in relation to Darwin's (1874) earlier observations on tribal relations.

An approach to understanding determinants of ethnocentrism that has perhaps been somewhat more fruitful than the biological approach is the search for *psychological* variables that may account for, or at least correlate with, ethnocentrism. Each of us is born into a culture, grows up in a culture, and experiences all the behavioral influences of that culture (e.g., parenting, education, social interplay, religion, and media). Researchers have looked to at least some of these influences for insight about the phenomenon of ethnocentrism.

One intriguing research domain has been the study of individual characteristics that might define a continuum of "open-mindedness." Working in Canada, Altemeyer (1996, 2003) found significant correlations between religious ethnocentrism, religious fundamentalism, and Manitoba ethnocentrism (i.e., people who scored high on religious fundamentalism also tended to be ethnocentric toward both other sociocultural groups and other religions). The religious fundamentalists, Altemeyer (2003) reported, had a very small "us" and a large "them" in terms of their religious views. In India, Hasnain (2007) reported that religious (Hindu and Muslim) adolescents were significantly more prejudiced and ethnocentric than were nonreligious individuals. In another study of Indian Hindu and Muslim students, Hassan (1978) found both groups of students to be ethnocentric, the Muslims more so than the Hindus. For both groups, ethnocentrism was significantly correlated with anxiety, authoritarianism, and rigidity.

At least two European studies have also shown significant correlations between ethnocentrism and authoritarianism. Todosijević and Enyedi (2002) found this connection among adolescents and parents in Hungary, and in the Netherlands, Van Ijzendoorn (2001) reported a similar relation between ethnocentrism and authoritarianism in both high school and university students. Thomas (1975), in a study of parenting styles in Pacific Island cultures, also found a positive relation between authoritarianism and ethnocentrism, and Epstein and Komorita (1966) reported that parental ethnocentrism and punitiveness were associated with ethnocentrism in children.

Several studies conducted in the middle of the twentieth century examined the relation between ethnocentrism and tolerance for ambiguity. In each case, tolerance (or intolerance) for ambiguity was significantly correlated with ethnocentrism. O'Connor (1952) and Block and Block (1951) confirmed this finding with samples of American students, and Taft (1956), studying Australians, came to a similar conclusion. In each case, intolerance for ambiguity was associated with higher levels of ethnocentrism.

In more recent work, de Oliveira, Braun, Carlson, and de Oliveira (2009) measured American university students' attitudes toward foreign-born instructors, as well as the students' performance on a measure of Big Five personality traits (McCrae & Costa, 1999). Their results indicated ethnocentric bias toward the foreign-born instructors. However, the Big Five traits of agreeableness and conscientiousness correlated positively with positive attitudes toward the instructors.

Taken together, research studies have suggested that ethnocentrism tends to be related to more rigid, authoritarian, intolerant ways of thinking, and that highly ethnocentric individuals prefer certainty to ambiguity. These individuals may be more likely to engage in thinking that Triandis (2009) has called *simple cognition*, thus reducing complex situations to simpler, discrete terms (e.g., right/wrong, like/dislike). It is possible, or perhaps even likely, that ethnocentrism has contributed, via an evolutionary function, to the survival of groups. Yet at the same time, it has also contributed to conflict and challenges as individuals and groups interact in the world, and people work to improve intergroup relations (Brewer & Brown, 1998). Are there ways to overcome the detrimental aspects of ethnocentrism?

Reducing Ethnocentrism

Allport (1954) suggested that contact between groups might serve to reduce tension between them – the so-called contact hypothesis. In a project aiming to reduce ethnocentrism, Borden (2007) arranged for university student contact with ethnic minorities and international students via service learning projects. Although this project had no control group, pre- and post-testing of students in two sections of an intercultural communication course, using the Generalized Ethnocentrism Scale (Neuliep, 2002), indicated a significant reduction in ethnocentrism. However, in a much larger test of the contact hypothesis, Dejaeghere, Hooghe, and Claes (2012) investigated the effect on ethnocentrism of experience in ethnically diverse schools; in a 2-year follow-up, student perceptions of the tensions they had experienced in school seemed to indicate increased (not decreased) prejudice. Dejaeghere et al. concluded, as have others (e.g., Brewer & Brown, 1998), that the quality of intergroup interaction is important to outcomes. More specifically, Brewer and Brown (1998) suggested that simple contact is unlikely to be effective in reducing ethnocentrism unless it also includes such added features as potential for meaningful relationships, institutional support, intergroup cooperation, and equal status between groups.

As early as the 1950s, Plant (1958a, 1958b) investigated the possibility that higher education might play a role in reduction of ethnocentrism. In one of these studies, Plant (1958a) administered a version of the Total Ethnocentrism Scale: Public Opinion Questionnaire E (Adorno, Frenkel-Brunswick, Levinson, & Sanford, 1950) to more than 1,000 entering college students, and later invited 315 of them to be retested upon completing their college work 4 years later. Of the 315 students, 271 completed the retest, and showed significantly reduced ethnocentrism scores compared to their entering scores. In a second study, again following up with students who had taken an ethnocentrism pretest, Plant (1958b) retested 755 students who had completed 2 years of college and 250 who had left college prior to the retest. Those who had stayed in college showed significant reductions in ethnocentrism, while those who had left showed no significant change. In both of Plant's studies, men showed higher levels of ethnocentrism than women – a finding consistent with other research (Hooghe, 2008).

Pettijohn and Naples (2009) used the Generalized Ethnocentrism Scale (Neuliep, 2002), as well as the US Ethnocentrism Scale (Neuliep & McCroskey, 1997), to evaluate the ethnocentrism of students before and after taking a course in introductory psychology or a course in cross-cultural psychology. Pettijohn and Naples reported significant decreases in ethnocentrism for the cross-cultural students, but not for the introductory students. Although the study had a number of design flaws, it nevertheless suggested the potential effect of cross-cultural education to reduce ethnocentrism.

In related work aimed toward identifying *how* education relates to ethnocentrism and tolerance, Bobo and Licari (1989) reported that education seemed to have a mitigating effect on intolerance, even for individuals with negative feelings toward a target group. Furthermore, an important contributor to the effect of education was cognitive sophistication (e.g., openness to new ideas, tolerance for uncertainty and ambiguity, intellectual interests). Hello, Scheepers, and Sleegers (2006) came to a somewhat different conclusion concerning the effects of education on ethnocentrism, finding that cognitive sophistication was not as important as perceived threat and authoritarianism. That is, more highly educated people saw ethnic groups as less threatening, and they were less authoritarian in their thinking, consistent with other research that I have discussed earlier in this chapter. Meeusen, de Vroome, and Hooghe (2013), analyzing data from 1,910 residents of the Netherlands, confirmed the negative relation between education and ethnocentrism, and concluded that cognitive ability and occupational status (as correlates of education) were key contributors.

Dong, Day, and Collaço (2008) studied the potential role of multiculturalism and intercultural communication sensitivity as predictors of ethnocentrism in a sample comprising mainly Caucasian and Asian Americans. They reported significant correlations between measures of ethnocentrism, multicultural ideology, and intercultural sensitivity, and pointed out the prospect that increasing appreciation for multiculturalism and improving intercultural sensitivity (perhaps through community cultural experiences) could reduce ethnocentrism. These ideas no doubt have promise, although the correlational nature of the research leaves unanswered questions concerning which of these measures may depend upon the other(s). Nevertheless, efforts to reduce ethnocentrism are perhaps one way to increase the likelihood that students will elect to study abroad, thus broadening their cultural experience (Goldstein & Kim, 2006).

Final Thoughts

Ethnocentrism, while universal, is more or less evident in different cultures. Some studies have suggested, for example, higher levels of ethnocentrism among Japanese (e.g., Neuliep et al., 2001) and Chinese (Li & Liu, 1975; Pan, 2007) students than among Americans. Pereira, Hsu, and Kundu (2002) measured ethnocentrism in business students from China, Taiwan, and India, and found the highest levels of ethnocentrism among those from mainland China, followed by Taiwan and India. These findings are consistent with the notion that, while individuals from collectivistic cultures may not have as many ingroups as individualists, they may be more strongly attached to their groups (Triandis, Bontempo, Villareal, Asai, & Lucca, 1988).

Although it may not appear in psychology courses as frequently as it could, the concept of ethnocentrism is an important, if often unrecognized, aspect of human behavior. Ethnocentrism is likely universal, existing, as numerous writers have observed, like the water surrounding a fish; the fish does not realize it is viewing the world through water, because it has never seen the world any other way. As teachers, a part of our role is to expand our students' horizons, to provide new experiences, and to offer new perspectives. If some of those experiences can open new cultural vistas, they have potential to change lives. Who knows, maybe we can help the frog in the well to see the ocean.

Teaching Activities

Ingroups and outgroups. Large automobile manufacturers are fierce competitors, and it is likely that personnel at one may well see those at other companies as members of outgroups. Yet in the early 1990s, an interesting thing happened. The heads of major American auto manufacturers banded together to travel to Japan to make the case for the marketing of American cars. This event illustrated the fact that ingroups and outgroups can be malleable in interesting ways. At home, the car makers were members of outgroups; but when they made their case abroad, they became members of the same ingroup.

Ask students to list various ingroups of which they are members. They are likely to identify themselves as members of a family, an academic class, clubs or organizations, their university, or perhaps their state and country. Then ask the students to select a few of their groups and attempt to portray them in Venn diagrams, identifying which groups are subsumed by others, which intersect with others, and which ones, like the automobile executives, might have interchangeable relations, depending upon circumstances.

Classroom discussion of this exercise can help students to see that ethnocentrism is not inevitably bad, that it can be changeable, and that being aware of ethnocentrism can be helpful. This activity may also help students to see the value of flexible (as opposed to rigid) ethnocentrism and of making the effort to understand what lies behind observable cultural differences.

Service learning. Service learning can present excellent, enriching opportunities for students to confront and overcome ethnocentrism *if* the activity has important learning goals, occurs in a properly supportive environment, and provides opportunity for reflection and analysis. Over many years, my students have completed service learning activities in numerous settings offering rich cultural experiences. Among these settings are a community center for Sudanese refugees; a community center providing after school activities for children of immigrant families in a neighborhood where 20 or more languages are spoken; and an alternative high school serving multicultural students whose personal or environmental situations make a typical high school experience difficult or impossible.

Students working in each of the field settings have benefit of a student mentor (a student who has previously taken the class and worked in the setting); assistance with scheduling and matching (whether from a service learning office or the faculty member); scheduled class time (perhaps a few minutes at the beginning or end of class a few times during the semester); assignment to maintain a journal or log, detailing observations, questions, and ideas; preparation of a final paper, relating observations and experiences to course content and research literature in a thoughtful, analytic way.

Properly managed and supported, the culture-based service learning experience provides students with opportunities and skills that are both personally and professionally rewarding. And people whom they may have seen as "the other" in the beginning can become friends, important people in the lives of the students, and vice versa. It is a useful way to reduce ethnocentrism, perhaps without ever saying the word.

Resources

Bronstein, P., & Quina, K. (Eds.). (2003). *Teaching gender and multicultural awareness*. Washington, DC: American Psychological Association.

This edited volume, in its twenty-five chapters, addresses integration of diversity in a variety of courses, and a number of the authors discuss infusion of their subject matters across the curriculum. Although ethnocentrism does not appear explicitly and the book's focus is multicultural (rather than cross-cultural), there is nevertheless much here that can be adapted to teaching in ways that will be helpful in addressing ethnocentrism.

Goldstein, S. (2016). *Cross-cultural explorations: Activities in culture and psychology* (2nd ed.). New York, NY: Routledge. (Original work published 2008)

This popular activities handbook contains exercises and demonstrations to accompany nearly any aspect of the teaching of culture and psychology. Several of the activities can be adapted to a discussion of ethnocentrism.

Gross, D., Abrams, K., & Enns, C. Z. (2016). *Internationalizing the undergraduate psychology curriculum: Practical lessons learned at home and abroad*. Washington, DC: American Psychological Association.

The chapters in this book cover a variety of approaches to internationalizing teaching. A number of the experiences these authors describe will serve to diminish the effects of ethnocentrism, both on campus and abroad.

Gurung, R. A. R., & Prieto, L. R. (Eds.). (2009). *Getting culture: Incorporating diversity across the curriculum*. Sterling, VA: Stylus.

This edited collection includes sections on a variety of issues related to the teaching of cultural diversity. Several of the chapters offer information or exercises (e.g., classroom games, activities) that will aid in grasping the reality of ethnocentrism and its role in understanding culture.

Palmer, N. (2010). *Sociology source: Teaching ethnocentricity.* Retrieved from https://thesocietypages.org/sociologysource/2010/07/26/teaching-ethnocentricity/

This online article describes classroom activities designed to break down ethnocentric views while increasing awareness of one's own culture.

References

Adorno, T., Frenkel-Brunswick, E., Levinson, D., & Sanford, N. (1950). *The authoritarian personality.* New York, NY: Harper.

Allport, G. W. (1954). *The nature of prejudice.* Reading, MA: Addison-Wesley.

Altemeyer, B. (1996). *The authoritarian specter.* Cambridge, MA: Harvard University Press.

(2003). Why do religious fundamentalists tend to be prejudiced? *International Journal for the Psychology of Religion, 13,* 17–28. doi:10.1207/S15327582IJPR1301_03

Banks, A. J. (2016). Are group cues necessary? How anger makes ethnocentrism among whites a stronger predictor of racial and immigration policy opinions. *Political Behavior, 38,* 635–657. doi:10.1007/s11109-016-9330-3

Banyasz, A. M., Tokar, D. M., & Kaut, K. P. (2014). Predicting religious ethnocentrism: Evidence for a partial mediation model. *Psychology of Religion and Spirituality, 8,* 25–34. doi:10.1037/rel0000020

Berry, J. W., Poortinga, Y. H., Segall, M. H., & Dasen, P. R. (2002). *Cross-cultural psychology: Research and applications* (2nd ed.). Cambridge: Cambridge University Press.

Beswick, D. G. (1972). A survey of ethnocentrism in Australia. *Australian Journal of Psychology, 24,* 153–163. doi:10.1080/00049537208255799

Bizumic, B., & Duckitt, J. (2007). Varieties of group self-centeredness and dislike of the specific other. *Basic and Applied Social Psychology, 29,* 195–202. doi:10.1080/01973530701332252

Block, J., & Block, J. (1951). An investigation of the relationship between intolerance of ambiguity and ethnocentrism. *Journal of Personality, 19,* 303–311. doi:10.1111/j.1467-6494.1951.tb01104.x

Bobo, L., & Licari, F. C. (1989). Education and political tolerance: Testing the effects of cognitive sophistication and target group affect. *Public Opinion Quarterly, 53,* 285–308. doi:10.1086/269154

Boer, D., Fischer, R., González Atilano, M. L., Hernández, J. G., Garcia, L. I. M., Mendoza, S., . . . Lo, E. (2013). Music, identity, and musical ethnocentrism of young people in six Asian, Latin American, and western cultures. *Journal of Applied Social Psychology, 43,* 2360–2376. doi:10.1111/jasp.12185

Borden, A. W. (2007).The impact of service-learning on ethnocentrism in an intercultural communication course. *Journal of Experiential Education, 30,* 171–183. doi:10.1177/105382590703000206

Brewer. M. B. (1999). The psychology of prejudice: Ingroup love or outgroup hate? *Journal of Social Issues*, *55*, 429–444. doi:10.1177/0022022107311843

Brewer, M. B. (2007). The importance of being we: Human nature and intergroup relations. *American Psychologist*, *62*, 728–738. doi:10.1037/0003-066X.62.8.728

Brewer, M. B., & Brown, R. J. (1998). Intergroup relations. In D. T. Gilbert, S. T. Fiske, & G. Lindzey (Eds.), *The handbook of social psychology* (Vol. 2, 4th ed., pp. 554–594). Boston, MA: McGraw-Hill.

Brislin, R. (2000). *Understanding culture's influence on behavior* (2nd ed.). Fort Worth, TX: Harcourt.

Cashdan, E. (2001). Ethnocentrism and xenophobia: A cross-cultural study. *Current Anthropology*, *42*, 760–765. doi:10.1080/00049537208255799

Chesler, M. A. (1965). Ethnocentrism and attitudes toward the physically disabled. *Journal of Personality and Social Psychology*, *2*, 877–882.

Darwin, C. (1874). *The descent of man and selection in relation to sex* (2nd ed.). New York, NY. A. L. Burt.

Dejaeghere, Y., Hooghe, M., & Claes, E. (2012). Do ethnically diverse schools reduce ethnocentrism? A two-year panel study among majority group late adolescents in Belgian schools. *International Journal of Intercultural Relations*, *36*, 108–117. doi:10.1016/j.ijintrel.2011.02.010

de Oliveira, E. A., Braun, J. L., Carlson, T. L., & de Oliveira, S. G. (2009). Students' attitudes toward foreign-born and domestic instructors. *Journal of Diversity in Higher Education*, *2*, 113–125. doi:10.1037/a0015746

Dong, Q., Day, K. D., & Collaço, C. M. (2008). Overcoming ethnocentrism through developing intercultural sensitivity and multiculturalism. *Human Communication*, *11*(1), 27–38. doi:

Durant, W. (1939). *The story of civilization: Part II. The life of Greece*. New York, NY: Simon and Schuster.

Epstein, R., & Komorita, S. S. (1966). Childhood prejudice as a function of parental ethnocentrism, punitiveness, and outgroup characteristics. *Journal of Personality and Social Psychology*, *3*, 259–264. doi:10.1080/00207597508247335

Fasel, N., Sarrasin, O., Green, E. G. T., & Mayor, E. (2016). Who is to blame? Official discourse and ethnic diversity attitudes during the 2011 riots in England. *Political Psychology*, *37*, 659–675. doi:10.1111/pops.12328

Faulkner, J., Schaller, M., Park, J. H., & Duncan, L. A. (2004). Evolved disease-avoidance mechanisms and contemporary xenophobic attitudes. *Group Processes and Intergroup Relations*, *7*, 333–353. doi:10.1177/1368430204046142

Fischer, P. M., & Zeugner-Roth, K. P. (2017). Disentangling country-of-origin effects: The interplay of product ethnicity, national identity, and consumer ethnocentrism. *Marketing Letters*, *28*, 189–204. doi:10.1007/s11002-016-9400-7

Freedman, D. G. (1984). Village fissioning, human diversity, and ethnocentrism. *Political Psychology*, *5*, 629–634. doi:10.2307/3791233

Gittler, J. B. (1972). Jews as an ethnic minority in the United States. *International Journal of Group Tensions*, *2*(4), 4–21.

Goldstein, S. B., & Kim, R. I. (2006). Predictors of US college students' participation in study abroad programs: A longitudinal study. *International Journal of Intercultural Relations, 30*, 507–521. doi:10.1016/j.ijintrel.2005.10.001

Gorman, D., & Cross, W. (2014). Cultural issues in mental health. In K.-L. Edward, I. Munro, A. Welch, & A. Robins (Eds.), *Mental health nursing: Dimensions of praxis* (2nd ed.). New York, NY: Oxford University Press.

Guo, G., & Zhou, X. (2017). Consumer ethnocentrism on product judgment and willingness to buy: A meta-analysis. *Social Behavior and Personality, 45*, 163–176. doi:10.2224/sbp.5548

Hammond, R. A., & Axelrod, R. (2006). The evolution of ethnocentrism. *Journal of Conflict Resolution, 50*, 926–936. doi:10.1177/0022002706293470

Hasnain, N. (2007). Does religiousness promote prejudice and ethnocentrism? *Psychological Studies, 52*, 123–125.

Hassan, M. K. (1978). A study of ethnocentrism, prejudice and related personality factors in Hindu and Muslim college students. *Psychologia: An International Journal of Psychology in the Orient, 21*(3), 150–154.

He, J., & Wang, C. L. (2015). Cultural identity and consumer ethnocentrism impacts on preference and purchase of domestic versus import brands: An empirical study in China. *Journal of Business Research, 68.* 1225–1238. doi:10.1016/j.jbusres.2014.11.017

Health Encyclopedia (2017). *The first trimester.* Rochester, NY: University of Rochester Medical Center. Retrieved from www.urmc.rochester.edu/encyclopedia/content.aspx?contenttypeid=85&contentid=P01218

Hello, E., Scheepers, P., & Sleegers, P. (2006). Why the more educated are less inclined to keep ethnic distance: An empirical test of four explanations. *Ethnic and Racial Studies, 29*, 959–985. doi:10.1080/01419870600814015

Herskovits, M. J. (1948). *Man and his works: The science of cultural anthropology.* New York, NY: Knopf.

Hooghe, M. (2008). *Ethnocentrism. International encyclopedia of the social sciences.* Philadelphia, PA: Macmillan Reference.

Hraba, J. (1972). The doll technique: A measure of racial ethnocentrism? *Social Forces, 50*, 522–527. doi:10.2307/2576794

Khan, S. S., & Liu, J. H. (2008). Intergroup attributions and ethnocentrism in the Indian subcontinent: The ultimate attribution error revisited. *Journal of Cross-Cultural Psychology, 39*, 16–36. doi:10.1177/0022022107311843

LeVine, R. A., & Campbell, D. T. (1972). *Ethnocentrism.* New York, NY: Wiley.

Li, W. L., & Liu, S. S. (1975). Ethnocentrism among American and Chinese youth. *Journal of Social Psychology, 95*, 277–278. doi:10.1080/00224545.1975.9918717

Matsumoto, D., & Juang, L. (2013). *Culture and psychology* (5th ed.). Belmont, CA: Wadsworth.

McCrae, R. R., & Costa, P. T., Jr. (1999). A five-factor theory of personality. In L. A. Pervin & O. P. John (Eds.), *Handbook of personality: Theory and research* (2nd ed., pp. 139–153). New York, NY: Guilford.

Meeusen, C., de Vroome, T., & Hooghe, M. (2013). How does education have an impact on ethnocentrism? A structural equation analysis of cognitive, occupational status and network mechanisms. *International Journal of Intercultural Relations, 37,* 507–522. doi:10.1016/j.ijintrel.2013.07.002

Mutisya, P. M., & Ross, L. E. (2005). Afrocentricity and racial socialization among African American college students. *Journal of Black Studies, 35,* 235–247. doi:10.1177/0021934704266597

Navarrete, C. D., & Fessler, D. M. T. (2006). Disease avoidance and ethnocentrism: The effects of disease vulnerability and disgust sensitivity on intergroup attitudes. *Evolution and Human Behavior, 27,* 270–282. doi:10.1016/j.evolhumbehav.2005.12.001

Navarrete, C. D., Fessler, D. M. T., & Eng, S. J. (2007). Elevated ethnocentrism in the first trimester of pregnancy. *Evolution and Human Behavior, 28,* 60–65. doi:10.1016/j.evolhumbehav.2006.06.002

Neuliep, J. W. (2002). Assessing the reliability and validity of the generalized ethnocentrism scale. *Journal of Intercultural Communication Research, 31,* 201–216.

Neuliep, J. W., Chaudoir, M., & McCroskey, J.C. (2001). A cross-cultural comparison of ethnocentrism among Japanese and United States college students. *Communication Research Reports, 18,* 137–146. doi:10.1080/08824090109384791

Neuliep, J. W., Hintz, S. M., & McCroskey, J. C. (2005). The influence of ethnocentrism in organizational contexts: Perceptions of interviewee and managerial attractiveness, credibility, and effectiveness. *Communication Quarterly, 53,* 41–56. doi:10.1080/01463370500055954

Neuliep, J. W., & McCroskey, J. C. (1997). The development of a U. S. and generalized ethnocentrism scale. *Communication Research Reports, 14,* 385–398. doi:10.1080/08824099709388682

O'Connor, P. (1952). Ethnocentrism, "intolerance of ambiguity," and abstract reasoning ability. *Journal of Abnormal and Social Psychology, 47,* 526–530. doi:10.1037/h0056142

Pan, S. (2007, Nov. 15). *Intercultural communication apprehension, ethnocentrism, and their relationship with gender: A cross-cultural comparison between the US and China.* Paper presented at the annual meeting of the National Communication Association, Chicago, Il. Retrieved from http://research.allacademic.com/one/www/www/index.php?cmd=www_search&offset=0&limit=5&multi_search_search_mode=publication&multi_search_publication_fulltext_mod=fulltext&textfield_submit=true&search_module=multi_search&search=Search&search_field=title_idx&fulltext_search=Intercultural+Communication+Apprehension%2C+Ethnocentrism+and+Their+Relationship+with+Gender%3A+A+Cross-cultural+Comparison+between+the+US+and+China

Park, J. H., Faulkner, J., & Schaller, M. (2003). Evolved disease-avoidance processes and contemporary anti-social behavior: Prejudicial attitudes and avoidance of people with physical disabilities. *Journal of Nonverbal Behavior, 27,* 65–87. doi:10.1023/A:1023910408854

Pereira, A., Hsu, C.-C., & Kundu, S. (2002). A cross-cultural analysis of ethnocentrism in China, India, and Taiwan. *Journal of International Consumer Marketing, 15*, 77–90. doi:10.1300/J046v15n01_05

Pettijohn, T. F., II, & Naples, G. M. (2009). Reducing ethnocentrism in U.S. college students by completing a cross-cultural psychology course. *Open Social Science Journal, 2*, 1–6.

Plant, W. T. (1958a). Changes in ethnocentrism associated with a four-year college education. *Journal of Educational Psychology, 49*, 162–165. doi:10.1037/h0041244

(1958b). Changes in ethnocentrism associated with a two-year college experience. *Journal of Genetic Psychology, 92*, 189–197. doi:10.1080/00221325.1958.10532392

Pratto, F., & Glasford, D. E. (2008). Ethnocentrism and the value of a human life. *Journal of Personality and Social Psychology, 95*, 1411–1428. doi:10.1037/a0012636

Price, W. F., & Crapo, R. H. *Cross-cultural perspectives in introductory psychology.* Pacific Grove, CA: Wadsworth.

Prothro, E. T. (1952). Ethnocentrism and anti-Negro attitudes in the Deep South. *Journal of Abnormal and Social Psychology, 47*, 105–108. doi:10.1037/h0060676

Raden, D. (2003). Ingroup bias, classic ethnocentrism, and non-ethnocentrism among American Whites. *Political Psychology, 24*, 803–828. doi:10.1046/j.1467-9221.2003.00355.x

Roberts, J. P. (1997). *A sociobiological examination of ethnocentrism between two ethnic units – Tamils and Guraratis – in the city of Pune, India.* (Unpublished doctoral dissertation). University of Wisconsin–Milwaukee.

Ross, M. H. (1991). The role of evolution in ethnocentric conflict and its management. *Journal of Social Issues, 47*, 167–185. doi:10.1111/j.1540-4560.1991.tb01829.x

Stephan, C. W., & Langlois, J. H. (1980). Physical attractiveness and ethnicity: Implications for stereotyping and social development. *Journal of Genetic Psychology, 137*, 303–304. doi:10.1080/00221325.1980.10532832

Strickland, B. S. (2000). Misassumptions, misadventures, and the misuse of psychology. *American Psychologist, 55*, 331–338. doi:10.1037/0003-066X.55.3.331

Sumner, W. G. (1906). *Folkways.* New York, NY: Ginn.

Taft, R. (1956). Intolerance of ambiguity and ethnocentrism. *Journal of Consulting Psychology, 20*, 153–154. doi:10.1037/h0047637

Taylor, D. M., & Jaggi, V. (1974). Ethnocentrism and causal attribution in a South Indian context. *Journal of Cross-Cultural Psychology, 5*, 162–171. doi:10.1177/002202217400500202

Thayer, B. A. (2004). *Darwin and international relations: On the evolutionary origins of war and ethnic conflict.* Lexington, KY: The University Press of Kentucky.

Thomas, D. R. (1975). Authoritarianism, child-rearing practices and ethnocentrism in seven Pacific Islands groups. *International Journal of Psychology, 10*, 235–246. doi:10.1080/00207597508247335

Todosijević, B., & Enyedi, Z. (2002). Authoritarianism vs. cultural pressure. *Journal of Russian and East European Psychology, 40*, 31–54.

Triandis, H. C. (2009). *Fooling ourselves: Self-deception in politics, religion, and terrorism.* Westport, CT: Praeger.

Triandis, H. C., Bontempo, R., Villareal, M. J., Asai, M., & Lucca, N. (1988). Individualism and collectivism: Cross-cultural perspectives on self-ingroup relationships. *Journal of Personality and Social Psychology, 4*, 323–338. doi:10.1037/0022-3514.54.2.323

Van Ijzendoorn, M. H. (2001). Moral judgment, authoritarianism, and ethnocentrism. *Journal of Social Psychology, 129*, 37–45. doi:10.1080/00224545.1989.9711697

Wilson, E. O. (1978). *On human nature.* Cambridge, MA: Harvard University Press.

CHAPTER 19

Cross-Cultural Attitudes toward Sexual Minorities

Mary E. Kite, LaCount J. Togans, and Kim A. Case

In contemporary times, the social change toward greater acceptance of sexual minorities has been striking. A recent review of global social attitudes, based on representative samples across fifty-one countries, showed clear movement toward greater acceptance of homosexuality (Smith, Son, & Kim, 2014). This social change has been accompanied by legislative changes, particularly in acceptance of same-sex marriage or civil unions. For example, same-sex marriage is legal in Canada, the United States, and most of Western Europe. Thus, when viewed through the lens of Western culture, the progress toward social justice for sexual minorities is both striking and heartening. However, when a broader, global perspective is adopted, the picture is bleaker. Same-sex couples' right to marry, for example, is notably absent in many parts of the world, including most of Africa and Asia and much of Central and South America (Freedom to Marry Internationally, 2015). Moreover, even in nations where the shift toward endorsing gay civil rights is largest, negative attitudes toward homosexual behavior and toward sexual minorities as individuals persist (Herek, 2016). For example, findings based on a recent representative sample of US adults revealed that the majority had negative views of lesbian, gay, bisexual, and transgender (LGBT) people (Norton & Herek, 2013).

In this chapter, we examine the psychological factors that influence cross-cultural attitudes toward homosexual behavior and toward lesbian women and gay men. We acknowledge at the outset an important limitation of our approach: Most of the available research primarily addresses attitudes toward the target group "homosexuals" to the exclusion of bisexual and transgender people. When possible, we include a discussion of the factors influencing the experiences of these individuals. We begin by explaining the advantages that accrue due to heterosexual privilege and how this links to prejudice against sexual minorities. Next, we discuss how cross-cultural attitudes toward homosexuality have been assessed in the literature and describe the results of international surveys assessing correlates of these views. Finally, we present three hands-on activities, based on data from the World Values Survey (2017), that are designed to provide students with a cross-cultural perspective on sexual prejudice.

Heterosexual Privilege

The backdrop for understanding sexual minorities' struggle for civil rights and legal protection begins with the recognition that heterosexuals, as the advantaged or normative group, are automatically granted these rights. Thus, when members of a marginalized and oppressed group face discrimination and disadvantage, members of the normative group experience advantage or "heterosexual privilege." Often, members of the normative group have little to no consciousness of this protected status. In fact, one of the main psychological consequences of belonging to a privileged group is the lack of awareness that one's ingroup enjoys advantaged treatment, even among those who fully recognize that the outgroup experiences discrimination (Case, 2013).

In her famous essay about white privilege, Peggy McIntosh (1988) also described heterosexual privilege as one form of advantage individuals are socialized not to acknowledge or even recognize. McIntosh (1988) outlined some of "the daily ways in which heterosexual privilege makes some persons comfortable or powerful, providing supports, assets, approvals, and rewards to those who live or expect to live in heterosexual pairs" (p. 16). Her personal reflections on privilege revealed that, among several advantages, she is allowed and encouraged to share her relationship status as a woman married to a man and that her children enjoy educational curricula that includes representations of their household makeup of one mother and one father. Thus, as heterosexuals, the two female authors of this chapter can interact with our faculty colleagues, students, university staff, and the local coffee shop baristas without a single worry that our sexual orientation or our male spouses will be viewed negatively. No one has ever asked us about our wives or excluded us for being in a relationship with a man. In fact, we have always had the right to marry a man, be covered on his insurance if needed, or meet his family without fear of being rejected for our heterosexuality. We can also discuss our relationships at work without fear of being ostracized or fired. As members of what Audre Lorde (1984) described as the "mythical norm," heterosexuals benefit from the privilege of being not only accepted, but also lauded as the idealized romantic version of sexuality.

Heterosexual privilege also includes institutional level policies and practices, along with public policy such as state legislation, that protect the privileged group but often target the LGBT community for discrimination and limit their civil rights. Although the US Supreme Court ruled in favor of same-sex marriage rights in June 2015, many states and local municipalities continue to attempt to enact same-sex marriage bans. For example, the Tennessee state legislature considered a 2016 bill (which failed) to restrict marriage to one man and one woman and approved 100 percent defunding of the University of Tennessee-Knoxville's Office for Diversity and Inclusion. The Pride Center, serving LGBT students, was funded by that office. Several states have also passed what have come to be known as "no promo homo" laws that restrict any positive discussion of LGBT issues, and, furthermore, some require that negative information be shared with students. For example, an Alabama state code requires health education to "emphasize, in a factual manner and from a public health perspective, that homosexuality is not a lifestyle acceptable to the general public and that homosexual conduct is a criminal offense under the laws of the state" (Responsible Sexual Behaviors Act, 1992). In contrast, it would be unthinkable to target services for heterosexual students or to pass laws restricting the rights of those with a heterosexual orientation.

Internationally, many countries have enacted antisodomy laws and broader laws that legally ban same-sex conduct while privileging heterosexual behavior. As one example, the Lebanon Penal Code Article 534 states that "any sexual intercourse contrary to the order of nature is punishable by up to one year in prison" (Reid, 2017). Thus, a full appreciation of the current status of lesbian, gay, and bisexual (LGB) rights internationally requires attention to international attitudes and to the institutional-level policies that continue to oppress sexual minorities and to privilege heterosexual individuals.

Consequences of Antigay Prejudice for Individuals

Systemic oppression and discrimination, including daily microaggressions and marginalization perpetrated against LGB individuals, result in negative consequences within educational, social, and workplace settings. The research on the daily microaggressions faced by LGB people within such settings reveals a consistent pattern of insults, verbal assaults, and psychological attacks (e.g., Nadal, 2013; Sue et al., 2011); experiencing these events creates "a toxic environment for lesbian, gay, and bisexual individuals" (Meyer & Frost, 2013, p. 255) that results in both acute and chronic stress. The continual experience of this stress has severe and far-reaching consequences for LGB people's mental and physical health (Meyer, 2003; Meyer & Frost, 2013).

Of course, heterosexuals, too, experience stressors, but the source of the strain is unrelated to their sexual orientation.

Within educational institutions, LGBT people face bullying that creates a hostile learning environment (Case & Meier, 2014; Nadal, 2013). In the absence of adult allies who intervene when bullying occurs, this social context has a negative impact on mental and physical health. Adolescent students who self-identify as a sexual minority or are bullied based on peers' perceptions that they are LGBT may skip school, drop out, and fail to continue on to college (Case, Kanenberg, Erich, & Tittsworth, 2012; Nadal, 2013; Sausa, 2002).

As these targeted LGBT students transition into workplace settings, the bullying continues in the form of further microaggressions, harassment, lower salaries, fear of being fired (or not being hired/promoted), and lack of spousal and dependent benefits as a result of discrimination based on sexual orientation (Schilt & Wiswall, 2008; Sears & Mallory, 2014). LGBT individuals may remain in, or return to, the closet and hide their sexuality or gender identity due to the threat of employment discrimination. Sexual minority individuals are also less likely to seek healthcare due to lack of affordable access, and they are more likely to delay care and to delay getting needed medications (Buchmueller & Carpenter, 2010; Ward, Dahlhamer, Galinsky, & Joestl, 2014). The number of suicide attempts by LGBT individuals is four times higher than that of heterosexual individuals, and the rates are even higher for LGBT people of color and for youth from families that reject them due to sexual or gender identity (Centers for Disease Control and Prevention, 2016; Family Acceptance Project, 2009). Given these cumulative negative effects, inclusion of these concerns within cross-cultural psychology will aid in raising awareness about the impact such stressors have on sexual minorities' everyday lives.

Why Teach Sexual Orientation within Cross-Cultural Psychology?

The main pedagogical benefits of infusing sexual orientation content into psychology courses include helping students understand the complexities of sexuality across cultures, challenging their assumptions of gay rights as an issue only within Western or industrialized nations, and disrupting categorical thinking about culture and sexuality as mutually exclusive. These benefits can be directly linked to undergraduate learning goals. According to the American Psychological Association's (2013) *Guidelines for the Undergraduate Psychology Major*, students majoring in psychological science at the baccalaureate level should develop understanding and skills to enact "Ethical and Social Responsibility in a Diverse World" (APA Goal 3, p. 26) and to contribute to a "society responsive to multicultural and global concerns" (p. 26). These specified learning goals cover student knowledge of privilege, discrimination, power, and global issues such as human rights and health. Because these factors interact to affect human rights on a global scale, we argue that full inclusion of sexual orientation, sexual minority individuals' lived experiences, and heterosexual privilege in the curriculum are required to fully meet this APA learning goal (see also Kite & Bryant-Lees, 2015).

Educators who address cross-cultural issues only within a normative frame of heterosexuality, and so leave out sexual minority concerns, present a privileged view of cross-cultural issues; the resulting curriculum designs support and maintain the erroneous assumption that cultures around the world do not include a diverse array of sexualities. Even silence on sexuality will support these assumptions because the default norm of heterosexuality remains when no further information is presented. Thus, without incorporating sexual minority experiences into cross-cultural studies, educators risk giving the impression that LGB issues are relevant only within the United States and similar European nations versus being present throughout all global societies.

Incorporating sexual minority concerns also allows faculty to bring intersectional theory and analysis into the psychological study of cross-cultural issues (Case, 2017; Cole, 2009; Dill & Zambrana, 2009). Rather than providing a description of cross-cultural beliefs, our approach also encourages students to analyze power and institutional-level forces, such as public policy, that affect lives at these often invisible intersections. For example, rather than simply describing attitudes in a buffet style across cultures, our approach challenges students to think critically about societal-level structures and their influence on attitudes toward sexual minorities. For example, how do cultures with greater access to Western television and Hollywood movies view LGBT people? How might attitudes of people from a particular culture be influenced by religion, state-sanctioned discrimination or equality, or economics?

Measuring Cross-Cultural Attitudes toward Homosexuals

When examining international attitudes toward sexual minorities, people should also make sure they are knowledgeable about how attitudes toward LGB individuals are measured across different cultural settings. In general, there are two approaches to conducting this cross-cultural research. The first approach is to select two or three countries that differ in cultural orientation and then ask a sample of individuals from these cultures to complete a questionnaire about their attitudes toward LGBTs or homosexual behavior (e.g., Furnham & Saito, 2009; Nierman, Thompson, Bryan, & Mahaffey, 2007). An advantage of this approach is that researchers can directly investigate whether there are meaningful cultural attitude differences.

The second method used to assess cross-cultural attitudes toward sexual minorities is to analyze existing survey data gathered by international research projects (e.g., the World Values Survey, the International Social Science Survey). These large-scale social science surveys measure respondents' attitudes regarding a myriad of different policies and social groups, including attitudes toward sexual minorities and homosexual behavior. Because the same items are used across representative samples of each country's citizens, researchers can examine global patterns of responses, such as whether attitudes differ by geographic region. Researchers can also explore whether culture-level variables, such as religion, gender roles, or political orientation, explain country-level attitudes.

Although both of these approaches are fruitful in generating more knowledge on this topic, they also present their own set of limitations. One concern is that the survey items utilized in these studies have to be translated into another language for at least one of the samples of interest. This can pose problems because, when these items are translated, the items' content validity can become compromised (Rogler, 1999). Back-translating items into the source language and then retranslating them does not guarantee that the items' original meaning and content are retained.

An additional limitation relates specifically to the international social surveys. Because these surveys assess a wide variety of social and political issues, they typically include only one or two items about sexual minorities and these items most often focus on homosexual behavior (e.g., is it wrong?) rather than on attitudes toward homosexual persons. For example, one item in data collection Wave 5 of the World Values Survey (WVS) assessed whether homosexuality was justifiable on a 10-point rating scale. A second item asked respondents to select from a list of group members (that included "homosexuals") they would not want as a neighbor. One limitation of this latter item is that the use of the term *homosexual* is linked to negative beliefs about this social group (Herek, Kimmel, Amaro, & Melton, 1991). Also, this term does not differentiate between attitudes toward lesbian women and gay men, although research consistently shows that attitudes are more negative toward the latter group (e.g., Whitley, Kite, Ballas, & Buxton, 2017). All of these concerns limit interpretation of the reported results.

Attitudes toward Homosexuality by World Region

Despite potential methodological shortcomings, headway has been made regarding understanding where attitudes toward homosexual behavior and sexual minorities differ globally. For example, in the most recent wave of the WVS (2017), researchers asked respondents from fifty-seven countries whether they believed homosexuality was justifiable. Results showed that the majority of citizens from fifty of those countries responded negatively. Respondents in the remaining seven countries (Australia, Germany, the Netherlands, New Zealand, Spain, Sweden, and Uruguay) were more positive. The most negative attitudes were reported by respondents from the Middle East (Qatar, Jordan), Western Asia (Azerbaijan, Armenia, Georgia), and Africa (Morocco, Tunisia).

The Pew Global Attitudes Project (PGAP; 2014) examined attitudes toward societal acceptance of homosexuality in thirty-nine countries. Respondents from North American countries, the European Union, and most of Latin America (with the exceptions of Bolivia, El Salvador, and Venezuela) were the most favorable. Less favorable attitudes were more prevalent in Eastern Europe and Russia. Respondents from Australia, the Philippines, and Japan reported fairly positive attitudes, but the respondents from the remainder of the Asia/Pacific region (South Korea, China, Malaysia, Indonesia, and Pakistan) reported more negative views. Both the WVS and the PGAP are noteworthy because they cataloged attitudes from individuals of African and Middle Eastern countries where people are generally strongly opposed to homosexuality. In most of these countries, fewer than 10 percent of respondents approved; exceptions were Israel, South Africa, and Lebanon with 40 percent, 32 percent, and 18 percent, respectively, of respondents being in favor of accepting homosexuality.

Factors Affecting Cross-Cultural Attitudes

The research on cross-cultural attitudes toward LGB individuals not only focuses on where differences in attitudes emerge, but also investigates what social psychological factors are correlated with these attitudes. One factor that has been found to consistently correlate with attitudes toward homosexuality is religion. For example, results of the PGAP (2014) found less acceptance of homosexuality in countries where residents reported that religion is important to their lives. However, there were a few exceptions: in Russia, a country that scored low on religiosity, only 16 percent of respondents reported favorable attitudes. In contrast, in the Philippines and Brazil, respondents scored high on religiosity, but also reported more positive attitudes. Adamczyk and Pitt (2009) examined responses to whether homosexuality can be justified across thirty-three countries. Their results indicated that individuals from predominately Protestant countries (e.g., Korea, South Africa, the United States) and predominately Catholic countries (e.g., Chile, Mexico, the Philippines) had more favorable attitudes toward homosexuality than those from predominately Muslim countries (e.g., Bosnia, Egypt, Tanzania). Additionally, the results by Adamczyk and Pitt also indicated no major difference in attitudes between predominately Muslim countries and predominately Buddhist countries (e.g., Vietnam, Japan), Hindu countries (India), and Christian orthodox countries (e.g., Moldova, Montenegro, Serbia). Similarly, Štulhofer and Rimac (2009) reported that attitudes toward homosexuality were more positive in predominantly Catholic or Protestant countries than in predominantly Eastern Orthodox countries.

The extent to which women's and men's attitudes differ appears to vary cross-culturally. For example, few gender differences appeared in the PGAP (2014), but when they emerged, it was women who were more accepting. Adamczyk and Pitt (2009) found stronger evidence for gender differences; looking across the thirty-three countries they evaluated, men were more sexually prejudiced than women. Specific countries that mirror this result include Germany (Steffens & Wagner, 2004), Italy (Lingiardi, Falanga, & D'Augelli, 2005), Canada (Andersen & Fetner, 2008), and the United States (Whitley et al., 2017). The available evidence also suggests that people from countries with more traditional gender roles also hold more negative attitudes toward homosexuality (e.g., Nierman et al., 2007).

An additional correlate of antigay prejudice is how much personal contact respondents have with sexual minorities. Although cross-cultural research examining this issue is limited, researchers have shown that people who report less contact with LGB people also report greater prejudice in China (Lin, Button, Su, & Chen, 2016), Germany (Steffens & Wagner, 2004), Italy (Lingiardi et al., 2005), Puerto Rico (Bauermeister, Morales, Seda, & González-Rivera, 2007), Turkey (Sakalli & Uğurlu, 2003), and the United States (Cullen, Wright, & Alessandri, 2002).

Activities

Based on our review of the cross-cultural literature on attitudes toward homosexuality and homosexual people, we developed three activities that use data from the World Values Survey (2017). There is no charge for using this resource and, although the data can be downloaded, it is not necessary to do so because there is an online analysis tool. The goal of all of our activities is to encourage students to explore how and why attitudes toward sexual minorities vary cross-culturally. Instructors can tailor the activities to focus on different subgoals, such as whether attitudes differ by culture-level variables (e.g., between individualistic and collectivist cultures) or individual difference variables (e.g., religiosity). The literature review we have provided can serve as a guide to choosing what instructors want their students to explore.

World Values Survey

The World Values Survey Association collects survey data from nationally representative samples on a variety of political and economic issues (www .worldvaluessurvey.org). The association is headquartered in Stockholm, Sweden, and its members are committed to conducting and making available high-quality research. Surveys have been conducted in nearly one hundred countries, representing almost 90 percent of the world's population. Funding partners include government ministries in several countries (e.g., the Netherlands, Libya, and Russia), the US National Science Foundation and the German Science Foundation, and nonprofit foundations (e.g., the Institute for Future Studies, Stockholm). These funds also allow data collection in developing countries that do not have the resources to participate.

Advance Preparation

Instructors will need to familiarize themselves with the Online Analysis Tool (www.worldvaluessurvey.org/WVSOnline.jsp). Data are available for six waves, each spanning 5 years, beginning in 1981; the countries included vary by wave. Because the number of countries in Waves 1 and 2 is relatively limited, we recommend focusing on Waves 3–6. To assist instructors in determining which results best meet their goals, we provide a summary of countries included by wave (Table 19.1) and the variable number for the two questions that address attitudes toward homosexuality in those waves (Table 19.2).

The online database is organized by tabs. By clicking on the tabs in order from left to right, students can get the data they need to complete the activities. See Activity A (in the Appendix to this chapter) for information about how to use the tab functions. Features of the tabs include (a) the ability to select a subset of countries, (b) the ability to limit results to one variable, (c) the option of listing a crossing variable (see Activity B.4), and (d) an interactive map on the website that shows

Table 19.1 *Selected Country Inclusion by World Region and Wave Number*

World Region	Wave 3 1995–1998	Wave 4 1999–2004	Wave 5 2005–2009	Wave 6 2010–2014
Africa	Nigeria South Africa	Morocco Tanzania Zimbabwe	Ethiopia South Mali South Africa	Ghana South Africa Tunisia
Asia	China Philippines Turkey	Bangladesh Jordan South Korea	Hong Kong Iran Malaysia	Azerbaijan Pakistan Singapore
Eastern Europe	Albania Bulgaria Czech Republic	Bosnia and Herzegovina Montenegro Serbia	Hungary Poland Russian Federation	Belarus Estonia Romania
North America	El Salvador Mexico United States	Canada Mexico United States	Guatemala Mexico Trinidad and Tobago	Mexico Trinidad and Tobago United States
Oceania	Australia New Zealand	–	Australia New Zealand	Australia New Zealand
South America	Argentina Chile Venezuela	Argentina Peru Venezuela	Argentina Brazil Chile	Argentina Chile Peru
Western Europe	Norway Spain Sweden Switzerland	Spain Sweden	Andorra France Italy United Kingdom	Germany Netherlands Spain

Table 19.2 *Variable Numbers for Questions Assessing Attitudes toward Homosexuality by Wave*

Question	Wave 3: 1995–1998	Wave 4: 1999–2004	Wave 5: 2005–2009	Wave 6: 2010–2014
Mentioned would not like to have as neighbors (negative attitude)	V60	V76	V38	V40
Think homosexuality can always be justified (10), never be justified (1), or something in between	V197	V208	V202	V203

Note: V = Variable number.

responses for the chosen variable for all countries in a wave (see Activity A.3 and Figure 19.1). For example, for the "neighbors" variable, the list on the right side of the screen shows the percentage of people by country (listed alphabetically) who mentioned "homosexuals" in the "would not want as" group. Note that you must select at least one country in Tab. 2 to get the map feature to work, but the map then shows the responses from all countries that responded to that variable. By using the map feature, students can click on the world map to see results for any included country and can show results for any by clicking on the outlined area above the map (see Figure 19.1). We provide instructions for three activities based

World Values Survey Wave 6: 2010–2014

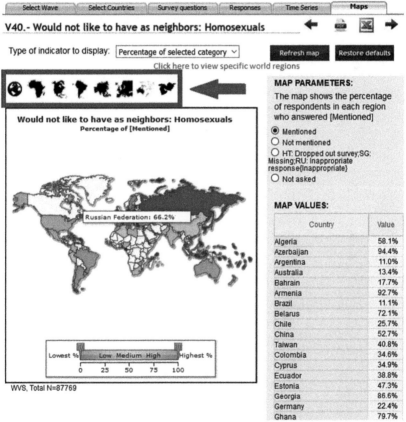

Figure 19.1   Map for attitudes toward homosexuals as neighbors [Wave 6]
Source: www.worldvaluessurvey.org/WVSOnline.jsp

on the WVS online database (see Activity A in the Appendix). All activities can be easily modified to meet specific course goals and to match students' level of statistical expertise.

Activity A: Cross-cultural Attitudes toward Homosexuality

Divide students into groups of four to six. Show students the list of countries included in the WVS (see Table 19.1) and ask them to predict which three countries hold the least accepting and which three hold the most accepting attitudes toward homosexuality. Ask them to justify their choices based on what they have learned about cross-cultural similarities and differences.

Next, provide the link for the online database and ask students to select the six countries they chose for one of the waves. Then, ask them to rank order a subset of the actual data for one of the attitudes toward homosexuality items. This can be easily done by clicking on the interactive map or by scrolling down the list by country name. Students can discuss how well the results match their predictions and the reasons for the match or mismatch. They can also discuss the cultural factors that might influence which countries' citizens are most and least accepting.

Activity B: Reflecting on Being a Sexual Minority

Assign each student to a different country from the most recent wave of the WVS database. Select a range of countries (e.g., very accepting to not at all accepting). Have students look up statistics regarding attitudes toward homosexuality in their assigned country. Students might also cross these attitudes by a number of participant demographic variables (e.g., sex or age) or by responses to variables that are generally correlated with attitudes toward homosexuality; possible variables from Wave 6 include human rights (V142), religiosity (V150–V156), sex before marriage (V206), couples living together before marriage (V43) and women's roles (V45, V47–V54).

As a homework assignment, ask students to write a one-page, single-spaced diary entry from the perspective of a sexual minority from their assigned country who is of their same age. The entry should address the hardships (or lack thereof) that a sexual minority in the student's assigned country might face. For the next class meeting, assign students to groups of four to six and ask them to role-play the person they wrote about. In each group, include students who were assigned to more or less accepting countries.

Activity C: Policy Recommendations

The goal of this activity is to have students make connections between science, policy, and their personal beliefs and how these factors can be translated into action. Have students identify five countries with the least accepting attitudes, using the map feature for either of the attitudes toward homosexuality variables. Have them also explore at least one other variable that has been found to be correlated with these attitudes (see Activity B). As a homework assignment, have students prepare a presentation that they would give to the United Nations about the experiences of LGB people in those countries. Although the WVS doesn't include attitudes toward transgender people, you may wish to have students include this group in their presentation. Their presentation should include recommendations for public policy changes that would support LGB(T) rights; these should be connected to the results of psychological science research and to concepts covered in your classes. For example, students could explain the contact hypothesis and discuss the research showing that individuals who have personal contact with sexual minorities show greater acceptance of homosexuality (e.g., Herek, 2016). This suggests that policies should be changed to make it safe for LGB(T) people to disclose their sexual orientation.

Suggestions for Discussion and Modification

We test drove Activity A in three classes on diversity-related topics. We first demonstrated how to use the website on a projection screen. We found that students, working in groups, were able to follow the instructions, but it was important to provide hard copies of Tables 19.1 and 19.2 to each group. Students were able to access the website on their cell phone, but this was not an ideal platform; we suggest encouraging students to bring a laptop on the scheduled day. Students had the most difficulty using the cross function because it presents data separately for each subgroup using a dropdown menu (see Figure 19.2).

Although we did not include this feature in our activity, students could statistically compare results across countries or by crossing variables. Based on the available data, advanced students could compute chi-square tests, t tests, or effect sizes. One feature we did not include in our activity is the Time Series feature, which produces graphs of the results across time and by country. We ourselves had difficulty getting consistent data from this Tab but encourage instructors of advanced students to explore this option because this feature can address questions such as whether acceptance is increasing over time (e.g., Smith et al., 2014).

World Values Survey Wave 6: 2010–2014

| Select Wave | Select Countries | Survey questions | **Responses** | Maps | Time Series |

V203.- Justifiable: Homosexuality   ← 🖨 ⊠ →

Breakdown by SEX   [Remove]   1. Click this drop-down menu to select a crossing variable ▊▋

Change crossing variable [-- Change -- ⌄] ⬅

Display [Show Column % (all responses) ⌄]

Choose a table

| Justifiable: Homosexuality x Country Code [Sex=Male] ⌄ |
| Justifiable: Homosexuality x Country Code [Sex=Male] |
| Justifiable: Homosexuality x Country Code [Sex=Female] |

⬅

Justifiable: Homosexuality		Azerbaijan	Spain	United States	
Never justifiable		36.2%	91.6%	7.7%	26.1%
2		3.1%	3.5%	1.4%	3.9%
3		3.2%	1.4%	1.7%	4.7%
4		2.8%	1.5%	3.3%	3.2%
5		16.1%	0.5%	15.4%	23.6%
6		5.0%	0.6%	8.5%	5.0%
7		3.9%	0.4%	8.5%	2.9%
8		5.3%	-	8.9%	5.8%
9		3.6%	0.3%	6.0%	3.8%
Always justifiable		17.8%	0.2%	33.7%	17.4%
No answer		2.1%	-	1.4%	3.5%
Don't know		0.9%	-	3.5%	-
(N) Male		2,154	495	577	1,083
Mean		4.68	1.23	7.14	5.02
Standard Deviation		3.49	0.95	2.85	3.28
Base mean		2,088	495	549	1,044

2. Once you've selected a crossing variable, click this drop-down menu to cross that variable with the chosen survey item

Selected samples: Azerbaijan 2011-2012, Spain 2011, United States 2011

Figure 19.2   Mean responses for the question of whether homosexuality is justifiable for [Wave 6] by country and participant sex

We believe students enjoyed the activity and many took time to explore additional variables. In the activity instructions, we provide a few questions for discussion but hope that instructors will modify this list based on the students' background and course goals. Issues reviewed in this chapter, such as the lack of attention to bisexuals and transgender people in these surveys or how results might differ if attitudes toward gay men and lesbians were evaluated separately, could be discussed. Measurement issues can also be considered; for example, are single-item attitude measures valid? Would the reliability of self-report data vary by country? Finally, we also note that this activity can be modified to explore a wide variety of social and political issues or personality variables, and we encourage instructors to consider its use in assessing other timely social attitudes.

APPENDIX

Student Instructions

Activity A

The goal of this activity is to explore cross-cultural attitudes toward homosexuality. This activity is based on the World Values Survey, which has data from representative samples in countries across the world. The survey questions cover a variety of social issues.

Instructions

1. Look at the list of countries that are included in one of the more recent waves of the survey in Table 19.1. As a group, choose one of the waves to explore. Before you look at the data, choose three countries that you believe will be *least accepting* and three countries you predict will be *most accepting* of homosexuality. Explain why you chose those countries.

2. Go to the Online Analysis Tool (www.worldvaluessurvey.org/ WVSOnline.jsp).

   Note that this tool is organized by tabs; by clicking on the tabs in order from left to right, you can get the data you need to test your hypothesis.

   a. Table 19.2 shows the two questions from the WVS that address attitudes toward homosexuality and the variable number for those questions for each wave. Choose the question your group wants to explore.

   b. In Tab. 1, select the wave you decided to examine.

   c. In Tab. 2, select all six countries you decided to include by checking the boxes before each country's name. Country names are listed alphabetically, reading horizontally.

   d. In Tab. 3, enter the variable number that matches the question you decided to explore. You can enter the variable in the provided box or you can scroll down to the variable and click on the variable number. This will give you the responses for your countries on your variable. Compare the actual answers to your predicted answers.

3. **Optional.** The Maps Tab has an interactive map that shows responses for the chosen variable for all countries in the wave you chose. For example, for the "neighbors" variable, a list on the right side of the page shows the percentage of people by country (listed alphabetically) that mentioned homosexuality in the "would not want as" group. Also on the Maps Tab, you can select responses for only one continent by clicking the outline of the continent on the top of the map.

   a. Use this interactive tool to find the three countries that are actually least and the three countries that are actually most accepting of homosexuality.

   b. What surprised you about the results? What country-level factors (e.g., religion, developing or developed country) might correlate with the results?

Activity B

The goal of this activity is to take the perspective of a sexual minority in one country and to think about the hardships that person might or might not face.

Instructions

1. Choose one of the countries from the most recent wave of the WVS database (see Table 19.1) or use the country that your instructor assigned you to. Go to the online database www.worldvaluessurvey .org/WVSOnline.jsp. Find the statistics regarding attitudes toward homosexuality in your assigned country.

2. Write a one-page, single-spaced diary entry from the perspective of a sexual minority you chose or your instructor assigned to you (e.g., gay man, lesbian, bisexual man, or bisexual woman) from your country who is of your same age. The entry should address the hardships (or lack thereof) that a sexual minority in your assigned country might face. Bring this entry to the next class meeting.

3. **Optional.** Under the Responses Tab, choose a crossing variable to examine (e.g., participant sex or participant age). Examine whether responses to the question differ between groups, such as women or men. Note that the results will appear in a drop-down menu; you must select each category separately to get the data.

4. **Optional.** Look up responses to questions for variables that research shows are correlated with attitudes toward homosexuality; possible variables from Wave 6 include human rights (V142), religiosity (V150–V156), sex before marriage (V206), couples living together before marriage (V43), and women's roles (V45, V47–V54). How might answers to these variables relate to country attitudes toward homosexuality? How might this affect a sexual minority's experiences in that country?

5. Your instructor will assign you to a group of four to six students. In that group, you will role-play the person you wrote about based on your diary entry. After each student has presented, discuss the similarities or differences between the experiences. Do you think those experiences would be similar or different for a sexual minority from your own country?

Activity C

The goal of this activity is think about how you can make connections between your personal beliefs, science, and public policy and how these factors can be translated into action.

Instructions

1. Identify five countries whose citizens report unaccepting attitudes toward homosexuality, using the map feature for either of the attitude toward homosexuality variables (see Activity A.1 and A.2). For example, in Wave 6, at least 80 percent of respondents from these countries mentioned homosexuals as a group they would not like to have as neighbors: Azerbaijan, Armenia, Georgia, Iraq, Morocco, Turkey, Rwanda, and Zimbabwe.

2. Explore at least one other variable that has been found to be correlated with these attitudes (see Activity B.4).

3. Prepare a presentation that you could give to the United Nations about the experiences of LGBs in at least one of the countries you chose. Your presentation should include recommendations for public policy changes that would support LGB rights.

Be sure to base your recommendations on psychological science research and theory. If possible, use concepts that have been covered in your class. For example, you might explain the contact hypothesis and discuss the research showing that individuals who have personal contact with LGBs show greater acceptance of homosexuality (e.g., Herek, 2016). This suggests that policies should be changed so that LGBs are safe in disclosing their sexual orientation.

References

Adamczyk, A., & Pitt, C. (2009). Shaping attitudes about homosexuality: The role of religion and cultural context. *Social Science Research, 39*, 338–351. doi:0.1016/j.ssresearch.2009.01.002

American Psychological Association. (2013). *APA Guidelines for Undergraduate Psychology Major, Version 2.0*. Washington, DC: Author.

Andersen, R., & Fetner, T. (2008). Cohort differences in tolerance of homosexuality: Attitudinal change in Canada and the United States, 1981–2000. *Public Opinion Quarterly, 72*, 11–330. doi:10.1093/poq/nfn017

Bauermeister, J. A., Morales, M., Seda, G., & González-Rivera, M. (2007). Sexual prejudice among Puerto Rican young adults. *Journal of Homosexuality, 53*, 135–161. doi:10.1080/00918360802103399

Buchmueller, T., & Carpenter, C. S. (2010). Disparities in health insurance coverage, access, and outcomes for individuals in same-sex versus different-sex relationships, 2000–2007. *American Journal of Public Health, 100*, 489–495. doi:10.2105/AJPH.2009.160804

Case, K. (Ed.). (2013). *Deconstructing privilege: Teaching and learning as allies in the classroom*. New York, NY: Routledge.

(Ed.). (2017). *Intersectional pedagogy: Complicating identity and social justice*. New York, NY: Routledge.

Case, K., Kanenberg, H., Erich, S., & Tittsworth, J. (2012). Transgender inclusion in university non-discrimination statements: Challenging gender-conforming privilege through student activism. *Journal of Social Issues, 68*, 145–161. doi:10.1111/j.1540-4560.2011.01741.x

Case, K., & Meier, S. C. (2014). Developing allies to transitioning and gender-nonconforming youth: Training for counselors and educators. *Journal of LGBT Youth, 11*, 62–82. doi:10.1080/19361653.2014.840764

Centers for Disease Control and Prevention. (2016). *Sexual identity, sex of sexual contacts, and health-risk behaviors among students in grades 9–12: Youth risk behavior surveillance*. Atlanta, GA: U.S. Department of Health and Human Services.

Cole, E. R. (2009). Intersectionality and research in psychology. *American Psychologist, 64*, 170–180. doi:10.1037/a0014564

Cullen, J. M., Wright, L. W., & Alessandri, M. (2002). The personality variable openness to experiences as it relates to homophobia. *Journal of Homosexuality, 42*, 119–134. doi:10.1300/J082v42n04_08

Dill, B. T., & Zambrana, R. E. (2009). Critical thinking about inequality: An emerging lens. In B. T. Dill & R. E. Zambrana (Eds.), *Emerging intersections: Race, class, and gender in theory, policy, and practice* (pp. 1–21). New Brunswick, NJ: Rutgers, The State University.

Family Acceptance Project. (2009). Family rejection as a predictor of negative health outcomes in White and Latino lesbian, gay, and bisexual young adults. *Pediatrics, 123*, 346–52.

Freedom to Marry Internationally. (2015). Retrieved from www.freedomtomarry .org/pages/the-freedom-to-marry-internationally

Furnham, A., & Saito, K. (2009). A cross-cultural study of attitudes toward and beliefs about, male homosexuality. *Journal of Homosexuality, 56*, 299–318. doi:10.1080/00918360902728525

Herek, G. M. (2016). The social psychology of sexual prejudice. In T. D. Nelson (Ed.). *Handbook of prejudice, stereotyping, and discrimination* (2nd ed., pp. 355–384). New York, NY: Psychology Press.

Herek, G. M., Kimmel, D. C., Amaro, H., & Melton, G. B. (1991). Avoiding heterosexist bias in psychological research. *American Psychologist, 46*, 957–963. doi:10.1037/0003-066X.46.9.957

Kite, M. E., & Bryant-Lees, K. B. (2016). Historical and contemporary attitudes toward homosexuality. *Teaching of Psychology, 43*, 164–170. doi:10.1177/ 0098628316636297

Lin, K., Button, D. M., Su, M., & Chen, S. (2016). Chinese college students' attitudes toward homosexuality: Exploring the effects of traditional culture and modernizing factors. *Sexuality Research and Social Policy, 13*, 158–172. doi:10.1080/19361653.2014.840764

Lingiardi, V., Falanga, S., & D'Augelli, R. (2005). The evaluation of homophobia in an Italian sample. *Archives of Sexual Behavior, 34*, 81–93. doi:10.1007/ s10508-005-1002-z

Lorde, A. (1984). *Sister outsider*. Freedom, CA: Crossing Press.

McIntosh, P. (1988). *White privilege and male privilege: A personal account of coming to see correspondences through work in women's studies*. Working Paper No. 189. Wellesley, MA: Wellesley Centers for Women.

Meyer, I. H. (2003). Prejudice, social stress, and mental health in lesbian, gay, and bisexual populations: Conceptual issues and research evidence. *Psychological Bulletin, 129*, 674–697. doi:10.1037/0033-2909.129.5.674

Meyer, I. H., & Frost, D. M. (2013). Minority stress and the health of sexual minorities. In C. J. Patterson & A. R. D'Augelli (Eds.), *Handbook of psychology and sexual orientation* (pp. 252–266). New York, NY: Oxford University Press.

Nadal, K. L. (2013). *That's so gay! Microaggressions and the lesbian, gay, bisexual, and transgender community*. Washington, DC: American Psychological Association.

Nierman, A. J., Thompson, S. C., Bryan, A., & Mahaffey, A. L. (2007). Gender role beliefs and attitudes toward lesbians and gay men in Chile and the U.S. *Sex Roles, 57*, 61–67. doi:10.1007/s11199-007-9197-1

Norton, A. T., & Herek, G. M. (2013). Heterosexuals' attitudes toward transgender people. Findings from a national probability sample of U.S. adults. *Sex Roles, 68*, 738–753. doi:10.1007/s11199-011-0110-6.

Pew Global Attitudes Project. (2014). *The global divide on homosexuality.* Retrieved from www.pewglobal.org/files/2014/05/Pew-Global-Attitudes-Homosexuality-Report-REVISED-MAY-27-2014.pdf

Reid, G. (2017). *Lebanon edges closer to decriminalizing same-sex conduct.* Human Rights Watch. Retrieved from www.hrw.org/news.

Responsible Sexual Behaviors Act. (1992). The Code of Alabama. § 16–40A-2c8.

Rogler, L. H. (1999). Methodological sources of cultural insensitivity in mental health research. *American Psychologist, 54,* 424–433. doi:10.1037/0003–066X.54.6.424

Sakalli, N., & Uğurlu, O. (2001). Effects of social contact with homosexuals on heterosexual Turkish university students' attitudes towards homosexuality. *Journal of Homosexuality, 42,* 53–62. doi:10.1300/J082v42n03_04

Sausa, L. A. (2002). Updating college and university campus policies. *Journal of Lesbian Studies, 6,* 43–55. doi:10.1300/J155v06n03_05

Schilt, K., & Wiswall, M. (2008). Before and after: Gender transitions, human capital, and workplace experiences. Article 39. *B.E. Journal of Economic Analysis and Policy, 8.*

Sears, B., & Mallory, C. (2014). Employment discrimination against LGBT people: Existence and impact. In C. M. Duffy & D. M. Visconti (Eds.), *Gender identity and sexual orientation discrimination in the workplace* (pp. 40-1–40-19). Arlington, VA: Bloomberg BNA.

Smith, T. W., Son, J., & Kim, J. (2014). *Public attitudes toward homosexuality and gay rights across time and countries.* Los Angeles: Williams Institute. Retrieved from https://williamsinstitute.law.ucla.edu/research/international/public-attitudes-nov-2014/

Steffens, M.C., & Wagner, C. (2004). Attitudes toward lesbians, gay men, bisexual women, and bisexual men in Germany. *Journal of Sex Research, 41,* 137–149. doi:10.1080/00224490409552222

Štulhofer, A., & Rimac, I. (2009). Determinants of homonegativity in Europe. *Journal of Sex Research, 46,* 24–32. doi:10.1080/00224490802398373

Sue, D. W., Nadal, K. L., Capodilupo, C. M., Lin., A. I., Torino, G. C., & Rivera, D. P. (2011). Racial microaggressions against Black Americans: Implications for counseling. *Journal of Counseling and Development, 86,* 330–338. doi:10.1002/j.1556-6678.2008.tb00517.x

Ward, B. W., Dahlhamer, J. M., Galinsky, A. M., Joestl, S. S. (2014). Sexual orientation and health among U.S. adults: National health interview survey, 2013. *National Health Stat Report, 77,* 1–10.

Whitley, B. E., Jr., Kite, M. E., Ballas, H., & Buxton, K. (2017, April). *Gender differences in heterosexuals' attitudes toward homosexuality: Twenty years later.* Poster presented at the Meeting of the Midwestern Psychological Association, Chicago.

World Values Survey Association. (2017). *World Values Survey.* Retrieved from www.worldvaluessurvey.org/wvs.jsp

CHAPTER 20

Peace Psychology: A Gateway and Path to Culture and Diversity

Linda M. Woolf and Michael R. Hulsizer

Around the globe and across communities, individuals deal daily with issues of distress, conflict, and, all too often, violence. From intrapersonal struggles to sweeping forms of mass destruction, such as war and genocide, issues of peace and conflict impact all of our lives. Additionally, institutional, societal, and structural forms of violence perpetuate injustices against marginalized individuals and communities based on differences such as income, gender, and ethnicity. Considering the influence of peace, conflict, and violence across the human condition, it is imperative that teachers integrate research and information concerning peace psychology across the curriculum.

At its core, peace psychology is cross-cultural in perspective with an eye toward addressing issues of diversity across all topics. As such, it is not difficult to ensure that teachers of peace psychology integrate culture into their classes. Rather, it is imperative that peace psychology teachers not neglect the dominant culture within the classroom as somehow exempt from course topics (e.g., human rights violations, structural violence). Although the topic of this chapter is the integration of culture into a peace psychology course, the chapter may be most useful to teachers of other courses. In fact, many peace psychology topics can easily be integrated across the psychology curriculum as a means to infuse issues of diversity and culture into more traditional psychology coursework. Hence, peace psychology is not just a path to understanding the importance of culture and diversity but also a gateway to integrate such topics across a range of psychology courses.

What Is Peace Psychology?

Peace psychology is a broad, interdisciplinary branch of psychology that synthesizes research and theory from both within and outside psychology. Indeed, peace psychologists draw on research from community, social, clinical, political, positive, media, trauma, developmental, and other branches of psychology as well as history, political science, international relations, religion, human rights, sociology, education, and peace studies. As a discipline, peace psychology aims to address peace on all levels, from the intrapersonal and interpersonal to broader issues impacting communities, nation-states, and international relations. Ultimately, the goal of peace psychology is to help build stable, just, and equitable cultures of peace. As such, peace psychologists not only address issues of global conflict but also recognize the importance of mindfulness, forgiveness, safe homes and families, meaningful employment, just social structures and institutions, recovery of trauma, social justice, and fundamental human rights.

Key concepts within peace psychology include the difference between negative and positive peace; direct and structural forms of violence; peacekeeping, peacemaking, and peacebuilding; psychosocial roots of mass violence; social justice; and human rights for all individuals. For example, negative peace focuses on interventions and strategies aimed at promoting a state of nonviolence and the elimination of direct forms of violence (e.g., crime, battering). Positive peace focuses on reducing and ameliorating the effects of structural forms of bias and violence. Cultures that do not aim to reduce ethnocentrism, nationalism, sexism, racism, ageism, homophobia, poverty, or other forms of social, political, economic, and ecological injustices cannot achieve positive peace. Ultimately, peacebuilding focuses on reducing structural violence and building communities characterized by conditions of social equality and social justice, and grounded in human rights. Of course, the creation of such communities may threaten the status quo and reduce the amount of privilege enjoyed by a majority culture. Hence, the steps to building communities of peace also must involve paths of critical self-evaluation both intra- and interpersonally, open dialogue, collaborative problem solving, peacemaking, diplomacy, and restorative justice.

Although the history of peace psychology can be traced to William James (1906) and his essay, *The Moral Equivalent of War*, as a discipline, it remains a relatively new distinct area of study within psychology. In 1990, the American Psychological Association (APA) established the Division of Peace Psychology (Division 48; The Society for the Study of Peace, Conflict, and Violence). Yet as of 2017, there was only one peace psychology graduate program – at the University of Massachusetts at Amherst: which was established in 2004. A perusal of the Division 48 webpage (http://peacepsychology.org/peace-course-syllabi/) reveals fewer than thirty peace psychology-related courses on its Teach Peace Courses web-page. Moreover, very few introductory psychology or social psychology textbooks include chapters or sections related to peace psychology or peace and conflict. Those texts directly related to peace psychology are primarily edited texts designed for professional audiences – making them difficult to use in the typical psychology course. These curricular impediments have made it a challenge for the field of peace psychology to become main-stream within psychology education, whether graduate or undergraduate.

Fortunately, there is an increasing number of resources available for psychology instructors to incorporate peace psychology into their courses. For example, Office of Teaching Resources in Psychology (http://teachp sych.org/page-1603066) of APA Division 2 (Society for the Teaching of Psychology) has a wealth of information related to topics of diversity, international psychology, and the psychology of peace and mass violence, which touch on most elements associated with peace psychology. The Society for the Psychological Study of Social Issues (www.spssi.org/) and the Peace Psychology Division (http://peacepsychology.org/) also include teaching resources on their websites. In addition, information about lecture suggestions, activities, and social learning projects appears at the end of this chapter.

Why the Integration of Culture Is Important to the Teaching of Peace Psychology

Peace psychologists often work in multicultural and international settings. Whether a peace psychologist is working with the survivors of genocide in Rwanda or addressing the effects of a police shooting in the United States, cross-cultural competence is imperative. Certainly, a psychologist cannot go into non-Western cultures and assume that what they have learned about Western psychological practices will translate into healing. For example, when working abroad, a peace psychologist must work with indigenous healers to create meaningful programs aimed at individual and community recovery, reconciliation, and reconstruction. Similarly, peace psychologists need to understand the communities they are entering when working throughout the United States. For example, when working with a group, neighborhood, or city in the aftermath of a police shooting, a psychologist needs local cultural awareness and competence. A lack of cultural sensitivity and failure to understand the consequences of margin-alization, social inequalities, and long-term structural forms of violence may lead a peace psychologist to incorrect, incomplete, or harmful responses to such a shooting. Understandably, most peace psychology courses focus heavily on issues of diversity and cultural competence.

Ironically, the biggest challenge in teaching peace psychology is ensuring that the course isn't identified as only being about "the other." Indeed, much of the work of peace psychologists occurs on the international stage and is, by its very nature, cross-cultural. For example, peace psychologists work with the victims of ecological disasters, war, and ethnocide, as well as child soldiers, individuals who are trafficked, and others who are victims of a host of human rights violations. Instructors need to be careful when coming up with examples of peace psychology in action, as they may unintentionally perpetuate the notion of American exceptionalism (Donnelly, 1998). Using examples of peace psychology in action from other countries may perpetuate the belief that the United States is superior to most other countries and that "human rights problems exist only in places that must be reached by crossing large bodies of salt water" (Donnelly, 1998, p. 88).

It is imperative that students recognize the significant issues of peace and conflict that occur in the United States. These conflicts and human rights violations are often grounded in inequitable but normalized social and political structures. Human rights violations and other forms of structural violence are ubiquitous and seemingly invisible, but no less important to study, understand, and seek to reduce. Our students need to recognize and critically evaluate such "at home" issues within a peace psychology course.

Key Concepts Most Likely to Be Misunderstood if Not Presented in Cultural Context

Almost any topic within peace psychology is likely to be misunderstood if not presented with an eye toward diversity and cultural context. One cannot understand or effectively respond to issues of direct violence (e.g., domestic violence, war) or structural violence (e.g., cultural acceptance of human rights violations, institutional forms of bias) without understanding the unique social, political, and cultural contexts of these harms. This section will highlight only a few key issues as well as practical examples.

Human Rights

The United Nations (UN; 1948) codified human rights under international law with the ratification of the Universal Declaration of Human

Rights (UDHR). This document outlined thirty articles grounded in social, cultural, economic, civil, and political rights. These rights are inherent in all individuals, indivisible and inalienable. The UN has further codified these rights through a range of additional conventions, principles, and protocols focusing on specific issues (e.g., International Covenant on Civil and Political Rights; the International Covenant on Economic, Social and Cultural Rights [ICESCR]; Convention against Torture and Other Cruel, Inhuman or Degrading Treatment or Punishment), and populations (e.g., Convention on the Rights of the Child [CRC]; Convention on the Elimination of All Forms of Discrimination against Women [CEDAW]; United Nations Principles for Older Persons; Convention on the Rights of Persons with Disabilities).

Although APA and other psychological societies have issued statements consistent with human rights as well as incorporated human rights mandates into their ethics codes, students of psychology receive very little human rights education. As such, students often perceive human rights violations as those committed by "others" in distant cultures and lands. They may be blind to those violations occurring in their own country. Instead, students may believe that the United States is the pinnacle of human rights (i.e., American exceptionalism). Upon entering the course, students may have only a cursory understanding of human rights violations or the structures that facilitate normalizing human rights violations within a society. Thus, teachers of psychology may want to begin a discussion of human rights with documents such as the CRC, CEDAW, or ICESCR, and analyze why the United States has not ratified these conventions. For example, students are often surprised to find that the United States is one of only two countries not to ratify the CRC or is one of a half dozen that is not a signatory to ending CEDAW.

These analyses can lead to fruitful discussions of what constitutes violations against these populations, particularly as identities intersect with other forms of diversity such as ethnicity/culture, race, gender identity, sexual orientation, or disability. Such discussions can lead to analyses of topics like healthcare, education, and housing from a human rights perspective and the barriers to attainment of full human rights that exist in society. Certainly, teachers can discuss with their students the issue of torture within the context of the Global War on Terror and the history of psychologists' roles in the facilitation of "enhanced interrogations" and torture (see Woolf, 2016a). Issues of homelessness, the death penalty, disparate rates of incarceration based on race, and a host of other topics can be discussed from a peace psychology and human rights perspective.

Terrorism

Students are exposed regularly to news about international terrorism. When these incidents occur, terrorism headlines and news stories often fill the airways and social media for days. Unfortunately, it is often difficult to find accurate, objective, nonbiased information about these incidents. The experience is much like standing in front of a fire hose that is coming from the hydrant associated with your political ideology. This onslaught of information is often biased and serves to confirm initial stereotypes. Ambiguous information is distorted to fit with preexisting beliefs. Any information contrary to one's ideology is often discarded. Complicating matters are legitimate examples of fake news, which further polarize the beliefs of recipients. Indeed, the misuse of the term "fake news" by those in positions of authority has further blurred the lines between objective and biased news.

Similarly, individuals exposed to information solely about international terrorism may come to believe that "radical Islamic terrorism" is the core problem and hence demonize an entire religion and the peoples practicing that religion. Yet many of the root dynamics and destructive outcomes of domestic terrorism (e.g., bombing of the Murrah Federal Building in Oklahoma City; hate crimes) are grounded in similar psychosocial foundations (Woolf & Hulsizer, 2002/2003, 2004). Through comparative analyses, students can come to understand the similarities and dangers of extremist beliefs and groups that impact not only those abroad but within a dominant culture as well. The Southern Poverty Law Center (SPL) provides a host of resources related to tracking domestic terrorism in the United States (see www.SPLCenter.org).

Post-Traumatic Stress Disorder (PTSD)

Psychologists have researched PTSD for decades and much is known about the causes and treatments for it with populations in the United States. However, such treatments may not work well with marginalized populations (Comas-Díaz, 2000), victims of human rights violations (Baker, 1995), differing cultural backgrounds (Kira, 2010), immigrants or refugees (Qureshi, Bagué, Ghali, & Collazos, 2015), or in response to large-scale disasters or atrocities (Hamber et al., 2015; Lykes, 1996; Marsella & Christopher, 2004). For example, Comas-Díaz (2000) argued that we cannot truly understand or respond to PTSD unless we further address the effects of racism as a form of long-term ethnopolitical violence.

Any treatment that fails to take into account ongoing structural violence and its influence on individuals and communities may lead to increased harm and marginalization.

Wessells and Monteiro (2001) worked with the reintegration of child soldiers into their communities following the protracted war in Angola. Children were often forced into service as soldiers and forced to kill members of their communities as a means of indoctrination and recruitment into militias. Following the war, and as part of postconflict reconstruction, it was necessary to reintegrate these traumatized children back into their communities. Western approaches to PTSD would not have taken into account the unique cultural and spiritual beliefs of these children and their communities. However, Wessells and Monteiro worked with indigenous healers to create meaningful approaches to facilitate healing that included the integration of knowledge concerning the psychosocial effects and treatment of trauma with traditional healing purification rituals.

In 1994, the Rwandan genocide resulted in the loss of over 800,000 Tutsi lives in just 100 days – deaths largely by clubbing or machete. It was one of the most intense and brutal genocides of the twentieth century. The Rwandan genocide was fueled by the use of radio as a component of genocide – radio personalities encouraged the genocide and identified the locations of individuals who fled into hiding. Indeed, radio announcers were charged and convicted of the crime of genocide.

Staub, Pearlman, Gubin, and Hagengimana (2005) used Radio La Benevolencija to facilitate healing and community reconciliation following the genocide using a radio drama and informational programming. Staub and colleagues partnered with La Benevolencija, a Dutch nongovernmental organization, to create the program Musekeweya (New Dawn). This program used radio as the means of communication, recognizing that radio is the dominant medium in Rwanda. Listeners followed the lives of the characters in the program as they struggled to deal with the aftermath of the genocide in their own lives as victims, perpetrators, and bystanders. Over the course of years, listeners learned more about what led to the genocide, the people as they healed, and the creation of a shared history leading to rebuilding of lives, a path to justice, and reconciliation. In 2010, an estimated 85 percent of the Rwandan population regularly listened to Musekeweya (Kogen & Price, 2014). The large-scale program was evaluated and determined to be successful as part of the country's ongoing efforts for reconciliation and reconstruction. Much of the program's success can be attributed to the fact that it was culturally embedded and grounded in research concerning the psychosocial roots of genocide.

For a brief vignette related to teaching about this project, which includes links to video, see Woolf (2016b).

Infusion of Cultural Concepts in the Teaching of Peace Psychology

The key to infusing cultural concepts into a peace psychology course is to ensure that issues are discussed from a comparative perspective inclusive of information from a host of cultural perspectives, including those peace and conflict issues within the dominant culture. For example, any examination of domestic violence is incomplete without a discussion of patriarchy, the division between public and private spheres within cultures, and/or a discussion of cross-cultural differences and values. In addition, any discussion of domestic violence must look at this behavior across genders, sexual orientation, age, and disability.

Similarly, issues related to lesbian, gay, bisexual, transgendered, queer, intersex, and asexual (LGBTQIA) populations can be discussed and compared in terms of laws and biases in the United States and around the globe. Although the United States, for example, now has achieved marriage equality, codified discrimination still exists in relation to credit, housing, employment, and a host of other civil rights (Woolf & MacCartney, 2014). Barriers to equality exist around the globe, including the criminalization of LGBTQIA individuals in some regions of the world, inclusive of torture and the death penalty. An understanding of the roots of such bias and hatred must be explored from a cross-cultural perspective and should involve an examination of the misuse of religion and ideology.

One hurdle associated with any discussion of aggression is the fact that students in the United States have been largely desensitized to violence. When compared to other similar industrialized countries in Europe and Asia, the United States has a much higher homicide rate. Not surprisingly, the United States typically has at least five major cities (e.g., New Orleans, St. Louis, Detroit, Baltimore, Oakland) in the top fifty most dangerous cities in the world. However, it is important to point out that crime is complex and that these top fifty most dangerous city lists tend to gloss over the multitude of reasons why one society may be more violent than another. For example, the United States does have a very unique type of violence, one not as prevalent elsewhere across the globe – gun violence.

Citizens in the United States, as compared to the rest of the world, have the greatest access to firearms. Gun rights activists claim that the solution to violence in the United States is more gun ownership by law-abiding citizens. They maintain that knowledge that a potential victim is carrying a firearm might deter a would-be criminal. There are reports, supporting this assertion, which suggest that concealed carry laws have reduced homicide rates (e.g., Lott, 2010). However, other studies have suggested that the link between concealed carry laws and crime reduction is false and the result of selective data mining (e.g., Wellford, Pepper, & Petrie, 2005).

Interestingly, there are cultural differences within the United States in the degree to which violence is perceived as an acceptable response to conflict. For example, researchers have noted that southern states have higher rates of violence as compared to the rest of the United States (Nisbett & Cohen, 1996). The researchers proposed that these differences were due to the cultural traditions associated with early settlers in this region. However, the tendency toward violence may have more to do with poverty, availability of firearms, and political ideology.

Although there is some controversy about the role culture plays in the higher incidence of violence associated with the US South, there is little controversy as to the role culture plays during times of war. Propaganda and the creation of enemy images has been an essential element in wartime throughout the ages. As noted by Urie Bronfenbrenner (1961) and peace psychologists such as Ralph White (1991), propaganda may involve the development of enemy mirror-images – the process by which each country or religion comes to view the other as evil, mad, the aggressor, and untrustworthy. White (1984) stated, "An exaggerated, literally diabolical image of another country – a country that is actually composed of human beings not so very different from the citizens of one's own country – is in my judgment the very taproot of war in the present-day world" (p. 121).

One interesting aspect of wartime propaganda that can be discussed in the classroom is the cultural variability that exists in the means by which countries portray their wartime counterparts. These often stereotypical images are important as they provide a rationale for engaging in violence but also highlight cultural beliefs and fears. Indeed, the main goal of wartime propaganda is to garner support for or enhance the likelihood of aggressive behavior directed toward another human being. To this end, wartime propaganda is extremely effective. For example, according to Keen (1991), during World War II, Japanese soldiers were portrayed as inhuman, treacherous, sly, sadistic, and unwilling to surrender. Unlike the propaganda used by the United States, Japanese propaganda focused on the political leadership in the United States. They portrayed President Franklin Roosevelt as demonic, bloodthirsty, and seeking the complete annihilation of the Japanese homeland. As a result, the Japanese continued to fight long after they had any chance at success.

Have we left this sort of *us versus them* propaganda behind since the end of WWII? Of course not. Our current political climate can be viewed as another real-time example of this us versus them mind-set. Since the beginning of the Global War on Terrorism, images in political cartoons and other media (e.g., television, film) have characterized individuals of Arab descent or Muslims as uncivilized fanatics, misogynists, and barbaric terrorists (Shaheen, 2003). Following the attacks of 9/11, anti-Muslim hate crimes went up over 1,600 percent (Federal Bureau of Investigation, 2001). In 2017, enemy images, often through political rhetoric, continued to fuel anti-Muslim and anti-Arab bias in the United States. Indeed, the Southern Poverty Law Center (Potok, 2017) noted a 197 percent increase in anti-Muslim hate groups in just 1 year's time, and CNN (Burke, 2017) reported that anti-Muslim hate crimes spiked over 67 percent, once again reaching 2001 levels. Teachers can foster discussion and analysis of such images and political rhetoric in the classroom, grounded in research concerning cultural stereotyping, prejudice, discrimination, political agenda setting and framing, and enemy images.

Teaching Activities

There are many activities or projects that students can engage in or do to explore cultural concepts within a peace psychology course. For example, students can learn about the impact of structural forms of violence in relation to education by examining videos such as *Waiting for Superman* (Guggenheim et al., 2011) and *The First Grader* (Feuer, Thompson, & Harding, & 20th Century Fox, 2011). *Waiting for Superman* described dropout factories in the United States and barriers to poor children's education – barriers that promote social injustice and equality in the United States. The film *The First Grader* highlighted the barriers to education in Kenya following implementation of free public school for children. Clips from these videos can be compared to highlight similar issues from different cultural perspectives. Students also can search for additional video clips to augment discussion and analysis from across cultures and incorporating information related to barriers to education based gender, sexual orientation, or disability.

It is not uncommon for students to express the belief that the United States is no more violent than other cultures. Indeed, they often argue that violence is a natural part of the human evolutionary process, misquoting

Spencer's (1864) idea of "survival of the fittest" (p. 474). If one examines such logic from an evolutionary perspective, it is clear that other factors such as prosocial behavior, cooperation for mutual survival, group organizational abilities, and language development played a more pivotal role in humanity's survival than aggressive behavior (Turnbaugh, Jurmain, Kilgore, & Nelson, 2001). A nice technique to illustrate how desensitized individuals in the United States are to violence is to discuss the findings of Bushman and Anderson (2001). In this meta-analysis, the authors provided the results of their examination of the violent media/aggression link. They also examined some well accepted cause/effect links, which should be familiar to students. For example, ask students if they think there is a connection between smoking cigarettes and lung cancer. Most will state yes. Then ask if they think it would be a good idea to inhale asbestos, ingest lead paint, or have unprotected sex. The vast majority will indicate these behaviors are unhealthy. Yet all but one of these relationships (smoking and cancer) is less well established than the link between media violence and aggression. Some students will really question these findings. After all, they have watched plenty of media violence and they have not gone out and killed anyone. This approach can lead to a very interesting discussion not only about media violence and aggression but also cultural perceptions of violence.

Additional ideas can include activities such as genocide case analysis, prejudice role playing exercises, survivors of conflict/genocide interviews, peacebuilding projects, etc. For more information about such activities in relation to teaching peace psychology, see Hulsizer and Woolf (2012), Woolf (2017), and Woolf and Hulsizer (2011). Kingston (2012) further developed a case for increasing human rights education at the undergraduate level.

Infusion into Traditional Psychology Courses

Peace psychology may be nicely integrated into traditional psychology courses as a path to increasing cross-cultural content. Many peace psychology topics and concepts also help students critically evaluate their world, their cultural perspectives, and biases. For example, as discussed, attitudes toward gun violence and the psychosocial meaning behind guns not only varies across the United States, but also within individual communities. In relation to guns, as well as a host of other structural violence factors such as prejudice and discrimination, individuals may live in the same community but have very different experiences of those communities and cultures.

The following brief lecture and activity suggestions do not represent a comprehensive listing of ideas. Rather, we present these ideas as a means to get teachers thinking about paths to integrating topics of peace and culture within their traditional psychology courses. Although some topics can be easily pigeon-holed into a specific psychology domain (e.g., learning, ethics), other topics may cut across different domains and hence be applicable in a range of lectures or courses. Ultimately, there are no limits as to how peace psychology can be integrated into the curriculum as a cross-cultural tool – it is largely a matter of one's imagination.

Hero rats. Operant conditioning is a staple in most introductory psychology courses. When it comes to providing students with examples of these concepts, teachers often resort to using pigeons in Skinner boxes or the application of these techniques to training one's dog to sit. A nice alternative is to introduce students to "hero rats" (see www.apopo.org/en/). Hero rats are African pouched rats trained to save lives. In such disparate places as Columbia and Tanzania, these rats sniff out landmines as well as detect tuberculosis in patients. Indeed, it is estimated that over 105,000 landmines have been detected and destroyed with millions of acres of land now usable to communities, thanks to these hero rats. Frantz (2016) authored a nice blog post discussing the use of hero rats to teach conditioning with links to useful videos and web pages.

SNAP challenge. Food insecurity is experienced by millions of individuals around the globe. Although some of our students may have experienced the challenges of hunger, most college students in the United States have had limited experience with famine, food scarcity, or ongoing hunger. Often, as an alternative extra credit assignment in developmental courses, the SNAP challenge can be introduced to students (Misyak, Helms, Mann, & Serrano, 2015; Webb, 2011). This exercise is designed to provide individuals a sense of what it would be like to live on the approximately $4.00 per day allotted by food stamps in the United States. Generally, the SNAP challenge lasts a week, but some churches, colleges, and other organizations have instituted longer challenges. Students should first review the basic rules (e.g., "Yes, Starbucks counts towards your daily total" and "No, you cannot just sponge off your friends for your meals"; you must drink and eat only what you purchased during that time). Most importantly, students should explore, discuss, and understand the context of food stamps as part of an individual's overall socioeconomic status.

Food stamps are designed to be a supplement covering about two-thirds of one's daily food costs. However, all too often, states have policies limiting assets (e.g., value of cars or other property) and severely limiting income. Hence, there may be days when one has a little extra money but many more days when one might have to make a choice between paying one's electric bill, purchasing medication, paying bus fare, or eating. It is important that students journalize about and discuss their experiences, placing their challenge in context. What is often most notable in this exercise is the amount of time that students report obsessing about food throughout their days as well as the impact on their cognitive processing. Such an activity is useful in contextualizing the impact of poverty on food security, ability for children to perform well in school, physical wellness, and a host of structural violence concerns. The SNAP Challenge Toolkit can be downloaded at http://frac.org/wp-content/uploads/take-action-snap-challenge-toolkit.pdf.

Responding to trauma. Many psychology courses examine the effect of trauma on the individual and community level. In clinical, counseling, positive, community, health, and other psychology courses, teachers can expand on trauma-related concepts, including discussions related to refugees and their families residing in the United States (e.g., American Psychological Association, 2010), the impact of trafficking (Task Force on Trafficking of Women and Girls, 2014), and the role of forgiveness in healing from trauma, including international conflict (Borris, 2011; Borris-Dunchunstang, 2007).

Truth and reconciliation commissions. When violent and hateful incidents divide communities, teachers can introduce the concepts associated with truth and reconciliation commissions (for a good overview, see Minow, 1998, 2008). Although students may have heard of the South African Truth and Reconciliation Commission, most may be unaware of the benefits of such programs around the globe, including countries such as the United States. Students can explore, contrast, and examine the goals associated with such commissions. For example, students can study the Greensboro Truth and Reconciliation Commission (2006; Jovanovic, 2012) and contrast this approach with another commission in South Africa (Fourie, Gobodo-Madikizela, & Stein, 2013), Peru (Espinosa et al., 2016), or other regions. Discussion of such programs can lead to further analyses related to the benefits of restorative justice programs. Such programs in the United States are particularly useful with youthful offenders who may otherwise find themselves in the poverty-to-prison pipeline (Umbreit & Armour, 2010).

Moral disengagement. Bandura's (1999; 2016) theory of moral disengagement is a useful gateway in social psychology, community, or political psychology classes to examine a host of topics from the death penalty to torture and genocide. Bandura described a process whereby reprehensible behavior becomes "acceptable" and perpetrators come to disengage from victims, often viewing them as less than human. Sadly, many of the greatest human rights violations that have been committed "for the greater good" and for all the "right" reasons can be traced through the process of moral disengagement. Students can expand on Bandura's ideas to additional harms such as homelessness, bullying, hate crimes, or other topics of relevance to their daily lives. This theory can be contrasted with Opotow's (2001) theory of moral exclusion, which highlights the role of structural violence in relation to the process of disengagement.

Ethics. Although most psychology courses provide material about research ethics, including informed consent, teachers often do not discuss the historical roots of such codes. For example, students can be introduced to the Nuremberg Code, which highlights ten fundamental tenets associated with research ethics. This code can be explored and examined within the context of more current codes. Although it is easy to highlight the creation of this code based on Nazi atrocities related to medical experimentation, that is an incomplete picture. Instead, the code can also be explored in relation to the Japanese biochemical warfare experimentation, primarily in China during World War II (Harris, 2002), the US Cold War experimentation (Goliszek, 2003), medical experimentation by US doctors and pharmaceutical companies around the globe (e.g., Subramanian, 2017), and the Tuskegee syphilis study (Jones, 1993; Washington, 2008). Tuskegee, in particular, can be examined to introduce the Belmont principles.

Through an examination of the disparate nature of these human rights violations occurring under the guise of medical experimentation, students can come to learn the underlying ideas and rationales for our current ethics codes – codes that are not simply a set of rules and procedures. Moreover, students can discuss the rationales for these experiments and why they were deemed "acceptable" based on the populations used as "participants." As discussed earlier, these violations can also be examined using Bandura's (2016) theory of moral disengagement. Finally, ethical dilemmas can be further explored in relation to conducting research across cultures where there may be issues of legal consent related to age, gender, citizenship status, disability, or other factors that may limit an individual's ability to give consent or expect confidentiality.

As noted, these examples highlight just some of the creative ways that culture and peace psychology topics can be integrated into traditional psychology courses. Additional ideas can range from evaluating online hate sites as part of media psychology classes to the development of peace-related service learning projects aimed at developing cross-cutting relationships on college campuses or within communities. An additional benefit of a service learning project is that social action can help move students from the possibility of potential despair, psychophysical numbing, and bystander inaction to involvement and recognition that they possess the tools to make a difference in the world.

Teaching Resources or Materials

Blumberg, H. H., Hare, A. P., & Costin, A. (Eds.). (2007). *Peace psychology: A comprehensive introduction*. Cambridge: Cambridge University Press.

Christie, D. J., Wagner, R. V., & Winter, D. D. (Eds.). (2001). *Peace, conflict, and violence: Peace psychology for the 21st century*. Englewood Cliffs, NJ: Prentice-Hall.

Hulsizer, M. R., & Woolf, L. M. (2012). Enhancing the role of international human rights in the psychology curriculum. *Psychology Learning and Teaching, 11*, 382–387. doi:10.2304/plat.2012.11.3.382

Mayton, D. (2009). *Nonviolence and peace psychology: Intrapersonal, interpersonal, societal, and world peace*. New York, NY: Springer. doi:10.1007/978-0-387-89348-8

Society for the Study of Peace, Conflict, and Violence. (Division 48, APA). (n.d.). Teach Peace web resources, http://peacepsychology.org/peace-course-syllabi/

United Nations. (2015a). The Core International Human Rights Instruments and their monitoring bodies. Retrieved from www.ohchr.org/EN/ProfessionalInterest/Pages/CoreInstruments.aspx

    (2015b). List of human rights issues. Retrieved from www.ohchr.org/EN/Issues/Pages/ListofIssues.aspx

Woolf, L. M. (2016). Teaching psychology: Infusing human rights. *Psychology Teacher Network, 26*(1). Retrieved from www.apa.org/ed/precollege/ptn/2016/02/human-rights.aspx

    (2017). Psychology education. A path to human rights and social responsibility. In R. L. Miller & T. Collette (Eds.), *Teaching Tips: A Compendium of Conference Presentations on Teaching, 2015–16*. Retrieved from http://teachpsych.org/ebooks/teachingtips

Woolf, L. M., & Hulsizer, M. R. (2004). Psychology of peace and mass violence – Genocide, torture, and human rights: Informational resources. *OTRP-Online*. Retrieved from the Society for the Teaching of Psychology website, http://teachpsych.org/resources/Documents/otrp/resources/woolf04genocide.pdf

    (2004). Psychology of peace and mass violence: Instructional resources. *OTRP-Online*. Retrieved from the Society for the Teaching of Psychology website, http://teachpsych.org/resources/Documents/otrp/resources/woolf04instr.pdf

(2004). Psychology of peace and mass violence – War, ethnopolitical conflict, terrorism, and peace: Informational resources. *OTRP-Online*, Retrieved from the Society for the Teaching of Psychology, http://teachpsych.org/resources/Documents/otrp/resources/woolf04war.pdf

(2011). Peace and war. In R. L. Miller, E. Balcetis, S. R. Burns, D. B. Daniel, B. K. Saville, & W. D. Woody (Eds.), *Promoting student engagement* (Vol. 2, pp. 225–229). Retrieved from the Society for the Teaching of Psychology, http://teachpsych.org/ebooks/pse2011/vol2/index.php

References

American Psychological Association. (2010). *Resilience and recovery after war: Refugee children and families in the United States.* Washington, DC: Author. Retrieved from www.apa.org/pubs/info/reports/refugees-full-report.pdf

Bandura, A. (1999). Moral disengagement in the perpetration of inhumanities. *Personality & Social Psychology Review*, *3*, 193–209. doi:10.1207/s15327957pspr0303_3

(2016). *Moral disengagement: How people do harm and live with themselves.* New York, NY: Worth.

Becker, D. (1995). The deficiency of the concept of posttraumatic stress disorder when dealing with victims of human rights violations. In R. J. Kleber, C. R. Figley, & P. R. Gersons (Eds.), *Beyond trauma: Cultural and societal dynamics* (pp. 99–110). New York: Plenum. doi:10.1007/978-1-4757-9421-2_6

Borris, E. R. (2011). Forgiveness and the healing of nations. *Dialogue & Alliance*, *25*, 59–64.

Borris-Dunchunstang, E. R. (2007) *Finding forgiveness: A 7-step program for letting go of anger and bitterness.* New York, NY: McGraw-Hill.

Bronfenbrenner, U. (1961). The mirror image in Soviet–American relations: A social psychologist's report. *Journal of Social Issues*, *17*(3), 45–56. doi:10.1111/j.1540-4560.1961.tb01682.x

Burke, D. (2017, January 30). Anti-Muslim hate crimes: Ignorance in action? Retrieved from www.cnn.com/2017/01/30/us/islamerica-excerpt-hate-crimes/

Bushman, B. J., & Anderson, C. A. (2001). Media violence and the American public: Scientific facts versus media misinformation. *American Psychologist*, *56*, 477–489. doi:10.1037//0003-066X.56.6-7.477

Comas-Díaz, L. (2000). An ethnopolitical approach to working with people of color. *American Psychologist*, *55*, 1319–1325. doi:10.1037/0003–066X.55.11.1319

Donnelly, J. (1998). *International human rights* (2nd ed.). Boulder, CO: Westview.

Espinosa, A., Páez, D., Velázquez, T., Cueto, R. M., Seminario, E., Sandoval, S., & . . . Jave, I. (2016). Between remembering and forgetting the years of political violence: Psychosocial impact of the truth and reconciliation commission in Peru. *Political Psychology.* Retrieved from www.academia.edu/28250224/Between_reme_mbering_and_forgetting_the_years_of_political_violence_

Psychosocial_impact_of_the_Truth_and_Reconciliation_Commission_in_
Peru

Federal Bureau of Investigation. (2001). FBI uniform crime reporting. Retrieved from https://ucr.fbi.gov/hate-crime/2001

Feuer, S., Thompson, D. M., Harding, R., & 20th Century Fox. (2011). *The first grader* [Film]. Hollywood, CA: 20th Century Fox.

Fourie, M. M., Gobodo-Madikizela, P., & Stein, D. J. (2013). Empathy, forgiveness, and reconciliation: The Truth and Reconciliation Commission in South Africa. In M. Linden, K. Rutkowski, M. Linden, & K. Rutkowski (Eds.), *Hurting memories and beneficial forgetting: Posttraumatic stress disorders, biographical developments, and social conflicts* (pp. 227–240). Amsterdam: Elsevier. doi:10.1016/B978-0-12-398393-0.00019-5

Frantz, S. (2016). *Hero rats: Trained to detect landmines and tuberculosis.* Retrieved from https://community.macmillan.com/community/the-psychology-community/blog/2016/07/20/hero-rats-trained-to-detect-landmines-and-tuberculosis

Goliszek, A. (2003). *In the name of science: A history of secret programs, medical research, and human experimentation.* New York, NY: St. Martin's.

Greensboro Truth and Reconciliation Commission. (2006). Final report. Retrieved from www.greensborotrc.org/

Guggenheim, D., Kimball, B., Chilcott, L., Strickland, B., Canada, G., Rhee, M., Weingarten, R., & Paramount Home Entertainment.. (2011). *Waiting for 'Superman'* [Film]. Hollywood, CA: Paramount Home Entertainment.

Hamber, B., Gallagher, E., Weine, S. M., Agger, I., Bava, S., Gaborit, M.,... Saul, J. (2015). Exploring how context matters in addressing the impact of armed conflict. In B. Hamber, E. Gallagher, B. Hamber, E. Gallagher (Eds.), *Psychosocial perspectives on peacebuilding* (pp. 1–31). New York, NY: Springer Science + Business Media. doi:10.1007/978-3-319-09937-8_1

Harris, S. (2002). *Factories of death: Japanese biological warfare, 1932–45, and the American cover-up* (2nd ed.). London: Routledge. doi.org/10.4324/NOE0415932141

Hulsizer, M. R., & Woolf, L. M. (2012). Enhancing the role of international human rights in the psychology curriculum. *Psychology Learning and Teaching*, 11, 382–387. doi:10.2304/plat.2012.11.3.382

James, W. (1910). The moral equivalent of war. *Popular Science Monthly*, 77. Retrieved from https://en.wikisource.org/wiki/Popular_Science_Monthly/Volume_77/October_1910/The_Moral_Equivalent_of_War

Jones, J. H. (1993). *Bad blood: The Tuskegee syphilis experiment.* New York, NY: Free Press.

Jovanovic, S. (2012). *Democracy, dialogue, and community action: Truth and reconciliation in Greensboro.* Fayetteville, AR: University of Arkansas Press.

Keen, S. (1991). *Faces of the enemy: Reflections of the hostile imagination.* San Francisco, CA: Harper Collins.

Kingston, L. N. (2012). Creating a "Human Rights Campus." *Peace Review*, 24(1), 78–83. doi:10.1080/10402659.2012.651028

Kira, I. A. (2010). Etiology and treatment of post-cumulative traumatic stress disorders in different cultures. *Traumatology, 16,* 128–141. doi:10.1177/1534765610365914

Kogen, L., & Price, M. E. (2014). Scholar-practitioner collaboration in media-related interventions: A case study of Radio La Benevolencija in Rwanda. *International Journal of Media and Cultural Politics, 10,* 301–312. doi:10.1386/macp.10.3.301_1

Lott, J. R., Jr. (2010). *More guns, less crime: Understanding crime and gun control laws* (3rd ed.). Chicago, IL: University of Chicago Press. doi:10.7208/chicago/9780226493671.001.0001

Lykes, M. B. (1996). Meaning making in a context of genocide and silencing. In M. B. Lykes, A. Banuazizi, R. Liem, M. Morris, & G. W. Albee (Eds.), *Myths about the powerless: Contesting social inequalities* (pp. 159–178). Philadelphia, PA: Temple University Press.

Marsella, A. J., & Christopher, M. A. (2004). Ethnocultural considerations in disasters: An overview of research, issues, and directions. *Psychiatric Clinics of North America, 27,* 521–539. doi:10.1016/j.psc.2004.03.011

Minow, M. (1998). *Between vengeance and forgiveness.* Boston, MA: Beacon.

(2008). Making history or making peace: When prosecutions should give way to truth commissions and peace negotiations. *Journal of Human Rights, 7,* 174–185. doi:10.1080/14754830802073295

Misyak, S., Helms, J., Mann, G., & Serrano, E. (2015). SNAP Challenge assignment: Preparing students for working with low-income populations. *Journal of Nutrition Education & Behavior, 47*(4), S12. doi:10.1016/j.jneb.2015.04.032

Nisbett, R. E., & Cohen, D. (1996). *Culture of honor: The psychology of violence in the South.* Boulder, CO: Westview.

Opotow, S. (2001). Social injustice. In D. J. Christie, R. V. Wagner, & D. D. Winter (Eds.), *Peace, conflict and violence: Peace psychology for the 21st century* (pp. 102–109). New York, NY: Prentice-Hall.

Potok, M. (2017, February 15). The year in hate. *Intelligence Report.* Retrieved from www.splcenter.org/fighting-hate/intelligence-report/2017/year-hate-and-extremism

Qureshi, A., Bagué, I. F., Ghali, K., & Collazos, F. (2015). Cultural competence in trauma. In M. Schouler-Ocak & M. Schouler-Ocak (Eds.), *Trauma and migration: Cultural factors in the diagnosis and treatment of traumatised immigrants* (pp. 159–175). Cham, Switzerland: Springer International. doi:10.1007/978-3-319-17335-1_11

Shaheen, J. G. (2003). Reel bad Arabs: How Hollywood vilifies a people. *The Annals of the American Academy of Political and Social Science, 588,* 171–193. doi:10.1177/0002716203588001011

Spencer, H. (1864). *The principles of biology.* London: Williams and Norgate.

Staub, E., Pearlman, L. A., Gubin, A., & Hagengimana, A. (2005). Healing, reconciliation, forgiving and the prevention of violence after genocide or mass killing: An intervention and its experimental evaluation in Rwanda. *Journal of Social & Clinical Psychology, 24,* 297–334. doi:10.1521/jscp.24.3.297.65617

Subramanian, S. (2017, February 26). Worse than Tuskegee. *Slate.* Retrieved from www.slate.com/articles/health_and_science/cover_story/2017/02/guatemala_syphilis_experiments_worse_than_tuskegee.html

Task Force on Trafficking of Women and Girls. (2014). *Report of the Task Force on Trafficking of Women and Girls.* Washington, DC: American Psychological Association. Retrieved from www.apa.org/pi/women/programs/trafficking/report.aspx

Turnbaugh, W. A., Jurmain, R., Kilgore, L. & Nelson, H. (2001). *Understanding physical anthropology and archaeology* (8th ed.). Belmont, CA: Wadsworth.

Umbreit, M., & Armour, M. P. (2010). *Restorative justice dialogue: An essential guide for research and practice.* New York, NY: Springer.

United Nations. (1948). Universal Declaration of Human Rights. Retrieved from www.un.org/en/universal-declaration-human-rights/

Washington H. A. (2008). *Medical apartheid: The dark history of medical experimentation on Black Americans from colonial times to the present.* New York, NY: Anchor Books.

Webb, L. E. (2011). Standing in the patient's shoes: Medical students take the SNAP Challenge. *Medical Education, 45,* 1135–1136. doi:10.1111/j.1365-2923.2011.04122.x

Wellford, C. F., Pepper, J. V., Petrie, C. V. (2005). *Firearms and violence: A critical review.* Washington, DC: National Academies Press.

Wessells, M. G., & Monteiro, C. (2001). Psychosocial interventions and post-war reconstruction in Angola: Interweaving Western and traditional approaches. In D. J. Christie, R. V. Wagner, & D. D. Winter (Eds.). *Peace, conflict, and violence: Peace psychology for the 21st century* (pp. 262–275). Englewood Cliffs, NJ: Prentice-Hall.

White, R. K. (1984). *Fearful warriors: A psychological profile of U.S.-Soviet relations.* New York, NY: Free Press.

  (1991). Enemy images in the United Nations-Iraq and East-West conflicts. In R. W. Rieber & R. W. Rieber (Eds.), *The psychology of war and peace: The image of the enemy* (pp. 59–70). New York, NY: Plenum Press. doi:10.1007/978-1-4899-0747-9_3

Woolf, L. M. (2016a). Peace psychology: A tapestry in history (Vignette 3: Peace psychology, APA, and torture). In W. D. Woody, R. L. Miller, & W. J. Wozniak (Eds.), *Psychological specialties in historical context: Enriching the classroom experience for teachers and students.* Retrieved from the Society for the Teaching of Psychology website, http://teachpsych.org/resources/Documents/ebooks/psychological-specialties-in-historical-context-2016.pdf

  (2016b). Peace psychology: A tapestry in history (Vignette 1: Recovery from genocide: Ervin Staub and Radio La Benevolencija). In W. D. Woody, R. L. Miller, & W. J. Wozniak (Eds.) *Psychological specialties in historical context: Enriching the classroom experience for teachers and students.* Retrieved from the Society for the Teaching of Psychology website, http://teachpsych.org/

resources/Documents/ebooks/psychological-specialties-in-historical-context-2016.pdf

Woolf, L. M., & Hulsizer, M. R. (2002/2003). Intra- and inter-religious hate and violence: A psychosocial model. *Journal of Hate Studies, 2,* 5–26.

(2004). Hate groups for dummies: How to build a successful hate group. *Humanity and Society, 28,* 40–62. doi:10.1177/016059760402800105

(2011). Peace and war. In R. L. Miller, E. Balcetis, S. R. Burns, D. B. Daniel, B. K. Saville, & W. D. Woody (Eds.), *Promoting student engagement* (Vol. 2, pp. 225–229). Retrieved from the Society for the Teaching of Psychology website, http://teachpsych.org/resources/e-books/pse2011/index.php

Woolf, L. M., & MacCartney, D. (2014). Sexual and gender minorities. In C. V. Johnson (Eds.). *Praeger handbook of social justice and psychology.* Westport, CT: Praeger.

Health and Well-Being

As Gurung (Chapter 21) explains, individuals trained in a number of subfields of psychology have made health their area of specialization. Both the definition and the reality of health may vary across cultural groups, and there remains a need for more integration of cultural concepts in health psychology research. In this chapter, readers will find good teaching content, teaching activities, and resources, and a discussion of the growth of the health psychology course in recent years.

Students may be surprised to find that well-being is more than simple happiness. As Kim-Prieto and Kukoff (Chapter 23) show, subjective well-being is complex and intimately tied to culture. A broad concept, well-being encompasses generally positive psychological functioning, satisfaction, and self-acceptance. In Chapter 23, the authors discuss variations in well-being across cultures, as well as teaching approaches that combine the teaching of well-being and culture.

CHAPTER 21

Health Psychology

Regan A. R. Gurung

Health psychology is an interdisciplinary subspecialty of psychology dedicated to promoting and maintaining health and preventing and treating illness (Leventhal, Weinman, Leventhal, & Phillips, 2008; Matarazzo, 1980). This area of psychology is perhaps one of the best places to discuss issues of culture. Our cultural backgrounds influence our health, shape healthy behaviors, prevent illness, and enhance our health and well-being. In this chapter, I first present a short history of the area of health psychology. I then review extant research on teaching health psychology followed by discussing how health varies across cultures. I end with pragmatic exercises to best teach about culture and health and resources for additional education.

Let's first be clear on what health psychology is. Health psychologists pay close attention to the way that thoughts, feelings, behavior, and biological processes all interact with each other to influence health and illnesses ranging from chronic heart disease and cancer to diabetes and obesity (Belar, McIntyre, & Matarazzo, 2003; Suls, Davidson, & Kaplan, 2010). A large proportion of health psychologists hold doctoral degrees in counseling and clinical psychology. Another substantial portion are trained as social psychologists. A smaller proportion of health psychologists are trained in developmental or experimental psychology. In many ways, health psychology is greater than a subfield within the discipline of psychology, as it is built on theoretical ideas and research findings from many other areas in psychology. This multidisciplinarity is evident when we look at the origins of the field.

A Brief History of the Field

Whereas one can argue that the ancient Greeks and Chinese knew the mind played a role in health, the first person to explicitly focus on the workings of the mind in disease was Freud. A name well known to most lay people, but one somewhat demonized in psychology, Freud nonetheless kick-started a focus on the role of thinking in health. Examining the role played by the mind continued later in the twentieth century by the psychoanalysts Franz Alexander and Helen Flanders Dunbar (Gurung, 2014a). Together they established the first formal gathering of individuals interested in studying the influences of the mind on health. This movement within the mainstream medical establishment was coined psychosomatic medicine. The new field of psychosomatic medicine had many supporters, which led to the formation of the first society specifically dedicated to the study of mind and body connections. The American Psychosomatic Society (APS) was formed to "promote and advance the scientific understanding of the interrelationships among biological, psychological, social, and behavioral factors in human health and disease, and the integration of the fields of science that separately examine each, and to foster the application of this understanding in education and improved health care" (American Psychosomatic Society, 2001, p. 1). In 1936, the New York Academy of Medicine's joint committee on religion and medicine, headed by Dunbar, assembled a collection of the psychosomatic medical literature, together with publications examining the relation of religion to health. Dunbar's early collection of articles led her to organize publication, in 1939, of the first journal for this field, *Psychosomatic Medicine*, which still publishes research today. Although the early movement faltered and received mixed attention because it was based heavily on Freudian ideas and case study methods of research, the APS survives and is still active with annual meetings and active members.

Another movement within the field of medicine, called *behavioral medicine*, looks at nonbiological influences on health. Doctors and healthcare specialists within the medical community were probably always aware that changes in behavior and lifestyle improve health, prevent illness, and reduce symptoms of illness, although they did not focus on this fact. The Society of Behavioral Medicine (SBM), a multidisciplinary, nonprofit organization founded in 1978, is dedicated to studying the influences of behavior on health and well-being. This organization brings together different disciplines – nursing, psychology, medicine, and public health – to form an interdisciplinary team. Similar to *Psychosomatic Medicine* for the APS, the SBM also has its own journal, *The Annals of Behavioral Medicine.*

Another important resource for health psychology, and for clinical health psychologists in particular, is the *International Classification of Diseases, Ninth Revision (ICD-9),* a classification of diseases and disorders. The connection between health psychology and medicine is strong. Today, health psychology and clinical health psychologists play an important role in the practice of medicine and management of disease (Nicholas & Stern, 2011). Modern health psychology has roots in philosophy, nineteenth-century scientific discovery, medical and clinical psychology, epidemiology and public health, medical sociology and anthropology, and psychosomatic medicine (Gurung, 2014a).

Teaching Health Psychology

Corresponding with the emergence of *Health Psychology*, the journal for Division 38 (Health Psychology) of the American Psychological Association, DiMatteo and Friedman (1982) developed a model course in social psychology and health. The course consisted of twelve units: the role of the health professional; the art of medicine: patient satisfaction with medical care, cooperation with medical regimens, nonverbal communication with patients, verbal communication with patients, illness behavior and the definition of illness, stress and illness, chronic illness, death and the process of dying, the family and health, the health professional, and institutions of healthcare. Of note, all of these topics are covered in contemporary classes and health psychology textbooks.

Whereas APA's Division 2 (Society for the Teaching of Psychology) has some resources on teaching health psychology, APA's Division 38 Education and Training Council has truly taken on the responsibility of reflecting on the health psychology course and capturing the contemporary state of the course. This group conducts periodic surveys of instructors teaching the course and posts recommendations for teachers of the course on the division website (www.health-psych.org/EducationCourses.cfm). Resources include course descriptions, typical course content, and sample syllabi.

There has been substantial growth of this course within the past two decades. In an early survey of 4,012 psychology courses, only 0.75 percent of courses focused on topics in behavioral medicine or health psychology (Scheirer & Rogers, 1985). By the late 1980s, 35 percent of universities (in a sample of 308) offered a health psychology course (Sarafino, 1988). More recently, one study showed 177 of 374 (48 percent) undergraduate psychology programs surveyed offered the course in 2005 (Stoloff et al., 2010) compared with only 112 of 400 programs surveyed (less than 26 percent) in a study conducted just 10 years earlier (Perlman & McCann, 1999). Similarly, 33 percent of schools in 2010 offered health psychology as a part of the psychology program (Brack, Kesitilwe, & Ware, 2010), compared with only 24 percent of departments in a national survey offering the course 20 years previously (Dorsel & Baum, 1989).

A number of researchers have studied how health psychology is taught. Brack et al. (2010) conducted a review of 300 university catalogs and showed the most common topics (with percentage of the sample who taught them) included the biopsychosocial model (93 percent), chronic illnesses (90 percent), adherence (87 percent), and behavior change (80 percent). Recently, Panjwani, Gurung, and Revenson (2017) conducted a large national survey of health psychology instructors. Each answered questions about how she or he taught and formatted the course and what readings and assignments she or he used; each rated the importance of major topics in the field. An analysis of topic importance ratings revealed five domains: chronic illness, stress and adjustment processes, health psychology in practice, health behavior change, and basics and background. Most instructors did not rely solely on a textbook, but used journal articles, videos, newspaper articles, and social media to augment their lessons. Central to this chapter, participants in the study noted that topics related to health disparities were often missing in textbooks.

The Need for a Cultural Approach to Health

The United States is a diverse nation with approximately 323 million citizens (US Census Bureau, 2017). Not all citizens of the United States are similarly healthy (Eshun & Gurung, 2009). For example, death rates for African Americans are significantly higher than those of Americans overall for heart disease, cancer, diabetes, HIV, and homicide (Gourdine, 2011). African Americans have higher mortality rates than European Americans in general (Williams, 2012). Even within ethnic groups, health varies. For example, health patterns and profiles differ within the various Latino groups (Zsembik & Fennell, 2005). Immigrants and refugees have unique health issues as well (Ciftci, Reid-Marks, & Shawahin, 2014; Nakeyar & Frewen, 2017) with acculturation playing a particularly important role (Abraido-Lanza, Echeverria, & Florez, 2016). Corresponding to such differences, the US healthcare system has been making active attempts to broaden approaches toward healthcare in order to fulfill the needs of the diverse population (Schooler & Baum, 2000) and advance cultural competence (Purnell et al., 2011). There are critical cultural variations in the conceptualization, perception, health-seeking behaviors, assessment, diagnosis, and treatment of abnormal behaviors and physical sickness.

In short, the answer to the simple question, "Are you healthy?" can vary according to where you live, how old you are, what your parents and friends think constitutes health, what your religious or ethnic background is, and what a variety of other factors indicate about you. If you live in

Seattle, Washington, where the skies are often cloudy, your health habits are probably different than if you live in Yuma, Arizona, one of the sunniest cities in the United States (see www.currentresults.com/Weather-Extremes/US/sunniest-cities.php for a full list). Factors such as where you live, your age, or your ethnicity interact with others to influence what you do and how healthy you will be. "Culture" is the term that adequately captures all these different elements that influence health.

Health across Cultures

Different cultures understand the etiology of health very differently (Gurung, 2014a). In Western medical circles, *health* is commonly defined as "the state in which disease is absent" (Galanti, 2014). Of course, this definition focuses primarily on the physical or biological aspect of life and correspondingly, this approach taken by Western medicine is often referred to as the *biomedical approach* to health. Non-Western societies have a different understanding of health. For example, in traditional Chinese medicine (TCM), health is the balance of yin and yang, the two complementary forces in the universe (Kaptchuk, 2000; Liao, 2011). Yin and yang are often translated into hot and cold (two clear opposites), referring to qualities, not temperatures. To be healthy, what you eat and drink and the way you live your life should have equal amounts of hot qualities and cold qualities. Balancing hot and cold is a critical element of many different cultures (e.g., Chinese, Indian, and even Mexican), although the foods that constitute each may vary across cultures. Some "hot" foods include beef, garlic, ginger, and alcohol. Some "cold" foods include honey, most greens, potatoes, and some fruits (e.g., melons, pears).

Other cultures also believe that health is the balance of different qualities (Galanti, 2014). Similarly, ancient Indian scholars and doctors defined health as the state in which "the three main biological units – enzymes, tissues, and excretory functions – are in harmonious condition and when the mind and senses are cheerful" (Svoboda, 2004, p. ix). Referred to as *Ayurveda*, or *knowledge of life*, this ancient system of medicine focuses on the body, the sense organs, the mind, and the soul. Another way of looking at health is the approach of Mexican Americans, the largest ethnic group in the United States. Mexican Americans believe that there are both natural biological causes for illness (similar to Western biomedicine) and spiritual causes (Tovar, 2017). Although Mexican American patients may go to a Western doctor to cure a biological problem, only *curanderos,* or healers, can be trusted to cure spiritual problems.

American Indians do not even draw distinctions between physical, spiritual, and social entities or between religion and medicine (Peters, Green, & Gauthier, 2014). Instead, most tribes (especially the Navajo) strive to achieve a balance between human beings and the spiritual world (Alvord & Van Pelt, 2000). The trees, the animals, the earth, the sky, and the winds are all players in the same game of life. Most of the world's cultures use a more global and widespread approach to assessing health instead of just looking at whether or not disease is absent to determine health (as the biomedical model and most Western approaches do).

Integrating Culture Is Important in the Teaching of Health Psychology

Teaching health psychology from and with a cultural perspective would be easier if the health psychology research on culture were adequate. Even in the face of increasing research on culture there are many areas of health psychology still lacking information about cultural differences (Keefe, Buffington, Studts, & Ramble, 2002). To be fair, cultural research is not always easy to do and there are many barriers. An examination of articles and books in the field shows that *culture* and *health psychology* have not been common key words (Kazarian & Evans, 2001), and even reviews of *Health Psychology* (the journal) have shown a limited number of articles on culture and health (Klonoff & Landrine, 2001), although the numbers are increasing.

There are clearly many different cultural approaches to health, and it is of great importance for healthcare workers and the administrations that support them to be culturally aware. Knowing about the different approaches to health can also help the lay consumer be better apprised of cultural differences, which in turn can lead to a reduction in stereotyping or prejudicial attitudes toward behaviors that may be seen as different from the norm. Millions of Americans hold very different health beliefs from mainstream Western biomedicine.

There are a number of different concepts that would be misunderstood if not presented in cultural context. For example, the three terms *cultural awareness, cultural sensitivity,* and *cultural competence* are frequently confused and/or used synonymously. *Cultural competence* incorporates, but goes beyond, cultural awareness and sensitivity; it is often defined as using a combination of culturally appropriate attitudes, knowledge, and skills that facilitate providing effective healthcare for diverse individuals, families, groups, and communities (Purnell & Pontious, 2014).

One of the best ways to see the importance of culture in understanding health is demonstrated by the Purnell model for cultural competence. Classified as a complexity and holographic theory, its organizing framework can be used in all practice settings and by all healthcare providers (Purnell, 2013). The model is a circle with major concepts such as global society, community, person, and family forming rims around the model. The outer rim represents global society, a second rim represents community, a third rim represents family, and the inner rim represents the person (see Figure 21.1). The interior of the circle is divided into twelve pie-shaped wedges depicting cultural domains

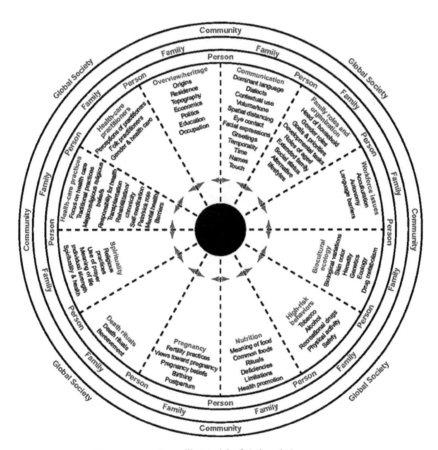

Figure 21.1   Purnell's Model of Cultural Competence.
Purnell, L. (2002). Updated figure and permission to post provided by Dr. Purnell
(personal email communication, June 2017)

(constructs) and their associated concepts. The dark center of the circle represents unknown phenomena.

Teaching health psychology using culture is aided by a focus on certain key areas. One of the most important is socioeconomic status. It is becoming one of the most important and widely studied constructs in health psychology (Adler & Rehkopf, 2008). Almost any study done on this topic shows that poverty and illness tend to go together, often linked by factors such as access to healthcare care and insurance. The poor (those with a yearly income equal to or less than $23,050 for a family of four (US Department of Health and Human Services, 2017) make up a large percentage of Americans without health insurance.

Of particular importance to taking a cultural approach to health is that the cultural makeup of those considered "poor" is changing. For example, Indiana's Manchester College and Bentley College in Massachusetts examined poverty rates and income levels from 1995 to 2006 for several groups in the US population. They found that the disparity in poverty rates between European Americans and other ethnic groups decreased 7 of the last 11 years, dropping 23 percent overall since 1995. Whereas European American poverty is remaining relatively stable (8.2 percent in 2006 versus 8.5 percent in 1995), the African American poverty rate dropped from 29.3 percent to 24.2 percent; Hispanics dropped from 30.2 percent to 20.6 percent; and Asians/Pacific Islanders dropped from 14.6 percent to 10.1 percent (Gurung, 2014a). Such changes can influence use of health services and consequently a number of other factors that health psychologists study.

Key Teaching Activities

Many of my students have grown up in small communities with minimal exposure to diversity. Even in large cities, many students are not well versed in the nuances of culture. Many clinicians and healthcare workers may not have received the necessary instruction to be culturally competent, but there are some easy ways to be prepared (Purnell & Pontious, 2014). It is critical to provide students with opportunities to experience cultural differences. I provide a number of demonstrations that are particularly useful in explaining cultural concepts in health psychology.

Who Am I? This is an activity I use on the very first day of class. Not only does it make a great ice breaker, but also it immediately alerts students to the variance existing in culture. In my classroom in Green Bay, Wisconsin, the majority of the students are White. Many of them are not fully aware of their rich cultural backgrounds. Given that health depends on culture, it is important to first recognize one's own cultural richness. I tell students to be ready to write down as many answers to my next question as possible. The question? Who am I?

I tell students to jot down the first thoughts that come to their minds, one below the other. I give them 1 minute and have them draw a line below the last word they wrote. I then have them write for another minute. Class then proceeds in one of a number of ways. When I am teaching thirty to forty students, I have each student read out his or her answers. I write the answers on the board and tell students to help me categorize responses. For example, if students say Muslim, Hindu, or Christian, I write down religion. If students mention their immigrant roots (e.g., part German, part Somalian) I write down ethnicity. The most common first answer is "American" (I write down nationality). Many students respond, "I'm just White" or "I only had American." Most also list responses such as "I am male," and "I am a daughter." If a student repeats a descriptor that is already on the board, I start tallying the responses. Soon the board is a picture of the cultural diversity in the class.

Most importantly, students notice that they often have the same items above the line I had them draw. Many of them think about themselves the same way in the first minute. As they think longer, deeper aspects of their culture are listed (i.e., below the line they drew). Many students see other students' responses and realize that they too see themselves the same way though they did not think about it at first.

At this juncture, I remind students that culture is broadly defined and that each of us has ethnicity, nationality, a gender and sexual orientation, geography, religion, and many more aspects that shape us and influence our health. After this discussion, students are more open to exploring cultural variances in health.

Culture and health book clubs. A number of books nicely unpack what happens when doctors take a Eurocentric/Western medicine approach without being fully open to cultural variance. A number of trade books nicely reveal what happens when cultures run into one another. In one of my classes, I require students to read three to four different trade books showcasing the interaction between culture and health. I divide students into groups of three to four and each student takes a turn at being a discussion leader for a book. Discussion leaders post their questions on the course management system website, and each group member responds to the questions. Discussion leaders then reply. Once students have had

sufficient time to read and discuss a book (often 2 weeks), I have a class
discussion of the book where I cull issues from the online discussion and
have the class as a whole reflect and discuss.

Using trade books provides students with affordable inroads into different cultures and the format, less intimidating than a textbook, often leads
to greater engagement with the material. Some good candidates for culture
and health book clubs are:

- *The Spirit Catches You and You Fall Down* **(Fadiman, 1994)**. This
  is a heart-wrenching story that captivates students while also educating
  them about Hmong Americans, refugees from the hills of Laos. A little
  Hmong American girl in Merced, California, develops epilepsy and
  due to a long series of miscommunications between her Western
  medical providers and her family, she lapses into a coma. The book
  is packed with examples of the clashes of cultures and provides ample
  fodder for classroom discussion. Each alternate chapter presents the
  history of the Hmong in America, shedding light on details few
  students are aware of. For example, students are surprised to learn
  the US government promised Hmong people citizenship in exchange
  for their assistance during the Vietnam war.
- *Coyote Medicine: Lessons from Native American Healing* **(Mehl-
  Madrona, 1998)**. This book portrays a different perspective on the
  practice of medicine. The author is a Western medicine-educated doctor
  who is trying to find a place in his practice for the approaches of his
  Native American people. His experiences starkly contrast how medicine
  is practiced in Western society with the cures and approaches to health of
  Native Americans. Along the way, students learn about the curative
  properties of the sweat lodge, vision quests, and many more ceremonies
  and practices. Mehl-Madrona also provides examples of shocking medical practices. One riveting anecdote involves OB-GYN doctors having
  races in the delivery room to see who could deliver a baby faster.
- *The Absolutely True Diary of a Part-Time Indian* **(Alexi, 1999)**.
  Although written for teenagers, this book is a student favorite. Alexi
  tells the story of a young Indian boy on the Spokane reservation who
  leaves to go to a White school. He is shunned by his Native American
  peers for leaving and treated badly by the White students at his new
  school. What makes this a must-read is the treatment of Native
  American stereotypes by Alexi (e.g., most Indians on the reservation
  drink). He states their existence, but also provides insights into their
  evolution from a circle of poverty. This discussion of the intersection of

low socioeconomic status and ethnicity is eye opening. The book also blends in development issues as the protagonist is experiencing many of the issues that growing children face. Health here is not so much sickness per se, but the lack of healthy behaviors and reasons why they exist in the Indian community.

Resources to Develop a Cultural Focus in Health Psychology Courses

With the variety of cultural differences in North America and the world, it is difficult for any single teacher or researcher to be well versed in them all. Fortunately, there is a rich set of resources to provide more information. Some of the places I find myself going most often are in the following list with a brief summary of what you will find:

Multicultural Approaches to Health (**Gurung, 2014b, 2014c**). This two-volume set contains twenty-four chapters, each providing in-depth summaries exploring different cultures. Whereas the level of writing makes this book more accessible to graduate students and faculty, upper-level undergraduates will also be able to glean nuggets of value. This series is geared toward providing health psychology with the cultural details that many introductory health psychology texts may not have the space for. Chapters cover key health psychological topics viewed through a cultural lens. For example, chapters cover health disparities among immigrants (Ciftci, Reid-Marks, & Shawahin, 2014), acculturation and health (Crawford & Avula, 2014), as well as specific approaches to health in different cultures (e.g., Native Americans; Peters et al., 2014)

Caring for Patients from Different Cultures (**Galanti, 2014**). Few resources bring home the importance of culture as well as this book that features actual examples from the healthcare field. Taking key topic areas from health psychology, such as pain and communication, Galanti (2014) describes how culture plays a role in the treatment of the concept. For example, students get engaged hearing about how in some cultures, the louder a woman screams during labor and delivery, the bigger the diamond ring she will get from her family. Why may a Chinese American man refuse treatment from a European American female doctor? How does culture influence staff interactions in a hospital? This resource makes a wonderful supplementary reading for health psychology classes, providing numerous cultural examples derived from the author's experiences and research in various healthcare settings.

Mexican American Health; Social, Cultural, and Clinical Perspectives
(Tovar, 2017). Perhaps one of the best examples of a growing focus on specific cultural groups within the United States, this book provides a rich history of Mexican Americans and clearly describes unique approaches to health; beliefs, values, and attitudes; and cures and treatments that differ significantly from Western medicine. The discussion of values, in particular, helps students see how whether one practices healthy behaviors can relate to what one's home culture believes should (or should not) be done.

Concluding Thoughts

It is important to acknowledge that many cultural variations exist within ethnic communities. Knowing how different cultural groups approach health and having a better understanding of why factors such as acculturation are important, and can help clinicians, healthcare workers, and others with an interest in how lifestyle decisions are made to be more culturally competent. Beyond these groups, understanding the role of culture on health is critical for every individual. Not only does understanding culture help explain the causes of many of our health behaviors, but also it helps us better understand the health behaviors of others around us.

The efforts to increase cultural competency in the treatment of mental and physical health are promising, but the wider healthcare arena and the general public need to pay attention to the causes of health disparities and the role played by multicultural approaches to health. We need a better connection between healthcare and the community, so that individuals can seek out treatments that best fit their cultural needs and the manifold health disparities can be reduced. A great place to start this process is in our classrooms. Every time we teach health psychology, we have an opportunity to open minds to the variance in culture.

References

Abraido-Lanza, A. F., Echeverria, S. E., & Florez, K. R. (2016). Latino immigrants, acculturation, and health: Promising new directions. *Annual Review of Public Health*, *37*, 219–236. doi:10.1146/annurev-publhealth-032315-021545

Adler, N. E., & Rehkopf, D. H. (2008) U.S. disparities in health: Descriptions, causes, and mechanisms. *Annual Review of Public Health*, *29*, 235–252. doi:10.1146/annurev.publhealth.29.020907.090852

Alexi, S. (2008). *The absolutely true diary of a part-time Indian*. New York, NY: Little Brown.

Alvord, L. A., & Van Pelt, E. C. (2000). *The scalpel and the silver bear: The first Navajo woman surgeon combines Western medicine and traditional healing.* New York, NY: Bantam.

American Psychosomatic Society. (2001). APS mission statement. Retrieved from www.psychosomatic.org/AnMeeting/PastEvents/archive/meet2001text.html

Belar, C. D., McIntyre, T. M., & Matarazzo, J. D. (2003). Health psychology. In D. K. Freedheim (Ed.), *Handbook of psychology: History of psychology* (Vol. 1, pp. 451–464). Hoboken, NJ: Wiley.

Brack, A. B., Kesitilwe, K., & Ware, M. E. (2010). Taking the pulse of undergraduate health psychology: A nationwide survey. *Teaching of Psychology, 37,* 271–275. doi:10.1080/00986283.2010.510962

Ciftci, A., Reid-Marks, L., & Shawahin, L. (2014). Health disparities and immigrants. In R. A. R. Gurung (Ed.), *Multicultural approaches to health and wellness in America: Major issues and cultural groups* (pp. 51–72). Westport, CT: Praeger.

Crawford, S., & Avula, K. (2014). Acculturation and health. In R. A. R. Gurung (Ed.), *Multicultural approaches to health and wellness in America: Major issues and cultural groups* (pp. 99–124). Westport, CT: Praeger.

DiMatteo, M. R., & Friedman, H. S. (1982). *Social psychology and medicine.* Cambridge, MA: Oelgeschlager, Gunn, & Hain.

Dorsel, T. N., & Baum, A. (1989). Undergraduate health psychology: Another challenge for an ambitious field. *Psychology & Health, 3*(2), 87–92. doi:10.1080/08870448908400368

Eshun, S., & Gurung, R. A. R. (2009). Introduction to culture and psychopathology. In S. Eshun & R. A. R. Gurung (Eds.), *Culture and mental health: Sociocultural influences, theory, and practice* (pp. 3–18). Chichester: Wiley-Blackwell.

Fadiman, A. (1998). *The spirit catches you and you fall down.* New York, NY: Farrar, Straus & Giroux.

Galanti, G. (2014). *Caring for patients from different cultures* (5th ed.). Philadelphia, PA: University of Pennsylvania Press.

Gourdine, M. A. (2011). *Reclaiming our health: A guide to African American wellness.* New Haven, CT: Yale University Press.

Gurung, R. A. R. (2014a). *Health psychology: A cultural approach* (3rd ed.). San Francisco, CA: Cengage.

Gurung, R. A. R. (Ed.). (2014b). *Multicultural approaches to health and wellness in America: Major issues and cultural groups.* Westport, CT: Praeger.

(Ed.). (2014c). *Multicultural approaches to health and wellness in America: Mental health and the mind-body connection.* Westport, CT: Praeger.

Kaptchuk, T. J. (2000). *The web that has no weaver: Understanding Chinese medicine.* Chicago, IL: Contemporary Books.

Kazarian, S. S., & Evans, D. R. (2001). *Handbook of cultural health psychology.* New York, NY: Academic Press.

Keefe, F. J., Smith, S. J., Buffington, A. L. H., Gibson, J., Studts, J. L., & Caldwell, D. S. (2002). Recent advances and future directions in the biopsychosocial assessment and treatment of arthritis. *Journal of Consulting and Clinical Psychology, 70*, 640–656. doi:10.1037/0022–006X.70.3.640

Klonoff, E. A., & Landrine, H. (2001). Depressive symptoms and smoking among US Black adults: Absence of a relationship. *Journal of Health Psychology, 6*, 645–649. doi:10.1177/135910530100600603

Leventhal, H., Weinman, J., Leventhal, E. A., & Phillips, L. A. (2008). Health psychology: The search for pathways between behavior and health. *Annual Review of Psychology, 59*, 477–505. doi:10.1146/annurev.psych.59.103006 .093643

Liao, Y. (2011). *Traditional Chinese medicine*. New York, NY: Cambridge University Press.

Matarazzo, J. D. (1980). Behavioral health and behavioral medicine: Frontiers for a new health psychology. *American Psychologist, 35*, 807–817. doi:10.1037/ 0003–066X.35.9.807

Mehl-Madrona, L. (1998). *Coyote medicine: Lessons from Native American healing*. New York, NY: Simon & Schuster.

Nakeyar, C., & Frewen, P. A. (2017). Evidence-based care for Iraqi, Kurdish, and Syrian asylum seekers and refugees of the Syrian civil war: A systematic review. *Immigrants and Refugees, 57*, 233–245.

Nicholas, D. R., & Stern, M. (2011). Counseling psychology in clinical health psychology: The impact of specialty perspective. *Professional Psychology: Research and Practice, 42*(4), 331–337. doi:10.1037/a0024197

Panjwani, A., Gurung, R. A. R., & Revenson, T. (2017). The teaching of undergraduate health psychology: A national survey. *Teaching of Psychology, 44*, 268–273. doi: 10.1177/0098628317712786

Perlman, B., & McCann, L. I. (1999). The most frequently listed courses in the undergraduate psychology curriculum. *Teaching of Psychology, 26*, 177. doi:10.1207/S15328023TOP260303

Peters, W. M. K., Green, J. M., & Gauthier, P. E. (2014). Native American medicine: The implications of history and the embodiment of culture. In R. A. R. Gurung (Ed.). *Multicultural approaches to health and wellness in America: Major issues and cultural groups* (pp. 171–198). Westport, CT: Praeger.

Purnell, L. (2002). The Purnell model for cultural competence. *Journal of Transcultural Nursing, 13*(3).

(2013). *Transcultural health care: A culturally competent approach* (4th ed.). Philadelphia, PA: F. A. Davis.

Purnell, L., Davidhizar, R. E., Giger, J., Strickland, O. L., Fishman, D., & Allison, D. M. (2011). A guide to developing a culturally competent organization. *Journal of Transcultural Nursing, 22*(1), 7–14. doi:10.1177/ 1043659610387147

Purnell, L., & Pontious, S. (2014). Cultural competence. In R. A. R. Gurung (Ed.), *Multicultural approaches to health and wellness in America: Major issues and cultural groups* (pp. 1–28). Westport, CT: Praeger.

Sarafino, E. P. (1988). Undergraduate health psychology courses. *Health Psychologist, 10*(3), 1–8.

Scheirer, C. J., & Rogers, A. M. (1985). *The undergraduate psychology curriculum: 1984*. Washington, DC: American Psychological Association.

Schooler, T. Y., & Baum, A. (2000). Neuroendocrine influence on the health of diverse populations. In R. M. Eisler & M. Hersen (Eds.), *Handbook of gender, culture, and health* (pp. 3–20). Mahwah, NJ: Lawrence Erlbaum.

Stoloff, M., McCarthy, M., Keller, L., Varfolomeeva, V., Lynch, J., Makara, K., ... Smiley, W. (2010). The undergraduate psychology major: An examination of structure and sequence. *Teaching of Psychology, 37*, 4–15. doi:10.1080/00986280903426274

Suls, J., Davidson, K., & Kaplan, R. (Eds.). (2010). *Handbook of health psychology and behavioral medicine*. New York, NY: Guilford.

Svoboda, R. E. (2004). *Ayurveda: Life, health, and longevity*. New Delhi: Penguin.

Tovar, M. (2017). *Mexican American health*. Westport, CT; Praeger.

US Census Bureau. (2017). *Quick facts: United States*. Retrieved from www.census.gov/quickfacts/fact/table/US/PST045216

US Department of Health and Human Services. (2017). HealthyPeople.gov. Retrieved from www.healthypeople.gov/2020/default.aspx

Williams, D. R. (2012). Miles to go before we sleep: Racial inequalities in health. *Journal of Health and Social Behavior, 53*, 279–295. doi:10.1177/0022146512455804

Zsembik, B. A., & Fennell, D. (2005). Ethnic variation in health and the determinants of health among Latinos. *Social Science and Medicine, 61*, 53–63. doi:10.1016/j.socscimed.2004.11.040

CHAPTER 22

Subjective Well-Being across Cultures: Some Universals and Many More Differences

Chu Kim-Prieto and Jaclyn Kukoff

Subjective well-being (SWB) encompasses both cognitive and affective dimensions. The cognitive dimension includes the evaluation of life as good and satisfying, and as lacking in regret. The affective dimension includes the experience of positive and pleasant emotions with greater frequency compared to negative and unpleasant emotions (Diener, Oishi, & Lucas, 2003). As such, SWB is more than simply the emotion of happiness; rather, it is the global sum of an individual's subjective assessment of her or his own well-being (Raibley, 2012). SWB includes positive psychological functioning and is correlated with self-acceptance, self-esteem, and mastery of one's environment (Ryff, 1989). Other similar constructs include positive interpersonal relationships, self-worth, optimism, frequency of positive feelings, and positive thinking (Diener et al., 2009).

Within this broad definition of SWB, however, are variations across different nations, cultures, language groups, and generations of people. The goal of this chapter is to make sense of, and account for, these differences in SWB so that they can inform our understanding and teaching of SWB. In doing so, we first provide a broad review of SWB, including the ways in which SWB varies across cultures. Then, we provide examples of the ways in which these differences may impact what and how SWB might be taught across different cultural contexts. Last, we conclude the chapter with an example of a classroom demonstration and lesson plan that contextualizes cultural differences in SWB and provides a jumping-off point for further classroom explorations.

Cultural Universals and Variations in SWB

Personality. Universals do exist in the domain of SWB, with personality traits, positive self-regard, and social support being some of the more robust predictors of SWB. For example, a meta-analysis by Steel, Schmidt, and Shultz (2008) found that personality could explain as much as 39 percent of the variability in SWB. Additional research indicates that much of the personality-SWB link can be explained by the role of extraversion and neuroticism in predicting positive and negative affect, respectively. That is, a large part of SWB is tied to the experience of positive and negative affect, and a large part of the trait variability in the experience of positive and negative affect is predicted by extraversion and neuroticism (DeNeve & Cooper, 1998; Hayes & Joseph, 2003; Lucas, Diener, Grob, Suh, & Shiao, 2000). The relation between the personality variables of extraversion and neuroticism and positive and negative affect has been replicated across cultures. For example, Lu and Shi (1997) demonstrated the link between extraversion and happiness in a study of Chinese residents of Taiwan; and analyzing a dataset of college students in forty-six nations, Kuppens, Realo, and Diener (2008) further found that positive emotions predicted SWB.

It must be noted, however, that even when discussing these broad universalities in SWB, caveats do exist. Although extraversion and neur-oticism are the best predictors of SWB overall, exceptions do exist. For example, Tanksale (2015) found that conscientiousness predicted SWB to a greater degree than extraversion or neuroticism in his sample of adults from India. In addition, culture-level differences in the valuation of positive and negative emotions further impact the link between personality and SWB. Suh, Diener, Oishi, and Triandis (1998) showed that the frequency of positive emotions was less predictive of SWB for Asians (Japanese and Korean), compared to European Americans. Indeed, the predictive power of positive emotions is weaker in cultures that value survival, compared to those that value self-expression (Kuppens et al., 2008). On the other hand, negative emotions have a higher impact on SWB in individualistic countries compared to more collectivistic countries (Bastian, Kuppens, De Roover, & Diener, 2014). This variability in the predictive power of positive emotions on SWB has further consequences when interventions for increasing well-being are considered. For example, an intervention that worked to increase optimism and gratitude had the effect of increasing SWB in Anglo American participants compared to the control condition, but no such effect was found for Asian American participants (Boehm, Lyubomirsky, & Sheldon, 2011).

Positive self-regard. Another variable that appears to have wide support in its importance to SWB is positive self-regard. Self-compassion, for example, is a robust predictor of SWB (for meta-analysis, see Zessin, Dickhäuser, & Garbade, 2015). In addition, Ryff (1989) found self-acceptance to positively predict SWB across thirty-one nations. However, as was the case for the personality factors of extraversion and neuroticism, important cultural caveats moderate and mediate this link. In further examining the strength of the relation between self-esteem and life satisfaction, Ryff (1989) found that this relation was moderated by culture, such that the relation was strongest in individualistic countries.

In addition, others have shown that the domains that provide the most boost for SWB seem to vary across cultures. For example, for South Asian participants, positive perceived social image predicted life satisfaction whereas for White British and White US participants, it was positive academic achievement (Rodriguez Mosquera, & Imada, 2013). Still others have shown that in some cultures, positive self-regard is fungible and context dependent. For example, Kim, Chiu, Cho, Au, and Kwak (2014) showed that Asians view themselves less positively compared to their beliefs about their parents' view of themselves. And when primed about their parents, Asians lowered the positivity of their self-views to match their perception of their parents' views. This interconnection of positive self-regard with perceptions of the ways in which others might perceive the self is also part of the Chinese concept of *mianzi*, personal positive status or esteem achieved through positive social interactions with others. Indeed, Huang and Wu (2012) found that having *mianzi* predicted life satisfaction in a sample of older Chinese adults. This interconnection and drawing of positive self-view from social connectedness provides a different view of sources of happiness compared to the standard Western lay beliefs.

Social support. The third variable to have widespread evidence of universality is social support. Social support can encompass support from family as well as friends and the community environment. For example, family embeddedness and perceived partner and spousal support are positively associated with positive affect (Brunstein, Dangelmayer, & Schultheiss, 1996; Siedlecki, Salthouse, Oisho, & Jeswani, 2014). Perceived social support is also positively linked to high life satisfaction and negatively linked to negative affect (Brunstein et al., 1996), and positive neighborhood environment is linked to positive affect and psychological well-being, controlling for socioeconomic status (Cutrona, Russell, Hessling, Brown, & Murry, 2000).

As is the case for positive self-regard, cultures vary in the domains of social support that predict SWB. For example, Asian American participants felt more "happy" and "good" when interaction partners were accurate in estimating social identity aspects of themselves (e.g., groups that they belong to, places where they grew up) compared to personal aspects of themselves (e.g., reliable, stubborn), whereas for European American participants, positive affect increased when personal selves were accurate compared to collective/social selves (Oishi, Koo, & Akimoto, 2008). Kreuzbauer, Chiu, Lin, and Bae (2014) further found a three-way inter-action effect, such that that for Asians, social identity signaling motivated by assimilation predicted life satisfaction whereas for European Americans, differentiation motivation predicted life satisfaction.

Religion. In addition to the three factors mentioned earlier, much research has noted the robust positive relation across cultures between religiosity/spirituality and SWB (for a review, see Kim-Prieto, 2014a). For example, in a study of students from Kuwait, Adbel-Khalek (2010) found that higher religiosity correlated with higher levels of well-being, and Pokimica, Addai, and Takyi (2011) similarly found religious affiliation and importance to be correlated with SWB in their sample of 1,200 participants from Ghana. Overall, religion and spirituality have consistently and robustly proven to be positively associated with well-being. Much of this link, however, can be explained by some of the factors outlined previously – positive affect, positive self-regard, and social support. For example, various religious practices, such as meditation and prayer, promote the production of positive affect, and provide social support as well as social capital to their adherents through organized communal worship and fellowship with other worshippers (for a review, see Kim-Prieto, 2014b).

Sources of Differences and Variations

As noted, whereas broad outlines of universality exist in predictors of SWB, many differences also exist across culture groups. It is not clear, however, why these differences exist. Current research provides evidence for multiple systems that explain, and also explain away, the cultural variation.

Culture-based sources of variation. One of the more consistent ways in which cultures differ in their mean levels of SWB is along the individualism-collectivism (I-C) dimension. For example, Basabe et al. (2002; Diener, Diener, & Diener, 1995) found that at the nation level, individualism significantly predicted SWB, even after controlling for other cultural dimensions such as femininity, power distance, and uncertainty avoidance. In their meta-analysis, Fischer and Boer (2011) further found that individualism predicted well-being at the national level, and was more predictive than national wealth.

Multiple investigations have attempted to untangle why I-C should have such a robust impact on SWB. One possibility is that individualistic cultures, such as Canada or New Zealand, place more focus on personal freedom, individual attainment, and other variables that are associated with SWB, compared to collectivistic cultures. Data, however, suggest that while these variables may be emphasized and valued more in individualistic cultures compared to collectivistic cultures, the variables also matter less to SWB in collectivistic cultures. For example, a meta-analysis of 108 samples of published and unpublished research found significant association between goal progress and SWB; but the research also found that this relation was moderated by I-C. That is, the relation between goal progress and SWB was stronger for individualistic cultures compared to collectivistic cultures (Klug & Maier, 2015). Similar moderation effects have also been found for other variables. For example, while power is positively correlated with SWB in US participants, it did not predict SWB for participants from the Philippines, a nation high on collectivism (Datu & Reyes, 2015).

In response, some have suggested that the difference in SWB across the I-C dimension could perhaps be due to the current measurement of SWB failing to capture the full range of the construct of SWB. Bond (2013) argued that well-being, as a construct, has different meanings across cultures, and that SWB therefore is not measurement invariant. That is, giving such a large weight to the affective dimension means that research may be tapping into only a limited component of SWB. Joshanloo (2013), for one, argued that the Islamic definition of happiness is derived from vitality, peacefulness, contentment, gratitude, and joy, and that the positive emotions of pleasure are only secondary to SWB. Ip (2014) proposed that social harmony may be just as important as happiness for SWB in Chinese societies. Uchida and Kitayama (2009) noted that for Japanese participants, the potential for social disruption caused by happiness was an important folk belief regarding SWB. Indeed, emerging data seem to support this proposal with Hitokoto and Uchida (2015) finding that interdependent happiness was a better predictor of SWB for Japanese students than for US students.

Others, however, have suggested that rather than a measurement error, it is individualism, more than collectivism, that accounts for the variability. For example, Hernandez et al. (2016) found that US Hispanic and Latino/a participants identified harmonious social relationships as an important factor in happiness. This finding is significant because unlike East Asian cultures, much of Latin American culture shows high SWB, even though both are considered high on collectivism (Diener et al., 1995). And still others have put forth relational mobility as a source of variability. For example, Yuki, Sato, Takemura, and Oishi (2013) noted that rather than collectivism accounting for US-Asian differences, it is the greater relationship mobility experienced in the United States, compared to many parts of Asia, that accounts for the difference.

Still others have suggested that perhaps another source of measurement error – cultural response bias (CRB) – may be responsible for some of the variability. CRB is the tendency of an individual to report a lower (or higher) score when rating personal dimensions, due to cultural norms or expectations of modesty. Everett, Krishnan, and Stening (1984) showed that Japanese managers were more likely to rate themselves with midpoint scores rather than higher ones, and Chen, Lee, and Stevenson (1995) demonstrated that Chinese and Japanese students reported lower scores when rating positive feelings. Oishi (2002) also found that Asian Americans rated their weekly life satisfaction more moderately and accurately than European Americans, who rated their weekly life satisfaction much higher and with a positivity bias when compared to the daily average of life satisfaction. Indeed, Kim, Schimmack, and Oishi (2012) replicated the higher evaluative bias for European Canadians compared to Asian Canadians, and further showed that this bias mediated the effect of culture on self-ratings of life satisfaction. This difference has been explained as one based on religious differences. Widespread religions in East Asia, such as Buddhism, Taoism, and Confucianism, emphasize modesty and moderation, and this may contribute to the reports of lower levels of SWB (Liu, Keeley, & Buskist, 2005). East Asian cultures emphasize low-arousal positive emotions, such as calm or relaxed, to a greater extent than Western cultures, and this can be traced to differences in religions – Buddhist versus Christian (Tsai, Miao, & Seppala, 2007).

Demographic factors. Outside of culture-based explanations, demographic factors, such as type of government, national wealth, and income, also account for cross-cultural and/or cross-national differences in SWB. For example, residents of countries that focus on human rights and social equality report higher levels of subjective well-being (Diener et al., 1995). Higher funding for welfare programs and greater social rights also significantly and positively predict life-satisfaction and happiness (Pacek & Radcliff, 2008).

In addition to type of government, wealth is another significant predictor of SWB. At the nation level, smaller GDP growth and greater income equality influence SWB, and also moderate the effect of both absolute and relative wealth on SWB at the individual level (Ball & Chernova, 2008). Similar to wealth, relative standard of living is also predictive of SWB, such that for a group of Asian countries – China, Hong Kong, Japan, Korea, Singapore, and Taiwan – relative standard of living was the strongest predictor of happiness (Shin & Inoguchi, 2009).

Culturally Responsive Teaching of SWB

Examples of Teaching Modules

Given the cultural variations in the predictors of SWB and their effects, it is important to consider the differences, as well as sources, of variability when teaching SWB. We recommend that cultural differences be integrated at every level of teaching. As seen from the review here, cultural variations affect the discussion of SWB at the predictor level as well as at the criterion level. We provide examples of different ways in which these differences can be brought into the classroom and used as a jumping-off point at which additional content can be integrated and expanded discussions can take place.

Pedrotti (2013) provided a discussion-based framework that can be used as a starting point for a discussion of cultural variation in SWB. While Pedrotti focused on positive traits, the framework provides a way to introduce the topic of culture and the ways in which our cultural background can be a source from which we can develop positive character strengths. Along with a summary of character strengths and their contribution to SWB, Pedrotti also provided a brief interactive guide for students to identify their own culture as a source of strength. This method provides a nonintimidating and inclusive way of introducing the topic because while it is easy for many students to think about culture as something that belongs to others and to identify cultural elements as something that differs or varies from their own background, it can be more difficult as well as more meaningful for students to identify the elements of their own culture. Starting with the self and one's own culture when introducing the topic of cross-cultural variation allows students to realize that all individuals are influenced by their own culture, whether they recognize it or not.

Once culture has been introduced as a source of individual-level variation, framing a wide-ranging discussion of the ways in which culture influences our everyday emotions, behaviors, and cognitions allows for an expanded discussion. And because one of the most reliable and widely researched differences across cultures is that of individualism-collectivism (I-C), it provides a framework from which further discussions about cultural differences can occur. Carducci (2012) provides a summary of key differences across the I-C domain, specifically focusing on emotions as well as a general pattern of differences across individuals. Although the framework is not specific to well-being, the focus on emotions provides a starting point for a discussion of SWB and ways in which culture serves as a source of differences. In addition, because the summaries are written with a non-expert in mind and are brief, they can be assigned to students as prior reading before the classroom discussion.

Activities that can accompany either of the discussions include a modified Twenty Statements Test (TST; Hartley, 1970). The TST gives twenty prompts that all begin with "I am _____," and is a method for generating self-descriptions. Students are instructed to fill in the twenty blanks to complete the sentences. Past research with White American college students shows that the majority of the nonconstrained and self-generated descriptions are traits (e.g., I am friendly) and other attribute descriptions (e.g., I like ice cream), as opposed to relational descriptions or group attributes (e.g., I am a mother, I am an American; Cousins, 1989; Trafimow, Triandis, & Goto, 1991). Administering the TST within the classroom and following up by discussing the differences in terms of levels of individualism and collectivism is a widely used teaching technique because the TWT is a robust and effective method.

A modification of the TST that uses a priming technique to show the further influence of culture and the ways in which cultural influence varies can also enhance the lesson. One I-C priming technique uses Brewer & Gardner's (1996) method of a word search that uses either "I" or "me" (individualistic) or "we" or "us" (collectivistic). This technique asks participants to read a descriptive passage that uses either singular or plural pronouns and asks participants to circle all pronouns. Lee, Aaker, and Gardner (2000) also report a similar method, using "I" or "me" versus "they" or "them" pronouns in their research. Trafimow et al. (1991) also describe a priming technique that can be used effectively in the classroom as a demonstration. As in other priming methods, participants are asked to read a story. But instead of using different pronouns, different versions of the story are used. In one story, the benefit accrues to the individual, whereas in the second story, the benefit accrues to the family group. The first story is expected to serve as the individualism prime, whereas the second story is expected to serve as the collectivistic prime (see Appendix to this chapter). Using the TWT in conjunction with one of the priming techniques mentioned here allows for an expanded discussion of not just cultural variations at the individual level but also of intra-individual variations along the dimensions of I-C.

Benefits of Cultural Understanding in the Classroom

The modules noted previously provide not only a way in which culture can be infused into the curriculum, but also provide a way for increasing learning by enhancing cultural understanding in the classroom. Adding cultural understanding to the course content can optimize learning outcomes by motivating students, especially through curriculum and pedagogy. Results show that in some cases, students are more motivated when learning about their own culture. For example, African American students showed increased motivation when learning about Afro-cultural themes and outperformed European American students when tested on the material (Boykin & Bailey, 2000).

Finally, providing cultural responsibility when teaching SWB is especially important because it has implications not just for the content of what is taught, but also the repercussions of that knowledge. As noted in the preceding review, cultural variation in the predictors and effects of SWB means that interventions for increasing SWB may not be equally effective across cultures. Thus, ensuring that what is taught includes cultural nuances can also ensure that ineffective and/or culturally inappropriate interventions are not undertaken. Such interventions would be damaging not only because they would be ineffective, but could also, in turn, cast doubt on the science of SWB and evidence-based attempts to enhance well-being.

APPENDIX

Written passages for priming individualism and collectivism as described in Trafimow et al. (1991, p. 652) follow.

Individualism

Sostoras, a warrior in ancient Sumer, was largely responsible for the success of Sargon I in conquering all of Mesopotamia. As a result, he was rewarded with a small kingdom of his own to rule. About 10 years later, Sargon I was conscripting warriors for a new war. Sostoras was obligated to send a detachment of soldiers to aid Sargon I. He had to decide whom to put in command of the detachment. After thinking about it for a long time, Sostoras eventually decided on Tiglath who was a talented general. This appointment had several advantages. Sostoras was able to make an excellent general indebted to him. This would solidify Sostoras's hold on his own dominion. In addition, the very fact of having a general such as Tiglath as his personal representative would greatly increase Sostoras's prestige. Finally, sending his best general would be likely to make Sargon I grateful. Consequently, there was the possibility of getting rewarded by Sargon I.

Collectivism

Sostoras, a warrior in ancient Sumer, was largely responsible for the success of Sargon I in conquering all of Mesopotamia. As a result, he was rewarded with a small kingdom of his own to rule. About 10 years later, Sargon I was conscripting warriors for a new war. Sostoras was obligated to send a detachment of soldiers to aid Sargon I. He had to decide whom to put in command of the detachment. After thinking about it for a long time, Sostoras eventually decided on Tiglath who was a member of his family. This appointment had several advantages. Sostoras was able to show his loyalty to his family. He was also able to cement their loyalty to him. In addition, having Tiglath as the

473

commander increased the power and prestige of the family. Finally, if Tiglath performed well, Sargon I would be indebted to the family.

References

Abdel-Khalek, A. M. (2010). Quality of life, subjective well-being, and religiosity in Muslim college students. *Quality of Life Research*, *19*, 1133–1143. doi:10.1007/s11136-010-9676-7

Ball, R., & Chernova, K. (2008). Absolute income, relative income, and happiness. *Social Indicators Research*, *88*, 497–529. doi:10.1007/s11205-007-9217-0

Basabe, N., Paez, D., Valencia, J., Gonzalez, J. L., Rimé, B., & Diener, E. (2002). Cultural dimensions, socioeconomic development, climate, and emotional hedonic level. *Cognition and Emotion*, *16*, 103–125. doi:10.1080/02699930143000158

Bastian, B., Kuppens, P., De Roover, K., & Diener, E. (2014). Is valuing positive emotion associated with life satisfaction? *Emotion*, *14*, 639–645. doi:10.1037/a0036466

Boehm, J. K., Lyubomirsky, S., & Sheldon, K. M. (2011). A longitudinal experimental study comparing the effectiveness of happiness-enhancing strategies in Anglo Americans and Asian Americans. *Cognition and Emotion*, *25*, 1263–1272. doi:10.1080/02699931.2010.541227

Bond, M. H. (2013). The pan-culturality of well-being: But how does culture fit into the equation?. *Asian Journal of Social Psychology*, *16*, 158–162. doi:10.1111/ajsp.12024

Boykin, A. W., & Bailey, C. T. (2000). The role of cultural factors in school relevant cognitive functioning: Synthesis of findings on cultural contexts, cultural orientations, and individual differences (Research Report No. 42). Center for Research on the Education of Students Placed at Risk. www.csos.jhu.edu.

Brewer, M. B., & Gardner, W. L. (1996). Who is this "we"? Levels of collective identity and self representations. *Journal of Personality and Social Psychology*, *71*, 83–93. doi:10.1037//0022-3514.71.1.83

Brunstein, J. C., Dangelmayer, G., & Schultheiss, O. C. (1996). Personal goals and social support in close relationships: Effects on relationship mood and marital satisfaction. *Journal of Personality and Social Psychology*, *71*, 1006–1019. doi:10.1037/0022-3514.71.5.1006

Carducci, B. J. (2012). Expressions of the self in individualistic vs. collective cultures: A cross-cultural-perspective teaching module. *Psychology Learning & Teaching*, *11*, 413–417. doi:10.2304/plat.2012.11.3.413

Chen, C., Lee, S. Y., & Stevenson, H. W. (1995). Response style and cross-cultural comparisons of rating scales among East Asian and North American students. *Psychological Science*, *6*, 170–175. doi:10.1111/j.1467-9280.1995.tb00327.x

Cousins, S. D. (1989). Culture and self-perception in Japan and the United States. *Journal of Personality and Social Psychology*, *56*, 124–131. doi:10.1037//0022-3514.56.1.124

Cutrona, C. E., Russell, D. W., Hessling, R. M., Brown P. A., & Murry, V. (2000). Direct and moderating effects of community context on the psychological well-being of African American women. *Journal of Personality and Social Psychology, 79,* 1088–1101. doi:10.1037//0022-3514.79.6.1088

Datu, J. A. D., & Reyes, J. A. S. (2015). The dark side of possessing power: Power reduces happiness in a collectivist context. *Social Indicators Research, 124,* 981–991. doi:10.1007/s11205-014-0813-5

DeNeve K., & Cooper, H. (1998). The happy personality: A meta-analysis of 137 personality traits and subjective well-being. *Psychological Bulletin, 124,* 197–229. doi:10.1037/0033-2909.124.2.197

Diener, E., Diener, M., & Diener, C. (1995). Factors predicting the subjective well-being of nations. *Journal of Personality and Social Psychology, 69,* 851–864. doi:10.1037/0022-3514.69.5.851

Diener, E., Oishi, S., & Lucas, R. E. (2003). Personality, culture, and subjective well-being: Emotional and cognitive evaluations of life. *Annual Review of Psychology, 54,* 403–425. doi:10.1146/annurev.psych.54.101601.145056

Diener, E., Wirtz, D., Biswas-Diener, R., Tov, W., Kim-Prieto, C., Choi, D. W., & Oishi, S. (2009). New measures of well-being. In E. Diener (Ed.), *Collected works of Ed Diener* (pp. 247–266). Netherlands: Springer. doi:10.1007/978-90-481-2354-4_12

Everett, J. E., Krishnan, A. R., & Stening, B. W. (1984). *South-East Asian managers: Mutual perceptions of Japanese and local counterparts.* Singapore: Eastern Universities Press.

Fischer, R., & Boer, D. (2011). What is more important for national well-being: Money or autonomy? A meta-analysis of well-being, burnout, and anxiety across 63 societies. *Journal of Personality and Social Psychology, 101,* 164–184. doi:10.1037/a0023663

Hartley, W. S. (1970). *Manual for the twenty statements problem.* Kansas City, MO: Greater Kansas City Mental Health Foundation.

Hayes, N., & Joseph, S. (2003). Big 5 correlates of three measures of subjective well-being. *Personality and Individual Differences, 34,* 723–727. doi:10.1016/s0191-8869(02)00057-0

Hernandez, R., Carnethon, M., Penedo, F. J., Martinez, L., Boehm, J., & Schueller, S. M. (2016). Exploring well-being among US Hispanics/Latinos in a church-based institution: A qualitative study. *Journal of Positive Psychology, 11,* 511–521. doi:10.1080/17439760.2015.1117132

Hitokoto, H., & Uchida, Y. (2015). Interdependent happiness: Theoretical importance and measurement validity. *Journal of Happiness Studies, 16,* 211–239. doi:10.1007/s10902-014-9505-8

Huang, Y., & Wu, L. (2012). Correlates of life satisfaction among older people in China: An examination of two cultural variables. *Aging & Mental Health, 16,* 1028–1038. doi:10.1080/13607863.2012.702727

Ip, P. K. (2014). Harmony as happiness? Social harmony in two Chinese societies. *Social Indicators Research, 117,* 719–741. doi:10.1007/s11205-013-0395-7

Joshanloo, M. (2013). A comparison of Western and Islamic conceptions of happiness. *Journal of Happiness Studies, 14,* 1857–1874. doi:10.1007/s10902-012-9406-7

Kim, Y. H., Chiu, C. Y., Cho, S., Au, E. W., & Kwak, S. N. (2014). Aligning inside and outside perspectives of the self: A cross-cultural difference in self-perception. *Asian Journal of Social Psychology, 17,* 44–51. doi:10.1111/ajsp.12042

Kim, H., Schimmack, U., & Oishi, S. (2012). Cultural differences in self- and other-evaluations and well-being: A study of European and Asian Canadians. *Journal of Personality and Social Psychology, 102,* 856–873. doi:10.1037/a0026803

Kim-Prieto, C. (2014a). Positive psychology of religion across traditions and beliefs. In C. Kim-Prieto (Ed.) *Religion and spirituality across cultures* (pp. 1–20). New York, NY: Springer.

(2014b) (Ed.). *Religion and spirituality across cultures.* New York, NY: Springer.

Klug, H. J., & Maier, G. W. (2015). Linking goal progress and subjective well-being: A meta-analysis. *Journal of Happiness Studies, 16,* 37–65. doi:10.1007/s10902-013-9493-0

Kreuzbauer, R., Chiu, C. Y., Lin, S., & Bae, S. H. (2014). When does life satisfaction accompany relational identity signaling: A cross-cultural analysis. *Journal of Cross-Cultural Psychology, 45,* 646–659. doi:10.1177/0022022113518369

Kuppens, P., Realo, A., & Diener, E. (2008). The role of positive and negative emotions in life satisfaction judgment across nations. *Journal of Personality and Social Psychology, 95,* 66–75. doi:10.1037/0022-3514.95.1.66

Lee, A. Y., Aaker, J. L., & Gardner, W. (2000). The pleasures and pains of distinct self-construals: The role of interdependence in regulatory focus. *Journal of Personality and Social Psychology, 78,* 1122–1134. doi:10.1037//0022-3514.78.6.1122

Liu, S., Keeley, J., & Buskist, W. (2015). Chinese college students' perceptions of characteristics of excellent teachers. *Teaching of Psychology, 42,* 83–86. doi:10.1177/0098628314562684

Lu, L., & Shi, J. B. (1997). Personality and happiness: Is mental health a mediator? *Personality and Individual Differences, 22,* 249–256. doi:10.1016/s0191-8869(96)00187-0

Lucas, R. E., Diener, E., Grob, A., Suh, E. M., & Shiao, L. (2000). Cross-cultural evidence for the fundamental features of extraversion. *Journal of Personality and Social Psychology, 79,* 452–468. doi:10.1037/0022-3514.79.3.452

Oishi, S. (2002). Experiencing and remembering of well-being: A cross-cultural analysis. *Personality and Social Psychology Bulletin, 28,* 1398–1406. doi:10.1177/014616702236871

Oishi, S., Koo, M., & Akimoto, S. (2008). Culture, interpersonal perceptions, and happiness in social interactions. *Personality and Social Psychology Bulletin, 34,* 307–320. doi:10.1177/0146167207311198

Pacek, A. C., & Radcliff, B. (2008). Welfare policy and subjective well-being across nations: An individual-level assessment. *Social Indicators Research, 89,* 179–191. doi:10.1007/s11205-007-9232-1

Pedrotti, J. T. (2013). *Culture and identity: Integrating an understanding of cultural context into a discussion of positive traits: Activities for teaching positive psychology: A guide for instructors.* Washington, DC: American Psychological Association, pp. 41–44. doi:10.1037/14042-007

Pokimica, J., Addai, I., & Takyi, B. K. (2012). Religion and subjective well-being in Ghana. *Social Indicators Research, 106*, 61–79. doi:10.1007/s11205-011-9793-x

Raibley, J. R. (2012). Happiness is not well-being. *Journal of Happiness Studies, 13*, 1105–1129. doi:10.1007/s10902-011-9309-z

Rodriguez Mosquera, P. M., & Imada, T. (2013). Perceived social image and life satisfaction across cultures. *Cognition & Emotion, 27*, 1132–1141. doi:10.1080/02699931.2013.767222

Ryff, C. D. (1989). Happiness is everything, or is it? Explorations on the meaning of psychological well-being. *Journal of Personality and Social Psychology, 57*, 1069–1081. doi:10.1037//0022-3514.57.6.1069

Shin, D. C., & Inoguchi, T. (2009). Avowed happiness in Confucian Asia: Ascertaining its distribution, patterns, and sources. *Social Indicators Research, 92*, 405–427. doi:10.1007/s11205-008-9354-0

Siedlecki, K. L., Salthouse, T. A., Oishi, S., & Jeswani, S. (2014). The relationship between social support and subjective well-being across age. *Social Indicators Research, 117*, 561–576. doi:10.1007/s11205-013-0361-4

Steel, P., Schmidt, J., & Shultz, J. (2008). Refining the relationship between personality and subjective well-being. *Psychological Bulletin, 134*, 138–161. doi:10.1037/0033-2909.134.1.138

Suh, E., Diener, E., Oishi, S., & Triandis, H. C. (1998). The shifting basis of life satisfaction judgments across cultures: Emotions versus norms. *Journal of Personality and Social Psychology, 74*, 482–493. doi:10.1037//0022-3514.74.2.482

Tanksale, D. (2015). Big Five personality traits: Are they really important for the subjective well-being of Indians? *International Journal of Psychology, 50*, 64–69. doi:10.1002/ijop.12060

Trafimow, D., Triandis, H. C, & Goto, S. G. (1991). Some tests of the distinction between the private self and the collective self. *Journal of Personality and Social Psychology, 60*, 649–655. doi:10.1037//0022-3514.60.5.649

Tsai, J. L., Miao, F. F., & Seppala, E. (2007). Good feelings in Christianity and Buddhism: Religious differences in ideal affect. *Personality and Social Psychology Bulletin, 33*, 409–421. doi:10.1177/0146167206296107

Uchida, Y., & Kitayama, S. (2009). Happiness and unhappiness in East and West: Themes and variations. *Emotion, 9*, 441–456. doi:10.1037/e633982013-243

Yuki, M., Sato, K., Takemura, K., & Oishi, S. (2013). Social ecology moderates the association between self-esteem and happiness. *Journal of Experimental Social Psychology, 49*, 741–746. doi:10.1016/j.jesp.2013.02.006

Zessin, U., Dickhäuser, O., & Garbade, S. (2015). The relationship between self-compassion and well-being: A meta-analysis. *Applied Psychology: Health and Well-Being, 7*, 340–364. doi:10.1111/aphw.12051

Personality, Disability, and Disorders

Personality theory in the West has typically employed theories and measures associated with mainstream psychology, and has dominated the teaching of personality. However, as Giordano (Chapter 23) shows, the Eastern philosophies of Buddhism and Confucianism have much to offer as systems for understanding personality and conceptualizing relationships. This chapter raises fundamental questions about the nature of personality, the self, and mental health, and offers ideas for readings and teaching approaches.

Integration of culture with the study of disability (Chapter 24) serves to raise students' consciousness about views of disability in their own culture as well as others, and to help students see that disability may be viewed quite differently across cultures. The authors discuss experiential approaches to teaching about disability and present case-based scenarios and study questions.

The imposition of Western standards and the failure to recognize the importance of indigenous views of mental health is likely to lead to a wide range of cultural syndromes and standards of normalcy. Similarly, cultures vary widely in their views of causes of psychological disorders. In Chapter 25, Tan discusses these issues and provides teaching exercises and activities designed to increase students' intercultural understanding.

Evidence-based and culturally sensitive therapies are key in psychotherapy, yet as Tanaka-Matsumi (Chapter 25) asks, is there evidence for particular therapies with differing cultural groups? This is the place for culturally adapted therapies, requiring cultural awareness and culturally informed treatment using specific professional skills of the sort presented in this chapter. The author describes culturally informed interview techniques and their use in education of graduate and undergraduate students, and the excitement inherent in introducing students to the importance of cultural awareness.

CHAPTER 23

Personality Is Culturally Constructed and Maintained: Helping Students Think Globally about Themselves and Others

Peter J. Giordano

It is difficult to imagine a time when psychologists did not study the intersections of psychological and cultural phenomena. In the not-too-distant past of our discipline, however, we erroneously assumed that principles of behavior, emotion, cognition, perception, and personality, the topic of this chapter, would apply in equal measure to persons living on all parts of the globe. What research participants revealed in a lab in California or North Carolina, for example, should be similar (we thought) to what participants exhibited in Beijing or Mumbai. Human experience and behavior do have many similarities across cultural landscapes, but there are also striking and important differences (Nisbett, Peng, Choi, & Norenzayan, 2001; see also Wang, 2017, for a brief but compelling summary of some of the similarities and differences).

In the domain of personality psychology, the interplay of culture and personality is of great interest to students and should be deeply explored in the personality course. An organizing theme of this chapter is that the construct of "personality" cannot be disentangled from cultural experience and therefore is *culturally constructed and maintained* over time. This notion is a sophisticated idea for undergraduate students to grasp, but the process of struggling with it has many intellectual rewards.

In this chapter, I identify four central issues in the personality course that are best understood when discussed in cultural context. I also offer suggestions for helping students understand these concepts and, at the end of the chapter, recommend reading resources to deepen your own or your students' appreciation for these ideas. The areas I discuss are by no means exhaustive. There are many others that could be explored in the personality course, and I encourage you to add to my list based on your own interests.

At this juncture, let me offer a confession, then an approach for introducing students to the cultural concepts I work with in the chapter, and finally several caveats. First, a confession. My perspective in this chapter is inspired by an interest in East Asian cultures, and particularly cultures that have been influenced by both Confucian and Buddhist traditions. I construe these perspectives not as religions, but as systems for understanding human personality and for conceptualizing relationships and optimal mental well-being. It some ways, it might seem strange to introduce these frameworks into the personality psychology course; in other ways it is not, and I hope to convince you that you can remain a scientific psychologist, while helping students think globally about their own and others' personalities.

Second, let me offer a strategy for introducing these ideas into a personality course. Any personality theory attempts to accomplish five things (Giordano, 2011). It (a) offers basic elements or components of personality, (b) suggests mechanisms by which personality develops, (c) proposes explanations for why people suffer or struggle psychologically, (d) recommends activities for alleviating suffering or changing personality, and (e) presents a model for a mature, healthy personality. Not all personality theories work with equal facility in all five domains. Freud's psychoanalytic perspective, for instance, has much to say about (a)–(d) but, relatively speaking, less to offer for understanding the mentally healthy person (is mental health merely the absence of neurosis?). Conversely, the Five Factor model and theory (McCrae & Costa, 2008) fully develop the most basic components (traits) of personality, but have little to suggest in terms of personality change. Confucian and Buddhist models of personhood and "personality" work with these same five dimensions to varying degrees, and you can use these elements to introduce students to these traditions, which may be quite foreign to them unless they have personal ties to Asia. And, as will become clearer in this chapter, both Confucianism and Buddhism have sophisticated analyses of the development of mental well-being and optimal personality functioning.

Finally, here are several caveats. The Confucian and Buddhist perspectives are extraordinarily complex, having evolved over a time span of over 2,500 years and across cultures, countries, and continents. Due to expanding globalization, however, these perspectives are ever more important for Western students to understand, at least in an introductory way. A person growing up in a Confucian heritage country such as China or South Korea, or in Japan, a culture steeped in Buddhist thought, for instance, may have culturally distinct ways of understanding selfhood, relationships with friends and family, and responsibilities to other people and to institutions. Because of these cultural underpinnings, these traditions raise interesting personality questions for students to explore.

One final caveat. When discussing the "East" and the "West," it is important not to dichotomize these two cultural heritages as completely distinct (Giordano, 2017; Hermans & Kempen, 1998). As I have already noted, there are many similarities *across* cultural boundaries and, conversely, *within* cultures, there are important distinctions that can be made. The cultural understanding and expression of Confucianism and Buddhism is not identical across East Asian countries.

How Should Personality Be Studied? (Corollary: What Groups of People Should Be Studied?)

As is the case with other psychological phenomena, personality is studied empirically in any number of ways. Most personality texts have a chapter on research methods to introduce descriptive, correlational, and experimental approaches to the study of personality. It is possible that the personality course you teach may also have a research methods course as a prerequisite as well as a laboratory component. These features of the course will obviously influence the depth of course discussions on research-related topics. Furthermore, personality courses may be organized in terms of theories or topics. The course I teach is organized around theoretical perspectives rather than topics, but the ideas I discuss can easily be incorporated into a topics-oriented framework.

When introducing the interconnections of personality and culture, students benefit from exploring how culture is best integrated into research activities. Many students born and raised in North America have never thought about these issues, especially if they grew up in communities lacking in cultural diversity. How should personality be studied in other cultures? Is it best to take a theory that was developed in Western Europe, for example, and then use it to study people in China, so as to compare Western Europeans (or North Americans) and Chinese on any number of personality dimensions? Or is it best to go to China and study Chinese people without any preconceived personality ideas? These are research-oriented questions for students to explore. These questions also tap into important research strategy distinctions. The former strategy views culture as a variable that can be studied independently of other aspects of the person in the search for personality universals. This approach is often adopted in cross-cultural research and is called an *imported* or imposed-etic research strategy (Giordano, 2013). The second question taps into an emic strategy, which asserts that culture can never be separated from the person being studied, leading to the development of indigenous theories of personality. Cultural psychologists tend to favor this way of studying culture and personality (Giordano, 2013). It is also possible, of course, to combine these two approaches with an eye toward the complementarity of universal and indigenous dimensions of personality (Matsumoto & Juang, 2008). These research issues can be either first introduced when the research methods chapter is the topic of discussion or the questions can be dealt with at a later time in the course schedule, for example, if these cultural discussions are addressed in a separate unit on culture and personality.

Another entry point for working with culture, personality, and research strategies is to question with students the demographics of participants in many psychological investigations, including personality studies. A compelling article for students to read is Henrich, Heine, and Noren-zayan's (2010) monograph in which the authors argued that much psy-chological science is built on samples of WEIRD participants – people who are Western, Educated, from Industrialized countries, who are also Rich (when compared to many around the globe) and from Democratic societies – who comprise roughly 15 percent of the world's population. If you teach in the United States and your students were part of a "subject pool" in an introductory psychology course, they will immediately resonate to this notion. The implications of this situation are readily apparent, and Henrich et al. (2010) discussed a number of research areas where this is problematic. This article is lengthy and challenging, so it might be worth assigning selected parts of it or giving students explicit guidelines on what to look for in the article. Generally speaking, the topics of research strategies and sample demographics are an excellent springboard for then working with other issues related to culture and personality.

What Is the Nature of the Self? (Corollary: Is There a Self?)

The construct of "self" is another area of intrinsic interest to students in a personality course. In their well-known theoretical and empirical work on self-construal, Markus and Kitayama (1991, 2010) drew attention to disparities in how persons construct their self-understanding as *independent* (the autonomous, rational self of the West) or *interdependent* (the relational self of the East). Construing oneself as autonomous is relatively typical in most North American and Western European countries. West-ern students often understand themselves and others in their social envir-onments in this way. The traditional or grand theories of personality also typically emphasize the value of younger people *separating* from their parents to establish their own *independent* identities and lives. This independence is a mark of psychological health. If this separation is fraught with problems, then the person may be seen as immature, neurotic, or somehow less than a fully functioning independent adult.

A fruitful area of discussion in the personality course is to explore with students the degree to which the independent self is a universal. The interdependent or relational self-construal is of interest to students since they may have never encountered this way of thinking. The core idea that the self does not exist autonomously but that it exists "in between" all of one's relationships is a conceptual idea that can take class discussion in any number of theoretical directions.

Working from the position of the interdependent self, what does this say about the importance or possibility of separating from one's parents? Is it healthy to do so? To what extent is separation needed or even beneficial? If one's identity is interdependent, what are one's responsibilities to family, close friends, or more distant acquaintances?

There are other interesting theoretical and empirical avenues to explore. First, discussion can center on whether the distinction between independent and interdependent self is reflected only in the West–East divide. There are data to suggest, for example, that persons living in the confederate states of the United States, as well as in Utah and Hawaii, endorse a relational self-construal to a greater degree than an independent self-construal (Vandello & Cohen, 1999). Second, Wang and Ross (2005) experimentally manipulated dimensions of self-construal in samples of Caucasian and Asian American college students and demonstrated memory recall effects from these manipulations. Discussion of data like these can lead to important questions about the instability or fluidity of the self, a topic to which I turn attention later in this chapter.

Finally, it can be useful for students to read and discuss some of the older literature in Western psychology arguing that the self can only be understood as relational. To this end, the work of John Dewey (1922) and George Herbert Mead (1934) can be enlightening for students. Their writing is more difficult for undergraduates to understand, but shorter passages are worth exploring alongside textbook material or more recent empirical articles. Mead (1934, p. 142; italics mine) asserted, for example, that "There are all sorts of different selves answering to all sorts of different social reactions. *It is the social process itself that is responsible for the appearance of the self; it is not there as a self apart from this type of experience.*" One might contend that personality psychology has advanced so far since 1934 that having students read such dated material is not needed. I would argue that there are still many intriguing conceptual resources in psychology's historical literature that can help students think critically about contemporary perspectives in the field. The important point for students to grasp is that the independent self is not held by all persons and therefore it is subject to both cultural and temporal influence.

Once students become familiar with self-construal as interdependent (i.e., they have been introduced to Markus and Kitayama's work), the door is opened to explore Confucian and Buddhist conceptions of the self and personality. Here I introduce basic ideas; the suggested readings at the end of the chapter provide more detailed discussions. The Confucian interpretation of personhood is inherently relational, as humans are understood to be "irreducibly social" (Fingarette, 1972). The Confucian tradition has been a dominant force in shaping the collectivism of East Asian cultures and in highlighting the relational self and the importance of social harmony. The relational or interdependent self is "common sense" in these cultural contexts.

Consistent with this theme, students also enjoy discussing the dynamics of family relationships in Confucian heritage cultures. The concept of *xiao* (孝; translated as filial piety or family reverence; Rosemont & Ames, 2009) emphasizes that family members are inextricably bound to one another and that it is in the family that persons first learn to be socially responsible. On this basis, they then learn to cultivate social harmony in ever-widening circles of social relationship, expanding from the family outward (Tu, 1989, 1994). The family, therefore, is not something that one strives to leave behind, thereby cultivating independence; rather, the family is the primary source of social connection, ethical education, and gratifying responsibility throughout one's life. Developmentally, traditional aged college students are often grappling personally with these issues, and therefore discussions on this topic can be lively. There are also important implications of this perspective for optimal personality functioning, a topic to which I return subsequently.

One final note on self-construal: Students may also find it of interest that recent studies of independent and interdependent selves are investigating neurological correlates of self-construal via neuroimaging techniques (Wang, Peng, Chechlacz, Humphreys, & Sui, 2017) in the relatively new area of cultural neuroscience (Kitayama & Tompson, 2010). As Kitayama and Uskul (2011) have argued, self-construal and other culturally important experiences become "embrained" or neurologically hard wired, so to speak.

If time permits in your personality course, Buddhist conceptions of the self also provide opportunity for discussion of the nature of the self.

Like Confucianism, Buddhist thought is extraordinarily complex with a cultural history spanning millennia. But there are accessible resources for students to read, which I mention at the end of the chapter, and which deemphasize metaphysics and instead offer clear explanations with little jargon. Wallace and Shapiro (2006) asserted that Buddhism is the most psychological of Eastern philosophical traditions, and many scholars are actively making connections between scientific psychology and a Buddhist perspective (Dahlgaard, Peterson, & Seligman, 2005; Wallace & Shapiro, 2006; Walsh & Shapiro, 2006).

In essence, Buddhism rejects the idea of an essential, organizing self that is the center of the personality or the "me" within personality (Markus & Kitayama, 2010). In fact, Buddhism asserts that the notion of an independent, autonomous self is the root of psychological distress and suffering. The independent self-construal creates a misguided self-centeredness, which in turn generates negative feelings of fear, envy, greed, narcissism, and so on. What we mistake as the self is really a conditioned, impermanent, always changing, dynamic flow of thoughts, feelings, and perceptions. If one pauses to carefully observe the cognitive activity of one's mind through meditative practices (e.g., mindfulness meditation), for example, one begins to see more clearly the cognitive patterns that lead to mental suffering. The key to psychological well-being, therefore, is to work to tame these mental states and to gain a clearer perception of one's conditioned self-centeredness, so as to recognize the interdependence of all persons and things. In so doing, one becomes less self-absorbed, more insightful, and more compassionate toward others. Stripped of its complex metaphysics (see Stephen Batchelor's *Buddhism without Beliefs* in the recommended readings), Buddhism is essentially an early form of cognitive psychology that can be accessible to undergraduates and can generate an important contrast with students' "common sense" endorsement of the independent self-construal.

Is Personality Best Understood as Structure or Process? (Corollary: What Is the Ontology of Personality?)

The philosophical foundations of personality theories are often overlooked in the personality course. Although the personality course is not a course in philosophy, it is important for students to see that theories of personality evolve in social, historical, and cultural contexts, all of which are anchored in *philosophical* traditions. It is common to discuss how personality perspectives derive in part from the personal histories of their intellectual architects, a topic that is sometimes covered in personality textbooks. These principles are seen clearly, for example, in the life and work of Freud. His understanding of persons and their personalities was influenced by his early life and family dynamics of the Victorian Era, his training as a physician, the events of World War I, and his encounters with the malevolence leading up to World War II (Gay, 1988). Importantly, social, historical, and cultural forces help shape all theoretical perspectives, including the most contemporary ones. In a half century, personality psychologists will be discussing the Big Five model and theory from a historical vantage point that will give a clearer understanding of the sociocultural forces that helped shape this important perspective.

Theoretical viewpoints can also be examined, however, in terms of the philosophical assumptions supporting them. Students in a personality course will benefit from this type of discussion even as they learn the theoretical nitty gritty of each perspective. These philosophical ideas are not easy for students to grasp, as they represent a sophisticated level of analysis. I recommend introducing these ideas slowly in the course so that over time students gain the ability to think in these ways. Because I organize my course into the dominant theoretical systems, I spend time in each perspective briefly addressing the philosophical underpinnings of each.

I explicitly work with culture and personality in a unit in the latter part of the course. It is at this point that I deal more deeply with the *ontological dimensions* of personality thinking. This unit approach is only one among many, of course. You may wish to incorporate ideas such as the ones I discuss here in a more integrated fashion throughout the course, rather than saving them for a component later in the semester. Whatever the organizational format, you can work with philosophical frameworks to help students deepen their understanding of how philosophical assumptions undergird theoretical (or topical) ideas.

Ontology is a branch of metaphysics that deals with the nature of being, reality, or existence. If we ask questions such as "What is the self like?" or "What is the nature of personality?" we are asking ontological questions. Scientific psychology answers these questions with the methods of empirical science. Philosophers approach these questions with different methods of inquiry, but both disciplines are interested in these questions.

The relevance of ontology to the personality course is that any system for understanding human personality is rooted in an ontological perspective. Western perspectives on personality typically derive from the world view of the classical Greek philosophers, which emphasizes a Being ontology (Ames, 2011, Giordano, 2014, 2015, 2017). Here again we are reminded that an East-West dichotomy does not always hold true, though it generally does. Comparative philosophers Ames and Rosemont (1998) articulated this dilemma of dichotomy as follows: "Proceeding from an awareness that the only thing more dangerous than making cultural generalizations is the reductionism that results from not doing so, we need to identify and elaborate [relevant] presuppositions" (p. 20; bracket mine). Construing personality as comprising structures such as a self, ego, proprium, or any number of traits or dispositions reflects a Being ontological tradition. Structures such as these are understood to be relatively stable and enduring and to have more than a nominal existence. These structures can therefore be measured and quantified, and used to make between individual and group comparisons. "Person A has more ego control than Person B," or "Group A is generally more conscientious than Group B" are assertions that illustrate these types of comparative statements. A Being ontology is common in the Western philosophical tradition and therefore is typically foundational in the development of Western personality theories. Students are certainly accustomed to thinking of personality in this way.

The dominant philosophical perspective in the East, however, is different, as it has evolved within philosophical traditions anchored in ancient cultures in Asia. The philosophical traditions of Daoism, Confucianism, and Buddhism have developed within a Becoming ontology (Ames, 2011), rather than a Being worldview. A Becoming ontology emphasizes process over structure, instability over stability, and change over stasis. From this event-oriented perspective, the world is best characterized as undergoing continuous dynamic change rather than as a stable network of structures. A Being or process ontology helps explain important notions in Eastern thought, such as an emphasis on impermanence, change, relationality, and the complementarity of opposites (see Nisbett et al., 2001). This way of thinking should not be understood as arcane and mystical. Seeing this perspective as esoteric is to interpret it through the common sense lens of a Being ontological perspective, rather than taking it on its own terms and within its own cultural context. To help students understand this way of thinking, it is useful for them to first recognize their own assumptions before working with a new set.

As one example that might make these ontologies more concrete for students, I use the illustration of success and failure. We might see these as steady states of being – I *am* a "success" or I *am* a "failure." Or I "failed" at that attempt whereas I "succeeded" in another endeavor. A Becoming ontology would instead seek to understand the *relation* between success and failure, the *impermanence* of each, and the *complementarity* of the two. From this perspective, success and failure can never exist on their own as independent – they are complementary and mutually entailing. Success, as soon as it is "achieved" is in the *process* of transitioning into failure, and vice versa. (The aphorism "failure is the mother of success" captures a process ontology quite nicely.)

Here again, I emphasize that this way of thinking is common sense in many Eastern cultures, although due to globalization and the Westernization of some cultures, the impact may be diminishing. Nevertheless, Confucianism and Buddhism developed within this type of processual thinking. Therefore, concepts within these traditions, including those related to personality, can only be grasped clearly when interpreted within this framework. For example, the relational self of Confucianism or the no-self of Buddhism makes sense only in this ontological context. The Confucian relational self is "located" between persons, not within this person or that person. Furthermore, the relational self must be understood as dynamic and fluid because the self changes as it moves into and out of different social contexts. Further still, personal roles and responsibilities change along with the particulars of various social relationships. Philosophers Ames and Rosemont (1998) clearly captured this sensibility when writing,

> In a world of substances [a Being ontology], people or things are related extrinsically, so that when the relationship between them is dissolved, they are remaindered intact. But relatedness defining of the Confucian worldview [a Becoming ontology] is intrinsic and constitutive . . . . Under such circumstances, the dissolution of relationships is surgical, diminishing both parties in the degree that this particular relationship is important to them. In such a world, people literally rather than figuratively change each other's minds. The point can be generalized still further perhaps: no-thing or nobody has an essence, but can be defined only "correlationally," at any given time, with differing relations holding at other times . . . . (p. 24; bracketed material mine)

Ontological perspectives also inform the scientific methods used to study personality, a topic that can be addressed with students. For example, measuring structures such as traits works well in studies with large sample sizes and where the goal of the investigation is to make between individual or group comparisons. But relational selfhood has significant implications for psychological inquiry. If the relational self is dynamic and changing, how do we compare one relational self with another? Or how do we study a relational self at Time 1 and then again at Time 2 in a different social context, if the relational self is dynamic and, to a degree, unstable? The most interesting level of analysis for relationally constructed selves may be at the level of the individual – to understand individual process and variation, not differences in group averages (Giordano, 2017). In this case, qualitative analyses (Gergen, Josselson, & Freeman, 2015) or subject-specific quantitative analyses may be most useful (Molenaar, 2004; Molenaar & Campbell, 2009; Molenaar, Huizenga, & Nesselroade, 2002; Molenaar & Valsiner, 2008; Nesselroade & Ram, 2004). Admittedly, discussion of person-specific analyses in an undergraduate personality course will remain at an introductory level, but students can grasp the conceptual notion behind these advanced techniques. Overall, introducing ideas such as these helps students think more deeply both about the cultural dimensions of personality construction and the methods we use to study personality phenomena. Gergen et al. (2015), in particular, did a nice job of arguing for the complementarity of qualitative and quantitative scientific strategies.

How Should We Best Understand Mental Health or Mental Well-Being? (Corollary: How Does One Attain Optimal Personality Functioning?)

The discussion of ontology can be used as a segue into considerations of mental health or mental well-being. This topic is of obvious significance in a personality psychology course. The inclusion of cultural perspectives on this topic is especially useful. Clearly, Western theorists such as Carl Rogers or Abraham Maslow have well-developed perspectives on mental well-being and healthy personality development. Even Bandura's work on self-efficacy has important implications for mental health. At the same time, both Confucianism and Buddhism offer mature and highly developed conceptual ideas for discussing mental health.

Buddhism is likely to be more familiar to students than Confucianism, yet unless they are Buddhist, students may have significant misconceptions about Buddhism. The tack I take is to help students see Buddhism not as a religion but as a philosophical approach to life that attempts to accomplish what most theories of personality do (see my earlier comments about the five domains that all personality theories address). Fortunately, contemporary scientific interest in mindfulness is contributing to an explosion of empirical studies on these cognitive practices that are closely aligned with the Buddhist tradition. A quick search of PsycINFO & PsycARTICLES with the keyword "mindfulness" will yield over 6,000 peer-reviewed journal articles since the year 2000. The same type of search for the previous 50 years yields slightly over 100 articles. There are now abundant theoretical and empirical resources to use in a personality course to help students think about the role of mindfulness practices in enhancing mental well-being.

Interestingly, one of the most popular personality textbooks of several decades ago contained an excellent chapter titled "Eastern Psychology." In this chapter, Hall and Lindzey (1978) made connections between existing Western theories and their Eastern counterparts that dealt with similar issues of mental suffering and mental well-being, drawing a good deal from Buddhist formulations. Anticipating the contemporary interest in mindfulness practices (a topic I will discuss), a subsection of this chapter was "Mindfulness Meditation: The Path to Personality Change." Perhaps Hall and Lindzey were ahead of their time, although by the fourth edition of this text, this chapter had been removed.

One avenue for working with these ideas in a personality course is for students first to gain an appreciation for the Buddhist conception of mental suffering and the way in which it arises. There are a number of good resources to use for this purpose, which present Buddhist ideas in a secular, nonreligious way. Using this formulation, mental well-being can be discussed in terms of lack of self-centeredness, clear and nonjudgmental perception of reality, open compassion toward oneself and others, and lack of negative mood states such as fear, anxiety, envy, greed, resentment, desire, and so on. Such ideas can then be compared to other Western personality approaches to psychopathology and mental health. It is useful in my view to focus discussion in this domain on enhancing and improving well-being rather than on a treatment approach for psychiatric problems.

Fortunately, there is a large and growing literature on the use of mindfulness practices for improving well-being in nonclinical populations. Moreover, students can benefit from seeing connections between age-old meditative traditions and modern cognitive science. Jankowski and Holas (2014), for example, drew upon clinical and nonclinical literature, as well as cognitive science and neuroscientific studies, to propose a metacognitive model of mindfulness. Shapiro, Carlson, Astin, and Freedman (2006) offered a theoretical model to explicate the mechanisms of action for the positive changes associated with mindfulness practices. Ideas from sources like these can easily be incorporated into discussions in a personality course, particularly when working with strategies of personality change within a Buddhist psychology.

Discussion of Confucian contributions to an understanding of mental health and well-being takes a bit more time because students are typically less familiar with the Confucian tradition. Like Buddhism, Confucianism is a rich and complex perspective, which has influenced East Asian culture in a variety of domains including education and politics as well as all dimensions of family life and other social systems. At its core, however, Confucianism emphasizes lifelong personal cultivation as a means to enhance not only oneself but, perhaps even more importantly, the lives of others. Therefore, Confucianism has many conceptual resources for working with notions of mental well-being.

Confucianism, as I discussed earlier, developed within a Becoming or process-oriented ontology. The self is inherently relational. Furthermore, establishing and maintaining harmonious relationships with others is a central human task that benefits all persons in the social context. The so-called Confucian project (Ames, 2011; Ivanhoe, 2000) is a lifelong commitment to work diligently to cultivate oneself in fulfilling all of one's roles and responsibilities in all domains of one's social life. In Confucianism, the paragon of this personal maturity is known as the *junzi* (君子; sometimes translated *authoritative person* or *exemplary person*), a virtuoso in interpersonal relationships. The *junzi* possesses a powerful blend of authority over and benevolence toward others. People respond to the influence of the *junzi* because it is noncoercive; the authority derives instead from the ability of the *junzi* in responding appropriately to the demands of the social situation, while ensuring the welfare of all. Importantly, becoming a *junzi* is not a trait that one acquires but a behavioral pattern of responding that develops continuously, or at least should, over the course of a lifetime. Additionally, the soil from which the *junzi* grows is first the family to whom one always is relationally loyal, and then extends outward into wider and wider social contexts (Tu, 1989).

The *junzi* as the exemplar of psychological health and mental well-being can be compared to other conceptions of mental health offered by Western personality theorists. To what extent does this formulation agree or disagree with similar models in the work of Freud, Jung, Allport, Rogers, Maslow, or others? Can one use the Five Factor model to capture the notion of the *junzi*? In Confucianism, how do the roles and responsibilities of family members compare to ideas in the Western perspectives? Earlier, I mentioned the Chinese concept of *xiao* (孝; filial piety or family reverence). When discussing the development of mental well-being in this context, you can generate a lively conversation around issues of family relationships and responsibilities toward family members. In these discussions, it is important always to link the comments to important theoretical ideas or to empirical findings. A free-wheeling discussion can be fun, but the intellectual work of building connections or identifying impasses across theoretical perspectives is important for student learning.

Summary and Conclusion

In this chapter, I have offered four domains in the personality psychology course that provide an opportunity to illustrate the intersection of cultural experiencing and human personality. Fortunately, any number of other areas can be explored, depending upon your own interests and inclinations. The important aim in all of these course discussions is to help students appreciate the rich contributions of cultural forces in shaping the construction and maintenance of human personality.

Suggestions for Further Exploration of the Confucian Tradition (with Brief Annotations)

Ames, R. T. (2011). *Confucian role ethics: A vocabulary*. Hong Kong: The Chinese University Press.

Ames is a gifted writer. This book provides an excellent overview of Confucianism, the Chinese philosophical tradition, and the dynamics of relational virtuosity. I would start, however, with other books I mention such as Littlejohn's or Van Norden's introductory books.

Ames, R. T., & Hall, D. L. (2001). *Focusing the familiar: A translation and philosophical interpretation of the Zhongyong*. Honolulu, HI: University of Hawai'i Press.

This beautifully written book has much to say about human relationships and skillful engagement with one's social context.

Ames, R. T., & Rosemont, H., Jr. (1998). *The analects of Confucius: A philosophical translation*. New York, NY: Ballentine.

Regarded as one on the best translations of the Analects with an excellent commentary to aid your understanding of the Chinese philosophical tradition.

Fingarette, H. (1972). *Confucius: The secular as sacred*. Long Grove, IL: Waveland.

This short monograph provides an informative perspective on the relational and social implications of Confucianism.

Ivanhoe, P. J. (2000). *Confucian moral self cultivation* (2nd ed.). Indianapolis, IN: Hackett.

This brief book is superb. It is well worth spending the time to grasp the interpersonal implications of the Confucian philosophers Ivanhoe discusses.

Littlejohn, R. L. (2011). *Confucianism: An introduction.* New York, NY: I. B. Tauris.

A very helpful historical overview and summary of central ideas in the Confucian tradition.

Rosemont, H., Jr., & Ames, R. T. (2009). *The Chinese classic of family reverence: A philosophical translation of the Xiaojing.* Honolulu, HI: University of Hawai'i Press.

This book has a wonderful commentary on this classic piece of Chinese literature. There is much here to generate discussion on ideas of relational skill in the family and in other important social relationships such as teachers and students.

Tu, W. (1989). *Centrality and commonality: An essay on Confucian religiousness.* Albany, NY: State University of New York Press.

This important monograph does a lovely job of interpreting the meaning of the Zhongyong (one of the most important texts in Confucian literature) and its emphasis on the relational self. Compare to the Ames and Hall (2001) book.

Van Norden, B. W. (2011). *Introduction to classical Chinese philosophy.* Indianapolis, IN: Hackett.

A very readable introduction to the major schools of thought in the classical period of Chinese philosophy.

Van Norden, B. W. (2008). *Mengzi: With selections from traditional commentaries.* Indianapolis, IN: Hackett.

Mengzi (or Mencius) is one of the leading classical Confucian philosophers after Confucius, and this excellent book provides an accessible overview of the virtue ethics of Mencius.

Suggestions for Further Exploration of Buddhism and Mindfulness (with Brief Annotations)

All of the following books are helpful for faculty wishing to expand their knowledge on these ideas. These books are also highly accessible to undergraduates (the Levine book is a bit more difficult) and could be assigned in a personality course as a way to introduce students to Buddhist psychology.

Batchelor, S. (1997). *Buddhism without beliefs*. New York, NY: Riverhead.

This book does an excellent job of summarizing basic Buddhist ideas, without complex metaphysics, on the sources of human suffering and the cultivation of mental well-being.

Brazier, D. (2002). *The feeling Buddha: A Buddhist psychology of character, adversity, and passion*. New York, NY: Palgrave Macmillan.

Like the Batchelor book, this book is a lucid and accessible explication of Buddhist psychology.

Gunaratana, B. H. (2011). *Mindfulness in plain English*. Somerville, MA: Wisdom.

As the title suggests, this book is a helpful introduction to mindfulness practice.

Harris, D. (2014). *10% happier*. New York, NY: Harper Collins.

This is an engaging, funny, and honest autobiographical account of the benefits of mindfulness meditation from someone who was initially a skeptic. Harris, a television journalist, also does a superb job of summarizing scientific data on the benefits of mindfulness practice. Students enjoy this book as an introduction to mindfulness and its connections to mental well-being.

Kabat-Zinn, J. (1994). *Wherever you go, there you are*. New York: Hyperion.

Another excellent introduction to mindfulness meditation by the founder of mindfulness-based stress reduction.

Levine, S. (1989). *A gradual awakening*. Garden City, NY: Anchor.

This book stays closer to Buddhist philosophy and is therefore a more advanced read.

Shapiro, S. L., & Carlson, L. E. (2009). *The art and science of mindfulness.* Washington, DC: American Psychological Association.

This book is written as a textbook for clinicians in training or who are currently practicing. Nevertheless, there are chapters that are quite readable for undergraduates, who will benefit from both the survey of empirical studies on mindfulness as well as from the recommendations for a mindful approach to cultivating mental health.

References

Ames, R. T. (2011). *Confucian role ethics: A vocabulary.* Hong Kong: The Chinese University Press.
Ames, R. T., & Rosemont, H., Jr. (1998). *The analects of Confucius: A philosophical translation.* New York, NY: Ballentine.
Dahlgaard, K., Peterson, C., & Seligman, M. E. P. (2005). Shared virtue: The convergence of valued human strengths across culture and history. *Review of General Psychology, 9,* 203–2013. doi:10.1037/1089–2680.9.3.203.
Dewey, J. (1922). *Human nature and conduct.* New York, NY: Henry Holt.
Fingarette, H. (1972). *Confucius: The secular as sacred.* Long Grove, IL: Waveland.
Gay, P. (1988). *Freud: A life for our time.* New York, NY: Norton.
Gergen, K. J., Josselson, R., & Freeman, M. (2015). The promises of qualitative inquiry. *American Psychologist, 70,* 1–9. doi:10.1037/a0038597
Giordano, P. J. (2011). Culture and theories of personality: Western, Confucian, and Buddhist perspectives. In K. D. Keith (Ed.), *Cross-cultural psychology: Contemporary themes and perspectives* (pp. 423–444). Malden, MA: Wiley-Blackwell.
(2013). Personality. In K. D. Keith, (Ed.), *Encyclopedia of cross-cultural psychology* (Vol. III, pp. 995–997). Chichester: Wiley-Blackwell.
(2014). Personality as continuous stochastic process: What Western personality theory can learn from classical Confucianism. *Integrative Psychological and Behavioral Science, 48*(2), 111–128. doi:10.1007/s12124–013–9250–2
(2015). Being or becoming: Toward an open-system, process-centric view of personality. *Integrative Psychological and Behavioral Science, 49*(4), 757–771. doi:10.1007/s12124–015–9329-z
(2017, February 6). Individual personality is best understood as process, not structure: A Confucian-inspired perspective. *Culture & Psychology,* 1–17. doi:10.1177/1354067X17692118
Hall, C. S., & Lindzey, G. (1978). *Theories of personality* (3rd ed.). New York, NY: Wiley.
Henrich, J., Heine, S. J., & Norenzayan, A. (2010). The weirdest people in the world. *Behavioral and Brain Sciences, 33,* 61–135. doi:10.1017/S0140525X0999152X
Hermans, H. J. M., & Kempen, H. J. G. (1998). Moving cultures: The perilous problems of cultural dichotomies in a globalizing society. *American Psychologist, 53,* 1111–1120. doi:10.1037/0003–066X.53.10.1111

Ivanhoe, P. J. (2000). *Confucian moral self cultivation* (2nd ed.). Indianapolis, IN: Hackett.

Jankowski, T., & Holas, P. (2014). Metacognitive model of mindfulness. *Consciousness and Cognition, 28,* 64–80. http://dx.doi.org/10.1016/j .concog.2014.06.005.

Kitayama, S., & Tompson, S. (2010). Envisioning the future of cultural neuroscience. *Asian Journal of Social Psychology, 13,* 92–101. doi:10.1111/ j.1467–839X.2010.01304.x

Kitayama, S., & Uskul, A. K. (2011). Culture, mind, and the brain: Current evidence and future directions. *Annual Review of Psychology, 62,* 419–449. doi:10.1146/annurev-psych-120709-145357

Markus, H. R., & Kitayama, S. (1991). Culture and the self: Implications for cognition, emotion, and motivation. *Psychological Review, 98,* 224–253. doi:10.1037/0033–295X.98.2.224

    (2010). Cultures and selves: A cycle of mutual constitution. *Perspectives on Psychological Science, 5,* 420–430. doi:10.1177/1745691610375557

Matsumoto, D., & Juang, L. (2008). *Culture and psychology* (4th ed.). Belmont, CA: Wadsworth.

McCrae, R. R., & Costa, P. T., Jr. (2008). The five-factor theory of personality. In O. P. John, R. W. Robbins, & L. A. Pervin (Eds.), *Handbook of personality: Theory and research* (3rd ed., pp. 159–181.). New York, NY: Guilford.

Mead, G. H. (1934). *Mind, self, and society.* Chicago, IL: University of Chicago Press.

Molenaar, P. C. M. (2004). A manifesto on psychology as idiographic science: Bringing the person back into scientific psychology, this time forever. *Measurement, 2*(4), 201–218.

Molenaar, P. C. M., & Campbell, C. G. (2009). The new person-specific paradigm in psychology. *Current Directions in Psychological Science, 18,* 112–117. doi:10.1111/j.1467–8721.2009.01619.x

Molenaar, P. C. M., Huizenga, H. M., & Nesselroade, J. R. (2002). The relationship between the structure of inter-individual and intra-individual variability: A theoretical and empirical vindication of developmental systems theory. In U. Staudinger & U. Lindenberger (Eds.), *Understanding human development* (pp. 339–360). Dordrecht: Kluwer.

Molenaar, P. C. M., & Valsiner, J. (2008). How generalization works through the single case: A simple idiographic process analysis of an individual psychotherapy. In S. Salvatore, J. Valsiner, S. Strout-Yagodzynski, & J. Clegg (Eds.), *Yearbook of idiographic science* (Vol. I, pp. 23–38). Rome: Firera.

Nesselroade, J. R., & Ram, N. (2004). Studying intraindividual variability: What we have learned that will help us understand lives in context. *Research in Human Development, 1,* 9–29. doi:10.1207/s15427617rhd0101&2_3

Nisbett, R. E., Peng, K., Choi, I., & Norenzayan, A. (2001). Culture and systems of thought: Holistic versus analytic cognition. *Psychological Review, 108,* 291–310. doi:10.1037//0033–295X.108.2.291

Rosemont, H., Jr., & Ames, R. T. (2009). *The Chinese classic of family reverence: A philosophical translation of the Xiaojing.* Honolulu, HI: University of Hawai'i Press.

Shapiro, S. L., Carlson, L. E., Astin, J. A., & Freedman, B. (2006). Mechanisms of mindfulness. *Journal of Clinical Psychology, 62,* 373–386. doi:10.1002/jclp.20237

Tu, W. (1989). *Centrality and commonality: An essay on Confucian religiousness.* Albany, NY: State University of New York Press.

   (1994). Embodying the universe: A note on Confucian self-realization. In R. T. Ames, W. Dissanayake, & T. P. Kasulis (Eds.), *Self as person in Asian theory and practice* (pp. 177–186). Albany, NY: State University of New York Press.

Vandello, J. A., & Cohen, D. (1999). Patterns of individualism and collectivism across the United States. *Journal of Personality and Social Psychology, 77,* 279–292. doi:10.1037/0022-3514.77.2.279

Wallace, B. A., & Shapiro, S. L. (2006). Mental balance and well-being: Building bridges between Buddhism and Western psychology. *American Psychologist, 61,* 690–701. doi:10.1037/0003-066X.61.7.690

Walsh, R., & Shapiro, S. L. (2006). The meeting of meditative disciplines and Western psychology. *American Psychologist, 61,* 227–239. doi:10.1037/0003-066X.61.3.227

Wang, F., Peng, K., Chechlacz, M., Humphreys, G. W., & Sui, J. (2017). The neural basis of independence versus interdependence orientations: A voxel-based morphometric analysis of brain volume. *Psychological Science, 28,* 519–529. doi:10.1177/0956797616689079

Wang, Q. (2017). Five myths about the role of culture in psychological research. *APS Observer, 30*(1), 20–24.

Wang, Q., & Ross, M. (2005). What we remember and what we tell: The effects of culture and self-priming on memory representations and narratives. *Memory, 13,* 594–606. doi:10.1080/09658210444000223

CHAPTER 24

Integration of Culture in Teaching about Disability

Elias Mpofu, James Athanasou, Debra Harley, Tinashe Dune,
Patrick Devlieger, and Chandra Donnell Carey

Disability is both a part of culture and influenced by culture. For that reason, an understanding of disability is enhanced when learning and teaching about disabilities addresses personal identity in the context of social roles and relations, including religious, economic, and political (Benedict, 1934; Devlieger, Miranda-Galarza, Brown, & Strickfaden, 2016; Ingstad & Whyte, 1995). Disability is a social category as well as an identity defined from and with social others and in social systems (Mpofu, 2016; Mpofu, Chronister, Johnson, & Denham, 2012). Integration of culture in teaching about disability enables students to gain an understanding of disability as a social construct often used for categorizing those with atypicality in human attributes, and particularly those associated with physical and mental functioning. Teaching about disability through a cultural lens also encourages students to gain an understanding of disability within the context of biopsychosocial diversity in the ways in which people function in major life domains, not just a quality of individual persons themselves. Students are therefore challenged with the premise that culture not only defines disability but also impacts how it is perceived (e.g., destiny, curse, punishment, misfortune, servitude) and the social responses some may have to the experience of disability by others.

Integration of culture in teaching about disability will equip students to acquire a heightened sense of awareness of the social oppressions that may come with disability ascription (Duan & Brown, 2016; Harley, 2009; Lee, 2008; Mpofu & Harley, 2015; Mpofu, Thomas, & Thompson, 1998) and of the discrimination and disenfranchisement that people with disability experience. Students of human services education programs need to understand disability in the context of culture to reduce prejudice and to make it more likely that they will improve their communication competencies across the disability spectrum. Unfortunately, disability ascription often carries culture-laden negative social connotations (Blacher, Begum, Marcoulides, & Baker, 2013; Lawson, 2001).

Teaching about culture and disability therefore requires an understanding of the category "disability" in time and space. For instance, the disability category as an expression of identity has evolved over time and its meaning has changed, continuing to show differences from one epoch to another and from one place to another. As students delve into the meaning of disability (e.g., as in the early Anglophone referent word "handicap": *hand-in-cap*), they are typically amazed at the meanings behind the term *handicap* and the semantic history of the terminology *intellectual disability*. From learning of disability in the context of culture, students achieve critical knowledge that understandings of disability are continuously evolving, and the construct of disability itself is valid in the context of the cultural setting in which it is appropriated. Students also acquire an understanding of the present tendencies toward homogenization of definitions of disability under the auspices of international conventions (Meekosha & Soldatic, 2011; Umeasiegbu, Mpofu, & Johnson, 2012). The latter development is aligned to the globalization of world cultures and need for policies for the humane treatment of people with disabilities.

When students are exposed to the ways that various cultures support or engage with people living with disability, they are more likely to engage in reflective learning about the ways their home culture defines disability (Ingstad & Whyte, 1995; Reid-Cunningham, 2009). In this context, students have the opportunity to examine their own society's framework of disability. Key questions relate to the extent of their society's disability social inclusiveness and the role this has on supporting healthier citizenship, less disability stigma, and opportunities for disability integration in a range of settings, including employment and intimate relationships. With integration of culture in teaching about disability, risks for cultural blind spots about different others diminish, and peddling of stereotypes and reductionist prototypes about different others is likely to be ameliorated.

Furthermore, the integration of culture in teaching about disability enables students to acquire knowledge that disability is one of the most typical of human experiences. For that reason, disability can easily be understood as a part of an individual's cultural identity. With a broader understanding of diversity in human attributes and functioning (as with universal design systems), students may understand disability as largely external to the person and closely defined by the cultural context. As such, students are likely to have some experiences or insights to contextualize their direct and/or indirect encounters with disability (Ariotti, 1999; Groce, 1985; Mpofu, 2016; Mpofu et al., 2012).

In learning about disability, students should be aware that not all cultures stigmatize atypicality in physical and mental functioning. As an example, Groce (1985) reported findings about people with deafness and hard of hearing on Martha's Vineyard, an island where early settlers carried a recessive gene for deafness. Over the years, hereditary deafness occurred with such frequency that it was not considered a disability (and nearly everyone spoke sign language). Some African proverbs explain how disability is captured in a greater existential awareness: *"Don't laugh at a disabled person, God keeps on creating you."* This proverb reiterates that being able-bodied is a temporary state for all people – with disability occurring at some point across the lifespan.

Integration of culture in teaching about disability can also reduce or mitigate stereotyping of people with atypicality on a particular biopsychosocial attribute. Stereotyping can have the pervasive effect of disenfranchising those to whom it is applied by virtue of the devalued status of disability (Galanti, 2001). A stereotype can result in less than adequate, appropriate, and culturally sensitive supports for those to whom it is applied. For example, a person with a disability ascription may be subjected to culturally inappropriate generalizations associated with her or his presumed disability in or about him or her to the exclusion of any apparent abilities that each may have.

Notably, infusing culture in teaching about disability is relevant and critical for students to understand the assumptions and processes behind rehabilitation programs aimed to support those with atypical functioning. For instance, international health agencies (e.g., the World Health Organization [WHO] and the United Nations Educational, Scientific, and Cultural Organization [UNESCO]) and accrediting health professional associations encourage universities to include understandings of disability within cultural competence in their health professional curricula. Similarly, international human rights treaties intended to promote, protect, and ensure people with disabilities equality under the law have been proposed, although "many of the everyday experiences of disabled people. . ." in the global south [are] outside the reach of human rights instruments" (Meekosha & Soldatic, 2011, p. 1383).

With this in mind, it is important that students learn of ethical responsibilities for cultural competence in working with diversity in human attributes inclusive of disability. Thus, understanding disability for competent health and human services provision requires knowledge of how communities of which people with disability are a part construct disability (Cartwright & Shingles, 2011; Mikkonen, Elo, Kuivila, Tuomikoski, & Kaariainen, 2016). For instance, people of traditionalist Mexican culture may believe that illness/disability results from three causes: sin, imbalance, and witchcraft (Cartwright & Shingles, 2011). From that cultural understanding in which life is about balance and imbalance, presumed failure to maintain balance may cause mental or physical illness. Without an appreciation of the cultural nuancing of explanations for disability, students may construct disability as primarily biomedical and secondarily social, which could result in failure to provide culturally competent human services.

Finally, in infusing culture in teaching disability, it is necessary to acknowledge that the disability as a lived experience has multilayered meanings, some of which aggregate into identifiable disability cultures. For that reason, there is a diversity of subcultures among the community of people with disabilities influenced by their historical evolution and contemporary experiences. Students learning about disability with cultural infusion can result in an appreciation of how human functioning with disability adds to the richness of cultural ways of being (Bryan, 2014).

Key Concepts about Disability That Would Be Misunderstood without Cultural Context

For quite some time, the integration of models of cultural diversity and disability have been marginalized by traditional education and resistance to "shift from a deficit-normative orientation predicated on assumptions about the desirability and undesirability of biological, anatomical, intellectual, physiological, psychological, and sociological traits" (Johnson & McIntosh, 2009, p. 75). Without infusion of culture in teaching about disability, students would likely misunderstand the implications of disability as a mundane human experience, the fact that disability is both an ascription and an identity, and that cultures differ in perspectives about disability. We briefly address each of these issues subsequently.

The universality of disability experience. In the absence of discussions about culture and disability, students may lack an understanding of its universality as well as its nuanced appreciation within cultures. For instance, students would not know that while disability is a universal and widely dispersed phenomenon (about 15 percent of the world's population has a disability; World Health Organization, 2011), about 90 percent of disabilities are not visible, and the extent to which those with invisible disabilities will identify with that exceptionality is influenced by cultural meanings ascribed to the disability. Without infusion of culture in teaching about disability, students may not know that more people with invisible disability self-identity with disability in cultures that do not exclude or marginalize those with disability.

Furthermore, without the infusion of culture in teaching about disability, students would not know that many indigenous (native) languages do not have words or phrases for terms like "disability," "handicap," "crippled," or other disability-specific conditions (Locus, 1986). For instance, the word *disability* does not exist among the Anangu culture on the borders of Western Australia, South Australia, and the Northern Territory (Ariotti, 1999). A person's sameness within the community is what defines him or her. A person with a physical or mental disability may be identified as having a "difference" but is not seen as a problematic or problematized "other" based on that disability. Therefore:

- The difference is only one element of the person.
- The individual is seen as an integral part of the community.
- The individual is seen as able to meet his or her negative obligation to do no harm as well as the positive obligation of assistance.
- The value of the individual is not lessened because of a physical or mental difference (disability; Lovern, 2008).

Disability identities. With no inclusion of culture in teaching about disability, students would likely not understand the fact that disability is a legitimate social identity, regardless of the fact that human attributes typically ascribed to disability are undervalued and that those identifying as having a disability risk being socially marginalized. Without this understanding, students lacking knowledge of the intersection of culture and disability would be ill-prepared advocates for the equitable and humane treatment of people with disability. Moreover, without learning about culture and disability, students will likely lack an understanding of how culture reifies and scapegoats certain human attributes through the use of language and social processes of disempowerment of persons through exclusion from activities ordinary for most citizens.

Culturally diverse perspectives of disability. Students learning about disability with no cultural infusion would have a narrow and unserviceable view of disability. For instance, students less exposed to culture and disability are unlikely to know that widely disseminated Western cultural perspectives on disability necessarily exclude eastern and oriental views of illness, such as traditional Chinese medicine, Unani medicine (India), or Muslim faith perspectives. For example, in the Islamic faith, emphasis is on disadvantaged people rather than disability. From this perspective, people with a psychiatric impairment or intellectual disability are "absolved from all the obligatory requirements in Islam" (Queensland Health and Islamic Council of Queensland, 2010, p. 17). Furthermore, students may lack an appreciation of the fact that some cultures hold views on disability that seem quaint and childish to Westerners. For instance, twins are not considered human by the Punan Bah of Borneo and are considered a greater social disgrace than the birth of a child with a disability; the Bariba in Benin (West Africa) do not consider that children born with teeth are normal; and premature infants among the Arunta of the Northern Territory, Australia, are viewed as the young of some other animal (e.g., kangaroo) that has entered the body of a woman in error (Landsman, 2009, p. 242).

Finally, the role of disability in one's life is also bound up with religion (a fundamental aspect of one's ethnocultural background). Disability can vary from being considered an instance of "bad luck" to having some existential meaning. Across all cultures, religiosity acts as a filter for interpretation of any event in one's life. This contrasts with mainstream Western medicine that adopts a secular view as its foundation.

Approaches to Teaching That Are Effective to Infuse Cultural Concepts in Teaching of Disability

Some traditional methods of infusing diversity into teaching are lectures, assigned readings, guest speakers, and field trips. Increasingly, community-engaged service learning is a major learning/teaching approach integrating culture and disability (Mpofu et al., 2015). In many universities, living-learning communities offer experiences of social inclusion and integration of disability and culture.

The interconnectedness of countries through globalization and internationalization of education and intercultural exchanges (as in study abroad programs; see Carlson & Wideman, 1988; Mpofu, Bracken, van de Vijver, & Saklofske, 2017; Tarrant, Rubin, & Stoner, 2013) provide great opportunities for inclusion of culture in teaching about disability. Carlson and Wideman (1988) found that "students with study abroad experience showed higher levels of international political concern, cross-cultural interest, and cultural cosmopolitanism than ... comparison group" with no study abroad placement (p. 13). And Tarrant et al. (2013) reported higher global citizenry with study abroad than with on-campus learning only. In the following, we explore several approaches to infusion of cultural concepts in teaching about disability.

Community-engaged service learning. Community-engaged service learning (Mpofu et al., 2015) is a disability-in-context approach to infusing a real-world learning experience component to academic or classroom-based learning. Students elect community participation activities with people with disabilities, adding to their disability and community living literacy. As part of the community-engaged service learning experience, students complete an experiential component with a person with a disability in which they identify and assist activities related to living with a disability. In addition, students complete one activity in which they will work with organizations/self-help groups for or of people with disabilities with a view to enhancing participation in their communities. Students receive ongoing mentoring by the course lecturer or field placement liaison staff using reflective journals or logs to support their learning from and with community partners.

While on community-engaged service learning, students work with people with disabilities in several ways; in particular, they

1. Offer volunteer service to organizations of and for people with disabilities in areas of public consciousness raising, community resource identification and mobilization
2. Help with the coordination and activity facilitation of self-help groups of people with disabilities
3. Enhance the resource awareness utilization profile of people with disabilities and their self-help groups
4. Assist people with disabilities in areas of need identified by or with individual(s) with disabilities or their agency
5. Assist individuals with disabilities in the community to monitor and support compliance with any medicinal, physiotherapy, and occupational therapy regimens that may be required

Ideally, students and community partners mutually elect each other for the community-engaged learning. To facilitate this, an on-campus orientation meeting is held by the third week of the semester for students to meet with community partners with whom they might elect to work. As part of the student orientation process, community partners will share regulatory compliances specific to their organization. Students must meet regulatory compliance requirements for the community partners they are engaged with prior to involvement in any activity with the community partners. Community partners will require proof of regulatory compliance with them for all students with service learning (details are provided during the on-campus orientation event).

Each student who completes the community-engaged learning experience component is likely to acquire a heightened sensitivity and capacity to work with people with disabilities in typical community health settings.

Study abroad experience. Typically, these programs are offered worldwide through a formal memorandum of understanding between two universities. This agreement gives students the chance to gain valuable course credits at their home university. More often than not, there is little if any additional tuition cost. Meanwhile, from a disability perspective, the immersion in another country reinforces the concept of disability as a sociocultural phenomenon. Typically, it provides:

1. New social perspectives on disability
2. Potential for the enhancement of interpersonal skills such as empathy or rapport building
3. Maturation and growth in overall personal adjustment
4. Heightened perception and understanding of disability

As an example, the University of Sydney offers elective study options that involve students working with a community-based organization in a health services field for a minimum of 4 weeks in Vietnam, Cambodia, India, and the Philippines (see http://sydney.edu.au/health-sciences/current-stu dents/fhs-abroad.shtml; retrieved April 2016). Other study abroad opportunities for students include experiences with families in the vocational training of persons with disabilities in Vietnam, cultural antecedents of poststroke depression in Singapore, biopsychosocial approaches in Pacific island cultures, and the effectiveness of return-to-work rehabilitation centers operated by the government in Malaysia (Olivier et al., 2012). The Singapore study abroad opportunity is with a local hospital providing care to people with depression following stroke and involves the role of family and other social supports in the recovery process.

Culture and disability case studies. The following are by way of example. Students are asked to consider the extent to which indigenous views of disability position disability in the individual and/or the community.

---

1. A Native American Indian Perspective

Background. Students take a case study pertaining to understanding of disability among Native American Indians. In presenting this case example, the instructor needs to acknowledge that there are some 565 American Indian communities with diversity in language and traditions.

Spring Flower is a 23-year-old female Navajo Indian living on a reservation in Arizona. She has always lived on the reservation and received her schooling there. She speaks English and Athabaskan. Spring Flower adheres to traditional beliefs and practices that the physical and spiritual world blend together. She was born with scoliosis. In accordance with Navajo beliefs, her condition is considered the result of a number of Yeis (evil spirits).

Spring Flower recalls that her family and community always accepted her. There was no "blame the victim" syndrome. Her family and community accept the "blame for this misfortune" and strive to restore harmony through proper ceremonies. At her high school graduation she remembers her parents' smile as she entered the room. Their smile signified acceptance and affection.

Her desire is to become a rehabilitation counselor. She states, "I want to help others find harmony in life. I want them to know that they can remove evil spirits from their path and find balance." She believes the lack of wellness is attributed to disharmony in mind, body, and spirit. According to Spring Flower, "each person is responsible for his or her own wellness by keeping him- or herself attuned to self, relations, environment, and universe." She wants to bring the practice of wellness into rehabilitation.

As believed in Navajo society, Spring Flower's condition is not a disability but a difference (not a deficit). The value of the individual is not lessened because of the difference. In her approach to service delivery, Spring Flower wants to incorporate the concept of disability as understanding "wholeness" as repeated constantly throughout Navajo culture, which optimizes the individual's humanity.

Study Questions

1. How does Navajo culture differ in its definition and concepts about disability from Western philosophy?
2. What are respectful ways to discuss disability with someone who is American Indian?
3. How can the Western approach to rehabilitation counseling incorporate American Indians' beliefs of wellness?
4. *Australian Aboriginal and Torres Strait Islander Views on disability*

Background. My name is Apanie. I am an Aboriginal woman from the Gamilaroi tribe, and I am 22 years old. Following a complicated birth in which I was without oxygen for some time, I acquired severe spastic quadriplegic cerebral palsy (CP) in the minutes following my birth; at least this is what the doctors tell me. This was diagnosed when I was 2 years of age, and has meant that I have always needed to live with a carer, as I have high-level care needs. As a child and teenager I lived with my mother, a Gamilaroi woman, and stepfather, an Anglo-Australian man. Both worked in mainstream health care services and did all the things the doctors and professionals advised them to do in supporting my health.

As I grew up and learnt more about my indigenous roots I learnt that Aboriginal people are more concerned about the quality of community living than with disability. My mother explained that when the harmony between Land, Lore, Language, and Law is disrupted the health of our people deteriorates persistently. This frightened me and made me want to know what my mother thought had caused my disability. When asked, she would explain that my 'condition' was perhaps an extension of how my totem (or spirit animal) experienced life. She explained that perhaps it had survived an attack from a predator which left it a bit scarred but resilient and tenacious (like Indigenous people have survived European invasion, which disrupted our Land, Lore, Language, and Law). She said I, like my totem, was a strong survivor who could do whatever I wanted – like all Aboriginal people. That story makes me feel proud and able.

My stepfather chuckled at this and said; "You don't believe all that folklore do you? The doctors have explained what caused your CP and there is nothing more to it." At 18 I left home and moved into a fully accessible residential building at the university, where I completed my undergraduate studies in law. At university I was provided with living support from nurses and nurse trainees within the university's attendant care program for students with disabilities.

After university, my mother (who was my primary carer when I lived at home) passed away and I now live in an aged-care facility, as it is the only place equipped to meet my health and daily needs within my community. I require daily assistance with all activities of daily living, including eating, bathing, getting dressed, getting out of bed and getting into bed.

On Facebook, I often see that my peers from university are dating, travelling, and trialing employment options. On the other hand, I am the youngest resident in the aged-care facility and have little opportunity for interaction with anyone my age, people outside the facility, or anyone from an Aboriginal background. I feel lost and confused.

I have a good relationship with the nursing staff at the aged-care facility and have told them that I am feeling quite negatively about myself, my prospects and how frustrating it is that I cannot be around other Aboriginal people or have opportunities to participate in indigenous events or celebrations. At least when I was at university there were opportunities to be supported outside of the residential colleges, as it was supported by the university and my fees. Now it is too expensive to have someone assist me outside of the aged-care facility. Without a job I can hardly do anything. Even then I do not feel like I belong anywhere. I sometimes think that there is no use for me except for being a good doorstop – perhaps the world and I would be better off without me.

I thought maybe I should have a chat with my stepfather, who pays for my stay at the aged-care facility, about all the issues I am having and how I don't have any friends or opportunities for intimate relationships. I asked him if he knew someone who could help me get in touch with my totem (spirit animal). He kindly told me that I "shouldn't worry about that nonsense" and should instead "work harder and make friends." He said that living with a severe disability moves a player from the field and onto the bench – I don't like when he uses sporting analogies for someone like me who is in a wheelchair most of the time.

Study Questions

1. What ethnocultural aspects were important to Apanie's understanding of disability, and why?
2. How may these personal factors explain Apanie's disability-related experiences?
   a. Age
   b. Sexuality
   c. Gender
   d. Community relationships
   e. Education
   f. Finances
3. *Violence and Disability in the City of Chicago, United States*

Background. In 1998 and in 2015, a documentary film was produced with spinal cord-injured patients in a rehabilitation hospital on the west side of Chicago. The first was *The Disabling Bullet,* the second *The Disabling Bullet Revisited.* The west side of Chicago is an area of ethnically specific and diverse neighborhoods; some areas were formerly inhabited by Jewish people, and others have traditional Italian characteristics, such as restaurants and memorials to important Italian people. Still others are now becoming more multicultural with immigrant groups from Arabic countries, and some neighborhoods are inhabited predominantly by African Americans or Mexican Americans. The documentary in 1998 featured only African-American men, of whom LaMar was one. His story goes as follows.

The Life Story of LaMar

I was incarcerated for 365 days at the very young age of 11. When I became free I decided to move back to Chicago and start over. But I became absorbed with the street life. Whatever was illegal, I was part of it. I dog fought, I gambled, and I was involved with stealing car parts. My father was always negative towards me. My important role model was a big-time drug dealer, GW.

When I got injured, I thought it was going to be an ordinary day. I picked up my girlfriend, and I was stopping for gas at the gas station. Suddenly, I fell and could not get up again. My friend asked, are you ok? I said, no I can't move. I got shot. I was picked up by an ambulance and taken to the hospital, and later transferred to a rehabilitation hospital. In 24 hours, my whole life had changed: moving, bowel, and sex. After a long period, I decided to pick up my life and move out to the suburbs, away from the city. I am currently studying to become a grade school teacher. When I now come out, I want to represent disabled people, and make it clear that life is not over. I also want to communicate that "when you are in the drug life, three things can happen and one will certainly happen: 'you will be dead, in jail, or disabled like me. One of these things will happen.'"

The story of LaMar painted a background of poverty but also illegal activity that led to profit making. It was this that LaMar explained as the cause of jealousy for which he became a target. He further explains that it was possible to radically leave his life style behind, and have a suburban life, as well as become a committed disabled person who is ready to share his story.

Some 17 years later we returned to Chicago to follow up on people like LaMar, but unfortunately, we could not find anyone. Instead, we worked with a new group of people. This time, we were surprised to work mostly with spinal cord injured women. Here are parts of the story of Vanessa.

The Life Story of Vanessa
I was shot at the age of 13. I should make it clear that my whole family is one of gangbangers and drug dealers. By the age of 10, I knew many skills of drug preparation and selling. I received little or no support from teachers in my school. For most teachers, I was dispensable, except for one teacher who saw some potential in me. Perhaps I should stress that kids like me need support. When I got shot, my mother was in shock and tried to protect me. She said: This is my baby and it should not happen to her. She moved me several times to other locations. But I brought more trouble to my home. One day they came to my home and were shooting at my house. The people in my house were taking their guns, but they had already left. All this stopped when I was 17 and became pregnant. I now have a beautiful daughter of 5 years, and I cannot imagine that anything would happen to her. Currently I have a nine-to-five job selling lottery tickets in the airport. I would like to retire at the age of 33, because Jesus died at this age. I would also like to write a book because I believe I have this potential and I would also like to be able to secure a future for my daughter by the age of 21. I would also like to move overseas.

Study Questions

1. What does the story of LaMar tell us of the social and cultural circumstances of his understanding of disability? How can we understand the worldview that emerges from his experiences? How does disability interact with ethnicity and gender?
2. What does the story of Vanessa tell us about violence and disability? How do religion, gender, motherhood fit in?
3. What do we understand of the way that disability has an impact on the future perspectives of LaMar and Vanessa?

Digital resources. One of the authors (P. D.) showed the documentary film *The Disabling Bullet* on a yearly basis between 1999 and 2014 and *The Disabling Bullet Revisited* beginning in 2016. The films follow a discussion about an understanding of disability, explained through etymology and models, and illustrate the presence and working of disability culture, viewing disability as a matter of identity with the potential of being transformative.

The film comes as a surprise, if not a shock, to an international audience of Belgian, other European, African, and Asian students. The surprise comes from the fact that it shows the socioracial disparities of the United States among its multiethnic population. It highlights not-so-easy to understand African American English, not-so-easy to understand life styles, surprising and paradoxical ways of living, and violence. The connection to violence alerts the students that disability should not be understood merely as a medical condition, but that social and cultural issues are paramount, with important psychological impact. In showing other digital resources, we continue to ask critical questions of disability and rehabilitation.

Typical resources include double amputee model Aimee Mullins's TED talk about her twelve pairs of legs, and Amanda Baggs' "In My Language" in which she addresses neurotypicals about how she understands her way of enjoying sensory experience. Students are pushed to address such confronting messages, as they do not dovetail with their experiences and with dominant discourses of disability in which they have been socialized. Many students go on to ask critical questions in the papers that they subsequently develop during the course.

Teaching Resources
Books and Book Chapters

Devlieger, P., Miranda-Galarza, B., Brown, S., and Strickfaden, M. (Eds.). (2016). *Rethinking disability: World perspectives in culture and society.* Antwerp: Garant.

Dune, T. (2012). *Constructions of sexuality and disability: Implications for people with cerebral palsy.* Saarbrücken: Lambert Academic Publishing.

Mpofu, E. (2016). The evolution of quality of life perspectives in the developing world. In R. L. Schalock & K. D. Keith (Eds.). *Cross-cultural quality of life: Enhancing the lives of persons with intellectual disability* (2nd ed., pp. 175–180). Washington DC: American Association on Mental Retardation.

Mpofu, E., Chronister, J., Johnson, E., & Denham, G. (2012). Aspects of culture influencing rehabilitation with persons with disabilities. In P. Kennedy (Ed.). *Handbook of rehabilitation*. New York, NY: Oxford. doi:10.1093/oxfordhb/9780199733989.013.0030

Mpofu, E., & Harley, D. A. (2015). Multicultural rehabilitation counseling: Optimizing success with diversity. In F. Chan, N. L. Berven, & K. R. Thomas (Eds.), *Counseling theories and techniques for rehabilitation and mental health professions* (2nd ed., pp. 417–441). New York, NY: Springer.

Stone, J. H. (2005). *Culture and disability: Providing culturally competent services.* Thousand Oaks, CA: Sage.

Journal Articles

Boston, Q., Dunlap, P. N., Ethridge, G., Barnes, E., Dowden, A. R., & Euring, M. J. (2015). Cultural beliefs and disability: Implications for rehabilitation counselors. *International Journal for the Advancement of Counseling, 37*, 367–374. doi:10.1007/s10447-015-9250-7

Meyer, H. D. (2010). Introduction – Culture and disability: Advancing comparative research. *Comparative Sociology, 9*, 157–164. doi:10.1163/156913210X12536181350999

Olson, R., Bidewell, J., Dune, T., & Lessey, N. (2016). Developing cultural competence through self-reflection in interprofessional education: Findings from an Australian university. *Journal of Interprofessional Care, 30*(3), 347–354. doi:10.3109/13561820.2016.1144583

Furler, J., & Kokanovic, R. (2010). Mental health cultural competence. *Australian Family Physician, 39*(4), 206–208. http://search.informit.com.au/documentSummary;dn=029962799397206;res=IELHEA

Weaver, H. N. (2015). Disability through a Native American lens: Examining influences of culture and colonization. *Journal of Social Work in Disability & Rehabilitation, 14*(3–4), 148–162. doi:10.1080/1536710X.2015.1068256

Journals

ALTER – European Journal of Disability Research. A peer-reviewed European journal that looks at disability and its variations.

Culture and Disability. An international and interdisciplinary forum for the publication of research related to the cross-cultural study of disability.

Journal of Literary & Cultural Disability Studies. Focuses on cultural and especially literacy representations of disability.

Digital Teaching Resources

A Native Winds TV Production – American Indian Disability Summit. (April 2009).

www.youtube.com/watch?v=N9sK3ecpeUg

An overview of an annual event to explore the lived experience of American
  Indian and Alaskan Natives who have disabilities.
National Council on Disability. (August 2013).
www.ncd.gov/publications/2003/Aug12003
A toolkit designed to improve various outcomes for American Indians and
  Alaskan Natives who experience a variety of different disabilities. It is
  designed to provide opportunities to increase awareness and to foster
  empowerment with information about disabilities, Indian tribes, and
  resources.
**Cultural Diversity Resource Kit for Disability Support providers
  (August 2005)**
www.prioletticonsultants.com.au/resources
**Diversity in Disability – Welcome to the Diversity in Disability
  Toolkit (July 2015).**
www.diversityindisability.org
This toolkit provides a cultural competency framework, a communication
  and engagement strategy for both the disability, ethnospecific, and
  mainstream community sectors together with supporting tools and
  resources.
  a. Virginia
      i.   Video 1: http://youtu.be/oYhCvNJjN_A
           Discussion of experiences with chronic health and disability.
  b. Farina:
      i.   Video 1: http://youtu.be/zkp2FmXICno
           Interview regarding experience with disability.
Video Documentaries
  a. *In My Language* **by Amanda Baggs (January 2007).** www.youtube
      .com/watch?v=JnylM1hI2jc
  b. *My 12 Pairs of Legs* **by Aimee Mullins** (January 2009)
      www.youtube.com/watch?v=JQoiMulicgg
These preceding two documentaries include high-impact messages on the
  construction of disability. Both videos illustrate perspectives of two
  persons with disabilities and how they navigate language, communication,
  and their bodies. The videos also discuss the limits that others' ideas about
  functionality can place on individuals with disability. The videos illustrate
  how societal constructions can be a major barrier to individuals with
  disabilities.

References

Ariotti, L. (1999). Social construction of Anangu disability. *Australian Journal of
    Rural Health*, *7*(4), 216–222. doi:10.1111/j.1440-1584.1999.tb00460.x
Benedict, R. (1934). Anthropology and the abnormal. *Journal of General
    Psychiatry*, *10*, 59–80. doi:10.1080/00221309.1934.9917714

Blacher, J., Begum, G. F., Marcoulides, G. A., & Baker, B. L. (2013). Longitudinal perspectives of child positive impact on families: Relationship to disability and culture. *American Journal on Intellectual and Developmental Disabilities, 118*(2), 141–155. doi:10.1352/1944-7558-118.2.141

Bryan, W. V. (2014). *Multicultural aspects of disabilities: A guide to understanding and assisting minorities in the rehabilitation process* (3rd ed.). Springfield, IL: Charles C. Thomas.

Carlson, J. S., & Wideman, K. F. (1988). The effects of study abroad during college on attitudes toward other cultures. *International Journal of Intercultural Relations, 12*(1), 1–17. doi:10.1016/0147-1767(88)90003-X

Cartwright, L. A., & Shingles, R. R. (2011). *Cultural competence in sports medicine.* Champaign, IL: Human Kinetics.

Duan, C., & Brown, C. (2016). *Becoming a multiculturally competent counselor.* Los Angeles, CA: Sage.

Galanti, G. (2001). The challenge of serving and working with diverse populations in American hospitals. *Diversity Factor, 9*(1), 21–27. Retrieved from http://hsc.unm.edu/community/toolkit/docs8/CulturalDiversity.pdf

Groce, N. E. (1985). *Everyone here spoke sign language: Hereditary deafness on Martha's Vineyard.* Cambridge, MA: Harvard University Press.

Harley, D. A. (2009). Multicultural counseling as a process of empowerment. In C. C. Lee, D. A. Burnhill, A. L. Butler, C. P. Hipolito-Delgado, M. Humphrey, O. Munoz, & H. Shin (Eds.), *Elements of culture in counseling* (pp. 127–147). Upper Saddle River, NJ: Pearson.

Ingstad, B., & Whyte, S. R. (1995). *Disability and culture.* Berkeley, CA: University of California Press.

Johnson, J. R., & McIntosh, A. S. (2009). Toward a cultural perspective and understanding of the disability and deaf experience in special education and multicultural education. *Remedial and Special Education, 30*(2), 67–83. doi:10.1177/0741932508324405

Landsman, G. H. (2009). *Reconstructing motherhood and disability in the age of "perfect" babies.* New York, NY: Routledge.

Lawson, J. (2001). Disability as a cultural identity. *International Studies in Sociology of Education, 11*, 203–222. doi:10.1080/09620210100200076

Lee, C. C. (2008). *Elements of culturally competent counseling (ACAPCD-24).* Alexandria, VA: American Counseling Association.

Locust, C. (1986). *American Indian beliefs concerning health and unwellness. Native American Research and Training Center.* Tucson, AZ: Native American Research and Training Center, University of Arizona.

Lovern, L. (2008). Native American worldview and the discourse on disability. *Essays in Philosophy, 9*(1), Article 14. Retrieved from http://commons.pacificu.edu/cgi/viewcontent.cgi?article=1300&context=eip

Meekosha, H., & Soldatic, K. (2011). Human rights and the global south: The case of disability. *Third World Quarterly, 32*(8), 1383–1397. doi:10.1080/01436597.2011.614800

Mikkonen, K., Elo, S., Kuivila, H.-M., Tuomikoski, A.-M., & Kaariainen, M. (2016). Culturally and linguistically diverse healthcare students' experiences of learning in a clinical environment: A systematic review of qualitative studies. *Nursing Studies, 54*, 173–187. doi:10.1016/j.ijnurstu.2015.06.004

Mpofu, E. (2016). The evolution of quality of life perspectives in the developing world. In R. L. Schalock & K. D. Keith (Eds.), *Cross-Cultural quality of life: Enhancing the lives of persons with intellectual disability* (2nd ed., pp. 175–180). Washington DC: American Association on Mental Retardation.

Mpofu, E., Bracken, B. A., van de Vijver, F. & Saklofske, D. H. (2017. Teaching about intelligence, concept formation, and emotional intelligence. In G. Rich, U. Gielen, & H. Takooshian (Eds.), *Internationalizing the teaching of psychology*. Charlotte, NC: Information Age.

Mpofu, E., Chronister, J., Johnson, E., & Denham, G. (2012). Aspects of culture influencing rehabilitation with persons with disabilities. In P. Kennedy (Ed.), *Handbook of rehabilitation*. New York, NY: Oxford. doi:10.1093/oxfordhb/9780199733989.013.0030

Mpofu, E., & Harley, D. A. (2015). Multicultural rehabilitation counseling: Optimizing success with diversity. In F. Chan, N. L. Berven, & K. R. Thomas (Eds.), *Counseling theories and techniques for rehabilitation and mental health professions* (2nd ed., pp. 417–441). New York, NY: Springer. doi:10.1017/jrc.2015.1

Mpofu, E., Mackey, M., Hossain, S.Z., Cordier, M. M., & Wilkes-Gillian, S. (2015). Pedagogical techniques in the health sciences. In O. Delano-Oriaran, M. W. Parks, and S. S. Fondrie. (Eds.), *Service-learning and civic engagement* (pp. 271–278). Thousand Oaks, CA: Sage. doi:10.4135/9781483346625.n49

Mpofu, E., Thomas, K. R., & Thompson, D. (1998). Cultural appropriation and rehabilitation counseling: Implications for rehabilitation education. *Rehabilitation Education, 12*, 205–216.

Olivier, M., Govindjee, A., Nyenti, M., Mohammed, M. A. B. A., & Huang, E. C. P. H. (2012). *SOCSO return to work programme in Malaysia*. Kuala Lumpur: Social Security Organisation.

Queensland Health and Islamic Council of Queensland. (2010). *Health care providers' handbook on Muslim patients* (2nd ed.). Brisbane: Division of the Chief Health Officer, Queensland Health.

Reid-Cunningham, A. R. (2009). Anthropological theories of disability. *Journal of Human Behavior in the Social Environment, 19*, 99–111. doi:10.1080/10911350802631644

Tarrant, M. A., Rubin, D. L., & Stoner, L. (2013). The added value of study abroad. Fostering a global citizenry. *Journal of Studies in International Education, 18*(2), 141–161. doi:10.1177/1028315313497589

Umeasiegbu, V. I., Mpofu, E., & Johnson, E. T. (2012). Disability and rehabilitation in the international context. In P. J. Toriello, M. Bishop, & P. D. Rumrill (Eds.), *New directions in rehabilitation counseling: Creative responses to professional, clinical, and educational challenges*. Linn Creek, MO: Aspen Professional Services.

World Health Organization. (2011). *World report on disability*. Geneva, Switzerland: Author.

CHAPTER 25

Cultural Issues in the Teaching of Psychological Disorders

Josephine C. H. Tan

Modern conceptualizations of psychopathology or psychological disorders are derived primarily from Western perspectives and have been influenced by notable figures such as William James, Emil Kraepelin, and Sigmund Freud (Daughtry, Keeley, Gonzales, & Peterson, 2016; Leong, Pickren, & Tang, 2012), to name a few. The etiological agents are posited to be biological, psychological, and/or psychosocial/environmental in nature (e.g., Kendler & Prescott, 2006; Kring & Sloan, 2010). Interventions that have been developed are based mostly on Western scientific evidence and are designed to address the effects of these causative factors (e.g., Barlow, 2014). However, there is widespread awareness that culture and psychology are inextricably linked. Although culture has been defined in different ways, the common theme is that it refers to a system of shared knowledge and meaning within a group that is transmitted from one generation to the next (Keith, 2011a). A cultural group would thus have shared beliefs, values, behaviors, and ways of life.

The mind develops within a cultural context (Ryder, Ban, & Chentsova-Dutton, 2011), and individuals within the same cultural group would interpret their life experiences through the same cultural lens. This has significant implications for the field of clinical psychology. The emergence of cultural clinical psychology, which integrates cultural and clinical psychology, enables us to study the interaction of culture and mind as it relates to psychological disturbances across different societies. This has led us to question whether the concept of psychological disorder or mental illness is a universal construct, and to examine how culture plays a role in the way that mental health and mental illness are understood, the way that psychopathology develops, and the manner in which psychological disturbances are displayed.

There is an abundance of excellent research on the different topics within the field of cultural clinical psychology. There are also many clinical textbooks that would provide a comprehensive coverage of the area (e.g., Bhugra & Bhui, 2007; Bhui & Bhugra, 2012; Tseng, 2003). For those who wish to gain some background familiarity with the topic of culture and psychology before progressing to culture and clinical psychology, there are also several excellent books (e.g., Keith, 2011b; Kitayama & Cohen, 2007; Valsiner, 2012) that would serve the purpose. This chapter begins with explanations for the importance of studying culture in clinical psychology followed by an overview of some of the basic issues in the field. It concludes with some suggested instructional exercises that might help students to relate to the course materials on a more personal and experiential level and to improve cultural literacy.

Relevance of Culture in Clinical Psychology

Traditionally, it was assumed that psychology offered a universal understanding of human behavior and dysfunctions. However, most of the research was carried out primarily in the United States and European countries by Western researchers with Western participants (Keith, 2011a), leading to questions about the generalizability of the findings to people in other countries. Today, the study of culture and psychology is becoming more prevalent as we appreciate that there are important psychological differences and similarities across cultures (Smith, Spillane, & Annus, 2006).

With globalization, contact between cultures increases significantly. As people become more mobile for work and study purposes, and immigrate or seek refugee status in other countries, the populations in many world regions become increasingly diverse. Contact with another culture vastly different from one's own can be psychologically stressful for those new to the host country, and for the citizens of the host country, particularly those who might not be familiar with the appearance, language, behavior, and traditions of the newcomers.

Adjustment problems can and do arise when one is faced with rapid cultural change (Tseng, 2003), even when the change is initiated by the individual. For example, international students and new immigrants who choose to travel to other countries often face a number of problems associated with cultural differences when they arrive (Berry, 1997; Mori, 2000). In situations when the displacement is not of one's choice, such as when refugees flee from conflict or discrimination, individuals might be faced with the additional burden of psychological trauma associated with having survived adverse environments and suffering losses in their relationships, community, jobs, and other meaningful aspects of their lives

(Kirmayer, 2007). Thus, clinical psychologists need to possess knowledge of cultural influences on human psychological functioning when they work with clients from different cultural backgrounds. Familiarity with cultural influences is important even for clinical psychologists who do not work with the new immigrant or refugee populations. Given the diversity among, for example, the US and Canadian citizenry, mental health professionals in those countries will very likely encounter clients from minority backgrounds who might present with different views on mental illness and treatment.

One of the most compelling arguments for cultural awareness and literacy in clinical psychology comes from Christopher, Wendt, Marecek, and Goodman (2014). These authors spoke to the adverse consequences of unintentionally imposing Western psychology on cultural groups that have their own cultural meanings or "folk psychology." Folk psychology consists of worldviews (how things are) and ethos (how things ought to be), and offers insight into the shared meanings within a cultural group. Christopher et al. also noted that Western psychology is not necessarily objective or value free, and called for psychologists to be open to learning from the psychology of other cultures. Thus, the need to include culture in the teaching of clinical psychology is indisputable. It can help clinicians increase their understanding of problems from the clients' viewpoints, improve communication, strengthen the therapeutic relationship, and reduce the likelihood of misinterpretation of assessment findings and misdiagnosis.

Teaching Cultural Clinical Psychology

The field of cultural clinical psychology is very broad and can be taught from different perspectives. One possible approach might be to examine the topic from an empirical and conceptual viewpoint, while another might emphasize the relevance of cultural factors in clinical practice. Still other instructors might teach about culture as part of diversity issues, or focus specifically on certain cultural groups, such as Asian Americans, African Americans, Latinos, Indigenous North American peoples, immigrants, or refugees. The amount of detail and depth of analysis may depend on whether the course is an undergraduate introductory course or is offered at a more advanced level.

Many instructors who are developing a course on cultural clinical psychology are likely to consult with colleagues in the area and review the syllabi of similar courses. One excellent online resource, which can be found at https://culturalclinicalpsych.org/, promotes cultural clinical psychology and offers teaching materials such as course syllabi submitted by instructors from the United States and Canada, teaching suggestions, readings, and class exercises. The site also provides conference information, publications, and a collaboration network for junior researchers in the field.

Courses that have indigenous psychology contents warrant special mention. There is substantial evidence to show that the poorer health status and disadvantaged socioeconomic conditions of Indigenous peoples are linked to their colonization by Europeans, and that in turn resulted in the loss of their culture, disintegration of the family and kinship system, intergenerational trauma, land dispossession, and sociopolitical oppression (e.g., Aho & Liu, 2010; Anderson et al., 2006; Bombay, Matheson, & Anisman 2011; Czyzewski, 2011; King, Smith, & Gracey, 2009; Reading & Wien, 2009; Wesley-Esquimaux & Smolewski, 2004). Self-determination and a return to their cultural roots and identity are important to healing and health of these Indigenous peoples (Chandler & Lalonde, 2008; Lavallee & Poole, 2009; McLennan & Khavarpour, 2004). Consequently, courses that cover Indigenous mental health usually take great care to ensure that the educational materials and discourse are culturally informed and that Indigenous points of view are also represented.

Topical issues. There are no standard guidelines for development and design of cultural clinical courses. However, professional psychology programs are mandated by their accreditation standards to include a diversity component, including culture, in their curriculum (e.g., American Psychological Association Commission on Accreditation, 2015; Canadian Psychological Association, 2011). Certain basic cultural issues are often covered in clinical courses and they are discussed briefly in the following. It is critical to keep in mind that this does not represent a complete or prescriptive list, that there are many other cultural questions that are not represented here and that might be similarly important, and that course contents are ultimately decided by instructors who design their courses to meet specific objectives and obtain specific outcomes.

Cultural perspectives on mental illness. The Cartesian distinction between mental and physical health is primarily a Western concept. It is reflected in the way that Western health professionals are trained and in the way the health system is set up. Thus, physical illnesses are treated by specially trained professionals in the biomedical fields, and psychological disorders are treated by specially trained psychiatrists and psychologists. However, this mind-body delineation is not one that is shared by all societies. Culture influences how individuals define, identify, and experience psychological difficulties and in some cases, the physical and psychological are one and the same (Kleinman & Good, 1985).

In some cultural groups, psychological distress might be expressed in the form of physical symptoms. Physical symptoms can be broadly clustered into gastrointestinal symptoms (e.g., diarrhea), pain symptoms (e.g., headaches), pseudoneurological symptoms (e.g., muscle weakness), reproductive organ symptoms (e.g., burning sensations in sexual organs), and other physical syndromes (e.g., temporo-mandibular joint syndrome) that affect different cultural groups to varying degrees (So, 2008). Some of the cultural syndromes that researchers have reported include *hwa-byung* in Korea that presents with heart palpitations, chest tightness, headache, indigestion, anxiety, and anger (Lee, Wachholtz, & Choi, 2014); *brain fag* in Nigeria that is associated with studying and presents with symptoms of unpleasant sensations in the head, memory and concentration problems, and visual impairments (Uchendu, Chikezie, & Morakinyo, 2014); *dhat* in India consisting of fatigue and other physical and psychological symptoms thought to be associated with semen loss (Perme, Ranjith, Mohan, & Chandrasekaran, 2005); *shenjing shuairuo* in China, consisting of fatigue, memory loss, cognitive and sleep problems, and aches and pains (Chang et al., 2005); and *ataque de nervios* in several Latino societies that presents with different symptom profiles depending on the geographical region (Baer et al., 2003). Tseng (2006) discussed other types of cultural syndromes and examined how their conceptualization has evolved from earlier times when they were considered "peculiar psychiatric disorders."

Cultural syndromes are ways in which individuals from specific societies communicate their distress, and many convey that distress primarily through physical complaints (Kirmayer & Young, 1998). Somatization among individuals from non-Western cultures might arise from a tendency to focus more on physical symptoms and less on concurrent psychological symptoms (Dere et al., 2013; Rao, Young, & Raguram, 2007). Some individuals might choose to report somatic instead of psychological symptoms because of their sensitivity to stigma associated with mental illness (Rao et al., 2007). A study of South Indian psychiatric patients indicated that those who were more Westernized reported a greater balance of psychological symptoms than those who were less Westernized (Rao et al., 2007), showing that familiarity with Western cultures could potentially exert an influence on symptom presentation.

Culture can also affect the threshold at which certain behaviors are perceived to be acceptable or abnormal. Mann et al. (1992) reported that Chinese and Indonesian clinicians gave higher scores than Japanese and

US clinicians for hyperactive behaviors when viewing the same standard-ized videotape vignettes of four boys engaging in individual and group activities. Thus, reports of the severity of certain behaviors are influenced by culturally related tolerance levels for those behaviors.

It is also important to note that certain behaviors that are accepted as pathological in some cultures might be considered otherwise in others. For example, some Hindus who participate in the religious festival Thaipusam fall into a dissociative trance while their bodies are pierced with needles, skewers, and hooks (Ward, 1984). From a Western perspective, such behaviors would be labeled as a form of psychotic break from reality, and a pathological form of self-mutilation. However, among the Thaipusam participants, this behavior is understood to be a religious ritual carried out for purposes of penance, honoring a vow made by the self or family member, overcoming bad karma, or spiritual enlightenment (Mellor et al., 2012).

Cultural perspectives on causes. Some societies attribute mental illness to spiritual or religious causes. Many Haitians, for example, see psychological difficulties as the result of a spell or a curse, one's failure to honor the spirits of family members who have died, or one's neglect of the voodoo gods (Desro-siers & St. Fleurose, 2002). In Thailand, possession by spirits as well as bad karma resulting from deeds and actions in present and past lives is thought by some to cause mental illness (Burnard, Naiyapatana, & Lloyd, 2006). Malays believe that mental illness is due to a loss of *semangat*, or soul substance, possession by a jinn (genie), black magic, or the neglect of Islamic values (Haque, 2008). Other societies invoke the impediment of natural substances in the body to explain mental illness. Some Asian societies believe that when the vital life force or energy does not flow properly in the body, illness results. The life force is known as *qi* in China, *ki* in Korea and Japan, *kwan* in Thailand, and *prana* in India (Tyson & Flaskerud, 2009). The Chinese consider interpersonal and intrapersonal harmony to be important to a sense of well-being (Kleinman, 1988) and harmony is achieved when there is a balance between the two opposing cosmic forces, the *yin* and the *yang*.

In the United States, some American Indian and Alaska Native groups see mental illness as spiritual possession, a special gift, or "an imbalance and disharmony with the inner and outer natural forces in the world" (Grandbois, 2005, p. 1005). It appears that the concept of mental illness may have been introduced to the Indigenous peoples during their earlier contact with Europeans (Walker & Ladue, 1986). Thus, it is not certain that any unusual behavior among Indigenous people would have been originally interpreted by them specifically as a mental or psychological problem, as opposed to a more general view that the behavior is atypical. Contemporary Indigenous health models that are widely accepted among American Indians in the United States, and First Nations in Canada conceptualize well-being as a balance among the physical, emotional, mental, and spiritual parts of a person and to connection to the family, kin system, community, and the land (Vukic, Gregory, Martin-Misener, & Etowa, 2011; Yurkovich & Lattergrass, 2008).

Culture as a contributing factor. Tseng (2003) described the various ways in which culture might contribute to psychological stress and psychopathology. Thus, certain cultural beliefs, such as excessive masturbation leading to loss of semen, might produce anxiety and cause the *dhat* syndrome (Grover et al., 2016). The degree to which such beliefs are shared by a group to which a person belongs can affect the severity of the anxiety. Some cultures have strictly prescribed roles and duties for certain members that can lead to psychological difficulties if the roles are of low social status. For instance, widowhood in India is often associated with social and economic sanctions, and in some cases, with various types of abuse (Varma, 2016). Stress might arise from cultural expectations of high or even perfectionistic performance (e.g., educational achievements among Asian students; Yoon & Lau, 2008), cultural limitations on behavior expression (e.g., restriction on expression of aversive emotions among Koreans might present as symptoms of *hwa-byung*; Pang, 1990), or cultural restrictions on choice (e.g., forced marriages in several countries; Seelinger, 2010).

Psychological problems arising from acculturative stress can also manifest when individuals experience rapid cultural change. The change can come about through voluntary migration (Hovey, 2000; Kirmayer et al., 2011; Mori, 2000; Mui & Kang, 2006; Pumariega, Rothe, & Pumariega, 2005; Thomas, 1995); forced relocation internal to a country (e.g., Indigenous peoples in North America; Denov & Campbell, 2002; Morris & Crooks, 2015; Walls & Whitbeck, 2012) or external to a country (e.g., refugees; Hassan et al., 2015; Porter & Haslam, 2005; Pumariega et al., 2005; Tempany, 2009); and cultural uprooting or destruction (e.g., Indigenous peoples; Kingston, 2015). The type and severity of psychological problems that emerge depend on the circumstances surrounding the rapid cultural change.

Culture as a protective factor. Cultural values can act as a protective factor against mental ill health. Key cultural values among Afghans (faith, family unity, service, effort, morals, and honor) promote social and moral order and a sense of hope (Eggerman & Panter-Brick, 2010). Stronger adherence to

Africentric cultural values (faith, unity, purpose, creativity, self-determination, collective work and responsibility, cooperative economics) among African American adolescent girls is associated with higher self-esteem that predicted greater life satisfaction (Constantine, Alleyne, Wallace, & Franklin-Jackson, 2006). Familism, which is a core cultural value for Latinos, is linked to lower conduct problems among Mexican-origin adolescents (Germán, Gonzales, & Dumka, 2009). *Inuit Quajimajatiqangit* (IQ) is the set of guiding principles of the Inuit people who live primarily in the arctic regions of Canada; IQ emphasizes respect, cooperation, and harmonious coexistence, and has implications for mental well-being (Wihak & Merali, 2003). Cultural resources, such as traditional activities, traditional spirituality, traditional languages, and traditional healing, contribute to resilience among Indigenous peoples (Fleming & Ledogar, 2008; McIvor, Napoleon, & Dickie, 2009). And cultural continuity serves as a protective factor against suicide among Indigenous youth in Canada (Chandler & Lalonde, 2008).

Culture and training in research and clinical skills. There is an abundance of research and articles on the incorporation of culture in clinical practice, clinical research, and graduate clinical training that are written from a primarily Western perspective. The reader is directed to the many excellent articles that speak to the issue of cultural competency in interventions (e.g., Castro, Barrera, & Steiker, 2010; Huey, Tilley, Jones, & Smith, 2014; Kalibatseva & Leong, 2014; Sue, Zane, Hall, & Berger, 2009), training and evaluation of students on multicultural competency (e.g., Jones, Sander, & Booker, 2013; Stuart, 2004), research (e.g., Kalibatseva & Leong, 2014), and teaching resources (e.g., Ryder & Chentsova-Dutton, 2014). Suggestions for clinical interviewing and clinical case formulation are offered by Caraballo et al. (2006), the *Diagnostic and Statistical Manual of Mental Disorders* (DSM-5; American Psychiatric Association, 2013), and by Tanaka-Matsumi in Chapter 26 of this book.

Exercises to increase cultural literacy. Instructors of cultural clinical psychology courses have developed different useful exercises to help students learn about the relevance of culture in clinical psychology. These might involve students responding to conceptual or empirical articles, written case studies, or videos within a cultural framework (e.g., see teaching exercises at https://culturalclinicalpsych.org/teaching/exercises/). The value of these exercises can be enhanced with some experiential activities to assist students to develop a deeper appreciation of how culture is woven into all aspects of human activities.

Self-reflection is an experiential activity that can help build self-awareness and cultural literacy. Students are asked to contemplate their own cultural background and upbringing, and to voluntarily share information on what they know about their cultural core values, traditions, and role expectations. Mundane acts that are often taken for granted, such as making appointments to visit a friend instead of dropping in unexpectedly, are examined to see whether they might be universal. Sharing voluntary self-reflections can be especially productive when the students in the class are from diverse cultural backgrounds or different parts of the country, have traveled widely, or have exposure to multiple cultures. One possible outcome of self-reflection is that students will become curious about their own culture and its influence on development of their personalities, attitudes, and beliefs. Becoming self-aware as a cultural being can help students see other cultures as unique in their own right instead of "other cultures" in relation to their own culture.

Guest speakers who are willing to share their life experiences and knowledge to bridge the cultural gap make excellent instructional resources. Examples are healthcare professionals and community care workers who work with diverse clientele, Indigenous Elders, traditional healers, and refugees. Such guest speakers typically require some information about the course and the class, and the aim of their presentation; the instructor learns in advance what the guest speakers need and makes the appropriate arrangements (e.g., preparing a tobacco pouch and arranging class seating in a circle for Indigenous Elders). Students should also be advised of what to expect and should have the opportunity if they wish to opt out of participating in any cultural activities or ceremonies that might be part of the presentation. Open exchange with presenters at the end of the class often leads to greater learning on the part of the students.

Field trips to facilities that offer culturally sensitive services provide students with the opportunity to learn about the clientele, the types of programs and services offered, and the ways in which culture is incorporated into the service. Instructors who have experience with providing culturally informed clinical care may find it useful to bring case studies (protecting client identity) to graduate-level classes for discussion. Students can also develop cultural literacy on their own by taking advantage of cultural events and activities that are held on campus and in their community, and by interacting with international students.

Sensitivity to student learning. Students who have limited exposure to other cultures might find the course to be somewhat daunting. Several might be reluctant to express themselves or ask questions for fear of coming across as culturally insensitive or ignorant, or expressing a perspective that runs counter to prevailing views. Caucasian students, in particular, might feel anxiety and guilt surrounding issues relating to colonialism of the Indigenous peoples and the destruction of their culture; these natural reactions might be heightened if there are Indigenous students in the same course. Instructors need to reflect on how to be supportive and provide a safe learning environment for all students, regardless of their cultural background. Sometimes, this can be accomplished by addressing the issue directly in a sensitive manner and allowing any concerns and reservations to be heard and discussed by everyone. This type of exchange in its own right can increase intercultural understanding among the students.

Concluding Comments

The field of cultural clinical psychology is very diverse. There is no consensus on how a course in this field should be taught, and there is no single course that can capture the full range of cultural variation in human behavior and functioning. Consequently, course syllabi will vary in their objectives, contents, and method of instruction. Nevertheless, all courses in cultural clinical psychology share a common purpose, and that is to increase the students' cultural awareness and knowledge and to prepare them to be culturally sensitive, if not competent, in their work and their daily life.

References

Aho, K. L., & Liu, J. H. (2010). Indigenous suicide and colonization: The legacy of violence and the necessity of self-determination. *International Journal of Conflict and Violence, 4,* 124–133. doi:10.4119/UNIBI/ijcv.65

American Psychiatric Association. (2013). *Diagnostic and statistical manual of mental disorders* (5th ed.). Arlington, VA: Author.

American Psychological Association Commission on Accreditation. (2015). Standards of accreditation for health service psychology. Retrieved from www.apa.org/ed/accreditation/about/policies/standards-of-accreditation.pdf

Anderson, I., Crengle, S., Kamaka, M. L., Chen, T.-H., Palafox, N., & Jackson-Pulver, L. (2006). Indigenous health in Australia, New Zealand, and the Pacific. *Lancet, 367*(9524), 1775–1785. doi:10.1016/S0140–6736(06) 68773–4

Baer, R. D., Weller, S. C., de Alba Garcia, J. G., Glazer, M., Trotter, R., Pachter, L., & Klein, R. E. (2003). A cross-cultural approach to the study of the folk illness nervios. *Culture, Medicine, and Psychiatry*, *27*, 315–337. doi:10.1023/A:1025351231862

Barlow, D. H. (Ed.). (2014). *Clinical handbook of psychological disorders: A step-by-step treatment manual* (5th ed.). New York, NY: Guildford.

Berry, J. W. (1997). Immigration, acculturation, and adaptation. *Applied Psychology*, *46*, 5–34. doi:10.1111/j.1464-0597.1997.tb01087.x

Bhugra, D., & Bhui, K. (2007). *Textbook of cultural psychiatry*. New York, NY: Cambridge University Press.

Bhui, K., & Bhugra, D. (2012). *Culture and mental health: A comprehensive textbook*. Boca Raton, FL: CRC.

Bombay, A., Matheson, K., & Anisman, H. (2011). The impact of stressors on second generation Indian residential school survivors. *Transcultural Psychiatry*, *48*, 367–391. doi:10.1177/1363461511410240 tps.sagepub

Burnard, P., Naiyapatana, W., & Lloyd, G. (2006). Views of mental illness and mental health care in Thailand: A report of an ethnographic study. *Journal of Psychiatric and Mental Health Nursing*, *13*, 742–749. doi:10.1111/j.1365-2850.2006.01028.x

Canadian Psychological Association. (2011). *Accreditation standards and procedures for doctoral programmes and internships in professional psychology – 5th revision*. Ottawa, Canada: Author. Retrieved from http://cpa.ca/docs/File/Accreditation/Accreditation_2011.pdf

Caraballo, A, Hamid, H., Lee, J. R., McQuery, J. D., Rho, Y., Kramer, E. J., . . . Lu, F. G. (2006). A resident's guide to the cultural formulation. In R. F. Lim (Ed.), *Clinical manual of cultural psychiatry* (pp. 243–269). Washington, DC: American Psychiatric Publishing.

Castro, F. G., Barrera, M., Jr., & Steiker, L. K. H. (2010). Issues and challenges in the design of culturally adapted evidence-based interventions. *Annual Review of Clinical Psychology*, *6*, 213–239. doi:10.1146/annurev-clinpsy-033109-132032

Chandler, M. J., & Lalonde, C. E. (2008). Cultural continuity as a protective factor against suicide in First Nations youth. *Horizons*, *10*(1), 68–72.

Chang, D. F., Myers, H. F., Yeung, A., Zhang, Y., Zhao, J., & Yu, S. (2005). Shenjing shuairuo and the DSM-IV: Diagnosis, distress, and disability in a Chinese primary care setting. *Transcultural Psychiatry*, *42*, 204–18. doi:10.1177/1363461505052660

Christopher, J. C., Wendt, D. C., Marecek, J., & Goodman, D. M. (2014). Critical cultural awareness: Contributions to a globalizing psychology. *American Psychologist*, *69*, 645–655. doi:10.1037/a0036851

Constantine, M. G., Alleyne, V. L., Wallace, B. C., & Franklin-Jackson, D. C. (2006). Africentric cultural values: Their relation to positive mental health in African American adolescent girls. *Journal of Black Psychology*, *32*, 141–154. doi:10.1177/0095798406286801

Czyzewski, K. (2011). Colonialism as a broader social determinant of health. Article 5 (pp. 1–14). *International Indigenous Policy Journal*, *2*(10). doi:10.18584/iipj.2011.2.1.5.

Daughtry, D. W., Keeley, J. W., Gonzales, C., & Peterson, K. (2016). The history of psychology. In W. D. Woody, R. L. Miller, & W. J. Wozniak (Eds.), *Psychological specialities in historical context: Enriching the classroom experience for teachers and students* (pp. 121–140). Retrieved from http://teachpsych.org/ebooks/index.php#/

Denov, M., & Campbell, K. (2002). Casualties of Aboriginal displacement in Canada: Children at risk among the Innu of Labrador. *Refuge. Canada's Journal on Refugees, 20*(2), 21–33.

Dere, J., Sun, J., Zhao, Y., Persson, T. J., Zhu, X., Yao., S.,...Ryder, A. G. (2013). Beyond "somatization" and "psychologization": Symptom-level variation in depressed Han Chinese and Euro-Canadian outpatients. *Frontiers in Psychology, 4,* 377. doi:10.3389/fpsyg.2013.00377

Desrosiers, A., & St. Fleurose, S. (2002). Treating Haitian patients: Key cultural aspects. *American Journal of Psychotherapy, 56,* 508–521.

Eggerman, M., & Panter-Brick, C. (2010). Suffering, hope, and entrapment: Resilience and cultural values in Afghanistan. *Social Science & Medicine, 71,* 71–83. doi:10.1016/j.socscimed.2010.03.023

Fleming, J., & Ledogar, R. J. (2008). Resilience, an evolving concept: A review of literature relevant to Aboriginal research. *Pimatisiwin: A Journal of Aboriginal and Indigenous Community Health, 6*(2), 7–23.

Germán, M., Gonzales, N. A., & Dumka, L. (2009). Familism values as a protective factor for Mexican-origin adolescents exposed to deviant peers. *Journal of Early Adolescence, 29,* 16–42. doi:10.1177/0272431608324475

Grandbois, D. (2005). Stigma of mental illness among American Indian and Alaska Native nations: Historical and contemporary perspectives. *Issues in Mental Health Nursing, 26,* 1001–1024. doi:10.1080/01612840500280661

Grover, S., Avasthi, A., Gupta, S., Dan, A., Neogi, R., Behere, P. B.,... Rozatkar, A. (2016). Phenomenology and beliefs of patients with Dhat syndrome: A nationwide multicentric study. *International Journal of Social Psychiatry, 62,* 57–66. doi:10.1177/0020764015591857

Haque, A. (2008). Culture-bound syndromes and healing practices in Malaysia. *Mental Health, Religion & Culture, 11,* 685–696. doi:10.1080/13674670801958867

Hassan, G., Kirmayer, L. J., Mekki-Berrada, A., Quosh, C., el Chammay, R., Deville-Stoetzel, J. B.,...Ventevogel, P. (2015). *Culture, context and the mental health and psychosocial wellbeing of Syrians: A review for mental health and psychosocial support staff working with Syrians affected by armed conflict.* Geneva: United Nations High Commissioner for Refugees.

Hovey, J. D. (2000). Acculturative stress, depression, and suicidal ideation in Mexican immigrants. *Cultural Diversity and Ethnic Minority Psychology, 6*(2), 134–151. doi:10.1037/1099-9809.6.2.134

Huey, S. J., Jr., Tilley, J. L., Jones, E. O., & Smith, C. A. (2014). The contribution of cultural competence to evidence-based care for ethnically diverse population. *Annual Review of Clinical Psychology, 10,* 305–338. doi:10.1146/annurev-clinpsy-032813-153729

Jones, J. M., Sander, J. B., & Booker, K. W. (2013). Multicultural competency building: Practical solutions for training and evaluating student progress. *Training and Education in Professional Psychology, 7*(1), 12–22. doi 10.1037/a0030880

Kalibatseva, Z., & Leong, F. T. L. (2014). A critical review of culturally sensitive treatments for depression: Recommendations for intervention and research. *Psychological Services, 11*(4), 433–450. doi:10.1037/a0036047

Keith, K. D. (2011a). Introduction to cross-cultural psychology. In K. D. Keith (Ed.), *Cross-cultural psychology: Contemporary themes and perspectives* (pp. 3–19). Malden, MA: Wiley-Blackwell.

Keith, K. D. (Ed.). (2011b). *Cross-cultural psychology: Contemporary themes and perspectives.* Malden, MA: Wiley-Blackwell.

Kendler, K. S., & Prescott, C. A. (2006). *Genes, environment, and psychopathology: Understanding the causes of psychiatric and substance use disorders.* New York, NY: Guildford.

King, M., Smith, A., & Gracey, M. (2009). Indigenous health part 2: The underlying causes of the health gap. *Lancet, 374*(9683), 76–85. doi:10.1016/S0140–6736(09)60827–8

Kingston, L. (2015). The destruction of identity: Cultural genocide and Indigenous peoples. *Journal of Human Rights, 14*(1), 63–83. doi:10.1080/14754835.2014.886951

Kirmayer, L. J. (2007). Foreword. In B. Drożdek & J. P. Wilson (Eds.), *Voices of trauma: Treating psychological trauma across cultures.* New York, NY: Springer.

Kirmayer, L. J., Narasiah, L., Munoz, M., Rashid, M., Ryder, A. G., Guzder, J., . . . & Pottie, K. (2011). Common mental health problems in immigrants and refugees: General approach in primary care. *Canadian Medical Association Journal, 183*(12), E959–67. doi:10.1503/cmaj.090292

Kirmayer, L. J., & Young, A. (1998). Culture and somatization: Clinical, epidemiological, and ethnographic perspectives. *Psychosomatic Medicine, 60,* 420–430. doi:10.1097/00006842–199807000–00006

Kitayama, S., & Cohen, D. (2007). *Handbook of cultural psychology.* New York, NY: Guildford.

Kleinman, A. (1988). *Rethinking psychiatry: From cultural category to personal experience.* New York, NY: Free Press.

Kleinman, A. M., & Good, B. (1985). Introduction: Culture and depression. In A. Kleinman & B. Good (Eds.), *Culture and depression. Studies in the anthropology and cross-cultural psychiatry of affect and disorder* (pp. 1–33). Berkeley, CA: University of California Press.

Kring, A. M., & Sloan, D. M. (Eds.). (2010). *Emotion regulation and psychopathology: A transdiagnostic approach to etiology and treatment.* New York, NY: Guildford.

Lavallee, L. F., & Poole, J. M. (2009). Beyond recovery: Colonization, health and healing for Indigenous people in Canada. *International Journal of Mental Health and Addiction, 8,* 271–281. doi:10.1007/s11469–009–9239–8

Lee, J., Wachholtz, A., & Choi, K. H. (2014). A review of the Korean cultural syndrome hwa-byung: Suggestions for theory and intervention. *Asia Taepyongyang Sangdam Yongu*, 4(1), 49. doi:10.18401/2014.4.1.4

Leong, F. T. L., Pickren, W. E., & Tang, L. C. (2012). A history of cross-cultural clinical psychology, and its importance to mental health today. In E. C. Chang & C. A. Downey (Eds.), *Handbook of race and development in mental health* (pp. 11–26). New York, NY: Springer Science + Business Media. doi:10.1007/978-1-4614-0424-8_2

Mann, E. M., Ikeda, Y., Mueller, C. W., Takahashi, A., Tao, K. T., Humris, E., . . . Chin, D. (1992). Cross-cultural differences in rating hyperactive-disruptive behaviors in children. *American Journal of Psychiatry*, *149*, 1539–1542. doi:10.1176/ajp.149.11.1539

McIvor, O., Napoleon, A., & Dickie, K. M. (2009). Language and culture as protective factors for at-risk communities. *Journal of Aboriginal Health*, 5(1), 6–25.

McLennan, V., & Khavarpour, F. (2004). Culturally appropriate health promotion: Its meaning and application in Aboriginal communities. *Health Promotion Journal of Australia*, *15*, 237–239.

Mellor, D., Hapidzal, F. M., Teh, K., Ganesan, R., Yeow, J., Abdul Latif, R., & Cummins, R. (2012). Strong spiritual engagement and subjective well-being: A naturalistic investigation of the Thaipusam festival. *Journal of Spirituality in Mental Health*, *14*, 209–225. doi:10.1080/19349637.2012.697375

Mori, S. (2000). Addressing the mental health concerns of international students. *Journal of Counseling & Development*, *78*, 137–144. doi:10.1002/j.1556-6676.2000.tb02571.x

Morris, M., & Crooks, C. (2015). Structural and cultural factors in suicide prevention: The contrast between mainstream and Inuit approaches to understanding and preventing suicide. *Journal of Social Work Practice*, *29*, 321–338. doi:10.1080/02650533.2015.1050655

Mui, A. C., & Kang, S. K. (2006). Acculturation stress and depression among Asian immigrant elders. *Social Work*, *51*, 243–55. doi:10.1093/sw/51.3.243

Pang, K. Y. (1990). Hwabyung: The construction of a Korean popular illness among Korean elderly immigrant women in the United States. *Culture, Medicine and Psychiatry*, *14*, 495–512. doi:10.1007/BF00050823

Perme, B., Ranjith, G., Mohan, R., & Chandrasekaran, R. (2005). Dhat (semen loss) syndrome: A functional somatic syndrome of the Indian subcontinent? *General Hospital Psychiatry*, *27*, 215–217. doi:10.1016/j.genhosppsych.2005.01.003

Porter, M., & Haslam, N. (2005). Predisplacement and postdisplacement factors associated with mental health of refugees and internally displaced persons: A meta-analysis. *Journal of the American Medical Association*, *294*, 602–612. doi:10.1001/jama.294.5.602

Pumariega, A. J., Rothe, E., & Pumariega, J. B. (2005). Mental health of immigrants and refugees. *Community Mental Health Journal*, *41*, 581–597. doi:10.1007/s10597-005-6363-1

Rao, D., Young, M., & Raguram, R. (2007). Culture, somatization, and psychological distress: Symptom presentation in South Indian patients from a public psychiatric hospital. *Psychopathology, 40,* 349–355. doi:10.1159/000106312

Reading, C.L., & Wien, F. (2009). *Health inequalities and social determinants of Aboriginal peoples' health.* Prince George: National Collaborating Centre for Aboriginal Health.

Ryder, A. G., Ban, L. M., & Chentsova-Dutton, Y. E. (2011). Towards a cultural-clinical psychology. *Social and Personality Psychology Compass, 5,* 960–975. doi:10.1111/j.1751–9004.2011.00404.x

Ryder, A. G., & Chentsova-Dutton, Y. E. (2014). Teaching and learning guide: Towards a cultural–clinical psychology. *Social and Personality Psychology Compass, 8,* 287–296. doi:10.1111/j.1751–9004.2011.00404.x

Seelinger, K. T. (2010). Forced marriage and asylum: Perceiving the invisible harm. *Columbia Human Rights Law Review, 42*(1), 55–117.

Smith, G. T., Spillane, N. S., & Annus, A. M. (2006). Implications of an emerging integration of universal and culturally specific psychologies. *Perspectives on Psychological Science, 1,* 211–233. doi:10.1111/j.1745–6916.2006.00013.x

So, J. K. (2008). Somatization as cultural idiom of distress: Rethinking mind and body in a multicultural society. *Counselling Psychology Quarterly, 21,* 167–174. doi:10.1080/09515070802066854

Stuart, R. B. (2004). Twelve practical suggestions for achieving multicultural competence. *Professional Psychology: Research and Practice, 35*(1), 3–9. doi:10.1037/0735–7028.35.1.3

Sue, S., Zane, N., Hall, G. C. N., & Berger, L. K. (2009). The case for cultural competency in psychotherapeutic interventions. *Annual Review of Psychology, 60,* 525–548. doi:10.1146/annurev.psych.60.110707.163651

Tempany, M. (2009). What research tells us about the mental health and psychosocial wellbeing of Sudanese refugees: A literature review. *Transcultural Psychiatry, 46,* 300–315. doi:10.1177/1363461509105820

Thomas, T. N. (1995). Acculturative stress in the adjustment of immigrant families. *Journal of Social Distress and the Homeless, 4*(2), 131–142. doi:10.1007/BF02094613

Tseng, W. S. (2003). *Clinician's guide to cultural psychiatry.* San Diego, CA: Academic Press.

(2006). From peculiar psychiatric disorders through culture-bound syndromes to culture-related specific syndromes. *Transcultural Psychiatry, 43,* 554–576. doi:10.1177/1363461506070781

Tyson, S., & Flaskerud, J. H. (2009). Cultural explanations of mental health and illness. *Issues in Mental Health Nursing, 31,* 650–651. doi:10.1080/01612840902838587

Uchendu, I. U., Chikezie, E. U., & Morakinyo, O. (2014). Brain fag syndrome among Nigerian university students in Abuja. *Journal of Psychiatry and Brain Functions, 1,* 1–6. doi:10.7243/2055-3447-1-1

Valsiner, J. (2012). *The Oxford handbook of culture and psychology.* New York, NY: Oxford University Press.

Varma, P. (2016). Abuse against widowhood in India. *International Journal of Indian Psychology, 4*(1), 131–146.

Vukic, A., Gregory, D., Martin-Misener, R., & Etowa, J. (2011). Aboriginal and Western conceptions of mental health and illness. *Pimatisiwin: A Journal of Aboriginal and Indigenous Community Health, 9*(1), 65–86.

Walker, R. D., & Ladue, R. A. (1986). An integrative approach to American Indian mental health. In C. B. Wilkinson (Ed.), *Ethnic psychiatry* (pp. 146–194). New York, NY: Plenum.

Walls, M. L., & Whitbeck, L. B. (2012). The intergenerational effects of relocation policies on Indigenous families. *Journal of Family Issues, 33*, 1272–1293. doi:10.1177/0192513X12447178

Ward, C. (1984). Thaipusam in Malaysia: A psycho-anthropological analysis of ritual trance, ceremonial possession and self-mortification practices. *Ethos, 12*, 307–334. doi:10.1525/eth.1984.12.4.02a00020

Wenzel, G. W. (2004). From TEK to IQ: *Inuit Qaujimajatuqangit* and Inuit cultural ecology. *Arctic Anthropology, 41*, 238–250. doi: 10.1353/arc.2011.0067

Wesley-Esquimaux, C. C., & Smolewski, M. (2004). *Historic trauma and Aboriginal healing*. Ottawa: The Aboriginal Healing Foundation.

Wihak, C., & Merali, N. (2003). Culturally sensitive counselling in Nunavut: Implications of Inuit traditional knowledge. *Canadian Journal of Counselling, 37*, 243–255.

Yoon, J., & Lau, A. S. (2008). Maladaptive perfectionism and depressive symptoms among Asian American college students: Contributions of interdependence and parental relations. *Cultural Diversity and Ethnic Minority Psychology, 14*(2), 92–101. doi:10.1037/1099-9809.14.2.92

Yurkovich, E. E., & Lattergrass, I. (2008). Defining health and unhealthiness: Perceptions held by Native American Indians with persistent mental illness. *Mental Health, Religion & Culture, 11*(5), 437–459. doi:10.1080/13674670701473751

CHAPTER 26

Culture-Infused Training in Clinical Psychology

Junko Tanaka-Matsumi

This chapter describes the author's experiences in the education of graduate and undergraduate students in culture-infused psychology courses in the United States and Japan. The overarching theme is cultural accommodation in psychological activities. I am a Japanese psychologist trained in clinical and cross-cultural psychology in the United States. I have taught clinical and cross-cultural psychology both in the United States and Japan. Diversity issues have always composed part and parcel of my own professional activities in teaching, research, and practice, which span nearly 40 years across Eastern and Western cultures.

Cultural and cross-cultural psychological perspectives are relevant to basic undergraduate psychology education programs as well as advanced graduate training programs in professional psychology. In the United States, the American Psychological Association (2003) established guidelines on multicultural education, training, research, and practice over a decade ago. In education, what types of activities can we provide students in order to nurture cultural awareness? It is important that we consider developing cultural awareness and interest in students as early as possible in psychology courses in high school (Keith, 2014) and undergraduate programs (Lonner & Murdock, 2012) by including interesting activities in culture and psychology (Goldstein, 2008). Ideally, prospective graduate students will have developed cultural awareness by the time they begin professional psychology training.

Definitions and Functions of Culture: Contextual-Interactive Approach

Culture is defined as "a unique meaning and information system, shared by a group and transmitted across generations, that allows the group to meet basic needs of survival, pursue happiness and well-being, and derive meaning from life" (Matsumoto & Juang, 2008, p. 12). Functions of culture include (a) adjustment, (b) ego defense, (c) value expression, and (d) knowledge (Triandis, 2007). Functional approaches to culture provide means to assess dynamic interactions between the person and the cultural environment. Emphasizing cultural context in interaction, Wang (2001) compared interactions of European American and Chinese mother–child conversations about four specific one-point-in-time events related to happiness, sadness, fear, and anger, in which both mother and child participated. The children were 3 years of age. Wang found different emotional styles and explanations between European American ("emotion explaining") and Chinese mothers ("emotion criticizing") that were attributed to cultural differences in early family narratives. Cultural sensitivity to learning styles (Tweed & Lehman, 2002) is particularly salient in cross-cultural psychotherapy situations. In psychotherapy, functional approaches require assessment of both the client and the therapist as they interact with each other in a particular setting.

Evidence-Based Practice and Cultural Context

Clinical scientists and practitioners are trying to promote evidence-based practice in order to develop efficacious and effective mental health programs for diverse groups of people. In fact, *evidence-based practice* and *cultural adaptation* have become key words in evaluating treatments for a variety of mental health problems (Draguns, 2013; Sue & Sue, 2008). Evidence-based psychotherapy refers to "a coherent and clinically expert process of assessment, case formulation, identification of goals, treatment planning, alliance building, research-informed intervention, monitoring of progress, adjustment as needed, and termination – all in the context of collaboration with the client (or parent, guardian, or caretaker of the client)" (Goodheart & Kazdin, 2006, p. 3).

However, in what specific ways does culture matter in the practice of psychotherapy and what can we do to accommodate cultural factors within specific psychotherapy such as cognitive behavior therapy (CBT)? For example, if a Chinese American is depressed, how does he or she experience depression and communicate the distress to others in the community (Kleinman, 1982)? Is there evidence for CBT to treat depression among Chinese Americans? What cultural modifications and adaptations of CBT are necessary in order to incorporate cultural beliefs, values, and behavioral norms associated with mental health concerns of ethnic minority groups? These and other questions have prompted scientist-practitioners to develop empirical research on cultural adaptations of psychotherapy

(Bernal, Jiménez-Chafey, & Domenech Rodríguez, 2009; Chu & Leino, 2017). As regards depression in Chinese-American clients, Hwang (2016) developed cultural accommodation strategies to include Chinese cultural values and behavioral norms into cognitive behavior therapy using the psychotherapy adaptation and modification framework (PAMF) and the formative method for adapting psychotherapy (FMAP) of his own development.

Studies on the cultural adaptations of empirically supported psychological interventions are clearly increasing in number, most notably in the United States, for diverse ethnocultural groups of clients (Bernal & Domenech Rodríguez, 2012; Chu, Leino, Pflum, & Sue, 2016). Significantly more positive outcome results have been reported for culturally adapted psychotherapies when compared with those of standard procedures based on meta-analyses of published studies (Benish, Quitana, & Wampold, 2011; Griner & Smith, 2006). Cultural adaptation refers to the systematic modification of an evidence-based treatment or intervention protocol to consider language, culture, and context in such a way that it is compatible with the client's cultural patterns, meanings, and values (Bernal et al., 2009; Chu et al., 2016).

Cross-cultural counseling and therapy is predicated on five basic points: (a) cultural adaptation of techniques, (b) reduction of cultural distance between the therapist and the client, (c) knowledge of culture-specific modes of self-presentation, (d) recognition of cross-cultural differences in the communication of distress, and (e) recognition of cross-cultural variations in normative stress coping styles (Draguns, 2002; Sue, 1998). Cognitive behavior therapy is a system of intervention whose proponents are making active efforts to accommodate culture into everyday practice and research (Hofmann, 2006; Tanaka-Matsumi, Higginbotham, & Chang, 2002)

Readers may recall the ADDRESSING model (Hays, 2016) as a framework to develop culturally informed case formulation for individual clients. The ADDRESSING acronym refers to the assessment of age and generational influences, developmental or other disability, religion and spirituality, ethnic and racial identity, socioeconomic status, sexual orientation, indigenous heritage, national origin, and gender. These culturally influencing factors contribute to the individual's current presenting problems and affect psychotherapy. The ADDRESSING model has been applied to cognitive behavior therapy to assist multicultural work, particularly to develop case formulation for each individual client (Wenzel, Dobson, & Hays, 2016). Culturally informed professionals seek methods of understanding interaction of the client and her or his environment, which includes the therapist within a particular professional context (Tanaka-Matsumi, 2008).

Developing Cultural Awareness in Psychology Education

"When we set aside any presumptions, we can better see that a cultural psychological perspective helps us recognize, reduce, and eliminate biases, uncover new mechanisms and develop new theories, and understand human cognition and behavior as a constructive process that takes place in the interaction between a person and her or his environment" (Wang, 2016, p. 593).

Education in cultural awareness should begin early and, ideally, it should be infused across all relevant courses, not just providing a separate course to increase cultural awareness, if psychologists are to function as cultural psychologists across settings in everyday activities (Lonner & Murdock, 2012). To set aside presumptions, academic courses can adapt activities in culture and psychology (Goldstein, 2008). Littleford and Nolan (2013) offered five questions and relevant activities to infuse cultural diversity into psychology courses. These include (a) curriculum-related activities to help students become more aware of their own cultural background, (b) introducing empirically based literature to increase knowledge-base, (c) developing skills to increase cultural competence in students, (d) presenting culture-inclusive research examples in class, and (e) highlighting the diversity among researchers. Littleford and Nolan (2013) stated that both the instructor and students would increase their own cultural awareness and develop culture-inclusive knowledge of psychology. I now review examples of specific curricular-related activities and literature that I have incorporated into cross-cultural psychology and applied clinical psychology courses.

Teaching Cross-Cultural Psychology

Increasing Academic Knowledge Base

I have emphasized developing academic awareness of the vast international knowledge base in cultural and cross-cultural psychology in undergraduate students in a course titled cross-cultural psychology. The knowledge base of cross-cultural, cultural, and indigenous psychology is solid, vast, and still growing (Keith, 2013). I have used *Culture and Psychology* (Matsumoto &

Juang, 2008) as a textbook in my undergraduate cross-cultural psychology course. Graduate-level textbooks of cross-cultural psychology highlight conceptual and methodological issues with reviews of empirical research on the relation between culture and psychology (e.g., Berry, Poortinga, Breugelmans, Chasiotis, & Sam, 2011). Through culture-infused texts and lectures, students grow familiar with the perspectives of cultural relativity and universality as two major conceptual frameworks to explain cultural variation in human activities.

To expand students' knowledge, in addition to the assigned textbooks, I have also used the *Online Readings in Psychology* (*ORPC*), a free online resource provided by the International Association for Cross-Cultural Psychology (IACCP) for researchers, teachers, students, and anyone who is interested in the interrelationships between psychology and culture. The ORPC contains eleven major units with over one hundred chapters contributed by cross-cultural scholars from all over the world. I introduce the ORPC in class by directly accessing the ORPC website and introduce the various topics comprising the eleven units (see Table 26.1 for topics and URL). I then give an assignment using the ORPC. Students are to access the ORPC web page, browse all eleven units, select articles of their preference, and read abstracts. To do this task, students need to skim many topics and make a choice. On a second assignment, students are to read one article, develop a short synopsis, and describe reasons for choosing a particular article. Students gradually become familiar with culture-inclusive research papers contributed by expert scholars from all over the world.

Table 26.1 *Major Fields of the Online Readings in Psychology and Culture (ORPC)*

Unit 1	Historical Perspectives on the Study of Psychology and Culture
Unit 2	Theoretical and Methodological Issues
Unit 3	Indigenous Approach
Unit 4	General Psychological Issues in Cultural Perspective
Unit 5	Social Psychology and Culture
Unit 6	Developmental Psychology and Culture
Unit 7	Applied Psychology and Culture
Unit 8	Migration and Acculturation
Unit 9	Biological Psychology, Neuropsychology and Culture
Unit 10	Health/Clinical Psychology and Culture
Unit 11	Teaching of Psychology and Culture

Note. http://scholarworks.gvsu.edu/orpc

This activity helps expanding students' psychological and cultural perspectives on human activities and institutions that are embedded in sociocultural context.

Developing Cross-Cultural Interviews

The cross-cultural interview project is another activity that I have incorporated into cross-cultural psychology courses at both undergraduate and graduate levels in both the United States and Japan. I encourage students to seek and apply academic knowledge in preparation for an interview with a person who is a native to a culture different from their own. I modeled this activity after Gabrenya (1998), who has taught a culture and psychology course at Florida Institute of Technology for many years. The intercultural interview in Gabrenya's class focuses on the respondents' subjective experience of being in the United States (host country), problems encountered by the international sojourner in adjustment, and adaptation to American society.

I explain to the students in the cross-cultural psychology class that the purpose of this cross-cultural interview is to appreciate the ups and downs of living in a different culture from their own. At first, students show hesitation about finding a respondent. Almost always, students find a respondent successfully either on the campus or off-campus through acquaintances. I instruct the students to prepare the following items for the interview: (a) information about the respondent's country and culture, (b) adjustment difficulties in the host country, (c) social networks, (d) impressions of the host country with specific examples highlighting cultural differences, (e) acculturation and stress coping, (f) predeparture orientations about the host country, and (g) elicitation of the respondent's plans for the future.

I also require students to consider (h) any particular precautions they exercised (e.g., religious customs, ethical considerations) and (i) self-knowledge they gained, including their own biases and values. They will also ask themselves (j) what they learned from the interview and what modifications they would make if they were to conduct another intercultural interview.

I begin giving the instructions for this assignment early in the course so students will read the relevant literature, start looking for prospective interviewees, and have enough time to make an appointment for the interview. Students are told to select a language to interview flexibly depending on the interviewee's native language. An interpreter could also accompany the student with permission of the interviewee. The cross-cultural interview has been one of the more rewarding exercises for the students. Students make individual class presentations and write a brief report on the interview. Class presentations contribute to creating an active learning environment.

Through class presentations of cross-cultural interviews, students discover culture first at a material level and then, depending on the preparation and interviewing skills, they find that culture becomes more subjective, reflecting values and meanings (Berry et al., 2011; Matsumoto & Juang, 2008). Furthermore, through oral presentations and discussions, students learn the value of individual differences and the danger of categorizing individuals. For example, East Asians are not all the same, and verbal communication styles are not uniformly of "high context" across East Asian cultures. Similarly, they note that the individualism-collectivism cultural dimension functions in relative terms within East Asian cultures.

Training in Professional Practice of Culturally Informed Clinical Interviews

The Culturally Informed Functional Assessment (CIFA) Interview

Having prepared students to gain academic knowledge in cross-cultural psychology and engagement in cross-cultural interactions in course work, I turn attention to the methods of clinically relevant interviews in a cross-cultural, professional context.

Contextual and functional frameworks can monitor the effectiveness of psychotherapy procedures with culturally different clients by employing generic principles of behavioral contingencies rather than considering a set of techniques to be adapted (Hayes, Muto, & Masuda, 2011; Masuda, 2016). The culturally informed functional assessment (CIFA) interview (Tanaka-Matsumi, Seiden, & Lam, 1996) was designed to facilitate the integration of cultural observations into cognitive-behavioral assessment and treatment planning (Tanaka-Matsumi et al., 2002). Specifically, it aims to increase the cultural relevance of a case formulation by generating detailed, culturally relevant information regarding observable events that are potentially connected to the client's presenting problem. The CIFA involves eight successive stages: (a) assessment of the client's cultural identity and level of acculturation, (b) assessment of the client's presenting problems, (c) elicitation of the client's conceptualization of the problems and possible solutions, (d) functional analysis of the antecedent-target-consequence sequence, (e) negotiation of similarities and differences between the functional analysis and the client's causal explanation of the problems, (f) development of a treatment plan that is acceptable to all parties involved, including culturally different individuals and reference groups, (g) data gathering that facilitates ongoing assessment of the client's progress, and (h) discussion of treatment duration, course, and expected outcome.

At each of these eight stages, the therapist compares and contrasts the perspectives of the client, the family, cultural reference groups, and the therapist's own emerging case formulation. The greater the therapist's knowledge of the client's cultural definitions of problem behavior and cultural norms regarding behavior, change strategies, and the change agents (i.e., the criteria for cultural accommodation to psychotherapy), the more accurate and useful an assessment will be. As part of practica in clinical psychology and counseling or professional workshops, the CIFA interview provides a functional analytic framework to assess clients' presenting problems contextually and develop a culturally informed case formulation.

Cultural Formulation Interview of the DSM-5

The fifth edition of the *Diagnostic and Statistical Manual of Mental Disorders* (DSM-5; American Psychiatric Association, 2013) introduced some major changes in the diagnostic system (Blashfield, Keeley, Flanagan, & Miles, 2014). The cultural case formulation interview (CFI), based on DSM-5, shows specific procedures and guidelines to assess cultural factors (Lewis-Fernández, Aggarwal, Hinton, Hinton, & Kirmayer, 2016). The CFI describes sixteen interview questions supplemented by twelve modules for further assessment. The sixteen questions of the CFI cover four domains of culturally relevant assessment: (a) cultural definitions of the clinical problem (three questions), (b) cultural perceptions of cause, context, and support (seven questions), (c) cultural factors affecting self-coping and past help-seeking (three questions), and (d) cultural factors affecting current help seeking (three questions).

The DSM-5-based CFI procedure gathers culture-relevant information surrounding the presenting problems and diagnosis: the patient's explanatory models of distress; the patient–clinician relationship; coping and help seeking; cultural identity; spirituality, religion, and moral traditions; psychosocial stressors; social networks; and level of functioning. Graduate students in clinical psychology in internship settings may practice the DSM-5 and CFI under proper supervision with diverse patients to develop case formulations. Because this is a new protocol published as a separate interview guideline, clinicians must be able to determine when to employ the DSM-5-CFI.

The Explanatory Model Interview Catalogue (EMIC)

Knowledge of indigenous views and explanatory models of illness is fundamental to understanding the cultural context of the individual's distress (Jenkins, 2015; Kleinman, 1980). The Explanatory Model Interview Catalogue (EMIC) consists of a semistructured interview for gathering data regarding patterns of distress and perceived causes, help-seeking behavior and treatment, general illness beliefs, and specific queries concerning the problem (Weiss, 1997). The culturally relevant, descriptive information gathered via the EMIC can assist case formulation. For example, Johnson, Chin, Kajumba, Kizito, and Bangirana (2017) interviewed in Uganda depressed patients in indigenous healing centers and Western-derived psychiatry settings in order to investigate possible differences in explanatory models of depression for patients and healers. These researchers trained local interviewers to develop a culturally informed knowledge base of depression in Uganda. Clearly, gathering narrative data is important for the therapist in order to develop an appropriate treatment plan through negotiations of explanatory models of therapists and their patients.

It is noted that the EMIC data-gathering steps are incorporated in the clinical modules that accompany DSM-5-CFI (Lewis-Fernandez et al., 2016). Trainers should be careful to distinguish conceptual differences between psychiatric diagnosis, such as the DSM-5, and the EMIC. The end purpose of the EMIC is to infuse assessment with local therapeutic practices, rather than developing a universal biomedical-psychiatric diagnosis.

Conclusion

Culture has come to the fore of professional activities of psychologists in education, research, and practice. Developing cultural awareness in students is an exciting professional task for psychology teachers. The present chapter focused on infusing interesting and challenging activities into formal academic psychology courses. Activity examples included cross-cultural interviews at the graduate and undergraduate levels, and practice in the CIFA interview. CIFA and the DSM-5 cultural formulation interviews may be compared for similarities and differences in underlying conceptual approaches to abnormal behaviors and psychopathology. Psychology instructors can make free and ubiquitous use of the online articles of the ORPC and other useful online resources. In the tradition of the scientist-practitioner model of training in applied psychology, cultural and cross-cultural perspectives will help in responding to the needs of diverse populations of the world.

References

American Psychiatric Association. (2013). *Diagnostic and statistical manual of mental disorders* (5th ed.). Washington, DC: Author.

(2003). Guidelines on multicultural education, training, research, practice, and organizational change for psychologists. *American Psychologist, 58*, 377–402. doi:10.1037/0003–066X.58.5.377

Benish, S. G., Quintana, S., & Wampold, B. E. (2011). Culturally adapted psychotherapy and the legitimacy of myth: A direct-comparison meta-analysis. *Journal of Counseling Psychology, 58*, 279–289. doi:10.1037/a0023626

Bernal, G., Jiménez-Chafey, M. I., & Domenech Rodriguez, M. M. (2009). Cultural adaptation of treatments: A resource for considering culture in evidence-based practice. *Professional Psychology: Research and Practice, 40*, 361–368. doi:10.1037/a0016401

Bernal, G., & Domenech Rodriguez, M. M. D. (Eds.). (2012). *Cultural adaptations: Tools for evidence-based practice with diverse populations.* Washington, DC: American Psychological Association.

Berry, J. W., Poortinga, Y. H., Breugelmans, S. M., Chasiotis, A., & Sam, D. (2011). *Cross-cultural psychology: Research and applications* (3rd ed.). Cambridge: Cambridge University Press.

Blashfield, R. K., Keeley, J. W., Flanagan, E. H., & Miles, S. R. (2014). The cycle of classification: DSM-I through DSM-5. *Annual Review of Clinical Psychology, 10*, 25–51. doi:10.1146/annurev-clinpsy-032813–153639

Chu, J., & Leino, A. (2017). Advancement in the mature science of cultural adaptations of evidence-based interventions. *Journal of Consulting and Clinical Psychology, 85*, 45–57. doi:10.1037/ccp0000145

Chu, J., Leino, A., Pflum, S., & Sue, S. (2016). A model for the theoretical basis of cultural competency to guide psychotherapy. *Professional Psychology: Research and Practice, 47*, 18–29. doi:10.1037/pro0000055

Draguns, J. G. (2002). Universal and cultural aspects of counseling and psychotherapy. In P. B. Pedersen, J. G. Draguns, W. J. Loner, & J. E. Trimble (Eds.), *Counseling across cultures* (5th ed., pp. 29–50). Thousand Oaks, CA: Sage.

(2013). Cross-cultural and international extensions of evidence-based psychotherapy: Toward more effective and sensitive psychological services everywhere. *Psychologia, 56*, 74–88. doi:10.2117/psysoc.2013.74

Gabrenya, W. K., Jr. (1998). The intercultural interview. In T. M. Singelis (Ed.), *Teaching about culture, ethnicity, and diversity: Exercises and planned activities* (pp. 57–63). Thousand Oaks. CA: Sage.

Goldstein, S. B. (2008). *Cross-cultural explorations: Activities in culture and psychology* (2nd ed.). Boston, MA: Allyn & Bacon.

Goodheart, C. D., & Kazdin, A. E. (2006). Introduction. In C. D. Goodheart, A. E. Kazdin, & R. J. Sternberg (Eds.), *Evidence-based psychotherapy: Where practice and research Meet* (pp. 3–10). Washington, DC: American Psychological Association.

Griner, D., & Smith, T. B. (2006). Culturally adapted mental health interventions: A meta-analytic review. *Psychotherapy: Theory, Research, Practice, Training, 43*, 531–548. doi:10.1037/0033-3204.43.4.531

Hayes, S. C., Muto, T., & Masuda, A. (2011). Seeking cultural competence from the ground up. *Clinical Psychology: Science and Practice, 18*, 232–237. doi:10.1111/j.1468-2850.2011.01254.x

Hays, P. A. (2016). *Addressing cultural complexities in practice: Assessment, diagnosis, and therapy* (3rd ed.). Washington, DC: American Psychological Association.

Hofmann, S. G. (2006). The importance of culture in cognitive and behavioral practice. *Cognitive and Behavioral Practice, 13*, 243–245. doi:10.1016/j.cbpra.2006.07.001

Hwang, W.C. (2016). *Culturally adapting psychotherapy for Asian heritage populations: An evidence-based approach.* Cambridge, MA: Elsevier Academic Press.

Jenkins, J. H. (2015). *Extraordinary conditions: Culture and experience in mental illness.* Oakland, CA: University of California Press.

Johnson, L. R., Chin, E. G., Kajumba, M., Kizito, S., & Bangirana, P. (2017). View of depression from traditional healing and psychiatry clinics in Uganda: Perspectives from patients and their providers. *Journal of Cross-Cultural Psychology, 48*, 243–261. doi:10.1177/0022022116675424

Keith, K. D. (Ed.). (2013). *The encyclopedia of cross-cultural psychology (3 vols.).* Chichester: Wiley-Blackwell.

  (2014). *Perspectives in psychological science.* (2014, July). American Psychological Association (APA), Education Directorate, Office of Precollege and Undergraduate Education. doi:10.1037/e521912014-001

Kleinman, A. 1980. *Patients and healers in the context of culture.* Berkeley, CA: University of California Press.

  (1982). Neurasthenia and depression: A study of somatization and culture in China. *Culture, Medicine, and Psychiatry, 6*, 117–189. doi:10.1007/BF00051427

Lewis-Fernández, R., Aggarwal, N. K., Hinton, L., Hinton, D. E., & Kirmayer, L. J. (Eds.). (2016). *DSM-5 handbook on the cultural formulation interview.* Washington, DC: American Psychiatric Publishing.

Littleford, L. N., & Nolan, S. A. (2013). Sphere of influence: How to infuse cultural diversity into your psychology classes. *Psychology Teacher Network, 23*(1). www.apa.org/ed/precollege/ptn/2013/05/index.aspx

Lonner, W. J., & Murdock, E. (2012). Introductory psychology texts and the inclusion of culture. *Online Readings in Psychology and Culture, 11*(1). doi:10.9707/2307-0919.1115

Masuda, A. (2016). Principle-based cultural adaptation of cognitive behavioral therapies: A functional and contextual perspective. *Japanese Journal of Behavior Therapy*, *42*, 11–19.

Matsumoto, D., & Juang, L. (2008). *Culture and psychology* (4th ed.). Belmont, CA: Wadsworth.

Sue, S. (1998). In search of cultural competence in psychotherapy and counseling. *American Psychologist*, *53*, 440–448. doi:10.1037/0003–066X.53.4.440

Sue, D., & Sue, D. M. (2008). *Foundations of counseling and psychotherapy: Evidence-based practices for a diverse society*. Hoboken, NJ: Wiley.

Tanaka-Matsumi, J. (2008). Functional approaches to evidence-based practice in multicultural counseling and therapy. In U. P. Gielen, J. G. Draguns, & J. M. Fish (Eds.), *Principles of multicultural counseling and therapy* (pp. 169–198). New York, NY: Routledge.

Tanaka-Matsumi, J., Higginbotham, N. H., & Chang, R. (2002). Cognitive-behavioral approaches to counseling across cultures: A functional analytic approach for clinical applications. In P. B. Pedersen, J. G. Draguns, W. J. Lonner, & J. E. Trimble (Eds.), *Counseling across cultures* (5th ed., pp. 337–354). Thousand Oaks, CA: Sage.

Tanaka-Matsumi, J., Seiden, D. Y., & Lam, K. (1996). Cross-cultural functional analysis: A strategy for culturally-informed clinical assessment. *Cognitive and Behavioral Practice*, *2*, 215–233. doi:10.1016/S1077–7229(96)80015–0

Triandis, H. C. (2007). Culture and psychology: A history of the study of their relationship. In S. Kitayama & D. Cohen (Eds.), *Handbook of cultural psychology* (pp. 59–76). New York, NY: Guilford.

Tweed, R. G., & Lehman, D. R. (2002). Learning considered within a cultural context: Confucian and Socratic approaches. *American Psychologist*, *57*, 89–99. doi:10.1037/0003–066X.57.2.89

Wang, Q. (2001). "Did you have fun?" American and Chinese mother–child conversations about shared emotional experiences. *Cognitive Development*, *16*, 693–715. doi:10.1016/S0885-2014(01)00055-7

(2016). Why should we all be cultural psychologists? Lessons from the study of social cognition. *Perspectives on Psychological Science*, *11*, 583–596. doi: 10.1177/1745691616645552

(2017). Five myths about the role of culture in psychological research. *Observer*, *30*(1). www.psychologicalscience.org/observer/five-myths-about-the-role-of-culture-in-psychological-research#.WSlAcZLyiUk

Weiss, M. (1997). Explanatory Model Interview Catalogue (EMIC): Framework for comparative study of illness. *Transcultural Psychiatry*, *34*, 235–263. doi:10.1177/136346159703400204

Wenzel, A., Dobson, K. S., & Hays, P. A. (2016). Culturally responsive cognitive behavioral therapy. In A. Wenzel, K. S. Dobson, & P. A. Hays (Eds.), *Cognitive behavioral therapy techniques and strategies* (pp. 145–160). Washington, DC: American Psychological Association. http://dx.doi.org/10.1037/14936–008

Epilogue
The Band Plays On
Kenneth D. Keith

Music has sometimes played a metaphorical role in discussions of teaching (e.g., Keith, 2006), and of the history and study of culture and psychology (Lonner, 2013). After all, orchestrating the complexities of the classroom, laboratory, or cultural observations can sometimes seem more daunting than conducting a large musical ensemble or untangling the plot of a complicated opera. Yet teaching and learning can clearly be aesthetic experiences (Hall, 1983; Kupfer, 1983), and what, we might wonder, could be more aesthetically pleasing than a classroom and a subject matter replete with a rainbow of diverse peoples and a panoply of rich cultural ideas. In some ways then, this final chapter might be considered a *coda*.

Music also, however, has at times carried unfortunate connotations. For example, we often hear the myth that Nero fiddled while Rome burned (although the fiddle had not yet been invented in the year 64 C.E.), and that while the Titanic sank, the band played on (true). Although the challenges we face today may not always seem as immediately perilous as those faced by Nero's Romans or the Titanic's passengers, they are nevertheless serious and sometimes daunting. And many of our most pressing challenges are global and behavioral in nature, and their solution depends upon behavior change across cultures.

Climate Change

Global climate change, according to climate scientists, is occurring rapidly and is driven by human behavior (Swim, Clayton, & Howard, 2011). Psychological scientists are studying the complex relations between human activity, population, socioeconomic status, carbon dioxide emissions, and other dimensions of the climate change problem, and they are engaged in assessment of public knowledge about climate change (Reynolds, Bostrom, Read, & Morgan, 2010). These psychologists recognize that climate change requires not just technological or economic understanding, but they also acknowledge that it is a behavioral and cultural issue (Hoffman, 2010).

Recently, scientists have addressed the need for a global social psychology to aid in dealing with global challenges. This would mean, among other things, the capacity for people to develop supranational identities – that is, the ability to identify with humanity in the broad sense, as opposed to a narrower national identity (Reese, Rosenmann, & McGarty, 2015). There is a need for an understanding of the cultural and perceptual basis of international agreements intended to advance the common good (Lipschutz, 1991) and recognition that solutions to climate change must also encompass social issues, including poverty (Van de Vliert, 2008).

The key point here is that mitigating climate change will require psychological solutions – behavior change. The research and the skills underlying that behavior change will come from a variety of perspectives within the broad scope of psychological science, among them cognitive science (Panno, Carrus, Maricchiolo, & Manetti, 2015); the study of emotional response (Chen, 2016); motivation, values, and communication (Howell, 2014); and behavior analysis (Todorov, 2010). Recognizing that narrative stories may sometimes be more effective than mere statistics, psychologists may help to improve those stories (Green, Strange, & Brock, 2013). Or perhaps psychological scientists will further enlighten the path to greater willingness to provide humanitarian aid across cultures (Andrighetto, Baldissarri, Lattanzio, Loughnan, & Volpato, 2014). The teaching approaches described in many of the chapters of this book represent potential contributions to development of the future psychologists whose skills will be essential to effective global responses to the challenge of climate change and its human consequences.

Global Conflict

As I write this chapter, conflicts exist in many places around the world. Some, as in the Middle East, are outwardly violent; others are potentially violent, allayed by tenuous diplomatic efforts; and still others are played out in political strife and bitter partisan debate. Chapter 20 in this volume presents the case for the teaching of the psychology of peace, and the psychological literature has addressed the issue of intractable conflict (Bar-Tal, Halperin, & Pliskin, 2015). Much conflict occurs not between states, but between religious or cultural groups within states (Bercovitch & Foulkes, 2012).

Marsella (2005) argued that differing views of reality between cultures can lead to conflict, and, if those views are embedded in fundamentalist religious, economic, and political views, the conflict can lead to violence, torture, war, and genocide. Individuals' constructions of reality, Marsella wrote, arise from their cultures, and conflict resolution may be achieved through cultural learning and understanding. Similarly, conflict resolution styles may differ according to culture, as Chua and Gudykunst (1987) found when comparing individuals from low-context and high-context cultures. Of particular cultural interest is the violence engendered by those individuals whom numerous countries have labeled terrorists. Sometimes, the attackers deliberately die in these incidents, and attempts to explain their behavior have at times proven contradictory, prompting Locicero and Sinclair (2008) to propose a model drawing upon developmental and ecological psychology There has also been cultural backlash against groups considered "barbarian" (particularly Muslims) and calls for defense of "civilization," sometimes resulting in a spiral of reciprocal hatred and violence (Vertigans, 2010). There have been allegations of involvement in such reciprocal retaliation by psychologists (Elkins, 2016; Pope, 2016) and efforts to use such actions as opportunities for the teaching of ethics in psychology (e.g., Handelsman, 2016).

Influenced by the classic research of Sherif et al. (1988/1961), Mayor (1995) argued that psychologists can play an important role in creation of a culture of peace. Mayor's idea was not new. More than six decades ago, a group of eminent psychologists produced a statement articulating the basis for peaceful relations among cultures. Known as *The Psychologists' Manifesto: Human Nature and the Peace: A Statement by Psychologists* (Allport et al., 1945), the document set forth several principles they believed to govern peace. Among them were these (Smith, 1999):

War can be avoided: War is not born in men; it is built into men.
Racial, national, and group hatreds can, to a considerable degree, be controlled.
Condescension toward "inferior" groups destroys our chances for a lasting peace.
Liberated and enemy peoples must participate in planning their own destiny.
The root desires of the common people of all lands are the safest guide to framing a peace.
The trend of human relationships is toward ever wider units of collective security. (p. 5)

Coming as it did on the heels of World War II, this statement was a powerful stand by a group of psychologists interested in culture and in peace. Unfortunately, however, their statement is as relevant and as essential today as it was in 1945. The resolution of conflict remains a major global need, and psychologists of the future will face the ongoing challenge of finding effective means to improve cultural understanding and facilitate peaceful behavior. As teachers of psychology, we must lead the way in developing and teaching the cultural awareness and psychological skills that students will need to grapple with conflict and to work toward a more peaceful world.

A Technological World

In my youth, I was a reader of the fictional comic strip detective Dick Tracy. Among his advanced techniques, Tracy used a "two-way wrist radio" to communicate with headquarters and to assist in his pursuit of criminals. In the mid-twentieth century, the two-way wrist radio was science fiction, a futuristic idea powered by an equally far-fetched atomic source. Today, people around the world carry small electronic devices far more powerful and complex than Tracy's creator could ever have imagined – and those devices have changed the world in ways that also would have seemed unimaginable in that earlier time.

The electronic age has been both boon and bane for cultures around the world. Twenty-four-hour television, for example, has made information of all sorts easily available to many people, but at the same time has some- times been associated with reductions in happiness or life satisfaction (Argyle, 1999; Schmiedeberg & Schröder, 2017) and lower socioeconomic status in women (Teychenne, Ball, & Salmon, 2012). Furthermore, sed- entary electronic activities may be disruptive in the lives of children (Granich, Rosenberg, Knuiman, & Timperio, 2011).

In a cross-cultural study of student use of technology beyond the classroom, Lai, Wang, Li, and Hu (2016) found that students' cultural values were correlated with self-directed technology use, and in a study of Lebanese students, researchers found measures of Hofstede's (1980) cul- tural dimensions to be related to perceptions of usefulness of technology and intentions to use electronic technology (Tarhini, Hone, Liu, & Tarhini, 2017). However, although culture may clearly influence attitudes toward technology, it is perhaps the reverse – the influence of technology on culture – that is even more important. Technological innovations have multiplied exponentially in the relatively recent historical past

(Heine, 2012), and information technology has become an essential tool as developing countries combat poverty and work to provide education and healthcare (Blaya, Fraser, & Holt, 2010; Kamssu, Siekpe, & Ellzy, 2004).

Many people in developing countries have benefited from availability of mobile telephones in personal communication (Horst, 2006), and trading practices (Overå, 2005), although hopes that internet-capable phones will relieve social exclusion among isolated people may depend upon afford-ability of appropriate devices (Chigona, Beukes, Vally, & Tanner, 2009). In Africa, widespread cell phone use, due to its contribution to ingroup coordination and cooperation, may have increased the potential for polit-ical violence (Pierskalla & Hollenbach, 2013), while in Malawi, commu-nity health workers have used phones to demonstrate the potential for improved effectiveness of healthcare communication with commensurate savings in hospital staff time and expense (Mahmud, Rodriguez, & Nesbit, 2010). Despite the fact that poverty levels in sub-Saharan Africa are high by world standards (Sembene, 2015), the proliferation of mobile phones has revolutionized many aspects of life in the region where two-thirds or more of people have phones (Pew Research Center, 2015).

The potential of electronic devices and electronic communication, especially mobile telephones, is great, yet researchers in numerous cultures have investigated a variety of social and psychological downsides to these technologies. These have included addiction to electronic devices (Güzeller & Coşguner, 2012), bullying (Jones, Manstead, & Livingstone, 2011), alcohol abuse (Burton, Dadich, & Soboleva, 2013), distracted driving (Vera-López et al., 2013), and depression (Lemola, Perkinson-Gloor, Brand, Dewald-Kaufmann, & Grob, 2015). For better or worse, and in cultures around the world, electronic technology has brought significant changes to the lives of people from all walks of life. The opportunities and the challenges afforded by these changes are mainly behavioral in character, and the nature of the technology transcends the boundaries of countries and continents. In the rapidly changing world of technology, psychology students of today will be the problem solvers of tomorrow, and the solutions they seek will require a wide range of cross-cultural skills.

The Role of Teachers

The global challenges I have briefly highlighted here may be among the most salient, but they are certainly not the only ones that students will face in a future that promises to be both complex and global. As we have always done, we must look to teachers to ready students for a future the teachers may never see, but that nevertheless demands preparation. The authors of the earlier chapters in this book have provided a wealth of information and ideas to aid in the task of preparing students, and in the process, they have shown how teachers can integrate cultural concepts with the traditional content of the many subfields of psychology. The prospect of teaching cross-cultural (and cultural, indigenous, or international) psychology is not new. Brislin (1975) discussed teaching about culture and psychology, Cushner (1987) characterized cross-cultural as the "missing link" in the teaching of psychology, and Cole (1984) lamented that the field had treated cross-cultural psychology as a "miscreant child."

Cole's (1984) commentary, based on his own experience, rings true today. He suggested (a) that the history of psychology, as he had encountered it (and as many might encounter it today), presented a variety of luminaries – such as Galton, Köhler, Koffka, Binet, Pavlov, Locke – from assorted cultural backgrounds, but without clarity about their relevance to education in psychology. (b) American psychology and American theories were dominant, to the extent that textbooks and undergraduate psychology curricula, even in countries with their own lengthy psychological histories, resembled those in the United States; happily, things have changed, and we have begun to recognize the limitations of US psychology and the contributions of others. (c) Methodologists have often mistrusted research carried out in cultural settings that violate standard experimental rules with the result that undergraduates have too infrequently learned about the psychological characteristics of people of other cultures. Although he offered these observations more than three decades ago and tremendous progress has since occurred in the study and teaching of culture (Lonner & Murdock, 2012), Cole's observations would still hit too close to home for comfort in too many of today's psychology classrooms.

In discussing integration of culture into the curriculum, Goldstein (1995) offered some useful guidelines, recommending:

1. Avoiding marginalization of cross-cultural materials and perspectives
2. Raising awareness about bias within the cross-cultural literature
3. Avoiding the creation or reinforcement of stereotypes
4. Using accurate terminology to make cross-cultural comparisons
5. Distinguishing between etics and emics
6. Creating a classroom environment in which diversity is valued (pp. 228–231)

Meeting these guidelines requires not only communication of knowledge but also of values. Matsumoto (2002) argued that effective teaching about culture involves accepting that it cannot be value free and that we must get beyond one-way didactic teaching approaches, instead exposing students to experiential cultural activities and exercises (e.g., simulations, role-playing). In this way, Matsumoto suggested, we may help students attain goals that will help them to adjust to and live in a changing, diverse world.

The authors of the chapters of this volume aspire to teach a psychology of all people, and to do it in all courses – culture across the curriculum. As Lonner and Murdock (2012, p. 14) noted, "World-wide we owe beginning students the challenge and pleasure of learning how the powerful forces of culture shape all of our lives." That challenge will be met only if students encounter great teachers. Benjamin (1987), writing about one of the great early teachers of psychology, Harry Kirke Wolfe, chose an apt title: "A Teacher Is Forever." Thousands of people, Benjamin noted, bear Wolfe's stamp without knowing his name. In the same way, we can hope to leave students a legacy that includes the skills to understand and to shape the rich tapestry and harmony of a diverse, multicultural world. Let the band play on.

References

Allport, G., Murphy, G., Crutchfield, R. S., English, H. B., Heidbreder. E., Hilgard, E.,...Tolman, E. C. (1945, March). The psychologists' manifesto: Human nature and the peace: A statement by psychologists. *Newsletter of the Society for the Psychological Study of Social Issues.*

Andrighetto, L., Baldissarri, C., Lattanzio, S., Loughnan, S., & Volpato, C. (2014). Humanitarian aid? Two forms of dehumanization and willingness to help after natural disasters. *British Journal of Social Psychology, 53,* 573–584. doi: 10.1111/bjso.12066

Argyle, M. (1999). Causes and correlates of happiness. In D. Kahneman, E. Diener, & N. Schwarz (Eds.), *The foundations of hedonic psychology* (pp. 353–373). New York, NY: Russell Sage Foundation.

Bar-Tal, D., Halperin, E., & Pliskin, R. (2015). Why is it so difficult to resolve intractable conflicts peacefully? A sociopsychological explanation. In M. Galluccio (Ed.), *Handbook of international negotiation: Interpersonal, intercultural, and diplomatic perspectives* (pp. 73–92). Cham: Springer.

Benjamin, L. T., Jr. (1987). A teacher is forever: The legacy of Harry Kirke Wolfe (1858–1918). *Teaching of Psychology, 14,* 68–74. doi:10.1207/s15328023top1402_1

Bercovitch, J., & Foulkes, J. (2012*). International Journal of Cross-Cultural Management, 12,* 25–47. doi:10.1177/1470595811413105

Blaya, J. A., Fraser, H. S. F., & Holt, B. (2010). E-health technologies show promise in developing countries. *Health Affairs, 29,* 244–251. doi:10.1377/hlthaff.2009.0894

Brislin, R. W. (1975). Teaching cross-cultural psychology: The United States, Asia and the Pacific. In J. Berry & W. Lonner (Eds.), *Applied cross-cultural psychology: Selected Papers from the Second International Conference, International Association for Cross-Cultural Psychology* (pp. 277–282). Amsterdam: Swets and Zeitlinger.

Burton, S., Dadich, A., & Soboleva, A. (2013). Competing voices: Marketing and counter-marketing alcohol on Twitter. *Journal of Nonprofit & Public Sector Marketing, 25,* 186–209. doi:10.1080/10495142.2013.787836

Chen, M.-F. (2016). Impact of fear appeals on pro-environmental behavior and crucial determinants. *International Journal of Advertising, 35,* 74–92. doi:10.1080/02650487.2015.1101908

Chigona, W., Beukes, D., Vally, J., & Tanner, M. (2009). Can mobile internet help alleviate social exclusion in developing countries? *Electronic Journal on Information Systems in Developing Countries, 36*(7), 1–16.

Chua, E. G., & Gudykunst, W. B. (1987). Conflict resolution styles in low- and high-context cultures. *Communication Research Reports, 4*(1), 32–37.

Cole, M. (1984). The world beyond our borders: What might our students need to know about it? *American Psychologist, 39,* 998–1005. doi:10.1037/0003-066X.39.9.998

Cushner, K. H. (1987). Teaching cross-cultural psychology: Providing the missing link. *Teaching of Psychology, 14,* 220–224. doi:10.1207/s15328023top1404_7

Elkins, D. N. (2016). The American Psychological Association and the Hoffman report. *Journal of Humanistic Psychology, 56,* 99–109. doi:10.1177/0022167815619064

Goldstein, S. B. (1995). Cross-cultural psychology as a curriculum transformation resource. *Teaching of Psychology, 22,* 228–232. doi:10.1207/s15328023top2204_3

Granich, J., Rosenberg, M., Knuiman, M. W., & Timperio, A. (2011). Individual, social, and physical environment factors associated with electronic media use among children: Sedentary behavior at home. *Journal of Physical Activity & Health, 8,* 613–625. doi:10.1123/jpah.8.5.613

Green, M. C., Strange, J. J., & Brock, T. C. (2013). *Narrative impact: Social and cognitive foundations.* New York, NY: Psychology Press.

Güzeller, C. O., & Coşguner, M. S. (2012). Development of a problematic mobile phone use scale for Turkish adolescents. *Cyberpsychology, Behavior, and Social Networking, 15,* 205–211. doi:10.1089/cyber.2011.0210

Hall, W. (1983). The aesthetics of teaching. *South Pacific Journal of Teacher Education, 11*(1),15–21. doi:10.1080/0311213830110102

Handelsman, M. M. (2016, May 25). Lessons from teaching about our latest scandal in psychology. The ethical professor [Blog post]. Retrieved from www.psychologytoday.com/blog/the-ethical-professor/201605/lessons-teaching-about-our-latest-scandal-in-psychology

Heine, S. J. (2012). *Cultural psychology* (2nd ed.). New York, NY: Norton.

Hoffman, A. J. (2010). Climate change as a cultural and behavioral issue: Addressing barriers and implementing solutions. *Organizational Dynamics, 39*, 295–305. doi:10.1016/j.orgdyn.2010.07.005

Hofstede, G. H. (1980). *Culture's consequences: International differences in work-related values.* Beverly Hills, CA: Sage.

Horst, H. A. (2006). The blessing and burdens of communication: Cell phones in Jamaican transnational social fields. *Global Networks, 6*, 143–159. doi:10.1111/j.1471-0374.2006.00138.x

Howell, R. A. (2014). Promoting lower-carbon lifestyles: The role of personal values, climate change communications and carbon allowances in processes of change. *Environmental Education Research, 20*, 434–435. doi:10.1080/13504622.2013.836624

Jones, S. E., Manstead, A. S. R., & Livingstone, A. G. (2011). Ganging up or sticking together? Group processes and children's responses to text-message bullying. *British Journal of Psychology, 102*, 71–96. doi:10.1348/000712610X502826

Kamssu, A. J., Siekpe, J. S., & Ellzy, J. A. (2004). Shortcomings to globalization: Using internet technology and electronic commerce in developing countries. *Journal of Developing Areas, 38*, 151–169. doi:10.1353/jda.2005.0010

Keith, K. D. (2006). Let the concert begin: The music of team teaching. In W. Buskist & S. F. Davis (Eds.), *Handbook of the teaching of psychology* (pp. 59–64). Malden, MA: Blackwell.

Kupfer, J. H. (1983). *Experience as art: Aesthetics in everyday life.* Albany, NY: State University of New York Press.

Lai, C., Wang, Q., Li, X., & Hu, X. (2016). The influence of individual espoused cultural values on self-directed use of technology for language learning beyond the classroom. *Computers in Human Behavior, 62*, 676–688. doi:10.1016/j.chb.2016.04.039

Lemola, S., Perkinson-Gloor, N., Brand, S., Dewald-Kaufmann, J. F., & Grob, A. (2015). Adolescents' electronic media use at night, sleep disturbance, and depressive symptoms in the smartphone age. *Journal of Youth and Adolescence, 44*, 405–418. doi:10.1007/s10964-014-0176-x

Lipschutz, R. D. (1991). Bargaining among nations: Culture, history, and perceptions in regime formation. *Evaluation Review, 15*, 46–74. doi:10.1177/0193841X9101500104

Locicero, A., & Sinclair, S. J. (2008). Terrorism and terrorist leaders: Insights from developmental and ecological psychology. *Studies in Conflict and Terrorism, 31*, 227–250. doi:10.1080/10576100701879638

Lonner, W. J. (2013). Foreword. In K. D. Keith (Ed.), *The encyclopedia of cross-cultural psychology* (Vol. I, pp. xl-li). Chichester: Wiley-Blackwell.

Lonner, W. J., & Murdock, E. (2012). Introductory psychology texts and the inclusion of culture. *Online Readings in Psychology and Culture, 11*(1). Retrieved from http://scholarworks.gvsu.edu/orpc/vol11/iss1/1/

Mahmud, N., Rodriguez, J., & Nesbit, J. (2010). A text message-based intervention to bridge the healthcare communication gap in the rural developing world. *Technology and Health Care, 18*, 137–144. doi:10.3233/THC-2010-0576

Marsella, A. J. (2005). Culture and conflict: Understanding, negotiating, and reconciling conflicting constructions of reality. *International Journal of Intercultural Relations, 29*, 651–673. doi:10.1016/j.ijintrel.2005.07.012

Matsumoto, D. (2002). Culture, psychology, and education. *Online Readings in Psychology and Culture, 2*(1). Retrieved from http://scholarworks.gvsu.edu/orpc/vol2/iss1/4/

Mayor, F. (1995). How psychology can contribute to a culture of peace. *Peace and Conflict: Journal of Peace Psychology, 1*, 3–9. doi:10.1207/s15327949pac0101_2

Overå, R. (2006). Networks, distance, and trust: Telecommunications development and changing trading practices in Ghana. *World Development, 34*, 1301–1315. doi:10.1016/j.worlddev.2005.11.015

Panno, A., Carrus, G., Maricchiolo, F., & Mannetti, L. (2015). Cognitive reappraisal and pro-environmental behavior: The role of global climate change perception. *European Journal of Social Psychology, 45*, 858–867. doi:10.1002/ejsp.2162

Pew Research Center. (2015). *Cell phones in Africa: Communication lifeline*. Washington, DC: Author.

Pierskalla, J. H., & Hollenbach, F. M. (2013). Technology and collective action: The effect of cell phone coverage on political violence in Africa. *American Political Science Review, 107*, 207–224. doi:10.1017/S0003055413000075

Pope, K. S. (2016). The code not taken: The path from guild ethics to torture and our continuing choices. *Canadian Psychology, 57*, 51–59.

Reese, G., Rosenmann, A., & McGarty, C. (2015). Globalisation and global concern: Developing a social psychology of human responses to global challenges. *European Journal of Social Psychology, 45*, 799–805. doi:10.1002/ejsp.2176

Reynolds, T. W., Bostrom, A., Read, D., & Morgan, M. G. (2010). Now what do people know about global climate change? Survey studies of educated laypeople. *Risk Analysis, 30*, 1520–1538. doi:10.1111/j.1539-6924.2010.01448.x

Schmiedeberg, C., & Schröder, J. (2017). Leisure activities and life satisfaction: An analysis with German panel data. *Applied Research in Quality of Life, 12*, 137–151. doi:10.1007/s11482-016-9458-7

Sembene, D. (2015). *Poverty, growth, and inequality in sub-Saharan Africa: Did the walk match the talk under the PRSP approach?* Washington, DC: International Monetary Fund.

Sherif, M., Harvey, O. J., White, B. J., Hood, W. R., & Sherif, C. W. (1988). *The Robbers Cave experiment: Intergroup conflict and cooperation.* Middletown, CT: Wesleyan University Press. (Original published in 1961)

Smith, M. B. (1999). Political psychology and peace: A half-century perspective. *Peace and Conflict: Journal of Peace Psychology, 5*, 1–16. doi:10.1207/s15327949pac0501_1

Swim, J. K., Clayton, S., & Howard, G. S. (2011). Human behavioral contributions to climate change: Psychological and contextual drivers. *American Psychologist, 66*, 251–264. doi:10.1037/a0023472

Tarhini, A., Hone, K., Liu, X., & Tarhini, T. (2017). Examining the moderating effect of individual-level cultural values on users' acceptance of E-learning in developing countries: A structural equation modeling of an extended technology acceptance model. *Interactive Learning Environments*, 25, 306–328. doi:10.1080/10494820.2015.1122635

Teychenne, M., Ball, K., & Salmon, J. (2012). Correlates of socio-economic inequalities in women's television viewing: A study of intrapersonal, social and environmental mediators. ArtID: 3. *International Journal of Behavioral Nutrition and Physical Activity*, 9. doi:10.1186/1479-5868-9-3

Todorov, J. C. (2010). On global warming and local indifference: Behavioral analysis of what persons can do about their own near environment. *Behavior and Social Issues*, 19, 48–52. doi:10.5210/bsi.v19i0.3223

Van de Vliert, E. (2008). *Climate, affluence, and culture.* Cambridge: Cambridge University Press.

Vera-López, J. D., Pérez-Núñez, R., Hijar, M., Hidalgo-Solórzano, E., Lunnen, J. C., Chandran, A., & Hyder, A. A. (2013). Distracted driving: Mobile phone use while driving in three Mexican cities. *Injury Prevention*, 19, 276–279. doi:10.1136/injuryprev-2012-040496

Vertigans, S. (2010). British Muslims and the UK government's "war on terror" within: Evidence of a clash of civilizations or emergent de-civilizing processes? *British Journal of Sociology*, 61, 26–44. doi:10.1111/j.1468-4446.2009.01300.x

Index